The SAGE Handbook of Child Development, Multiculturalism, and Media

Joy Keiko Asamen dedicates this book to the memory of her parents, Keigi and Kiyo Asamen.
Mesha L. Ellis dedicates this book to her parents, Linda and Eugene Ellis.
Gordon L. Berry dedicates this book to his wife, G. Juanita Berry.

The SAGE Handbook of Child Development, Multiculturalism, and Media

Edited by
Joy Keiko Asamen
Pepperdine University
Mesha L. Ellis
Vanderbilt University
Gordon L. Berry
University of California, Los Angeles

SAGE
Los Angeles • London • New Delhi • Singapore

For information:

SAGE Publications, Inc.
2455 Teller Road
Thousand Oaks, California 91320
E-mail: order@sagepub.com

SAGE Publications India Pvt. Ltd.
B 1/I 1 Mohan Cooperative
Industrial Area
Mathura Road, New Delhi 110 044
India

SAGE Publications Ltd.
1 Oliver's Yard
55 City Road
London EC1Y 1SP
United Kingdom

SAGE Publications Asia-Pacific Pte. Ltd.
33 Pekin Street #02–01
Far East Square
Singapore 048763

Printed in the United States of America

Library of Congress Cataloging-in-Publication Data

Asamen, Joy Keiko, 1953-
The SAGE handbook of child development, multiculturalism, and media/Joy Keiko Asamen, Mesha L. Ellis, Gordon L. Berry.
p. cm.
Includes bibliographical references and index.
ISBN 978-1-4129-4915-6 (cloth)
1. Child development—Handbooks, manuals, etc. 2. Child psychology—Handbooks, manuals, etc. 3. Multiculturalism. 4. Mass media and children. 5. Internet and children. I. Ellis, Mesha L. II. Berry, Gordon L. III. Title. IV. Title: Handbook of child development, multiculturalism, and media.

HQ767.9.A83 2008
305.231089—dc22 2007050204

Printed on acid-free paper

08 09 10 11 12 10 9 8 7 6 5 4 3 2 1

Acquiring Editor: Todd R. Armstrong
Editorial Assistant: Aja Baker
Production Editor: Sarah K. Quesenberry
Copy Editor: Brenda Weight
Typesetter: C&M Digitals (P) Ltd.
Proofreader: Sally Jaskold
Indexer: Kathy Paparchontis
Marketing Manager: Carmel Schrire

Contents

Foreword

Multiculturalism, Media, and Money

JOHN P. MURRAY

FARRELL J. WEBB

The interrelationship of "the three Ms"—multiculturalism, media, and money—is a dominant theme in this outstanding collection of essays in the *Handbook of Child Development, Multiculturalism, and Media.* Doctors Asamen, Ellis, and Berry have performed a heroic service for media scholars and human development professionals by assembling a set of 28 essays, involving 50-plus authors from diverse backgrounds and professional experience, to address the issues of multiculturalism and media.

Media are a central feature in this *Handbook,* but the goals, functions, and outcomes of media for children's development turn on the influences of the other two "Ms"—money and multiculturalism. To the extent that diverse cultures are "valued" by those in the production and distribution of media products, then the depictions of various ethnic and racial groups will be accurate and informed. Money, as represented in the perceived economic value of various consumers of media, is an important component in determining whether, and how, ethnic identities and concerns will be portrayed in drama, advertising, sporting activities, or news.

Much has changed since the late 1940s when television burst on the American scene (and indeed, the world scene). For example, the families portrayed on the television screens of America in the post–WWII 1950s were White, middle-class, two-parent/two-child, suburban, striving consumers of the "good life," busily acquiring and maintaining a white house and a manicured lawn, two cars, multiple home appliances, and upward mobility (think Ozzie and Harriet). Gradually, the portrayal of families changed in ways that began to reflect, albeit in a somewhat distorted fashion, the changes in family structure in the late 1950s and '60s, namely, the rise in divorce and the increase in single-parent families. But, even in this area, the changes in TV families in the 1960s and '70s were peculiar. True, there were more single-parent families portrayed on television, but the single-parent families were predominantly *male*-headed households that resulted from the death of the mother and produced a smooth-functioning, moderately wealthy household, with few child care problems—such as the programs *My Three Sons* and the long-running (1959–69) Western, *Bonanza,* in which the three sons were each born to a different mother who conveniently died during childbirth or shortly thereafter (Huston et al., 1992). Meanwhile, back on the real ranch or in the gritty urban landscape, most of the single-parent families were *female*-headed households, living in near poverty, with intractable child care problems following divorce, not death, of the spouse.

In the late 1960s and through the '80s, television did begin to portray a greater diversity of families, both ethnically diverse and economically diverse (Cole, 1981). For example, one of the first portrayals of a female-headed household on American television was the program *Julia,* which began in 1968, and portrayed a young Black woman who was widowed when her husband was killed in Vietnam and was raising a young school-age son in Los Angeles while working full-time as a nurse. Erik Barnouw (1975) notes that *Julia* was the first romantic comedy stylistically similar to *I Love Lucy,* starring a Black actress, Diahann Carroll, but despite the nurse's salary, it was a "high-society" lifestyle. By 1973–74, the Black heroes and heroines lived in a different world of economic struggle, such as those portrayed in *Good Times,* where the family lived in absolute poverty; *Sanford & Son,* where the family business, a junkyard, was both their home and their livelihood; and *The Jeffersons,* considered the one family that had made a class transition from lower-middle to upper-middle class.

Despite these changes in the 1970s, '80s, and '90s, in those years and on into the 21st century, there have been continuing concerns about the *nature, frequency,* and *validity* of portrayals of ethnic and racial diversity. This idea was reinforced by the periodic portrayal of very successful African American families, such as the Huxtables in *The Cosby Show* and the families portrayed in the sequel, *A Different World.* Although these were positive portrayals of African Americans, there were few positive portrayals of other groups, for example, Asian Americans and Latinos, during this time. In effect, American media has not yet accurately portrayed families of color.

Yet, if we examine the social context and history of modern media in America, it is clear that there is a prevailing hegemony that goes unchallenged largely because it goes unnoticed. In other words, media are able to generate images, exaggerate characteristics, and eliminate others through sheer product quantity. Often those who lack power over the most mundane activities in their own lives can hardly find time to challenge the images generated by more powerful and sustaining institutions, such as media. Nowhere is this idea more obvious than in the area of family images created by media. In fact, some of the works in this book point directly at this issue. It is important to note that the subtle nature and the very overpowering effect of media on children can and does lead them to accept images that can be less flattering. Some of the works in this volume provide the basis for which ideas about people of color developed and were perpetuated through history. It is that history that has been redefined, reshaped, and retold in media packages that may or may not reflect the accuracy of the events because the priority of the story is more important than the facts. The simple definition of what is a family vis à vis a created perspective, as is often done with media, changes the way in which some groups are seen and valued.

On the surface, these media constructs appear nonproblematic; however, a careful examination will show that these approaches assume certain qualities are more desirable, and that these qualities, as a rule, are not present for people of color. That is to say, these ideas prescribe ideals that are often available to some groups but not others. For example, these ideals prescribe that individuals must be heterosexual, male dominated, Eurocentric, Christian, wealthy, free of problems, and able to resolve life issues with little effort, as well as must enjoy good relationships with law enforcement, live in large clean spaces, not be hungry, and be free of mental health problems (Webb, 2005).

Some of the most important issues that need to be addressed by those using this volume center on understanding what will the new families look like and what should be the role of media in portraying and promoting these family types. Recent trends, based on our observations and study of various public and private data sources, show that children in America will grow up in families with the following characteristics:

- At least one half of all children will spend at least one quarter of their lives in a female-headed household.
- The new families will have severely limited economic growth and growth opportunities.
- The new families will be characterized by a semiextended family form, often made up of fictive kin who have some ties to the original homeland of these new families.
- The new families will more than likely have two primary languages within their household for at least two generations.
- The new families will involve at least a definite recognition of sexually variant relatives and/or parents.
- The new families will consist primarily of people of color.
- The new families will have social customs, beliefs, attitudes, and communication forms that have not been previously examined in the current theoretical constructs.
- The new families will have unique adaptations to the *soi-disant* religious beliefs—they may not all be "Christians."
- The new families will probably have some major involvement with a governmental institution (not by choice in most cases), for example, immigration, homeland security, criminal justice, public welfare, and social services.
- The new families will likely have one or more family members suffering from a major mental illness at one time during their lives, most notably depression.

How families will be portrayed in the modern media landscape remains a large question. The new families, and especially the children in these families, will be stigmatized if adjustments in how media present families are not made. In short, media must become more multicultural and inclusive as suggested by the works in this book. Media must also become more responsible. Gone are the days when one image would suffice—parents and children have to be discussed and shown in a variety of situations, and these images have to reflect the people as accurately as possible.

The changes in media will come in part from a larger social change. The irony of this is that the contemporary media can play a very important role in fostering such social change. The effect of media on society is well known, particularly in the area of violence. Yet, it is this subhegemonic position maintained by media that must be harnessed if we are to see an elimination of the subtle microagressions (Sue et al., 2007) in language, images, beliefs, and attitudes that all the chapters in this volume address as important issues. The danger comes from the difficulty in measuring these problems because they require a buildup over time. Media images quicken the pace through repetition and frequency—the outcome is the same but achieved in less time.

The notion of multiculturalism cannot exist without an understanding and acceptance of differences and the importance of these differences in our lives. The differences should be understood as features unique to particular groups. They should not be reviled or treated as problematic. How to achieve such an understanding of these unique statuses is one of the critical and essential points of this volume. Worldviews involve more than gathering information about others; they also require that a deeper understanding of and respect for those not like us be developed. It is here where the parents, teachers, and families, along with the media, can be used to help shape a critical multicultural worldview. What should be involved in this worldview is one task taken on by the writers in this volume. It is no easy task. Yet, it is clear that with time, and some important paradigm shifts in modern media, the multicultural worldview is not far off. The advent of the Internet, text messaging, YouTube, instant messaging, and the belief that we are all connected, or can become connected, has major implications for modern media. Apple computer's release of the i-Phone has altered the future of communications and media. Each of these media innovations causes us to rethink our social policies, whether we agree with them or not. Clearly, the use of these devices has already altered many social agreements between people. The ability to take photos at will and communicate with others from around the world without speaking, as well as the blending of ideas from different cultures, are all part of the new worldview that multiculturalism specialists will have to address in the ever-changing world. The present volume is a great attempt at making headway in addressing this new world.

The editors and authors of the *Handbook of Child Development, Multiculturalism, and Media* are well suited to the task of changing the face of the multicultural communication scene. Professor Gordon Berry and Professor Joy Asamen have produced several landmark publications (Asamen & Berry, 1998; Berry & Asamen, 1993) that have moved research and public policy in the direction of major changes during the past two decades. Some of these changes have already taken place, such as the changes in children's television in the late 1960s and early 1970s as a result of Newton Minow's famous "Vast Wasteland" speech as the new Commissioner of the Federal Communications Commission in the early 1960s—although he and others have clearly noted the slow pace of change (Minow, 1991; Palmer, 1988). However, we must not forget that there are many other changes afoot—from the post-1960s civil rights era that is still being tentatively assimilated (Blair, 2008), to the broadening of America's worldview and the enlargement of cultural diversity in a world that is very, very different from the comfortable beliefs concerning the Anglo-Saxon foundation myths of American culture. Indeed, as a recent study group convened by the Guggenheim Foundation (2007) noted, "imagining the next war" must involve a realistic assessment of the depth of cultural divides in the world and the dangers in failing to appreciate the importance of differing worldviews.

We have had over a half-century of research on the issue of children and television in America (Huston et al., 1992; Murray & Salomon, 1984; Pecora, Murray, & Wartella, 2007), and yet we are still struggling to come to grips with the meaning of media in the lives of our fellow citizens. This *Handbook of Child Development, Multiculturalism, and Media* will force all serious students of culture and communication to focus their attention on the central issue of the way in which our society chooses to shape its future.

REFERENCES

Asamen, J. K., & Berry, G. L. (Eds.). (1998). *Research paradigms, television, and social behavior.* Thousand Oaks, CA: Sage.

Barnouw, E. (1975). *Tube of plenty: The evolution of American television.* New York: Oxford University Press.

Berry, G. L., & Asamen, J. K. (Eds.). (1993). *Children and television: Images in a changing sociocultural world.* Newbury Park, CA: Sage.

Blair, C. (2008). *Civil rights/civil sites: ". . . Until Justice Rolls Down Like Waters."* National Communication Association Conference—The Carroll C. Arnold Distinguished Lecture, San Antonio, TX, November 2006. New York: Pearson Education Publishing.

Cole, B. (Ed.). (1981). *Television today: A close-up view—readings from TV Guide.* New York: Oxford University Press.

Guggenheim Foundation. (2007). *Imagining the next war.* New York: Harry Frank Guggenheim Foundation.

Huston, A. C., Donnerstein, E., Fairchild, H., Feshbach, N. D., Katz, P. A., Murray, J. P., et al. (1992). *Big world, small screen: The role of television in American society.* Lincoln: University of Nebraska Press.

Minow, N. N. (1991). *How vast the wasteland now?* New York: Freedom Forum Media Studies Center at Columbia University.

Murray, J. P., & Salomon, G. (Eds.). (1984). *The future of children's television: Results of the Markle Foundation/Boys Town Conference.* Boys Town, NE: Boys Town Press.

Palmer, E. L. (1988). *Television and America's children: A crisis of neglect.* New York: Oxford University Press.

Pecora, N., Murray, J. P., & Wartella, E. A. (Eds.). (2007). *Children and television: Fifty years of research.* Mahwah, NJ: Lawrence Erlbaum.

Sue, D. W., Capodilupo, C. M., Torino, G. C., Bucceri, J. M., Holder, A. M. B., Nadal, K. L., et al. (2007). Racial microagressions in everyday life: Implications for clinical practice. *American Psychologist, 62*(4), 271–286.

Webb, F. J. (2005). The new demographics of family. In V. L. Bengston, A. C. Acock, K. R. Allen, P. Dilworth-Anderson, & D. M. Klein (Eds.), *Sourcebook of family theory and research* (pp. 101–102). Thousand Oaks, CA: Sage.

Acknowledgments

The editors would like to express our sincere appreciation to Todd Armstrong, our acquisition editor at Sage Publications, who offered guidance and support throughout the process and expeditiously shepherded the volume to its completion.

We also wish to extend a special thanks to Katie Grim and Sarah Quesenberry of Sage for their indispensable assistance throughout the course of this project, and to Brenda Weight, who copyedited the volume.

Most importantly, we are grateful to the prospectus reviewers, James A. Graham (Department of Psychology, the College of New Jersey), Gail Ritchie Henson (Department of Communication, Bellarmine University), Carolyn Stroman (Department of Communication and Culture, Howard University), and L. Monique Ward (Department of Psychology, University of Michigan), who saw the merit in the proposed volume, allowing us to actualize this project.

The senior editor, Joy Keiko Asamen, especially thanks her husband, Ron Kishiyama, for his continued support of her career.

Mesha L. Ellis, coeditor, would like to thank the members of her family for their endless encouragement and support throughout the years.

And finally, Gordon L. Berry, coeditor, would like to acknowledge Harvey Lehman and Stanley Robertson, two former television executives who were champions for multicultural ideals in the media industry.

Introduction

The Interface of Child Development, Multiculturalism, and Media Within a Worldview Framework

GORDON L. BERRY

THE DEVELOPING CHILD, MULTIMEDIA, AND A CULTURALLY DIVERSE SOCIETY

There are in our scholarly discourses certain areas of study with constructs that are composed of systematically arranged theories, ideas, and concepts that, whether expressed separately or together, carry their own set of historical and contemporary complexities. This introductory section of the *Handbook* considers three such complex areas of study and sociocultural constructs. These three areas discussed flow naturally from the title of the *Handbook* and include child development within the principles of human development; multiculturalism and its relationship to pluralism and cross-cultural attitudes and beliefs; and various types of media as they provide information, models, and experiences that assist developing children to learn about the world within a broad-based multimedia landscape. The term *interface* was selected as a concept in the title of the introduction in order to emphasize the connected and common boundaries that can emerge between and among areas of study. At the same time, this term also serves to highlight the fact that there are often points at which seemingly independent systems or diverse sociocultural concepts might interact with each other. Such an interaction of concepts can serve to bring together a focus on a number of complex principles, behaviors, and policies related to the early development of children who are growing up in an ever-changing multicultural and multimedia world.

The culturally diverse and media-rich environments, today, challenge children to acquire and understand a world where the press of a button, the pointing of a remote, or perhaps even the blinking of the eyes can expose them to a mosaic of customs, languages, religions, values, and sociopolitical beliefs that are similar to and different from their own. Indeed, the multicultural and multimedia shifts taking place in our society even challenge the adults in the home or family, school, religious institutions, and other agents of socialization for the hearts and minds of developing children. Such a shifting cultural and media-rich landscape suggests that children, adolescents, and adults will need to be more open and understanding to those worldviews different from their own. A worldview is generally related to how an individual perceives his or her relationship to the world. Not only are worldviews composed of our attitudes, values, opinions, and concepts, but they also may affect how an individual thinks, makes decisions, behaves, and defines events (Sue, 1981). The attitudes and behaviors held by an individual help shape the personality constructs that are used to influence a worldview (Asamen & Berry, 2003). Thus, the worldview becomes for individuals a construct that directly affects and mediates their belief systems, assumptions, modes of problem solving, and conflict resolution (Ibrahim, 1991). Metaphorically, each person tends to view the world through a different pair of glasses, and multiple lenses that can reflect racial, ethnic, gender, cultural, religious, and other contextual factors (Ivey, Ivey, & Simek-Morgan, 1993). Clearly, children growing and developing in the 21st century, which is partly defined by its multimedia and vast communication resources, face a special challenge as they are bombarded by value and belief systems that play a role in the continuing process of shaping their worldviews (Asamen & Berry, 2003).

The major theories, concepts, opinions, and research based on the knowledge growing out of this *Handbook* reflect on the importance of understanding more about how children grow, learn, and develop within a sociocultural context of a changing technological and culturally diverse country and world. Ernest Boyer (1991), drawing on the early work of James Agee, wrote that "in every child who is born, under no matter what circumstances, and of no matter what parents, . . . the potentiality of the human race is born again" (p. 15). It was within the context of children and both the historical and contemporary complexities of the issues related to child development, multiculturalism, and media studies from which this introduction was framed.

CHILDREN AND DEVELOPMENT

The United Nations Convention on the Rights of the Child was adopted in 1989. It broadly defined a child as every human being to the age of 18 unless, under the law of his or her state, he or she has reached a majority earlier (Geddes, 1997). Considering the vital role of children in the lives of adults and their place in determining the future direction of humankind, this statement was a long time in coming and broad in its meaning. At the time the United Nations issued its statement on children, the scientific studies of child development and psychology were actively exploring a number of theories about them. Although the field of child development is extensive and complex, it was important to establish a brief framework for it in order to form a bridge to the other major themes in the *Handbook*.

One obvious way to begin the process of bridging some of the themes in this book is to see child development as encompassing the specialties of developmental psychology and child psychology, as well as the attention given to the intellectual, personal, and social aspects of individual development (Jeffrey, 2005). Child development includes physical, psychological, social, and all human growth from birth to adolescence, and is rooted in what we know as human behavior. Specialists in child development study virtually everything about children: the way their personalities are formed; the way they think and learn; and the way they acquire, understand, and respond to the special demands of their culture (Eggen & Kauchak, 1997; Wood, Wood, & Boyd, 2006).

The field of child development, as might be expected, has not escaped the push and pull of the many theories and schools of thought that have emerged over the years. One premier area of professional debate has been the controversy related to the issue of whether inherited or acquired traits have the greatest influence on certain developmental characteristics and behaviors. Although some of the so-called nature-nurture issues are active today, there is now a recognition that both processes have a role to play in human development. That is to say, human beings are the products of both heredity and environment and these processes tend to be interrelated. Similar controversial issues have centered on the types of research paradigms and evaluation models that are necessary to measure some of the physical, cognitive, and psychosocial developmental aspects of children. Whether one is looking at nature-nurture issues or the research models, however, developmental specialists seem to agree that there can be some individual variations from child to child, but human development tends to involve a somewhat predictable process. Wendell Jeffrey (2005) provided a contemporary perspective on this consensus in the field of child development by pointing out "that given minimally adequate nourishment, reasonable protection from illness, and other hostile aspects of the environment, a relatively orderly pattern and sequential process of physical growth, as well as behavioral and motor skills can be observed in children" (p. 450).

The cognitive and behavioral changes found within the developmental processes are at the core of what is known as learning. Learning, among other factors, will depend on the level of maturation of the learner's related stages of development. The implications of the biological aspects of this maturational process are that whether your theory of learning is based on a cognitive perspective, behavioral views, social learning concepts, or others, learning is interrelated with development and it also assists in guiding it (Eggen & Kauchak, 1997). The National Association for the Education of Young Children (NAEYC) identified a set of developmentally appropriate principles that provided a foundation for understanding in theory and practice many of the consensus points found among the specialists in child development and learning (Bredekamp & Copple, 1997). Six of the principles are identified here because they are succinct and yet comprehensive enough to form a point of departure for linking the learning aspects of child development with the multicultural and multimedia constructs in this introduction, and those same areas of study that are woven throughout the *Handbook*. The selected principles from the NAEYC are the following:

1. Domains of children's development—physical, social, emotional, and cognitive—are closely related. Development in one domain influences and is influenced by development in other domains.
2. Development occurs in a relatively orderly sequence, with later abilities, skills, and knowledge building on those already acquired.
3. Development proceeds at varying rates from child to child as well as unevenly within different areas of each child's functioning.
4. Development and learning occur in and are influenced by multiple social and cultural contexts.
5. Children are active learners, drawing on direct physical and social experience as well as culturally transmitted knowledge to construct their own understandings of the world around them.
6. Development and learning result from interaction of biological maturation and the environment, which includes both the physical and social worlds that children live in. (Bredekamp & Copple, pp. 10–13)

I submit that the linear listing of these principles from the NAEYC cannot explain all the complexities associated with learning and development. The six points do, however, provide a framework for understanding that just as the many domains of child development are interrelated, so too are the relationships among these principles.

CHILDREN AND MULTICULTURALISM

At a juncture in the history, according to some estimates, humans left Africa around 1.9 million years ago (Wong, 2006). There is, of course, still some question and mystery as to where the migrations took these early ancestors. What we do know is that from those very early migrations and over thousands of years, the world became a rich mosaic of people and cultures whose human development includes the ability to visit distant planets, transplant organs in the body, paint beautiful pictures, compose complex musical scores, sail to great depths under the sea, and communicate over vast distances across the globe. Humankind is also at a point in history where the world is being made smaller by technological advances, the forces of geopolitics, and the present multicultural migrations taking place on a global scale. Sociocultural and political changes large and small can always have some impact on the lives of children, as do the culturally diverse demographic patterns developing in the United States.

The multicultural and multiethnic nature of the changes in the country can be seen in the large number of people who are reported to be using multiple categories to describe their racial/ethnic group (Asamen & Berry, 2003). Immigrants have settled into a broad array of American communities, and this has brought about an unprecedented level of ethnic diversity. Robin Fields (2006) highlighted the changing demographic pattern in the United States by pointing out the following data since 2000:

> The nation remains about two-thirds white, but minorities make up an increasing share of the population in every state but Virginia. . . . Latinos, who became the country's largest minority in 2000, continue to outpace other groups. They now constitute 14.5% of the population, up from 12.5% five years ago. (p. A12)

Indeed, the demographic future tends to suggest that sometime in the middle of the 21st century, the United States will become what is called a "minority-majority society," and that is a society in which the various minority groups of color will constitute a majority (Asamen & Berry, 2003; Chisman, 1998). This demographic picture of the number of people of color is already present in many urban cores, in some suburbs, and in the entire metropolitan areas of a few cities.

The half-decade since 2000 has brought gradual and predictable ethnic changes to a state like California where, of the 35 million residents, a third are Latino, and where Asians outnumber African Americans more than 2 to 1 (Fields, 2006; Maton, Kohout, Wicherski, Leary, & Vinokurov, 2006). The change in the ethnic makeup of the country becomes very clear when one observes so many aspects of everyday life. It is safe to say that every aspect of society in the United States, ranging from schools and urban life to media and business, has been influenced by the rapidly increasing ethnic diversity in the country (Maton et al., 2006). The diversification of the United States can be seen more dramatically by data showing that the population is increasingly aging, people with disabling conditions are seeking more opportunities, and women presently represent one of the growing groups entering the labor force today.

Any analysis of changing demographic patterns and cultural diversity frequently moves race and ethnicity to the center of the discussions. Jon Meacham (2000) pointed out that the national conversation about race must now shift, and there is a need to think more broadly about the changing face of America. At the same time, there has also been an issue with the meaning of race that has always caused a discussion of it to be scientifically problematic. Race is, after all, a social construct. Thus, Henze, Katz, Norte, Sather, and Walker (2002) supported the proposition that from a biological framework the concept of race and the continuance of race classification are erroneous and indeed obsolete. A term such as *ethnicity* is a better descriptor because it refers to groups of people who perceive themselves as constituting a community because of a common culture, ancestry, language, history, religion, and customs. At the same time, ethnicity does not mean that there are a constant or uniform set of social experiences either for individuals or for groups (Riggins, 1992).

The reference to the concept of culture related to changing demographic patterns and a theme of multiculturalism also needs, albeit difficult to define, some brief explanation. Culture in the ideational sense is a product of learning, and it consists of what the members of a human group have to know in order to function acceptably as members of that group in the practices, customs, beliefs, and other activities in which they engage (Fowers & Davidov, 2006). A broader way to frame the elements of culture is by identifying some of the contemporary concepts that are meeting a level of understanding among social scientists. They are the following:

1. There is tremendous variation in the cultural repertoire within a given cultural group, depending on age, gender, occupation, economic niche, and many other factors.

2. Cultural borderlands, with much sharing and borrowing, are more the rule than the exception these days, especially among industrialized nations and in our increasingly interconnected cyberspaces.

3. We all actively construct and change culture, as well as acquire parts of it through socialization—the only culture that remains static is a culture that has died.

4. Much of culture is implicit—foods and festival depictions give a false picture of culture as a visible, ritualized set of practices and ignore the less-visible aspects of culture, such as the way we respond to a compliment or how we know when it is appropriate to hug somebody. (Henze et al., 2002, p. 11)

Some other capsule views agreed on among social scientists are that culture is learned, it is dynamic, it has multiple meanings, it is not an inherited trait, and we now live in a culturally plural and multicultural world (Henze et al., 2002; Murphie & Potts, 2003).

Multicultural concepts and issues, although a part of the literature and national debate in this country today, have been at the core of human thought from its early beginnings. Morris Jackson (1995) noted that this concept was recognized in ancient Mediterranean civilizations from the new kingdom of pharaonic Egypt through the collapse of the Roman Empire. A framework for understanding multiculturalism in the United States is to see it as having some elements of cultural pluralism. That is to say, a culturally pluralist society that promotes the principles of what John Axelson (1993) broadly referred to as having unity in diversity, and where various cultural groups in this country develop through equal cooperation and interaction. To endorse cultural diversity and cultural pluralism within this framework of multiculturalism is to understand and appreciate the differences that exist among the citizens of the United States, to affirm cultural differences, to profess a wholesome respect for the intrinsic worth of every individual, and to reject separatism (Asamen & Berry, 2003; American Association of Colleges of Teacher Education, 1973).

Some of the early debates among scholars, researchers, educators, and various types of media groups were related to cross-cultural conflicts involving assimilationist, cultural pluralist, and multiculturalist ideologies. At the center of these early discussions and debates were the issues related to the role each ideology might play in the socialization of the child, the ethnic identity of the child, the nature of schooling, and certainly how individuals would see their place and values as members of society. While there were other ideologies in the cross-cultural debates, a quick summary of some of the beliefs is the following: (a) the assimilationist envisions a society in which ethnicity and race are not important identities, and group affiliations would be based primarily on such variables as social class, politics, education, and other interests; (b) the pluralist tended to view the ethnic group as very important in the socialization of the individual, and it is within their own particular ethnic groups that children and adolescents develop their language, lifestyle, and values; (c) the multicultural theorist envisions an open society in which individuals from diverse ethnic, cultural, and social class groups have equal opportunities, as well as a place where various ethnic groups will have some unique cultural characteristics as they share and are influenced by common national traits (Banks, 1994). The debates involving the ideologies of these three groups and others, especially related to cross-cultural and multicultural beliefs, are active in some quarters today. For example, some critics of multiculturalism charge that it tends to classify people according to categories, oversimplifies the source of human identity, and encourages division and tensions among ethnic groups.

Multiculturalism as conceptualized in a more contemporary framework suggests a type of cross-cultural balance and inclusiveness related to within-group differences and between-group differences. One advantage of using multicultural concepts in this way is that it implies and includes a wide range of multiple groups without grading, comparing, or ranking them as better or worse than one another, and without denying the very distinct and complementary, or even contradictory, perspectives that each group brings with it (Asamen & Berry, 2003; Pederson, 1991). The perspective of multiculturalism advanced here does not mean that there are no standards applied to the concepts and practices of individuals and groups. Clearly, there are such factors as common obligations and common civic standards of conduct that are expected of people living in a country, state, city, and community. What is called for when cross-cultural issues arise is the need for a type of sociocultural narrative that looks at customs, behaviors, and beliefs that grow out of an *emic*, or from within a cultural context, and not exclusively from an *etic*, or outside of it.

This introduction perceives its tenets of multiculturalism as trying to bridge some of the philosophical and sociopolitical fissures that have been a part of the past and present debates. That is to say, the conceptual framework articulated recognizes the legitimacy of the multicultural debates. It also recognizes the often-complex nature of the relationships between and among so many diverse groups in the United States. At the same time, the framework also embraces a belief system that seeks cross-cultural common ground to foster unity, respect, open dialogue, civility, and intergroup understanding, while striving for a commitment to common national goals within a spirit of cultural diversity.

The *Handbook* uses a broad-base approach to understanding the multicultural concepts by including racial/ethnic groups, gender/women, social class, religious groups, the elderly, persons with disabilities, and lesbian/gay/bisexual/transgender individuals under its multicultural tent. Much of the thought, especially related to children and media, has centered on African Americans, Native American Indians/Alaska Natives, Asian/Pacific Islander Americans, Hispanic/Latino Americans, and women. In this connection, it is also important to recognize the long history of stereotyping and bigotry aimed at certain religious groups and immigrant populations. Consistent with the inclusive perspective argued for here is the description of multiculturalism advanced by the organization Visions Incorporated (2005) of Arlington, Massachusetts, which offered the following statement:

> Multiculturalism refers to the process of recognizing, understanding, and appreciating one's own culture as well as the culture of others. It stresses an appreciation of the impact of differences—race, gender, class/status, age, sexual/affectional orientation, religion, military experience, language, ethnicity, country of birth and physical ability. (p. 1)

It is axiomatic to observe that the United States is a country where historically and traditionally people differ not only in the areas of ethnicity, gender, class, and religion, but also in family composition, lifestyle, political outlook, and their general worldview. David Meyers (2007) captured a perspective on some cultural differences and what might be referred to as the common humanness of our similarities in the following observation:

> Because we are so mindful of how others differ from us, we often fail to notice the similarities predisposed by our shared biology. Cross-cultural research can help us by leading us to appreciate both our cultural diversity and human kinship. Compared with the person-to-person differences within groups, the differences are small. Regardless of our culture—and culture is itself something that shapes us . . . we humans share the same life-cycle. (p. 125)

Finding new ways of working together will require teaching and thinking about people's differences so as not to divide, separate, or exclude, but rather to learn from the differences (Xanthopoulos, 2006).

CHILDREN AND MEDIA

The culturally diverse United States and the world are long past the issues of whether mass media are dynamic forces in shaping the lives of children, adolescents, and adults in a global society. That genie is metaphorically off the printing press, out of the electronic box, free of the printed circuits, and media worldwide are a fact of life. Of course, the globalization of mass media must be understood within the reality that two thirds of the world's population who live in regions referred to as developing countries enjoy only 15% of the world's income, and this imbalance in resources naturally defines the state of mass media in certain parts of the world (Musa & Okoli, 2001). Mass media as used in this context generally means the system of information for reaching a large, diversified, anonymous, and widely scattered audience (Thomas & Carpenter, 2001). These media are represented by the press, broadcast television, radio, Internet services, websites, advertising, cable, cinema, video-recorded music, computers, satellite services, electronic games, photography, photocopiers, billboards, and other emerging forms of communication and media devices. They are the media that supply our cultural icons and stereotypes, suggest consumer demands and wishes, and convey much of the news and information people use on a daily basis (Asamen & Berry, 2003; Firestone & Garmer, 1998).

Pertti Alasuutari (1999) noted that the media are an essential part of our everyday life and social reality, and they unproblematically provide us with some level of common ground for discourse in modern society.

"Radio, television, film and the other products of media culture provide materials out of which we forge our identities, our sense of class, of ethnicity and race, of nationality, of sexuality, of us and them" (Kellner, 1995, p. 10). The implications of the positions by Alasuutari and Kellner are that media and its technologies are not neutral or benign because their messages embody the ideas, needs, and possibilities in our culture.

Steven Lubar (1993) referred to the media as a part of the "information culture" at least as much as ethnicity, race, or geography. Understanding the media means we must increasingly do so within the context of an information society, and to realize that the term no longer refers to a single coherent set of theoretical or empirical constructs (Curran & Gurevitch, 2005). Every medium comprises and is shaped by technologies, social relationships (institutions), and cultural forms (Grossberg, Wartella, & Whitney, 1998). These writers further concluded that "each of these ways of thinking about the media is important, for each contributes something unique to how we understand the media and their relationship to society and social reality" (p. 10). The implications of the social reality of this emerging media environment are that the people who are studying, creating, producing, and broadcasting various types of media need to be aware of some of the special complexities they bring to society and learning experiences of the developing child.

The unique and special attributes of media and the healthy development of children from birth to age 12, teenage, and early adult years are major themes of this *Handbook*. Special attention to children who are younger than 12 is especially important because of a need to assist them toward the sound social and emotional developmental tasks during the early childhood years, as well as to help in their cross-cultural experiences and media usage. These are the children for whom the electronic media are thoroughly integrated in the fabric of their life, with television, movies, videos, music, video games, and computers being a natural part of their everyday lives (Kaiser Family Foundation Center on the Media and Child Health, 2005). It is interesting to note that in a typical day, 83% of children ages 6 months to 6 years use some form of screen media, including 75% who watch television, 32% who watch videos or DVDs, 16% who use a computer, and 11% who play either console or handheld video games (Rideout & Hamel, 2006). In a study of young people with a sample from ages 8 to 18, the conclusions were that they live media-saturated lives by spending an average of nearly 6½ hours a day on media; television and music dominated these activities (Rideout, Roberts, & Foehr, 2005). Television, computers, radio, and other forms of media are now converging so that they will have a greater impact on the child's attitudes, beliefs, and information base. For example, with high-speed Internet connections provided either by telephone wire, a cable television line, or a satellite link, new entertainment options such as movies-on-demand, radio, television, and live online games against many players scattered around the globe have become a reality (Paik, 2001).

Children's and adolescents' usage of various types of media at such saturated levels naturally becomes the concern of those specialists and groups interested in their social development and learning. Media have their greatest effect when they are used in a manner that reinforces and channels attitudes and opinions that are consistent with the psychological makeup of the person and social structure of the groups with which the child identifies (Wilson & Gutierrez, 1995). Consistent with the psychosocial makeup of children and similar to other learning experiences, social cognitive theory suggests that cross-culture attitudes related to gender, ethnic, religious, class, and other beliefs can be acquired from observations growing out of television and other media through the process of modeling (Bandura, 1986; Berry & Asamen, 2001; Eggen & Kauchak, 1997). The learning experiences drawn from both positive and negative cross-cultural media images provided to children can become a part of their stored bits of information or schemata that will help them draw relationships and understandings from the content and its messages.

Children are a special audience for television as well as special users of video games, the Internet, and other media (Bryant & Bryant, 2003). In the further words of these two researchers: "Because of a lack of previous experiences and limited cognitive schemata, children are not able to interpret present circumstances in a sophisticated manner, but instead rely on their senses in the here and now" (p. 198). One way to attempt to get some understanding of television and the other media might well be to introduce the concept of "scripts" as constructs for ascertaining how sexist, ageist, and other cross-cultural views are acquired by children. A script consists of a "vignette" of both an image and a conceptual representation, as well as observations made by the child and programs for how to solve problems (Bushman & Huesman 2001; Condry, 1989). The television content can, for example, provide scripts for how children should behave, comprehend sex roles, and view health-related behavior (Condry, 1989). Scripts as a type of schema can also play a part in the way in which children and adults perceive the ethnic, gender, social class, religious, and other social roles they experience in their daily activities and the multimedia world. The unique nature and attractiveness of various types of media make the exploration of them in this *Handbook* especially important when we consider their impact on the special developmental needs of children. These are, after all, the children who can spend a great deal of time with content that has no known value to their development, but they can also learn preacademic skills from well-designed television programs that can have lasting association with their academic achievement (Huston, Bickham, Lee, & Wright, 2007).

THE ORGANIZATION OF *THE SAGE HANDBOOK OF CHILD DEVELOPMENT, MULTICULTURALISM, AND MEDIA*

The nexus of understanding how children grow and develop in a changing multicultural and multimedia-rich society presented a special set of challenges for both the scope of this book and its organization. As editors, we attempted to bring the three major themes together and explore their complexities from a multidisciplinary perspective. We believe the contributors to this book did an excellent job of providing scholarly, research-based, and practical content that will assist academics, public policy groups, foundations, teachers, parents, media professionals, and especially college students at all levels to better understand the major themes identified in this volume.

The *Handbook* is divided into four major parts:

1. Part I (Chapters 1–6) provides a foundation for understanding the roots and key concepts of multiculturalism, the cognitive processes involved in child development, and the principles associated with the early acquisition of a worldview. This part also addresses the methodological challenges relevant to the study of multicultural issues. The chapters in the first part of the volume provide the prerequisite theoretical context for critically reading the chapters in the following three parts.

2. Part II (Chapters 7–12) focuses on the traditional institutional influences that contribute toward the socialization of children

and their view of self and others (home and family, community and sociopolitical context, school, religion, and peers). The authors who contribute to this part of the *Handbook* not only offer an overview of the scholarly literature on how these agents of socialization may contribute to the development of a multicultural worldview, but also provide suggestions for how these institutions may promote the development of this perspective.

3. Part III (Chapters 13–24) concentrates on one of the most influential agents of socialization among children—television and other electronic and print media forms. Given their powerful influence on children, these media forms help shape the multicultural worldview of children. The chapters in this part of the *Handbook* discuss the various media forms in relation to the development of multicultural awareness as well as attitudes toward self and others.
4. Part IV (Chapters 25–28) offers chapters relevant to promoting a multicultural perspective among children by various constituencies. The authors who contribute to this part of the volume offer research and programs related to the role of parents, public policy groups, government agencies, broadcasters, advocacy groups, and others interested in the media, cross-cultural issues, and the needs of developing children.

Professor Ronald Takaki (1993), in the book *A Different Mirror,* presented a series of observations that are still viable to close the introduction to this book. He wrote the following:

> Whatever happens we can be certain that much of our society's future will be influenced by which "mirror" we choose to see ourselves. America does not belong to one race or one group, . . . and Americans have been constantly redefining their national identity from the moment of first contact on the Virginia shore. By sharing their stories they invite us to see ourselves in a different mirror. (p. 17)

Thus, our theories, scholarly research, well-thought-out practices, and good old common sense need to be aware of the importance of having healthy and media-literate children in a country and world trying to see and understand through a prism of many multicultural reflections.

REFERENCES

Alasuutari, P. (1999). Cultural images of the media. In P. Alasuutari (Ed.), *Rethinking the media audience, the new agenda* (pp. 86–104). London: Sage.

American Association of Colleges of Teacher Education. (1973). No model American: A statement on multicultural education. *Journal of Teacher Education, 14,* 264.

Asamen, J. K., & Berry, G. L. (2003). The multicultural worldview of children through the lens of television. In E. L. Palmer & B. M. Young (Eds.), *The faces of televisual media teaching, violence, selling to children* (pp. 107–123). Mahwah, NJ: Lawrence Erlbaum.

Axelson, J. A. (1993). *Counseling and development.* Belmont, CA: Wadsworth.

Bandura, A. (1986). *Social foundations of thought and action: A social cognitive theory.* Upper Saddle River, NJ: Prentice Hall.

Banks, J. (1994). *Multiethnic education theory and practice.* Boston: Allyn & Bacon.

Berry, G. L., & Asamen, J. K. (2001). Television, children, and multicultural awareness: Comprehending the medium in a complex multimedia society. In D. G. Singer & J. L. Singer (Eds.), *Handbook of children and the media* (pp. 359–373). Thousand Oaks, CA: Sage.

Boyer, E. L. (1991). *Ready to learn a mandate for the nation.* Princeton, NJ: Carnegie Foundation for the Advancement of Teaching.

Bredekamp, S., & Copple, C. (Eds.). (1997). *Developmentally appropriate practice in early childhood.* Washington, DC: Association for the Education of Young Children.

Bryant, J. A., & Bryant, J. (2003). Effects of entertainment televisual media on children. In E. L. Palmer & B. M. Young (Eds.), *The faces of televisual media teaching, violence, selling to children* (pp. 195–217). Mahwah, NJ: Lawrence Erlbaum.

Bushman, B. J., & Huesmann, L. R. (2001). Effects of televised violence on aggression. In D. G. Singer & J. L. Singer (Eds.), *Handbook of children and the media* (pp. 223–254). Thousand Oaks, CA: Sage.

Chisman, F. P. (1998). Delivering on diversity: Serving the media needs and interests of minorities in the twenty-first century. In A. K. Garmer (Ed.), *Investing in diversity: Advancing opportunities for minorities and the media* (pp. 1–30). Washington, DC: Aspen Institute.

Condry, J. (1989). *The psychology of television.* Hillsdale, NJ: Lawrence Erlbaum.

Curran, J., & Gurevitch, M. (2005). Introduction to the fourth edition. In J. Curran & M. Gurevitch (Eds.), *Mass media and society* (pp. 1–4). London: Hodder Arnold.

Eggen, P., & Kauchak, D. (1997). *Educational psychology: Windows on classrooms.* Upper Saddle River, NJ: Prentice Hall.

Fields, R. (2006, August 15). A dispersion of new minorities to new places. *Los Angeles Times,* p. A12.

Firestone, C. M., & Garmer, A. K. (1998). Foreword. In C. M. Firestone & A. K. Garmer (Eds.), *Digital broadcasting and the public interest* (pp. vii–xx). Washington, DC: Aspen Institute.

Fowers, B. J., & Davidov, B. J. (2006). The virtue of multiculturalism personal transformation, character and openness to the other. *American Psychologist, 61,* 581–594.

Geddes, J. B. (1997). *Childhood and children: A compendium of customs, superstitions, theories, profiles, and facts.* Phoenix, AZ: Oryx Press.

Grossberg, L., Wartella, D., & Whitney, C. (1998). *Media making: Mass media in a popular culture.* Thousand, Oaks, CA: Sage.

Henze, R., Katz, A. N., Norte, E., Sather, S. E., & Walker, E. (2002). *Leading for diversity: How school leaders promote positive interethnic relations.* Thousand Oaks, CA: Corwin Press.

Huston, A. C., Bickham, D. S., Lee, J. H., &Wright, J. C. (2007). From attention to comprehension. In N. Pecora, J. P. Murray, & E. A. Wartella (Eds.), *Children and television: Fifty years of research* (pp. 41–63). Mahwah, NJ: Lawrence Erlbaum.

Ibrahim, F. A. (1991). Contribution of cultural worldview to generic counseling and development. *Journal of Counseling and Development, 70,* 13–19.

Ivey, A. E., Ivey, M. B., & Simek-Morgan, L. (1993). *Counseling and psychotherapy: A multicultural perspective.* Boston: Allyn & Bacon.

Jackson, M. L. (1995). Multicultural counseling: Historical perspectives. In J. C. Ponterotto, J. M. Casas, L. A. Suzuki, & C. M. Alexander (Eds.), *Handbook of multicultural counseling* (pp. 3–16). Thousand Oaks, CA: Sage.

Jeffrey, W. E. (2005). Child development. In *The encyclopedia Americana* (Vol. 6, pp. 450–459). Danbury, CT: Encyclopedia Americana.

Kaiser Family Foundation Center on Media and Child Health. (2005, January). *The effects of electronic media on children ages zero to six: A history of research* (Issue Brief No. 7239). Menlo Park, CA: The Henry J. Kaiser Foundation.

Kellner, D. (1995). Cultural studies, multiculturalism, and media culture. In G. Dines & J. M. Humez (Eds.), *Gender, race, and class in media* (pp. 5–17). Thousand Oaks, CA: Sage.

Lubar, S. (1993). *Infoculture: The Smithsonian book of inventions of the information age.* Boston: Houghton Mifflin.

Maton, K. L., Kohout, J. L., Wicherski, M., Leary, G. E., & Vinokurov, A. (2006). Minority students of color and graduate pipeline, disquieting and encouraging, 1989–2003. *American Psychologist, 61,* 117–131.

Meacham, J. (2000, September 18). The new face of race. *Newsweek, 12,* 38–41.

Meyers, D. (2007). *Psychology.* New York: Worth.

Murphie, A., & Potts, J. (2003). *Culture and technology.* New York: Palgrave Macmillan.

Musa, B. A., & Okoli, E. J. (2001). Developing nations. In E. K. Thomas & B. H. Carpenter (Eds.), *Mass media in 2025: Industries, organizations, people, and nations* (pp. 167–179). Westport, CT: Greenwood Press.

Paik, H. (2001). The history of children's use of electronic media. In D. G. Singer & J. L. Singer (Eds.), *Handbook of children and the media* (pp. 1–27). Thousand Oaks, CA: Sage.

Pedersen, P. B. (1991). Introduction to the special issue on multiculturalism as a fourth force in counseling. *Journal of Counseling and Development, 70,* 4.

Rideout, V., & Hamel, E. (2006, May). *The media family: Electronic media in the lives of infants, toddlers, preschoolers and their parents.* Menlo Park, CA: Henry J. Kaiser Family Foundation.

Rideout, V., Roberts, D., & Foehr, U. G. (2005, March). *Generation M: Media in the lives of 8- to 18-year olds, executive summary.* Menlo Park, CA: Henry J. Kaiser Family Foundation.

Riggins, S. H. (Ed.). (1992). *Ethnic minority media: An international perspective.* Newbury Park, CA: Sage.

Sue, D. W. (1981). *Counseling the culturally different: Theory and practice.* New York: John Wiley & Sons.

Takaki, R. (1993). *A Different mirror: A history of multicultural America.* Boston: Little, Brown and Company.

Thomas, E. K., & Carpenter, B. H. (Eds.). (2001). *Mass media in 2025: Industries, organizations, people and nations.* Westport, CT: Greenwood Press.

Visions Incorporated. (2005). *A personal approach to multiculturalism* [Brochure]. Arlington, MA: Author.

Wilson, C. C., & Gutierrez, F. (1995). *Race, multiculturalism, and the media: From mass to class communication.* Newbury Park, CA: Sage.

Wong, K. (2006). Strangers in a new land. *Scientific American, 16,* 48–57.

Wood, S. E., Wood, E. G., & Boyd, D. (2006). *Mastering the world of psychology.* Boston: Pearson Educational.

Xanthopoulos, J. A. (2006). Multiculturalism. In H. J. Birx (Ed.), *The encyclopedia of anthropology* (pp. 1636–1641). Thousand Oaks, CA: Sage.

Part I

Foundations for Multicultural Concepts, Child Development Principles, and an Emerging Worldview

Part I of this *Handbook* begins at the most appropriate point by providing a historical foundation for understanding the key concepts of multiculturalism, ethnic identity, and cognitive processes involved in child development, and the principles associated with the early acquisition of an individual's worldview. This part of the volume also addresses some of the research and methodological challenges relevant to the study of multicultural issues. Thus, the principles and concepts of the first part of the *Handbook* form a type of historical and theoretical framework for the remainder of this volume.

Part I begins with a chapter by Ronald Takaki that provides historical insight into the "Master Narrative of American History" in which America has been defined as "White." His treatise challenges this notion by providing an account of the diverse cultures that compose and have contributed to what we know as America.

The chapters by Mesha Ellis and John Lochman, Khiela Holmes, and Mary Wojnaroski focus on the cognitive processes in regards to the developmental factors that facilitate knowledge acquisition and the relevance of social cognition and social information processing in the function and development of children's social schema, respectively. These chapters provide the theoretical bases for understanding the cognitive processes relevant to the multicultural development of children.

Sha'kema Blackmon and Elizabeth Vera move the discussion to a more specific exploration of ethnic and racial identity development among children of color. In this chapter, a recommendation for more ethnic-racial socialization research on groups of contemporary interest is suggested.

Finally, Part I ends with a chapter by Frederick Leong, Desirée Baolian Qin, and Jason Huang that offers an overview of the conceptual issues underlying multicultural research methods, such as approaches to differences; defining race, ethnicity, and culture; studies across cultures; and planning research. Furthermore, measurement equivalence issues, data collection challenges, cultural moderators, and the use of mixed methods are considered in conducting culturally appropriate and relevant research.

CHAPTER 1

Multiculturalism as a Cornerstone of Being in the 21st Century

A Historical Perspective

RONALD TAKAKI

THE MASTER NARRATIVE OF AMERICAN HISTORY

When I was a child, I lived in Palolo Valley on the island of Oahu, Hawaii. My neighbors were Japanese, Chinese, Portuguese, Korean, and Hawaiian. Across the stream that flowed down the middle of the valley lived Puerto Rican and Filipino families. As children, we played with each other, speaking in pidgin English. "Da kind *tako* [octopus in Japanese] *ono* [delicious in Hawaiian]." In the homes of our families, we heard an immense variety of languages. We thought of ourselves as Americans, and said the Pledge of Allegiance to the flag each morning. Our teachers did not teach us why peoples from around the world had come to be living together in our valley. But it was not their fault: they themselves had never had the opportunity to learn about the history of Hawaii's sugar industry and its insatiable need for laborers. Missing in their education and ours was the study of our multicultural roots—a cornerstone of our identity and being.

As a teenager, I became a surfer. Today, when my Berkeley students find out about my past, they become very curious: How did a surfer become a scholar?

A high school teacher changed my life. I attended Iolani High School, an Episcopalian institution, and during my senior year in 1956, I was in a class taught by Dr. Shunji Nishi, PhD. As his students, we were impressed. There were other Asian American doctors in Hawaii, but they were all MDs. This one was a PhD. I remember going home and asking my mother, who had been born on a plantation and had only an eighth-grade education. "Mom," I said, "my teacher's name is Dr. Shunji Nishi, PhD. Mom, what's a PhD?" She looked at me and said, "I don't know, but he must be very smart." A light went on in my head. Maybe someday I could become Ronald Takaki, PhD.

Dr. Nishi became a role model for me, and I began studying hard. He made his students write short papers every 2 weeks, essays about the problems of the world and the human condition. He taught us that to write is to think. My essays were returned with extensive marginal comments. Many of them were epistemological questions. A critical thinking skill, epistemology asks the question, "How do you know, you know, what you know?" In other words, the "how" of knowing is more important than the "what." How you know something determines what you know about it. Dr. Nishi and I developed a relationship with one another, through my essays and his marginal comments.

One day in April, Dr. Nishi flagged me on campus. "Ronald, I think it would be good for you to go away to college—good for your personal growth and your intellectual development. There is this fine liberal arts college in Ohio, called the College of Wooster. Would you like to go to the College of Wooster?" I blurted out, "No." I had already been accepted to the University of Hawaii, and Ohio seemed so far away, for I had never been off the islands. Dr. Nishi replied, "Would it be okay for me to write to the college and tell them about you?" I said fine, walked away, and forgot about this conversation. A month later, I received a letter from the dean of the College of Wooster, which read: "Dear Mr. Takaki, you have been accepted to the College of Wooster. But please fill out the application form."

After arriving on campus in the fall, I experienced a culture shock. My fellow students asked me questions like "How long have you been in this country?" and "Where did you learn to speak English?" My grandfather had come here in 1886, before many European immigrants. To the Wooster students, however, I did not look like an American and did not have an American-sounding name.

Reflecting later on my Wooster experience, I realized that my fellow students had learned nothing about Asian Americans in courses called U.S. history. They had also learned nothing or very little about Mexican Americans, African Americans, and Native Americans.

The Wooster students perceived me through a filter—what I call the Master Narrative of American History. This narrative is the pervasive and popular but mistaken story that our country was settled by European immigrants and that Americans are White or European in ancestry. "Race," Toni Morrison (1992, p. 47) explained, has functioned as a "metaphor" necessary to the "construction of Americanness": in the creation of our national identity, "American" has been defined as "White."

This widely shared assumption lies hidden beneath our conscious thinking. However, once we become aware of the Master Narrative, we can find it not only in everyday conversations and the curriculum but also in statements of policymakers as well as the entertainment media.

The Master Narrative has often been innocent. The Wooster students did not intend to isolate or insult me. President Ronald Reagan was not seeking to exclude anyone when he offered a metaphor in his appeal for funding the space program. "We landed on these eastern shores," he declared in a televised speech, "and we advanced civilization westward against the frontier. And space exploration is our latest frontier." However, many of us asked, "Who are 'we'?" Some of us were already here on these eastern shores when the English strangers first landed. Others of us landed on these western shores. In his powerful and vivid depiction of heroic White soldiers fighting the Nazis during the D-Day invasion, Steven Spielberg did not intentionally leave out the presence of African American soldiers unloading the ships on the beaches of Normandy and feeding the White combat troops. But their presence was absent from *Saving Private Ryan* because the film was seeking to entertain rather than to present accurate history. *Saving Private Ryan* was Hollywood's portrayal of World War II.

But the Master Narrative has frequently been injurious. It led to the enslavement of Africans in 17th-century Virginia; the 1790 law restricting naturalized citizenship to "Whites" only; the Indian removal of the

1830s; the U.S. war against Mexico in 1846 under the banner of manifest destiny; the Jim Crow laws denying dignity to African Americans; the 1882 Chinese Exclusion Act; the 1924 National Origins Immigration Act, which restricted immigration from southern and eastern Europe and totally closed the gates to Asia; the World War II internment of 120,000 Japanese Americans, including U.S. citizens by birth; today's racially tinged nativism aimed at "illegal immigrants" from Mexico; and the government's detention and deportation of Muslims after the 9-11 terrorist attack.

Whether innocent or injurious, the Master Narrative's narrow and exclusive definition of who is an American leaves many of us feeling left out.

After graduating from Wooster in 1961, I entered the PhD program in American history at the University of California, Berkeley. However, even the completion of the PhD was not fulfilling intellectually. I still found myself asking, How do I know, I know, what I know about the history of the diverse peoples of the United States of America? My pursuit for answers lasted for decades and led to the writing of an abundance of books—*Iron Cages: Race and Culture in 19th Century America* (Takaki, 1979); *Pau Hana: Plantation Life and Labor in Hawaii* (Takaki, 1983); *Strangers From a Different Shore: A History of Asian Americans* (Takaki, 1989); *A Larger Memory: A History of Our Diversity, With Voices* (Takaki, 1998); *Double Victory: A Multicultural History of America in World War II* (Takaki, 2000); and most important, *A Different Mirror: A History of Multicultural America* (Takaki, 1993).

ROOTS: THE "VARIED CAROLS"OF AMERICA

While researching and writing a more inclusive and hence more accurate history, I discovered the plantation origins of Palolo Valley's diversity.

In the 19th century, as the planters took lands from the Hawaiian people in order to cultivate sugar cane, they declared, "Get labor first, and capital will follow." To get laborers, they looked everywhere, especially in Asia. Requisitions sent to the mercantile houses in Honolulu reveal their frenzied scramble for laborers. In a letter to a plantation manager, July 2, 1890, the Davies Company of Honolulu (Laupahoehoe Plantation Records, 1890) acknowledged receipt of a list of orders:

bonemeal

canvas

Japanese laborers

macaroni

Chinaman

A letter, May 5, 1908, from the vice president of H. Hackfield and Company to manager George Wilcox of the Grove Farm Plantation (Grove Farm Plantation Records, 1908) had itemized sections, listed alphabetically, for

fertilizer

Filipinos

Though they placed orders for workers along with supplies, planters were conscious of the nationalities of their laborers. An ethnically diverse labor force was designed to create divisions among the workers and reinforce control over them. Plantation managers devised a policy: "Keep a variety of laborers, that is different nationalities, and thus prevent any concerted action in case of strikes, for there are few, if any, cases of Japs, Chinese, and Portuguese entering into a strike as a unit" (Fairfield, 1895).

However, these immigrants from many different countries had their own ideas, feelings, and dreams for their lives in plantation

Hawaii. They, too, were actors in history, making choices and taking action. In their own words, they told stories of working in the cane fields and creating new communities in the camps.

On the plantations, the laborers found themselves in a world of regimented labor. Early in the morning, they were jarred from their sleep by the loud scream of the plantation siren. A song captured the beginning of their workday:

> Awake! Stir your bones! Rouse up!
>
> Shrieks the Five o'Clock Whistle.
>
> Don't dream you can nestle
>
> For one more sweet nap.
>
> Or your ear-drums I'll rap
>
> With my steam-hammer tap
>
> Till they burst.
>
> Br-r-row-aw-i-e-ur-ur-rup!
>
> Wake up! wake up! wake up! w-a-k-e-u-u-u-up!
>
> Filipino and Japanee;
>
> Porto Rican and Portugee;
>
> Korean, Kanaka and Chinese;
>
> Everybody whoever you be
>
> On the whole plantation—
>
> Wake up! wake up! wake up! w-a-k-e-u-u-u-up!
>
> Br-r-row-aw-i-e-ur-ur-rup! ("The Five O'Clock Whistle," 1910)

After waking up, the workers assembled in front of the mill where they were organized into gangs, each one supervised by a *luna*, or White overseer. The ethnicity of the gangs varied: some were composed of one nationality, whereas others reflected a mixture of Hawaiians, Filipinos, Puerto Ricans, Chinese, Japanese, Portuguese, and Koreans. For everyone, fieldwork was punishing and brutal. "We worked like machines," a laborer complained. "For 200 of us workers, there were seven or eight lunas and above them was a field boss on a horse. We were watched constantly" (Ethnic Studies Oral History Project, 1981, p. 360). Harvesting the cane was dirty and exhausting work. The workers whispered to the wind, come, please come and cool our sweaty backs. But the breezes often could not reach them because they were surrounded by the green thicket. Twelve feet in height, the cane was like a formidable forest, and the workers were like miniature soldiers as they cut the stalks (Ethnic Studies Oral History Project, p. 360).

Fighting back against the cane, workers refused to be intimidated by the managers. Contrary to the stereotype of Asians as quiet and accommodating, they repeatedly engaged in strikes, inspired by fierce visions of what their labor and lives in Hawaii should be.

The first major strike was organized in 1909 by Japanese laborers, who constituted 70% of the workforce. In their strike demands, the laborers called for equal pay for equal work: they wanted the same pay as workers from Puerto Rico and Portugal. "It is not the color of his skin or hair, or the language he speaks, or manners and customs that grow cane in the field," the strikers declared. "It is labor that grows cane." Their strike demands reflected the transformation of these sojourning laborers into settlers. "We have decided to permanently settle here [and] to unite our destiny with that of Hawaii, sharing the prosperity and adversity of Hawaii with other citizens of Hawaii" (Commissioner of Labor on Hawaii, 1910, p. 76). Significantly, these Japanese immigrants were framing their demands in "American" terms. They argued that the deplorable conditions on the plantations perpetuated an "undemocratic and un-American" society of "plutocrats and coolies."

Fair wages would encourage laborers to work more industriously and productively and enable Hawaii to enjoy "perpetual peace and prosperity." They were seeking to create "a thriving and contented middle class—the realization of the high ideal of Americanism" (Commissioner of Labor on Hawaii, p. 76).

However, the planters crushed the strike and then began importing Filipino laborers in a divide-and-rule strategy. By 1920, the Japanese workers represented only 44% of the labor force, and the Filipino workers constituted 30%. Pitted against one another, the laborers of both nationalities quickly realized that their struggle for better conditions and higher pay would have to be based on interethnic working-class solidarity.

In 1920, demanding higher wages, Japanese and Filipino laborers went out on strike together. The Filipino Laborers Association initiated the action. "This is the opportunity that the Japanese should grasp," declared the leader of the Filipino strikers, "to show that they are in harmony with and willing to cooperate with other nationalities in this territory, concerning the principles of organized labor. We should work on this strike shoulder to shoulder" (Tsutsumi, 1922, pp. 194–198). Three thousand Filipino workers stopped working. Japanese newspapers urged the Japanese laborers to join the Filipino strikers: "Laborers from different countries" should take "action together." Between Filipinos and Japanese, there should be "no barriers of nationality, race, or color." The Japanese Laborers Association joined the work stoppage. United in struggle, the strikers of both nationalities combined into a new union—the Hawaii Laborers Association, an identity based on region and class (Tsutsumi, pp. 194–198).

Though the strikers held out for months, they were finally forced to return to work. Nevertheless, they had learned valuable lessons. The strike had demonstrated the making of an American identity, the transforming of immigrants into Americans. At their rallies, Japanese and Filipinos waved the flag of their adopted nation. Moreover, the strike had revealed a new multicultural consciousness being created in plantation communities.

Coming from different countries, these immigrants had been transplanting their customs and traditions to the islands. Living together in plantation camps, the workers and their families had been hosting ethnic holidays and celebrations. One of the most colorful and noisy festivals was Chinese New Year, with firecrackers filling the plantations with explosions and smoke. During the midsummer, Japanese held their traditional *obon,* or festival of souls, with dancers stepping in circles to the beat of *taiko* drums. The most important celebration for Filipino laborers was Rizal Day—December 30, the anniversary of the Spanish execution of the famous revolutionary Jose Rizal in 1896. Together, families of different nationalities had been creating a community of a fusion of many cultures.

In the camps, these immigrants from many countries had also been exchanging different ethnic foods. The daughter of a Portuguese laborer remembered how her mother would make gifts of "little buns for the children in the camp. The Japanese families gave us sushis and the Hawaiians would give us fish." "Everybody took their own lunches" to school, Lucy Robello of the Waialua plantation said, and they would trade their foods with one another. Meanwhile, in the fields, their parents were sharing their lunches. Together, workers of different ethnicities would taste each other's foods and exclaim, "*Ono, ono!*" "Tasty, tasty!" (Ethnic Studies Oral History Project, 1977, p. 223).

Initially, the laborers of each ethnic group spoke only their native tongue. Soon they began to acquire a common language.

Planters had wanted the immigrant laborers to be taught a functional, spoken English so they could give commands to their multilingual work force. "By this," explained a planter, "we do not mean the English of Shakespeare but the terms used in everyday plantation life. A great many of the small troubles arise from the imperfect understanding between overseers and laborers." Over the years, a plantation dialect developed called "pidgin English"—a basic English that incorporated Hawaiian, Japanese, Portuguese, and Chinese phrases as well as the rhythms and intonations of these languages. Though it had begun as "the language of command," this hybrid language, with its luxuriant cadences, lyrical sounds, and expressive hand gestures, soon became the language of the community. "The language we used had to be either pidgin English or broken English," explained a Filipino laborer. "And when we don't understand each other, we had to add some other words that would help to explain ourselves. That's how this pidgin English comes out beautiful" (Ethnic Studies Oral History Project, 1977, p. 11).

Gradually, over the years, the immigrants were planting roots in Hawaii through their children. The planters did not want the laborers' children to be educated beyond the sixth or eighth grade. A visitor from the mainland noticed the presence of Japanese children on the plantations and asked a manager whether he thought the coming generation of Japanese would make intelligent citizens. "Oh, yes," he replied, "they'll make intelligent citizens all right enough, but not plantation laborers—and that's what we want" (Aller, 1958, p. 39).

In the schools, however, the children were being taught lessons that made them critical of the plantation system. From their teachers, many of whom were Whites from the mainland, they learned about freedom and equality as they recited the Declaration of Independence. "Here the children learned about democracy or at least the theory of it," said a University of Hawaii Japanese-American student. They were taught that honest labor, fair play, and industriousness were virtues. But they "saw that it wasn't so on the plantation." Seeing their parents suffer from drudgery, low wages, and discrimination, many of the second generation did not want to be tracked into plantation labor. Education, they believed, was the key to employment opportunity as well as freedom from the plantation. "My father did everything in his power," said the daughter of a Japanese immigrant, "to make us realize that going to school would be to our advantage" (Smith, 1937, p. 52).

Indeed, the immigrant parents believed their children were entitled to educational advantages. After all, they had transformed the islands into a profitable sugar economy. "With my bare hands and calloused heart and patience," a worker boasted, "I helped build Hawaii" (Felipe, 1972, p. v). "When we first came to Hawaii," the 1920 strikers proudly declared, "these islands were covered with ohia forests, guava fields and areas of wild grass. Day and night did we work, cutting trees and burning grass, clearing lands and cultivating fields until we made the plantations what they are today" (Hawaii Laborers' Association, 1920, p. 1).

As they worked to enrich Hawaii's economy, the peoples of the plantations were reinventing themselves. Ethnic identities based on national origins were being transformed in a multicultural crucible. A culturally diverse society was being created, and its people were becoming American. At one of their rallies during the 1920 strike, Japanese and Filipinos held high a portrait of Abraham Lincoln, and in the schools, their children memorized the Gettysburg Address. These "strangers from a different shore" were insisting that their adopted nation live up to its founding principles.

The story of the immigrant plantation laborers of Hawaii is only one of the missing chapters in America's epic history. Others abound. In what Walt Whitman (1958, p. 9) celebrated as "the varied carols" of America, the people of many different races and ethnicities tell a refreshing and revealing history of our country.

Like Hawaii, beneath the making of the larger society's diversity was an economic reality. After landing on "these eastern shores" in the 17th century, the English colonizers seized lands from Indians. In Massachusetts, they established a farming and commercial economy, and in Virginia, they cultivated tobacco as an export crop dependent on the exploitation of slaves from Africa. After the American Revolution, the economy was transformed into what historian Douglass C. North called inter-regional specialization. The expanding and industrializing economy tied together a broad range of different peoples. In the textile mills of Lowell, Providence, Fall River, and other towns in New England, Irish immigrant women labored in noisy and dusty factories. The demand for cotton from the South ignited the expansion of cotton agriculture into upcountry Georgia and South Carolina, then into Alabama, Mississippi, and Louisiana. To clear the path for cotton cultivation, entire tribes of Cherokees and Choctaws were taken from their homelands and removed to Oklahoma. Black slaves planted and picked cotton grown on lands previously inhabited by Indians. Cotton agriculture crossed the border into Texas, a region of Mexico, and paved the way to the U.S. war against Mexico, which ended with the annexation of half of Mexico and the incorporation of its inhabitants into the United States. One of the aims of the war was the possession of the San Francisco Bay, and the opening of trade with Asia, which, in turn, opened the way to the migrations of Chinese to America.

Connecting the different regions of an industrializing economy, the railroad system was an achievement of a diversity of workers. Hired out by their owners, 20,000 slaves were used to build the rail lines of the South—the Mississippi Railroad, the Georgia, the South Carolina, the Raleigh and Gaston, and others. Laying railroad ties, Black laborers sang:

> Down the railroad, um-huh
>
> Well, raise the iron, um-huh
>
> Raise the iron, um-huh (Bunton, 1940, as cited in Grossman, 1989, p. 192)

Irish railroad construction laborers heard their foremen yelling, "Now Mick do this, and Mick do that." And the Irish shouted back, "The divil take the railroad!" As they laid tracks for the Union Pacific, they tuned their bodies to the rhythms of a work song:

> Then drill, my Paddies, drill—
>
> Drill, my heroes, drill,
>
> Drill all day, no sugar in your tay
>
> Workin' on the U. P. railway. (Wittke, 1956, p. 39)

While falling asleep at night, the Irish workers continued to feel the vibrations of the sledge hammers in their hands and to hear the pounding ringing in their heads. Then they felt the merciless biting of insects:

> When I lay me down to sleep,
>
> The ugly bugs around me creep;
>
> Bad luck to the wink that I can sleep,
>
> While workin' on the railroad. (Wittke, 1956, p. 39)

During the early 20th century, 10,000 Japanese laborers worked in railroad construction, many of them for the Northern Pacific. Shuttled from one construction site to another, they lived in boxcars, sleeping in double-decked bunks. "We slept in the freight cars," one of them recalled, "suffering a lot from troops of bedbugs. In order to protect ourselves from these despicable insects we each made a big sleeping sack out of cotton cloth, crawled in with our comforter and blanket, and then pulled the string tight at the top to close up the sack." Japanese workers complained about the fickle and fierce weather in song:

> A railroad worker—
>
> That's me!
>
> I am great.
>
> Yes, I am a railroad worker.
>
> Complaining:
>
> "It is too hot!"
>
> "It is too cold!"
>
> "It rains too often!"
>
> "It snows too much!"
>
> They all ran off.
>
> I alone remained.
>
> I am a railroad worker! (Ito, 1973, p. 343)

Mexican laborers laid tracks in the Southwest and California. When they began working in Santa Barbara, a local newspaper reported that the "Chinamen section hands" of the Southern Pacific Railroad had been replaced by "a gang of Mexicans." By 1900, this company had 4,500 Mexican workers. A song in Spanish told what it was like to work on the railroad:

> Some unloaded rails
>
> Others unloaded ties . . .
>
> Those who knew the work
>
> Went repairing the jack
>
> With sledge hammers and shovels,
>
> Throwing earth up the track.
>
> And others of my companions
>
> Threw out thousands of curses. (Gamio, 1930, pp. 84–85)

In this multicultural America of a dynamic economy, interethnic crisscrossings occurred. The Irish workers of the Union Pacific and the Chinese workers of the Central Pacific together built the transcontinental railroad, laying the last rails at Promontory Point, Utah, in 1869 (Roediger, 1991). A year later, Chinese immigrant laborers were transported to Massachusetts as scabs to break an Irish immigrant strike at a shoe factory; in response, the Irish recognized the need for interethnic working-class solidarity and tried to organize a Chinese lodge of the Knights of St. Crispin. After the Civil War, Mississippi planters recruited Chinese immigrants to discipline the newly freed Blacks (Caldwell, 1971). In 1903, Mexican and Japanese farm laborers went on strike together in Oxnard, California (Almaguer, 1984). Their union officers had names like Lizarras and Yamaguchi, and strike meetings were conducted in Spanish and Japanese. The Mexican strikers declared that they were standing in solidarity with their "Japanese brothers" because the two groups had toiled together in the fields and were now fighting together for a fair wage. Speaking in impassioned Yiddish during the 1909 "uprising of twenty-thousand" strikers in New York, the charismatic Clara Lemlich compared the abuse of Jewish female garment workers to the experiences of Blacks: "[The bosses] yell at the girls and 'call them down' even worse than I imagine the Negro slaves were in the South" (Sachar, 1992, p. 183).

For the different communities of this expanding diversity, America came to represent a new world where promising possibilities could be pursued and seemingly impossible achievements realized. Immigrants had made bold and dangerous crossings, pushed by political events and economic hardships in their homelands and pulled here by America's demand for labor as well as by their own hopes for a better life. A poem captured the expectations felt by Japanese newcomers:

> Day of spacious dreams!
>
> I sailed for America,
>
> Overblown with hope. (Ito, 1973, p. 20)

"By all means let me go to America," a young man in Japan begged his parents (Ito, 1973, p. 33). He had calculated that in 1 year as a laborer here he could save almost 1,000 yen—an amount equal to the income of a governor in Japan. "My dear Father," wrote an immigrant Irish girl living in New York, "Any man or woman without a family are fools that would not venture and come to this plentyful Country where no man or woman ever hungered" (Schrier, 1970, p. 24). Facing anti-Semitic persecution and violence in Russia, the cry "To America!" roared like "wild-fire" in Jewish communities (Cahan, 1960, pp. 59–61). In the shtetels, a song floated in the air:

> As the Russians, mercilessly
>
> Took revenge on us,
>
> There is a land, America,
>
> Where everyone lives free. (Slobin, 1982, p. 155)

"America was in everybody's mouth," a Jewish immigrant recalled. "Businessmen talked [about] it over their accounts; the market women made up their quarrels that they might discuss it from stall to stall; people who had relatives in the famous land went around reading their letters" (Antin, as quoted in Howe, 1983, p. 27). Similarly, for Mexican immigrants crossing the border in the early 20th century, El Norte became the stuff of fantasies:

> If only you could see how nice
>
> the United States is;
>
> that is why the Mexicans
>
> are crazy about it. (Cardoso, 1980, p. 80)

Beyond the economy and beyond the variety of cultures, race was knotted into America's most catastrophic crisis: the Civil War was fought over slavery. In his First Inaugural Address, presented on March 4, 1861, President Abraham Lincoln declared, "One section of our country believes slavery is *right* and ought to be extended, while the other believes it is *wrong* and ought not to be extended" (Adler, 1968, p. 255). Southern secession, he argued, would mean anarchy. Lincoln sternly warned the South that he had taken a solemn oath to defend and preserve the Union. Americans were one people, he explained, bound together by "the mystic chords of memory, stretching from every battlefield and patriot grave to every living heart and hearthstone all over this broad land." In the South, however, Lincoln's appeal for unity fell on deaf ears, and the war came.

Two years later, in the spring of 1863, the armed struggle was reaching a terrifying turning point. The Union Army had suffered defeats, and its soldiers were completing their terms of enlistments and returning home. "There were almost no new volunteers," wrote historian David Donald (1995, pp. 429–431). "It would be months before the new conscription act could bring in recruits." Until then, Lincoln had been reluctant to turn to Blacks as a source of military might. Frederick Douglass appealed to the President: "Let the slaves and free colored people be called into service, and formed into a liberating army, to march into the South and raise the banner of emancipation among the slaves." Lincoln realized he had no choice. In a letter to the military governor of Tennessee, he wrote, "The colored population is the great *available* and yet *unavailed* of, force for restoring the Union. The bare sight of 50,000 armed and drilled Black soldiers on the banks of the Mississippi would end the rebellion at once." Lincoln urged his generals to recruit Black men, and within months, there were 200,000 Black troops.

At Gettysburg, on November 19, 1863, Lincoln declared, "Four score and seven years ago, our fathers brought forth, upon this continent, a new nation, conceived in Liberty, and dedicated to the proposition that all men are created equal" (Adler, 1968, pp. 462–463). Lincoln had made equality a war aim, alongside the preservation of the Union. Shortly after the bloody battle at Gettysburg, Lincoln wrote a letter to an old friend, James C. Conkling: "There will be some black men who can remember that with silent tongue, and clenched teeth, and steady eye, and well-poised bayonet, they have helped mankind on to this great consummation" (p. 439). Lincoln acknowledged the military significance of the 200,000 Black soldiers: Without them, the commander in chief told his advisers, "we would be compelled to abandon the war in three weeks." These Black men in blue were making the decisive difference in determining that our "government of the people, by the people, for the people" would "not perish from the earth" (Donald, 1995, p. 327).

"DON'T BE FOOLED"

The telling of stories, such as the one about the 200,000 Black men in blue, can be healing. "Everybody remembers the first time they were taught that part of the human race was Other," observed Toni Morrison (Angelo & Morrison, 1989, p. 121). "That's a trauma. It's as though I told you that your left hand is not part of your body." Storytelling can help restore our wholeness. By writing about the people on Mango Street, Sandra Cisneros (1991, pp. 109–110) explained, "the ghost does not ache so much."

Storytelling can also lead to changes in society. "I hope this survey do a lot of good for Chinese people," an immigrant told an interviewer from Stanford University in the 1920s. "Make American people realize that Chinese people are humans. I think very few American people really know anything about Chinese" (Burnett, 1924, p. 6). After she escaped from slavery, Harriet Jacobs (1987, p. xiii) wrote in her autobiography, "[My purpose] is not to tell you what I have heard but what I have seen—and what I have suffered." What oppressed individuals like the Chinese immigrant and Jacobs were seeking was a transformation of our nation that would, as Langston Hughes (1951, p. 106) sang, "let America be America, again, where equality is in the air we breathe."

The remembering can also enable children to embrace their ethnic identities. "This story is dedicated to the descendants of Lazar and Goldie Glauberman," Jewish immigrant Minnie Miller (n.d.) wrote in her autobiography. "My history is bound up in their history and the generations that follow should know where they came from to know better who they are." Similarly, Tomo Shoji (1988), an elderly Japanese American woman, urged Asian Americans to learn more about their roots: "We got such good, fantastic stories to tell. All our stories are different." Seeking to know how they fit into America, many young people want to become listeners, eager to learn about the hardships and humiliations as well as the hopes and happiness of their parents and grandparents. They want to hear stories of the past, unwilling to remain ignorant or ashamed of their ethnic identity.

Storytelling can also enable the people of America's diversity to become the owners of their history and to challenge the Master Narrative of American history. Native American novelist Leslie Marmon Silko (1978, p. 2) cautioned,

> I will tell you something about stories.
>
> They aren't just entertainment.
>
> Don't be fooled.

History is storytelling, and we need to be careful not to be "fooled." While the study of the past seeks enlightenment, it reflects the scholar's particular perspective or view of the world. What happens when historians leave out many of America's peoples? What happens, to borrow the words of Adrienne Rich (1986, p. 199), "when someone with the authority of a teacher" describes our society, and "you are not in it"? Such an experience can be disorienting—"a moment of psychic disequilibrium, as if you looked into a mirror and saw nothing." But what should we do about our exclusion from history? Audre Lorde (as cited in Gates, 1992, p. 192) answers:

> It is a waste of time hating a mirror
>
> or its reflection
>
> instead of stopping the hand
>
> that makes glass with distortions.

To free ourselves from distortions, we have to unlearn much of what we have been taught about America's past. "To finally recognize our own invisibility," declared Mitsuye Yamada (1983, p. 40), "is to finally be on the path toward visibility."

Reflected in "a different mirror" of a more inclusive history, our visibility can empower us to discern what Melville (1969, p. 169) observed over 100 years ago: "America has been settled by the people of all nations. You can not spill the blood of an American, without spilling the blood of the whole world. We are not a narrow tribe." This truth has been the transcendent theme of our history. Like the Palolo Valley community of my childhood, America is a nation peopled by the world.

In the new century, the changing colors of our society are compelling us as educators and scholars in the field of child development to recognize and practice multiculturalism as a cornerstone of our identity and our being. We can no longer say, "It's not our fault."

REFERENCES

Adler, M. J. (Ed.). (1968). *The annals of America* (Vol. 9, The Crisis of the Union). Chicago: Encyclopedia Britannica.

Aller, C. (1958). *The evolution of Hawaiian labor relations.* Unpublished doctoral dissertation, Harvard University, Boston.

Almaguer, T. (1984). Racial domination and class conflict in capitalist agriculture: The Oxnard sugar beet workers' strike of 1903. *Labor History, 25*(3), 334–347.

Angelo, B., & Morrison, T. (1989, May 22). The pain of being Black. *Time Magazine, 133*(21), 121.

Burnett, C. H. (1924, July 5). *Social document of Pany Lowe* (Survey of Race Relations Box No. 28–242, Major Documents, 1905–1926). Palo Alto, CA: Hoover Institution Archives, Stanford University.

Cahan, A. (1960). *The rise of David Levinsky.* New York: Harper. (Original work published 1917)

Caldwell, D. (1971). The negroization of the Chinese stereotype in California. *Southern California Quarterly, 33,* 123–131.

Cardoso, L. A. (1980). *Mexican emigration to the United States, 1897–1931.* Tucson: University of Arizona Press.

Cisneros, S. (1991). *The house on Mango Street.* New York: Vintage.

Commissioner of Labor on Hawaii. (1910). *The higher wage question.* Washington, DC: Bureau of Labor Statistics.

Donald, D. (1995). *Lincoln.* New York: Simon and Schuster.

Ethnic Studies Oral History Project. (1977). *Waialua and Haleiwa* (Vol. 9). Honolulu: University of Hawaii at Manoa.

Ethnic Studies Oral History Project. (1981). *Uchinanchu.* Honolulu: University of Hawaii at Manoa.

Fairfield, G. H. (1895). *Report of the Labor Commission on strikes and arbitration.* Honolulu: Government Printing Office.

Felipe, V. (1972). *Hawaii: A Pilipino dream.* Unpublished master's thesis, University of Hawaii.

Gamio, M. (1930). *Mexican immigration to the United States.* Chicago: University of Chicago Press.

Gates, H. L., Jr. (1992). *Loose canons: Notes on the culture wars.* New York: Oxford University Press.

Grossman, J. R. (1989). *Land of hope: Chicago, Black sojourners, and the great migration.* Chicago: University of Chicago Press.

Grove Farm Plantation Records. (1908, May 5). [Letter from H. Hackfield and Company to G. N. Wilcox]. Lihue, HI: Grove Farm Plantation.

Hawaii Laborers' Association. (1920). *Facts about the strike.* Honolulu: Author.

Howe, I. (1983). *World of our fathers.* New York: Simon and Schuster.

Hughes, L. (1951). Let America be America again. In L. Hughes & A. Bontemps (Eds.), *The poetry of the Negro, 1746–1949.* Garden City, NY: Doubleday.

Ito, K. (1973). *Issei.* Seattle, WA: Executive Committee for Publication of Issei.

Jacobs, H. A. (1987). *Incidents in the life of a slave girl.* Cambridge, MA: Harvard University Press. (Original work published 1857)

Laupahoehoe Plantation Records. (1890, July 2). [Letter from Theo. H. Davies and Company to C. McClennan, microfilm]. Honolulu: University of Hawaii Library.

Melville, H. (1969). *Redburn.* Chicago: Northwestern University Press. (Original work published 1849)

Miller, M. (n.d.). [Autobiography]. Unpublished manuscript.

Morrison, T. (1992). *Playing in the dark: Whiteness in the literary imagination.* Cambridge, MA: Harvard University Press.

Rich, A. (1986). *Blood, bread, and poetry: Selected prose, 1979–1985.* New York: W. W. Norton.

Roediger, D. R. (1991). *The wages of whiteness: Race and the making of the American working class.* London: Verso Books.

Sachar, H. M. (1992). *A history of the Jews in America.* New York: Knopf.

Schrier, A. (1970). *Ireland and the American emigration, 1850–1900.* New York: Russell and Russell.

Shoji, T. (1988, March 4). [Presentation]. Ohana Cultural Center, Oakland, CA.

Silko, L. M. (1978). *Ceremony.* New York: New American Library.

Slobin, M. (1982). *Tenement songs: The popular music of the Jewish immigrants.* Urbana: University of Illinois Press.

Smith, W. C. (1937). *Americans in the making.* Ann Arbor: University of Michigan.

Takaki, R. (1979). *Iron cages: Race and culture in 19th century America.* New York: Oxford University Press.

Takaki, R. (1983). *Pau hana: Plantation life and labor in Hawaii.* Honolulu: University of Hawaii Press.

Takaki, R. (1989). *Strangers from a different shore: A history of Asian Americans.* Boston: Little, Brown and Company.

Takaki, R. (1993). *A different mirror: A history of multicultural America.* New York: Little, Brown and Company.

Takaki, R. (1998). *A larger memory: A history of diversity, with voices.* New York: Little, Brown and Company.

Takaki, R. (2000). *Double victory: A multicultural history of America in World War II.* New York: Little, Brown and Company.

The five o'clock whistle. (1910, April 27). *Kohala Midget,* p. 1.

Tsutsumi, T. (1922). *History of Hawaii laborers' movement.* Honolulu: University of Hawaii Archives.

Whitman, W. (1958). *Leaves of grass.* New York: New American Library.

Wittke, C. (1956). *The Irish in America.* Baton Rouge: Louisiana State University Press.

Yamada, M. (1983). Invisibility is an unnatural disaster: Reflections of an Asian American woman. In C. Moraga & G. Anzaldua (Eds.), *This bridge called my back: Writings by radical women of color* (pp. 35–40). New York: Kitchen Table/Women of Color Press.

CHAPTER 2

Children and the Principles of Learning

Implications for Multicultural Development

MESHA L. ELLIS

Multiculturalism has received a great deal of attention over the past 15 to 20 years. Many have advocated that true inclusion and multiculturalism cannot occur if the traditions, perspectives, and voices of nonmainstream and/or non-Western communities are not heard, appreciated, or incorporated within mainstream society's value system. Although a general consensus among social scientists exists that globalization requires a more authentic valuing and understanding of diverse perspectives, very little attention has been paid to the mechanisms by which a multicultural perspective is developed.

With the progressive trends in globalization, it is crucial that our nation's youth be able to fully interact with individuals from diverse backgrounds. Multiculturalism facilitates this process. Development of a multicultural perspective, hence, is the mechanism by which an acknowledgement of diversity is transformed into an ideological process that fully extends substantive inclusion of multiple cultural perspectives into a society. This chapter explores the cultural basis of knowledge acquisition and introduces a model to explain the process by which a multicultural worldview can be developed. The current chapter will consequently survey developmental factors (i.e., biological, psychological, and environmental) that facilitate childhood knowledge acquisition.

A DEVELOPMENTAL PERSPECTIVE OF LEARNING

Development is a process by which systematic changes occur within an individual over the course of the life cycle. The developmental process is additionally marked by characteristics (e.g., biological sex, some physical features, preferences) that remain constant across the lifespan. Although learning and development share a number of common underlying mechanisms, they are not the same. Learning promotes development and refers to changes in behavior that simultaneously result from experiences and practices (Rogoff, 1990). Exploring learning and knowledge acquisition from a developmental perspective requires a purposeful incorporation of both individual and contextual factors. This is highlighted because it is nearly impossible to divorce human development as well as the process of learning from the social, historical, and cultural contexts in which they occur (Bailey & Pransky, 2005; Wertsch, 1991). Weisner (2002) explains that cultural communities create developmental pathways that are shaped by community-specific learning opportunities that are provided through daily routines and activities. Weisner adds that it is through daily routines and cultural activities that children learn community values and goals that ultimately influence interactional styles, attachment patterns, conceptions of self, gender roles, and modes of relating to the larger environment.

Human learning occurs as the result of the interplay among biological maturation, psychological processes, and environmental context (Keller & Greenfield, 2000). Although many theoretical conceptualizations contribute to our understanding of human development and learning, the sociohistorical tradition founded by Vygotsky (1968/1988) comprehensively addresses the multi-influenced nature of cognitive development and provides a substantive foundation on which to base an exploration of childhood learning and worldview development. According to the sociohistorical perspective, "social, historical, and cultural circumstances help shape a person's view of the world and give rise to the ways of functioning within that world" (Sanchez, 1999, p. 352).

One of the primary strengths of the sociohistorical approach is that it incorporates environmental factors such as historical influence, cultural context, and social interaction in its conceptualization of cognitive development. This perspective holistically reflects the reality in which learning and development occur. Viewing children's actions as embedded in social context, cognitive growth is conceptualized as being constructed through cultural practices and is regarded as a social activity (Gauvain, 2005; Greenfield, Maynard, & Childs, 2000). The emphasis within the sociohistorical conceptualization of development resides in the social constructive nature of learning and cognitive development. Within this conceptualization, historical processes function to impact and direct cultural activities, making cognitive development a situation-specific endeavor. Because learning is embedded within environmental context, it is facilitated through apprenticeship or guided participation in social experience and represents a transformation of one's role and involvement in cultural activities and cultural creation (Rogoff, 1990; Rogoff, Paradise, Arauz, Correa-Chávez, & Angelillo, 2003; Tomasello, Carpenter, Call, Behne, & Moll, 2005).

Principles of Learning

Within the sociohistorical approach, a distinction is made between higher and lower mental functions. Lower, or elementary, mental functions are conceptualized as natural mental abilities that are involuntary and genetically inherited (Wertsch, 1991). Lower mental functions relate to primary biological functions that form a foundation for higher mental functions. Higher mental functions, conversely, facilitate the development of complex intellectual activities (e.g., voluntary attention, logical memory, concept formation) and incorporate the use of symbols (i.e., cultural tools) (Wertsch, 1991). Higher mental functions develop through social interaction and are socially and/or culturally mediated. Higher mental functions, then, are conceptualized to consist "of a variety of cognitive skills, each independently acquired in socially organized activities, forever tied to the contexts in which they develop" (Guberman & Greenfield, 1991, p. 240). Thus, learning serves as the mechanism by which cognitive processes move from the level of lower mental functioning to higher mental abilities.

Learning transpires through a variety of modalities (e.g., visual, auditory, kinesthetic, mixed) and follows irregular paths. Research suggests certain forms of learning occur via the same pathway regardless of age (e.g., Chen & Siegler, 2000; Kuhn, Garcia-Mila, Zohar, & Andersen, 1995; Siegler & Chen, 1998), whereas other styles of learning arise from multiple pathways that change over time (Spencer, Vereijken, Diedrich, & Thelen, 2000). The process of learning involves progress, inconsistent patterns of generalization, regressions, and momentary transitional approaches, as well as qualitative and quantitative changes (Amso & Casey, 2006; Schauble, 1996; Siegler, 2005). Learning is dependent on prior knowledge and appears to be most productive when the constraints of tasks are clearly known and when learners are encouraged to seek causal understanding of phenomena (Hausfather, 1996; Siegler, 2005).

Learning strategies allow children to encode, recall, and process information. The strategies used by children vary with age and experience. Research suggests that children not only use both active and passive learning strategies to solve novel problems, but they contemplate and adjust their strategies based on previous experiences, reflection, or the environmental feedback they receive, whether the feedback is provided by a mentor or from the success or failure of solving the task itself (Shrager & Siegler, 1998; Siegler, 2005; Siegler & Araya, 2005). The learning endeavor is impacted by factors that are both internal and external to the learner.

Rogoff (1995) suggests that development occurs on three planes: personal, interpersonal, and institutional. The personal plane involves both biological and psychological processes that influence learning and development. The interpersonal plane includes the tools used by cultures (e.g., communication patterns and interaction modes/assumptions) to set the rules of engagement for interpersonal interactions with family members, peers, teachers, and community members. The institutional plane is composed of the larger societal factors that provide a context for the individual (e.g., societal rules, nationalistic identities, shared history, societal customs and beliefs). A discussion of learning and development cannot be regarded as comprehensive if the contributions provided by each of these planes of existence are not considered (Rueda, Gallego, & Moll, 2000). Consequently, personal, interpersonal, and institutional contributions to learning and development will now be evaluated in light of their contribution to worldview development.

THE PERSONAL PLANE: BIOLOGICAL FOUNDATIONS OF LEARNING

Infants enter the world biologically prepared to learn (Carey & Gelman, 1991). Tomasello, Carpenter, Call, Behne, and Moll (2005) suggest that humans are the only species biologically adapted to create shared goals and participate in coordinated action plans. These species-specific accomplishments could not occur if it were not for the motivation humans possess to interact with others (Tomasello et al., 2005). This motivation serves an evolutionary function to help maintain infant life through contact with caregivers. In fact, from their time of birth, infants are equipped with an inherent inclination for relating to others. Because voices (DeCasper

& Fifer, 1980) and faces (Keller & Greenfield, 2000; Nelson, 2001) are among the first stimuli to capture a newborn's attention, caregivers begin introducing their offspring to the world by capitalizing on these modes of interest. The biologically based proclivity to interact with others not only increases the probability for infant survival but also forms one of the many biological building blocks of learning. Biological building blocks of learning consist of inherited genetic instructions, biologically programmed processes, and inherent preferences that, inevitably, when contextually influenced, promote learning and cognitive development.

Biological Building Blocks

Biological processes, at a basic level, provide the foundation upon which lower mental functions (i.e., rudimentary cognitive processes) operate. The ability to learn, maintain cognitive control, and engage in goal-directed behavior is a function of neural processes that lie at the center of brain development (Brown, Zoccoli, & Leahy, 2005; Thomas et al., 2004). Impressive advances observed in cognition (e.g., sensation, schema creation, perceptual development, coordination of memory processes) and in the control of actions (e.g., visual tracking, motor skill development) throughout childhood occur as a result of the formation of neural pathways (Sigelman & Rider, 2006). Neural pathways provide the means by which the processing, incorporation, and reliance on sensory information facilitate learning and cognitive development. Neural pathways are strengthened by repeated use. Cortical changes as a result of neural development appear to be associated with learning (Amso, Davidson, Johnson, Glover, & Casey, 2005; Epstein, 1980). Thus, changes in brain organization correspond to the refinement of specialized brain regions and enhancement of memory structures and processes, as well as programmed neuronal anatomical modifications (Kagan, 2003). Amso and Casey (2006) explain that "development and learning correspond to a fine-tuning of neural systems with enhanced recruitment of task-relevant regions and suppression of less task-relevant regions" (p. 28).

The sights, sounds, smells, tastes, tactile sensations, and kinesthetic experiences to which infants are exposed shape the formation of unique neural pathways (Amso & Casey, 2006). Whether the sensory experiences are provided by caregivers or individually sought out by infants, processing of sensory information is facilitated through neural pathways that link sensory input with memory structures. As a result of the associations made between sensory input and memory structures, the brain facilitates a process by which cognitive representations of events, called schemata, are created (Kagan, 2003). Schemata are organizational structures that allow for the categorization of information. Perception is a cognitive process highly reliant upon context that involves the selection, organization, and interpretation of perceptual schemata (Kagan, 2003; Mandler, 2004; Sigelman & Rider, 2006). Advances in working memory and retrieval strategies provide the apparatus on which basic perception relies. It is through perception that meaningful objects and events are recognized.

With the array of the sources of information provided through sensory, motor, and perceptual experiences, infants use schemata to construct categories to assist them in learning and interpreting their world (Mandler, 2004; Newman & Newman, 2006). It has long been argued that infants develop categories on multiple levels and that the process of developing categories occurs throughout infancy. Perceptual categories represent a basic cognitive ability that assesses perceptual similarity. According to Mandler, perceptual categories are formed through procedural learning and allow infants to recognize and identify objects.

Procedural learning relies on the acquisition of rules, is automatic, and is not under the conscious awareness of the learner (Thomas et al., 2004). This form of learning is promoted through extended practice and exposure. Mandler highlights that, like procedural learning upon which they are based, perceptual categories are created outside of the control and awareness of infants.

Conceptual categories, on the other hand, evaluate class membership, distinguish kinds, and tend to develop more slowly than perceptual categories as they are informed by experience and cognitive maturation. Conceptual categories allow for the recall of information as well as "making inductive generalizations" (Mandler, 2004, p. 22). Mandler proposes that conceptual categories are created through the use of declarative learning. The intentional nature of declarative learning requires a more sophisticated level of cognitive processing than does procedural learning. Declarative learning occurs rapidly and involves the acquisition of factual knowledge. Early in infancy, conceptual categories appear to contain fewer details than perceptual categories.

The psychological tools and culturally mediated frames of reference available to infants significantly influence the perceptual and conceptual categories initially created. These categories, refined through experience, physical development, and cognitive advances, become more sophisticated with age. In a series of studies conducted in the 1960s, Segall, Campbell, and Herskovits (1966), while evaluating culturally distinct influences of illusions, demonstrated that cultural differences in visual perception were a function of the availability and familiarity of specific environmental experiences. In a review of research conducted to evaluate perceptual preferences in African American and Indian American children, Shade (1989) found that the cultural frame in which perceptual experiences occur impact higher-order cognitive processes and influence the types of learning strategies children select as well as the amount of cognitive engagement (i.e., mental effort) they dedicate to solving problems. Shade's research suggests that the biological mechanisms that underlie higher cognitive processes such as joint attention, language development, concept formation, and theory of mind do not operate outside of the influence of cultural context. In fact, the meanings infants and children ascribe to perceptual and conceptual categories are created, shaped, and refined through everyday experiences with caregivers.

THE PERSONAL PLANE: PSYCHOLOGICAL FOUNDATIONS OF LEARNING

Although the learning endeavor would be insurmountable were it not for the foundation provided by biological development, complex thinking and learning activities would not occur without higher-order psychological processes. Biological and psychological processes are complementary (Kagan, 2003) and provide learners with the means to engage in worldview development. Psychological processes rely and build upon the foundation provided by biological building blocks to promote the development of higher mental abilities. This next section will highlight a few of the psychological processes that serve to provide support for learning across childhood.

Attention

The ability to selectively focus provides a foundation for learning experiences as it facilitates the encoding of information into memory systems. Attending to sensory stimuli provides the mechanism by which basic perception occurs. At advanced levels, attention provides the means to support the learning needed to function within one's larger society. Sustained attention facilitates the ability to persist on tasks and ultimately leads to advances in the strategies used to increase the efficiency of memory and learning processes. Through sustained attention, nuances about the environment, interactions with others, and knowledge about self are more readily understood. Attention processes, like all other cognitive processes, are shaped by evolutionary, environmental, and cultural factors. The learning opportunities available to members of a given society affect how attention and learning develop, as what is attended to inevitably shapes one's conception of reality.

Joint attention has been heralded as the cornerstone of psychological development because of the role it plays in facilitating the social cognitive development of infants and children (Mundy & Acra, 2006). Infants become social beings through joint attention, as it contributes to the development of an understanding of "others as intentional beings" (Goswami, 2006, p. 545). It is through joint attention and social engagement that infants gain access to the available cultural tools that shape not only learning opportunities but also cognitive development (Goswami, 2006). Joint attention integrates the use of objects with social exchanges. It involves coordinating attention with social partners (Mundy, Card, & Fox, 2000). Social partners, in collaboration with infants, shape, follow, and direct attention to promote learning opportunities.

Joint attention plays a crucial role in learning through pretend play with partners (Tomasello, 1995). Young children have been noted to make tremendous advances in pretend play when the play occurs with social partners when compared to solitary pretend play. Joint attention skills also contribute significantly to language acquisition and development (Baldwin, 1993; Mundy & Gomes, 1998; Paterson, Heim, Friedman, Choudhury, & Benasich, 2006). The social exchanges facilitated through joint attention help infants understand the nuances of spoken language, experiment with communication modalities, and gain exposure to concepts that were previously outside of awareness.

Language

In interactions with others, language serves as a bridge between knowledge and understanding. Words create the base upon which experiences are not only defined but shaped. While most infants become effective communicators, a number of psychological and biological processes are at work to support language production, comprehension, and utilization (Sirois, Buckingham, & Shultz, 2000). For example, language relies on the coordination of linguistic, cognitive, and social skills (Im-Bolter, Johnson, & Pascual-Leone, 2006). Attention, visual, and auditory processing, as well as memory resources, also influence the effective use of language (Im-Bolter et al., 2006). Language is not developed in isolation, for it is through context that children learn how to use words and determine "the role that mental terms play in various circumstances" (Astington & Peskin, 2004, p. 65). Ultimately, language provides a powerful medium that promotes higher mental abilities. Language affords the means by which self-awareness moves from a sensory level to a cognitive level.

Language is the primary psychological tool that mediates thoughts, feelings, behavior, and cognitive development (Wertsch, 1991). Even advanced categorization schemes emerge through the use of language. Although language is initially used as a means of communication, over time its internalization becomes a means by which thinking and voluntary activity control occurs to promote cognitive advances such as concept formation. Astington and Peskin (2004) explain that "language both structures the concepts and provides the medium in which such structures can be conveyed" (p. 67). It is through language that cultural values and abstract concepts are learned and become available for consideration (Hoffman, 1989; Nelson, 1996; Sellami, 2000). Culturally specific naming practices direct infant attention to salient details, processes, and categorization schemes to influence conceptual development (Mandler, 2004). Consequently, one's concept of reality rests upon the perceptual, behavioral, and experiential framework provided by language.

Concept Formation

The ability to create meaning systems based on categorical associations among sensations, memories, ideas, and experiences develops throughout infancy and childhood. This ability is called *concept formation.* Concept formation, like categorization creation, requires the utilization of abstract rules and is dependent on both active engagement and environmental experience (Astington & Peskin, 2004). Conceptual formation enhances the learning endeavor by creating generalization strategies that increase the efficiency of problem solving, abstract reasoning, understanding of language, language utilization, and creativity. It is through concept formation that infants learn to form interpretations of what they experience as well as what they see others experience (Mandler, 2004).

Guberman and Greenfield (1991) suggest that concepts can be formed, expanded, or refined through a process called conceptual transfer, in which a concept from one area is applied and used to facilitate understanding in a new area. Conceptual transfer occurs laterally when an infant or child spontaneously and flexibly applies preexisting concepts to new areas with similar features. Conceptual transfer also occurs vertically when infants and children learn to apply preexisting concepts to new areas with assistance from a parent, teacher, or more knowledgeable partner. Concept formation begins to develop quite early during infancy and contributes to an eventual appreciation for a number of mental states such as desire, belief, and intention.

Facility with abstract concepts such as mental states provides an avenue for great advances in cognitive development, interpersonal learning, and worldview development. Initially, experiential knowledge provides the basis on which rudimentary concepts are formed (Astington & Peskin, 2004). Rudimentary concepts not only provide a means by which awareness of one's own feelings, intentions, and abilities is developed, but rudimentary concepts also provide infants with a capacity to begin to infer intentions and feelings to others (Kagan, 2003). With time, language and social interaction play pivotal roles in expanding rudimentary concepts to more sophisticated analogues.

Theory of Mind

Children gain insight into and speculate about the intentions of others by using information acquired through concept formation. Tomasello et al. (2005) suggest that discerning and generating hypotheses about the intentions of others is one of the most important skills children learn because it provides a means to interpret the actions of others. Coull, Leekam, and Bennett (2006) explain that the development of social interaction skills, emotional understanding, and communication rests on children's ability to create theories about their own mental states as well as the mental states of others. This ability has been termed *theory of mind* (Premack & Woodruff, 1978). Theory of mind lies behind one's ability to predict and/or explain the behaviors of others (Kail & Cavanaugh, 2000; Zahavi & Parnas, 2003). Theory of mind, accordingly, sets the stage for the view of human nature one ultimately develops.

While theory of mind appears to develop as a function of the learning opportunities provided by parents, family members, teachers, and more knowledgeable partners, it influences what is learned as well as the methods used to learn (Lucariello, 2004). Theory of mind, thus, contributes significantly to cognitive development as it provides a means by which cultural understandings of worldview are transmitted, interpreted, and advanced. Theory of mind provides a culturally imparted context to understand the behaviors of others. The degree to which one is able to engage in new and advanced modes of thinking lies in direct proportion to his or her conceptual understanding. The process by which theory of mind develops is largely influenced by the learning opportunities and conceptual supports provided within one's cultural frame of reference. Guberman and Greenfield (1991) highlight that cognitive processes and learning strategies do not occur outside the context of socioculturally influenced practices. That is, socialization practices transmitted through interpersonal relationships greatly influence the type and process by which theory of mind is developed.

THE INTERPERSONAL PLANE: CONTEXTUAL FOUNDATIONS OF LEARNING

"One reason that infants may develop psychological understanding relatively early in life is that their caretakers treat them as social partners" (Goswami, 2006, p. 545). In fact, infants and children are often expected to participate in cultural activities, understand cultural modes of communication, and adopt cultural mores well before the meanings and intentions of these activities are understood (Gauvain, 2005). Infants learn to express and read emotions through back-and-forth interactions with caregivers, a process referred to as synchrony. Through synchrony, infants begin to develop the basic skills of social interaction and self-control, as well as symbolic play and language (Feldman & Greenbaum, 1997). The cultural values, roles, rules, and beliefs caregivers hold heavily influence their interactions and socialization practices with offspring (Barrera & Corso, 2002; Keller & Greenfield, 2000). Parental conceptions of obedience, cooperation, aggression, dependence, independence, and so forth, help to shape the social development, theory of mind, and cognitive processing displayed by their offspring. The organization of learning processes provided by caregivers flows from the cultural frame out of which they emerge (McKeon, 1994; Rogoff, 2003).

According to the sociohistorical perspective, a zone of proximal development exists for all humans at every skill level. The zone of proximal development is the range of ability, skills, or knowledge that are within the potential of a learner but are not yet mastered (Guberman & Greenfield, 1991). Mastery is obtained in the zone of proximal development through social interaction with willing mentors who teach more inexperienced group members how to use the psychological tools available to them. Psychological tools are the cultural artifacts that mediate a learner's thoughts, behaviors, and feelings and ultimately socialize one's progress through culturally specific developmental pathways (Greenfield, Keller, Fuligni, & Maynard, 2003). Examples of psychological tools include counting systems, mnemonic devices, maps, diagrams, art, writing, language, and learning strategies. Cognitive development transpires as a result of mastery and incorporation of psychological tools.

Mentors can take many forms (e.g., parents, teachers, siblings, peers) and always represent a more experienced learner or teacher who, during the mentoring process, continuously assesses and adjusts the task at hand to a range that is within the less experienced learner's ability (Dasen, 2005). The mentoring process is frequently referred to as scaffolding. A mentor provides a scaffold by structuring participation in learning encounters for the purpose of fostering the development of a learner's emerging capabilities. "By solving the task under the guidance of more knowledgeable partners, learners restructure their task definition in accord with that provided by the tutor" and coconstruct, along with the mentor, the learning experience (Guberman & Greenfield, 1991, p. 250).

The psychological tools transmitted to children to promote cognitive development occur via formal and informal learning experiences. Formal educational experiences tend to be hierarchical and organized, and occur in structured educational settings such as schools. Formal learning experiences, in general, are compulsory and curriculum driven. The environments in which formal learning experiences occur tend to rely on the transmission of subject matter by an expert. Formal learning experiences contribute to cognitive development through purposeful transmission of psychological tools through lectures, activities, and exercises.

Informal learning experiences, on the other hand, occur within the context of everyday activities. Informal learning experiences are dynamic in nature and tend to rely on the active participation of learners. These activities may not be recognized as those that promote "learning" by the learner because the educational experiences tend to be facilitated in everyday modes of information transmission (e.g., communication with parents/relatives/peers, video games, television, computers, books, magazines, work groups). Informal educational experiences may occur unintentionally, as they are frequently not organized in a manner where information is presented in systematic ways (Fobih, 1986). Although informal learning experiences may occur within formal classroom settings, they tend to arise out of the interests and activities of the learner that frequently are associated with the acquisition of the skills, knowledge, and psychological tools that make everyday life possible. Informal learning experiences have been found to substantially contribute to cognitive development. For example, in a sample of 57 fifth-, seventh-, and ninth-grade students, McClurg and Chaillé (1987) found that video games requiring the use of spatial skills improved student scores on a spatial ability measure regardless of grade level or sex.

Another powerful mode of informal education occurs through observing and listening-in on community undertakings with the ultimate goal of eventually collaborating by assisting in shared activities (Rogoff et al., 2003). This form of learning has been termed intent participation (Rogoff et al., 2003). It is through intent participation that children learn syntax rules, how to communicate (Akhtar, Jipson, & Callanan, 2001), the rules of games, and categorization schemes (Rogoff et al., 2003). In all, informal learning experiences frequently cannot occur without the assistance of others. That is, informal learning is most often facilitated through mentoring relationships that provide the means by which everyday skills, knowledge, and psychological tools are acquired within each child's zone of proximal development.

THE INSTITUTIONAL PLANE: SOCIETAL FOUNDATIONS OF LEARNING

Ethnicity, regional affiliation, and societal institutions (e.g., churches, schools, government, courts) provide powerful contexts for learning and worldview development. Each of these and the subcultures they possess mold parenting practices, formal educational goals and experiences, media experiences, religious experiences, occupational opportunities, values, beliefs, and interactional patterns. All of these cultural communities help children understand themselves, themselves in relation to others, and themselves in relation to the larger society. Greenfield et al. (2003) highlight that the developmental pathways and learning opportunities available to children are constrained by the existing social structures that are subject to both economic and environmental conditions.

Formal education has been described as one of the major socializing agents for children. Bailey and Pransky (2005) suggest that "education serves to orient children to distinct worldviews consistent with the unique goals, histories, and material realities of those cultural entities" (p. 20). Aikenhead (1997) explains that ideologically neutral teaching strategies do not exist and that the learning experiences provided through formal education expose children to culturally embedded instruction where teachers, in many ways, serve as culture brokers (Jegede & Aikenhead, 1999). It is argued that because students enter the academic environment with preexisting cultural frames, they must engage in a process of cultural border crossing when confronted with academic material (Aikenhead & Jegede, 1999).

The thesis behind cultural border crossing assumes that each academic subject taught in schools has a subculture of its own. This assumption is based on the premise that each course of study promotes subject-specific values, norms, expectations, beliefs, and conceptions of the world (Krogh & Thomsen, 2005). Jegede and Aikenhead (1999) maintain that the academic endeavor is a cross-cultural experience that requires students to manage and negotiate multiple cultural contexts daily. Rogoff (1995) highlights that the cultural contexts to which children are exposed can be complementary, overlap, or conflict with one another. Children's preexisting learning and coping strategies contribute significantly to their ability to cross cultural borders. The facility with which children are able to learn (i.e., cross cultural borders) within the academic environment is also highly dependent on whether or not the values, customs, and belief systems inherent in the subject-specific cultural communities are consistent with, complement, and/or respect those brought from the student's home cultural community (Lee, 2002). Likewise, the facility with which children are able to develop worldviews that incorporate multiculturalism will be dependent on the skill mentors demonstrate in teaching and providing learning opportunities that not only introduce new forms of cultural thinking but reinforce, acknowledge, and respect the ways of knowing indigenous to each student's cultural frame.

CONCLUSION: WORLDVIEW DEVELOPMENT AND MULTICULTURAL PERSPECTIVES

The process by which a worldview is developed is complex and multi-influenced, and occurs across the span of the life cycle. Humans, by nature, seek to understand their surroundings. As such, comprehensive yet personal conceptualizations of life, the world, and the relationship one holds with the larger environment have been created, adapted, and transmitted by various cultural groups. Strongly influenced by culture, worldview consists of the beliefs and assumptions one holds about the world. These beliefs and assumptions inevitably influence the goals, behaviors, problem-solving methods, conflict resolution activities, and decision-making processes that shape interactions and practices within the larger environment (Ibrahim, 1991). Sue (1978) highlighted that the perceived relationship one develops with nature, institutions, people, and objects is a function of worldview.

The process of worldview development is a function of internalization of the information learned through mentored learning experiences and historical context. A child's biological predisposition interacts with his or her psychological processes to influence how the information provided through social and cultural interaction is absorbed, internalized, and acted on. Within the present historical context, learning experiences have been supplemented by various technological advances that have facilitated exposure to "other" ways of knowing and a diverse array of mentors. Within the United States of America, not only do parents, teachers, and peers serve as mentors, but entertainers, politicians, and journalists provide models for societally constrained "acceptable" behavior and discourse.

The present historical context necessitates that we, as potential socializing agents, engage in a thoughtful consideration of the means by which we can help children develop worldviews that incorporate a multicultural perspective. It is within the current context that globalization has dismantled the boundaries that once contributed to an ethos of egocentrism. Children are confronted with multiple cultural contexts on a daily basis. No longer are homogeneous neighborhoods, schools, churches, and families the norm. As our country becomes more diverse, it is imperative that shifts occur in the socialization practices used to ready children for successful incorporation in the larger society. Because cultural processes are socially negotiated, interactive, cumulative, internal to group members (Greenfield et al., 2003), and evolve as cultures and value systems change over time (Greenfield et al., 2000), children in consort with socializing agents have an opportunity to actively correspond to the changing historical, economic, and environmental demands.

Helping youth develop a worldview that incorporates and acknowledges multiculturalism is linked to the processes by which cultural learning occurs. Cultural learning flows from the culturally specific transmission methods utilized to teach and forward information to future generations of cultural group members. Learning and, in particular, cultural learning lies at the crux and forms the foundation upon which the development of a multicultural perspective, that is, a worldview that incorporates multiculturalism, is based.

REFERENCES

Aikenhead, G. S. (1997).Toward a First Nations cross-cultural science and technology curriculum. *Science Education, 81,* 217–238.

Aikenhead, G. S., & Jegede, O. J. (1999). Cross-cultural science education: A cognitive explanation of a cultural phenomenon. *Journal of Research in Science Teaching, 36*(2), 269–287.

Akhtar, N., Jipson, J., & Callanan, M. A. (2001). Learning words through overhearing. *Child Development, 72*(2), 416–430.

Amso, D., & Casey, B. J. (2006). Beyond what develops when: Neuroimaging may inform how cognition changes with development. *Current Directions in Psychological Science, 15*(1), 24–29.

Amso, D., Davidson, M. C., Johnson, S. P., Glover, G., & Casey, B. J. (2005). Contributions of the hippocampus and the striatum to simple association and frequency-based learning. *Neuroimage, 27,* 291–298.

Astington, J. W., & Peskin, J. (2004). Meaning and use: Children's acquisition of the mental lexicon. In J. M. Lucariello, J. A. Hudson, R. Fivush, & P. J. Bauer (Eds.), *The development of the mediated mind: Sociocultural context and cognitive development* (pp. 59–78). Mahwah, NJ: Lawrence Erlbaum.

Bailey, F., & Pransky, K. (2005). Are "other people's children" constructivist learners too? *Theory Into Practice, 44*(1), 19–26.

Baldwin, D. A. (1993). Early referential understanding: Infants' ability to recognize referential acts for what they are. *Developmental Psychology, 29*(5), 832–843.

Barrera, I., & Corso, R. M. (2002). Cultural competency as skilled dialogue. *Topics in Early Childhood Special Education, 22*(2), 103–113.

Brown, A. S., Zoccoli, S. L., & Leahy, M. M. (2005). Cumulating retrieval inhibition in semantic and lexical domains. *Journal of Experimental Psychology: Learning, Memory, and Cognition, 31*(3), 496–507.

Carey, S., & Gelman, R. (1991). *The epigenesis of mind: Essays on biology and cognition.* Hillsdale, NJ: Lawrence Erlbaum.

Chen, Z., & Siegler, R. S. (2000). Intellectual development in childhood. In R. J. Sternberg (Ed.), *Handbook of intelligence* (pp. 92–116). New York: Cambridge University Press.

Coull, G. J., Leekam, S. R., & Bennett, M. (2006). Simplifying second-order belief attribution: What facilitates children's performance on measures of conceptual understanding? *Social Development, 15*(2), 260–275.

Dasen, P. R. (2005). Socio-historical change and cognitive development. *Human Development, 48*(6), 371–375.

DeCasper, A., & Fifer, W. (1980). Of human bonding: Newborns prefer their mothers' voices. *Science, 208*, 1174–1176.

Epstein, H. T. (1980). Some biological bases of cognitive development. *Bulletin of the Orton Society, 30*, 46–62.

Feldman, R., & Greenbaum, C. W. (1997). Affect regulation in mother-infant play as precursors to the development of symbolic competence. *Infant Mental Health Journal, 18*(1), 4–23.

Fobih, D. K. (1986). The influence of different educational experiences on classificatory behavior of some Ghanaian children. *Nigerian Journal of Guidance and Counseling,* 2(2), 82–94.

Gauvain, M. (2005). Sociocultural contexts of learning. In A. E. Maynard & M. I. Martini (Eds.), *Learning in cultural context: Family, peers, and school* (pp. 11–40). New York: Kluwer Academic/Plenum.

Goswami, U. (2006). Developmental science review: The foundations of psychological understanding. *Developmental Science* 9(6), 545–550.

Greenfield, P. M., Keller, H., Fuligni, A., & Maynard, A. (2003). Cultural pathways through universal development. *Annual Review of Psychology, 54*, 461–490.

Greenfield, P. M., Maynard, A. E., & Childs, C. P. (2000). History, culture, learning, and development. *The Journal of Comparative Social Science, 34*(4), 351–374.

Guberman, S. R., & Greenfield, P. M. (1991). Learning and transfer in everyday cognition. *Cognitive Development,* 6(3), 233–260.

Hausfather, S. J. (1996). Vygotsky and schooling: Creating a social context for learning. *Action in Teacher Education, 18,* 1–10. Retrieved August 12, 2006, from http://chd.gse.gmu.edu/immersion/knowledgebase/theorists/constructivism/vygotsky.htm

Hoffman, D. (1989). Language and culture acquisition among Iranians in the United States. *Anthropology and Education Quarterly, 20*(2), 118–132.

Ibrahim, F. A. (1991). Contribution of cultural worldview to generic counseling and development. *Journal of Counseling & Development, 70*(1), 13–19.

Im-Bolter, N., Johnson, J., & Pascual-Leone, J. (2006). Processing limitations in children with specific language impairment: The role of executive function. *Child Development, 77*(6), 1822–1841.

Jegede, O. J., & Aikenhead, G. S. (1999). Transcending cultural borders: Implications for science teaching. *Research in Science and Technological Education, 17*(1), 45–66.

Kagan, J. (2003). Biology, context and developmental inquiry. *Annual Review of Psychology, 54*, 1–23.

Kail, R. V., & Cavanaugh, J. C. (2000). *Human development: A lifespan view.* Belmont, CA: Wadsworth.

Keller, H., & Greenfield, P. M. (2000). History and future of development in cross-cultural psychology. *Journal of Cross-Cultural Psychology, 31*(1), 52–62.

Krogh, L. B., & Thomsen, P. V. (2005). Studying students' attitudes towards science from a cultural perspective but with a quantitative methodology: Border crossing into the physics classroom. *International Journal of Science Education, 27*(3), 281–302.

Kuhn, D., Garcia-Mila, M., Zohar, A., & Andersen, C. (1995). Strategies of knowledge acquisition. *Monographs of the Society for Research in Child Development, 60*(4, Serial No. 245).

Lee, C. D. (2002). Interrogating race and ethnicity as constructs in the examination of cultural processes in developmental research. *Human Development, 45*, 282–290.

Lucariello, J. M. (2004). New insights into the functions, development, and origins of theory of mind: The functional multilinear socialization (FMS) model. In J. M. Lucariello, J. A. Hudson, R. Fivush, & P. J. Bauer (Eds.), *The development of the mediated mind: Sociocultural context and cognitive development* (pp. 33–57). Mahwah, NJ: Lawrence Erlbaum.

Mandler, J. M. (2004). Two kinds of knowledge acquisition. In J. M. Lucariello, J. A. Hudson, R. Fivush, & P. J. Bauer (Eds.), *The development of the mediated mind: Sociocultural context and cognitive development* (pp. 13–32). Mahwah, NJ: Lawrence Erlbaum.

McClurg, P. A., & Chaillé, C. (1987). Computer games: Environments for developing spatial cognition? *Journal of Educational Computing Research, 3*(1), 95–111.

McKeon, M. (1994). The role of science in the reversal of the trend of failure in children with emotional and behavioural difficulties. *Therapeutic Care & Education, 3*(1), 68–71.

Mundy, P. C., & Acra, C. F. (2006). Joint attention, social engagement, and the development of social competence. In P. J. Marshall & N. A. Fox (Eds.), *The development of social engagement: Neurobiological perspectives* (pp. 81–117). New York: Oxford University Press.

Mundy, P., Card, J., & Fox, N. (2000). EEG correlates of the development of infant joint attention skills. *Developmental Psychobiology, 36*(4), 325–338.

Mundy, P., & Gomes, A. (1998). Individual differences in joint attention skill development in the second year. *Infant Behavior & Development, 21*(3), 469–482.

Nelson, C. A. (2001). The development and neural bases of face recognition. *Infant and Child Development, 10,* 3–18.

Nelson, K. (1996). *Language in cognitive development: Emergence of the mediated mind.* New York: Cambridge University Press.

Newman, B. M., & Newman, P. R. (2006). *Development through life: A psychosocial approach.* Belmont, CA: Thomson Wadsworth.

Paterson, S. J., Heim, S., Friedman, J. T., Choudhury, N., & Benasich, A. A. (2006). Development of structure and function in the infant brain: Implications for cognition, language and social behaviour. *Neuroscience & Biobehavioral Reviews, 30*(8), 1087–1105.

Premack, D., & Woodruff, G. (1978). Does the chimpanzee have a theory of mind? *Behavioral and Brain Sciences, 1*(4), 515–526.

Rogoff, B. (1990). *Apprenticeship in thinking: Cognitive development in social context.* New York: Oxford University Press.

Rogoff, B. (1995). Observing sociocultural activity on three planes: Participatory appropriation, guided participation, and apprenticeship. In J. V. Wertsch, P. del Río, & A. Alvarez (Eds.), *Sociocultural studies of mind* (pp. 139–164). New York: Cambridge University Press.

Rogoff, B. (2003). *The cultural nature of human development.* New York: Oxford University Press.

Rogoff, B., Paradise, R., Arauz, R. M., Correa-Chávez, M., & Angelillo, C. (2003). Firsthand learning through intent participation. *Annual Review of Psychology, 54*, 175–203.

Rueda, R., Gallego, M. A., & Moll, L. C. (2000). The least restrictive environment. *Remedial and Special Education, 21*(2), 70–78.

Sanchez, S. Y. (1999). Learning from the stories of culturally and linguistically diverse families and communities: A sociohistorical lens. *Remedial and Special Education, 20*(6), 351–359.

Schauble, L. (1996). The development of scientific reasoning in knowledge-rich contexts. *Developmental Psychology, 32*(1), 102–119.

Segall, M. H., Campbell, D. T., & Herskovits, M. J. (1966). *The influence of culture on visual perception.* Oxford, UK: Bobbs-Merrill.

Sellami, A. L. (2000, March). *Teaching towards cultural awareness and intercultural competence: From what, through how, to why culture is?* Paper presented at the annual meeting of Teachers of English Speakers of Other Languages, Vancouver, BC, Canada.

Shade, B. J. (1989). The influence of perceptual development on cognitive style: Cross ethnic comparisons. *Early Child Development and Care, 51,* 137–155.

Shrager, J., & Siegler, R. S. (1998). SCADS: A model of children's strategy choices and strategy discoveries. *Psychological Science, 9*(5), 405–410.

Siegler, R. S. (2005). Children's learning. *American Psychologist, 60*(8), 769–778.

Siegler, R. S., & Araya, R. (2005). A computational model of conscious and unconscious strategy discovery. In R. V. Kail (Ed.), *Advances in child development and behavior* (Vol. 33, pp. 1–42). Oxford, UK: Elsevier.

Siegler, R. S., & Chen, Z. (1998). Developmental differences in rule learning: A microgenetic analysis. *Cognitive Psychology, 36*(3), 273–310.

Sigelman, C. K., & Rider, E. A. (2006). *Life-span human development* (5th ed.). Belmont, CA: Wadsworth/Thomson Learning.

Sirois, S., Buckingham, D., & Shultz, T. R. (2000). Artificial grammar learning by infants: An auto-associator perspective. *Developmental Science, 3*(4), 442–456.

Spencer, J. P., Vereijken, B., Diedrich, F. J., & Thelen, E. (2000). Posture and the emergence of manual skills. *Developmental Science, 3*(2), 216–233.

Sue, D. W. (1978). Eliminating cultural oppression in counseling: Toward a general theory. *Journal of Counseling Psychology, 25*(5), 419–428.

Thomas, K. M., Hunt, R. H., Vizuetal, N., Sommer, T., Durston, S., Yang, Y., et al. (2004). Evidence of developmental differences in implicit sequence learning: An MRI study of children and adults. *Journal of Cognitive Neuroscience 16*(8), 1339–1351.

Tomasello, M. (1995). Joint attention as social cognition. In C. Moore & P. J. Dunham (Eds.), *Joint attention: Its origins and role in development* (pp. 103–130). Hillsdale, NJ: Lawrence Erlbaum.

Tomasello, M., Carpenter, M., Call, J., Behne, T., & Moll, H. (2005) Understanding and sharing intentions: The origins of cultural cognition. *Behavioral and Brain Sciences, 28*(5), 675–735.

Vygotsky, L. S. (1988). The genesis of higher mental functions. In K. Richardson & S. Sheldon (Eds.), *Cognitive development to adolescence: A reader* (pp. 61–79). Hillsdale, NJ: Lawrence Erlbaum. (Original work published 1968)

Weisner, T. S. (2002). Ecocultural understanding of children's development pathways. *Human Development, 45*(4), 275–281.

Wertsch, J. V. (1991). A sociocultural approach to socially shared cognition. In L. B. Resnick, J. M. Levine, & S. D. Teasley (Eds.), *Perspectives on socially shared cognition* (pp. 85–100). Washington, DC: American Psychological Association.

Zahavi, D., & Parnas, J. (2003). Conceptual problems in infantile autism research: Why cognitive science needs phenomenology. *Journal of Consciousness Studies, 10*(9–10), 53–71.

CHAPTER 3

Children and Cognition

Development of Social Schema

JOHN E. LOCHMAN

KHIELA J. HOLMES

MARY WOJNAROSKI

This chapter will overview key issues in the functions and development of children's social schema. Within a social information processing (SIP) framework (e.g., Crick & Dodge, 1994), online processing of social events involves attributions and decisions of encountered problems, and is distinguished from children's latent mental structures that can influence SIP. These latent mental structures can be conceptualized as schemas (Lochman & Dodge, 1998) or scripts (Huesmann, 1988).

SCHEMAS

Children's cognitive schemas have evident effects on their social adjustment (Salmivalli, Ojanen, & Peets, 2005), their information processing (Crick & Dodge, 1994; Lochman, Powell, Whidby, & FitzGerald, 2006), and their attention and memory retrieval (Koriat, Goldsmith, & Pansky, 2000). People are better at recalling information that is congruent with their schemas than information that is incongruent with their schemas (Szentagotai et al., 2005), and some schemas come to be more readily accessible than others (Bruner, 1992). Schemas account for how organisms actively construct their perceptions and experiences, rather than merely being passive receivers and processors of social information. However, individuals are not clearly aware of their schemas, but only have vague concepts of what their schemas are or should be (Tilden & Dattilio, 2005).

Authors' Note: The preparation of this chapter has been supported by grants to the first author from the National Institute for Drug Abuse (DA 16135; DA 08453), the Office of Juvenile Justice and Delinquency Prevention (2006JLFX0232), and the Centers for Disease Control and Prevention (R49/CCR418569).

Schemas have been defined in somewhat different ways by various theoreticians and researchers, but they are commonly regarded as consistent, core beliefs and patterns of thinking with affective elements (Lochman & Lenhart, 1995; Tilden & Dattilio, 2005). These underlying cognitive structures form the basis for individuals' specific perceptions of current events. Similar to Adler's (1964) concept of "style of life" and Kelly's (1955) "personal constructs," schemas are cognitive blueprints or master plans that construe, organize, and transform peoples' interpretations and predictions about events in their lives (Mischel, 1990). Stable schemas originate in childhood, and selectively filter a person's perception of his or her environment when the schemas are activated by life events.

Attributes of Schemas

Schemas have certain basic attributes. First, a distinction can be made between *active* schemas, which are often conscious and govern everyday behavior, and *dormant* schemas, which are typically out of individuals' awareness and emerge only when the individuals are faced with specific events or stressors. The dormant schemas are in a state of "chronic accessibility" (Mischel, 1990) or state of potential activation, ready to be primed by minimal cues. Thus, individuals' beliefs and expectations, which emerge when they are intensely stressed or aroused, may not be at all apparent when they are calm and not aroused.

Second, existing schemas can be either compelling or noncompelling. Noncompelling schemas are not strongly held by a person, and can be given up easily. In contrast, compelling schemas are strongly entrenched in the person's way of thinking. They promote more filtering and potential distortions of the person's perceptions of self and others (Fiske & Taylor, 1984). The compelling schemas lead to more rapid judgments about the presence of these schema-related traits in self and others, and they often operate outside of conscious awareness (Erdley, 1990).

Third, schemas can be more or less permeable. Permeable schemas permit a person to alter his or her interpretation of events through successive approximations, a process identified as "constructive alternativism" by Kelly (1955). A person with relatively permeable schemas can readily adapt his or her schemas to the specific situations and conditions he or she encounters, thereby adding new elements and complexity to the schema. Schemas are typically more permeable and situational as individuals develop and have experiences in a number of situations (Mischel, 1990; Rotter, Chance, & Phares, 1972). Relatively nonpermeable schemas are preemptive, and promote rigid black-white thinking (Kelly, 1955).

Origins of Schemas

Schemas evolve out of the child's interactions with parents and other significant others, and can be influenced by the child's broader community and cultural context. Schemas about one's relationships are learned early in life from children's families-of-origin and their other relationship experiences, as well as from cultural traditions and mass media (Tilden & Dattilio, 2005). The scaffolding models of self in relation to others as articulated in attachment theories can be conceptualized as schemas that affect individuals' automatic thoughts and emotional responses to others (Tilden & Dattilio, 2005). From an attachment theory perspective (Bowlby, 1982), children's experiences within their families can lead them to acquire positive and constructive schemas about themselves and their social environment, or negative and potentially counterproductive schemas. If a child experiences a parent who is warmly attentive, anticipates her child's needs in a flexible manner, and responds to the child in consistent ways, the child's social schemas can involve expectations that others are reliable and trustworthy. Thus, when the child begins to interact with other adults and peers, the child is interested in developing positive interactions with others and expects that others can be motivated to interact in reciprocally positive ways.

In contrast, experiences such as chronic child maltreatment can lead a child to develop schemas of the social world as a hostile, threatening place with relationships oriented toward establishing dominance (Burks, Laird, Dodge, Pettit, & Bates, 1999). Early maladaptive schemas developed through adverse experiences with parents, siblings, and peers can also affect children's schemas about themselves, such as when parental criticism leads to a child's schema that he or she is not loveable (Hoffart et al., 2005).

Aversive social experiences are stored thus in memory in schemas. For example, children who attend to and interpret early violent social experiences in a hostile manner will develop hostile schemas of others (Burks et al., 1999). Such schemas then increase the likelihood that the child will begin to display chronic externalizing problems. Burks et al. (1999), in fact, found that children who had developed hostile schemas of parents and peers behaved in more aggressive ways themselves, and that their hostile schemas served to maintain their aggressive behavior over time.

Schemas and Emotional Arousal

It is important to recognize that social information processing might both influence, and be aversely impacted by, heightened levels of the negative affect and emotional arousal associated with individuals' schemas. Emotions have been hypothesized to mediate the relation between attributions and behavior (Weiner, 1990) and serve as an adaptive system that motivates individuals to solve their perceived problems. For example, when a child attributes blame for a social conflict to another person's hostility, the child will tend to experience frustration or anger; but when the child attributes a social conflict to personal flaws or imperfections, the child will tend to experience sadness or depression (Weiner). These cognition-emotion linkages can then result in different decisions about social goals (e.g., revenge vs. conflict avoidance) and appropriate behavioral responses in interpersonal situations (e.g., aggression vs. withdrawal). Once schemas are activated, emotional reactions often persist across time, which can negatively influence social attributions and response styles throughout an extended social exchange (Lochman & Dodge, 1998). Along these lines, a recent laboratory investigation found that young boys who experience increased heart rate as the result of provocation also experience increases in hostile attributional biases (Williams, Lochman, Phillips, & Barry, 2003).

Automatic and Controlled Processing

When evaluating the schemas and SIP of children and adolescents, it is often useful to differentiate between more automatic versus controlled processing problems (Lazarus, 1991). Automatic processing is commonly described as occurring outside of conscious awareness and is fast, effortless, and unintentional. Effortful processing, on the other hand, occurs within conscious awareness and is depicted as slow and deliberate. Individuals' use of schemas, such as stereotypes one has, increases under conditions of constrained processing capacity (Dijksterhuis & Nordgren, 2006). Even though schematic stereotypes are activated automatically, they are applied when an individual is consciously thinking about a person or group (Dijksterhuis & Nordgren, 2006). Research suggests that schemas mainly affect conscious and intentionally activated memories rather than unconscious and unintentional memories (Szentagotai et al., 2005). Thus, schemas, which can activate goals that operate preconsciously (Gollwitzer & Moskowitz, 1996) and are activated automatically, have an impact, in particular, on controlled information processing. Whereas a vast majority of research with children and adolescents has focused on effortful information processing, studies have begun examining the association between emotional problems and more automatic processing of social stimuli. For example, trait anxiety in adults has been associated with increased skin conductance responses to threatening pictures in comparison to neutral pictures, even when these stimuli are presented outside of conscious awareness (Najstrom & Jansson, 2006). While this suggests that relatively automatic attentional biases to fear and threat cues may be associated with anxiety problems in adults, studies examining how automatic processes are related to child and adolescent anxiety, as well as other forms of psychopathology, are needed.

SPECIFIC AREAS OF SCHEMATIC FUNCTIONING AND CHILDREN'S SOCIAL BEHAVIOR

Self-Esteem

One aspect of an individual's self-schema is self-esteem, which is defined as an individual's subjective evaluation of the self (that is, his or her feelings of worth) and is fairly established at age 8 (Harter, 1982). Children evaluate their competence in several domains including academic, social, and physical. These evaluations are associated with future behavior and subsequent psychological adjustment. Furthermore, self-schemas have been found to regulate behavior particularly when self-awareness is present (Froming, Nasby, & McManus, 1998). Children who have a poor self-worth may attempt to compensate for that feeling by engaging in antisocial behaviors (Fryrear, Nuell, & White, 1977). Studies have found that aggressive boys had lower levels of self-worth than nonaggressive boys (Lochman & Dodge, 1994). Aggressive behavior can be partially attributed to cognitive schemata that children develop as a result of their social status in society and their global self-worth (McMahon & Watts, 2002). Social self-esteem (i.e., the extent to which children feel they are accepted and popular among their peers; De Bruyn & Van Den Boom, 2005) includes how children perceive their relationships with peers.

Social Goals

Social goals are an element of schemas as well, and can have positive or negative effects on children's peer relations (Arsenio & Lemerise, 2004). Therefore, social goals can be conceptualized as motivational factors that influence children's subsequent responses to social situations (Lochman et al., 2006). Positive social adjustment (i.e., prosocial behavior or peer popularity) is significantly related to the likelihood that the child will select goals that will build upon a relationship with his or her peers (e.g., being helpful to peers); however, social maladjustment (i.e., aggressive behavior or peer rejection) is related to the selection of goals that are likely to be detrimental to a peer relationship (e.g., dominance and revenge; Crick & Dodge, 1994). Rabiner and Gordon (1992) found that aggressive-rejected children were less able to integrate self-oriented and other-oriented concerns than average and popular boys. In another study documenting aggressive children's self-oriented goals for dominance, Boldizar, Perry, and Perry (1989) used the Rotter et al. (1972) social learning framework to examine outcome values. In their goal-oriented outcome values, aggressive children were found to place more value on achieving control of the victim, and less value on suffering by the victim, retaliation from the victim, peer rejection, or negative self-evaluation.

Although a child's goals can be consciously accessed and applied to his or her decision making in a particular social problem that he or she encounters, goals are also important components of schemas. Thus, goals at a situationally specific level operate as a step within SIP. However, at a global cross-situational level, goals are part of overarching schemas. This conceptualization parallels the two general classes of theories accounting for goal effects on action and cognition (Gollwitzer & Moskowitz, 1996). In the first case, goals directly affect responses, and in the second case, goals are part of self-regulation and the focus is on how goals regulate cognition and behavior. Individuals develop values for certain outcomes and goals, and the affective preferences can operate preconsciously to narrow the individual's attention (Gollwitzer & Moskowitz, 1996).

Ethnic Identity, Religiosity, and Spirituality

Cultural variables such as ethnic identity and religiosity/spirituality can also be conceptualized as schemas. Moreover, when preference is attached to schemas, they can be conceptualized as attitudes (Dodge, 1993). Religion can be conceptualized as a schema that guides decisions and motivates behavior (Ozorak, 2005) and can be defined as an organized activity that is characterized by specific behaviors, doctrine, and denominations.

> Spirituality is the personal quest for understanding answers to ultimate questions about life, about meaning, and about relationship to the sacred or transcendent, which may (or may not) lead to or arise from the development of religious rituals and the formation of community. (Koenig, McCullough, & Larson, 2001, p. 18)

Research has demonstrated that religiosity (i.e., the importance of religion, relying on religious teachings during a problem, praying when facing a personal problem, and relying on religious beliefs in day-to-day living) serves as a buffer against the negative effects of significant life events including cigarette smoking, heavy drinking, and marijuana use (Wills, Yaeger, & Sandy, 2003). Studies have also found a negative relation between religiosity (i.e., frequency of religious service attendance, importance of religion, time spent in religious activities over the weekend, and importance of involvement in community-based religious activities) and delinquent behaviors (Johnson, Jang, Larson, & De Li, 2001). Abbot-Chapman and Denholm (2001) concluded that adolescents who endorsed higher levels of religiosity (i.e., religious belief and church-going) had lower levels of risk in several categories, including smoking marijuana and binge drinking. Some argue that religious behaviors deter individuals from engaging in criminal behavior (Baier & Wright, 2001). This notion is partially due to the fact that religion promotes moral behavior and encourages social control (Fitzpatrick, 1967).

Because race and ethnicity are salient in society, children and adolescents must perceive in which racial and ethnic category they belong. Naturally, in order to process, store, and retrieve knowledge more efficiently regarding these categories, children develop schemas. Specifically, feelings of attachment or closeness to a particular ethnic group may increase the likelihood that the values and stereotypes associated with that group will be internalized (Hogg, 2003). Children's schema regarding their ethnic identity may have implications for achievement, educational attitudes, adjustment, and behavior. Ethnic identity refers to one's sense of belonging to an ethnic group and the part of one's thinking, perceptions, feelings, and behavior that is due to one's ethnic group membership (Rotheram & Phinney, 1987). Ethnic identity also includes having a sense of pride, which focuses on having positive feelings toward one's ethnic group (Phinney, 1990). Other group orientation, an attitude toward ethnic groups other than your own, is not considered an aspect of ethnic identity, but is important in an individual's overall social identity (Phinney, 1992). Phinney argues that individuals' attitudes toward their ethnic group are important in their psychological adjustment. Ethnic identification has been found to be positively associated with academic performance (Wong, Eccles, & Sameroff, 2003) and feelings of academic efficacy (Oyserman, Harrison, & Bybee, 2001). Furthermore, there is a positive association between adolescents' strength of ethnic identification and academic attitudes in that those adolescents with stronger ethnic identification are more positive about education and their school and believe it is useful for their future (Fuligni, Witkow, & Garcia, 2005).

Paschall and Flewlling (1997) found that a higher level of ethnic identity was associated with a lower level of violent behavior among African American adolescent males. Research examining the impact of ethnic identity on aggressive behavior has concluded that these variables are negatively associated with one another among child and adolescent populations (McMahon & Watts, 2002). Arbona, Jackson, McCoy, and Blakely (1999) concluded that a higher score on ethnic identity was associated with nonfighting attitudes among youth ages 10 to 13 who were African American and Latino/a. A strong sense of ethnic identity is associated with fewer aggressive behaviors (McMahon & Watts, 2002).

Holmes and Lochman (2007) investigated the relations among schematic variables (ethnic identity, self-worth, and social goals) and aggression for European American and African American aggressive preadolescents (ages 9–13). A primary goal of the study was to determine the extent to which self-worth and social goals mediated the relation between ethnic identity and aggressive behavior. For European American preadolescents, ethnic identity was significantly positively correlated with self-worth and negatively significantly correlated with aggression. Furthermore, self-worth was negatively significantly correlated with aggression. For African American preadolescents, ethnic identity was significantly negatively correlated with dominance and revenge-oriented social goals and had a nonsignificant trend negative association with aggression. In addition, there was a nonsignificant trend positive association between dominance and revenge social goals and aggression. Holmes and Lochman found that ethnic identity served as the full mediator between self-worth and aggression for European American aggressive preadolescents. Moreover, ethnic identity and dominance and revenge social goals produced main-effect trends when predicting aggression for African American aggressive preadolescents. These findings suggest that schemas involving children's ethnic identity, self-esteem, and social goals are interrelated, and that these relations differ for various ethnic groups.

SCHEMAS AND SOCIAL INFORMATION PROCESSING

Social information processing (SIP) is a process of encoding and interpreting social cues and choosing a behavior based on individual interpretation. SIP has been used to explain facets of human experience including aggression (Crick & Dodge, 1994), depression (Pössel, Baldus, Horn, Groen, & Hautzinger, 2005), and morality (Narvaez, Lapsley, Hagele, & Lasky, 2006).

Social Information Processing

Research accepts the influence of children's social cognitions in social encounters (Lochman

& Dodge, 1994; Lochman & Wells, 2002). Crick and Dodge (1994) developed a model of SIP that stated that children enter social interactions with genetically dictated abilities and memories for past experiences. Externally, they receive a set of cues that are also used to determine behavior. The steps of the model are (1) encoding of external and internal cues, (2) interpretation and mental representation of those cues, (3) clarification or selection of a goal, (4) response access or construction, (5) response decision, and (6) behavioral enactment. In Steps 1 and 2, children attend to certain cues, encode, and interpret them in a manner consistent with previous experiences and internal representations of those involved and of what is expected to occur. During Step 3, children choose a desired outcome for the encounter. Children enter social situations with characteristic goal orientations based on beliefs about social encounters, as well as their typical responding tendencies. However, children also modify previous goals and create new ones germane to the circumstances. During Step 4, children generate possible solutions either from memory, or in new situations, novel solutions, to achieve the desired goal. At Step 5, children evaluate the list of possible responses and choose the option they feel will produce the most positive outcome. The choice is affected by the expected outcome after performing the response, the confidence they have in themselves to enact the response, and the suitability of the response. Finally, in Step 6, children enact the chosen response. Therefore, a child's reaction to an event is not solely based on the actual event itself, but also the child's interpretation of the event.

Social Information Processing of Aggressive Children

Often, SIP is distorted in socially maladjusted children, especially aggressive youth. Lochman and Dodge (1998) described a conceptual model where aggressive children expect interpersonal relations to be aggressive based on schemas of themselves and others, which then influence their in-the-moment interpretations (SIP). Research has found that aggressive children often have characteristic ways of thinking or acting at each step of the social information process (Crick & Dodge, 1994; Lochman & Dodge, 1998). It is important to note that these tendencies occur more often in ambiguous situations than when a peer is intentionally and obviously acting aggressively toward another child, as most children, aggressive or not, will interpret the actions as aggressive. Aggressive children scan for hostile cues more frequently than nonaggressive children (Lochman et al., 2006). This leads them, during Step 1, to remember more cues that seem hostile than nonaggressive children (Dodge, Petit, McClasaky, & Brown, 1986). In Step 2, children must interpret others' intentions. Lochman and Dodge (1994) found support for a hostile attribution bias, or the tendency to see other's intentions as hostile as opposed to benign or neutral, in aggressive boys. In addition, aggressive boys tend to underestimate their own aggressiveness and place responsibility for the encounter on the other child (Lochman & Dodge, 1998).

During Step 3, aggressive children choose dominance and revenge goals more often than nonaggressive children (Lochman, Wayland, & White, 1993). When children generate possible solutions to the problem at Step 4, aggressive children create less verbal assertion and compromise solutions than nonaggressive children, as well as more direct action solutions and physically aggressive solutions (Lochman et al., 2006). Often, aggressive children make an attempt to resolve the situation prosocially but when questioned for a second and third response, return to aggressive solutions. During Step 5, children evaluate their list of choices. Aggressive children are more likely to believe that aggression will reduce aversive treatment and produce tangible rewards than nonaggressive children (Lochman & Dodge, 1994; Perry, Perry, & Rasmussen, 1986), and also believe that aggression will create a positive image of them, not cause others to suffer (Lochman et al., 2006). Last, during Step 6, children must enact their chosen behavior. Aggressive children are less skilled in performing prosocial acts than nonaggressive children (Dodge et al., 1986).

Ethnic Differences in Social Information Processing

When testing cognitive models, it is necessary to examine the generalizability of such models. Although SIP likely has an impact on all social situations, much of the research has been conducted in the child aggression area. Despite frequent research on the effect of SIP on aggressive behavior, relatively few studies have examined how the relation between SIP and aggression might differ among ethnic groups. When it has been examined, researchers have found small or no differences in the relation between characteristic aggressive choices in the social information process and aggressive behavior for a variety of races. Graham, Hudley, and Williams (1992) found that hostile attributional biases were related to children's aggressive behavior in the same manner for African American youth as in previous samples. Lochman and Dodge (1998) found no differences in aggressive children's tendency to underestimate their own aggression and overestimate others' aggression between Black and White children. Zelli, Dodge, Lochman, Laird, and The Conduct Problems Prevention Research Group (1999) found that a relation between normative beliefs and subsequent aggression was mediated by social cognitions in similar ways for Black and White children.

However, there is some limited research on different social cognitions held by different ethnicities, as well as differences in SIP. Bellmore, Witkow, Graham, and Juvonen (2005) examined racial differences in social cognitions. Black adolescents were more likely than White, Latino, and Asian adolescents to approve of aggression. White adolescents were less likely to approve of hostile responses than the other three ethnicities. They then examined the relation between normative beliefs regarding aggression (schema) and response selection (SIP). Their research demonstrated that normative beliefs impacted response selection for all four racial/ethnic groups. However, the relation was somewhat weaker, but still significant, for Black students. Although the researchers hypothesized the reason for this difference (Black children may rely on different schemas in a school context), this hypothesis has not been tested.

Integration of Schemas and Social Information Processing

During the encoding and interpretation stages of the model (Steps 1–2), schemas of what other children are like and self-schemas are activated (Dodge & Rabiner, 2004). When encoding social cues, schemas can narrow children's attention to specific facets of the social environment at the expense of other social cues (e.g., Lochman, Nelson, & Sims, 1981). For example, a child with a general expectancy that others will try to dominate him or her may be hypervigilant to verbal and nonverbal signals about a peer's control efforts, while missing signs of the peer's friendliness, or attempts to negotiate. Children's schema about control and aggression will also heavily influence the second stage of processing, as the child interprets the malevolent meaning and intentions in others' behavior (Lochman & Lenhart, 1995). Children notice information that is schema consistent, or events that correspond with their idea of other children, and often ignore schema-inconsistent information. Beliefs about others help children assign meaning to the actions of those involved in the social encounter. Children's self-schemas also impact the first two steps of the model. People are much quicker and more efficient at noticing and processing behavior of others that is consistent with their own self-schema (Baldwin, 1992). Again, they are more likely to interpret the information in ways that support their self-schema.

During the action steps of the model (3–6), the child selects a goal and enacts a response to achieve it. The other schema and self-schema are again helpful in understanding the child's goal selection. A child will choose a situational goal based on schematic stored social goals; if the child has experienced positive relationships with peers, he or she may be more likely to emphasize relational goals than one who has had negative experiences. Furthermore, the knowledge of one's own typically desired outcome in social encounters will determine the child's goal selection (Baldwin, 1992). After the determination of a goal, the child generates possible solutions and chooses one. The schema of normative beliefs about the appropriateness of solutions can be activated (Huesmann & Guerra, 1997) and influence choice selection. Again, a child's self-schema, specifically what he or she typically does in similar encounters, has an impact on behavioral choice. In addition, people are more likely to enact responses that are held in their relational schema of what will produce successful outcomes (Lochman et al., 2006). In a study of the direct effect of adolescents' social goals on their solutions to social problems, Lochman et al. (1993) used a social learning theory framework (Rotter et al., 1972) to examine boys' ratings of (a) the value of four social goals in a conflict situation (avoidance, dominance, revenge, affiliation), (b) the solution they would use to accomplish each goal, and (c) their level of expectations that they could attain the goals with their selected responses. Aggressive boys had significantly higher value ratings for the dominance and revenge goals and lower ratings for an affiliation goal, in comparison to nonaggressive boys, consistent with research by Erdley and Asher (1996). The dominance-oriented pattern of social goals was found to be associated with adolescents' delinquency and substance use rates. Although aggressive and nonaggressive boys endorsed similar patterns of behavioral solutions to attain each of the goals, aggressive boys had substantial differences from nonaggressive boys in solutions they would use to gain their main goal. This suggests the direct effect of goals (schematic proposition) on problem solutions (cognitive products). Due to their overvaluing of dominance and revenge goals, aggressive boys had more aggressive and fewer bargaining solutions than did nonaggressive boys.

Several studies have examined the linkage between schemas and SIP with aggressive children. Zelli et al. (1999) found that the relation between normative beliefs regarding aggression and subsequent aggression was mediated by hostile attribution, greater generation of aggressive solutions, and positive evaluation of aggressive solutions. Dodge, Laird, Lochman, Zelli, and The Conduct Problems Prevention Research Group (2002) found that the relation between emotion understanding and aggression was partially mediated by hostile attributions, hostile response generation, positive aggression evaluation, and instrumental goals. These preliminary studies have provided some support for the relation between social schemas and SIP; however, much more research is needed to achieve greater understanding.

Although schemas and SIP affect behavior in social situations, they do so in different ways. Crick and Dodge (1994) differentiated "between the rapid real-time processing of social information and the representations of earlier social events stored in long-term memory." In other words, schemas are latent cognitive structures developed over time from previous experiences, whereas SIP is an actual event that occurs in the moment of the social encounter. The schemas represent knowledge and beliefs about social encounters and guide and determine the interpretation of new circumstances. Crick and Dodge (1994) offered this characteristic of SIP as an advantage that schema theories do not have, as it has a more direct link to behavior. Most likely, SIP is automatic and children do not consciously engage in each step of the model. However, this automaticity is likely what leads to errors in processing and inappropriate behavioral responses. Research has shown that some socially maladjusted children were able to accurately process social information in reflective conditions, but not automatic ones (Rabiner, Lenhart, & Lochman, 1990).

Research suggests that schematic effects on SIP are evident in minority children as well as in Caucasian children. Graham and Hudley (1994) used a priming experimental paradigm to find that African American male adolescents have beliefs about the hostile intentions of others that remain active in their memory and that guide their subsequent information processing. For aggressive children who have been targets of aggressive behavior, having a low threshold for assuming negative intentions from others may represent an acquired survival strategy.

CONCLUSION

To date, most of the research on schemas and SIP has been separate. The integration of the two aspects of social cognition is an important and necessary step to better understand social interactions. Little is empirically known about the effects each has on the other, although the proposed theories have received some support. Even less is known about the generalizability of the model, because most of the research on SIP has been conducted on aggressive children. Furthermore, diverse samples have been used in previous research, but there is a lack of comparison research on SIP with different ethnicities. The examination of these differences, as well as race/ethnicity as a contextual factor, will give further insight into the choices of maladjusted youth. Last, the field of psychology has evidence that altering schemas and SIP can produce long-lasting change in children and adolescents with a distorted self- and worldview. Applying an integrated model to an intervention program can only enhance the results the two have found separately.

REFERENCES

Abbott-Chapman, J., & Denholm, C. (2001). Adolescents' risk activities, risk hierarchies and the influence of religiosity. *Journal of Youth Studies, 4,* 279–297.

Adler, A. (1964). *Social interest: A challenge to mankind.* New York: Capricorn.

Arbona, C., Jackson, R. H., McCoy, A., & Blakely, C. (1999). Ethnic identity as a predictor of attitudes of adolescents toward fighting. *Journal of Early Adolescence, 19,* 323–340.

Arsenio, W. F., & Lemerise, E. A. (2004). Aggression and moral development: Integrating social information processing and moral domain models. *Child Development, 75,* 987–1002.

Baier, C. J., & Wright, B. R. E. (2001). "If you love me, keep my commandments": A meta-analysis of the effect of religion on crime. *Journal of Research in Crime and Delinquency, 38,* 3–21.

Baldwin, M. W. (1992). Relational schemas and the processing of social information. *Psychological Bulletin, 112,* 461–485.

Bellmore, A. D., Witkow, M. R., Graham, S., & Juvonen, J. (2005). From beliefs to behavior: The mediating role of hostile response selection in predicting aggression. *Aggressive Behavior, 31,* 453–472.

Boldizar, J. P., Perry, D. G., & Perry, L. C. (1989). Outcome values and aggression. *Child Development, 60,* 571–579.

Bowlby, J. (1982). *Attachment and loss, Vol. 1: Attachment* (2nd ed.). New York: Basic Books.

Bruner, J. S. (1992). Another look at New Look 1. *American Psychologist, 47,* 780–783.

Burks, V. S., Laird, R. D., Dodge, K. A., Pettit, G. S., & Bates, J. E. (1999). Knowledge structures, social information processing, and children's aggressive behavior. *Social Development, 8,* 220–236.

Crick, N. R., & Dodge, K. A. (1994). A review and reformulation of social information-processing mechanisms in children's social adjustment. *Psychological Bulletin, 115,* 74–101.

De Bruyn, E. H., & Van Den Boom, D. C. (2005). Interpersonal behavior, peer popularity, and self-esteem in early adolescence. *Social Development, 14,* 555–573.

Dijksterhuis, A., & Nordgren, L. F. (2006). A theory of unconscious thought. *Perspectives on Psychological Science, 1,* 95–109.

Dodge, K. A. (1993). Social-cognitive mechanisms in the development of conduct disorder and depression. *Annual Review of Psychology, 44,* 559–584.

Dodge, K. A., Laird, R., Lochman, J. E., Zelli, A., & The Conduct Problems Prevention Research Group. (2002). Multidimensional latent-construct analysis of children's social information processing patterns: Correlations with aggressive behavior problems. *Psychological Assessment, 14,* 60–73.

Dodge, K. A., Petit, G. S., McClasky, C. L., & Brown, M. M. (1986). Social competence in children. *Monographs of the Society for Research in Child Development, 51* (2, Serial No. 213).

Dodge, K. A., & Rabiner, D. L. (2004). Returning to roots: On social information processing and moral development. *Child Development, 75,* 1003–1008.

Erdley, C. A. (1990). *An analysis of children's attributions and goals in social situations: Implications of children's friendship outcomes.* Unpublished manuscript, University of Illinois.

Erdley, C. A., & Asher, S. R. (1996). Children's social goals and self efficacy perceptions as influences on their responses to ambiguous provocation. *Child Development, 67,* 1329–1344.

Fiske, S. T., & Taylor, S. E. (1984). *Social cognition.* Reading, MA: Addison-Wesley.

Fitzpatrick, J. P. (1967). The role of religion in programs for the prevention and correction of crime and delinquency. In *Task force report: Juvenile delinquency and youth crime.* Washington, DC: Government Printing Office.

Froming, W. J., Nasby, W., & McManus, J. (1998). Prosocial self-schemas, self-awareness, and children's prosocial behavior. *Journal of Personality and Social Psychology, 75,* 766–777.

Fryrear, J. L., Nuell, L. R., & White, P. (1977). Enhancement of male juvenile delinquents' self-concepts through photographed social interactions. *Journal of Clinical Psychology, 33,* 833–838.

Fuligni, A. J., Witkow, M., & Garcia, C. (2005). Ethnic identity and the academic adjustment of adolescents from Mexican, Chinese, and European backgrounds. *Developmental Psychology, 41,* 799–811.

Gollwitzer, P. M., & Moskowitz, G. (1996). Goal effects on action and cognition. In E. T. Higgins & A. W. Kruglanski (Eds.), *Social psychology: Handbook of basic principles* (pp. 361–399). New York: Guilford Press.

Graham, S., & Hudley, C. (1994). Attributions of aggressive and nonaggressive African-American male early adolescents: A study of construct accessibility. *Developmental Psychology, 30,* 365–373.

Graham, S., Hudley, C., & Williams, E. (1992). Attributional and emotional determinants of aggression among African American and Latino early adolescents. *Developmental Psychology, 28,* 731–740.

Harter, S. (1982). The perceived competence scale for children. *Child Development, 53,* 87–97.

Hoffart, A., Sexton, H., Hedley, L. M., Wang, C. E., Holthe, H., Haugum, J. A., et al. (2005). The structure of maladaptive schemas: A confirmatory factor analaysis and a psychometric evaluation of factor-derived scales. *Cognitive Therapy and Research, 29,* 627–644.

Hogg, M. (2003). Social identity. In M. R. Leary & J. P. Tangney (Eds.), *Handbook of self and identity* (pp. 462–479). New York: Guilford Press.

Holmes, K. J., & Lochman, J. E. (2007). *Ethnic identity in African American and European American preadolescents: Relation to self-worth, social goals, and aggression.* Manuscript submitted for publication.

Huesmann, L. R. (1988). An information-processing model for the development of aggression. *Aggressive Behavior, 14,* 13–24.

Huesmann, L. R., & Guerra, N. G. (1997). Children's normative beliefs about aggression and aggressive behavior. *Journal of Personality and Social Psychology, 72,* 408–419.

Johnson, B. R., Jang, S. J., Larson, D. B., & De Li, S. (2001). Does adolescent religious commitment matter? A reexamination of the effect of religiosity on delinquency. *Journal of Research in Crime and Delinquency, 38,* 22–43.

Kelly, G. A. (1955). *The psychology of personal constructs.* New York: Norton.

Koenig, H. G., McCullough, M. E., & Larson, D. B. (2001). *Handbook of religion and health.* New York: Oxford University Press.

Koriat, A., Goldsmith, M., & Pansky, A. (2000). Toward a psychology of memory accuracy. *Annual Review of Psychology, 51,* 481–537.

Lazarus, R. (1991). Cognition and motivation in emotion. *American Psychologist, 46,* 352–367.

Lochman, J. E., & Dodge, K. A. (1994). Social-cognitive processes of severely violent, moderately aggressive, and nonaggressive boys. *Journal of Consulting and Clinical Psychology, 62,* 366–374.

Lochman, J. E., & Dodge, K. A. (1998). Distorted perceptions in dyadic interactions of aggressive and nonaggressive boys: Effects of prior expectations, context, and boys' age. *Development and Psychopathology, 10,* 495–512.

Lochman, J. E., & Lenhart, L. (1995). Cognitive behavioral therapy of aggressive children: Effects of schemas. In H. P. J. G. Van Bilsen, P. C. Kendall, & J. H. Slavenburg (Eds.), *Cognitive behavioral approaches for children and adolescents: Challenges for the next century* (pp. 145–166). New York: Plenum.

Lochman, J. E., Nelson, W. M., & Sims, J. P. (1981). A cognitive behavioral program for use with aggressive children. *Journal of Clinical Child Psychology, 13,* 146–148.

Lochman, J. E., Powell, N. R., Whidby, J. M., & FitzGerald, D. P. (2006). Cognitive-behavioral assessment and treatment with aggressive children. In P.C. Kendall (Ed.), *Child and adolescent therapy: Cognitive-behavioral procedures* (3rd ed., pp. 33–81). New York: Guilford.

Lochman, J. E., Wayland, K. K, & White, K. J. (1993). Social goals: Relationship to adolescent adjustment and to social problem solving. *Journal of Abnormal Child Psychology, 21,* 135–151.

Lochman, J. E., & Wells, K. C. (2002). Contextual social-cognitive mediators and child outcome: A test of the theoretical model in the Coping Power program. *Development & Psychopathology, 14,* 945–967.

McMahon, S. D., & Watts, R. J. (2002). Ethnic identity in urban African American youth: Exploring links with self-worth, aggression, and other psychosocial variables. *Journal of Community Psychology, 30,* 411–431.

Mischel, W. (1990). Personality disposition revisited and revised: A view after three decades. In L. Pervin (Ed.), *Handbook of personality: Theory and research* (pp. 111–134). New York: Guilford.

Najstrom, M., & Jansson, B. (2006). Unconscious responses to threatening pictures: Interactive effect of trait anxiety and social desirability on skin conductance responses. *Cognitive Behaviour Therapy, 35,* 11–18.

Narvaez, D., Lapsley, D. K., Hagele, S., & Lasky, B. (2006). Moral chronicity and SIP: Tests of a social cognitive approach to the moral personality. *Journal of Research in Personality, 40,* 966–985.

Oyserman, D., Harrison, K., & Bybee, D. (2001). Can racial identity be promotive of academic efficacy? *International Journal of Behavioral Development, 25,* 379–385.

Ozorak, E. W. (2005). Cognitive approaches to religion. In R. F. Paloutzian & C. L. Park (Eds.), *Handbook of the psychology of religion and spirituality* (pp. 216–234). New York: Guilford Press.

Paschall, M. J., & Flewlling, R. L. (1997). Measuring intermediate outcomes of violence prevention program targeting African-American male youth: An exploratory assessment of the psychometric properties of six psychological measures. *Health Education Research: Theory and Practice, 12,* 117–128.

Perry, D. G., Perry, L. C., & Rasmussen, P. (1986). Cognitive social learning mediators of aggression. *Child Development, 57,* 700–711.

Phinney, J. S. (1990). Ethnic identity in adolescents and adults: Review of research. *Psychological Bulletin, 108,* 499–514.

Phinney, J. S. (1992). The Multigroup Ethnic Identity Measure: A new scale for use with diverse groups. *Journal of Adolescent Research, 7,* 156–176.

Pössel, P., Baldus, C., Horn, A. B., Groen, G., & Hautzinger, M. (2005). Influence of general self-efficacy on the effects of a school-based universal primary prevention program of depressive symptoms in adolescents: A randomized and controlled follow-up study. *Journal of Child Psychology and Psychiatry, 46,* 982–994.

Rabiner, D. L., & Gordon, L. V. (1992). The coordination of conflicting social goals: Differences between rejected and nonrejected boys. *Child Development, 63,* 1344–1350.

Rabiner, D. L., Lenhart, L., & Lochman, J. E. (1990). Automatic versus reflective social problem solving in relation to children's sociometric status. *Developmental Psychology, 26,* 1010–1016.

Rotheram, M. J., & Phinney, J. S. (1987). *Children's ethnic socialization: Pluralism and development.* Newbury Park, CA: Sage.

Rotter, J. B., Chance, J. E., & Phares, E. J. (1972). *Applications of a social learning theory of personality.* New York: Holt, Rinehart, and Winston.

Salmivalli, C., Ojanen, T., & Peets, K. (2005). "I'm ok but you're not" and other peer-relational schemas: Explaining individual differences in children's social goals. *Developmental Psychology, 41,* 363–375.

Szentagotai, A., Schnur, J., DiGiuseppe, R., Macave, B., Kallay, E., & David, D. (2005). The organization and the nature of irrational beliefs: Schemas or appraisal. *Journal of Cognitive and Behavioral Psychotherapies, 5,* 139–158.

Tilden, T., & Dattilio, F. M. (2005). Vulnerability schemas of individuals in couples relationships: A cognitive perspective. *Contemporary Family Therapy, 27,* 139–162.

Weiner, B. (1990). Attribution in personality psychology. In L. Pervin (Ed.), *Handbook of personality: Theory and research* (pp. 609–637). New York: Guilford.

Williams, S. C., Lochman, J. E., Phillips, N. C., & Barry, T. D. (2003). Aggressive and nonaggressive boys' physiological and cognitive processes in response to peer provocations. *Journal of Clinical Child & Adolescent Psychology, 32,* 568–576.

Wills, T. A., Yaeger, A. M., & Sandy, J. M. (2003). Buffering effect of religiosity for adolescent substance use. *Psychology of Addictive Behaviors, 17,* 24–31.

Wong, C. A., Eccles, J. S., & Sameroff, A. (2003). The influence of ethnic discrimination and ethnic identification on African American adolescents' school and socioemotional adjustment. *Journal of Personality, 71,* 1197–1232.

Zelli, A., Dodge, K. A., Lochman, J. E., Laird, R. D., & The Conduct Problems Prevention Research Group. (1999). The distinction between beliefs legitimizing aggression and deviant processing of social cues: Testing measurement validity and the hypothesis that biased processing mediates the effects of beliefs on aggression. *Journal of Personality and Social Psychology, 77,* 150–166.

CHAPTER 4

Ethnic and Racial Identity Development in Children of Color

SHA'KEMA M. BLACKMON

ELIZABETH M. VERA

Children's racial and ethnic cognitions have been topics of investigation for more than half a century. Such research has been linked to the study of ethnic prejudice and discrimination in children (Aboud, 1988; Allport, 1954; Clark & Clark, 1940; Katz, 1973; Quintana & Vera, 1999; Ramsey, 1987) and has influenced public policy on interracial relations, for example, Brown v. Board of Education (Benjamin & Crouse, 2002). Ethnic and racial identities for ethnic minority children are believed to be particularly important in not only the development of identity in general, but as a self-protective strategy for coping with prejudice, discrimination, and stigmatization (Crocker & Major, 1989; Cross, 1995; Parham & Helms, 1985). In this chapter, ethnic and racial identity development will be discussed as well as the major contextual influences that affect such identity development. Specifically, key components of ethnic and racial identities such as ethnic awareness and ethnic-racial socialization will be presented. Future directions for racial and ethnic identity research will also be discussed with regard to Arab and Muslim American children, transracially adopted children, and assessing the impact of alternative forms of socialization on urban youth of color.

ETHNIC AND RACIAL IDENTITIES IN CONTEXT

It is important to understand ethnic and racial identities in the broader context of identity development. Ethnic and racial identities are part of a more complex construct referred to as social identity. Tajfel (1974) defined social identity as a contextual understanding of the self based on the social realms in which one interacts. Contexts that influence social identity include cultural group memberships (i.e., race, ethnicity, and gender) and familial, educational, and peer contexts. Thus, social identity is a multifaceted perspective of the self that influences the way individuals explain and make sense of their lives. Social identity theory provides a framework for understanding how group membership influences interpersonal relations with members of one's own group and other groups (Bernal, Saenz, & Knight, 1991). Understanding the development of social identity in children is critical to the work of psychologists and other mental health professionals. Childhood and adolescence, in particular, are life stages in which identity is very much a "work in progress"; working effectively with youth of color, in particular, requires being grounded in the literature that has explored these issues.

Defining Ethnic and Racial Identities

Ethnic identity is an important part of self-identity that differentiates members of one ethnic group from another (Bernal, Knight, Garza, Ocampo, & Cota, 1990). In addition to the formation of the self-concept, ethnic identity is also thought to be influential in the development of values, attitudes, and behaviors. For example, one's ethnic group membership might influence languages spoken, preferences for foods, rituals practiced, and holidays observed. Racial identity refers to one's self-identification as a member of a racial group or groups (Helms, 1990). Racial group membership is not the same as ethnic group membership, which is evidenced by the following examples. A child might racially be Black but have an ethnic identity as a Haitian American. Likewise, a child might identify racially as White but ethnically as Arab American. Race most certainly has implications for one's view of the world, experience of privilege or discrimination, and interactions with others. Race also influences the development of values, attitudes, and behaviors, but it is largely accepted that many important ethnic group differences exist among individuals who are members of the same racial group (Helms, 1990).

Furthermore, the sociopolitical histories of many ethnic groups include racial group mixtures. For example, for Mexican Americans, their ethnic heritage is composed of the mixture of White Spaniards with conquered indigenous peoples. Because of the history of slavery, many African Americans are racially a mixture of Black and White or indigenous peoples. Although ethnicity and race are often used interchangeably in the literature, they are in fact distinct concepts, both of which have psychological relevance. All individuals possess both racial and ethnic group memberships that influence their identity development. It is also easier for children to learn to categorize people based on race than ethnicity because oftentimes ethnic groups have racial similarities that are difficult for children to discern (e.g., Filipinos versus Puerto Ricans). However, by middle childhood, most children are capable of correctly identifying people based on both race and ethnicity (Bernal et al., 1990).

Within specific ethnic groups, physical appearances vary by race, which further complicates identity development, for children in particular. For example, Mexican American children who are darker-skinned and appear more phenotypically indigenous may experience discrimination differentially than those who are lighter-skinned, with more European features. Research seems to indicate that these racial differences within ethnic groups can have important influences on quality-of-life indices. For example, Relethford, Stern, Gaskill, and Hazuda (1983) investigated the influence of race on a sample of Mexican Americans and Puerto Ricans and found that skin color became progressively lighter as they moved from lower socioeconomic status to higher socioeconomic status in their sample. Arce, Murguia, and Frisbie (1987) also examined phenotypical differences among Mexican Americans and found correlations among skin tone, income level, and education level. Thus, one's racial and ethnic identities appear to have significant psychological and socioeconomic implications that extend into adulthood.

Ethnic and identity development begins in childhood and serves as the mechanism through which children attain an understanding of themselves as members of cultural groups. However, as children develop cognitively and socially and interact with the important contexts in their world, their understanding of identity matures. Hence, ethnic and identity development are dynamic processes influenced by context and social-cognitive abilities.

Components of Ethnic and Racial Identities

Leading scholars have identified a number of key components of ethnic and racial identity development in children (Aboud, 1987; Bernal et al., 1990; Rotheram & Phinney, 1987). Perhaps the simplest form of ethnic and racial identity involves self-identification with ethnic and racial groups. Although rudimentary, the process of identifying oneself as a member of a group has critical implications for the formation of identity (Tajfel, 1974). Identification with social groups tends to produce a psychological or social connection to other group members. Members of social groups, including racial and ethnic groups, may show preferences toward others of the same groups. These processes stem from universal human needs to affiliate with one or more human groups (Allport, 1954). Although most children begin to self-identify as members of a racial group relatively early in life (i.e., 3–4 years of age), the identification with ethnic groups occurs later in childhood (i.e., 5–8 years of age) (Bernal et al., 1990). However, this may vary among ethnic groups. For example, Quintana (1994) found that some Mexican American children ages 7 and 8 were not able to accurately identify their ethnic group membership. Self-identification of ethnicity is complicated for young children because not only are they learning to identify with groups in which they are members, but they also must learn to differentiate themselves from groups in which they are not members. In exploring children's reasoning for racial and ethnic self-identifications, Quintana found that many second graders who identified both as White and Mexican American did so because, in the words of one child, they were not "Black."

One reason that children are believed to self-identify racially before self-identifying according to ethnicity is because most of the racial terms commonly used in the United States also have chromatic connotations (e.g., White or Black; Hirschfeld, 1994). There is some debate over whether children who use racial terms that also have chromatic connotations are using the terms to refer to race per se or to color. However, it is clear that such literal associations between labels and their connotations are helpful to the learning process of children.

For example, Quintana (1994) reasoned that during middle elementary school, children understood nonchromatic racial and ethnic terms when the terms were reflective of literal or descriptive features of race and ethnicity, such as marking appearance (e.g., Black) or geographical heritage (e.g., Mexican American or African American). Hence, existing research suggests that the developmental sequencing of children's understanding of racial and ethnic terms is based on the ontologic complexity of the terms. Racial terms that are also chromatic are learned before ethnic terms, which are less literal, but are still understandable to children (e.g., being Mexican means that your family comes from Mexico). Following this logic, it would seem that children's understanding of the social implications underlying the terms they use as self-referents would occur later in their development because understanding political connotations is ontologically more complex.

Another component of racial and ethnic identity development involves an understanding that one's membership in such groups is both unchangeable and permanent. In preschool and early elementary school, many children may not yet have acquired this knowledge, termed ethnic or racial constancy, which is the understanding that ethnic or racial status remains constant despite superficial changes (e.g., changes in hair or skin tones). Racial and ethnic constancy have been studied in conjunction with gender constancy, and it has been found that by middle childhood, most children have both accurate understanding of their gender, racial, and ethnic group memberships and comprehend that it is not possible to change these identities (Ocampo, Bernal, & Knight, 1993).

Contextual Influences on Ethnic/Racial Awareness

Ethnic/racial awareness is an individual's recognition of his or her own racial and ethnic distinctiveness as well as that of other individuals (Rotheram & Phinney, 1987). It includes both self-identification and constancy, but it also has psychological meaning in that it is related to the development of racial and ethnic pride, feelings of belongingness, and ultimately achievement of a positive identity. For children of color in the United States, ethnic/racial awareness can occur through personal recognition and discovery, experiences of oppression (e.g., stigma, discrimination, stereotyping), ethnic-racial socialization, and so forth. It can occur in the context of peers, family, the media, and community interactions. It also occurs at conscious and unconscious levels.

Research by Van Ausdale and Feagin (1996) suggests that elements of ethnic/racial awareness are present as early as age 3. In a long-term child-centered observational study of preschoolers in a school setting, these authors found that children understand and use racial/ethnic concepts in varying ways. They found that children were able to use racial and ethnic concepts to exclude peers who were members of stigmatized groups, socially control the behavior of peers based on race/ethnicity, define themselves and others, and use ethnicity/race as a way to include peers in play. Van Ausdale and Feagin's findings are important in that they demonstrate young children are not only aware of racial-ethnic differences, but they incorporate race and ethnicity into their early social lives.

Ethnic/racial awareness can be demonstrated anecdotally by a situation that arose while one of the authors of this chapter was working for a preschool-based mental health program and was approached by a preschool employee who described a parent's concern about her child's questions regarding her physical features and complexion. The following is a brief summary of the situation.

Janel was a 4-year-old, tan-complexioned, African American child who lived with her mother and younger brother. Her mother and brother had lighter skin complexions and different hair textures than Janel. At home, Janel began to make comments to her mother that reflected her awareness of these differences between herself and her mother and brother. Janel's mother reported that Janel was very sad about looking different from her family members and that she was concerned about her. As a psychoeducational intervention to increase this child's sense of racial awareness and pride, Janel's mother was encouraged to obtain a copy of a book titled *Shades of Black* (Pinkney & Pinkney, 2005), which depicts African American children with an array of complexions, hair textures, and eye colors. Janel's mother later reported that after reading the book to her child, Janel felt better about herself and her physical characteristics.

Janel's experience exemplifies that ethnic/racial awareness is often first detected in the context of one's own family. Her story also demonstrates that although children of color may not be able to fully verbalize and explain their racial/ethnic awareness, it can be an emotionally distressing process, especially if not actively addressed. The intervention represented an opportunity to reframe Janel's developing negative perceptions of her physical features (i.e., I am not like my mother and brother) by helping her develop a more accurate understanding of ethnic and racial belonging and a positive sense of ethnic and racial pride.

Ethnic/racial awareness is important to youth of color throughout their development because they are often the targets of both explicit and ambiguous discrimination, which can hinder their developing self-concept. Oftentimes the discrimination that children inflict on other children reflects their understanding of racial and ethnic stereotypes. Research on stereotype consciousness during middle childhood suggests that children's awareness of stereotypes increases with age but begins for some children at age 6 (McKown & Weinstein, 2003). Among a diverse sample of children, African American and Latino children were found to be most aware of widely held stereotypes in comparison to White and Asian youth. It was further found that stereotype consciousness interfered with cognitive performance as a function of stereotype threat for children who were aware of stereotypes. Stereotype threat is defined as the fear of personally validating a negative stereotype about an individual's social group, a fear that can lead to poor academic performance (Steele & Aronson, 1995). Though stereotype threat can have a deleterious effect on youth as they develop, recent research has found that having a strong connection to one's racial identity can moderate the effects of stereotype threat among African American college students (Davis, Aronson, & Salinas, 2006). Hence, growing ethnic and racial awareness also results in an understanding of stereotypes that can impact psychological and academic well-being.

Adolescence is a pivotal time in the development of ethnic/racial awareness because by adolescence, youth have developed the cognitive structures necessary to understand their life experiences in a more nuanced manner. Ethnic/racial awareness is not a stepwise linear process that smoothly flows from one developmental stage to the next. Rather, it is best thought of as a process that changes from one where children are attempting to figure out how ethnicity and race define who they are to a process whereby adolescents and young adults develop feelings and attitudes about their group memberships. Jean Phinney, a pioneer in the area of ethnic identity in adolescence, suggests that ethnicity is a particularly salient construct for understanding psychological and academic development among adolescents (Phinney, 1996). Overall, her research suggests that varying degrees of attachment to one's ethnic identity has important consequences for youth's self-concept and self-esteem and that these consequences are most significant for youth of color in the United States (Phinney, 1992; 1996; Phinney & Devich-Navarro, 1997). This is due to the fact that there is a history of oppression in the United States that has stigmatized non-White ethnic groups. Thus, her research has shown that adolescents' ethnic identities range from well-explored, positive identities to unexplored neutral or negative identities.

Other researchers have examined the range of ethnic and racial identity statuses found among adolescents (Oyserman, Kemmelmeier, Fryberg, Brosh, & Hart-Johnson, 2003). In a domestic and international sample of African American, Native American, and Palestinian Israeli youth, Oyserman et al. (2003) found that when youth were asked, "What does it mean to you to be a member of your race or ethnic group?" the content of adolescents' responses reflected a variety of identity development statuses. Specifically, the researchers categorized their participants into four statuses: aschematic, in-group only, dual, or minority identities. An aschematic identity reflected an individual that responded in a manner that suggested that group membership was not important to how the self was viewed. The in-group only self-schema did not include conceptualizations of the self related to larger society. Dual-identity responses reflected a form of bicultural identity in which adolescents view themselves as members of the in-group and larger society. Minority-identity adolescents responded in a manner that suggests being a member of their group was associated with seeking to overcome societal barriers relevant to their in-group. It was additionally found that there were developmental differences in these identifications among the students. The older students were less likely to possess an aschematic self-schema.

Oyserman et al. (2003) hypothesized that as youth develop, it may become more challenging to maintain an aschematic schema because they are consistently confronted by experiences that are best explained by racial/ethnic factors. Most notably, students with an in-group only or aschematic racial and ethnic schemas demonstrated lower grades than their dual-identity and minority-identity peers. Oyserman et al.'s (2003) work is consistent with recent research that suggests that youth with a positive sense of themselves and others are less susceptible to stereotype threat in academic settings (Davis et al., 2006) as well as racial socialization research that shows that African American youth who had a high degree of awareness about racial issues received higher grades than peers who received fewer messages about race (Sanders, 1997). Thus, varying degrees of ethnic/racial awareness may impact a variety of childhood outcomes.

At later stages of development, factors beyond cognitive development play a role in racial/ethnic awareness, because cognitive structures become more "adult-like" during adolescence. For example, a recent line of research has examined the temporal salience and context-dependent nature of ethnic and racial awareness. Kim-Ju and Liem's (2003) research explored ethnic self-awareness in college students by measuring the impact of social contexts that consisted of racially mixed, predominantly majority, and predominantly minority situations represented in vignettes. They found that across these contexts, Asian Americans when compared to Whites were more aware of their ethnicity. Interestingly, Asian Americans reported the highest level of ethnic awareness when they were presented with predominantly minority and predominantly majority vignettes. Thus, ethnic self-awareness may fluctuate as a function of social context.

RACIAL AND ETHNIC SOCIALIZATION: COPING WITH DISCRIMINATION

There is an ever-present struggle among people of color in the United States to maintain cultural values, attitudes, and behaviors that reflect healthy, positive ethnic and racial identities in a multiculturally diverse larger society (Constantine & Sue, 2006). One method of encouraging positive ethnic and racial identities is through the process of ethnic-racial socialization. Ethnic-racial socialization is the practice and process that parents use to promote positive cultural identity while preparing youth for possible experiences of individual, cultural, or institutional oppression (Peterson, 1985; Umana-Taylor & Yazedjian, 2006). It can further be viewed as an intervening factor that affects ethnic and racial identity formation and self-concept development.

Historically, parents raising children in the context of oppression have provided ethnic-racial socialization to their children (e.g., McGill, 2000). Ethnic-racial socialization is a dynamic process that has changed over time (Brown & Lesane-Brown, 2006) and across generations (Umana-Taylor & Yazedjian, 2006) in terms of themes and messages (Coard & Sellers, 2005). Hughes et al. (2006) suggest the most frequently occurring ethnic-racial socialization messages address cultural socialization, preparation for bias, promotion of mistrust, and promotion of egalitarian values. Cultural socialization is the practice of teaching children about their ethnic/racial heritage and culture. Preparation for bias is the act of preparing children to cope with discrimination. Promotion of mistrust is the practice of teaching youth to be cautious during interracial encounters. Egalitarianism is the practice of encouraging children to appreciate individual traits (Hughes & Chen, 1997). Socialization messages also vary as a function of self-reported ethnicity (Anglin & Whaley, 2006; Biafora, Taylor, Warheit, Zimmerman, & Vega, 1993) and age (Hughes & Chen, 1997). Methods of racial and ethnic socialization include oral communication, modeling, role-playing (Coard, Wallace, Stevenson, & Brotman, 2004), and not discussing race at all (Hughes et al., 2006). A recent review of literature suggests the predictors of racial-ethnic socialization attitudes and behaviors have thus far included age and gender of children, parental immigration status, socioeconomic status, region, neighborhood, and parental racial identity, as well as parental and child experiences with discrimination (Hughes et al., 2006).

Though ethnic-racial socialization is an important, positive experience for many youth, it is often a challenging process for parents in that it is influenced by the racial and ethnic attitudes they, themselves, possess. An overabundance of negative messages about racial discrimination and mistrust can have the potential to affect a child's ability to function in multicultural settings (Biafora et al., 1993). For instance, a child who hears consistent messages about cultural mistrust in the absence of other positive racial socialization messages (e.g., coping strategies) may become angry or depressed about the harsh realities of racism and have difficulty functioning in multicultural social contexts. Youth who receive little or no socialization may struggle to understand their racial experiences and lack the coping mechanisms necessary to appropriately deal with such experiences. These youth may blame themselves and internalize stereotypes about their particular social group.

Yet, despite parents' attempts to racially and ethnically socialize their children in ways they believe will help them survive in the world, it is clear that by adolescence, youth individualize their identities and strategies for coping with racism, which often are quite different from what they were taught by their parents (Phinney & Chavira, 1995). This is likely because important aspects of socialization occur outside the family.

Extrafamilial Ethnic-Racial Socialization

Ethnic-racial socialization can also occur in contexts beyond the family. People in the community or alternative caregivers, such as fictive kin, can also be involved. These individuals can include teachers (Ladson-Billings, 1997), therapists/counselors (Greene, 1992; Thomas, 2005), peers (Constantine & Blackmon, 2002; Diemer, Kauffman, Koenig, Trahan, & Hsieh, 2006), mentors, social service employees, and community members. Extrafamilial ethnic-racial socialization processes can take place in a variety of domains. These domains often serve as cultural "shelters" in which youth of color can be immersed in their respective cultures and receive an abundance of culturally affirming messages and experiences. These locations include but are not limited to schools, places of worship, culturally centered community agencies or programs, and culturally centered educational institutions (e.g., historically Black colleges and universities, culture-centered private schools, home schooling).

For example, in 2002, Constantine and Blackmon explored ethnic-racial socialization in Black adolescents attending an African-centered parochial school. They hypothesized that Black parents may place their children in such schools to expose them to their culture, promote cultural practices, and protect their children from oppression-related experiences until they have matured to develop the necessary coping skills. Interventions that provide youth with ethnic-racial socialization experiences have been found to reduce problem behaviors (Whaley & McQueen, 2004), reduce relational aggression, and increase ethnic identity (Belgrave et al., 2002).

Neighborhoods can also be important contexts in identity development for youth because they can contain socializing agents and institutions for youth that reinforce or negate socialization messages provided to youth at home. Important findings about African American and Latino youth have emerged that suggest that neighborhood is an important factor in ethnic-racial socialization, the ethnic identity development process, and behavioral adjustment (Bennett, 2006; Caughy, Nettles, O'Campo, & Lohrfink, 2006; Supple, Ghazarian, Frabut, Plunkett, & Sands, 2006). For instance, negative neighborhood climate has been found to moderate the relationship between parental socialization messages and externalizing behavior among children, suggesting that negative neighborhood attributes (e.g., crime, lack of social capital) may weaken the strength of ethnic-racial socialization messages (Caughy et al., 2006). Other findings suggest that ethnic-racial socialization can mediate the relationship between negative neighborhood effects and ethnic identity content (Bennett, 2006). Similar research with Latino adolescents suggests that neighborhood risk moderates the relationship between family ethnic-racial socialization practices and ethnic affirmation (Supple et al., 2006).

The effects of neighborhood on ethnic-racial socialization are understandable when one considers that many American children spend significant amounts of time outside the home. One important element of neighborhoods is the dominant peer groups that live in neighborhoods. Constantine and Blackmon (2002) theorized that ethnic-racial socialization messages provided to children by African American parents are reinforced among Black youths' peer groups. Underresourced neighborhoods are significantly related to deviant peer affiliation (Brody et al., 2001), whereas other research suggests that ethnic identity is a moderator between parental monitoring and deviant peer affiliation (Hanawahine, 2004). Thus, ethnic and racial identities are influenced by purposeful socialization that children receive from their families, cultural institutions, and educational settings as well as inadvertent socialization that may come from neighborhood influences.

Ethnic-Racial Socialization and Mental Health Outcomes

The potential that exists for experiencing racial- and ethnic-based discrimination represents a continuous risk factor that affects the development of youth of color (LaFromboise, Hoyt, Oliver, & Whitebeck, 2006). Constantine and Sue (2006) argued that developing positive mental health is difficult for people of color, suggesting that "separating public and private evaluations may be a vital survival strategy for many Blacks and other people of color" (p. 233). Thus, without the process of positive ethnic-racial socialization, children of color may be far more susceptible to negative psychological and environmental effects on their mental health. Several recent studies have established connections between socialization and mental health outcomes.

Research with Asian American immigrant parents and their children highlights the importance of ethnic-racial socialization as a potential buffer for mental health difficulties. Kim, Gonzales, Stroh, and Wang (2006) found that fathers' self-reported experiences of marginalization were significantly associated with their adolescents' depressive symptoms. They further found that Asian American adolescents' own experiences of marginalization were significantly associated with depressive symptoms. These findings suggest that both personal and familial experiences of oppression may contribute to childhood depression. The authors argued that being ill equipped to cope with discrimination may be the pathway through which negative mental health outcomes occur.

In another study of Native American adolescents ages 10 to 15 experiencing adversity living on or near reservations, LaFromboise and her colleagues (2006) found that resiliency (i.e., the lack of negative mental health outcomes) markedly decreases with age; perceived discrimination was identified as a "primary risk factor". Interestingly, the authors found that Native American youth who had received positive cultural socialization were 1.8 times more likely to be resilient in the face of adversity. Thus, while there is a need for future research in this area, initial findings suggest that ethnic-racial socialization has significant implications for mental health status, not just identity development.

FUTURE DIRECTIONS IN ETHNIC-RACIAL SOCIALIZATION RESEARCH

Arab American and Muslim American Youth

Some youth may require unique ethnic-racial socialization experiences given the contexts in which they exist. For instance, recent research has found a causal relationship between discriminatory events and psychological distress for many Arab Americans (Moradi & Hassan, 2004). Since September 11th, the social climate within the United States has changed for many Americans, but for Arab Americans, there has been a significant increase in racial victimization such as racial and religious profiling. These experiences represent a contemporary stressor and psychological burden for Arab American parents and children, which may demand an increase in ethnic-racial socialization of these youth. Muslim youth may also experience similar challenges in the wake of September 11th. Some Muslim Americans have reported intolerant acts that include racial epithets, negative looks and gestures, avoidance by others, intimidation, defacement of property, and physical attacks (Livengood & Stodolska, 2004). Many Muslim women have also experienced gendered discrimination as a function of style of dress and clothing that readily identifies them to others. Research with Muslim adolescents has found that students felt their peers did not understand Islam and the cultural differences that exist between groups; and harmful stereotypes about Islam are insidious in schools (Ahmad & Szpara, 2003). The students further reported that they were negatively affected by such stereotypes. Hence, for Muslim American parents, socialization may include a combination of ethnic, racial, and religious messages. Future research should seek to document and understand the socialization processes of Arab and Muslim American parents, especially as they may relate to child outcomes.

Transracial and International Adoptees

Similar to their nonadoptive peers, transracial and internationally adopted youth of color are also vulnerable to the effects of oppression (Lee, 2003). Lee, Grotevant, Hellerstedt, Gunnar, and The Minnesota International Adoption Project Team (2006) suggest that transracial cultural socialization, a subcategory of ethnic-racial socialization, is the process and purposeful effort of transmitting messages about children's birth culture. Transracial and international adoptions represent an interesting challenge for majority parents, who may struggle with how to culturally socialize their children. Lee (2003) suggests that cultural socialization is a more complex process when adoptees and their parents are of a different race and/or ethnicity. He further suggests that White parents may not always have the cultural repertoire to prepare youth for life as a person of color. Research indicates that many White adoptive parents are less engaged in ethnic-racial socialization processes than parents of color (Hamm, 2001). Other research on internationally adopted children and White parents further confirms these findings. Lee and his colleagues (2006) found, in a study of White adoptive parents, that parents who adopted children from Russia reported lower ethnic socialization efforts than parents who had adopted children from China, Columbia, India, and Korea. These findings may speak to the salience of racial issues for White parents who adopt children. Because there are fewer visible differences between White parents and adopted children from similar racial groups, parents may feel less of a need to ethnically socialize their children than those who adopt children with visible racial differences.

Yet, these findings may be related to research with nonadopted children that suggests ethnic-racial socialization is largely influenced by parents' own ethnic and racial identities (Thomas & Speight, 1999). White adoptive parents may not have the same degree of racial and ethnic identification as many of their ethnic minority counterparts, which is influenced by their own socialization experiences. As a result, many transracially adoptive parents may be challenged in helping their children develop a healthy ethnic-racial identity. It is also conceivable that these parents may vicariously experience racism-related stress as a function of raising a child of color. These special challenges for transracial and international adoptive parents will demand new research from the field and new intervention strategies. The first stages in this research are being conducted by Lee (2003), who has specified specific socialization strategies for adoptive parents raising racially dissimilar children (i.e., finding opportunities for cultural assimilation, enculturation, and racial inculcation).

"Street" Culture and the Media

For youth who do not receive positive and consistent ethnic-racial socialization messages from traditional sources such as family, school, or community leaders, other forms of socialization may subvert healthy identity development. Oliver (2006) highlighted "street socialization" as an alternative form of socialization to which urban, underclass/low-income Black males may be exposed. Through street socialization, youth learn ways of obtaining social status and value; it takes place in locales such as street corners, parks, and other public spaces. Street socialization is further proliferated through some forms of rap music and the hip-hop culture, which are disseminated through the media. Thus, youth do not necessarily have to directly participate in street socialization (e.g., gangs and crews) to be influenced by such messages.

The messages of street socialization can include toughness, the sexual subjugation of women, and the glorification of illegal activities, which may result in stereotyped cultural and gender identities. Street socialization is a legitimate form of socialization that influences the ways adolescents living in high-risk neighborhoods view themselves racially, ethnically, and in terms of gender, but it is not a well-studied phenomenon. The content of many music videos and other forms of media tends to glorify aspects of "street life," but it is not clear whether these types of influences have the potential to nullify competing socialization messages that come from family and other sources. Some have argued that despite the fact street socialization often confirms stereotypes that exist about youth of color, such lifestyle messages reflect survival mechanisms utilized in various communities (Kubrin, 2005). Nonetheless, children and adolescents, as consumers of music videos, television, and movies, are vulnerable to the depiction of members of their ethnic and racial groups, whether the depictions are positive or negative. Therefore, it is important to further study the impact of these media images on the development of racial and ethnic identities.

CONCLUSION

Understanding the complexity of ethnic and racial identities of children and adolescents has been a major focus of psychological research for several decades. The findings from these investigations have been valuable to professionals who endeavor to promote the healthy identity development of youth, particularly children and adolescents of color. It is also important to acknowledge the need for further research that addresses the contemporary needs of children and adolescents. Yet, it is apparent that familial and nonfamilial socialization that fosters positive racial and ethnic identities is important to the psychological well-being of all children.

REFERENCES

Aboud, F. E. (1987). The development of ethnic self-identification and attitudes. In J. S. Phinney & M. J. Rotheram (Eds.), *Children's ethnic socialization* (pp. 32–55). Newbury Park, CA: Sage.

Aboud, F. E. (1988). *Children and prejudice.* Cambridge, UK: Basil Blackwell.

Ahmad, I., & Szpara, M. (2003). Muslim children in urban America: The New York City schools experience. *Journal of Muslim Minority Affairs, 23*(2), 295–301.

Allport, G. W. (1954). *The nature of prejudice.* Cambridge, MA: Addison-Wesley.

Anglin, D., & Whaley, A. L. (2006). Racial/ethnic self-labeling in relation to group socialization and identity in African-descended individuals. *Journal of Language and Social Psychology, 25*(4), 457–463.

Arce, C. H., Murguia, E., & Frisbie, W. P. (1987). Phenotype and life chances among Chicanos. *Journal of Behavioral Sciences, 9*(1), 19–32.

Belgrave, F. Z., Reed, M. C., Plybon, L. E., Butler, D. S., Allison, K. W., & Davis, T. (2002). An evaluation of the Sisters of Nia: A cultural program for African American girls. *Journal of Black Psychology, 30*(3), 329–343.

Benjamin, L. T., & Crouse, F. M. (2002). The American Psychological Association's response to Brown v. Board of Education: The case of Kenneth B. Clark. *American Psychologist, 57,* 38–50.

Bennett, M. D. (2006). Culture and context: A study of neighborhood effects on racial socialization and ethnic identity content in a sample of African American adolescents. *Journal of Black Psychology, 32*(4), 479–500.

Bernal, M. E., Knight, G. P., Garza, C. A., Ocampo, K. A., & Cota, M. K. (1990). The development of ethnic identity in Mexican-American children. *Hispanic Journal of Behavioral Sciences, 12,* 3–24.

Bernal, M. E., Saenz, D. S., & Knight, G. P. (1991). Ethnic identity and adaptation of Mexican American youths in school settings. *Hispanic Journal of Behavioral Sciences, 13*(2), 135–154.

Biafora, F. A., Taylor, D. L., Warheit, G. J., Zimmerman, R. S., & Vega, W. A. (1993). Cultural mistrust and racial awareness among ethnically diverse Black adolescent boys. *Journal of Black Psychology, 19*(3), 266–281.

Brody, G. H., Ge, X., Conger, R., Gibbons, F. X., Murry, V. M., Gerrard, M., et al. (2001). The influence of neighborhood disadvantage, collective socialization, and parenting on African American children's affiliation with deviant peers. *Child Development, 71*(4), 1231–1246.

Brown, T. N., & Lasane-Brown, C. L. (2006). Race socialization messages across historical time. *Social Psychology Quarterly, 69*(2), 201–213.

Caughy, M. O., Nettles, S. M., O'Campo, P. J., & Lohrfink, K. F. (2006). Neighborhood matters: Racial socialization of African American children. *Child Development, 77*(5), 1120–1236.

Clark, K. B., & Clark, M. P. (1940). Skin color as a factor in racial identification and preferences in Negro children. *Journal of Negro Education, 19,* 341–350.

Coard, S. I., & Sellers, R. M. (2005). African American families as a context for racial socialization. In V. C. McLoyd, N. E. Hill, & K. A. Dodge (Eds.), *African American family life: Ecological and cultural diversity* (pp. 264–284). New York: Guilford Press.

Coard, S. I., Wallace, S. A., Stevenson, H. C., & Brotman, L. M. (2004). Toward culturally relevant preventive interventions: The consideration of racial socialization in parent training with African American families. *Journal of Child and Family Studies, 13*(3), 277–293.

Constantine, M. G., & Blackmon, S. M. (2002). Black adolescents' racial socialization experiences: Their relations to home, school, and peer self-esteem. *Journal of Black Studies, 32*(3), 322–335.

Constantine, M. G., & Sue, D. W. (2006). Factors contributing to optimal human functioning in people of color in the United States. *The Counseling Psychologist, 34*(2), 228–244.

Crocker, J., & Major, B. (1989). Social stigma and self-esteem: The self-protective properties of stigma. *Psychological Review, 96,* 608–630.

Cross, W. E., Jr. (1995). Oppositional identity and African American youth: Issues and prospects. In W. D. Hawley & A. W. Jackson (Eds.), *Toward a common destiny: Improving peace and ethnic relations in America* (pp. 185–204). San Francisco: Jossey-Bass.

Davis, C., Aronson, J., & Salinas, M. (2006). Shades of threat: Racial identity as a moderator of stereotype threat. *Journal of Black Psychology, 32*(4), 399–417.

Diemer, M. A., Kauffman, A., Koenig, N., Trahan, E., & Hsieh, C. (2006). Challenging racism, sexism, and social injustice: Support for urban adolescents' critical consciousness development. *Cultural Diversity and Ethnic Minority Psychology, 12*(3), 444–460.

Greene, B. (1992). Racial socialization as a tool in psychotherapy with African American children. In L. A. Vargas & J. D. Koss-Chioino (Eds.), *Working with culture: Psychotherapeutic interventions with ethnic minority children and adolescents* (pp. 63–81). San Francisco: Jossey Bass.

Hamm, J. V. (2001). Barriers and bridges to positive cross-ethnic relations: African American and White parent socialization beliefs and practices. *Youth and Society, 33,* 62–98.

Hanawahine, G. L. (2004). Ethnic identity as a moderator in the relationship between parental monitoring and deviant peer affiliation. *Dissertation Abstracts International, 65*(11-B). (UMI No. 3153788)

Helms, J. (1990). *Black and white racial identity: Theory, research, and practice.* New York: Greenwood.

Hirschfeld, L. A. (1994). The child's representation of human groups. *The Psychology of Learning and Motivation, 31,* 133–185.

Hughes, D. L., & Chen, L. (1997). When and what parents tell children about race: An examination of race-related socialization among African American families. *Applied Developmental Science, 1*(4), 200–214.

Hughes, D., Rodriguez, J., Smith, E. P., Johnson, D. J., Stevenson, H. C., & Spicer, P. (2006). Parents' ethnic-racial socialization practices: A review of research and directions for future study. *Developmental Psychology, 42*(5), 747–770.

Katz, P. A. (1973). Stimulus predifferentiation and modification of children's racial attitudes. *Child Development, 44,* 232–237.

Kim, S. Y., Gonzales, N. A., Stroh, K., & Wang, J. L. (2006). Parent-child cultural marginalization and depressive symptoms in Asian American family members. *Journal of Community Psychology, 34*(2), 167–182.

Kim-Ju, G. M., & Liem, R. (2003). Ethnic self-awareness as a function of ethnic group status, group composition and ethnic identity orientation. *Cultural Diversity and Ethnic Minority Psychology, 9*(3), 289–302.

Kubrin, C. E. (2005). Gangstas, thugs, and hustlas: Identity and the code of the street in rap music. *Social Problems, 52*(3), 360–378.

Ladson-Billings, G. (1997). *Dreamkeepers: Successful teachers of African-American children.* San Francisco: Jossey-Bass.

LaFromboise, T. D., Hoyt, D. R., Oliver, L., & Whitebeck, L. B. (2006). Family, community, and school influences on resilience among American Indian adolescents in the upper midwest. *Journal of Community Psychology, 34*(2), 193–209.

Lee, R. M. (2003). The transracial adoption paradox: History, research and counseling: Implications of cultural socialization. *The Counseling Psychologist, 31*(6), 711–744.

Lee, R. M., Grotevant, H. D., Hellerstedt, W. L., Gunnar, M. R., & The Minnesota International Adoption Project Team. (2006). Cultural socialization in families with internationally adopted children. *Journal of Family Psychology, 20*(4), 571–580.

Livengood, J. S., & Stodolska, M. (2004). The effects of discrimination and constraints negotiation on leisure behavior of American Muslims in the post September 11 America. *Journal of Leisure Research, 36*(2), 183–208.

McGill, A. (2000). *In the hollow of your hand: Slave lullabies.* Boston: Houghton Mifflin Company.

McKown, C., & Weinstein, R. S. (2003). The development and consequences of stereotype consciousness in middle childhood. *Child Development, 74*(2), 498–515.

Moradi, B., & Hasan, N. T. (2004). Arab Amerian persons' reported experiences of discrimination and mental health. *Journal of Counseling Psychology, 51*(4), 418–428.

Ocampo, K. A., Bernal, M. E., & Knight, G. (1993). Gender, race, and ethnicity: The sequencing of social constancies. In M. E. Bernal & G. P. Knight (Eds.), *Ethnic identity* (pp. 11–30). New York: State University of New York Press.

Oliver, W. (2006). "The streets": An alternative Black male socialization institution. *Journal of Black Studies, 36*(6), 918–937.

Oyserman, D., Kemmelmeier, M., Fryberg, S., Brosh, H., & Hart-Johnson, T. (2003). Racial-ethnic self schemas. *Social Psychology Quarterly, 66*(4), 333–347.

Parham, T., & Helms, J. (1985). Attitudes of racial identity and self-esteem of Black students: An exploratory investigation. *Journal of College Student Personnel, 26,* 143–147.

Peterson, M. F. (1985). Racial socialization of young black children. In H. P. McAdoo & J. L. McAdoo (Eds.), *Black children: Social, educational, and parental environments* (pp. 159–173). Newbury Park, CA: Sage.

Phinney, J. S. (1992). The multigroup ethnic identity measure: A new scale for use with diverse groups. *Journal of Adolescent Research, 7*(2), 156–176.

Phinney, J. S. (1996). When we talk about American ethnic groups, what do we mean? *American Psychologist, 51*(9), 918–927.

Phinney, J. S., & Chavira, V. (1995). Parental ethnic socialization and adolescent coping with problems related to ethnicity. *Journal of Research on Adolescence, 5,* 31–53.

Phinney, J. S., & Devich-Navarro, M. (1997). Variations in bicultural identification among African American and Mexican American adolescents. *Journal of Research on Adolescence, 7*(1), 3–32.

Pinkney, S. L., & Pinkney, M. C. (2005). *Shades of Black: A celebration of our children.* New York: Scholastic.

Quintana, S. M. (1994). A model of ethnic perspective taking ability applied to Mexican-American children and youth. *International Journal of Intercultural Relations, 18,* 419–448.

Quintana, S. M., & Vera, E. M. (1999). Latino children's understanding of ethnic prejudice: Educational implications. In S. Tomlinson (Ed.), *Building multicultural communities: Contributions from counseling psychology and higher education* (pp. 102–120). Newbury Park, CA: Sage.

Ramsey, P. G. (1987). Young children's thinking about ethnic differences. In J. S. Phinney & M. J. Rotheram (Eds.), *Children's ethnic socialization* (pp. 56–72). Newbury Park, CA: Sage.

Relethford, J., Stern, M., Gaskill, S., & Hazuda, H. (1983). Social class, admixture, and skin color variation among Mexican Americans and Anglo Americans living in San Antonio, Texas. *American Journal of Physical Anthropology, 62,* 97–102.

Rotheram, M. J., & Phinney, J. S. (1987). Introduction: Definition and perspectives in the study of childrens' ethnic socialization. In J. S. Phinney (Ed.), *Children's ethnic socialization: Pluralism and development* (pp. 10–31). Beverly Hills, CA: Sage.

Sanders, M. G. (1997). Overcoming obstacles: Academic achievement as a response to racism and discrimination. *Journal of Negro Education, 66*(1), 83–93.

Steele, C. M., & Aronson, J. (1995). Stereotype threat and the intellectual test performance of African Americans. *Journal of Personality and Social Psychology, 69*(5), 797–811.

Supple, A. J., Ghazarian, S. R., Frabut, J. M., Plunkett, S. W., & Sands, T. (2006). Contextual influences on Latino adolescent ethnic identity and academic outcomes. *Child Development, 77*(5), 1427–1433.

Tajfel, H. (1974). Social identity and intergroup behaviour. *Social Science Information/sur les Sciences Sociales, 13*(2), 65–93.

Thomas, A. J. (2005). Family counseling and psychotherapy in racial-cultural psychology: Case applications. In R. J. Carter (Ed.), *Handbook of racial-cultural psychology and counseling* (Vol. 2, pp. 364–391). Hoboken, NJ: John Wiley and Sons.

Thomas, A. J., & Speight, S. (1999). Racial identity and racial socialization attitudes of African American parents. *Journal of Black Psychology, 25*(2), 152–170.

Umana-Taylor, A. J., & Yazedjian, A. (2006). Generational differences and similarities among Puerto Rican and Mexican mothers' experiences with familial ethnic socialization. *Journal of Social and Personal Relationships, 23*(3), 445–464.

Van Ausdale, D., & Feagin, J. R. (1996). Using racial and ethnic concepts: The critical case of very young children. *American Sociological Review, 61*, 119–793.

Whaley, A. L., & McQueen, J. P. (2004). An Afrocentric program as primary prevention for African American youth: Qualitative and quantitative exploratory data. *The Journal of Primary Prevention, 25*(2), 253–269.

CHAPTER 5

Research Methods Related to Understanding Multicultural Concepts

FREDERICK T. L. LEONG

DESIRÉE BAOLIAN QIN

JASON L. HUANG

With the increasing globalization and the aftermath of September 11th, social scientists in the United States have begun to pay more attention to the impact of multiculturalism on what they study and how they study the phenomena in question. In this chapter, we seek to facilitate this movement by providing an overview to the key challenges in applying research methods to multicultural concepts and multicultural populations.

We begin with an overview of the conceptual issues underlying multicultural research followed by a review of measurement equivalence issues. Next we examine the special challenges involved in data collection, discuss significant cultural moderators, and end with a review of the importance of mixed methods in multicultural research in child development. It is our view that an increased understanding of these issues and challenges by social scientists will result in more culturally appropriate and culturally relevant research being conducted.

CONCEPTUAL ISSUES

Approaches to Differences

A clarification of the conceptual issues surrounding multicultural perspective in psychology is a necessary foundation for the understanding of methodological issues. Multicultural perspective counters the long-held universality assumption that the mainstream American experience is universal and the research findings in the field are equally applicable to all populations. Burlew (2003) summarized the flaws of the universality assumption, stating that such an assumption (a) fails to recognize the possibility that theories developed from one culture may not generalize to another, (b) limits researchers from developing alternative theories and variables that contribute to the study of the psychology of ethnic minorities, (c) neglects the existence of culture-related protective mechanisms, and (d) leads to the deviational view of minority differences from the mainstream White culture. More specifically, in the field of child development, the mainstream developmental theories may be able to provide a heuristic general framework to assist specific model development, but they fail to contribute to the understanding of the developmental processes in children of color (Garcia Coll et al., 1998).

Recognizing the need to address differences in the psychology of different ethnic groups, however, may not necessarily translate into appropriate approaches in actual research studies. The way that differences between cultures are viewed may differ. One conceptual approach interprets cultural differences from the dominant cultural standard as less developed (Bourne, 1991). The nature of the hierarchy may be attributed to genetic factors or cultural influences. The genetically deficient model views physical, intellectual, and psychological differences as genetic inferiority in ethnic groups, whereas the culturally deficient model views ethnic group differences as the consequences of a lack of access to social and cultural resources. Another approach to difference attributes cultural differences to the effects of racism and social oppression, but such an approach tends to overemphasize the trauma and neglect cultural heritages and resilience of the minorities (Potts & Watts, 2003). In contrast, the culturally diverse/difference model sees differences across ethnic groups as complementary and equivalent. This model rejects the notion that differences from the White middle-class mainstream are inferior or deviant; rather, it accepts differences as legitimate and valuable (Garcia Coll et al., 1998).

Definition of Race, Ethnicity, and Culture

There is a general lack of clarification in the use of the terms *race*, *ethnicity*, and *culture*, and researchers often use them interchangeably (Okazaki & Sue, 1995). In general, race has been used to denote a subgroup of people who share some genetically based physical characteristics that are somewhat distinct from other subgroups (Jones, 1997). Ethnic group can be defined as "a group socially distinguished or set apart, by others or by itself, primarily on the basis of cultural or nationality characteristics" (Feagin, 1989, p. 9).

Arguing that researchers use race and ethnicity as proxy variables to capture some common psychological characteristics shared among people from the same ethnic groups, Okazaki and Sue (1995) suggested that researchers directly measure the underlying psychological variables that produce the cultural differences in the phenomena at hand. To the extent that these psychological variables associated with culture are identifiable, this approach may help to circumvent the methodological issues in culture-related research such as nonrandom assignment of cultures. For example, variables such as individualism-collectivism, Confucianism and its derivatives, and face and its derivatives may be relevant in the study of Asian Americans (Okazaki, Lee, & Sue, 2006). However, depending on the types of studies being conducted, it is often true that researchers are unable to specify the underlying psychological variables and, thus, they may have to resort to the use of race or ethnicity as proxy variables.

Types of Studies Across Cultures

Depending on the existence or absence of a priori hypotheses and contextual cultural variables, four types of research paradigms are generally adopted in comparisons between cultures (Van de Vijver, 2002). The first two types of studies are mostly concerned with hypothesis testing. Generalizability studies examine the degree to which research findings in one culture may generalize in other cultures, without involving specific contextual cultural factors. Contextual theory studies explicitly investigate the relations between cultural variables and psychological outcomes. A large number of cultures differing on the culture factors of interest will be sampled to test the hypothesized relations. In contrast, two other types of cross-cultural studies do not have a priori hypotheses. Psychological differences studies examine the comparability of psychometric properties of a certain measure across different cultures, such as means, standard deviations, and reliability coefficients. Ecological linkage studies seek to understand cross-cultural differences by exploring relations with a large number of contextual variables.

Cultural researchers have started to examine the influences of individual and cultural variables simultaneously using multilevel analysis. According to Leung and Van de Vijver (2006), two types of multilevel studies are relevant to cross-cultural studies. The first type of study examines the influences of variables from different levels of analysis in terms of their mean levels. The second type examines differences in psychological meanings across different levels. In addition to these two kinds of multilevel studies, culture has also been conceptualized from a within-individual perspective. G. T. Chao and Moon (2005) proposed the metaphorical view of culture as a mosaic so that (a) different cultural elements influence an individual just as "tiles" of a mosaic, and (b) individual tiles are organized by certain rules into a localized structure to influence the individual as a whole "picture." Some tiles may dominate others, some tiles may self-organize into localized structures, and others may remain independent and influence the individual rather unpredictably. Such a *bottom-up* approach does not assume the similarity and aggregation of culture-related variables within an ethnic group, and it acknowledges the possibility that the same cultural factors may have quite different effects on different individuals.

Planning for Research

Leung and Van de Vijver (2006) proposed two different approaches to cross-cultural research design. To maximize the relevance of measures to the local culture and avoid the dominance of one culture over the others, the decentered approach based on a diverse culture orientation is advocated in the conceptualization and design of a multicultural research study. The decentered approach solicits input from multiple cultures, so that the core construct being measured represents a culture-general set instead of a single culture.

In contrast to the decentered approach, the convergence approach does not involve local cultural inputs in the study design; instead, it seeks to maximize the cultural distance so that the constructs of interests would be novel to the cultures where it is investigated. When the patterns of relationship between constructs originated in one foreign culture are replicated in local cultures, convergence is found and the original culture is deemed to have exerted an influence on such relationship. If the patterns of relationship are not found in local cultures, it is quite likely that the original culture has a unique influence on such relationship.

MEASUREMENT EQUIVALENCE

An often-quoted dictum in psychological research is that "If something exists, it must exist in some amount and can therefore be measured." A multicultural corollary to that is that "Measures of social and psychological constructs are usually culturally relative and their equivalence in meaning and application should not be assumed." Best practices in multicultural research require that we evaluate if our selected instruments are indeed applicable to all cultural groups (Leung & Van de Vijver, 2006). When measuring constructs in multicultural contexts or across cultures, equivalence in measurement needs to be systematically evaluated rather than assumed. As observed by Leung and Van de Vijver, construct validation is possible only after measurement equivalence has been established.

Types of Measurement Equivalence

Berry (1980) provided a critical review of measurement equivalence issues in cross-cultural research. Conceptually, he argued that meaningful comparison of two phenomena presupposes the same underlying dimension. Therefore, comparison requires dimensional identity (Duijker & Frijda, 1960), which, in turn, needs to be established through demonstration of universality or equivalence. According to Berry, the seemingly contradictory stance between equivalence and variation can be resolved by the levels of analysis perspective: there can be identity for structure or function at one level, and variation for observable phenomena at another. Berry suggested two ways to establish dimensional identity. First, researchers may adopt the demonstration of universals from disciplines such as biology, linguistics, anthropology, or sociology. Second, researchers may use empirical demonstration of equivalence through data.

In earlier work, Berry and Dasen (1974) suggested that cross-cultural researchers pay attention to three forms of measurement equivalence. First, functional equivalence may be established by showing that two or more behaviors in different cultures are functionally related to similar problems. Second, conceptual equivalence may be established by demonstrating across cultures the equivalence of meaning of research materials or of behaviors. Three methods fall under conceptual equivalence: (a) translation equivalence (Brislin, 1976; Werner & Campbell, 1970), (b) semantic differential analyses (Osgood, 1965), and (c) linguistic analyses and object classification. Third, metric equivalence may be shown if psychometric properties of two sets of data are the same for different cultural groups. In order to demonstrate metric equivalence, researchers need to demonstrate that statistical relationships are similar among variables across cultures. They also need to show that the patterns of statistical relationships among dependent variables are similar in different cultures. This can be achieved by showing similarity in correlation matrices (Poortinga, 1975) or by common factor structures (Buss & Royce, 1975).

Marsella and Leong (1995) provided some examples to illustrate the different types of measurement equivalence. Using the notion of conceptual equivalency as referring to the similarity in the nature and meaning of a concept, they provided the following example. In the United States, the word *dependency* is associated with immaturity, childishness, helplessness, and many other derogatory terms. This is because American society has always valued individual "independence." Mainstream European American culture socializes children to be independent, self-sufficient, and autonomous. Children are encouraged to move away from home and to establish lives that are relatively independent of their family. Marsella and Leong contrasted this view with Japanese culture, in which children are socialized to be interdependent and to be an integral part of the family. The Japanese value of *amae* encourages people to impose on other's benevolence for assistance (e.g., Doi, 1971). It is said that in Japan, "the nail that sticks out must be hammered in." The emphasis is on interdependency and conformity. Thus, giving American personality scales on dependency to Japanese subjects will result in the latter evidencing high scores. But, the implications and consequences of these scores are not the same as in American culture, because in Japanese culture, dependency does not have the same negative connotations.

In terms of linguistic equivalence, Marsella and Leong (1995) proposed that this term acknowledges the importance of administering tests in the language preferences of the subjects under study. Linguistic equivalence is mainly concerned with translation. Thus, back-translation is used to develop an accurate foreign language translation of an English language instrument. However, it makes no assumption about the validity of the instrument. As a process, it merely attempts to provide an accurate linguistic translation, thus permitting comprehensibility. The authors noted that the simple translation of materials from one language into another language is no guarantee that the instrument is valid or appropriate for use in another culture (e.g., asking Vietnamese subjects whether they "like mechanics magazines" can be translated, but it may not be a valid question).

In summary, whereas authors such as T. P. Johnson (1998) have identified over 50 types of measurement equivalence, most cross-cultural researchers subscribe to these four major types of measurement equivalence: (a) conceptual, (b) functional, (c) linguistic, and (d) metric.

Strategies for Dealing With Measurement Equivalence

In their classic article discussing measurement in cross-cultural research, Hui and Triandis (1985) provided further clarification of measurement equivalence by pointing out that "conceptual equivalence of the construct is the first requirement for cross-cultural comparison" (p. 133). In other words, two cultures need to have the same concept if the measurement and comparison of that concept is to take place. In terms of functional equivalence, they proposed that this form of equivalence needs to be understood in terms of similarity of the goals of these two sets of behaviors. In addition, behaviors can be considered to be functionally equivalent only if they share similar precursors (antecedents), consequences, and correlates. They also added the concept of equivalence in construct operationalization, where the procedures used to measure a construct in different cultures need to be similar. Their last clarification of measurement equivalence was to divide metric equivalence into item equivalence (the items in our measures have the same meaning across cultures) and scalar equivalence (our measures have the same metrics across cultures).

In the rest of their paper, Hui and Triandis (1985) went on to suggest various strategies for improving and demonstrating different types of measurement equivalence. They begin by noting that psychological constructs differ in levels of abstraction. The abstraction continuum is related to universality-cultural difference distinction, as well as to the detection of cross-cultural differences on a given construct. According to the authors, commonality can be achieved by increasing the level of abstraction, often by sacrificing precision. Researchers often start out from abstraction toward specificity, assuming commonality and universality first, until the assumptions can no longer be met.

Hui and Triandis (1985) went on to delineate the typical approaches to measurement in cross-cultural research. Many researchers use direct comparisons and crude translations. This approach translates the test first, and then uses simple t-test or

MANOVA to test for cultural difference. However, the underlying assumption that equivalences exist is highly questionable. Other researchers use regression methods to evaluate if regression parameters of the criteria are the same. Although being economical and simple, the differences in subjects, variability, and measure reliability may lead to fluctuations in parameters.

Another common approach involves using coscoring methods to try to arrive at a common metric for the groups to be compared. Cattell's (1957) transcultural method is most widely known. It factors a sample of people by taking "one representative from each culture" (pp. 853–854). There are three variations of this approach. The first method randomly selects a representative from each culture. Factor analysis will yield the factors that subjects from each culture can be scored on, but such factors may not be interpretable because the factors show both individual differences and cultural differences. The second method randomly selects individuals from each culture, but it only factors the standard scores for each person relative to the local culture. This method removes between-group variance from factoring and leaves only within-group variance. The third method factors the mean score on each variable for each group. It removes within-group variance and retains only between-group difference. Such a method is problematic in presupposing conceptual/functional and operational equivalence.

The item response theory (IRT) method represents a more recent approach to measurement in multicultural research. Item and scalar equivalence can be assessed by examining item characteristic curves in different cultures. Two methods may be used: (a) use bilinguals to respond to both versions of the same scale, and (b) use the same scale on two different populations. Yet another recent method is the response pattern method. Irvine (1965; Irvine & Carroll, 1980), as a proponent of this method, proposed using *delta-plot* for aptitude and ability testing (Angoff, 1972). Under the assumption of conceptual/functional and operational equivalence, this method correlates the order rankings of item difficulty for each pair of cultures to assess whether the item taps the same attribute in the two cultures. However, there is no objective standard to evaluate the correlation coefficient. In addition, the coefficient only indicates overall similarity in the relative endorsement frequency of each item, but will not show difference if the frequency in one culture is uniformly higher or lower than in another culture.

With regards to linguistic equivalence, different translation techniques have been proposed. Brislin (1976) proposed methods such as back-translation, bilingual and committee approach, decentering, and pretests. There are two limitations to this approach. First, conceptual equivalence should be established before meaningful comparison. Second, cultural difference in terms of extraneous factors such as social desirability and motivation to respond may be problematic. The back-translation method has become the de facto approach to dealing with linguistic equivalence in multicultural research.

Examining the internal structure congruence of measures is another approach to evaluating measurement equivalence. The underlying rationale of this approach is that an equivalent construct should have the same components and the same relations among components across cultures. Multiple methods can be employed to investigate internal structure, such as factor analysis, multidimensional scaling, and maximum likelihood factor analysis, as well as comparison of correlation matrices of components. It should be noted that internal structure congruence cannot be taken as indicative of scalar equivalence.

Hui and Triandis (1985) also discussed the combined etic-emic approach. This approach identifies an etic construct first, and then develops and validates emic measures for such a construct. Then, the "emically defined etic construct" can be used in cross-cultural comparisons (Davidson, Jaccard, Triandis, Morales, & Diaz-Guerrero, 1976). There are two limitations to this approach: (a) constructs investigated are usually more abstract; and (b) item and scalar equivalences are absent, so there can be no direct comparison of cultures.

Finally, Hui and Triandis (1985) discussed the validation by nomological network approach. This approach is based on the notion that a construct should show similar empirical relationships if it has the same meaning across cultures. However, such an approach is insensitive to nonequivalence at the item and scalar levels. Moreover, it requires the equivalence of criteria.

In view of the advantages and disadvantages associated with the different approaches, Hui and Triandis proposed a multiple strategies approach to dealing with measurement equivalence issues in multicultural research. Specifically, they suggested the use of a combination of several methods to establish equivalence in most, if not all, levels of abstraction.

DATA COLLECTION

Basic Sampling Strategy

It should be noted that sampling is not the only approach to obtaining data in multicultural research. Reports of national censuses reveal important demographic information that may assist researchers to test the research question. In addition, demographic information shown in census materials may be central to the research question itself.

However, most multicultural studies involve the selection of representative samples of respondents to represent the populations of interest. The choice of sampling strategy in multicultural research is both determined by the research question being investigated and constrained by the accessibility of samples to the researcher. Sampling strategies can be divided into two broad groups, probability sampling versus nonprobability sampling. Probability sampling ensures that every person of the population has an equal opportunity to be selected in the sample. In contrast, nonprobability sampling does not guarantee the probability of inclusion in the study for each person.

Multicultural research studies using probability sampling are usually done on a large scale. Large-scale studies entail great investment of resources; therefore, nonprobability sampling is adopted more often, partly due to practical constraints.

Nonprobability sampling may take several forms. Purposive sampling selects the participants into the sample by certain characteristics deemed relevant to the study by the researcher. Snowball sampling is another form of nonprobability sampling. It solicits future participants via the help of current participants, and, thus, gradually reaches out to a network of people.

Convenience sampling is yet another form of nonprobability sampling. By selecting participants primarily on the basis of their availability and willingness to participate, a convenience sample is created. It should be noted that most psychological studies involve the use of convenience sampling to a certain extent. The use of college students in psychological research is a familiar example of convenience sampling to psychologists. Okazaki and Sue (1995) cautioned the use of college samples and community samples in multicultural studies, noting that the former tends to underestimate the diversity of the larger minority populations, whereas the latter limits the generalizability of research findings.

Recruitment and Retention of Participants

The solicitation of an appropriately large sample of ethnic minorities has long been acknowledged as a challenge. This challenge is, in part, due to the overall small population of some ethnic minorities (Sue & Sue, 2003). Sometimes the researcher has to compromise by combining the respondents from different ethnic groups sharing some common origin, treating the resultant data as if they were one ethnic group (e.g., combining Chinese American, Korean American, and Japanese American into one group). Okazaki and Sue (1995) cautioned against such practice on the basis that there may be substantial variability between the different ethnic groups and the combination may lead to large within-sample heterogeneity.

The difficulty in recruiting ethnic minorities originates not only from the limited population size, but also from cultural and ethnic differences in people's willingness to participate in psychological research (Okazaki & Sue, 1995). The cultural norms in responding and participating in research should be fully considered in the beginning of sampling.

Cauce, Ryan, and Grove (1998) proposed several strategies to recruit participants from ethnic minority groups, including (a) providing monetary incentives, (b) gaining support from organizational or community leaders of an ethnic group, (c) creating and utilizing personal contacts, (d) collecting information at the respondent's place of convenience, (e) using a neutral name for the study to avoid stigmatization, and (f) using follow-up calls. In addition, there are some other ways to increase the response rate, such as familiarizing ethnic minority respondents with the informed consent process (Sue & Sue, 2003), ensuring confidentiality, and accommodating the time available for possible participants.

In longitudinal studies, or studies that involve multiple administrations of data collection, the retention of participants is as important as the recruitment. Burlew (2003) suggested that lower socioeconomic status might lead to higher dropout rates in ethnic minorities, but she also noted the general success of researchers in retaining large percentages of participants. A few strategies are available to maintain a high retention rate, including collecting accurate personal information, maintaining interim or regular contacts, and implementing gradually increasing incentives toward the end of the study (Cauce et al., 1998).

Other Issues Relevant to Sampling

Some methodological issues with regard to sampling in multicultural studies are summarized. First, the assumptions about the use of ethnicity should be made explicit. Second, there is a need to classify persons of mixed racial or ethnic background. Third, self-perceived ethnicity may not be the same as cultural identification (Okazaki & Sue, 1995).

Finally, a caveat of the use of ethnicity is in order. Although it is sometimes assumed that diversity within an ethnic group is small or negligible (e.g., when race or ethnicity is used as a control variable), this may not be the case. Diversity within the four large ethnic minority groups may be due to the within-group difference in social condition and lifestyles (Burlew, 2003). Therefore, the level of specificity in the measure of ethnicity is contingent on the research question. Furthermore, identifying the aspects of culture that are related to the research question not only captures the within-group variation, but also enables the researcher to better understand the psychological influence beyond the overly broad concept of culture.

CULTURAL MODERATORS

In this section, we focus our discussion of methods related to cultural moderators in child development. More specifically, we examine what researchers need to pay attention to in an effort to capture the impact of culture on the development of children from diverse backgrounds. We examine the fluid nature of culture and discuss methods related to the study of the cultural moderators (e.g., ethnic identity and acculturation). We also highlight the context of large-scale immigration for studies of child development.

Cultural context plays a critical role in child development (Bronfenbrenner, 1979). A critical aspect of child development is the process of "children and families engaged in activities within a cultural and community context" (Weisner, 2005, p. 1). However, it was not until the last few decades that developmental psychologists have begun to recognize culture as an important context exerting critical influence on developmental outcomes in children (Quintana et al., 2006). There was a significant lack of attention to culture and other key factors that dictate the contexts and moderate the experiences of child development (Garcia Coll et al., 1998). Earlier research on child development was based almost exclusively on the experience of children (mostly boys) from White middle-class families (Erikson, 1968). Models of development based on White middle-class male samples were then established as norms that were expected to cut across different class, gender, ethnic, and cultural backgrounds (Gilligan, 1982).

The interest in culture has grown in child development given the increasingly diverse profile of the American child population as a result of large-scale immigration. With post-1965 immigration has come the largest wave of immigrant children in U.S. public schools, speaking over 100 different languages (C. Suarez-Orozco & M. Suarez-Orozco, 2001). Immigrant children are the fastest growing sector in the U.S. child population. Currently, one out of five children under 18 in the United States is either an immigrant child or a child with immigrant parents (Qin, Feinauer, & Quiroz, 2001). As a result, researchers are beginning to pay more attention to culture.

However, when culture is considered in the field of developmental psychology, another set of problems emerges. First, differences and divergences from the White middle-class "norm" have often been interpreted as biological or cultural deficiency (Garcia Coll, 2005). This is largely due to "a long history of antagonist attitudes toward difference" in Western psychology (Potts & Watts, 2003). Asian American parenting, for example, has been depicted unfavorably when compared to European American parenting, characterized as more authoritarian and restrictive than White middle-class parenting (Kim & Wong, 2002). However, when examined closely, R. K. Chao (1994) found that, rooted in the Confucian culture, "authoritarian" parenting is used by parents out of concern for the children; it does not necessarily lead to negative developmental outcomes in children. Similarly, in their study, Bornstein and colleagues (1998) found that Japanese mothers rate themselves as least competent and satisfied with their parenting compared to any of the other non-Asian groups. However, this does not necessarily indicate that the Japanese mothers are worse mothers; instead, the high value placed on modesty in the Japanese culture makes it culturally inappropriate for the Japanese mothers to assert their competence and satisfaction in parenting. It is, therefore, critical to take appropriate expression of behaviors in a particular culture into consideration when interpreting research findings on multicultural samples (Bornstein et al., 1998).

There is a need to examine the developmental constructs from the indigenous cultural-specific perspective. For example, Gorman (1998) has argued that Asian immigrant parenting should be examined as its own entity, "as qualitatively distinct and dissimilar from either Asian or European American parenting" (Kim & Wong, 2002, p. 193). Garcia Coll and Magnuson (1997) also argued that immigrant children's development should be examined as its own entity rather than using the models of White middle-class children as a benchmark. The culturally different model should be the guiding conceptual principle. Similarly, after reviewing the literature on Asian American parenting, Kim and Wong concluded that

> unfortunately, the bulk of the research on Asian/Asian American parenting have blindly applied Western parenting concepts to Asian/Asian Americans. Some have proceeded with great care in translating . . . despite such efforts, there is an appalling lack of indigenous and culture-specific Asian parenting concepts in the studies examined. (p. 189)

Second, in studies that attempt to focus on a specific ethnic group, culture is often *essentialized,* depicted as fixed and frozen (Okazaki et al., 2006; Qin, 2004). This approach ignores the changing and fluid nature of culture. Studies on the Asian and Asian American population, for example, overwhelmingly use the constructs of Markus and Kitayama's (1991) individual-collective or independent-interdependent framework (Okazaki et al.). There has been an overreliance on these cultural traits in interpretation of findings related to the Asian American population. Little attention has been paid to the changing economic, social, and cultural forces of Asian societies today and how these forces are shaping traditional values like collectivism or interdependence. For example, in Chen and his colleagues' (1998) study of Chinese and Canadian toddler socialization and parental beliefs, findings suggested that while there were some differences in Canadian and Chinese mother's beliefs in socialization, there were a lot of similarities; in particular, they found that Chinese parents encourage independence as much as Canadian parents. They concluded that because of the changing social milieu in China, parents are increasingly aware of the importance for children to be independent. As anthropologist James Watson (2004) points out, culture should no longer be "perceived as a preprogrammed mental library—a knowledge system inherited from ancestors" (p. 145). We should instead treat culture as "a set of ideas, attributes, and expectations that is constantly changing as people react to changing circumstances" (p. 145). Chen and his colleagues' study is an example of the cultural values illustrated by changing parental beliefs and socialization strategies as responses to social change. This is particularly important for studies of recent immigrant families. Researchers need to consider the contemporary cultural context of their countries of origin and interpret findings based on this knowledge rather than relying on "traditional," essential cultural values and beliefs depicted in earlier research.

The importance of understanding fluidity and changing processes of culture also extends to the examination of well-established developmental constructs such as ethnic identity (Qin, under review). Erikson (1968) suggested that identity implies the "resiliency of maintaining essential patterns in the process of change" (p. 96). In minority child development, ethnic identity has been examined as a linear, stage-wise progression from moratorium to achievement of an ethnic identity (Phinney, 1989). However, in the development of identity formation in immigrant children, the inherent conflicts in their environment lead to potential development of multiple identities, or multiple aspects of identity, which are not consistent with each other (Qin, under review). As Marcelo Suárez-Orozco (2000) contended,

> the idea that there is a single, coherent, and continuous identity, that is the product of a series of crises unfolding in a unilinear, stage-specific process of change can no longer explain the lived experiences of many, if not most, children. (p. 14)

Along this line, Rumbaut (2005) defines ethnic identity not as inevitable outcomes, but as "complex products of people's ongoing efforts to interpret, understand, and respond to the social structural, cultural, and historical situations in which they find themselves within their sets of resources and vulnerabilities" (p. 160). In this definition, ethnic identity is a fluid negotiation process. Qin's (2004) research with Chinese immigrant adolescents also shows that identity formation is a dynamic, complex, and multifaceted process shaped by different factors that cannot be adequately characterized by simple categories like "Chinese," "American," or "Chinese American" (Qin, 2004, 2006). It is important for future research to take into consideration the situational, dynamic nature of identity.

Third, there has been an overemphasis on negative developmental outcomes in children from diverse cultural backgrounds. For example, in studies on immigrant children, there has been an overwhelming emphasis on the negative impact of migration and acculturation on children. Acculturation refers to the process whereby immigrants must learn new cultural parameters and interpersonal expectations in their negotiation of two or more cultures (C. Suárez-Orozco, Todorova, & Qin, 2006). Developmental psychologist Garcia Coll and her colleague Magnuson (1997) pointed out that the reason research on immigrant children's psychological development has focused so much on acculturation is that research on immigrant adults is dominated by the belief that adjustment differences in adults are due either to the self-selection of migrants or to acculturative stress. Because children do not self-select their migration, research thus focuses heavily on acculturation. This focus has led nearly all researchers to examine the negative impact of migration and acculturation on children (Garcia Coll & Magnuson).

However, migration can also be a resilient factor in child development. Indeed, recent research shows that first-generation immigrants have better health indicators than those who have lived longer in the United States, while foreign-born members of the ethnic group are generally healthier than those of the second and third generation (Iannotta, 2003; Morales, Lara, Kington, Valdez, & Escarce, 2002). Immigrant optimism (resulting from favorable comparison of their situation in the new country after migration), family cohesion, and selective population of people who chose to migrate to the United States may contribute to this "immigrant health paradox" (C. Suárez-Orozco et al., 2006). As social scientists, we need to recognize the specific strengths and challenges of immigrant youth and strive to conduct quality research that considers the multiplicity of factors—structural, cultural, familial, and individual—that contribute to differential outcomes (C. Suárez-Orozco et al., 2006).

Fourth, researchers have yet to clearly delineate culture, race, ethnicity, and immigration in child development. In studies of immigrant children, Garcia Coll and Magnuson (1997) contended that it is difficult to disentangle the effects of the simultaneous and various processes in conducting research with immigrant children. In a recent special issue on multicultural child development, Quintana and colleagues (2006) pointed out that it is difficult to disentangle race and ethnicity from culture, and it is challenging to disentangle immigration status from culture. Other child development psychologists have also called for more research efforts to unpack immigration in child development. For example, psychologist Tseng (2006) contends that

> studies . . . need to identify, measure, and test the immigration-related constructs (i.e., language acquisition, acculturation, changing family roles, etc.) that can explain generational differences. Doing so takes researchers beyond documenting *that* immigration matters to examining *how* immigration matters for development. (p. 1434)

Another critical problem in the field of child development is an overreliance on quantitative methods. In the next section, we discuss why this may be and call on developmental researchers to utilize mixed methods in their research. We believe this is particularly important for understanding multicultural concepts in child development.

MIXED METHODS

Much improvement has been made in terms of methods used to study processes and contexts of child development, most prominently in the wider adoption of longitudinal methods (Quintana et al., 2006). However, as a result of prioritizing outcome over process of development, the discipline of developmental psychology has been dominated by the scientific, positivist paradigm, which aims to clearly delineate and define variables under consideration and to achieve objectivity (Garcia Coll & Magnuson, 1997; C. Suárez-Orozco & Qin, 2006). The resulting dependence on experimental designs and quantitative methods can be quite limiting, particularly in capturing the cultural processes and contexts of child development (C. Suárez-Orozco et al., 2006).

When the "paradigm wars" or "method wars" (quantitative and qualitative purists see the two methods as incompatible and cannot be mixed) ended in the late 1990s, researchers realized that "a purist approach would not get much research done" (R. B. Johnson & Onwuegbuzie, 2004, p. 14). Using multiple methods in research design is increasingly recognized as important in the field of child development. As psychological anthropologist Tom Weisner (2005) asked, "How can one conceptualize development as such a journey on a pathway consisting of activities in some specific cultural/ecological context and imagine that we could use only one method to find out about it?" (pp. 1–2). There is a growing consensus among researchers studying multicultural concepts that mixed-method research design is essential to this kind of endeavor (Garcia Coll, 2005; Okazaki & Sue, 1995; C. Suárez-Orozco & Qin, 2006). As Greene and Caracelli (1997) contended, "that children's development occurs in a complex context, a mix of interpenetrated ecological and cultural factors that challenge even the most sophisticated and richly funded research design, provides the basis and justification for mixed-methods investigations" (p. 255).

Mixed-method research is defined as a class of research in which quantitative and qualitative research techniques, methods, approaches, concepts, or language are mixed and combined in a single study or a series of studies (Bazeley, 2003; Johnson & Onwuegbuzie, 2004; Tashakkori & Creswell, 2007). There are generally two types of mixed-method approaches: (a) mixed methods (inclusion of a quantitative phase and a qualitative phase in an overall research study), and (b) mixed model (mixing qualitative and quantitative approaches within or across various stages of the research process) (Johnson & Onwuegbuzie, 2004; Tashakkori & Teddlie, 1998).

So why do we mix methods in our research? What are the added benefits of using mixed-method research design? What is gained in combining multiple approaches in one study? Greene, Caracelli, and Graham (1989) articulated five main benefits of mixed-method research: (a) *triangulation*, which allows the researcher to seek convergence in results through different approaches; (b) *complementarity*, clarifying and illustrating results from one method with the use of another method; (c) *development,* which allows the researcher to use findings from one method to help shape the other methods or steps in the research process; (d) *initiation,* that is, discovering contradictions or paradoxical findings that may challenge and lead to a reframe of the original research question; and (e) *expansion,* using different methods to expand the breadth and range of research. Overall, researchers believe that using a mixed-method approach can enhance the validity or credibility of findings and allow for a "broader, deeper, more inclusive" understanding of child development (Greene, 2005, p. 409; Rossman & Wilson, 1994). As Weisner (2005) pointed out, "for some fundamental questions in our field, the use of mixed methodology may bring about a deeper understanding of developmental processes" (p. 299).

Research with children from different cultural backgrounds necessitates multimodal methodologies. Questions and measures that are valid for one group may not be valid for another group (McLoyd & Steinberg, 1998; C. Suárez-Orozco & M. Suárez-Orozco, 1995). Hence, instruments that capture the experiences of individuals from a variety of backgrounds are a challenge to develop (C. Suárez-Orozco & Qin, 2006). Qualitative approaches, in conjunction with quantitative approaches, lend themselves to closer and deeper understanding than compared to other methodologies. For example, in the Harvard Immigration Projects directed by Carola and Marcelo Suárez-Orozco (1997–2002), which followed 400 immigrant children (from five different countries/areas) for 5 years, ethnographic fieldwork and face-to-face interviews were used to gain the informants' point of view, guiding the researchers in the development of systematic strategies of assessment, which then allowed them to interpret findings in a locally relevant cultural context. Psychological techniques were used to systematically follow up on the tentative theoretical constructions that emerge from the ethnographic process (C. Suárez-Orozco & Qin, 2006). In this study design, triangulation of different methods helps the researchers deal with the challenges of validity in conducting research with children from diverse cultural backgrounds. It also served to counteract the limitations of self-report data—a problem that might have been exaggerated among immigrant youth. By sifting through self-reports, parent reports, teacher reports, and researchers' own observations, researchers were able to establish both congruence and discongruence in what immigrant children say they do, what others say they do, and what researchers see them do (C. Suárez-Orozco et al., 2006).

It is important to point out that the choice of methods should be driven by the research question. Researchers and research methodologists need to question "when each research approach is most helpful and when and how they should be mixed or combined in their research studies" (Johnson & Onwuegbuzie, 2004, p. 15). Yoshikawa and colleagues (2008) point out five types of research in the field of developmental psychology for the use of mixed-method research design: (a) to assess developmental or contextual constructs (e.g., school climate, parent-child relations) that are difficult to measure using either quantitative or qualitative alone; (b) to integrate the study of beliefs, goals, and practices in socialization and development; (c) to estimate and understand developmental change at multiple time scales; (d) to examine reciprocal relationships between contextual and individual-level factors; and (e) to explore causal associations and their mechanisms. A key question researchers need to ask themselves before embarking on a mixed-method design is whether they can achieve results that they cannot achieve with only a quantitative or a qualitative component (Johnson & Onwuegbuzie, 2004).

Mixed-method research design remains relatively new in social science research. Currently, there are still major challenges for researchers to truly mix methods in their research. It is especially difficult for researchers to genuinely integrate their findings (Bryman, 2007). As Niglas (2004) pointed out for educational research, "substantial integration of qualitative and quantitative data during the analyses was exercised very rarely" (p. 98). Often quantitative and qualitative components are treated separately in the design, collection, analysis, and reporting of the data. In his interview with researchers who adopt mixed-method approaches, Bryman found that there are some common barriers for integration: researchers tend to have stronger training and faith in one or the other, the *timeline* in conducting qualitative and quantitative components is another realistic issue, and publication issues are also important to many. Nonetheless, the U.S. child population is becoming increasingly diverse. To understand the cultural contexts of child development, it is crucial for child development scholars to have a solid understanding of multiple methods and take advantage of the benefits offered by mixed-method research design to answer the specific research questions they have.

REFERENCES

Angoff, W. H. (1972, August). *A technique for the investigation of cultural differences.* Paper presented at the convention of the American Psychological Association, Honolulu, HI.

Bazeley, P. (2003). Teaching mixed methods. *Qualitative Research Journal, 3,* 117–126.

Berry, J. W. (1980). Introduction to methodology. In H. C. Triandis & J. W. Berry (Eds.), *Handbook of cross-cultural psychology* (Vol. 2, pp. 1–28). Boston: Allyn & Bacon.

Berry, J. W., & Dasen, P. (Eds.). (1974). *Culture and cognition.* London: Methuen.

Bornstein, M. H., Haynes, O. M., Azuma, H., Galperin, C., Maital, S., Ogino, M., et al. (1998). A cross-national study of self-evaluations and attributions in parenting: Argentina, Belgium, France, Israel, Italy, Japan, and the United States. *Developmental Psychology, 34*(4), 662–676.

Bourne, E. J. (1991). Does the concept of the person vary cross-culturally? In R. A. Shweder (Ed.), *Thinking through cultures: Expeditions in cultural psychology* (pp. 113–155). Cambridge, MA: Harvard University Press.

Brislin, R. (1976). Comparative research methodology: Cross-cultural studies. *International Journal of Psychology, 11*(3), 215–229.

Bronfenbrenner, U. (1979). *The ecology of human development: Experiments by nature and design.* Cambridge, MA: Harvard University Press.

Bryman, A. (2007). Barriers to integrating quantitative and qualitative research. *Journal of Mixed-Methods Research, 1,* 8–22.

Burlew, A. K. (2003). Research with ethnic minorities: Conceptual, methodological, and analytical issues. In G. Bernal, J. E. Trimble, A. K. Burlew, & F. T. L. Leong (Eds.), *Handbook of racial and ethnic minority psychology* (pp. 179–197). Thousand Oaks, CA: Sage.

Buss, A., & Royce, J. B. (1975). Detecting cross-cultural commonalities and differences: Intergroup factor analyses. *Psychological Bulletin, 82,* 128–136.

Cattell, R. B. (1957). *Personality and motivation structure and measurement.* New York: Harcourt Brace Jovanovich.

Cauce, A. M., Ryan, K. D., & Grove, K. (Eds.) (1998). *Children and adolescents of color, where are you? Participation, selection, recruitment, and retention in developmental research.* Mahwah, NJ: Lawrence Erlbaum.

Chao, G. T., & Moon, H. (2005). The cultural mosaic: A metatheory for understanding the complexity of culture. *Journal of Applied Psychology, 90*(6), 1128–1140.

Chao, R. K. (1994). Beyond parental control and authoritarian parenting style: Understanding Chinese parenting through the cultural notion of training. *Child Development, 65,* 1111–1119.

Chen, X., Hastings, P., Rubin, K., Chen, H., Cen, G., & Stewart, S. L. (1998). Child-rearing attitudes and behavioral inhibition in Chinese and Canadian toddlers: A cross-cultural study. *Developmental Psychology, 34*(4), 677–686.

Davidson, A. R., Jaccard, J. J., Triandis, H. C., Morale, M. L., & Diaz-Guerrero, R. (1976). Cross-cultural model testing: Toward a solution of the etic-emic dilemma. *International Journal of Psychology, 11,* 1–13.

Doi, T. (1971). *The anatomy of dependence.* Tokyo, Japan: Kodansha Press.

Duijker, H. C. J., & Frijda, N. H. (1960). *National character and national stereotypes.* Amsterdam: Noord-Hollandse.

Erikson, E. H. (1968). *Identity: Youth and crisis.* New York: Norton.

Feagin, J. R. (1989). *Racial and ethnic relations* (3rd ed.). Englewood Cliffs, NJ: Prentice-Hall.

Garcia Coll, C. (2005). Editorial. *Developmental Psychology, 41*(2), 299–300.

Garcia Coll, C., Lamberty, G., Jenkins, R., McAdoo, H. P., Crnic, K., Wasik, B. H., et al. (Eds.). (1998). *An integrative model for the study of developmental competencies in minority children.* Philadelphia: Brunner/Mazel.

Garcia Coll, C., & Magnuson, K. (1997). The psychological experience of immigration: A developmental perspective. In A. Booth, A. C. Crouter, & N. S. Landale (Eds.), *Immigration and the family: Research and policy on U.S. immigrants* (pp. 91–131). Hillsdale, NJ: Lawrence Erlbaum.

Gilligan, C. (1982). *In a different voice.* Cambridge, MA: Harvard University Press.

Gorman, J. C. (1998). Parenting attitudes and practices of immigrant Chinese mothers of adolescents. *Family Relations, 47*(1), 73–80.

Greene, J. C. (2005). Synthesis: A reprise on mixing methods. In T. S. Weisner (Ed.), *Discovering successful pathways in children's development: Mixed methods in the study of childhood and family life* (pp. 405–419). Chicago: University of Chicago Press.

Greene, J. C., & Caracelli, V. J. (Eds.). (1997). *Advances in mixed-method evaluation: The challenges and benefits of integrating diverse paradigms.* San Francisco: Jossey-Bass.

Greene, J. C., Caracelli, V. J., & Graham, W. F. (1989). Toward a conceptual framework for mixed-method evaluation design. *Educational Evaluation and Policy Analysis, 11*(3), 255–274.

Hui, C. H., & Triandis, H. C. (1985). Measurement in cross-cultural psychology: A review and comparison of strategies. *Journal of Cross-Cultural Psychology, 16*(2), 131–152.

Iannotta, J. (2003). *Emerging issues in Hispanic health: A summary of a workshop.* Washington, DC: National Research Council.

Irvine, S. H. (1965). Adapting tests to the cultural setting: A comment. *Occupational Psychology, 39,* 13–23.

Irvine, S. H., & Carroll, W. K. (1980). Testing and assessment across cultures: Issues in methodology and theory. In H. C. Triandis & J. W. Berry (Eds.), *Handbook of cross-cultural psychology methodology* (Vol. 2, pp. 181–244). Boston: Allyn & Bacon.

Johnson, R. B., & Onwuegbuzie, A. J. (2004). Mixed methods research: A research paradigm whose time has come. *Educational Researcher, 33*(7), 14–26.

Johnson, T. P. (1998). Approaches to equivalence in cross-cultural and cross-national survey research. *ZUMA Nachrichten Spezial,* 1–40.

Jones, J. M. (1997). *Prejudice and racism.* San Francisco: McGraw-Hill.

Kim, S. Y., & Wong, V. Y. (Eds.). (2002). *Assessing Asian and Asian American parenting: A review of the literature.* New York: Kluwer Academic/Plenum.

Leung, K., & Van de Vijver, F. J. R. (2006). Cross-cultural research methodology. In F. T. L. Leong & J. T. Austin (Eds.), *The psychology research handbook* (pp. 443–454). Thousand Oaks, CA: Sage.

Markus, H. R., & Kitayama, S. (1991). Culture and the self: Implications for cognition, emotion, and motivation. *Psychological Review, 98*(2), 224–253.

Marsella, A. J., & Leong, F. T. L. (1995). Cross-cultural issues in personality and career assessment. *Journal of Career Assessment, 3*(2), 202–218.

McLoyd, V., & Steinberg, L. (1998). *Studying minority adolescents: Conceptual, methodological, and theoretical issues.* Mahwah, NJ: Lawrence Erlbaum.

Morales, L., Lara, M., Kington, R., Valdez, R., & Escarce, J. (2002). Socioeconomic cultural and behavioral factors affecting Hispanic health outcomes. *Journal of Healthcare for the Poor and Underserved, 13,* 477–503.

Niglas, K. (2004). *The combined use of qualitative and quantitative method in educational research.* Tallinn, Estonia: Tallinn Pedagogical University Dissertation on Social Sciences.

Okazaki, S., Lee, R. M., & Sue, S. (2006). Theoretical and conceptual models: Toward Asian Americanist psychology. In F. T. L. Leong, A. Inman, A. Ebreo, L. Yang, L. Kinoshita, & M. Fu (Eds.), *Handbook of Asian American psychology* (2nd ed.; pp. 29–46). Thousand Oaks, CA: Sage.

Okazaki, S., & Sue, S. (1995). Methodological issues in assessment research with ethnic minorities. *Psychological Assessment, 7*(3), 367–375.

Osgood, C. E. (1965). Cross-cultural comparability in attitude measurement via multilingual semantic differentials. In I. Steiner & M. Fishbein (Eds.), *Current studies in social psychology* (pp. 95–107). Chicago: Holt, Rinehart and Winston.

Phinney, J. S. (1989). Stages of ethnic identity development in minority group adolescents. *Journal of Early Adolescence, 9,* 34–49.

Poortinga, Y. H. (1975). Some implications of three different approaches to intercultural comparison. In J. W. Berry & W. J. Lonner (Eds.), *Applied Cross-Cultural Psychology* (pp. 329–332). Amsterdam: Swets and Zeitlinger.

Potts, R. G., & Watts, R. J. (2003). Conceptualization and models: The meaning(s) of difference in racial and ethnic minority psychology. In G. Bernal, J. E. Trimble, A. K. Burlew, & F. T. L. Leong (Eds.), *Handbook of racial and ethnic minority psychology* (pp. 65–75). Thousand Oaks, CA: Sage.

Qin, D. B. (2004). Dragons and phoenixes in the new land: The role of gender in the adaptation of immigrant Chinese children. *Dissertation Abstracts International Section A: Humanities and Social Sciences, 65*(5-A), 1664.

Qin, D. B. (2006). Our child doesn't talk to us any more: Alienation in immigrant Chinese families. *Anthropology and Education Quarterly, 37,* 162–179.

Qin, D. B. (under review). Being 'good' or being 'popular': Gendered and ethnic identity formation of Chinese immigrant adolescents. *Journal of Adolescent Research.*

Qin, D. B., Feinauer, E., & Quiroz, B. (2001). Immigration and education special issue: Introduction. *Harvard Educational Review, 71*(3), v–x.

Quintana, S. M., Aboud, F. E., Chao, R. K., Contreras-Grau, J., Cross, W. E., Jr., Hudley, C., et al. (2006). Race, ethnicity, and culture in child development: Contemporary research and future directions. *Child Development, 77*(5), 1129–1141.

Rossman, G. B., & Wilson, B. L. (1994). Numbers and words revisited: Being "shamelessly eclectic." *Quality and Quantity, 28,* 315–327.

Rumbaut, R. G. (2005). The melting and the pot: Assimilation and variety in American life. In P. Kivisto (Ed.), *Incorporating diversity: Rethinking assimilation in a multicultural age* (pp. 154–173). Boulder, CO: Paradigm.

Suárez-Orozco, C., & Qin, D. B. (2006). Gendered perspectives in psychology: Immigrant origin youth. *International Migration Review, 40,* 165–198.

Suárez-Orozco, C., & Suárez-Orozco, M. (1995). *Transformations: Immigration, family life, and achievement motivation among Latino adolescents.* Stanford, CA: Stanford University Press.

Suárez-Orozco, C., & Suárez-Orozco, M. (2001). *Children of immigration.* Cambridge, MA: Harvard University Press.

Suárez-Orozco, C., Todorova, I., & Qin, D. B. (2006). The well-being of immigrant adolescents: A longitudinal perspective on risk and protective factors. In F. Villarruel & T. Luster (Eds.), *The crisis in youth mental health: Volume II. Disorders in adolescence* (pp. 53–84). Westport, CT: Praeger.

Suárez-Orozco, M. (2000). Everything you ever wanted to know about assimilation but were afraid to ask. *Journal of the American Academy of Arts and Sciences, 129*(4), 1–30.

Sue, S., & Sue, L. (2003). Ethnic research is good science. In G. Bernal, J. E. Trimble, A. K. Burlew, & F. T. L. Leong (Eds.), *Handbook of racial and ethnic minority psychology* (pp. 198–207). Thousand Oaks, CA: Sage.

Tashakkori, A., & Creswell, J. W. (2007). Editorial: The new era of mixed methods. *Journal of Mixed Method Research, 1*(1), 3–7.

Tashakkori, A., & Teddlie, C. (1998). *Mixed-methodology: Combining qualitative and quantitative approaches.* Thousand Oaks, CA: Sage.

Tseng, V. (2006). Unpacking immigration in youths' academic and occupational pathways. *Child Development, 77*(5), 1434–1445.

Van de Vijver, F. J. R. (2002). Types of cross-cultural studies in cross-cultural psychology. In W. J. Lonner, D. L. Dinnel, S. A. Hayes, & D. N. Sattler (Eds.), *Online readings in psychology and culture* (http://www.wwu.edu/~culture). Bellingham, WA: Center for Cross-Cultural Research, Western Washington University.

Watson, J. (2004). Globalization in Asia: Anthropological perspectives. In M. Suárez-Orozco & D. B. Qin-Hilliard (Eds.), *Globalization: Culture and education in the new millennium* (pp. 141–173). Berkeley: University of California Press.

Weisner, T. S. (Ed.). (2005). *Discovering successful pathways in children's development: Mixed methods in the study of childhood and family life.* Chicago: University of Chicago Press.

Werner, O., & Campbell, D. T. (1970). Translating, working through interpreters, and the problem of decentering. In R. Narroll & R. Cohens (Eds.), *A handbook of method in cross-cultural anthropology* (pp. 398–420). New York: Natural History Press.

Yoshikawa, H., Weisner, T. S., Kalil, A., & Way, N. (2008). Mixing qualitative and quantitative research methods in developmental science: Uses and methodological choices. *Developmental Psychology, 44*, 344–354.

Part II

Institutions of Socialization and the Development of a Child's Multicultural Worldview

There are a core set of concepts and developmental constructs that provide a basis for researching, understanding, and indeed dissecting the sociocultural factors related to what social scientists refer to as socialization. Part II of this *Handbook* examines, from several dimensions, these institutions that contribute to the socialization of children and youth. These institutions, or agents of socialization, are represented, in part, by the home and family; community, sociopolitical system, and religious organizations; educational institutions; and even the peer group. Each institution has an intervening economic, social, and emotional way of affecting the behavior and belief systems of developing children and their multicultural worldview.

Part II begins with a chapter by Daren Graves and Sherryl Browne Graves in which they highlight some of the major issues relevant to growing up in the multiculturally rich 21st century, such as the development of self and self in relation to others, racial/ethnic identity development, and the agents of socialization that influence children's development. The chapter also offers some intervention strategies that prepare children to effectively negotiate the diverse world in which they exist.

The remainder of the chapters in Part II focus on specific agents of socialization, starting with home and family with Sinead Younge and Harriette Pipes McAdoo. Although their chapter focuses on African American children and families, some of the issues raised about varied forms of family types (i.e., single- and two-parent households, blended families, heterosexual and same-sex households, and extended kinships) have relevance to other children and families as well.

In broadening the discussion from family to the community and sociopolitical system, Shelly Harrell and Miguel Gallardo argue that understanding the development of a multicultural worldview among racial/ethnic minority groups must recognize the extent to which sociopolitical and community dynamics contribute toward a view of inferiority and powerlessness, which, in turn, influences attitudes and behaviors within and between groups. For White Americans, the development of a multicultural worldview means recognizing the inequities that exist in society that privilege them and deny racial/ethnic minorities. They propose strategies for maximizing successful intergroup relations and coalition building.

Another community influence that can affirm the value of multiculturalism is religious leadership. Erylene Piper-Mandy and Daryl Rowe provide a unique discussion on the intersection of social consciousness and religious leadership among the various ethnic communities as well as the spiritual discourse on multiculturalism and the emergence of liberation theology. Although the contributors are speaking from their own religious perspective, the overall premise of the chapter has takeaway points for religious leadership from diverse faiths.

It is without question that schools play a major role in the socialization of children and youth. Robert Cooper and Cheong Huh provide a conceptual framework for empowering and transforming the school experience of students transitioning from middle school to high school, a time period that has been associated with negative academic outcomes for students of color, in particular. Although a considerable amount of research has addressed the educational experiences of students of color who attend underresourced schools in urban settings, less is known about the educational experiences of college-bound high school students of color who attend racially diverse, affluent suburban schools. Evellyn Elizondo, Kimberly White-Smith, and Walter Allen attempt to address this gap by presenting the findings from their study of the social and educational experiences of African American and Latino students in a high-resourced school.

Finally, Cynthia Hudley rounds out Part II of this volume by exploring the influence of peers on the multicultural worldview development of children. Her chapter takes into account attitude research, contact effects, social identity, and racial/ethnic identity.

CHAPTER 6

Multicultural Issues in the Lives of Developing Children in the 21st Century

DAREN A. GRAVES

SHERRYL BROWNE GRAVES

Growing up in 21st-century America will challenge children in many different ways. The need to use renewable natural resources versus reliance on carbon-based resources will continue as an ongoing environmental crisis. Digital technologies with the potential to connect children globally while isolating them in their homes will be a challenge. Information overload will be commonplace as children have 24-hour-a-day access to knowledge from the past and instant access to breaking news. However, one of the most pressing challenges but at the same time an enriching opportunity for 21st century American children will be learning to live, learn, work, and play with others whose backgrounds and experiences may be different than their own.

With the arrival of the 21st century, American society is and will continue to be more diverse such that by 2050, Americans of European descent will no longer be in the majority (U.S. Census Bureau, 2002). These dramatic changes in the population have also changed the racial/ethnic composition of schools. The percentage of students from visible racial and ethnic groups is expected to rise to 50% or more of the school population by 2035 (Meece & Kurtz-Costes, 2001; U.S. Census Bureau, 2004). Furthermore, while students of color are likely to attend schools in which there are large groups of students from diverse ethnic and cultural groups, students of European descent are more likely to have K–12 educational experiences in which their group is in the majority (Snyder, Tan, & Hoffman, 2004). Thus, students from visible racial/ethnic groups are more likely to be faced with the challenge of getting along with diverse groups of individuals while in the school setting (Tracey, Sunderman, & Orfield, 2005). With the ethnic and cultural diversity reflected in schools and the number of nonnative students, there is also variation in linguistic background. By 2050, it is projected 40% of students will arrive at school speaking a language other than English (Ladson-Billings, 2000; Lindholm-Leary, 2000). With entry into a century in which the United States is rich with demographic diversity, children need the knowledge, attitudes, skills, and behaviors to participate meaningfully in a multicultural society.

The remainder of this chapter is devoted to a discussion of the issues that are relevant to the multicultural development of children. Included in this discussion is the development of self and self in relation to others, racial/ethnic identity development, and the agents of socialization that influence the development of children. The chapter ends with a discussion of intervention strategies that prepare children to effectively negotiate the diverse world in which they exist.

MULTICULTURAL DEVELOPMENT IN THE LIVES OF CHILDREN

Self and Identity Development

One of the important developmental tasks children negotiate is to come to an understanding about themselves and how they view themselves in relation to other people (Shantz, 1975). Identity development is largely a task of adolescence, according to Erikson (1968), although the process starts during the preschool years (Harter, 2006). It is through this socioemotional developmental process that children come to understand the complexities of the social contexts in which they exist. The development of a sense of self includes a child's self-concept, which are the perceptions and beliefs about his or her characteristics, strengths, and weaknesses, whereas self-esteem refers to the child's judgments and feelings about his or her value and worth (Harter, 2006).

At an early age, children are aware of the physical differences among humans and are capable of acknowledging these differences (Katz & Kofkin, 1997). From preschool through adolescence, children and youth have racial and ethnic attitudes that vary by race, ethnicity, and age (Aboud, 1988; Bigler & Liben, 1993; Graves, 1999b; Joyner & Kao, 2000). At the younger ages, there is a stronger tendency for African, Asian, Latino, and Native American children to display a range of attitudes toward same- and other-race groups (Cramer & Anderson, 2003; Kowalski & Lo, 2001; Lovelace, Scheiner, Dollberg, Segui, & Black, 1994). There is a tendency for young children of color to express pro-White bias (Lovelace, Freund, & Graves, in press; Spencer & Markstrom-Adams, 1990). White children are more consistently pro-White in their attitudes, with a greater likelihood of expressing negative attitudes toward other race groups (Bigler & Liben, 1993; Katz, 2003; McGlothlin & Killen, 2006).

In a recent study, European American first- and fourth-grade students attending racially and ethnically homogeneous schools completed two measures of multicultural attitudes (McGlothlin & Killen, 2006). One measure, the Ambiguous Situations Task, presented participants with eight brightly colored picture cards showing a situation in which a wrongdoing may or may not have occurred. The misbehavior included ambiguous situations with money, toys, school, and swings. In the school situation, for example, there are two children in a class sitting beside each other. Each child has sheets of paper and one child looks at a sheet with "2 + 2 = 4" written on it. The other child has a paper with "2 + 2 = _" written on it and is looking in the direction of the other child's paper. Each card contains a White child and a Black child. Each card has two versions: one version in which the White child could be considered the perpetrator and another version in which the Black child could be the perpetrator. In addition, the participants were asked how much contact they had with African Americans by presenting cards with a group of six individuals. The cards varied from one card in which all six individuals were European Americans (card 1) to a group of six African Americans (card 5), with varying numbers of African Americans to European Americans in cards 2 through 4. Children were asked to select the card that most looked like their town, neighborhood, school, teams, friendships, and family. Their rating of intergroup contact was low, with participants reporting "none" or "not many" African Americans in their environment, as was expected from the U.S. Census data of their community. When given an ambiguous situation, the European American children rated African Americans perpetrators more negatively than they did same-race perpetrators. The ratings were most evident in the swing situation, in which one child is seen on the ground, and the toy situation, in which one child has all the toys and the other has no toys. The children displayed their bias by attributing intentions to children in interracial peer interactions. Their bias was most evident when there was the possibility of aggression. In these situations, the White children were more likely to attribute aggressive intentions to African American children.

With increasing age, same-race preference increases among students of color (Spencer & Markstrom-Adams, 1990). During adolescence, teens tend to evaluate racial interactions positively though their actual participation in cross-race interactions may be quite infrequent (Joyner & Kao, 2000). It is against this racially conscious social context that children are developing a sense of self and an identity.

The process by which a child will be able to effectively navigate the multicultural United States society is mediated by the development of his or her racial/ethnic, class, and gender identities. Identity is important because it is a crucial component in how people acquire and understand culture, whether it is their own or that of others. As Grant and Sleeter (2007) state, "All of us learn behavior patterns, beliefs, language, and ways of making sense of the world in the context of webs of human relationships in which we participate and with which we identify" (p. 10). Furthermore, they indicate that the context of these human relationships is defined by, among other things, race, class, and gender. In other words, individuals cannot divorce their sense of identity from how they experience the world, and how the world experiences them.

Racial/Ethnic Identity Development

Racial or ethnic identity is one of the many components of identity that will frame how children experience culture (in general) and a multicultural society. Racial identity is one's sense of self in relation to one's racial or ethnic group, and is multidimensional in nature (Spencer, Noll, Stoltzfus, & Harpalani, 2001). Racial/ethnic identity changes in response to the process and context in which development occurs. It is not a static construct. Rather, it develops over time as one encounters new and different experiences (Spencer, Noll, Stoltzfus, & Harpalani, 2001). Various models of racial or ethnic identity development exist that facilitate an understanding of how individuals frame and navigate a multicultural society. For example, Cross (1971, 1978, 1999) developed the *nigrescence* model to describe African American racial identity development that posits a process whereby African Americans develop more sophisticated views of themselves and society. Cross (1991) refers to the process as a "resocializing experience, which moves beyond the narrow confines of an oppressed identity to more positive conceptions of oneself and one's 'Blackness'" (p. 190). Helms (1990) proposed a similar model for White racial identity development. One of the major distinctions between the two models is that African Americans grow more aware of racism and White privilege through their encounters with acts of personal and structural racism whereas Whites come to understand and acknowledge racial privilege and may even experience guilt during the developmental process for the privilege they have at the expense of other marginalized racial groups.

There are other racial/ethnic identity models that parallel the models of Cross and Helms for other ethnic groups, such as Arce's (1981) model for Chicano identity and Kim's (1981, as cited in Sue et al., 1998) model for Asian American identity. Other models take a more general approach on racial/ethnic development, for example, Phinney (1990, 1992) and Helms' (1995) People of Color Racial Identity Model. There are also models of biracial and multiracial identity development, as well as gay and lesbian identity development (Ponterotto, Utsey, & Pedersen, 2006).

Overall, the various racial/ethnic identity models share some similar assumptions. How the individual makes sense of racial or ethnic identity can affect (a) the extent to which the individual internalizes positive and/or negative framings of the individual's own racial culture; (b) how the individual emotionally responds to these framings; (c) with whom the individual decides to form meaningful relationships; and (d) the extent to which the individual politically aligns with the belief that there are benefits to achieving a socially just, multicultural society.

Socialization Agents and Identity Development

The development of identity requires an examination of the role that others play in helping children learn about themselves. The "others," also referred to as socialization agents, include family, peers, schools, and the larger society as expressed through mass media.

Family

Families, especially parents, are important contributors to children's development of their identity. Parents provide children with feedback about who they are by signaling the acceptability of their behavior in and out of the home (Harter, 2006). Parents and family members also provide children with examples of how issues of self and identity can and have been achieved. The use of examples starts children on a process of comparing their characteristics and behaviors to those of others in their experience. This set of evaluative activities is known as the social comparative process, and the individuals or groups to which children compare and with which they evaluate their behavior and characteristics change with age and with other demographic features (Harter, 2006).

For parents from visible racial and ethnic groups, it is an important child-rearing goal that their children develop a positive sense of self, making the selection of the comparison group important for the healthy development of their offspring (Hughes, Rodriguez, et al., 2006). Research suggests that members of these groups do not use the majority culture as the comparison group (Harter, 2006). Rather, children identify with their racial/ethnic group and use that connection as the basis for the development of a positive self-concept and high self-esteem. Another mechanism that helps explain the high levels of self-esteem from members of groups devalued by the larger society is the search for positive social identity based on unique or distinctive characteristics (Gray-Little & Hafdahl, 2000). From this perspective, if children of color accept a positive racial/ethnic identity and if they evaluate their racial/ethnic heritage as positive and meaningful, then that aspect of identity enhances their sense of self-worth. Given these two social comparison approaches, it is important to identify the different ways in which parents and families influence children's development of a strong sense of identity and, with that foundation, the ability to engage with people different from themselves.

Prejudice is a negative opinion directed at an individual or a group based on faulty or unsubstantiated data, resulting in an inflexible generalization (Ponterotto, 1991). Parental racial or ethnic socialization is a protective factor against the prejudice and racism experienced by children in the larger society. The protective factor is most evident for children from racial and ethnic minority groups but inconsistent for Caucasian children whose parents may endorse a color-blind perspective on issues of race (Hamm, 2001). This color-blind perspective causes Caucasian parents to not engage in socialization activities around issues of race and ethnicity. Ethnic/racial socialization is the process by which parents teach their children about their own racial or ethnic group and about the relations between racial and ethnic groups (Hughes & Johnson, 2001). Racial/ethnic socialization encourages racial and ethnic pride by (a) cultural socialization, that is, teaching children about their culture, heritage, and history (Hughes, Bachman, Ruble, & Fuligiani, 2006); (b) preparation for experiences of racism, prejudice, and discrimination (Hughes & Chen, 1999); (c) promotion of mistrust, that is, encouraging distrust or caution in interracial interactions (Hughes, Bachman, et al., 2006); and (d) egalitarianism and silence about race, that is, valuing individual characteristics over racial/ethnic group membership and avoiding the mention of race (Spencer, 1983).

A number of racial/ethnic-group parents (African, Japanese, Mexican, Dominican, Puerto Rican, Haitian, and West Indian Americans) report engaging in racial/ethnic socialization with their children (Biafora, Warheit, Zimmerman, & Gil, 1993; Hughes & Chen, 1999; Phinney & Chavira, 1995), particularly those parents who themselves are strongly identified with their racial/ethnic group (Hughes, 2003; Romero, Cuellar, & Roberts, 2000; Thomas & Speight, 1999). White parents, however, are the least likely to engage in racial/ethnic socialization, and when they do engage in the practice, they largely use egalitarian or color-blind strategies (Hamm, 2001; Phinney & Chavira, 1995).

Generally, the research indicates that racial/ethnic socialization is associated with favorable outcomes in regards to racial/ethnic identity development (Constantine & Blackmon, 2002; Hughes, Rodriguez, et al., 2006; Scott, 2003; Stevenson, 1995).

Peers

In addition to parents and families, peers are major socializing agents who contribute to the development of a child's identity. The influence peers have on children's sense of identity increases as they get older and can become the most powerful socializing agent when children reach adolescence (Erikson, 1968).

Adolescents begin to have a heightened awareness, understanding, and sensitivity to society's values, as it is during these years that society begins to prepare them for assimilation into the adult work world. In order to make this transition smooth, schools, for the most part, make the adolescents aware of society's values and expectations (Erikson, 1968). Because finding one's role in the adult work world can be a daunting task, they experience what Erikson refers to as an identity crisis. To cope with this crisis, adolescents often attach themselves to specific groups and/or an "adolescent subculture" (Erikson, 1968, p. 128), which allows them to be among a group of peers who accept them for who they are as well as influence how they define themselves. This adolescent subculture provides a safe space for adolescents to begin integrating the skills and knowledge they learned in the earlier stages of development with the values and responsibilities that society will expect of them as adults (Erikson, 1968).

The peers of adolescents of color can have a profound impact on how youth see themselves within the context of the United States' multicultural society. For example, Fordham and Ogbu (1986) found African American students from a predominately Black, working-class high school reported anxiety about being called "brainiacs" (i.e., students who did well in school), which was viewed as equivalent to being called "White." The potential of being ostracized by peers encouraged students to not do well in school, or at least appear disinterested in school, in order to avoid such ostracism. However, African American students in a predominately White, private college prep high school formed informal social networks with other African American students who shared valuing high academic effort and outcomes to help them navigate the social and psychological challenges of the context (Datnow & Cooper, 1996). In other words, these African American youth were not made to feel "White" by their Black peers for achieving academically and working hard in school.

Wong, Eccles, and Sameroff (2003) found that children who experience racial discrimination by their peers were more likely to experience a decline in grades, a lowered perception of doing well in school, and a decrease in self-esteem, as well as an increase in depression. Furthermore, Gonzalez (2003) found that Mexican American students who perceived relating positively to peers were more likely to maintain a high value of schooling, even if faced with discrimination from school staff.

Friendship choice is one way to assess the extent to which children's racial/ethnic attitudes are influencing their intergroup relations with others. Generally, children and adolescents have fewer cross-race friendships than same-race friendships (Aboud, Mendelson, & Purdy, 2003; Joyner & Kao, 2000). When there are opportunities for cross-race friendships, White children are less positive than children from other groups about these relationships (Aboud et al., 2003). However, when White and Black elementary students from schools in which they were numerical majorities developed cross-race friendships, they were more popular and socially satisfied than students without a cross-race friend (Lease & Blake, 2005). Furthermore, Latinos and Native Americans were more likely than Whites to have a friend from a different race/ethnicity, whereas African and Asian Americans were less likely than Whites to have a friend from a different race/ethnicity (Joyner & Kao, 2000).

Overall, the research appears to indicate that peers, whether of one's own racial/ethnic group or from other groups, have a role in determining whether children process and make sense of multicultural contexts in adaptive and/or maladaptive ways.

Schools

Schools are a very important socialization agent for children in preparing them for a multicultural society. Just as other socialization agents, schools can prepare children for living in a multicultural society in ways that are both adaptive and maladaptive. For example, Solomon (1992) discusses how a Black separatist culture can emerge when African American students recognize the inequities of their school experience (e.g., being disproportionately placed in lower-track courses) that are tied to their Black identity. These students may challenge those in authority who, in turn, elect to punish the Black students rather than hear their concerns. These authority figures may also limit their interactions with the Black students, further marginalizing them. In response, the Black students withdraw from dominant-group activities as well as pull away from interactions with other groups. Hence, a separatist culture is created. To minimize the potential for such a contentious relationship between students of color in the school context, Ladson-Billings (1995) advocates implementing culturally relevant pedagogy to better serve the educational lives of African Americans and other students of color. Ladson-Billings (1995) defines culturally relevant pedagogy as "a pedagogy of opposition not unlike critical pedagogy but specifically committed to collective, not merely individual, empowerment" (p. 160). Ladson-Billings (1992) has found that teachers who use culturally relevant pedagogy have students, especially students of color, who are actively engaged in their classrooms and schools, while also becoming more empowered to help themselves and invested in achieving a socially just, multicultural society.

To engage students of color in their school experience, schools need to forge connections between the home and school cultures of these students. For example, Moll, Amanti, Neff, and Gonzalez (1992) found when teachers drew on the "funds of knowledge" of their Southwestern Latino students, it resulted in their students being more engaged in their schooling. Funds of knowledge were defined as "historically accumulated and culturally developed bodies of knowledge and skills essential for household or individual functioning or well being" (Moll et al., 1992, p. 133). The "teachers assume the role of the learner" (Moll et al., 1992, p. 139) by visiting the homes of their students, interviewing their parents, and bringing this knowledge back to the classroom as credible forms of information that provide further impetus for inquiry by students. The connection created between the home and the school encouraged students to become highly engaged in their projects and committed overall to their schooling.

MacPhee (1997) found that White students also benefit from schools that value a multicultural perspective. In her study, she introduced literature that featured African Americans as central characters to White first-grade students as a way to teach lessons about equity and social justice. "The students frequently addressed issues of racial prejudice and called them unjust," and by being introduced "to the life experiences of others, [they could not] help but make them more conscious of their own experiences and the diversity of human experience" (MacPhee, 1997, p. 39). She argues that although many feel that first graders are too young to talk about issues of equity and multiculturalism, her students were actively engaged in such issues and were able to make connections to their own lives.

Given the increasing racial and ethnic diversity in the United States, schools are increasingly becoming sites where multicultural frames of reference are necessary for the academic and psychosocial well-being of the students and families they serve. Therefore, those who create the cultures of schools serve as gatekeepers for our children, who are growing up in an increasingly diverse society.

Media

Media, including television, video games, computers, and the Internet, have the capacity to influence the attitudes, behaviors, beliefs, perceptions, and knowledge of children and adolescents on issues of diversity (Bakagiannis & Tarrant, 2006; Graves, 1996, 1999b). Media representations can suggest the value and standing of groups in the larger society, a factor that we previously suggested can influence self-concept and identity (Branscombe, Schmitt, & Harvey, 1999; Crocker, Luhtanen, Blaine, & Broadnax, 1994). For example, research on television viewing appears to support the positive influence exposure to Black programs and identification with Black characters has on the self-esteem of African American children and adolescents (McDermott &

Greenberg, 1984; Ward, 2004), and this effect seems most noticeable in feelings of competence and satisfaction with personal looks among adolescents (Ward, 2004). However, research on the influence of music videos on African American adolescents found that gender stereotypes were reinforced among those youth who identified with the video characters, and this was particularly true for the younger adolescent (Ward, Hansbrough, & Walker, 2005). In contrast, research with Latino children did not find a relationship between self-concept and the amount of television viewing or access to Spanish-language television content (Subervi-Velez & Necochea, 1990).

One might argue, at least among African American children and adolescents, access to positive media representations of one's own race can serve as a protective factor against stigma and stereotyping, similar in process to racial socialization.

INTERVENTION STRATEGIES WITHIN A MULTICULTURAL FRAMEWORK

So what do we know about preparing children to negotiate, in effective ways, the diverse world in which they live? There have been a wide variety of intervention strategies developed to reduce prejudice and to increase social inclusion of diverse children. Many of these efforts take place in schools, because this is where children spend a large part of their daily lives. The interventions include a focus on curriculum and materials, instructional organization and practices, direct training, and media presentation.

Multicultural Education

One of the most important and wide-ranging school-based interventions that can help children develop a greater ability to understand and work with those from cultures differing from their own is multicultural education. Although the term *multicultural education* may mean different things to different people, Nieto and Bode (2007) provide a comprehensive definition of the term as well as delineate its purpose. Among the multiple purposes of multicultural education, according to Nieto and Bode, is to "confront not only issues of difference but also issues of power and privilege. This means challenging racism and other biases as well as the inequitable structures, policies, and practices of schools and, ultimately, of society itself" (p. 4). Inherent in Nieto and Bode's purpose of multicultural education is the notion that among the many challenges of successfully inducting children into a socially just, multicultural society is to prepare children to confront and defy both interpersonal and structural forms of oppression that they will inevitably face.

Given this goal of multicultural education, Nieto and Bode (2007) put forth a framework of multicultural education with seven key components. "The seven basic characteristics of multicultural education . . . are as follows: Multicultural education is antiracist . . . basic education . . . important for all students . . . pervasive . . . education for social justice . . . a process . . . [and] critical pedagogy" (p. 44). Nieto and Bode make "antiracist education" the first component of their definition because "antiracism, indeed antidiscrimination in general, is at the very core of a multicultural perspective" (p. 45). They stress the importance of multicultural education being "basic education" to prevent some from believing that there is a dichotomy between multicultural education and the basic skills that have come to be associated with education (i.e., reading, writing, and arithmetic). Rather, multicultural education is a critical component of basic education.

Dispelling the myth that multicultural education only serves and benefits students of culturally marginalized backgrounds, Nieto and Bode (2007) assert that multicultural education's intended target is students of all backgrounds, including those associated with cultural privilege. Nieto and Bode state, "Although it is true that the primary victims of biased education are those who are invisible in the curriculum, everyone misses out when education is biased" (p. 50). In other words, multicultural education is not effective if those with privilege are not being made aware of their own privilege, while those with less privilege are simultaneously gaining privilege through a more just representation of their lived experiences in the curriculum. In addressing the importance of multicultural education being "pervasive," Nieto and Bode emphasize that multicultural education must be dispersed through all the content and pedagogy of a given classroom or school. Instead of being a stand-alone subject, multicultural education should be "a philosophy, a way of looking at the world, not simply a program or a class or a teacher" (p. 52).

Another key component of Nieto and Bode's (2007) definition of multicultural education is the notion that it is "education for social justice." Given the goal of multicultural education mentioned previously, Nieto and Bode posit that it is important that education not be transmitted in a vacuum. Rather, multicultural education needs to couch all the learning and teaching in the context of combating the interpersonal and structural inequities that a multicultural society must combat throughout its development into a more just society. It is also important to note that because society is dynamic, and the fabric of a multicultural society will change given the fluidity of cultures over time, multicultural education is "a process," according to Nieto and Bode. Whereas one might believe that the facts and figures that one transmits via multicultural education are the most important aspect, Nieto and Bode state that "the sensitivity and understanding teachers show their students are more crucial" (p. 54). In this regard, multicultural education involves more than specific content knowledge. It involves teachers being aware of the ever-changing issues affecting their students, as well as serving as agents of change in dismantling oppressive structures in and out of schools. Finally, Nieto and Bode assert that multicultural education is "critical pedagogy." Ira Shor (1992) defines critical pedagogy as

> habits of thought, reading, writing, and speaking which go beneath surface meaning, first impressions, dominant myths, official pronouncements, traditional cliches, received wisdom, and mere opinions, to understand the deep meaning, root causes, social context, ideology, and personal consequences of any action, event, object, process, organization, experience, text, subject matter, policy, mass media, or discourse. (p. 129)

In this vein, critical pedagogy is a teaching approach that attempts to help students question and challenge domination, and the beliefs and practices that dominate. Furthermore, critical pedagogy poses a reciprocal relationship between the teacher and the students. This is important in multicultural education because "a multicultural perspective does not simply operate on substituting one 'truth' or perspective for another. Rather, it reflects on multiple and contradictory perspectives to understand reality more fully" (Nieto & Bode, p. 57). Simply because multicultural education is a process that is intended to help dismantle structures of oppression, it is in the best interest of multicultural educators to empower students to recognize, question, and combat these structures. Critical pedagogy gives students the tools and practice within the classroom setting that enables them to take these tools outside the classroom to achieve justice in society-at-large.

Research on the effectiveness of multicultural curricula to reduce prejudice or develop positive racial attitudes is inconsistent (Pfeifer, Brown, & Juvonen, 2007). Most efforts focus on changes in attitudes, with little attention to interracial interaction and friendship relationships (e.g., Katz & Zalk, 1978; Slone, Tarrasch, & Hallis, 2000). More effective uses of multicultural curricula employ extended contact with the materials (Cameron & Rutland, 2006; Slone et al., 2000).

Bilingual Education

Aside from the preparation of children to speak English in addition to their first language, one of the interests in bilingual education has been the incidental development of positive intergroup relations (Genesee & Gandara, 1999), although more recent descriptions of two-way or dual-language programs include cross-cultural understanding as one of the major goals of this approach to bilingual education (Center for Applied Linguistics, 2001).

Dual-language bilingual education, in which children from two different language groups are in class together learning in two different languages, increases proficiency in learning the second language (Marsh, Hau, & Kong, 2002). Dual-language programs are also thought to provide a laboratory for reducing prejudice, discrimination, and stereotyping because of four factors: (a) there is equal and prolonged contact between both groups of children; (b) both groups of children are at an equal disadvantage in one of the languages, thereby both groups have the same standing within the classroom; (c) both groups are more likely to perceive the different-language colleagues as similar because they are both learning a new language and acquiring academic knowledge in that language; and (d) the curriculum materials recognize the culture and heritage of both groups of students (Center for Applied Linguistics, 2001).

There is evidence in Canadian and U.S. dual-language programs that supports positive outcomes in intergroup relations. For example, students were found to experience positive changes in racial/ethnic attitudes (Cazabon, Lambert, & Hall, 1993), identification and self-esteem (Lindholm, 2001), language use (Clement, 1995), and to a lesser extent affiliation and contact (Genesee, 1981) after participation in dual-language programs. However, there is also evidence that some of the changes were not sustained over time in either the Canadian or U.S. environment (Genesee & Gandara, 1999). The inability to sustain change over time may be the result of how much an emphasis the program placed on facilitating positive intergroup interaction, because this goal is not the principal focus of the academic program.

Instructional Approaches

There is evidence that the use of specific instructional approaches can enhance multicultural knowledge, attitudes, and behaviors. The most investigated instructional approach is the use of cooperative learning to improve intergroup relations (Slavin, 2001). Using various formats to create cooperative learning groups, there is evidence that supports that intergroup relations improve through an increase in cross-race friendships across different age groups and racial/ethnic groups (Slavin & Cooper, 1999). Cooperative learning is effective because it focuses on the conditions that are most effective in supporting prejudice reduction. The focus on the role of interdependence is crucial for team members to experience positive outcomes. This approach also requires clear and strong teacher support for interracial contact (Slavin, 2001).

In addition to cooperative learning, other instructional approaches enhance multicultural attitudes in children. For example, the use of role-playing and antiracist teaching is associated with prejudice reduction (MacGregor, 1993). These techniques are also associated with higher levels of achievement for the participants.

Classroom Contact

The seminal work by Allport (1954) presented the idea that prejudice reduction would take place when there was contact between members of different racial and ethnic groups, an infrequent occurrence at the time his theory emerged. Over the years, there has been extensive work trying to identify the conditions under which contact is most effective for a range of subjects in diverse settings (Pettigrew & Tropp, 2006; C. W. Stephan & W. G. Stephan, 2004; W. G. Stephan, 1999). For children, school is a setting where contact does take place. Which raises the question—How effective are classroom contact interventions in improving intergroup interaction among children?

In a study of White, Latino, and Asian American seventh and ninth graders, using classroom contact to reduce prejudice was examined (Molina & Wittig, 2006). Prejudice reduction under conditions of contact was more likely (a) when students perceived that there were opportunities to get to know students from the different groups in the classroom, (b) when students had decreased feelings of anxiety and threat regarding the diverse groups, and (c) when students perceived all students to be part of a single group in which cooperative interdependence was important. Racial/ethnic-group membership appeared to make a difference in the effectiveness of this intervention. Perceived opportunities to get to know diverse students and opportunities for cooperative interdependence were associated with more positive racial attitudes for White and Asian students but not for their Latino counterparts. This finding suggests the need for closer examination of how race and ethnicity influence young people's development of multicultural attitudes and behaviors.

Diversity Training

Another approach has been the development of peer models of tolerance and social inclusion with the help of diversity training. This approach has generally been used in business but has more recently been implemented in school settings (Paluck & Green, 2006). In an experimental test of diversity training, adolescent participants demonstrated improved awareness of and attitudes toward prejudice against various groups. The training did not affect participants' personal feelings of comfort with members of the same group. The participants were able to influence their friends' and classmates' knowledge of policies and structures that promoted prejudice and attitudes toward speaking out against prejudice in their school. There is evidence that direct training on issues of prejudice can influence attitudes and behaviors of participants and, under the right conditions, these effects can generalize to the social networks of those trained.

Media Interventions and Multicultural Programming

Explicit efforts to use media, particularly television, to reduce prejudice include broadcast materials for use by children in the home and video materials to be used with adults in schools or community-based settings. These media products have been created by developers associated with the production of educational television for children, like Sesame Workshop (formerly Children's Television Workshop) and Family Communications, the producers of *Mister Rogers' Neighborhood*.

Research suggests that viewing educational programs can influence children's racial attitudes (Bogatz & Ball, 1971), willingness to interact with children from different racial groups (Lovelace et al., 1994), and use of positive characteristics to describe children from different ethnic groups (Cole et al., 2003). These results were found for diverse preschool children in the United States and children in Israel (the West Bank and Gaza). Similarly, research on *Different and the Same*, a video prejudice-reduction series developed by Family Communications, demonstrated that exposure to the series was associated with increased cross-race friendship selections (Graves, 1999a; Katsuyama, 1997) and an increased willingness to help a child from different racial groups. Children learned specific strategies for conflict resolution through the use of these videos (Graves, 1999a; Katsuyama, 1997). This discussion offers support for the potential of media materials designed to improve intergroup relations to influence different aspects of children's preferences, strategies, and attitudes toward children from groups different from their own.

CONCLUSION

In the future, children will more likely encounter children and adults from racial and ethnic groups different from their own. As children negotiate this diverse world, they will, as part of normal development, engage in the process of self-definition and identity development. As a part of that process, not only do children learn about themselves but themselves in relation to others. This understanding is mediated by one's racial/ethnic, class, and gender identities, and this is of particular importance for children of color.

In order for children to more effectively negotiate multicultural experiences, they will require preparation to engage productively and have their lives enriched by the diverse world in which they exist. To this end, we have offered some broad categories of intervention strategies for the reduction of prejudice, discrimination, and stereotyping in which concerned adults can engage and promote to help children learn to live, play, learn, and work in the multicultural society of the 21st century.

REFERENCES

Aboud, F. E. (1988). *Children and prejudice.* New York: Basil Blackwell.

Aboud, F. E., Mendelson, M. J., & Purdy, K. T. (2003). Cross-race peer relations and friendship quality. *International Journal of Behavioral Development, 27*(2), 165–173.

Allport, G. W. (1954). *The nature of prejudice.* Reading, MA: Addison-Wesley.

Arce, C. A. (1981). A reconsideration of Chicano culture and identity. *Daedalus, 110,* 177–192.

Bakagiannis, S., & Tarrant, M. (2006). Can music bring people together? Effects of shared musical preference on intergroup bias in adolescence. *Scandinavian Journal of Psychology, 47,* 129–136.

Biafora, F. A., Warheit, G. J., Zimmerman, R. S., & Gil, A. G. (1993). Racial mistrust and deviant behaviors among ethnically diverse Black adolescent boys. *Journal of Applied Social Psychology, 23,* 891–910.

Bigler, R., & Liben, L. (1993). A cognitive-developmental approach to racial stereotyping and reconstructive memory in Euro-American children. *Child Development, 64,* 1507–1518.

Bogatz, G. A., & Ball, S. (1971). *The second year of Sesame Street: A continuing evaluation.* Princeton, NJ: Educational Testing Service.

Branscombe, N. R., Schmitt, M. T., & Harvey, R. D. (1999). Perceiving pervasive discrimination among African Americans: Implications for group identification and well-being. *Journal of Personality and Social Psychology, 77,* 135–149.

Cameron, L., & Rutland, A. (2006). Extended contact through story reading in school: Reducing children's prejudice toward the disabled. *Journal of Social Issues, 62,* 469–488.

Cazabon, M., Lambert, W., & Hall, G. (1993). *Two-way bilingual education: A progress report on the Amigos Program* (Research Rep. No. 7). Washington, DC: National Center for Research on Cultural Diversity and Second Language Learning.

Center for Applied Linguistics. (2001). *Directory of two-way immersion programs in the U.S.* Washington, DC: Author.

Clement, R. (1995). The acquisition of French as a second language in Canada: Towards a research agenda. In J. W. Berry & J. Laponce (Eds.), *Ethnicity and culture in Canada* (pp. 410–434). Toronto: University of Toronto Press.

Cole, C. F., Arafat, C., Tidhar, C., Tafesh, W. Z., Fox, N. A., Killen, M., et al. (2003). The educational impact of *Rechove Sumsum/Shara'a Simsim:* A *Sesame Street* television series to promote respect and understanding among children living in Israel, the West Bank and Gaza. *International Journal of Behavioral Development, 27*(5), 409–422.

Constantine, M. G., & Blackmon, S. M. (2002). Black adolescents' racial socialization experiences: Their relations to home, school, and peer self-esteem. *Journal of Black Psychology, 32,* 322–335.

Cramer, P., & Anderson, G. (2003). Ethnic/racial attitudes and self-identification of Black Jamaican and White New England children. *Journal of Cross-Cultural Psychology, 34,* 395–416.

Crocker, J., Luhtanen, R., Blaine, B., & Broadnax, S. (1994). Collective self-esteem and psychological well-being among White, Black and Asian college students. *Personality and Social Psychology Bulletin, 20,* 503–513.

Cross, W. E. (1971). Negro to Black conversion experience. *Black World, 20,* 13–17.

Cross, W. E. (1978). The Thomas and Cross models of psychological Nigrescence: A review. *Journal of Black Psychology, 5*(1), 13–31.

Cross, W. E., Jr. (1991). *Shades of Black diversity in African-American identity.* Philadelphia: Temple University Press.

Cross, W. E. (1999). *Shades of Black diversity in African-American identity.* Philadelphia: Temple University Press.

Datnow, A., & Cooper, R. (1996). Peer networks of African-American students in independent schools: Affirming academic success and racial identity. *Journal of Negro Education, 65*(4), 56–72.

Erikson, E. (1968). *Identity and youth crisis.* New York: W. W. Norton.

Fordham, S., & Ogbu, J. (1986). Black student's school success: Coping with the burden of acting White. *Urban Review, 18,* 176–206.

Genesee, F. (1981). Bilingualism and biliteracy: A study of cross-cultural contact in a bilingual community. In J. Edwards (Ed.), *The social psychology of reading* (pp. 147–172). Silver Spring, MD: Institute of Modern Languages.

Genesee, F., & Gandara, P. (1999). Bilingual education programs: Cross-national perspective. *Journal of Social Issues, 55*(4), 665–686.

Gonzalez, R. (2003). Reconciling academic and ethnic identity: Mexican-American adolescents' encounter experiences. *Dissertation Abstracts International, 64*(5-A), 1525.

Grant, C. A., & Sleeter, C. (2007). *Doing multicultural education for achievement and equity.* New York: Taylor and Francis.

Graves, S. B. (1996). Diversity on television. In T. M. MacBeth (Ed.), *Tuning in to young viewers* (pp. 61–86). Newbury Park, CA: Sage.

Graves, S. B. (1999a). *Different and the same: A final report.* New York: Carnegie Corporation.

Graves, S. B. (1999b). Television and prejudice reduction: When does television as a vicarious experience make a difference? *Journal of Social Issues, 55*(4), 707–725.

Gray-Little, B., & Hafdahl, A. R. (2000). Factors influencing racial comparison of self-esteem: A quantitative review. *Psychological Bulletin, 126,* 26–54.

Hamm, J. (2001). Barriers and bridges to positive cross-ethnic relations: African-American and White parent socialization beliefs and practices. *Youth and Society, 33,* 62–98.

Harter, S. (2006). The self. In N. Eisenberg (Ed.), *Handbook of child psychology: Vol. 3. Social, emotional and personality development* (pp. 505–570). Hoboken, NJ: Wiley.

Helms, J. E. (Ed.). (1990). *Black and White racial identity: Theory, research and practice.* Westport, CT: Greenwood Press.

Helms, J. E. (1995). An adaptation to Helms' White and people of color racial identity models. In J. G. Ponterotto, J. M. Casas, L. A. Suzuki, & C. M. Alexander (Eds.), *Handbook of multicultural counseling* (pp. 181–198). Thousand Oaks, CA: Sage.

Hughes, D. (2003). Correlates of African-American and Latino parents' messages to children about ethnicity and race: A comparative study of racial socialization. *American Journal of Community Psychology, 31,* 15–33.

Hughes, D., Bachman, M., Ruble, D., & Fuligiani, A. (2006). Tuned in or tuned out: Children's interpretations of parents' racial socialization messages. In L. Balter & C. Tamis-Lemonda (Eds.), *Child psychology: A handbook of contemporary issues* (2nd ed., pp. 591–610). Philadelphia: Psychology Press.

Hughes, D., & Chen, L. (1999). The nature of parents' race-related communications to children: A developmental perspective. In L. Balter & C. S. Tamis-Lemonda (Eds.), *Child psychology: A handbook of contemporary issues* (pp. 467–490). Philadelphia: Psychology Press.

Hughes, D., & Johnson, D. (2001). Correlates in children's experiences of parents' racial socialization behaviors. *Journal of Marriage and Family, 63,* 981–995.

Hughes, D., Rodriguez, J., Smith, E. P., Johnson, D., Stevenson, H. C., & Spicer, P. (2006). Parents' ethnic-racial socialization practices: A review of research and directions for future study. *Developmental Psychology, 42*(5), 747–770.

Joyner, K., & Kao, G. (2000). School racial composition and adolescent racial homophily. *Social Science Quarterly, 81*(3), 810–825.

Katsuyama, R. M. (1997). *An evaluation of the Springfield city schools "Reaching Our Children" (ROC) program.* Dayton, OH: University of Dayton, Social Science Research Center.

Katz, P. A. (2003). Racists or tolerant multiculturalists? How do they begin? *American Psychologist, 58*(11), 897–909.

Katz, P. A., & Kofkin, J. A. (1997). Race, gender, and young children. In S. S. Luthar, J. A. Burack, D. Cicchetti, & J. Weisz (Eds.), *Developmental psychopathology: Perspectives on adjustment, risk, and disorder* (pp. 51–74). New York: Cambridge University Press.

Katz, P. A., & Zalk, S. R. (1978). Modification of children's racial attitudes. *Developmental Psychology, 14,* 447–461.

Kowalski, K., & Lo, Y.-F. (2001). The influence of perceptual features, ethnic labels and sociocultural information on the development of ethnic racial bias in young children. *Journal of Cross-Cultural Psychology, 32,* 444–455.

Ladson-Billings, G. (1992). Liberatory consequences of literacy: A case of culturally relevant instruction for African American students. *Journal of Negro Education, 61*(3), 378–390.

Ladson-Billings, G. (1995). But that's just good teaching! The case for culturally relevant pedagogy. *Theory Into Practice, 34*(3), 159–165.

Ladson-Billings, G. (2000). Fighting for our lives: Preparing teachers to teach African American students. *Journal of Teacher Education, 51*(3), 206–214.

Lease, A. M., & Blake, J. J. (2005). A comparison of majority-race children with and without a minority race friend. *Social Development, 14*(1), 20–41.

Lindholm, K. (2001). *Dual language education.* Avon, UK: Multilingual Matters.

Lindholm-Leary, K. (2000). *Biliteracy for a global society: An idea book on dual language education.* Washington, DC: National Clearinghouse on Bilingual Education.

Lovelace, V., Freund, S., & Graves, S. B. (in press). Race relations and *Sesame Street*: Racial knowledge, attitudes and understanding in preschool children. In M. B. Spencer & G. K. Brookins (Eds.), *Ethnicity and diversity: Minorities no more.* Westport, CT: Greenwood Press.

Lovelace, V., Scheiner, S., Dollberg, S., Segui, I., & Black, T. (1994). Making a neighborhood the *Sesame Street* way: Developing a methodology to evaluate children's understanding of race. *Journal of Educational Television, 20,* 69–77.

MacGregor, J. (1993). Effectiveness of role playing and antiracist teaching in reducing student prejudice. *Journal of Educational Research, 86*(4), 215–226.

MacPhee, J. (1997). "That's not fair!" A White teacher reports on White first graders' responses to multicultural literature. *Language Arts, 74*(1), 33–40.

Marsh, H. W., Hau, K.-T., & Kong, C. K. (2002). Multilevel causal ordering of academic self-concept and achievement: Influence of language of instruction (English compared with Chinese) for Hong Kong students. *American Educational Research Journal, 39,* 727–763.

McDermott, S., & Greenberg, B. S. (1984). Black children's esteem: Parents, peers, and television. In R. N. Bostrom (Ed.), *Communication yearbook 8* (pp. 164–177). Beverly Hills, CA: Sage.

McGlothlin, H., & Killen, M. (2006). Intergroup attitudes of European American children attending ethnically homogeneous schools. *Child Development, 77*(5), 1375–1386.

Meece, J. L., & Kurtz-Costes, B. (2001). The schooling of ethnic minority children and youth. *Educational Psychologist, 36*(1), 1–7.

Molina, L. E., & Wittig, M. A. (2006). Relative importance of contact conditions in explaining prejudice reduction in a classroom context: Separate and equal? *Journal of Social Issues, 62*(3), 489–509.

Moll, L. C., Amanti, C., Neff, D., & Gonzalez, N. (1992). Funds of knowledge for teaching: Using a qualitative approach to connect homes and classrooms. *Theory Into Practice, 31*(2), 132–141.

Nieto, S., & Bode, P. (2007). *Affirming diversity.* Boston: Allyn & Bacon.

Paluck, E. L., & Green, D. P. (2006). *Anti-bias education and peer influence as two strategies to reduce prejudice: An impact evaluation for the anti-defamation league peer training program.* New York: Yale University, Anti-Defamation League.

Pettigrew, T. F., & Tropp, L. R. (2006). A meta-analytic test of intergroup contact theory. *Journal of Personality and Social Psychology, 90,* 751–783.

Pfeifer, J. H., Brown, C. S., & Juvonen, J. (2007). Teaching tolerance to schools: Lessons learned since Brown v. Board of Education about the development and reduction of children's prejudice. *Social Policy Report, 21*(2), 1–24.

Phinney, J. S. (1990). Ethnic identity in adolescent and adults: Review of research. *Psychological Bulletin, 108,* 499–514.

Phinney, J. S. (1992). The multigroup ethnic identity measure: A new scale for use with diverse groups. *Journal of Adolescent Research, 7,* 156–176.

Phinney, J. S., & Chavira, V. (1995). Parental ethnic socialization and adolescent coping with problems related to ethnicity. *Journal of Research on Adolescence, 5,* 31–54.

Ponterotto, J. E. (1991). The nature of prejudice revisited: Implications for counseling interventions. *Journal of Counseling and Development, 70,* 216–224.

Ponterotto, J. G., Utsey, S. O., & Pedersen, P. B. (2006). *Preventing racism: A guide for counselors, educators and parents.* Thousand Oaks, CA: Sage.

Romero, A. J., Cuellar, L., & Roberts, R. E. (2000). Ethnocultural variables and attitudes toward cultural socialization of children. *Journal of Community Psychology, 28,* 79–89.

Scott, L. D. (2003). The relation of racial identity and racial socialization to coping with discrimination among African American adolescents. *Journal of Black Psychology, 33,* 520–538.

Shantz, C. U. (1975). The development of social cognition. In E. M. Hetherington (Ed.), *Review of child development research* (Vol. 5, pp. 257–323). Chicago: University of Chicago Press.

Shor, I. (1992). *Empowering education: Critical teaching for social change.* Chicago: University of Chicago Press.

Slavin, R. E. (2001). Cooperative learning and intergroup relations. In J. A. Banks & C. A. M. Banks (Eds.), *Handbook of research on multicultural education* (pp. 628–634). San Francisco: Jossey-Bass.

Slavin, R. E., & Cooper, R. (1999). Improving intergroup relations: Lessons learned from cooperative learning programs. *Journal of Social Issues, 55*(4), 647–664.

Slone, M., Tarrasch, R., & Hallis, D. (2000). Ethnic stereotypic attitudes among Israeli children: Two intervention programs. *Merrill-Palmer Quarterly, 46*(2), 370–389.

Snyder, T. D., Tan, A. G., & Hoffman, C. M. (2004). *Digest of education statistics 2003* (NCES No. 2005–025). Washington, DC: Government Printing Office.

Solomon, P. R. (1992). *Black resistance in high school: Forging a separatist culture.* Albany: State University of New York Press.

Spencer, M. B. (1983). Children's cultural values and parental child rearing strategies. *Developmental Review, 3,* 351–370.

Spencer, M. B., & Markstrom-Adams, C. (1990). Identity processes among racial and ethnic minority children in America. *Child Development, 61,* 290–310.

Spencer, M. B., Noll, E., Stoltzfus, J., & Harpalani, V. (2001). Identity and school adjustment: Revisiting the "acting White" assumption. *Educational Psychologist, 36*(1), 21–30.

Stephan, C. W., & Stephan, W. G. (2004). Intergroup relations in multicultural education programs. In J. A. Banks & C. A. M. Banks (Eds.), *Handbook of research on multicultural education* (pp. 782–798). New York: Jossey-Bass.

Stephan, W. G. (1999). *Reducing prejudice and stereotyping in schools.* New York: Teachers College Press.

Stevenson, H. C. (1995). Relationships of adolescent perceptions of racial socialization to racial identity. *Journal of Black Psychology, 33,* 49–70.

Subervi-Velez, F. A., & Necochea, J. (1990). Television viewing and self-concept among Hispanic American children: A pilot study. *Howard Journal of Communications, 2,* 315–329.

Sue, D. W., Carter, R. T., Casas, J. M., Fouad, N. A., Ivey, A. E., Jensen, M., et al. (1998). *Multicultural counseling competencies: Individual and organizational development.* Thousand Oaks, CA: Sage.

Thomas, A. J., & Speight, S. L. (1999). Racial identity and racial socialization attitudes of African American parents. *Journal of Black Psychology, 25,* 152–170.

Tracey, C. A., Sunderman, G. L., & Orfield, G. (2005). *Changing NCLB district accountability standards: Implications for racial equity.* Cambridge, MA: Harvard University.

U.S. Census Bureau. (2002). *Statistical abstracts of the United States: 2002* (122nd ed.). Washington, DC: Author.

U.S. Census Bureau. (2004). *U.S. interim projections by age, sex, race, and Hispanic origin.* Retrieved August 2, 2007, from http://www.census.gov/ipc/www/usinterimproj/natprojtab01a.xls

Ward, L. M. (2004). Wading through the stereotypes: Positive and negative associations between media use and black adolescents' conceptions of self. *Developmental Psychology, 40*(2), 284–294.

Ward, L. M., Hansbrough, E., & Walker, E. (2005). Contributions of music video exposure to black adolescents' gender and sexual schemas. *Journal of Adolescent Research, 20*(2), 143–166.

Wong, C. A., Eccles, J. S., & Sameroff, A. (2003). The influence of ethnic discrimination and ethnic identification on African American adolescents' school and socioemotional adjustment. *Journal of Personality, 71*(6), 1197–1232.

CHAPTER 7

Home and Family in the Development of a Multicultural Worldview

SINEAD N. YOUNGE

HARRIETTE PIPES MCADOO

The operational definition of multiculturalism is context specific. For the purposes of this chapter, multiculturalism will be defined as the inclusion and respect for the diversity of race, gender, class, and sexual orientation. Multiculturalism is a relatively new field, which works to empower and validate its participants, and it is heavily influenced by a number of different sociocultural factors. The 1950s and 1960s were a pivotal time in United States history because in a country where racial segregation was sanctioned by law, the 1950s were marked by a period of integration that necessitated change in the physical, sociological, and psychological perspective of many Americans. Because modern multiculturalism, as practiced in the United States, emerged from the civil rights movement, African Americans have been placed in the unique position of being an integral part of the dialogue *on* multiculturalism, yet little is known about the multicultural influences, attitudes, and perceptions *of* African Americans. Consequently, the 1954 *Brown v. Board of Education* decision dictated that children of all races and ethnicities would be among the pioneers of this new social experiment in integration. More than half a century later, many questions regarding multiculturalism and African American youth remain.

WORLDVIEW AND THE FAMILY

Multiculturalism attempts to foster understanding and appreciation of ethnic diversity by acknowledging and respecting diverse group identities and cultures. Multiculturalism has its roots in social psychology, which for decades has been investigating group identification and intergroup relations, primarily as cognitive and affective processes. The family plays a pivotal role in these aforementioned processes.

Generally, the role of the family is to act as the primary socialization agent and provide support and codes of conduct of social competence for children within a given network. Interestingly, the family can act as a protective factor and/or risk factor for various outcomes. Normative codes of conduct enable children to interpret cues and adopt normative behaviors that are adaptive in relationships with parents, peers, and other external forces.

Socialization is a dynamic and complex process that is often multidirectional and involves multiple systems (e.g., family, church, school, society, media). Western concepts of family functioning and, in turn, socialization tend to be culturally bound and, when inappropriately applied to diverse forms of family functioning, can make misinformed or erroneous generalizations about what is considered "healthy" functioning. It must be noted that some universal patterns of socialization do exist across families and cultures (i.e., connectedness, achievement, social skills); however, the manner in which specific cultural values or competencies are passed down differs according to each culture. This chapter will focus on the traditional and contemporary socialization of African American[1] children. Although African Americans are not a monolithic group, race remains a salient factor in some of the ways in which African American families rear their children (Miller, 1999). An in-depth discussion that defines *family* in its various forms, including single-parent households, blended families, and gay/lesbian families, is explored and practical suggestions are offered as to how various agents of socialization can nurture the development of a multicultural worldview in African American children.

According to Billingsley (1968), there are five general statements that characterize families of all people of African descent: (a) they are extended in form, (b) they have fictive kin who become as close to the family as blood kin, (c) they have supportive family patterns, (d) they have flexible family boundaries, and (e) they have flexible gender roles in child rearing. In order to understand the process of African American familial socialization practices, the composition of the African American family is discussed.

DEMOGRAPHIC CHARACTERISTICS OF THE AFRICAN AMERICAN FAMILY

In the year 2000, African Americans constituted 12.3% of the total U.S. population (McKinnon, 2001). Over the past couple of decades, the proportion of African Americans who live in heterosexual married-couple families has declined sharply. Marriage is becoming a minority lifestyle for many African American families (McAdoo, 2007). Currently, 44% of African American adults are married, which is significantly lower than the marriage rates for other ethnic groups in the United States (Administration for Children and Families, 2006). Forty-seven percent of Black males are single in comparison with their White single male counterparts (28%). Overall, Black males are more likely than their White counterparts to be divorced or widowed, and the slight gender imbalance of Black males to Black females is further compounded by the homicide, incarceration, and poverty rates, which place a strain on Black male–Black female relations (Blackman, Clayton, Glenn, Malone-Colon, & Roberts, 2005). The majority of Black children (82%) are currently living in homes without the biological father present; however, Black nonresident fathers have a higher rate than White and Latino nonresident fathers of visiting their children and partaking in primary care duties (Coles, 2001). Data from the National Survey of Families and Households indicate that Black males are more likely to be single, full-time fathers than their White and Latino counterparts (Eggebeen, Snyder, & Manning, 1996);

therefore, although a significant proportion of African American children come from "single parent" homes, father or "father" figures are often present. Subsequently, the family structure of African Americans often extends beyond the nuclear family, yet little research is conducted on alternative forms of family structure or functioning.

Same-Sex Unions and Parenting

To date, little is known about the experiences of the African American lesbian, gay, bisexual, transgendered (LGBT) community or same-sex unions, and, consequently, African American same-sex parenting. The lack of data on this group may be due to a number of factors. In the past, LGBT individuals were regularly denied the right to adopt, which limited the number of same-sex parents (excluding those with biological children) (Dang & Frazer, 2004). Although legislation has changed or eased in some states, lesbian and gay parents of all races continue to face social stigmatization and may have fears of being too openly public about their parenting statuses because of custody concerns (Rooney, 2001).

In order to better inform the debate on the impact of same-sex marriage in the United States, particularly on Black same-sex couples, the National Gay and Lesbian Task Force Policy Institute, in collaboration with the National Black Justice Coalition, conducted an analysis of data from the 2000 U.S. Census Bureau (Dang & Frazer, 2004). Data demonstrated that Black same-sex households constituted 14% of all same-sex households in the U.S., and according to the 2000 U.S. Census, Black and Latino same-sex households are nearly twice as likely as White non-Latino same-sex households to be parenting, which means that antigay parenting policies directly and disproportionately impact Black and Latino same-sex couples (Dang & Frazer, 2004). U.S. Census data also demonstrate that Black male same-sex couples are almost twice as likely to be living with a biological child as White male same-sex couples, and Black female same-sex couples are just as likely to be living with an adopted or foster child as Black married heterosexual couples (Dang & Frazer, 2004). On average, Black same-sex couples earn less and are less likely to own a home than their White and heterosexual Black counterparts, and their inability to access the legal protections of marriage disproportionately impacts their earning power and diminishes their ability to provide for their children (Dang & Frazer, 2004). In addition, Black LGBT parents experience a double, and in some instances a triple, minority status by being confronted with "racism in the [majority] White gay events and venues; and experience with homophobia in Black heterosexual organizations, from their families of origin, from straight friends, and also in churches and religious organizations" (Dang & Frazer, 2004, p. 11).

African American Same-Sex Parents and Religion

African American child rearing, in general, has a strong religious orientation (Taylor, Chatters, Tucker, & Lewis, 1990); however, with few exceptions, the Christian church does not traditionally condone homosexual behavior and many churches do not recognize same-sex unions. With spirituality/religiosity playing a key role in the socialization of African American children, this can place bisexual and homosexual parents or parents in same-sex unions in a quandary. Eighty-five percent of Black LGBT individuals surveyed in the 2000 U.S. Census indicated that they were affiliated with a religion (Dang & Frazer, 2004). About half reported that their church or religious institution influences their daily lives (Dang & Frazer, 2004). These findings support the claim that many Black lesbian and gay parents, similar to Black heterosexual parents, want to pass down the spiritual/religious values in which they themselves were raised to their children, but are confronted with the challenge of an institution [the church] that condemns their lifestyle.

The role of religiosity among African Americans and lack of positive or nonstereotypical mainstream representations of African American lesbian and gay individuals or same-sex unions influences the way in which African American children view these individuals, and, in some instances, may perpetuate the lack of cultural sensitivity to or identification with "sexual minorities" by African American youth. This lack of identification or sensitivity toward individuals with different sexual orientations may inhibit the ability of African Americans to identify with a common struggle against another marginalized group (Garnets, 2002). Subsequently, identity development can be difficult for young African American LGBT individuals, who must contend with a dual racial- and sexual-orientation minority status and are confronted with the challenge of deciding with which group they should identify or, alternatively, actively working to build a healthy model of sexual orientation based on multiplicity, which is inclusive of the intersections of minority statuses.

There has been an increasing amount of debate over lesbian and gay parenting in general. With the proportion of Black same-sex parents and the growing number of lesbian and gay White parents adopting Black children (Dang & Frazer, 2004), more research on African American children raised by same-sex parents is warranted. Among the small body of research on lesbian and gay parenting that does exist, many of the empirical research findings are consistent with the conclusion that lesbian and gay individuals can be fit and effective parents (Rooney, 2001).

ROLE OF THE EXTENDED FAMILY IN AFRICAN AMERICAN FAMILIES

Whether a child is raised in a single-parent, two-parent, heterosexual, or same-sex household, African American parents rely on relatives and friends to play supportive roles in their child-rearing practices. Extended kinship support has been characterized as a key adaptive strategy and traditional family resource for African Americans (Demo & Cox, 2000; Johnson, 2000; Taylor, 1996). For many African Americans, extended kinship support is an adaptive strategy that allows for the sharing of resources and the opportunity for extended kin to provide social capital to help influence children's growth toward positive developmental pathways. In a recent study by Pollack and Lamborn (2006), adolescents' perceptions of parenting practices and extended kinship support in relation to academic adjustment were examined in a sample of African American and European American high school students. Although extended family networks or *fictive kin* have most commonly been examined in reference to African Americans, the results from this study demonstrate that extended kinship support related to adolescents' academic adjustment, including attitudes about school, aspirations and expectations, and school engagement, were nearly equally beneficial for both African American and European American students; however, this study also demonstrated that there are some parenting style differences between African American and European American parents.

African American Parenting Style

African Americans have generally been characterized as having an *authoritative* parenting style. According to Baumrind's (1971) model of parenting styles, an authoritative parenting style is characterized as being highly demanding and highly responsive, otherwise stated, high in both warmth and control. Moreover, authoritative parents remain receptive to the child's view but take responsibility for firmly guiding the child (Baumrind, 1996). Authoritative parenting styles have been linked to positive adolescent development; however, comparative studies of Black and White parenting styles demonstrate that the Baumrind's model may be applicable to racial ethnic minorities, but only when considered with caveats, because the parenting styles are qualitatively different across racial groups (Attaway & Bry, 2004; Baumrind, 1971, 1996; Hill, 1997). Thus, when Whites are utilized as the standard, Black parenting styles may be interpreted inaccurately. Moreover, parenting style must be examined within the contexts that children are raised, and differences between social class and ethnic groups among African Americans do exist.

African American Socialization of Gender Roles

Biological gender differences transcend race, class, and sexual orientation; however, gender roles are socially constructed and vary depending on cultural norms (Lips, 2006). Some have argued that the emphasis on race and ethnicity in multiculturalism has eclipsed the discourse on the role of gender. Although gender does play an important role in the discourse on multiculturalism, a disparate proportion of economic deprivation in the African American community, along with racism, has made it difficult and impractical for many African Americans to create sharply defined divisions between male and female gender roles. Hill (2001) postulates that Black parents have embraced most of the values of the dominant society; however, she argues that their American experiences and African heritage have led to some distinctive socialization patterns, most of which revolve around race, class, and gender. There is some evidence that African American women have escaped the narrow confines of the restrictive gender roles assumed by a Eurocentric worldview. African American women have had to assume heavy responsibility for paid work, family, and community and have incidentally circumvented Eurocentric ideas of male privilege and power (Dill, 1988).

As a result of African American women's unique experiences in the United States, Ossanna, Helms, and Leonard (1992) developed a *womanist identity model*, which was an adaptation from Cross's (1971) nigresence model. Ossanna and colleagues' stages include preencounter, encounter, immersion/emersion, and internalization. Similar to Cross's model, the fourth and final stage is characterized by the woman defining her womanhood in her own terms and is not bound by external definitions about what it means to be a woman. There is a small but growing body of research to support women's differential identity development based on race (Boisnier, 2003). In addition to society, families play an important role in the gender role development of children. African American daughters, from an early age, are taught to assume strong family roles and to be strong, self-reliant, and independent individuals who are part of and play an integral role in a larger group, the family (Collins, 1987). Some studies support the view of gender neutrality in socializing children in Black families such that parents have similar role expectations for sons and daughters (Nobles, 1985; Peters, 1988; Scott, 1993) and that the child's gender does not dictate these expectations. Other scholars have argued that child rearing in the African American community is gender specific. hooks (1981) and Pinderhughes (1986) have written about the protective stance that many African American women take toward their fathers, brothers, husbands, and sons. Institutionalized racism has made many African American women reluctant to hold African American men to a feminist standard of accountability in the private world of the family. Black parents support competence and self-reliance more in daughters than in sons (McAdoo, 1988; Staples & Johnson, 1993) and may have higher expectations for daughters because they view them as having a greater opportunity to survive and succeed in mainstream society (Staples & Johnson, 1993). Conversely, lower expectations for sons may be shaped by the "extra" barriers commonly faced by Black men. Yet, this stance ignores the double burden of sexism and racism that constructs the lives of African American women (Silverstein, 2006).

African American Racial Socialization

In addition to gender, an important aspect of socialization for Black parents and children is racial socialization, defined as parents' "attempts to prepare their children for the realities of being Black in America" (Taylor et al., 1990, p. 994). Hughes (2003) examined the frequency and correlates of two dimensions of racial socialization among urban African American, Puerto Rican, and Dominican parents: messages about ethnic pride, history, and heritage (cultural socialization) and messages about discrimination and racial bias (preparation for bias). Her findings demonstrated that there were no significant ethnic group differences in the frequency of cultural socialization. However, African American parents reported more frequent preparation for bias than did Dominican parents, who, in turn, reported more frequent messages of preparation for bias than did Puerto Rican parents (Hughes, 2003). These findings demonstrate that the frequency and correlates of racial socialization depend on the dimension of racial socialization, parents' ethnic group membership, and children's ages. The aforementioned factors are all imperative for the development of a healthy self-esteem in addition to equipping children of color for future, perhaps adverse, experiences based on race.

Ethnic/Racial Identity

In order to combat adverse experiences based on race, one strategy used by some African American parents is to instill a sense of racial and ethnic identity in their children to combat the effects of racism. William Cross (1971) developed a stage model in an article titled "The Negro to Black Conversion Experience." Cross outlines four stages that African Americans go through in moving from self-hatred to self-acceptance, referred to as *nigrescence,* or the process of becoming Black. These stages include the preencounter, the encounter, immersion/emersion, and internalization. This final stage is where individuals feel more positive and secure about their Black identity but also exhibit increased comfort with and acceptance of other cultures. Cross's model supports the view that affirmation toward one's ethnic group leads to a positive ethnic identity and higher levels of acceptance toward ethnic out-groups. Despite the substantial body of research on intragroup relations, specifically ethnic/racial identity and African American youth, there exists little empirical evidence on African American youths' intergroup relations, specifically their influences on and attitudes toward diversity and multiculturalism.

Cross's model has engendered a number of other models for African Americans and other ethnic groups. Interestingly, whereas most models of ethnic identity use Whites as the referent group, it is imperative to examine the relationship between African Americans and other individuals of color. Cross's early stages may be characterized by lack of understanding or negating other groups' experiences of oppression. In contrast, the later stages of the nigrescence model are characterized by African American individuals reaching out to different ethnic groups in order to understand their cultural values and ways of life.

Intergroup Relations

Until recently, African Americans constituted the largest ethnic minority group in the United States, and research on interethnic group relations traditionally focused on Whites and Blacks or Whites and members of other ethnic groups (i.e., Latinos, Asians, Native Americans) (Berry, 1988, 1997; Birman, 1994; LaFromboise, Coleman, & Gerton, 1993). Large metropolitan cities, and more recently smaller suburban cities, that have traditionally been populated by Blacks are seeing a rise in newly arrived immigrants (e.g., Latinos and Asians) who are in direct competition with African Americans for jobs and resources (Randall & Delbridge, 2005). Theorists have purported that when individuals from different ethnic groups come into contact with one another, assimilation (taking on the values of a host group while rejecting his or her original values) (Berry, 1988) will occur or the two groups will remain distinct and separate. These processes have been examined within an "Anglo conformist" model and are not appropriate for individuals who share a minority-group status. The competition and lack of cross-cultural understanding that often occurs between groups can contribute to tension and animosity, which can manifest itself in racial violence between Blacks and Latinos such as that recently reported in cities like Los Angeles (Hernandez, 2007). Latinos have exceeded Blacks as the largest ethnic minority group in the United States, and Los Angeles County comprises the largest proportion of Mexicans than any other county in the United States (U.S. Census Bureau, 2001). Although Latinos and Blacks share many of the same socioeconomic deprivations and reside in the same or similar neighborhoods, there remains a significant amount of "social distancing"[2] between these two groups (Hernandez, 2007). On January 7, 2007, the *Los Angeles Times* published an editorial on the racial strife between Blacks and Latinos residing in Los Angeles. The recent rise in violence was attributed to both a competition for economic resources and the legacy of White supremacy that is deeply ingrained in Latin America and possibly reinforced in the beliefs of Mexican immigrants residing in Los Angeles (Hernandez, 2007). The article cited findings from the 1999–2000 Lilly Survey of American Attitudes and Friendships (LSAF). The survey found that African Americans, in comparison with Latinos, reported feeling less hostility toward Latinos than Latinos felt toward them, and African Americans also reported being more accepting of intermarriage with Latinos than Latinos. The recent reports of strife between Blacks and Latinos should not overshadow the history of these two groups residing harmoniously (though not completely absent of incident) side by side in cities across the United States for several generations. Rather than assimilation, acculturation (the changing of two groups that come into contact with one another) has often occurred. Rather than an assimilation model, a *cultural mosaic* model should be promoted where, rather than rejecting their cultural heritage, groups that come into contact with one another are altered to form a novel new culture. Aspects of this perspective are demonstrated in multicultural communities across the United States, with a generation of different cultures raised in proximity with one another creating shared forms of music, dance, style of dress, and other important vestiges of culture. Due to the dearth of research, further investigation on the intergroup relations between African Americans and other groups is warranted.

A SYSTEMS APPROACH TO PROMOTING A MULTICULTURAL PERSPECTIVE

Taking Bronfenbrenner's (1977, 1979, 1989) systems approach to human behavior, it is known that children do not develop in isolation. Rather, they develop in a variety of contexts and environments that surround the individual and with which the child is in constant interaction (e.g., Bridge, Judd, & Moock, 1979; Bronfenbrenner, 1977, 1979, 1989). The microlevel of the ecological model of human development includes the immediate and earliest influences, such as the family. The higher levels include local neighborhood or community institutions such as the school, religious institutions, and peer groups, as well as the specific culture with which individuals identify. The relationships between these levels are multidirectional and work to socialize the child in a particular manner.

This chapter has focused on the role of the family, religious institutions, culture, and policy in the development and socialization of African American children. In order for a child to develop in a healthy and optimal manner, the child must adopt multiple identities in different contexts (i.e., student, daughter or son, employee). The home and family become the primary agents and perhaps the most significant agents of socialization. The complexity of managing multiple identities becomes most apparent when children enter the educational system, and even more complex as they age and later leave the homes of their parents. In order to develop and/or hone a multicultural perspective, practitioners must take a strength-based approach. This approach should use and promote the preexisting strengths within the African American community. The family, which has traditionally been viewed as the primary socialization agent of children, can engender a sense of cultural relativism and appreciation for the diversity that exists among individuals of other races, religious beliefs, genders, political orientations, and sexual orientations.

NOTES

1. For the purposes of this chapter, the terms *African American* and *Black* will be used interchangeably.
2. Social distancing was originally conceptualized as the unease one ethnic or racial group has with interacting with another ethnic group (Bogardus, 1925).

REFERENCES

Administration for Children and Families. (2006). *Marriage, divorce, childbirth, and living arrangements among African American or Black populations.* Retrieved December 8, 2006, from http://www.acf.hhs.gov/healthymarriage/about/aami_marriage_statistics.htm

Attaway, N. M., & Bry, B. H. (2004). Parenting style and Black adolescents' academic achievement. *Journal of Black Psychology, 30*(2), 229–247.

Baumrind, D. (1971). Current patterns of parental authority [Monograph]. *Developmental Psychology, 4,* 1–103.

Baumrind, D. (1996). Parenting, the discipline controversy revisited. *Family Relations, 45*, 405–414.
Berry, J. W. (1988). Psychology of acculturation: Understanding individuals moving between cultures. In. J. W. Berry & R. C. Annis (Eds.), *Ethnic psychology: Research and practice with immigrants, refugees, native peoples, ethnic groups and sojourners* (pp. 1–40). Lisse, Netherlands: Swets & Zeitlinger.
Berry, J. W. (1997). Immigration, acculturation, and adaptation. *Applied Psychology: An International Review, 46*, 5–34.
Billingsley, A. (1968). *Black families in White America.* Englewood Cliffs, NJ: Prentice Hall.
Birman, D. (1994). Acculturation and human diversity in a multicultural society. In E. J. Trickett, R. J. Watts, & D. Birman (Eds.), *Human diversity: Perspectives on people in context* (pp. 261–284). San Francisco: Jossey-Bass.
Blackman, L., Clayton, O., Glenn, N., Malone-Colon, L., & Roberts, A. (2005). *The consequences of marriage for African Americans: A comprehensive literature review.* Retrieved December 8, 2006, from http://americanvalues.org/consequences_report.pdf
Bogardus, E. S. (1925). Social distance and its origins. *Journal of Applied Sociology, 9*, 216–226.
Boisnier, A. D. (2003). Race and women's identity development: Distinguishing between feminism and womanism among Black and White women. *Sex Roles: A Journal of Research, 49*(5/6), 211–219.
Bridge, R., Judd, C., & Moock, P. (1979). *The determinants of educational outcomes: The impact of families, peers, teachers, and schools.* Cambridge, MA: Ballinger.
Bronfenbrenner, U. (1977). Toward an experimental ecology of human development. *American Psychologist, 32*, 513–530.
Bronfenbrenner, U. (1979). *The ecology of human development.* Cambridge, MA: Harvard University Press.
Bronfenbrenner, U. (1989). Ecological systems theory. In R. Vasta (Ed.), *Annals of child development* (Vol. 6, pp. 187–251). Greenwich, CT: JAI Press.
Coles, R. L. (2001). The parenting roles and goals of single Black full-time fathers. *The Western Journal of Black Studies, 25*(2), 101–116.
Collins, P. H. (1987). The meaning of motherhood in Black culture and Black mother-daughter relationships. *Sage: A Scholarly Journal on Black Women, 4*(2), 3–10.
Cross, W. E. (1971). The Negro to Black conversion experience: Towards the psychology of Black liberation. *Black World, 20*, 13–27.
Dang, A., & Frazer, S. (2004). *Black same-sex households in the United States: A report from the 2000 census.* New York: National Gay and Lesbian Task Force Policy Institute and the National Black Justice Coalition.
Demo, D. H., & Cox, M. J. (2000). Families with young children: A review of research in the 1990s. *Journal of Marriage & the Family, 62*, 876–895.
Dill, B. T. (1988). Our mother's grief: Racial ethnic women and the maintenance of families. *Journal of Family History, 13*, 415–431.
Eggebeen, D., Snyder, T., & Manning, W. D. (1996). Children in single-father families in demographic perspective. *Journal of Family Issues, 17*, 441–465.
Garnets, L. D. (2002). Sexual orientations in perspective. *Cultural Diversity and Ethnic Minority Psychology, 8*(2), 115–129.
Hernandez, T. K. (2007, January 7). *Roots of Latino/Black anger: Longtime prejudices, not economic rivalry, fuel tensions.* Retrieved February 18, 2007, from http://www.latimes.com/news/opinion/la-op-hernandez7jan07,0,2489.story?call=la-opinion-rightrail

Hill, N. E. (1997). Does parenting differ based on social class? African American women's perceived socialization for achievement. *American Journal of Community Psychology, 25*(5), 675–697.

Hill, S. A. (2001). Class, race, and gender dimensions of child rearing in African American families. *Journal of Black Studies, 31*(4), 494–506.

hooks, b. (1981). *Ain't I a woman? Black women and feminism.* Boston: South End Press.

Hughes, D. (2003). Correlates of African American and Latino parents' messages to children about ethnicity and race: A comparative study of racial socialization. *American Journal of Community Psychology, 31(*1/2), 15–33.

Johnson, C. L. (2000). Perspectives on American kinship in the later 1990s. *Journal of Marriage and the Family, 62,* 623–639.

LaFromboise, T., Coleman, H. L. K., & Gerton, J. (1993). Psychological impact of biculturalism: Evidence and theory. *Psychological Bulletin, 114,* 395–412.

Lips, H. M. (2006). *A new psychology of women: Gender, culture, and ethnicity.* New York: McGraw-Hill.

McAdoo, H. (Ed.). (2007). *Black families.* Thousand Oaks, CA: Sage.

McAdoo, J. L. (1988). The roles of Black fathers in the socialization of Black children. In H. P. McAdoo (Ed.), *Black families* (2nd ed., pp. 257–269). Newbury Park, CA: Sage.

McKinnon, J. (2001). *The Black population: 2000.* Retrieved November 12, 2006, from http://www.census.gov/prod/2001pubs/c2kbr01–5.pdf

Miller, D. (1999). Racial socialization and racial identity: Can they promote resiliency for African American adolescents? *Adolescence, 34*(135), 493–502.

Nobles, W. W. (1985). *Africanity and the Black family: The development of a theoretical model* (2nd ed.). Oakland, CA: Institute for the Advanced Study of Black Family Life and Culture.

Ossana, S. M., Helms, J. E., & Leonard, M. M. (1992). Do "womanist" identity attitudes influence college women's self-esteem and perceptions of environmental bias? *Journal of Counseling and Development, 70,* 402–408.

Peters, M. F. (1988). Parenting in Black families with young children: A historical perspective. In H. P. McAdoo (Ed.), *Black families* (2nd ed., pp. 227–241). Newbury Park, CA: Sage.

Pinderhughes, E. (1986). Minority women: A nodal position in the functioning of the social system. In M. Alt-Riche (Ed.), *Women and family therapy* (pp. 51–63). Rockville, MD: Aspen Systems.

Pollack, L. L., & Lamborn, S. D. (2006). Beyond parenting practices: Extended kinship support and the academic adjustment of African-American and European-American teens. *Journal of Adolescence, 29,* 813–828.

Randall, N. H., & Delbridge, S. (2005). Perceptions of social distance in an ethnically fluid community. *Sociological Spectrum, 25,* 103–122.

Rooney, S. C. (2001). Examining Redding's (2001) claims about lesbian and gay parenting. *American Psychologist, 57*(4), 298–299.

Scott, J. W. (1993). African American daughter-mother relations and teenage pregnancy: Two faces of premarital teenage pregnancy. *Western Journal of Black Studies, 17,* 73–81.

Silverstein, L. B. (2006). Integrating feminism and multiculturalism: Scientific fact or science fiction? *Professional Psychology: Research and Practice, 37*(1), 21–28.

Staples, R., & Johnson, L. B. (1993). *Black families at the crossroads: Challenges and prospects.* San Francisco: Jossey-Bass.

Taylor, R. D. (1996). Adolescents' perceptions of kinship support and family management practices: Associations with adolescent adjustment in African American families. *Developmental Psychology, 32,* 687–695.

Taylor, R. J., Chatters, L. M., Tucker, M. B., & Lewis, E. (1990). Developments in research on Black families: A decade review. *Journal of Marriage & Family, 52*(4), 993–1014.

U.S. Census Bureau. (2001). *The Hispanic population: Census 2000 brief.* Retrieved December 13, 2006, from http://www.census.gov/prod/2001pubs/c2kbr01–3.pdf1

CHAPTER 8

Sociopolitical and Community Dynamics in the Development of a Multicultural Worldview

SHELLY P. HARRELL

MIGUEL E. GALLARDO

> *There is a fable of a big white dog sitting on a porch with a large loaf of bread, and a group of black, brown, and yellow dogs yapping outside the fence, coveting the bread. Whenever the colored dogs got close enough to the fence to annoy the big white dog, he'd pull off a morsel of bread, hardly more than a crumb, and throw it out to the howling hordes. Then, enjoying his own bread, he'd sit back and disparagingly watch the other dogs fight over crumbs.*
>
> —Author Unknown

This fable about the big white dog on the porch reminds us of the significant role community and sociopolitical dynamics have in shaping behavior. Sociopolitical contexts, characterized by the dynamics of power and privilege, inclusion/exclusion, us/them, belonging/alienation, stratification and access to resources, reflect the larger sociopolitical system within which we are socialized and live our daily lives. Community contexts include both physical communities (e.g., neighborhood, school, workplace) and identity communities that extend beyond physical boundaries and reflect a more psychological sense of community (e.g., "the Black community," "the Korean community"). The dynamics of these sociopolitical and community contexts reflect the macrosystemic and ideological influences that contribute to the shapes and colors of the lenses through which we view ourselves, others, and the world around us. Ultimately, it is these lenses that determine our behavior and interactions, our understanding of our own social locations, and our worldview. These lenses not only influence individual and group behavior, but also contribute to the extent and pace of our collective progress toward a just world where all of humanity is honored and can live with dignity and self-determination. An inclusive, multicultural worldview is necessary for this progress to occur, and socialization of this multicultural worldview during childhood and adolescence is a critical ingredient.

WORLDVIEW AND CULTURE IN A SOCIOPOLITICAL CONTEXT

Worldviews are "sets of beliefs and assumptions that describe reality" (Koltko-Rivera, 2004, p. 3). One's worldview contains ideas about human nature, the purpose and meaning of life, and the ultimate causes of phenomena. Koltko-Rivera goes on to describe worldview as

> a way of describing the universe and life within it, both in terms of what is and what ought to be. . . . A worldview defines what can be known or done in the world, and how it can be known or done . . . what goals can be sought in life . . . what goals should be pursued. . . . Worldviews include assumptions that may be unproven, and even unprovable, but these assumptions are superordinate, in that they provide the epistemic and ontological foundations for other beliefs within a belief system. (p. 4)

In his comprehensive review and integration of worldview theories, Koltka-Rivera identifies several worldview dimensions that can be thought of as part of a larger multicultural worldview. These include otherness, relation to humanity, interaction, interpersonal justice, sociopolitical justice, and world justice. Each of these can take different forms. For example, within the dimension of otherness, one's worldview can be characterized by accepting and welcoming of otherness or by the sensibility that otherness is intolerable and unacceptable.

Ibrahim and Kahn (1987) conceptualized worldview as beliefs, values, and assumptions that are directly related to the cultural context in which they emerge. The complexity of understanding worldview is rooted in the social reality that each individual is exposed to multiple cultural contexts throughout his or her lifetime. These cultural contexts include both the larger societal culture as well as the smaller group cultures within which we are socialized. Every culture has a set of beliefs and attitudes that are *lived* by the group. They do not need to be stated, questioned, or defended. These beliefs and attitudes often cannot even be easily articulated, and may not be within conscious awareness, until a different culture is encountered that presents a contrast to one's own way of living. Abney (1996) further states that culture is dynamic and changing, not static; it changes as the condition of the people changes and as their interaction with the larger society changes. Falicov (1983) defines culture as

> those sets of shared world views, meanings, and adaptive behaviors derived from simultaneous membership and participation in a variety of contexts, such as language; rural, urban or suburban setting; race, ethnicity, and socioeconomic status; age, gender, religion, nationality; employment, education and occupation, political ideology, stage of acculturation. (pp. xiv–xv)

A child's defining worldview inevitably reflects multiple cultural contexts, including ethnic/racial culture of origin, school culture, neighborhood culture, peer culture, and religious culture, among many other dimensions of culture.

It is also important to recognize *sociopolitical culture* as an important influence on the development of worldview. Sociopolitical culture refers to those beliefs, attitudes, and behaviors associated with membership in groups defined by social stratification, "isms," and the dynamics of oppression (Harrell, 2000). At the most fundamental level, there are two primary expressions of sociopolitical culture: *majority culture* and *minority culture*. These refer to the values, beliefs, and behaviors that are characteristic of belonging to a dominant, privileged group (majority) or to a nondominant, marginalized group (minority). These sociopolitical cultures are important determinants of the lens through which one sees the world and one's place in it. Sociopolitical culture suggests that there are shared dimensions of worldview that can be commonly found across diverse racial/ethnic groups who share similar status in larger society.

In the United States, race is a central determinant of sociopolitical culture. Race is not simply the color of one's skin, but more the way in which we designate certain groups into socially ranked or stratified places in society. Although the socially constructed concept of race does not provide a valid system of classification biologically, phenotypic expression (e.g., skin color, eye color and shape, hair color and texture) continues to influence status and privilege in societies throughout the world. White or lighter complexion, lighter eyes, straight hair, and thin body shape continue to be prized characteristics while darker skin color, darker eyes, tightly curled hair, and thick body shape are devalued. Valued physical characteristics continue to characterize a larger portion of those with more power and privilege in a society, whereas the devalued characteristics are more commonly seen among those with less societal privilege. Different phenotypic expressions, manifested in physical appearance, have direct implications and directly influence the local social worlds of the individuals and groups who occupy them. Socialization messages about what is attractive and desirable from within racial/ethnic groups, as well as from larger society, often mirror dominant-culture values and preferences. It is this ideology of White supremacy that saturates systems of socialization and makes race a determinant of the social hierarchy. Simultaneously, this ideology erects barriers to developing (at individual, group, organizational, and societal levels) a multicultural worldview where the rainbow of phenotypic expressions are equally valued.

Ogbu (1994) defines racial stratification as the "hierarchical organization of socially defined 'races' or groups symbolized by skin color" (p. 268). Skin color has direct implications for the status afforded to certain groups in society as defined by members of the dominant group. Ogbu (1994) states, "In a system of racial stratification people are prohibited from changing their group membership" (p. 269). The relative permanence of this assigned social strata results in systematic asymmetric distribution and access to resources, limited social mobility, and a disproportionate segment of racial/ethnic groups of color living in barrios and "hoods" with substandard housing, ineffective education systems, and unequal access to good healthcare. Consequently, as a reflection of this sociopolitical cultural context, ways of coping, interpreting, and making sense of the world develop as a means of survival and as a way to counter any forms of stigmatization, subjugation, and marginalization imposed upon them. Members of disenfranchised groups establish cultural and familial adaptations in the spirit of the survival of the group's people and traditions. Therefore, socialization processes for children of color are a reflection of social conditions rooted in racial stratification. Ultimately, sociopolitical forces and racial stratification impact the formation of worldview beliefs and can present obstacles to the development of a positive multicultural worldview.

A multicultural worldview requires (a) a central consciousness of diversity and global citizenship; (b) an attitude of inclusion; (c) an assumption that difference is not deviance but is to be valued, honored, and affirmed; (d) a view of people of all cultures as fully human with dignity and a right to self-determination; (e) an awareness of social and economic asymmetries that confer privilege based on social location; and (f) a belief in the power of the interdependencies and interconnectedness across cultures. These fundamental assumptions and beliefs of a multicultural worldview are likely to be strongly related to behaviors contradictory to discrimination and the maintenance of oppression.

Unfortunately, this multicultural worldview involves assumptions and values about the nature of reality that are in stark contrast to the dominant worldview that characterizes the United States. For example, autonomy, competition, profit, acquisition of material resources, and "being #1" are elements of the defining worldview orientation of the dominant culture. Deviance from an idealized societal norm (i.e., White, male, assertive, ambitious, rational, emotionally controlled) is associated with pathology, or at best, inferiority. Independence and superiority are core cultural assumptions of the dominant worldview in the United States, and the stated belief in equality is translated into a correct attitude of ignoring "color" and valuing people to the degree that they are "like us."

This dominant cultural worldview, which stands in opposition to a multicultural worldview, is manifested through the dominant cultural narratives of any society. Rappaport (1995) describes dominant cultural narratives as stories that are told repeatedly through social institutions such as media and our system of education. These narratives become overlearned by all members of a society (majority and minority) and are internalized to such an extent that they become "reality." A common narrative is that of the African American male as a violent criminal and threat to the safety of innocent people. A related narrative is the White American male hero whose courage and integrity "saves the day." However, these narratives are sociopolitically determined in that the decisions of which choice of stories to tell through media and within our system of education are controlled by those in positions of power and privilege. This suggests that it is the dominant worldview that defines social reality as communicated and learned through mainstream socialization agents. The cultural and community narratives that tell stories of the strengths of people of color must often be learned through alternative and intragroup socialization agents (i.e., racial socialization). These stories are not frequently told through mainstream socialization agents and are often not accessible as socialization messages outside of the particular culture or community. These cultural and community narratives can also be taken, distorted, and "retold" in ways that perpetuate the view of reality embedded in dominant cultural narratives.

With respect to issues of worldview and culture, it is also important to consider the specific dimensions of worldview that differ between mainstream, dominant culture and underrepresented, marginalized groups in society. A review of the literature indicates that the historically oppressed racial/ethnic groups in the United States frequently come from cultures of origin that view the world through a collectivistic lens. These groups historically have included African Americans (Nobles, 1986; Parham, 2002), Asian Americans (Mio, Barker-Hackett, & Tumambing, 2006; Sue & Sue, 2002; Yeh, 2000), Latinos (Falicov, 1998; Santiago-Rivera, Arredondo, & Gallardo-Cooper, 2002), Native Americans (Duran, 2006; Trimble & Thurman, 2002), and Middle Easterners (Dwairy, 2006; Jalali, 1996). The collectivistic cultural paradigm for these groups implies that group identity supersedes individual identity. This orientation differs from the dominant cultural worldview, which encourages a more individualistic lens whereby individual needs supersede that of the larger group. This distinction becomes important when delineating group differences in the process of developing a multicultural worldview. An individualistic worldview is in contradiction to the development of an inclusive multicultural worldview. Collectivist values, such as interconnectedness and cooperation, are more compatible with a multicultural worldview orientation. This suggests that developing a multicultural worldview may be a naturally better "fit" for many individuals from racial/ethnic groups of color because there is already a foundation in collectivistic thinking. However, caution should be taken here because it is quite possible to have a very rigid collectivist orientation simultaneously with an intolerance toward "otherness."

Embracing a multicultural worldview for racial/ethnic minority groups in the United States means recognizing the extent to which one views the world through a lens of inferiority and powerlessness and how this view influences attitudes and behaviors within and between groups (e.g., the colored dogs fighting over morsels of bread). Internalized racism and intragroup colorism are manifestations of the absence of a multicultural worldview among people of color. Developing a multicultural worldview for White Americans means recognizing the asymmetries that exist in larger society that grant privileges to them that are not enjoyed by racial/ethnic minorities. Belief in the myth of a color-blind society and an unquestioned assumption of one's own group as the standard for what is normal, healthy, and "better" reflect the absence of a multicultural worldview among many Whites. Strong sociopolitical and self-awareness of the ways in which one colludes with the sociopolitical and community dynamics that perpetuate racial stratification is an important element of a multicultural worldview for both Whites and people of color.

ECOLOGICAL THEORY, PSYCHOLOGY, AND HUMAN DEVELOPMENT

Ecological theory provides a foundational conceptual framework for examining sociopolitical and community contexts in the development of a multicultural worldview. Characterized by multiple levels of analysis, the ecological paradigm serves to illuminate the role of sociopolitical and community dynamics. Thus, a multicultural worldview should not just be viewed as a characteristic of individuals, but also of groups, organizations, and broader macrosystems. The ecological paradigm provides a critical alternative to the medical model and individual person emphasis that has dominated conceptions of human development. Ecological theory, with origins in the person-environment theory of Kurt Lewin in the 1930s (Dalton, Elias, & Wandersman, 2006), has had increasing influence in many disciplines, including public health, education, and psychology. Two areas within psychology have been particularly influenced by ecological theory: developmental psychology and community psychology.

Developmental psychology has been profoundly influenced by the work of researchers such as Urie Bronfenbrenner (1977, 1979, 1986), James Garbarino (Garbarino, 1982), and Margaret Beale Spencer (1999, 2006), who have brought attention to the inextricable link between social context and child development. Developmental psychologist Urie Bronfenbrenner is well known for his ecological systems model (Bronfenbrenner 1977, 1979, 1986). Bronfenbrenner's landmark contribution is characterized by his articulation of ecological systems theory, which identifies the multiple, nested systems that must be considered in a comprehensive understanding of child development. The theory proposes that the individual is nested within four systems: the *microsystem* (the child's most immediate contexts such as the family and peer group); the *mesosystem* (intermediate contexts where different microsystems interact, such as the neighborhood or school); the *exosystem* (social networks and institutions that indirectly affect development, such as parental place of employment); and the *macrosystem* (ideologies and systems of the broader social context reflecting core values and structures, such as gender roles, social policy, and the global economy). The concept of the *chronosystem,* an important contribution of Bronfenbrenner's later thinking, involves issues of continuity and change in social contexts, sociohistorical conditions, and the patterning of events and transitions over the life course. A family's movement from working class, to poverty, and into homelessness is an example of the importance of incorporating chronosystemic factors in a comprehensive understanding of child development. Bronfenbrenner's human ecology holds that these five ecological systems interact with and influence each other, and collectively exert influence on human development.

Of particular relevance to development of a multicultural worldview is Spencer's extension of this general ecological systems approach, which she terms "the phenomenological variant of ecological systems theory." This theory underlies the use of an identity-focused cultural ecological perspective to better understand risk and protective factors among children of color and the identity-context linkages. For example, the social context consists of socialization messages that perpetuate bias, prejudice, and discrimination. Identity development is linked to the meaning that children make of their social contexts (Spencer, 1999, 2006).

Community psychology is the area of psychology that emphasizes the importance of understanding human behavior in its cultural, environmental, social, historical, and sociopolitical contexts (Dalton et al., 2006). Multiple levels of analysis are integral to a community psychology approach to human behavior with an emphasis on the role of the diverse settings in which we live and develop. Empowerment and well-being are relevant constructs from the field of community psychology that inform our analysis of sociopolitical and community processes in the development of a multicultural worldview. The creation of empowering settings that facilitate personal, relational, and collective well-being is a necessary strategy to mobilize individuals and communities to challenge dominant-culture worldview orientations and move society toward a multicultural worldview. As long as the well-being of racial/ethnic minorities is jeopardized, there will be little systematic progress toward the socialization of a multicultural worldview.

Empowerment is both a process and an outcome (Zimmerman, 2000). Settings and organizations can be empowering and/or empowered. Groups and individuals can be characterized by their degree of psychological and behavioral empowerment. Community psychology conceptualizes empowerment as involving the identification and nurturing of strengths and resources of individuals, organizations, and communities to become change agents in their own lives and contexts and to be involved in activities that exert influence in the broader social and political environment. Empowerment-oriented interventions bridge multiple levels of analysis. At the intrapersonal and interpersonal level, empowerment includes motivation, commitment to values, self-efficacy, skills, and competencies. At the group level, empowerment involves a sense of connectedness, interdependence, and collective action. An organization or community can be empowering of its members by nurturing both individual and group empowerment. An organization can also be empowered to effect change within, as well as to influence external systems. From a community psychology perspective, nurturing a multicultural worldview within individuals, groups, and society requires attention to modifying the social contexts within which people develop as well as the larger macrosystemic and sociopolitical processes that influence the structure and operations of social, organizational, community, and institutional settings. Social justice is conceptualized as a necessary condition for optimal personal, relational, and collective well-being (Prilleltensky, 2003), and social justice is not possible in the absence of a widespread multicultural worldview.

SOCIALIZATION IN THE CONTEXT OF SOCIOPOLITICAL AND COMMUNITY DYNAMICS

An examination of sociopolitical influences on socialization processes requires an attention to the central characteristics of the dominant worldview that influences all agents of socialization in varying degrees. It is important to examine the influence of broader macrosystemic factors, the more direct and proximal agents of socialization (e.g., family, school, media). Lloyd (2002) notes that mass communication outlets (i.e., the media) are children's primary connection to the world outside of their local contexts. They are the primary sources of information about people, places, and situations that are not within personal experience. Because we continue to live in communities that are largely segregated by race, ideas about other racial/ethnic groups come largely from the multitude of media available to youth, including video gaming, the Internet (e.g., MySpace, YouTube), television, movies, and music. All of these agents of socialization exist in a broader sociopolitical context that influences both the process and content of socialization messages transmitted by families, schools, and media.

For racial/ethnic minority group children, socialization involves a process of learning how to negotiate the social world while attempting to simultaneously balance the mainstream, the minority, and their own specific cultural group influences. Socialization occurs with respect to the values and customs of ancestral cultures, the anticipatory socialization provided to teach children appropriate responses to racism, and exposure to the values and behaviors of the dominant culture. As Ogbu (1981) reminds us, to understand child-rearing practices, we must understand such practices within the context they occur. Knight, Cota, and Bernal (1993) suggest that members of the same ethnic group draw from the cultural models available to them to influence positive child-rearing practices.

Tong (2004) found that through the internment era, Japanese children received a socialization process that negated individualism. These children were taught that family came before personal needs. This socialization process was also used as a means to pass down through the generations a more cohesive and collective ethnic identity that served as a barrier to the social stigmatization associated with their "differentness." Similarly, studies have also found that Latino parents place a higher value on being respectful and less on individual autonomy in comparison to Caucasians (Arcia & Johnson, 1998; Harwood, Schoelmerich, Ventura-Cook, Schulze, & Wilson, 1996). Despite these studies, there is a paucity of literature addressing these groups, and less so for Native Americans and Middle Eastern populations.

Much of the racial socialization literature has focused on African Americans. The work of Howard Stevenson (1994) to develop an empirical measure and factor analytically derived types of racial socialization has made a vitally important contribution to advancing empirical work on racial socialization. Many other researchers have examined socialization in an African American context. For example, Hamm (2001) found that African American parents were more proactive in socializing their children and believed that they needed to be the primary means of socializing their children in order to protect and buffer their children against racism. These parents did not trust the school system and viewed the school as possibly contributing to poor cross-ethnic relations rather than bridging any gaps. Caughy, O'Campo, Randolph, and Nickerson (2002) state that "for African American parents, preparing children to function in the U.S. society necessitates a special consideration of the unique social position of African Americans in this country" (p. 1611). Interestingly, Caughy et al. found that the socialization of racial pride was associated with less behavior problems, leading to potentially higher academic achievement. Racial socialization has important implications for the empowerment of children of color to resist societally proscribed roles of failure and minimal functioning. Racial socialization research further reinforces the need for intentional and positive racial socialization practices for racial/ethnic minority children of color in the United States.

A search of the literature uncovers a lack of research identifying child-rearing practices with respect to the racial socialization process for White Americans. Being a group with relative societal power and privilege suggests that individuals pay less attention to aspects of social identity with dominant-group status (Tatum, 2000). It can be deduced from this that there is very little intentional socialization of dominant-group children with respect to their social location as Whites in a system of racial stratification. In addition, there is not widespread evidence supporting dominant-group socialization of their children to have a multicultural worldview valuing the development of more cross-ethnic relationships and understanding (Hamm, 2001).

Strong socialization messages within the media influence perceptions of different racial/ethnic groups. The media portrayal of Whites in positions of power and privilege, while frequently depicting Blacks and Latinos in menial or service positions or engaging in illegal or illegitimate behaviors, continues to perpetuate the challenges of socializing children with a well-balanced multicultural worldview. As another example, although children's television has included more diverse characters (e.g., the African American, Asian, or Latino friend of the main White character), one could argue that the racial/ethnic minority children portrayed are typically "colorized" versions of the White characters. Despite these admirable attempts to defy stereotypes, these characters often lack cultural identification. This depiction reinforces the assimilationist idea that dominant culture is the norm that other cultures must adopt. It also furthers the misconception that Whites do not have to challenge their worldview or get out of their comfort zone to fully embrace cultural diversity.

Despite the efforts of parents to socialize their children in positive ways to combat the discriminatory environments and cultural contexts in which they live, the umbrella of unequal social ranks based on one's physical appearance and place in society are, at times, more powerful. Children of color may, too frequently, feel as though they have limited choices to change their social position and existence. Historically, the two primary avenues to a better life presented to young males of color have been the military or a "gangsta" lifestyle. These may provide more immediate changes in their lives and appear more realistic than achieving "the good life" through traditional routes of education and employment. Similarly, young women and girls of color may see motherhood as the primary pathway and most realistic route to a satisfying and meaningful life. These frequently traveled paths for youth of color appear to reflect a feeling of powerlessness in their own life journey and a perception that no matter what they do, there are few options that promise a change in their circumstances or their well-being. Families of color with unequal access to higher-quality social resources (e.g., schools, health care) may develop mistrust of mainstream institutions and not learn strategies to successfully negotiate systems. Cycles and experiences of working hard and having hope, then encountering barriers that result in disappointment, disillusionment, and exhaustion, can take a toll on families. These obstacles to sustained parental socialization efforts to promote empowerment highlight the need for broader community and sociopolitical intervention.

It is evident that the big white dog's desire to not be annoyed by the yapping colored dogs can result in unfulfilled hunger, intra- and intergroup fighting, and learned helplessness. Communities of color are often left competing with one another for the same resources, rendering these communities split and disorganized. In the book *Black-Brown Relations and Stereotypes,* Mindiola, Niemann, and Rodriguez (2002) describe the state of affairs between Blacks and Latinos. In their account of the social relations of these two communities, they describe the growing tensions and challenges these communities face at the peril of both cultural groups. Many would argue that this is not coincidental. As a result, many communities of color are attempting to find common ground to form alliances, work together, and initiate a steady process of empowered, collaborative action toward the shared goal of social transformation. Such transformation is necessary if the vision of a multicultural worldview is to be realized.

SOCIOPOLITICAL AND COMMUNITY FACTORS IN WORLDVIEW CHANGE

Published in his 1999 book of poetry titled *The Rose That Grew From Concrete,* Tupac Shakur wrote the following "Untitled Poem":

> Please wake me when I'm free
>
> I cannot bear captivity
>
> Where my culture I'm told holds no significance
>
> I'll whither and die in ignorance
>
> But my inner eye can c a race
>
> Who reigned as kings in another place
>
> The green of trees were rich and full
>
> And every man spoke of beautiful
>
> Men and women together as equals
>
> War was gone because all was peaceful
>
> But now like a nightmare I wake 2 c
>
> That I live like a prisoner of poverty
>
> Please wake me when I'm free
>
> I cannot bear captivity
>
> 4 I would rather be stricken blind
>
> Than 2 live without expression of mind (p. 15)

Tupac, considered a "gangsta thug" by mainstream media, wrote about a lived cultural, contextual experience with great intelligence and insight. Like so many of his peers within racial/ethnic groups of color, Tupac called out for the removal of the shackles and chains from the mind. While racial/ethnic minority groups are physically and legally free in the United States, many members of these groups are still prisoners of an ideology of White supremacy and a system of racial stratification that influence beliefs and assumptions about oneself and one's place. The gangster hip-hop, rap mogul has become a pie in the sky for children of color across diverse racial/ethnic groups. This, along with governmental efforts to specifically target people of color for recruitment into the armed forces in the United States, are routes to worldviews that collude with the maintenance of racial oppression. However, these two options become viable realities and can provide immediate relief from the sobering recognition of the relative permanence of one's social location. Removal of shackles and chains imprisoning the minds of racial/ethnic minority youth requires empowerment strategies that weaken the grip of dominant worldview beliefs and assumptions.

Dr. Martin Luther King, Jr., in his 1967 keynote address at the annual convention of the American Psychological Association, offered the concept of "creative maladjustment." King noted that standing up for justice and standing against prevailing norms of an oppressive status quo can appear "abnormal" (King, 1968). However, this type of maladjustment is necessary if a multicultural worldview is to be nurtured and spread. Similarly, in his 1999 address to this same organization, the Reverend Jesse Jackson (2000) stated, "Learning to live in a diverse social order requires that we question the prevailing precepts of our society and not seek the comfort of isolation within our own small group" (p. 328). Consistent with the observations of King and Jackson, developing a multicultural worldview requires attention to changing the structures and ideologies that perpetuate the status quo. Changing those structures and ideologies requires the empowerment of individuals, groups, and organizations as well as attention to sociopolitical and community processes.

As described earlier, worldview develops through various agents of socialization. However, beginning in childhood and throughout life, worldview can be modified or shifted substantially. Worldview change can happen slowly and passively through larger sociopolitical changes that gradually shift dominant ideologies, directly through an intentional process initiated by parents and other agents of socialization, or more dramatically through a transformative life event. In addition, during adolescence and adulthood, worldview shifts can be self-initiated through a process of introspection and awareness. Community and sociopolitical contexts can facilitate or hinder a multicultural worldview throughout the life span. Although a multicultural worldview can be understood at multiple levels of analysis, our focus is largely on strategies implemented within or targeted toward the exosystemic and macrosystemic systems that ultimately influence the content of messages from more proximal agents of socialization, such as parents, peers, teachers, and media.

There are numerous strategies that can facilitate individual, group, and organizational empowerment necessary to change exosystem and macrosystem factors. These include (a) critical consciousness and sociopolitical development, (b) pedagogical and educational interventions, (c) citizen participation and activism, (d) leadership development, (e) community-based intergroup relations initiatives, and (f) the building of cross-racial/cross-ethnic alliances and coalitions. The successful implementation of any of these strategies is challenged by the individualism and racial stratification characteristic of dominant culture. They each involve "swimming upstream," battling against the strong push of social forces that operate continuously to maintain the status quo. They all involve the "creative maladjustment" that Dr. King (1968) described.

A challenge for communities populated by historically oppressed racial/ethnic groups is the lack of a critical mass of community members willing or able to participate in the process of social change. This may be related to a lack of trust in the "system," a need to focus attention on day-to-day survival needs, and the apathy that develops as a result of failed attempts to make changes that breeds an attitude of "no matter what

I do, nothing is going to change." The absence of strong leadership within communities of color has also been noted as an important factor in low levels of participation in social activism. Intergroup relations initiatives can provide a broader sense of community across groups that lay a foundation for the formation of alliances, coalitions, and community support for citizen participation in social justice work. However, an important prerequisite for maximizing the success of intergroup initiatives, leadership development, community organizing for increased civic participation, and coalition building is that the mind is free from the shackles of the dominant cultural worldview of which Tupac (1999) spoke. This requires attention to sociopolitical development, critical consciousness, and a pedagogy that nurtures them.

Critical Consciousness, Sociopolitical Development, and Liberation Psychology

Critical consciousness and sociopolitical development are rooted in the Latin American traditions of liberation theology and liberation psychology (Martín-Baró, 1996). Several scholars have pointed to the need for a "psychology of liberation" to address the effects of oppression (Comas-Díaz, 2000; Watts, Williams, & Jagers, 2003). Liberation psychology informs the development of interventions to enhance awareness of one's social condition and the multiple contexts that determine that condition. This awareness is often referred to as critical consciousness and is rooted in the process of *conscientização* (critical consciousness) developed by Paolo Freire in his classic 1970 work *Pedagogy of the Oppressed.* Comas-Díaz, Lykes, and Alarcon (1998) suggest that critical consciousness reflects a deep and multileveled understanding of one's surrounding environmental circumstances that influence the development of behaviors and feelings contributing to the perpetuation of oppression, discrimination, and subjugation. It involves recognition of the forces that shape and exert influence on the physical, psychological, spiritual, relational, and collective aspects of well-being. The process of facilitating a critical consciousness involves inviting silenced voices to share personal, cultural, and community narratives that bring into question the legitimacy of the dominant cultural narratives that limit opportunities and prescribe rigid social roles. This awareness also involves helping our children and youth better understand their culture of origin and native language; explore the dynamics of the past, current, and anticipated circumstances; and discover how their life experiences impact how they engage current situations and mentally plan for future ones. A possible end result of such critical consciousness might be the development of more active participation in changing one's community and life circumstances. Watts, Griffith, and Abdul-Adil (1999) offer a model of sociopolitical development that describes the phases of becoming critically conscious and empowered to participate in social change. The articulation of such a model has direct implications for intervention approaches to nurture sociopolitical development among youth.

Pedagogical and Educational Approaches

Freire (1970) described a revolutionary approach to pedagogy that involves the incorporation of life experience, dialogue, and a critical thinking process necessary to participate in liberation efforts. He described the commonly used "banking system of education," where schools are instruments of the status quo and the primary pedagogical methods are ones of deposit and withdrawal (i.e., the teacher deposits information and then expects to withdraw it, exactly as deposited, at a later date). Freire advocates for a more humanizing education that honors the experience of groups that are oppressed in society by breaking the culture of silence around the dehumanizing effects of oppression. Freire suggests that this liberatory educational process will contribute to the dismantling of systems of oppression and free both the oppressor and the oppressed. Freire describes this pedagogy as having a problem-posing orientation with a goal of critical consciousness. His pedagogy involves an authentic process of critical dialogue leading to dialogic cultural action. Essentially, he describes a system of emancipatory education that would change systems of education so that children of all races and ethnicities can find their own voice, listen to the voices of others, and ultimately contribute to the development of a multicultural worldview.

The school context plays a tremendous role in socialization, including the socialization of worldview. Bazron, Osher, and Fleischman (2005) describe the need for a culturally responsive system of education that does not alienate or marginalize communities of color nor perpetuate current sociopolitical dynamics that maintain social asymmetries. They recommend five principles toward the promotion of this culturally responsive education:

> (a) match classroom instruction to cultural norms for social interaction to enhance students' social skill development and problem-solving ability; (b) when asking questions or giving directions, adjust wait time for students from cultures to enhance classroom participation and critical thinking skills; (c) be sensitive to the cultural shifts that immigrant students, or other students with minority family and community cultures, must make as they move between school and home; (d) help parents gain cultural capital, to develop the skills to negotiate the education system and knowledge of the norms of behavior that govern schools and social system; and (e) use culturally responsive and respectful approaches in character education, social skill instruction, and discipline. (Bazron et al., pp. 83–84)

The model the authors outline addresses several goals toward the remediation of the disempowerment of people of color as well as an equalization of power and resources. The program fosters the development of more critically thinking citizens from both the racial/ethnic minority and dominant Caucasian communities, empowers students toward leadership development, and educates both the parents and children toward the unification of solid decision-making skills. School-based programs such as this would also help foster the interconnectedness of cross-ethnic group relations by enhancing a deeper understanding of cultural differences, while concurrently creating superordinate goals to work toward collaboratively. Ultimately, these changes could do much to promote a more balanced multicultural worldview in society, and contribute to the creation of intergroup relationships characterized by respect, equality, and dignity.

CONCLUSION

Challenges to developing a multicultural worldview bring us back to the fable of the big white dog on the porch, feeding the colored dogs morsels of bread, motivated by his own self-interest of not being annoyed by them. An individualistic worldview that runs counter to a collaborative and connected multicultural worldview is symbolized by the white dog's behavior. The power to influence the conditions of others is afforded to those with the social, economic, and political resources. For the colored dogs, fighting over morsels of bread is their reality. They may not even be aware of other alternatives to getting fed, leaving fighting with each other as their "reality." Racial/ethnic groups of color risk the same fate as the colored dogs. The prevailing sociopolitical dynamics socialize a perceived reality where one must "look out for #1" in order to survive and obtain valued societal resources. A multicultural worldview requires a fundamental shift in sociopolitical and community dynamics. This shift involves movement toward true social justice such that equal access to resources is driven by beliefs of inclusion, interconnectedness, and social responsibility; values that embrace diversity as a natural and positive social resource; and an assumption of the dignity, worth, and right to self-determination of all human beings regardless of phenotypic expression or ethnic ancestry.

The issues raised in this chapter make it clear that developing a multicultural worldview requires attention to the broader sociopolitical and community dynamics that influence the more immediate agents of socialization. The diverse media outlets available are critical points of intervention that can contribute to the process of developing a multicultural worldview and infusing it into broader society. The structure and content of these media outlets are determined by those in positions of power and privilege and motivated by profit and encouraging an acquisition mentality to stimulate the purchasing of various products and services. The racial stratification reflective of dominant cultural ideology permeates macrosystemic influences on socialization agents and presents a formidable challenge to transforming society toward a more multicultural worldview. However, it is necessary to engage this goal—one mind, one community, one music video, one television program at a time—until the dominant worldview *is* a multicultural worldview. This is a critical direction for the sake of our children and their descendents and, indeed, for the future of our world. As Jesse Jackson (2000) stated in his 1999 American Psychological Association address, "The challenges of our day are to oppose hatred and the violence it spawns, to rectify injustices that result from the status quo, and to learn to live in the new world order" (p. 328). A multicultural worldview is fundamental to this new world order defined by social justice, inclusion, and peace.

REFERENCES

Abney, V. D. (1996). Cultural competency in the field of child maltreatment. In J. Briere, L. Berliner, J. A. Bulkley, C. Jenny, & T. Reid (Eds.), *The APSAC handbook on child maltreatment* (pp. 409–419). Thousand Oaks, CA: Sage.

Arcia, E., & Johnson, A. (1998). When respect means to obey: Immigrant Mexican mothers' values for their children. *Journal of Child and Family Studies, 7,* 79–95.

Bazron, B., Osher, D., & Fleischman, S. (2005). Creating culturally responsive schools. *Educational Leadership, 63*(1), 83–84.

Bronfenbrenner, U. (1977). Toward an experimental ecology of human development. *American Psychologist, 32,* 513–531.

Bronfenbrenner, U. (1979). *The ecology of human development.* Cambridge, MA: Harvard University Press.

Bronfenbrenner, U. (1986). Ecology of the family as a context for human development: Research perspectives. *Developmental Psychology, 22,* 723–742.

Caughy, M. O., O'Campo, P. J., Randolph, S. M., & Nickerson, K. (2002). The influence of racial socialization practices on the cognitive and behavioral competence of African American preschoolers. *Child Development, 73*(5), 1611–1625.

Comas-Díaz, L. (2000). An ethnopolitical approach to working with people of color. *American Psychologist, 55,* 1319–1325.

Comas-Díaz, L., Lykes, M. B., & Alarcon, R. (1998). Ethnic conflict and psychology of liberation in Guatemala, Peru, and Puerto Rico. *American Psychologist, 53,* 778–792.

Dalton, J. H., Elias, M., & Wandersman, A. (2006). *Community psychology: Linking individuals and communities* (2nd ed.). New York: Wadsworth.

Duran, E. (2006). *Healing the soul wound: Counseling American Indians and other native peoples.* Williston, VT: Teachers College Press.

Dwairy, M. (2006). *Counseling and psychotherapy with Arabs and Muslims: A culturally sensitive approach.* New York: Teachers College Press.

Falicov, C. J. (Ed.). (1983). *Cultural perspectives in family therapy.* Rockville, MD: Aspen.

Falicov, C. J. (1998). *Latino families in therapy: A guide to multicultural practice.* New York: Guilford.

Freire, P. (1970). *Pedagogy of the oppressed.* New York: Continuum.

Garbarino, J. (1982). *Children and families in the social environment.* New York: Aldine de Gruyter.

Hamm, J. V. (2001). Barriers and bridges to positive cross-ethnic relations: African American and White parent socialization beliefs and practices. *Youth and Society, 33*(1), 62–98.

Harrell, S. P. (2000). *Integrative sociocultural assessment (ISA).* [Unpublished training materials]

Harwood, R. L., Schoelmerich, A., Ventura-Cook, E., Schulze, P. A., & Wilson, S. P. (1996). Culture and class influences on Anglo and Puerto Rican mothers' beliefs regarding long-term socialization goals and child behavior. *Child Development, 67,* 822–839.

Ibrahim, F. A., & Kahn, H. (1987). Assessment of worldviews. *Psychological Reports, 60*(1), 163–176.

Jackson, J. (2000). What ought psychology do? *American Psychologist, 55,* 328–330.

Jalali, B. (1996). Iranian families. In M. McGoldrick, J. Giordano, & J. K. Pearce (Eds.), *Ethnicity and family therapy,* (2nd ed., pp. 347–363). New York: Guilford Press.

King, M. L., Jr. (1968). The role of the behavioral scientist in the civil rights movement. *American Psychologist, 23,* 180–186.

Knight, G. P., Cota, M. K., & Bernal, M. E. (1993). The socialization of cooperative, competitive, and individualistic preferences among Mexican American children: The mediating role of ethnic identity. *Hispanic Journal of Behavioral Sciences, 15,* 291–309.

Koltko-Rivera, M. E. (2004). The psychology of worldviews. *Review of General Psychology, 8*(1), 3–58.

Lloyd, B. T. (2002). A conceptual framework for examining adolescent identity, media influence, and social development. *Review of General Psychology, 6,* 73–91.

Martín-Baró, I. (1996). *Writings for a liberation psychology.* Cambridge, MA: Harvard University.

Mindiola, T., Niemann, F. Y., & Rodriguez, N. (2002). *Black-Brown relations and stereotypes.* Austin: University of Texas.

Mio, J. S., Barker-Hackett, L., & Tumambing, J. (2006). *Multicultural psychology: Understanding our diverse communities.* Boston: McGraw-Hill.

Nobles, W. W. (1986). *African psychology.* Oakland, CA: Black Family Institute.

Ogbu, J. U. (1981). Origins of human competence: A cultural ecological perspective. *Child Development, 52,* 413–429.

Ogbu, J. U. (1994). Racial stratification and education in the United States: Why inequality exists. *Teachers College Record, 98*(2), 264–298.

Parham, T. A. (Ed.). (2002). *Counseling persons of African descent: Raising the bar of practitioner competence.* Thousand Oaks, CA: Sage.

Prilleltensky, I. (2003). Understanding, resisting, and overcoming oppression: Towards psychopolitical validity. *American Journal of Community Psychology, 31,* 195–201.

Rappaport, J. (1995). Empowerment meets narrative: Listening to stories and creating settings. *American Journal of Community Psychology, 25,* 795–807.

Santiago-Rivera, A. L., Arredondo, P., & Gallardo-Cooper, M. (2002). *Counseling Latinos and la familia: A practical guide.* Thousand Oaks, CA: Sage.

Shakur, T. (1999). *The rose that grew from concrete.* New York: Pocket Books.

Spencer, M. B. (1999). Social and cultural influences on school adjustment: The application of an identity-focused cultural ecological perspective. *Educational Psychologist, 34,* 43–57.

Spencer, M. B. (2006). Phenomenology and ecological systems theory: Development of diverse groups. In R. M. Lerner & W. Damon (Eds.), *Handbook of child psychology: Volume 1, Theoretical models of human development* (6th ed., pp. 829–893). Hoboken, NJ: John Wiley and Sons.

Stevenson, H. (1994). Racial socialization in African American families: Balancing intolerance and survival. *Counseling and Therapy for Couples and Families, 2,* 190–198.

Sue, D. W., & Sue, D. (2002). *Counseling the culturally diverse: Theory and practice* (4th ed.). New York: Wiley.

Tatum, B. D. (2000). The complexity of identity: "Who am I?" In M. Adams, W. J. Blumenfeld, R. Castaneda, H. Hackman, M. L. Peters, & X. Zuniga (Eds.), *Readings for diversity and social justice: An anthology on racism, antisemitism, sexism, heterosexism, ableism, and classism* (pp. 9–15). New York: Routledge.

Tong, B. (2004). Race, culture, and citizenship among Japanese American children and adolescents during the internment era. *Journal of American Ethnic History, 23*(3), 3–40.

Trimble, J., & Thurman, P. (2002). Ethnocultural considerations and strategies for providing counseling services for Native American Indians. In P. Pedersen, J. Draguns, W. Lonner, & J. Trimble (Eds.), *Counseling across cultures* (5th ed., pp. 53–91). Thousand Oaks, CA: Sage.

Watts, R., Griffith, D., & Abdul-Adil, J. (1999). Sociopolitical development as an antidote to oppression: Theory and action. *American Journal of Community Psychology, 27,* 255–272.

Watts, R. J., Williams, N. C., & Jagers, R. J. (2003). Sociopolitical development. *American Journal of Community Psychology, 31*(1/2), 185–194.

Yeh, C. J. (2000). Depathologizing Asian-American perspectives of health and healing. *Asian American and Pacific Islander Journal of Health, 8,* 138–149.

Zimmerman, M. (2000). Empowerment theory: Psychological, organizational, and community levels of analysis. In J. Rappaport & E. Seidman (Eds.), *Handbook of community psychology* (pp. 43–64). New York: Kluwer Academic.

CHAPTER 9

Changing Drum Rhythms

How Religious Leaders Can Affirm the Value of Multiculturalism in Their Communities

ERYLENE PIPER-MANDY

DARYL M. ROWE

The dancers must change their steps according to the change in the rhythm of the drum

—Ewe Proverb

The purpose of this chapter is to discuss the cultural lens through which religious leaders in the 21st century must interpret sacred texts and religious tenets in order to help children embrace multiculturalism. As children of the 1960s, arguably the most definitive epoch of American social change to date, the authors grew up in an era in which we witnessed firsthand the importance of socially conscious spirituality on the development of social change, and the impact of determined religious leadership on the development of socially committed children. Because we were both raised in church (the first author, Seventh-day Adventist, and the second author, Methodist), we know personally the church's extraordinarily rich and textured effect, its power to inform and to transform not only individual lives, but the life of a community, of a nation as well. As children, we learned to dream from King, and to speak truth from Malcolm. As we matured into our careers, our professional allegiances—to cultural plurality, to social justice, to community empowerment, to ethnic diversity—have been steeped in the potent swirls of these Christian religious and spiritual experiences. We both attribute our current dedication to multiculturalism to the impact of the spiritually rooted, socially directed moral education that characterized our childhoods. Although our ideas are rooted in our foundational Christian experiences, it is our belief that religious leaders from all faiths may discover meaningful insights from this chapter.

The original drum message of American social and political philosophy—*we the people; we hold these truths; a more perfect union; all men [and women] are created equal*—continues as a percussive tempo in the lives of 21st-century American citizens, just as it did in the 1960s. But this latest interpretation of the original sociopolitical philosophy—multiculturalism—demands a change, a new pulse in American cultural history. Like a perpetual life dance, every generation of young Americans must appropriate the deepest truths—and confront the most blatant violations—in the foundation of American society and governance in its own way, building on the accomplished dance patterns of the generations that precede them. As the Ewe proverb suggests, every new historical troupe of dancers must change their steps to the change in the rhythm of the drum. The current drum cadence of social justice and inclusion must have its own dance rhythms, and its own dance champions.

The aim of this chapter is to consider a design through which current and future religious leaders can advocate a spirit-filled, compassionate multiculturalism. We begin by grounding our thinking in the social consciousness of the era of the 1960s, examining its impact on intergroup relations and the resulting development of multiculturalism. Second, we will reflect on the nature of religious leadership in the 1960s, which was both impacted by social consciousness of that era and which also influenced and informed the moral center of its movements. We will study that leadership through the multifaceted lenses of African American, Latino, and Asian American theologues, and the organizations that shielded them from more virulent assault and through which they were able to mobilize larger masses of everyday peoples to pick up the banner of a spirit-grounded social consciousness. Third, we will examine the roles that religious leaders embrace to further social change in the 1960s.

Finally, given the powerful influence that religious leadership enjoys within any community, we will conclude our discussion with the development of programs through which the clergy from a number of religious traditions can affirm the value of multiculturalism among their communities and children.

Before we can begin to discuss effective frameworks for spiritual discourse and pragmatic strategies for religious programming, however, we should examine and analyze the lessons in social activism and religious leadership from the quintessential era in which to study them—the 1960s.

THE ROLE PARADIGM—LESSONS OF 1960S ACTIVISM

Modern concepts of multiculturalism find their origins in the 1960s (Bannerjee, 2002; Smedley, 1999). For that reason alone, it would be important to examine spiritual activism in that era to identify models and methods with which to inform our 21st-century discourse and duty. But the 1960s also offer modern American sensibilities a unique view of activism among religious leaders, an activism so extensive that religious and spiritual leaders became social and political leaders as well (Perry & Rolland, 1999). It is this fusion that will form the prototype from which we can then frame new paradigms for the current decades.

A close examination of the leadership of the four major movements of that period—the civil rights/Black power movement (including the black studies movement), the antiwar movement, the women's movement, and the antipoverty movement (Karenga, 2002)—offers at least three important lessons that provide a paradigm on the *role* religious leaders must engage in their advocacy of multiculturalism.

Lesson 1: Religious Leaders as Social Activists

The first lesson in religious initiatives that we learned from the 1960s reveals the power and efficacy of religious leaders as social activists. The importance of religious leaders in the development of social justice has a long history in the United States (Carson, 1994). For example, Carson discusses the importance of Martin Luther King's father's and grandfather's involvement in a "distinctively African American version of social gospel Christianity"—which he defines as addressing the everyday social concerns of the congregation—on King's accepting his call to the ministry (p. 161). The era of the 1960s offers perhaps the best example, however, of religious leaders effectively positioned within each ethnic group to bridge the ideas and ideologies of the scholarly intelligentsia and the political elite to the masses of poor people by proclaiming social justice from the unique cultural perspective of that ethnic group (Perry & Rolland, 1999). They might not have termed it as such, but these leaders and their organizations were engaged in a transformative multicultural social justice enterprise.

The clergy who had been by and large distanced from the masses of their parishioners by their social status and class now embraced the everyday struggles of ordinary people, and they used their education, their status, and their weekly forum to elevate the issues of common people to collective popular concern (Jones, 1989). Religious leaders undertook a new spiritual consciousness by linking the themes of spiritual significance with themes of social injustice (Cooper-Lewter & Mitchell, 1986).

When preachers began to link the religious themes in which they were immersed with icons and idioms in which their people were immersed, a new set of symbols emerged. The Reverend Albert Cleague at the Shrine of the Black Madonna in Boston, Massachusetts, commissioned a statue of the Virgin Mary and the Christ Child with dark skin, proclaiming that a people's view of their deity could not reflect their oppressors (Karenga, 2002). The fusion of theological icon and indigenous ideology shifted religious focus in favor of African American activism, and bound the clergy to the largest support base possible among its congregants.

Similarly, Falicov (1999) examines how the Virgin of Guadalupe has served as an honored symbol for Latino social activists, fusing indigenous Aztec and European Catholic elements into a brown-hued Catholic Virgin who champions the needs of the downtrodden.

Native American indigenous theology had traditionally linked the social and the sublime (Kidwell, Noley, Tinker, & Weaver, 2001), but now Christianity, the religion of their conversion, began to shift toward Native social focus. As the call for Black power of the 1960s found its analogue in the call for Red power in the 1970s, Native American religious orators argued for a return to indigenous spiritual symbols that incorporated liberation images reflective of Native people, while pressing for sociopolitical mobilization (Hraba, 1994). When Lakota Catholic parishes use sage or cedar during services, they are infusing Christianity with Native symbolism. In Rapid City, South Dakota, "a purification rite may be used during the penitential rite of the liturgy, and the four-direction song is sung. A Native deacon may burn a cedar or sage blessing before the gospel reading and during the presentation of the gifts at offertory" (Howarth, 1999). This emphasis on indigenous spiritual systems sparked a significant break with Western religious hegemony and provided a new point of departure by elevating indigenous systems to the authority previously reserved for dominant religious traditions.

Lesson 2: Organizing for Mass Social Actions

The second lesson we learned from the era outlines the processes that educated and organized masses of penitents into social change agents. The activity of God is always focused on the poor, the neglected, the silenced, the oppressed; God is therefore first and foremost God of the *least*. The 1960s clergy mobilized this support base in their own churches in pursuit not only of spiritual journey but also of social and political empowerment (Cone, 1969). In the African American national community, the Southern Christian Leadership Conference (SCLC) was organized around the destruction of segregation and the promotion of integration, with particular emphasis on creating opportunities for African Americans (Jones, 1989). As an alternative to Christian perspectives, the Nation of Islam (NOI) was initially committed to secession, because they believed that it allowed African Americans and Euro-Americans to control their own territories. NOI leaders did not believe that true equality between the races within the same national boundaries was possible, even though there was a strong push for economic development (Karenga, 2002). Thus, although it might appear that these two organizations were in diametric opposition, careful analysis reveals the beginning of a multicultural perspective in both the SCLC focus on racial and ethnic parity and the NOI insistence on the preservation of African American cultural inheritance and economic empowerment.

In Latino communities, the League of United Latin American Citizens (LULAC), the oldest organization in the United States representing Spanish-speaking communities, was comparable to SCLC and NOI in that its objective was the destruction of segregation and the promotion of integration (Kaplowski, 2005). Clergy joined the organization and offered their support in the organization's efforts. Las Hermanas and PADRES, both Christian organizations, were instrumental in influencing numerous public and private policymakers in favor of Latino inclusion (Medina, 2005).

Within the Native American community, the American Indian Civil Rights Council (AICRC), United Native Americans (UNA), and the American Indian Movement (AIM) had similar objectives to that of SCLC, Core, and LULAC—the removal of destructive social policies on and off the reservation and the restoration of treaty integrity (Hraba, 1994). These organizations resurrected dependence on traditional spiritual practices, such as the Dream Dance, Sun Dance, and Peyote cults that emphasized penitence, atonement, and a restoration of an Indian lifestyle.

Within Pan-Asian communities, Christian churches were also effective in bridging the twin goals of worship and social activism. For example, within the Korean American community, churches were instrumental in providing educational and literacy services that not only afforded mutual assistance, but supported Korean nationalism in the 1950s. The overwhelming majority of Korean independence movement leaders were affiliated with Christian churches in the United States (Hraba, 1994).

Lesson 3: Ecumenical Unity

The third critical lesson of the 1960s encompasses the ecumenical unity that refined and consolidated often similar but distinct ethnic agendas. In addition to organizing their communities, religious leaders of the 1960s also organized themselves. In this significant era in American cultural history, Christian and Muslim, shaman and Jew, Catholic and Protestant suspended territorial and doctrinal divisiveness in favor of a unified platform upon which to communicate and dedicate social vision to racial harmony, social justice, and economic parity. The Interdenominational Theological Center, the then–National Council of Christians and Jews (now the National Council for Community and Justice) and the National

Council of Churches all represent the enduring thrust of ecumenical agency.

A summary of the lessons derived from the activism and scholarship in the 1960s provides clear guidelines for social change agency among modern clergy. First, religious leaders in the 1960s gained efficacy as cadres of leaders worked together to create social change. Current prominent clerics began to institutionalize so that they could continue to effectively mobilize. Using the religious networks already in place, leadership cadres educated and inspired masses of people in specific collective projects, which must be the modern analogues of the sit-ins, boycotts, marches, and social change ventures of the 1960s. Second, religious leaders grasped and grappled with the varied stages of relationship between the dominant group and the subordinate groups, as well as the relationships among the subordinate groups. They directed their congregants to conceive both spiritual and social needs based on the relationship of their particular ethnic/cultural group to the other groups within the political and economic hierarchy. Finally, religious leaders continually and accurately analyzed the current moral climate and adapted their theology and their activism to promote the substantive shifts in "business-as-usual" race perspectives.

THE RHETORIC PARADIGM—SPIRITUAL DISCOURSE OF THE 1960S

One of the most important models from the social activism of the civil rights era and subsequent decades involves identifying and articulating effective *frameworks* for spiritual discourse on multiculturalism. Perhaps the most enduring and abundant legacy of the era is composed of its sermons: the moving sacred rhetoric of King; the powerful moral logic of Malcolm; the uncompromising positions of James Cone; the fierce oratory of theologues Gustavo Gutierrez and Emilio Castro; the biting wit of Standing Rock Sioux religious leader Vine Deloria, Jr.; or the *rice-roots* water buffalo theology of theologue Kosuke Koyama (1974). In each case, their genius lies in the cultural specificity of their hermeneutic insight, their ability to situate their exegesis of sacred text within the cultural center and social mission of their people. The body of work that arose from these scholar-activists became known as *liberation theology*.

The liberation theologies that found their genesis and arguably their apotheosis in the movements of the 1960s and 1970s are based on a shift in exegetical schema. These movements inspired religious thinkers to *reread* their sacred texts in terms of the particular struggles of their own people. They developed a critical exegesis that both informed and was informed by other critical perspectives—a critical theory. At its most basic level, all critical theory is directed at critiquing and transforming the social world, rather than simply explaining and understanding it. Historically, critical theory was based on the examination of such dominant discourse in macrosocial systems as class (Horkheimer & Adorno, 1974). But the critical examination of race led ethnic theorists in the United States to explore critical theory from their own alternate cultural discourses. African American, Chicano-Latino, and Asian American theologues were particularly adept at providing the theological relevance that advanced a new direction for religious thought based on critical exegesis and a new model of religious commitment based on critical moral consciousness.

Exegesis is essentially the examination and explanation of the literal, consequent, and typical sense of sacred text. Its central assumption is that there is a material and a mystical character to any scriptures. The material character reflects the actual lived-in experience of the writer and of the generation in which the writer is situated. The mystical character reflects the divine intention, the nature and constitution of truth. The mystical character of a sacred text refers to the spiritual principles that underlie the particular historical specificity of the community and the culture through which the divine intention is realized. This assumption leads to the understanding that it is possible to detect the mystical content from the material example; it is also possible for religious thinkers steeped in a particular historical moment and immersed in a specific cultural community to apply mystical content from the original context to a new hermeneutic context—their own.

The liberation theologians reread their sacred texts and developed a critical theology. Each religious pundit worked within the social, economic, and political world of their own community, and the critical theology that emerged was labeled *liberation,* as a statement of the need to escape the religious as well as social, political, and economic hegemony of the dominant culture in which they were embedded. This rereading was occurring simultaneously among Latin American and African American theologians during the 1960s, although they started from different ends of the race/class continuum (Cone, 1984). Although this rereading has been documented within Christian theology, it seems likely that other religious/spiritual leaders have followed a similar process.

Latino Liberation Theology

Latino concepts of social justice and religious obligation begin outside the territorial United States. Dominican priest Gustavo Gutierrez of Lima, Peru, is generally acknowledged as the father of the Latino *liberation theology;* although Cone defined Black theology as a theology of liberation in 1969. Gutierrez's (1971/2000) seminal text, *A Theology of Liberation: History, Politics and Salvation,* outlines the three basic concepts of liberation theology: the liberation of the poor and the oppressed from poverty and privation, the elevation of the downtrodden and the marginalized from all those systems that impose on and benefit from their loss of dignity and empowerment, and finally the freedom from acquisitive selfishness associated with the upper classes. In *We Drink From Our Own Wells,* Gutierrez (1983/1984) establishes an incontrovertible link between the Christian's relationship with God and with the Biblical *least*—the oppressed (cf. Matthew 25:40). He continues to articulate an indigenous-centered theology, rooted in emancipatory social activism.

African American Liberation Theology

African American liberation theology is the first of its kind that is indigenous to the United States. James Cone's (1975) *God of the Oppressed* is the clearest expression of the spiritual platform he initiated with *Black Theology and Black Power* (Cone, 1969) and continued in *A Black Theology of Liberation* (Cone, 1986). The principal theological premise of this trilogy asserted that God, in order to *be* God, was first and foremost God of the oppressed, and that all activity aimed at unmasking and alleviating oppression was actually God inspired and God approved. The association between the heavenly concerns and human conditions elevated the struggles of the poor, the wounded, the silenced, and the abused to unprecedented importance, in the minds of the theologues and of their people; striving to better the earthly conditions of the downtrodden became a central act of piety, not only for them, but especially for those who had been blessed with measures of wealth. Like the work of Gutierrez, the genius of this concept, in one stroke, both inaugurated social justice as a divine imperative and obligated those in upper socioeconomic classes to attend to the lower classes.

Asian Liberation Theology

Asian liberation theology, like its Latino counterpart, has its genesis outside the United States. As such, it is inextricably situated within Asian cultural systems. Because Western religious systems, such as Christianity, are generally imported in conjunction with American political, military, and economic agenda, these spiritual traditions are presented in the Western worldview. The proselytization of Western religious systems, no matter how piously intended, acts as a major source of Western political and social infiltration because it provides the justification for imperialist activity (Ani, 1994).

Furthermore, Asian liberation theology, like its ethnic counterparts, originated from an understanding that Euro-American theology was insufficient for grasping universal concepts of religious knowledge (Cone, 1979). In his groundbreaking text, *Water-Buffalo Theology* (1974), Japanese theologian Kosuke Koyama outlines the profound need to situate religious discourse in the icons, images, and interests of the Thai people to whom he dedicated his career. He emphasizes the importance of the simple sentence and concrete thought development; influenced by the concept of *parable,* he discards the language and ideation of abstracts derived from years of seminary training and actually strives to think in the terms of the people he serves. Koyama defines religious praxis in terms of the daily lives of the Thai people; in emphasizing a spiritually practical as opposed to religiously theoretical approach, he situated piety within a particular cultural milieu. *Three Mile an Hour God* (1980) advances Koyama's incursion into indigenous faith systems. He argues forcibly that Christian practice must be informed by centuries-old Asian religious systems, and that the confluence between the two must be forged in the everyday, "rice-roots" experience.

LIBERATION THEOLOGY AND THE DEVELOPMENT OF OTHER CRITICAL THEORIES

Liberation theologies developed within a crucible of at least three other critical theories, which shaped the development of religious thought, even as they were informed by it: *critical social theory, critical race theory,* and *critical cultural theory.*

Critical Social Theory

The first critical theory that informs social justice issues of the 1960s concerns developments in intergroup relations in the United States. The civil rights era marks advancement in the relationship between the dominant and the subordinate racial/ethnic groups along the continuum from segregation toward integration, the political and social aim of the movement. Schaefer (2001) has argued that dominant and subordinate group relations in any society will fall into one of seven categories in a scale that runs from profound exclusion to profound inclusion. The first three (extinction, expulsion, secession) are categories of exclusion, with each being a method of physically separating the dominant and subordinate groups not only in terms of sociopolitical distance but also in terms of geopolitical domains. The fourth category—segregation—is a bridge category in that it is both inclusive, in the sense that the subordinate groups are maintained alive within the dominant group's territory, but also exclusive, in its separation of social, economic, and political access. According to Schaefer, the last three categories (assimilation, fusion, pluralism) are further advancements in inclusion; Schaefer represents all seven categories as a linear progression.

But our current vantage point, that is, post-1965, allows us to critically examine the linearity of the Schaefer (2001) model. If we investigate the last three categories in terms of their impact on the cultures of the groups, we see that each of these three categories is in fact a distinctive endpoint possibility for intergroup relations. *Assimilation* refers to the state and process by which the subordinate groups take on the characteristics of, and are in fact absorbed into, the dominant group—Group A + Group B = Group A. Assimilation allows for the members of the subordinate group to physically survive, but *the culture of the group must be surrendered. Fusion,* which can be represented as Group A + Group B = Group C, alters the culture of both, destroying the unique character of the contributing cultures. *Pluralism* signifies the only category of the three that involves the *preservation* of the original cultural categories—Group A + Group B + Group C = Group A+B+C. There are two essential assumptions inherent in this concept. First, the cultural hegemony (control over the discursive space) of the dominant group is replaced by the inclusion and infusion of multiple cultural narratives, so that a fluid and flexible system of values—ideals, interests, and icons—becomes inherent in the rhetoric of the nation. This shift in cultural contributions must, however, also be accompanied by a corresponding assumption—the massive shift in the power relations between the dominant and subordinate groups. The power of dominance is gradually subsumed into a system of interlocking equities in which each group exercises appropriate control not only over national political and economic agendas, but also over the cultural life and social destiny of its own people. The final three categories, according to Schaefer, are part of the relations continuum; they are actually, however, three different endpoints of the relations trajectory. Pluralism is, therefore, the political correlate to the social category we know as multiculturalism; neither assimilation nor fusion results in the preservation of the original cultures.

As the era of the 1960s began, the relationship between the dominant group in the United States and most of the minority groups in the United States—especially the racialized ethnic minorities—was based on segregation (Schaefer, 2001). The struggle for integration resulted in a move along the continuum from segregation toward a new paradigm in intergroup relations. But even as the country labored toward integration, other voices condemned the cultural absorption that was integration's mandate and the continued racial disparities that were segregation's social legacy. Tensions arose as integration's ideal and its limitation collided in real-life experience. The seeds of multiculturalism grew from the tensions associated with this shift.

Critical Race Theory

Another way of examining late 20th-century critical theory emerges from within a broader social political analysis. Delgado (1995) advances critical race theory as a framework for analyzing issues associated with race in the United States, and offers a method for examining how to infuse multiculturalism with a spiritual perspective. As an eclectic system of thought emerging out of civil rights law, critical race theory argues that progress toward more equitable allocation of power among ethnic/racial groups in the United States has been needlessly difficult, and that strategies for ameliorating racism have increasingly led to inadequate outcomes.

Delgado (1995) identifies a number of beliefs that sustain critical race theorists. First, as opposed to seeing racism as a peculiar way of thinking/acting held by a few, critical race theorists see racism as the prevailing foundation of U.S. society. As such, awareness of racism must be superimposed on any analysis exploring the advent of multiculturalism. Because of the insidious nature of racism and race-based identifications—preferences for or against persons based on their presumed phenotypic characteristics (see Smedley, 1999, for a fuller discussion)—only severe bias is emphasized, and the everyday, "business-as-usual forms of racism" (p. xiv) permeating the social fabric of American society are ignored. It is this common, pervasive degree of racism that can impact ethnic groups' religious leadership because of an occasionally superficial struggle among themselves for a delimited piece of the sociopolitical pie.

Second, critical race theorists believe that to develop new perspectives about race, the prevalent beliefs, conventions, and practices of this society must be examined. They recommend using more person-centered forms of expression—storytelling, autobiography, and myth deconstruction—as strategies for recreating a collective reality centered in the life experiences of those racial/ethnic groups that have been historically disenfranchised. The aim is to empower the voices of those who have been discounted, dismissed, disregarded. Third, critical race theorists believe that *interest convergence*—the idea that powerful Whites only support the concerns of persons of color when those concerns converge with the interests of the powerful—operates in race-related issues in the United States. Furthermore, critical race theorists develop and organize conceptual frameworks by emphasizing the specific details of the lives of people of color.

Finally, critical race theory asserts that the current approach to multiculturalism typifies the power relations between the *objective* scholar (theorist, researcher, practitioner) and the subject matter (the cultural others)—the intent is to understand *them* so that *they* can be better served by *us*. In this vein, the study, understanding, knowledge, and evaluation of other embedded cultures are simply more sophisticated examples of conquest and dominion (Bulhan, 1985). The net result has been that the systems of thought, which define the features and functioning of human behavior, have remained relatively unaltered.

Liberation theologies build on many of the assumptions of critical race theory. Specifically, they base their work on nontraditional methods, focusing on the multivocal harmonic symphony of perspectives and advocacy within their own ethnic groups.

Critical Cultural Theory

Research into the indigenous sacred thought informs us that each indigenous culture constructs its own spiritual systems, that is, explanations of metaphysical reality that are internally consistent with and drawn from that culture. In this context, the words *religious* and *spiritual* are not necessarily synonymous; the former refers to those ritualized, institutionalized theories and practices, rituals, and rites associated with a particular theology, which can be imported or imposed (Ani, 1994), and the latter to the essential characteristic of human beingness which is indigenous to and conjured from a particular cultural cosmology (Ani, 1994). Even whenever a non-indigenous religion is imported or imposed on a people, it is transformed so that it conforms to the indigenous cultural system (e.g., the Virgin of Guadeloupe in the Chicano/Latino church; the ecstatic praise in the African American church). The imported religion becomes primarily a cultural expression of the people who practice it. Even worldwide religious systems, such as Christianity and Islam, are expressed and experienced through their appropriation into a particular people's spiritual system.

It will become important to note that the teaching of moral development is also a cultural act; that is, the manner as well as the content of such instruction is rooted in the cultural traditions of a people. Different ethnic groups construct different moral systems that are taught differently in different systems of moral development (Ani, 1994).

THE ADVENT OF MULTICULTURALISM

In the social sciences, the advent of multiculturalism has been heralded as a *new force,* similar in impact to behavioral and humanistic approaches in psychology, functionalism and symbolic interactionism in sociology, or cultural materialism in anthropology (Pedersen, 1999). Multiculturalism has been described as attempting to see humans in a broader social and historical context, which affects cognition, emotion, and behavior, and as a process in which trained professionals "from one cultural, ethnic, racial background interact with a client of a different cultural, ethnic, or racial background for the purpose of promoting the client's cognitive, emotional, psychological, and/or spiritual development" (D'Andrea & Daniels, 1995, p. 18). This perspective regarding the lived experiences of *cultural others* can serve as a model for the challenges confronting multiculturalism within religious communities.

Unfortunately, the majority of the work subsumed under the paradigm of multiculturalism in applied social sciences has been myopic in both scope and vision. There has been a failure to adequately define the philosophical assumptions and reluctance to address the broader issues related to definitions of health and mental health (Nobles, King, & James, 1995). Instead, most of the work has adhered to the underlying Eurocentric assumptions regarding the conceptions of human beingness, features of functioning, and methods for defining and restoring health and order, which have throughout Western academic history been allied with discussions of spirit and the highest levels of human functioning.

The problem is structural in nature. Multiculturalists in all fields begin as trained social scientists, adhering to the fundamental assumptions inherent in their field of training, who simply attempt to apply their acquired disciplinary knowledge to cultural *others* (cf. Said, 1978; italics added). Rarely are there attempts to immerse oneself into the study of the languages, culture, institutions, and political ambiance of cultural *others.* On the contrary, legitimacy is generally granted to the existing systems for comprehending human nature, features of functioning, and methods for restoring health, and accolades are most often afforded to those who simply apply and impose the assumptions and paradigms of existing systems to the cultural *others,* with little infusion of the cultural assumptions that are the foundations of those *others'* ways of life. As a result, the representations (read as theories, strategies, and interventions) are less illustrative of the particular manifestations of humanity out of which cultural others emerge, but simply representations of existing psychological notions about what is considered normal and abnormal behavior.

Even where thought is given to the underlying assumptions of the theoretical models, the conclusion of scientists steeped in their own cultural centers is that there is no substantive difference between the Euro-American models and those of other cultures, *nor in fact can there be.* Western scientific proponents assert that the Western world is considered to have produced the only true science and all other peoples provide variation in the application of science, but not in the very structure and definitions of science. For example, Moll (2002), in his discourse on the South African psychology, has argued that African psychology is mythical; "there is no such thing as psychology which is essentially African, rather a psychology that is engaged in the issues and problems of Africans" (p. 9). Thus, the challenge for religious leaders is to frame their spiritual practices from within the cultural contours of their multinuanced and multivoiced communities.

MULTICULTURALISM AND THE TRIANGULATION OF CRITICAL PERSPECTIVES

Modern religious proponents must be informed by the development of exegetical foundations, because these theories form the basis for triangulating the central definitions of multiculturalism. Critical social theory frames multiculturalism as a dynamic tension between cultural specificity and cultural unity. Pluralism demands that the unique threads representing the ethnic cultures that create the American tapestry be conserved, as opposed to fused or assimilated. Multiculturalism must be deeply engaged in preserving each ethnic culture distinctly and individually, as well as in presenting them as a complex, unified whole.

Critical race theory demands that multiculturalism confront its racist potential by elevating and focusing on the voices that have been previously marginalized or silenced. Multiculturalism must examine cultural specificities by focusing on the real-life experiences of that culture's members, ensuring a rich, multilayered, multidimensional, multivocal representation of that cultural experience.

Critical cultural theory demands a new conceptualization of culture, by articulating that each ethnic group has a specific cultural center—a set of assumptions that informs cultural transformations. Multiculturalism must examine cultural unity as a requirement to view any event, action, policy, or perception—including (perhaps especially) religion—from several different cultural centers simultaneously.

CHANGING DRUM RHYTHMS—MULTICULTURALISM IN THE 21ST CENTURY

Although there is certainly powerful discourse coming from the religious communities around social issues, its most vocal adherents have been given either to simply restating past dictums or reviving past dogma. Multiculturalism deserves and needs fresh commitment and fresh direction for the spiritual community. It requires us to examine the meaning of multiculturalism, the true intent of multiculturalism, and finally the most effective practices that multiculturalism demands. From our perspective, the true *meaning* of multiculturalism is concerned with representation at the level of system of thought. *Multiculturalism* must begin at the level of definitions and paradigms.

Multiculturalism in the 21st century offers a new challenge to a new generation of theologians. This challenge is exactly analogous to the challenge of the 1960s—an imperative to shift to a new intergroup relationship for American majority and minority groups. Where the mission of the 1960s thrust intergroup relations in the United States forward from segregation toward integration, the emergence of multiculturalism, with all its incorporated critical perspectives, heralds a new step toward political pluralism as the true endpoint of a just society.

The new challenge presented by multiculturalism will demand new rhetoric and new roles. In a curious swing of a religious pendulum, the modern church rhetoric has centered on individual struggles toward right-doing, toward values for individual families, and toward a spiritual base for material acquisition. But the focus of new spiritual discourse must shift toward mobilizing protracted struggle for collective response to the macrosystemic analysis of social justice, economic parity, and political empowerment.

The new rhetoric must inform several directives gleaned from the old-school rhetorical discussion. First, it is clear that for religious leaders to reclaim full responsibility for inculcating an ethos of multiculturalism to children, they must work to translate existing scriptures into, and situate spiritual instruction in, the lived experiences of the people to whom they attend. This is the effect of a multicultural hermeneutics and exegesis that seeks to fuse multidimensionality into religious leadership. Second, religious leaders must ground their teaching aims in the sociocultural milieu of their congregants; the purpose is to extensively study the indigenous symbols of the people, incorporate those symbols into their understanding and instruction of religious doctrine, and through the use of the peoples' cultural symbols transform both their religious tenets *and* the people *and* the political and economic macrosystem.

Third, religious leaders must integrate the multivocal and subtlety-hued language systems of congregants into the delivery of messages of inspiration, transformation, and perseverance. To be effectively mobilized, the congregants must hear the rhythmic timbre of their own voices reflected back to them through song and sermon, homily and liturgy. Last, a critical goal for current religious leaders is to infuse their preaching with the richly textured stories of heroes and heroines from a broader cultural mix into a viable social, political, and religious discourse.

The true *intent* of multiculturalism is to create an American mosaic instead of an American melt. Thus, from the perspective of *role responsibilities,* religious leadership must coalesce into nationwide movements to promote and sustain a multicontextual and multidimensional multiculturalism. In each ethnic group, there have been those who have argued for the right of any people within American society to preserve their cultural inheritance, as well as the right to have that inheritance influence the direction of the larger social order.

There has also been an extensive critique of the dominant group aims concerning the continued positioning of what is clearly worldwide power dynamics in the control of human and material resource. Thus, a second imperative from the perspective of role responsibilities is for religious leadership to work fervently for social equality, political pluralism, and economic redistribution.

Finally, the moral core of multiculturalism dictates that local, denominational, and ecumenical efforts of the clergy provide the mobilizing vigor for a new movement. Modern theologians must make use of new applications of old-school mobilization tactics. Boycotts and fund-raising must now be initiated on the Internet. Organizational Web pages dedicated to multicultural content can be used to organize virtual letter-writing campaigns advocating for or against political platforms and socioeconomic policies, as well as position papers on current events.

Our current thrust toward multiculturalism arises as a response to the critique of vulgar assimilationism. Discourse and action must move away from fad-like, one-shot attempts at the appeasement of consciousness to a continual, communal agitation of the status quo. The question that must be answered by the children of this century is, Will postmodern multiculturalism be an assimilation tactic, a fusion tactic, or a pluralist tactic?

The dancers must change their steps according to the change in the rhythm of the drum

REFERENCES

Ani, M. (1994). *Yurugu: An African-centered critique of European cultural thought and behavior.* Lawrenceville, NJ: Africa World Press.

Bannerjee, L. (2002). Psychology and the reach of multiculturalism in American culture. In E. Davis-Russell (Ed.), *Multicultural education, research, intervention and training* (pp. 3–19). San Francisco: Jossey-Bass.

Bulhan, H. A. (1985). *Franz Fanon and the psychology of oppression.* New York: Plenum.

Carson, C. (1994). Martin Luther King, Jr., and the African-American social gospel. In P. E. Johnson (Ed.), *African-American Christianity: Essays in history.* Berkeley: University of California Press.

Cone, J. H. (1969). *Black theology and the Black church.* Maryknoll, NY: Orbis Books.

Cone, J. H. (1975). *God of the oppressed.* New York: Seabury Press.

Cone, J. H. (1979, May 23). Asian theology today: Searching for definitions. *Christian Century, 96,* 589–591.

Cone, J. H. (1984). *For my people: Black theology and Black power.* Maryknoll, NY: Orbis Books.

Cone, J. H. (1986). *A Black theology of liberation.* Maryknoll, NY: Orbis Books.

Cooper-Lewter, N., & Mitchell, H. H. (1986). *Soul theology: The heart of American Black culture.* Nashville, TN: Abingdon Press.

D'Andrea, M., & Daniels, J. (1995). Promoting multiculturalism and organizational change in the counseling profession: A case study. In J. G. Ponterotto, J. M. Casas, L. A. Suzuki, & C. M. Alexander (Eds.), *Handbook of multicultural counseling* (pp. 17–33). Thousand Oaks, CA: Sage.

Delgado, R. (1995). *Critical race theory: The cutting edge.* Philadelphia: Temple University Press.

Falicov, C. J. (1999). Religion and spiritual folk traditions in immigrant families: Therapeutic resources with Latinos. In F. Walsh (Ed.), *Spiritual resources in family therapy* (pp. 104–120). New York: Guilford Press.

Gutierrez, G. (1984). *We drink from our own wells: The spiritual journey of a people.* (Matthew J. O'Connell, Trans.). Maryknoll, NY: Orbis Books. (Original work published 1983)

Gutierrez, G. (2000). A theology of liberation: History, politics and salvation (12th printing; Matthew J. O'Connell, Trans.). Maryknoll, NY: Orbis Books. (Original work published 1971)

Horkheimer, M., & Adorno, T. (1974). *Dialectic of enlightenment (cultural memory in the present).* New York: Continuum International.

Howarth, R. (1999, December). *Shining through: Native spirituality sheds a new light on Christianity.* American Indian Report. Retrieved May 29, 2007, from http://www.bluecloud.org/shiningthrough.html

Hraba, J. (1994). *American ethnicity* (2nd ed.). Itasca, IL: F. E. Peacock.

Jones, W. A. (1989). Confronting the system. In G. S. Wilmore (Ed.), *African American religious studies: An interdisciplinary anthology* (pp. 429–455). Durham, NC: Duke University Press.

Kaplowski, C. (2005). *Lulac, Mexican Americans and national policy.* College Station: Texas A & M University Press.

Karenga, M. (2002). *Introduction to Black studies* (3rd ed.). Los Angeles: University of Sankore Press.

Kidwell, C. S., Noley, H., Tinker, G., & Weaver, J. (2001). *A Native American theology*. Maryknoll, NY: Orbis Books.

Koyama, K. (1974). *Water-Buffalo theology*. London: Orbis Books and SCM Press.

Koyama, K. (1980). *Three mile an hour God: Biblical reflections*. Maryknoll, NY: Orbis Books.

Medina, L. (2005). *Las hermanas: Chicana/Latina religious-political activism in the U.S. Catholic Church*. Philadelphia: Temple University Press.

Moll, I. (2002). African psychology: Myth and reality. *South African Journal of Psychology, 32*(1), 9–16.

Nobles, W. W., King., L., & James, C. B. (1995). *Health promotion and disease prevention: Strategies in the African American community*. African American professionals health promotion and disease prevention focus group report submitted to the Congress of National Black Churches. Washington, DC: The Association of Black Psychologists.

Pedersen, P. (1999). *Multiculturalism as a fourth force*. Philadelphia: Brunner/Mazel.

Perry, A. V., & Rolland, J. S. (1999). Spirituality expressed in community action and social justice: A therapeutic means to liberation and hope. In F. Walsh (Ed.), *Spiritual resources in family therapy* (pp. 272–292). New York: Guilford Press.

Said, E. W. (1978). *Orientalism*. New York: Vintage Books.

Schaefer, R. T. (2001). *Race and ethnicity in the United States* (2nd ed.). Upper Saddle River, NJ: Prentice Hall.

Smedley, A. (1999). *Race in North America: Origin and evolution of a worldview*. Boulder, CO: Westview Press.

CHAPTER 10

Improving Academic Possibilities of Students of Color During the Middle School to High School Transition

Conceptual and Strategic Considerations in a U.S. Context

ROBERT COOPER

CHEONG R. HUH

Ensuring both excellence (quality schooling) and equity (access, participation, and benefit) in American public education remains one of the greatest challenges of the 21st century. Fifty years after the Supreme Court's landmark decision in the 1954 *Brown v. Board of Education of Topeka, Kansas*, the educational landscape in this country has remained virtually unchanged. Although more non-White students are attending elementary and secondary schools and they are graduating from high school at higher rates than in 1954, a larger percentage of students are being educated in segregated public schools today than in the early 1970s (Garibaldi, 1998; Orfield & Yun, 1999). Education in this country remains separate and unequal (Cooper, 1996; Kozol, 1991; Orfield & Yun, 1999). Orfield and Yun (1999) note that

> resegregated schools have not occurred by accident; rather they are partly the result of out migration of Whites from urban to suburban school districts and the ineffective implementation of court orders designed to increase the school integration in the late 1960s and 1970s. The 1954 Brown decision notwithstanding, it is discomforting to realize that many of the schools attended by African American [Students of Color] are still inherently unequal. (p. 14)

Authors' Note: Special thanks to the following colleagues for their thoughtful input in the development of the EASE Transitional Choice Model and ongoing commitment to the UCLA EASE Project: Shiv Desai, Daniel Liou, Pedro Nava, and Erica Yamamura.

Despite the myriad of educational reform efforts over the past five decades to ensure high-quality schooling experiences for students in general, and students of color more specifically, far too many schoolchildren continue to fare poorly in our nation's public schools. In high schools throughout the country, for example, African American and Latino students lag behind their White and Asian counterparts in academic achievement (Conchas, 2001; Kober, 2001), graduation (Orfield, Losen, Wald, & Swanson, 2004; Rumberger, 1987, 1995; U.S. Department of Education, 1997), and college enrollment (Harvey & Anderson, 2005). Research suggests that students who underperform in high school eventually disengage from the learning process altogether and fail to obtain a high school diploma (Bryk, 1994; Cooper & Yamamura, 2005; Lee & Burkam, 2003). Although starting high school should represent the coming of age for a young person, this transition for many students of color results in feelings of isolation, disconnection, and an immeasurable sense of loneliness. We argue in this chapter that the negative outcomes associated with the middle to high school transition—poor attendance, decline in student achievement, discipline-related problems, and decrease in extracurricular activities (Newman, Lohman, Newman, Myers, & Smith, 2000)—can be mitigated by the development of what we are calling a critical third space. A *critical third space* is a metaphorical space of empowerment and transformation. It is in this metaphorical space, we argue, where students learn, through the development of a multicultural worldview, to exert their individual agency and harness the social and political capital from the educators who work in their schools.

This chapter presents a conceptual framework for improving the academic possibilities of students transitioning from middle school to high school through the development of a critical third space. Borrowing from the college choice literature (Hossler & Stage, 1992), we've coined the term *transitional choice* to describe the emergent conceptual framework. The transitional choice model is an attempt to capture the range of educational decisions with which adolescents are challenged at a critically important transitional point in the educational pipeline. This framework brings together both theory and practice in a way that can help educators and policymakers fundamentally change the schooling experience of students, particularly students of color, and begin to close the persistent achievement gap in this country between students of color and their White counterparts. Building upon the work of educational theorists who argue that schools play a critical role in socializing students to understand who they are and their role in society, one of the important features of the model is that it is an attempt to capture the relationship between school policy, practice, and culture and the mental models students employ to make sense of the world in which they live. Implicit in this framework is the idea that educators must create the conditions within schools for students to identify the metaphorical space that allows them to become critical of the systematic inequalities found in society in general and in schools more specifically, and use that information to inspire and motivate themselves to pursue their academic and career aspirations.

IMPROVING THE ACADEMIC POSSIBILITIES OF STUDENTS OF COLOR

Demographic projections suggest that the children populating our urban centers are disproportionately students of color and represent one of the largest-growing segments of this country's population. This influx of students has created a beautiful mosaic of racial and ethnic diversity. However, this influx of students is also exacerbating and highlighting all that is wrong with the failing educational system. For example, Ream and Castillo (2001), in a recent study, cite data from the National Center for Educational Statistics that indicate test scores in reading, mathematics, and science for students of color have lagged behind those of Whites on the National Assessment of Educational Progress for the past two decades. They report that by the age of 9, performance differences have emerged in all academic subjects and, by the age of 13, students of color are approximately 2 years behind White students in both reading and math.

In a recent study, Balfanz and Legters (2004) concluded that the underachievement of the economically disadvantaged and students of color can be attributed to the large number of urban students who drop out of high school. It is important to note that the high school dropout rate is not just a high school problem. Students intellectually disengage from the learning process long before they physically leave. However, it is the period of transition from one school level to another, a point of great vulnerability, that serves as the catalyst for students to choose to exit the schooling process. This transition takes place at the time of several important concurrent changes in their lives and in the lives of all adolescents. These changes include physical, social, and environmental changes. In the school context, this is a time when students' attitudes toward school become more negative (Epstein & McPartland, 1976), self-esteem and academic self-concept decline (Marsh, 1989; Wigfield, Eccles, MacIver, Reuman, & Midgley, 1991), and students drop out of the educational process altogether.

The transition from middle school to high school plays a significant role in the future academic trajectory and career choice of students. Depending on the ease of the transition, students choose to pursue their academic and career goals with vigor and enthusiasm or they disengage from the schooling process and eventually drop out. For example, students who get involved in the culture and activities of the school develop a greater sense of belonging, which is positively associated with motivation toward school, effort, and eventual achievement (Felner, Ginter, & Primavera, 1982; Goodenow, 1993). The difficulties related to the transition from middle school to high school are well documented. The large, bureaucratic nature of most high schools challenges students to adjust to new rules and new expectations, while providing them little, if any, adult support and nurturing. As students struggle to fit in socially, poor prior academic preparation in core subjects exacerbates the anxiety associated with the transition (Legters & Kerr, 2001).

We argue that improving the academic possibilities of students of color has to take as its starting point, what several scholars have referred to as the *social distribution of possibilities,* a term used to describe unequal distribution of opportunities to participate in different social and institutional contexts (Stanton-Salazar, 1997; Wellman, 1983). Students of color, by virtue of the schools they attend, are systematically denied access to the types of people, experiences, skills, funds of knowledge, and discourse—support networks—that middle-class nonurban students consistently depend on to secure their successful and privileged participation in the schooling process in this country (Cooper & Jordan, 2003; Cooper & Williams-Chizhik, 2004).

Implicit in the transitional choice framework is the notion that the academic possibilities of students of color are determined by a complex navigational process among three spheres of influences. To capture and promote the academic possibilities of students of color, we must better understand how the tensions among these spheres serve as both facilitators and barriers to the intellectual development and occupational exploration of high school students at a critical juncture in their academic careers. This emergent conceptual model incorporates and emphasizes the three most significant sources of influence of a student's academic development through their adolescent years: the family, peer networks, and the school itself. Although discussion regarding these three spheres of influence is not unique, the proposed model differs from previous sociodevelopmental frameworks and models in that the emphasis is on the interplay and interaction of these three spheres of influence as opposed to exploring the distinct and unique contributions of each sphere to the learning process. Additionally, this model suggests that individual agency as well as group identification and agency are important to push the boundaries of schools and expand the learning opportunities afforded students to discover their full academic possibilities.

It is our contention that until we are able to more successfully ease the transition from middle to high school and increase the number of schools that create a space for students to grapple with their doubly marginalized status in society (poor and minority), communities of color, and society at large, will fail to cultivate the substantial reservoir of human talent that is needed to sustain the democracy upon which this country rests. Education in this country must evolve to the point where students are developing the social and political capital needed to be full participants in the labor market. Labor market projections suggest that the next generation of students must obtain higher levels of skills and training if they are to be productive participants in the capitalistic structures and systems of American society. Therefore, students must be exposed early and often to the endless educational and occupational possibilities and challenges that await them. They must endeavor to understand the tensions among the multiple forces that will influence, shape, and dictate their future academic and career trajectories. Students are border crossers who must navigate and negotiate among the multiple spaces in which they operate (Phelan, Davidson, & Yu, 1993).

DEVELOPING A CRITICAL THIRD SPACE THROUGH A MULTICULTURAL WORLDVIEW

Although the three spheres of influence on the transition into high school are distinct and separate, there are facets of their socialization processes that overlap. Each sphere has embedded within it a socialization process by which students come to understand and value the importance of success in school. Socialization in this context is defined as the process of change or development that occurs as a result of a student's exposure and interactions. In the United States, there are classical models of socialization that delineate the process by which students come to internalize, identify with, and conform to the cultural norms, values, and ideals of their environment (Boykin & Toms, 1985; Sampson, 1977). However, within the context of this model, the focus is placed on the socialization process that leads to the development of the critical third space.

The point at which these spheres overlap depends on the age and developmental stage of the student. One area of overlap, providing the intellectual and emotional support for the development of a critical third space is an area that can significantly increase the academic possibilities of students. The development of the critical third space is perhaps the most prominent feature of the transitional choice model. When students have a positive and realist perspective of who they are in relationship to people and things around them, as well as having a historical, political, and cultural understanding of the events and traits that contribute to their individual and group identity, students are in a better position to make informed decisions about their future education and careers.

Following the lead of several scholars who have written about the development of a third space (Bhabha, 1994; Gutierrez, Baquedano-Lopez, Alvarez, & Chiu, 1999), we call the intersection and integration of the three spheres the critical third space. Embedded in the concept of a third space is the recognition of a first and second space. The first space represents the convergence of the three spheres of influence. The first space is where students have to struggle to negotiate the demands of each of the spheres upon their educational and career trajectories. It is in this space adolescents make the difficult choice of how to respond to the demands and expectations of each sphere.

The second space is where students metaphorically come to terms with their doubly marginalized status in this society. This space is a navigational space, a space where students begin to make sense of the world around them. This space not only symbolically represents the transition from adolescence to young adulthood, but also the transition into becoming a racialized intellectual being, meaning that the second space is used to understand the social constructs such as race and class, which, some would argue, determine social and economic policies in the United States.

This second space is used by adolescents to develop the skills and resources to go between the multiple spheres of influence with little conflict. The challenge of negotiating the three spheres of influence is heightened for many students of color because of the doubly marginalized status of being both poor and minority. Contemporary scholars who study minority students have suggested that there is a lack of attention to and knowledge of how race and class influence the socialization process within schools. This lack of evidence suggests that students must learn how to participate in multiple and often conflicting and contradictory social systems and contexts (Boykin, 1986; Phelan et al., 1993; Stanton-Salazar, 1997). For many students, participation in multiple social systems and contexts is made easier by being introduced and exposed to people and ideas that are reflective of the diversity of society and not being confined to the social norms of their family and immediate community. For many students of color, this means bringing issues of race, ethnicity, culture, and social class into the foreground of their individual and group identity. It means examining social systems, such as health care, the criminal justice system, and schools, with an eye on who in society benefits from them and how these benefits are tied to inequalities associated with race, social class, language, gender, and other social categories (Rogers & Quartz, 2000).

Successful navigation in the second space leads to a critical third space. The critical third space is the place where students are empowered to be critical of institutional systems and institutions, which they are both products of and participants in. It is in this metaphorical space where urban students develop the aspirations, motivations, and resiliency to overcome the adversities that stand between them and their desired objectives. Whereas our use of the concept of the third space differs from other scholars who view the third space as a way to build bridges between the multiple worlds of students (Bhabha, 1994; Gutierrez, et al., 1999; Hudicourt-Barnes, 2003), we see the critical third space as the interactions of students' multiple worlds. The third space can be viewed as a space of cultural, social, and epistemological change in which the competing and sometimes conflicting values, cultural norms, and societal pressures of the three spheres are brought into "conversation" to determine the influence each sphere will have on the academic and career trajectory of the student (Barton, 2001; Hammond, 2001; Morrel, 2002). We see the interaction of the home, school, and peer network as generating a third space that provides the mediational contexts and tools necessary for future academic and career development. Although the relative importance of each sphere to students changes over time, it is not the degree of importance or influence of any one sphere at any given time that creates the opportunities or barriers to a student's educational pursuit. It is, however, a student's ability to navigate, negotiate, and balance the tensions and demands between the spheres that facilitate the creation of a critical third space. It is in this space that the student decides how and when he or she will be influenced by the spheres. We argue that it is the successful navigation among the three spheres that creates the space for students to pursue their educational interest and achieve their educational goals. The third space is important because it provides opportunities for success in school, while also giving voice to students who are often silenced because of their marginalization in this society (Moje, Ciechanowski, & Ellis, 2004).

Despite the importance of the three spheres of influence on the development of young adolescents, very few educational reform efforts over the past three or four decades have attempted to create the conditions necessary for such a space to develop. Stanton-Salazar (1997) argues that decades of educational reform, particularly in urban schools, where the vast majority of students of color attend school, has failed to facilitate the development of positive student social support networks that produce the social and political capital that create lifelong academic and career opportunities. He goes on to argue that these support networks play a vital role in society:

> While they [schools] function primarily as conduits for transmitting the effects of socioeconomic background, race, and gender, they [schools] may also function as lifelines to resources that permit low-status individuals to overcome social structural barriers and to experience healthy human development, school achievement, and social mobility. (p. 5)

If urban schools are to serve as vehicles of healthy human development, school achievement, and social mobility, a new data-driven framework (Barton, Drake, Perez, Louis, & George, 2004) for understanding the influences that shape the academic possibilities of urban high school students during the middle to high school transition is warranted. We must move away from deficit notions of students of color to make sense of the ongoing underachievement of urban students. Deficit thinking leads to the blaming of students for the failure of schools.

Drawing on our collective research experiences—Cooper both as an associate research scientist at the Center for the Social Organization of Schools at the Johns Hopkins University and now at the University of California, Los Angeles, and Huh as an educator at several of the University of California campuses—we use our extensive research experiences in the field to ground the discussion of the theoretical constructs we present in the model (see Figure 1). We begin the discussion by first laying out the theoretical model that can help us conceptualize how to improve the academic possibilities of urban students. Within that discussion, we draw on Phelan's notion of students as border crossers. We use this concept as a way to illuminate the interconnectedness of and interaction among the major spheres of influences on adolescent development.

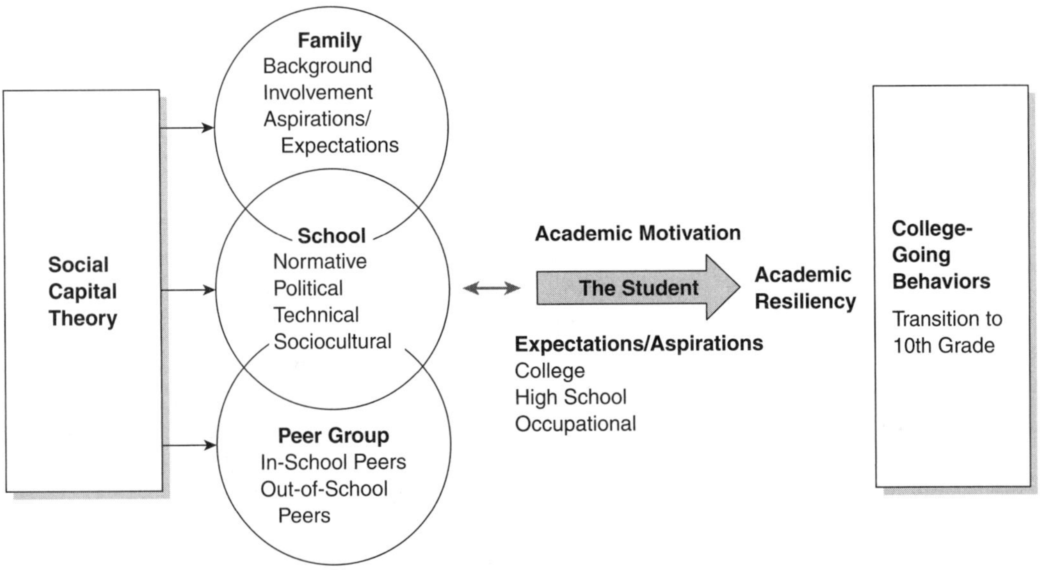

Figure 1 EASE Transition Model

THREE SPHERES OF INFLUENCE ON THE DEVELOPMENT OF A CRITICAL THIRD SPACE

Sphere I—The Family

In the early life of adolescents, the most influential socialization agent is the family. Parents and adolescents typically share similarity in values and attitudes with regards to such concepts as the importance attributed to school and education (Newman et al., 2000). The family equips children with the values, skills, and knowledge necessary to be successful in school. Of the three spheres, the influence of the family is perhaps the most underestimated force impacting the transition from middle school to high school. Although there is a general acceptance that family involvement enhances student academic performance, low-income families and families of color, however, are thought of as not having the social and political capital to be influential in this process.

Although it is widely accepted that family involvement can greatly influence the development and educational achievement of students, the specific family behaviors that enhance school performance are not well understood. Some research concludes that it is a family's ability to stimulate, reinforce, and encourage high expectations that contributes to student success (Clark, 1983). Other findings underscore the contributions of parental values and attitudes (Sewell & Shah, 1968), and yet others conclude that parental involvement in the school is the important factor (Lightfoot, 2004). Despite the relatively limited understanding of how families are important in the schooling process, there is a body of research that confirms that family involvement in the schooling process influences student achievement, motivation, and other educational outcomes (Epstein, 2005; Greenwood & Hickman, 1991; Hoover-Dempsey & Sandler, 1997).

In a recent study, Newman and his colleagues (2000) concluded that if we are to ensure a successful transition from middle school to high school and improve the ability of students of color to succeed in high school, we must do more to engage the family in the schooling process. For most high schools, this requires a change in how parental involvement is defined. Moreover, there must be a change in the climate that would make interacting with school personnel more comfortable, more meaningful, and less intimidating (Newman et al., 2000).

Although parental involvement tends to dwindle during high school, it serves a very important function. Parental involvement has been said to be an important form of social and political capital (Cooper & Nava, 2006; McNeal, 1999), with middle-class parents having a better understanding of the school's expectations of parent involvement (Lareau, 1987). Yet, although influential, McNeal determined that parents with a lower socioeconomic status and of minority status made less strides in the school with the same level of involvement as their White and higher SES counterparts. Therefore, this leads us to hypothesize that while parental involvement is critical to a successful transition from middle school to high school for students of color, parental involvement must be targeted to specific activities that gain their student's access to high-status knowledge, opportunities, and experiences.

Sphere II—Peer Networks

The second sphere that promotes the development of the third space and successful transition from middle school to high school among students of color is the relationships they develop with each other. Peer networks often play a particularly significant role in adolescents' attitudes, including their orientation toward school (Berndt, 1982; Felner et al., 1982; Kelly & Hansen, 1987). Fuligini and Eccles (1993) found that adolescents whose parents were perceived as restrictive and did not foster developmentally appropriate levels of intimacy and individuality turned to peer networks for support and advice more than they turned to their parents during the transition into high school. Peers provide the support adolescents need to successfully face the new challenges associated with transitioning into a new schooling environment.

Peer group association plays a significant role in both the social and academic transition into high school. Research repeatedly demonstrates the connections between peer group association and academic performance (Green, Forehand, Beck, & Vosk, 1980). Research suggests that academic performance can be both positively and negatively affected by peer group association, depending on the dominant value within the peer group (Brown, Lohr, & McClanahan, 1986; Roberts & Peterson, 1992).

In one of the most well-cited research studies looking at urban students and peer group influence, Fordham and Ogbu (1986) suggest that many African American students, responding to the systematic exclusion of African Americans in the political, social, economic, and educational systems of the larger society, develop an oppositional social identity. They maintain that African American students refrain from displaying certain behaviors or engaging in certain activities because they characterize White culture (Datnow & Cooper, 1996). In their study, academic success was viewed as "White people's prerogative" and striving for success in school was viewed as "acting White." Consequently, Fordham and Ogbu maintained that African American students, for fear of betraying the collective group identity, resisted or opposed the idea of achieving success in their academic pursuits (Datnow & Cooper, 1997).

In contrast to Fordham and Ogbu (1986), Mehan and his colleges in an untracking program found that the African American students in their study were able to confirm their cultural identity while simultaneously recognizing the importance of academic achievement (Mehan, Villanueva, Huberman, & Lintz, 1996). This study presented data that suggest that for the African American students in this study, their academic ideology was neither oppositional nor conformist. Instead of succumbing to the tensions between academic success and the oppositional demands of their peers, the African American students in this study formed new, academically oriented peer groups that also promoted a respect for cultural maintenance (Datnow & Cooper, 1997).

Like the African American students in the Mehan et al. study, we hypothesize that low-income students of color can develop academically oriented peer networks that support academic success, cultural integrity, and a positive transition from middle to high school.

Sphere III—School Structures, Policies, and Practices

The third sphere of influence on the intellectual developmental and academic trajectory of students is schooling structures. Because students spend more waking hours in school than anywhere else, including with their families, the values, expectations, and opportunities students are exposed to are greatly determined by the institutional values of the school they attend. The school's funds of knowledge in many ways determine which students will pursue postsecondary opportunities and which students will occupy positions in careers and industries that are not highly sought after. Research suggests that students who develop a positive sense of belonging to their school are more likely to report experiences positively associated with motivation toward school, high levels of participation, and eventual achievement (Newman et al., 2000).

The unique challenge of schools serving students of color is to prepare them to recognize and to deal with their doubly marginalized status in society. Whereas some schools confront the issues of race and class explicitly, others choose a more subtle approach. However, given the historical legacy of exclusion, segregation, and social inequalities found in schools, research in other school settings suggests that these issues must be confronted openly (Datnow & Cooper, 1996). Open dialogue regarding racism and classism is critical for American youth. These types of discussion assist in the development of a positive ethnic self-identity and a critical third space.

Despite extensive civil rights efforts, true integration in American society has yet to be realized. Consequently, American society remains stratified by both race and class (Cooper & Williams-Chizhik, 2004). Research has argued that given these social conditions, students of color, and we would argue urban youth in general, must develop a positive sense of ethnic identity in order to be successful in school (Boykin, 1986). When living in a society where being poor and minority have negative connotations and consequences, it is important that students of color see themselves as intellectual, competent in academic and social circles, and able to enter and graduate college.

MODELING TRANSITIONAL CHOICE: CONCEPTUAL CONSIDERATIONS

"Transitional life events" (Bloom, 1978), such as transition from middle school to high school, often require changes in ideas, attitudes, and behaviors (Reyes, Gillock, Kobus, & Sanchez, 2000). How students adapt to new environments is greatly influenced by the interaction between previous life experiences and the new environment (Bronfenbrenner, 1979; Kelly, Ryan, Altman & Stelzner,

2000). Previous research has identified numerous factors that are predictive of achievement in high school among early adolescents (Cooper, 2000; Eccles & Midgley, 1989). As previously discussed, these factors can be broadly categorized into three spheres of influence: (a) family (Cooper & Nava, 2006); (b) peer networks (Berndt & Keefe, 1995); and (c) school structures, policies, practices, and culture (Anderman & Anderman, 1999; Goodenow, 1993). In the conceptual model that is presented in this chapter, we focus on these three general domains within the educational context because of their significant ability to influence students' expectations for and valuing of educational achievement. Although research on the transition from middle to high school has yielded information about the important factors associated with a positive transition, few models have been developed.

Drawing on the high school transition literature as well as the work of sociologists who study social capital theory, we present a conceptual model that helps illuminate the multiple factors that influence the transition from middle to high school for students of color. As a simple recursive model, we hypothesize unidirectional causal relations among the variables, as indicated by arrows in Figure 1. The variables in the model are operationally defined by composite constructs that emerged from the literature, as well as our experiences in working with the targeted population. Borrowing from the college choice literature (Hossler & Stage, 1992), we use the term *transitional choice* to define as a range of educational decisions at a critical transitional point in the educational pipeline (a) the decision of students to continue their education at the next level (academic predisposition), (b) the decision to engage intellectually in the coursework at the new school (academic transition); (c) the decision to pursue one's academic goals despite barriers (academic resiliency); (d) the decision to get involved in both the official and unofficial culture of the school, which is most apparent through a student's participation in extracurricular activities (social transition); and (e) the decision to abide by the rules and policies of the new school (social adjustment). The constructs that make up the transitional choice model are an attempt to illuminate and capture the multitude of concurrent changes that are taking place in the academic life of adolescents during a very volatile period of their lives (Eccles, Lord, & Buchanan, 1996; Simmons & Blyth, 1987). To maximize the academic potential of students of color, we must first fully understand the factors that contribute to their positive academic self-identity (Bereiter, 1985; Wang, 1990) and how these factors exert their positive influence (Cool & Keith, 1991; Linney & Seidman, 1989).

As depicted in the model, the influence of student background characteristics is expected to affect the criterion variables of academic predisposition, academic transition, academic resiliency, social transition, and social adjustment, both directly and indirectly through the three spheres of influences: the family, the school, and the students' peer network (see Figure 1). The three spheres are posited to have a direct influence on the transition process of urban students at the beginning of the high school career.

According to the maxim, "what you learn determines what you earn." However, for minorities and women, educational attainment does not directly translate into earning potential. Nonetheless, increasing the educational possibilities of students of color is the key for many of our urban youth trapped in a cycle of school failure. Consequently, educators, policymakers, and researchers must diligently search for new ways to understand the persistent age-old problems that confront public education. The model we present here is not a new way of conceptualizing the problem, but perhaps a different way of seeking the solution.

ASSUMPTIONS AND UTILITY OF THE MODEL

Assumption 1: Students are embedded in multiple contexts in multiple ways. The first assumption of the model is that students are in a perpetual state of self-assessment and self-identification. For example, within a family context, a student is not a student, but a son, brother, or cousin. Embedded in each of these roles is a set of expectations, responsibilities, and family and cultural aspirations. The response to life situations differs depending on the particular role the student assumes. Building on the notion of embedded contexts, the conceptual model attempts to account for the complex developmental tasks, challenges, and relationships that must be negotiated by adolescents during the transition from middle school to high school. The tasks, identified in previous research, include physical maturation; cognitive advancements; emotional development, including becoming more self-reliant and autonomous from parents; expanding relationships with peers; and gaining the ability to have intimate friendships. Although there are many theoretical models that attempt to account for students' adaptations to high school, few consider concurrent changes in the students' relationships with their peers, family, and school context during the transition to ninth grade (Eccles et al., 1996; Simmons & Blyth, 1987). We argue that although these spheres are separate and distinct, it is a student's ability to navigate and negotiate the borders of each of these spheres that creates the "third space" that is needed for him or her to capitalize on the social, political, and human capital that facilitates his or her educational dreams into a reality.

Assumption 2: Students are border crossers. Educational research focusing on families; peer networks; and school structures, policy, and practice is not new, nor revolutionary. In fact, the research is voluminous on family involvement in education and its relationship to educational attainment (Barton et al., 2004; Gutman & McLoyd, 2000; Hoover-Dempsey & Sandler, 1997). Voluminous also is the research on peer groups and school policies and practices and their relationship to educational attainment. Phelan and colleagues (1993), however, argue that we know a great deal about the influences of peers, family, and school independently, but little is known about how these worlds combine in the day-to-day lives of adolescents.

The analytic approach that the model represents moves beyond separate lines of inquiry by focusing on the interplay and interaction of the three spheres as well as the students' ability to successfully navigate across and between them. Phelan and her colleagues (1993) introduce the notion of border crossing, navigating across the multiple worlds that students must negotiate as they move through adolescence to adulthood. Phelan et al. developed this notion in a study where they sought to understand student perceptions of boundaries and borders among the multiple worlds in which they live. The use of *world* is to mean, as Phelan et al. suggested, "the cultural knowledge and behaviors found with the boundaries of students' particular families, peer groups, and schools" (p. 56). It is presumed both by Phelan et al. and by us that each world contains values and beliefs, expectations, actions, and emotional responses familiar to those who participate in the day-to-day activities of that world.

Phelan et al.'s (1993) work examined how students of different racial and ethnic groups and socioeconomic status navigated the multiple worlds they encountered in their high school careers. These investigators focused on the border crossing in grades 9–12. This model departs from Phelan et al.'s work in two very fundamental ways. First, our work focuses on perhaps one of the most critical junctures in the educational pipeline and in a student's academic career, the transition from middle school to high school. It is at this transition where students, for the first time in their academic careers, can act upon the emotional disengagement from the educational process that has occurred over time, which could lead to physical disengagement at the end of the ninth-grade year. Second, this work focuses on urban youth. Given the unique social, cultural, political, and historical contexts in which urban youth are situated, the transition to high school is not just about navigating and negotiating between and across multiple worlds, it is also about creating a third space where they have voice to articulate and shape how and when these worlds interact, mesh, and remain separate.

Assumption 3: The critical third space is where the academic possibilities are realized for students, and particularly for students of color. The third assumption of the model is the critical third space, which is where the academic possibilities are realized for students. If educators and caring adults want to help students of color realize and materialize their full academic possibilities, the focus must be on helping them successfully navigate and negotiate the tensions among the three distinct, yet overlapping, spheres of influence. For many students of color, these spheres not only become more distinct over time, but often conflict with one another. Students who are successful in the current educational enterprise are those who find ways to create a voice in all three spheres and articulate and shape the influence of the spheres on their academic trajectory.

IMPLICATIONS FOR POLICY AND PRACTICE

The conceptual model presented in this chapter suggests that rather than focusing exclusively on one of the three important dimensions of schools—families; peer networks; or school policies, practices, and culture—exploring the intersection of these three dimensions may prove more effective in supporting the academic and social transition of students of color into the high school environment.

Whereas there is a multiplicity of factors that contribute to why students are being failed by the educational system in this country, research looking specifically at the transition into high school suggests that if students are to be successful in the schooling process, they must feel connected to caring adults, engaged in the culture of the school, and experience a curriculum that is intellectually rigorous and culturally relevant. As school communities grapple with the increasing numbers of students who struggle during the transition into high school and eventually drop out, developing a curriculum that reflects the lived experiences of the students has become a focal point for many urban school reform efforts. In most cases, when educators seek to make their teaching more culturally relevant, they alter the curriculum in ways that make it more reflective of the multicultural nature of the United States. In many schools, these changes occur under the auspices of multicultural education.

Multicultural education has emerged as an umbrella concept that deals with race, culture, language, social class, and disability (Sleeter & Grant, 1994). A multicultural curriculum is attractive as it provides a curriculum that is more representative of the increasingly diverse world we live in. Implemented properly, multicultural education can significantly enhance the development of the critical third space in that students are trained to synthesize, analyze, and question information from multiple perspectives. One of the important goals of multicultural education is to generate, expand, and disseminate knowledge about various individuals and groups that have contributed to the development of world cultures. Unfortunately, traditional school structures and curricula have led to inaccuracies and omissions concerning the contributions and life conditions of major ethnic groups within our society and from nations across the globe (Bennett, 1995, 2001). Multicultural education offers great hope as it seeks to empower students in developing confidence in their ability to understand the multiple cultures, ideas, and people that make up our global community. Multicultural education also seeks to prepare students academically to influence, manage, and lead the social, political, and economic institutions of our society in the future (Delpit, 2003).

Contrary to the beliefs of some educators, multicultural education is not an attempt to replace the curriculum traditionally taught in our public schools. Rather, it seeks to augment the curriculum. The goal of education from a multicultural perspective is to be inclusive, not exclusive. According to Banks (1989, 1991), the focus of multicultural education is to reform those variables in the school environment that prevent students from having effective, enriching, and stimulating learning experiences. Banks and other theorists argue that the implementation of "true" multicultural education requires a total transformation of the current school environment. This transformation must include not only changes in the technical aspect of the learning environment, such as curriculum, pedagogy, and assessment, but also in attitudes, perceptions, and behaviors of educators who organize and structure those environments. Multicultural education is an attempt to get educators to move beyond rhetoric and tradition and see that the "potential for brilliance is sprinkled evenly across all ethnic groups" (Bennett, 1995, p. 17).

Before educators can effectively implement a multicultural approach to teaching and learning, they must first grapple with their own personal and cultural values, assumptions, and beliefs about students and student learning (Chizhik & Chizhik, 2002a, 2002b). This is a critical component of multicultural education, given that the distribution of opportunities for learning is more a function of the beliefs and behaviors of educators than a function of true differences in the abilities and motivations of students. The degree to which "true" multicultural education becomes a reality in America's classrooms depends largely on the attitude and behavior of the individual teachers. As students develop more positive academic and racial identities in multicultural school settings, the propensity for having hatred, hostility, and prejudice toward other students simply because they are different diminishes greatly (Cooper & Slavin, 2001).

CONCLUSION

The transition from middle school to high school can be overwhelming for many students. The challenges of developing new relationships, being prepared for academic rigor, negotiating the physical plant, and fitting in can all serve to make a natural part of life's course seem too daunting, and feelings of isolation, rejection, and alienation can arise. These feelings are only exacerbated for youth in urban areas from families with low-income levels, who are ethnic minorities, immigrants, and without a family history of success in the schooling environment. The conceptual model presented in this chapter suggests that bringing the three significant spheres of influence on the academic and emotional development of adolescents during their transition into high school into conversation with one another creates an important metaphorical space for urban youth. This space, the critical third space, helps students make sense of the multicultural world in which they live. This space is a place of empowerment and transformation. Students develop a sense of agency and confidence by acquiring the social and political capital needed to successfully navigate high school and prepare for their future academic and career endeavors.

The process of developing this critical third space is captured in the transitional choice model. The goal of the transitional choice model is to contribute to a growing body of research that seeks to identify possible strategies and relationships that increase the number of students of color who discover their academic potential and successfully transition into high school and eventually make what is often a long journey to college. For affluent students who are the children of college graduates, the primary goal of secondary education is often to reproduce for students the level of knowledge, skills, and abilities their parents already have. For example, it is not uncommon for doctors, lawyers, and business leaders to be the sons and daughters of such professionals. In middle-class households, college is often perceived as a birthright and the focus of decision making is placed on "which" college a student should attend, rather than whether or not she or he should go to college. The psychological orientation of the families and schools serving middle-class students gives them a competitive edge in higher education. However, among poor, urban students, a different situation is more prevalent. Many of these students belong to families where neither parent attended college; indeed, many have not finished high school. In order for urban students to discover their full academic potential, the schooling process within the urban context must become transformative. Students must be encouraged and prepared to move beyond the educational level of their families and reconcile their fears of both failure and success. Urban schools must work in partnerships with families and students to build supportive and nurturing, yet challenging, learning environments that help students transition into high school, college, and beyond with ease.

REFERENCES

Anderman, L. H., & Anderman, E. M. (1999). Social predictors of changes in students' achievement goal orientations. *Contemporary Education Psychology, 25,* 21–37.

Balfanz, R., & Legters, N. (2004). *Locating the dropout crisis.* Retrieved April 24, 2006, from http://www.csos.jhu.edu/tdhs/rsch/Locating_Dropouts.pdf

Banks, J. (1989). Multicultural education: Characteristics and goals. In J. Banks & C. M. Banks (Eds.), *Multicultural education: Issues and perspectives* (pp. 2–26). Boston: Allyn & Bacon.

Banks, J. A. (1991). Multicultural education: Its effects on students' racial and gender role attitudes. In J. P. Shaver (Ed.), *Handbook of research on social studies teaching and learning* (pp. 459–469). New York: Macmillan.

Barton, A. C. (2001). Science education in urban settings: Seeking new ways of praxis through critical ethnography. *Journal of Research in Science Teaching, 38,* 899–917.

Barton, A., Drake, C., Perez, J., Louis, K., & George, M. (2004). Ecologies of parental engagement in urban education. *Educational Researcher, 33*(4), 3–12.

Bennett, C. (1995). *Comprehensive multicultural education: Theory and practice.* Needham, MA: Allyn & Bacon.

Bennett, C. (2001). Genres of research in multicultural education. *Review of Educational Research, 71*(2), 171–217.

Bereiter, C. (1985). The changing face of educational disadvantagement. *Phi Delta Kappan, 67,* 538–541.

Berndt, T. J. (1982). The features and effects of friendships in early adolescence. *Child Development, 53,* 1447–1460.

Berndt, T. J., & Keefe, K. (1995). Friends' influence on adolescents' academic achievement motivation: An experimental study. *Journal of Educational Psychology, 82,* 664–670.

Bhabha, H. (1994). *The location of culture.* London: Routledge.

Bloom, B. L. (1978). Marital disruption as a stressor. In D. G. Forgays (Ed.), *Primary prevention of psychopathology* (Vol. 2, pp. 81–101). Hanover, NH: University Press of New England.

Boykin, A. W. (1986). The triple quandary and the schooling of Afro-American children. In U. Neisser (Ed.), *School achievement of minority children: New perspectives* (pp. 95–130). New York: Academic Press.

Boykin, A. W., & Toms, F. (1985). Black child socialization: A conceptual framework. In H. McAdoo & J. McAdoo (Eds.), *Black children* (pp. 33–51). Beverly Hills, CA: Sage.

Bronfenbrenner, U. (1979). *The ecology of human development.* Cambridge, MA: Harvard University Press.

Brown, B. B., Lohr, M. J., & McClanahan, E. L. (1986). Early adolescents' perceptions of peer pressure. *Journal of Early Adolescence, 6,* 139–154.

Bryk, A. S. (1994). *More good news that school organization matters. Issues in restructuring schools* (Issue Report No. 7). Madison: University of Wisconsin, Center on Organization and Restructuring of Schools.

Chizhik, E. W., & Chizhik, A. W. (2002a). A path to social change: Examining students' responsibility, opportunity, and emotion toward social justice. *Education and Urban Society, 34,* 283–297.

Chizhik, E. W., & Chizhik, A. W. (2002b). Decoding the language of social justice: What do "privilege" and "oppression" really mean? *Journal of College Student Development, 43,* 792–808.

Clark, R. M. (1983). *Family life and school achievement: Why poor Black children succeed or fail.* Chicago: University of Chicago Press.

Conchas, G. (2001). Structuring failure and success. Understanding the variability in Latino school engagement. *Harvard Educational Review, 71,* 475–504.

Cool, V. A., & Keith, T. Z. (1991). Testing a model of school learning: Direct and indirect effects on academic achievement. *Contemporary Educational Psychology, 16,* 28–44.

Cooper, R. (1996). De-tracking reform in an urban California high school: Improving the schooling experience of African American students. *Journal of Negro Education, 65*(2), 190–208.

Cooper, R. (2000). Urban school reform from a student of color perspective. *Urban Education, 34*(5), 597–622.

Cooper, R., & Jordan, W. (2003). Cultural issues in comprehensive school reform. *Urban Education, 38*(4), 380–397.

Cooper, R., & Nava, P. (2006, April). *"Es lo mas importante": Examining perceptions of parent involvement of Mexican-American parents and students at Valley High School.* Paper presented at the annual meeting of the American Educational Research Association, San Francisco, CA.

Cooper, R., & Slavin, R. E. (2001). Cooperative learning programs and multicultural education: Improving intergroup relations. In F. Salili & R. Hoosain (Eds.), *Research on multicultural education and international perspectives* (pp. 15–33). San Francisco: Jossey-Bass.

Cooper, R., & Williams-Chizhik, E. (2004). Talking about race in schools post-Brown: A public relations challenge. *Journal of School Public Relations, 25,* 203–119.

Cooper, R., & Yamamura, E. (2005, April). *Latino adolescent peer groups: Academic supporters or suppressors?* Paper presented at the annual meeting of the American Educational Research Association, Montreal, Canada.

Datnow, A., & Cooper, R. (1996). Peer networks of African Americans in independent schools: Affirming academic success and racial identity. *Journal of Negro Education, 60*(2), 219–228.

Datnow, A., & Cooper, R. (1997). Peer networks of African American students in independent schools: Affirming academic success and racial identity. *Journal of Negro Education, 66*(1), 56–72.

Delpit, L. (2003). Educators as "seed people" growing a new future. *Educational Researcher, 32*(7), 14–21.

Eccles, J. S., Lord, S., & Buchanan, C. M. (1996). School transition in early adolescence: What are we doing to our young people? In J. Graber, J. Brooks-Gunn, & A. Petersen (Eds.), *Transitions through adolescence* (pp. 251–284). Hillsdale, NJ: Lawrence Erlbaum.

Eccles, J. S., & Midgley, C. (1989). Stage-environment fit: Developmentally appropriate classrooms for your adolescents. In C. Ames & R. Ames (Eds.), *Research on motivation in education* (Vol. 3, pp. 139–186). San Diego, CA: Academic Press.

Epstein, J. L. (2005). School, family, and community partnerships in the middle grades. In T. O. Erb (Ed.), *This we believe in action: Implementing successful middle level schools* (pp. 77–96). Westerville, OH: National Middle School Association.

Epstein, J. L., & McPartland, J. M. (1976). The concept and measurement of the quality of school life. *American Educational Research Journal, 13,* 15–30.

Felner, R. D., Ginter, M., & Primavera, J. (1982). Primary prevention during school transitions: Social support and environmental structure. *American Journal of Community Psychology, 10,* 277–290.

Fordham, S., & Ogbu, J. U. (1986). Black students' school success: Coping with the "burden of 'acting White.'" *Urban Review, 18*(176).

Fuligini, A. J., & Eccles, J. S. (1993). Perceived parent-child relationships and early adolescents' orientation towards peers. *Developmental Psychology, 29,* 622–632.

Garibaldi, A. M. (1998). Four decades of process . . . and decline: An assessment of African American educational attainment. *Journal of Negro Education, 66*(2), 105–120.

Goodenow, C. (1993). Classroom belonging among early adolescent students: Relationships to motivation and achievement. *Journal of Early Adolescence, 13*(1), 21–43.

Green, K., Forehand, R., Beck, S., & Vosk, B. (1980). Person-environment congruence as a predictor of adolescent health and behavioral problems. *American Journal of Community Psychology, 10,* 511–526.

Greenwood, G. E., & Hickman, C. W. (1991). Research and practice in parent involvement: Implications for teacher education. *Elementary School Journal, 91,* 278–288.

Gutierrez, K. D., Baquedano-Lopez, P., Alvarez, H., & Chiu, M. (1999). Building a culture of collaboration through hybrid language practices. *Theory Into Practice, 38,* 87–93.

Gutman, L. M., & McLoyd, V. C. (2000). Parents' management of their children's education with the home, at school, and in the community. An examination of African-American families living in poverty. *Urban Review, 32*(1), 1–24.

Hammond, L. (2001). Notes from California: An anthropological approach to urban science education for language minority families. *Journal of Research in Science Teaching, 38,* 983–999.

Harvey, W. B., & Anderson, E. L. (2005). *Minorities in higher education 2003–2004: Twenty-first annual status report.* Washington, DC: American Council on Education.

Hoover-Dempsey, K., & Sandler, H. (1997). Why do parents become involved in their children's education? *Review of Educational Research, 67*(1), 3–43.

Hossler, D., & Stage, F. K. (1992). Family and high school experience influences on the postsecondary educational plans of ninth-grade students. *American Educational Research Journal, 29*(2), 425–451.

Hudicourt-Barnes, J. (2003). The use of argumentation in Haitian Creole science classrooms. *Harvard Educational Review, 73,* 73–93.

Kelly, J. A., & Hansen, D. J. (1987). Social interactions and adjustment. In V. B. Van Hass & M. Hersen (Eds.), *Handbook of adolescent psychology* (pp. 131–146). Elmford, NY: Pergamon.

Kelly, J. G., Ryan, A. M., Altman, B. E., & Stelzner, S. P. (2000). Understanding and changing social systems: An ecological view. In J. Rappaport & E. Seidman (Eds.), *The handbook of community psychology* (pp. 133–159). New York: Kluwer Academic/Plenum.

Kober, N. (2001). *It takes more than testing: Closing the achievement gap.* Washington, DC: Center on Education Policy.

Kozol, J. (1991). *Savage inequalities: Children in America's schools.* New York: HarperPerennial.

Lareau, A. (1987). Social class differences in family-school relationships: The importance of cultural capital. *Sociology of Education, 60,* 73–85.

Lee, V., & Burkam, D. T. (2003). Dropping out of high school: The role of school organization and structure. *American Educational Research Journal, 40*(2), 353–393.

Legters, N., & Kerr, K. (2001). *Easing the transition to high school: An investigation of reform practices to promote ninth grade success.* Baltimore, MD: Center for Social Organization of Schools, Johns Hopkins University.

Lightfoot, D. (2004). "Some parents just don't care": Decoding the meanings of parental involvement in urban schools. *Urban Education, 39*(1), 91–107.

Linney, J. A., & Seidman, E. (1989). The future of schooling. *American Psychologist, 44,* 336–340.

Marsh, H. W. (1989). Age and sex effects in multiple dimensions of self-concept: Preadolescence to early adulthood. *Journal of Educational Psychology, 81,* 417–430.

McNeal, R. (1999). Parental involvement as social capital: Differential effectiveness on science achievement, truancy, and dropping out. *Social Forces, 78,* 117–144.

Mehan, H., Villanueva, I., Huberman, M., & Lintz, A. (1996). *Constructing school success: The consequences of untracking low-achieving students.* Cambridge, UK: Cambridge University Press.

Moje, E., Ciechanowski, K., & Ellis, L. (2004). Working toward third space in content area literacy: An examination of everyday funds of knowledge and discourse. *Reading Research Quarterly, 39*(1), 38–70.

Morrel, E. (2002). Toward a critical pedagogy of popular culture: Literacy development among urban youth. *Journal of Adolescent & Adult Literacy, 46,* 72–77.

Newman, B. M., Lohman, B., Newman, P. R., Myers, M. C., & Smith, V. L. (2000). The transition to high school for academically promising, urban, low-income African American youth. *Adolescence, 35*(7), 45–66.

Orfield, G., Losen, D., Wald, J., & Swanson, C. (2004). *Losing our future: How minority youth are being left behind by the graduation rate crisis.* Cambridge, MA: The Civil Rights Project at Harvard University.

Orfield, G., & Yun, J. (1999). *Resegregation in American schools.* Retrieved July 22, 2003, from http://www.civilrightsproject.harvard.edu/research/deseg/reseg_schools99.php

Phelan, P., Davidson, L., & Yu, H. C. (1993). Students' multiple worlds: Navigating the boarders of family, peer, and school cultures. In P. Phelan & A. Davidson (Eds.), *Renegotiating cultural diversity in American schools* (pp. 52–83). New York: Teachers College Press.

Ream, R., & Castillo, S. (2001, December). *Does peer social capital moderate the impact of student mobility on the mathematics achievement of Mexican Americans across immigrant generations?* Paper presented at the UC Accord Conference, San Jose, CA.

Reyes, O., Gillock, K. L., Kobus, K., & Sanchez, B. (2000). A longitudinal examination of the transition into senior high school for adolescents from urban low-income status and predominantly minority backgrounds. *American Journal of Community Psychology, 28*(4), 519–544.

Roberts, L., & Petersen, A. C. (1992). The relationship between academic achievement and social self-image during early adolescence. *Journal of Early Adolescence, 12*(2), 197–219.

Rogers, J., & Quartz, K. (2000, April). *Teaching for social justice: Framing the complexity and contradiction.* Paper presented at the annual meeting of the American Education Research Association, New Orleans, LA.

Rumberger, R. W. (1987). High school dropouts: A review of issues and evidence. *Review of Educational Research, 57,* 101–121.

Rumberger, R. W. (1995). Dropping out of middle school: A multilevel analysis of students and schools. *American Educational Research Journal, 32,* 538–625.

Sampson, E. (1977). Psychology and the American ideal. *Journal of Personality and Social Psychology, 35,* 767–778.

Sewell, W. H., & Shah, V. P. (1968). Parents' education and children's educational aspirations and achievements. *American Sociological Review, 33,* 191–209.

Simmons, R. G., & Blyth, D. A. (1987). *Moving into adolescence: The impact of pubertal change and school contact.* Hawthorne, NY: Alain de Gruyter.

Sleeter, C., & Grant, C. (1994). *Making choices for multicultural education: Five approaches to race, class and gender.* New York: Macmillan.

Stanton-Salazar, R. D. (1997). A social capital framework for understanding the socialization of racial minority children and youth. *Harvard Educational Review, 67*(1), 1–40.

U.S. Department of Education, National Center for Educational Statistics. (1997). *The condition of education, 1997*. Washington, DC: U.S. Government Printing Office.

Wang, M. C. (1990). Programs that promote educational equity. In H. P. Baptiste, H. C. Waxman, J. Walker de Felix, & J. E. Anderson (Eds.), *Leadership, equity, and school effectiveness* (pp. 132–154). Newbury Park, CA: Sage.

Wellman, B. (1983). Network analysis: Some basic principles. In R. Collins (Ed.), *Sociological theory* (pp. 155–200). San Francisco: Jossey-Bass.

Wigfield, A., Eccles, J. S., MacIver, D., Reuman, D. A., & Midgley, C. (1991). Transition during early adolescence: Changes in children's domain-specific self-perceptions and general self-esteem across the transition to junior high school. *Development Psychology, 27*, 552–565.

CHAPTER 11

Do Integration and Belonging Go Hand in Hand?

Adolescents' Social and Educational Experiences in a Multicultural Learning Environment

EVELLYN ELIZONDO

KIMBERLY A. WHITE-SMITH

WALTER R. ALLEN

> *Schooling, like education in general—never liberates without at the same time limiting. It never empowers without at the same time constraining. It never frees without at the same time socializing. The question is not whether one or the other is occurring in isolation but what the balance is, and to what end, and in light of what alternatives.*
>
> (Cremin, 1977, p. 37)

The creation of free publicly funded schools was intended to solve the issues of stimulating social mobility and establishing cultural stability in a growing and changing America during the 1800s (Sadovnik, Cookson, & Semel, 2001). Horace Mann called education "the great equalizer of the conditions of men" and saw *the common school* as a means of preparing new immigrants to be productive citizens and good workers (as cited in Sadovnik et al., 2001). Research has shown that American public schools are among the best in the world (Berliner & Biddle, 1995).

However, it is apparent that America's public schools have not lived up to the promise of providing equal access for all students to the rigorous education necessary for becoming an asset in today's job market (Berliner & Biddle, 1995). For instance, in the state of California, affluent and White American students receive a higher-quality education than their low-income and minority peers in the form of more financial resources and highly prepared teachers (Shields et al., 1999). Furthermore, despite the large socioeconomic advances that ethnic and linguistic minorities have made in American society, there is still a wide gap in their educational attainment and achievement compared to White Americans. According to Franklin (2004), "African Americans are the wealthiest, most highly educated, and most influential African people in the world" (p. 159). Nonetheless, 69% of African American and 64% of Latino students demonstrate deficits in reading, whereas only 33% of White American students face comparable difficulties (Snow, Burns, & Griffin, 1998). Additionally, in a report of the College Board (1999), the achievement gap between middle-class African American and White students is even greater than the achievement gap between low-income African American and White students.

Much has been written on the inadequacies of low-income, high-minority urban schools (English, 2002; Oakes, 2005; Shields et al., 1999). In his current book, Kozol (2005) details the atrocities endured by low-income and minority students in schools across the country. He reports that inner-city schools are typically racially segregated, insufficiently funded, and staffed with ill-prepared teachers and administrators. Correspondingly, there is a solid body of literature that examines the elements that support minority student achievement in underresourced, urban schools (Foster, 1997; Gonzalez et al., 1995; Howard, 2001; Ladson-Billings, 1994; Stanton-Salazar, 2001). However, we argue that due to context, the obstacles that hinder school success and the features that support achievement for African Americans and Latinos in suburban, high-resourced schools are completely different from those endured by students attending inner-city schools. The purpose of this study is to contribute to the body of scholarship examining the resiliency factors that support Latino and African American college-bound high school students in a racially diverse and affluent school setting.

BACKGROUND

The rigor and intensity of the secondary school curriculum is the most accurate predictor of postsecondary school success (Adelman, 1999). However, evidence that schools still engage in legal discriminatory practices, like tracking and labeling, is found in the overrepresentation of Latinos and African Americans in special education and their underrepresentation in gifted and Advanced Placement (AP) programs (English, 2002; Oakes, 2005; Oakes & Guiton, 1995; Welner, 2001). Further, a study conducted by the Education Trust (1999) demonstrated that Asian and White American students were far more likely to be enrolled in college preparatory classes (42.1% and 34.1%) than Latinos (22.6%) and African Americans (25.7%). This is significant when looking at demographic trends, which indicate that by 2010, 50% of the youth in California, New York, and Texas will be people of color, and a third of the nation's youth will reside in those three states (Balz & Esten, 1998).

English (2002) suggests that the achievement gap between ethnic minorities and White Americans will never be resolved because the tools used to measure student outcomes are fundamentally flawed. Measurements of intelligence, ability, and achievement are inherently biased in content against socioeconomic status and race (Perkins, 1995). In addition, school and district administrators tend to overlook the advantage that White students have over their Latino and African American peers regarding access to information, mentors, and social networks available to them via the vast number of same-race teachers and counselors.

According to the results of a survey conducted by the National Education

Association (2003), during the 2000–2001 academic year, 90% of the teaching force nationwide was White. In another study, Monica A. White (2004) interviewed Black teachers and students who experienced the transition between de jure segregation and de facto segregation (1950s–1960s). From their perspectives, African American students lost more than they gained in terms of social supports, access to rigorous academics, and role models.

This begs the question: Presently, what resiliency factors support and propel Latino and African American students to excel academically in high-resourced, predominantly White high schools? The concept of resiliency emerged from the field of developmental psychopathology (Masten, Best, & Garmezy, 1990) and postulates that the developmental processes at work in students are the same regardless of their abilities to overcome life obstacles (Pianta & Walsh, 1998). Therefore, the idea of being resilient is not a phenomenon reserved only for a small group of fortunate people. In fact, resilience is a common response that comes out of ordinary adaptive processes (Masten & Curtis, 2000). According to Rutter (1981), resilience is a "positive role of individual differences in people's responses to stress and adversity" (p. 316). Thus, it is important to reveal the methods of resiliency so that it can be developed in others.

Benard (1996) provides a practical and holistic conceptual framework for examining the phenomenon as it is operationalized. Evidence of resilience can be observed in both personal strengths and environmental protective factors. Personal strengths can be categorized into four intersecting domains: social competence, problem solving, autonomy, and sense of purpose (Benard, 1996). Environmental protective factors can be found in schools, communities, or families and include close relationships, opportunities to participate, and clear and positive expectations for achievement.

Although there are numerous frameworks available to study resiliency as a concept (see Wang, Haertel, & Walberg, 1994; Waxman, 1992; Wolin & Wolin, 1993), most tend to focus solely on student capability and neglect other factors such as school and family context (Stanton-Salazar, 2001; Wang, Haertel, & Walberg, 1994). The intent of this study is to make transparent not only the characteristics and coping strategies of college-bound Latino and African American students, but the environmental factors that support and develop resilience in students.

The present study is part of a larger research project aimed at addressing educational access, equity, and diversity issues in higher education. The main goal of the project is to identify factors related to educational successes among African American and Latino students residing in Southern California. This research carried out a cross-sectional, mixed-method design. Quantitative and qualitative data were collected from teachers, parents, counselors, and students at 10 Los Angeles Basin high schools varying in school characteristics and demographics.

For the purposes of this study, we selected 1 of the 10 school sites, *Cove High School* (institutional name is fictitious), because of its unique school environment. The student population is not only the most racially and socioeconomically diverse of all our schools but also among the highest academically credentialed public schools in the state of California.

METHOD

Cove High School Profile and the Sample

Cove High School is an academically above-average-performing school located in a large coastal community with a population of approximately 90,000. The community is largely composed of college-educated (50%), White-collar professionals (75%). During the 2001–2002 academic year, Cove enrolled over 3,000 students. Given that Cove High buses Latino and Black students from lower-income neighborhoods, the student body represents a diverse ethnic and socioeconomic community comprising 50% White, 34% Latino, 10% Black, and 7% Asian. The families at Cove range from affluent to low income. The distribution of wealth and parental education among minority and majority students depicts a bimodal trend, with Latino and Black students reporting considerably lower income and parental education than White and Asian students.

Academically, Cove considers itself a college-going community, producing higher-than-state-average college-going rates for Blacks and Latinos. During the 2001–2002 academic year, slightly over half (58%) of the senior class were UC/CSU eligible. Compared to average statewide college eligibility rates (68% Asian, 34% White, 19% Black, and 16% Latino), Cove High eligibility rates across most groups were greater (73% White, 66% Asian, 37% Black, and 36% Latino) (California Postsecondary Education Commission, 2002). On average, 2002 Cove graduates scored higher SAT I Math (550) and Verbal (518) scores than both the statewide (517 Math/498 Verbal) and nationwide (514 Math/506 Verbal) averages. Although the school offers the largest number of Advanced Placement classes across all of our 10 participating schools, the representation of Latino and Black students enrolled in AP courses remains disproportionately low compared to their Asian and White counterparts.

In this study, we present student data for 109 Cove High juniors and seniors who volunteered to participate in focus group discussions concerning their academic experiences and college plans. Of these participants, 47 were Latino, 35 were White, 18 were Black, and 9 were Asian American. A total of 12 focus groups were conducted and generally varied by race, gender, and class. Of these focus groups, four were all Latino, two were all White, and six were mixed ethnicity. Given the nature of these data, not all participants responded to each question.

Data Collection Methods

All volunteering participants were read a standardized introduction to the study by staff researchers and had an opportunity for questions. Following the introduction, a 15-minute survey was completed by participants prior to the focus group discussion. Survey items consisted of demographic information and general impression of quality of education, campus climate, and students' rapport with school counselors and staff. These data were used to broadly contextualize students' qualitative responses and to allow for a point of reference from which to interpret their unique experiences. Completed surveys were collected by researchers and stored in a locked briefcase. Focus group interviews were broadly structured, using open-ended questions designed to tap into college readiness, social expectations to attend college, and availability of resources, as well as school-related support networks and barriers to higher education.

Design and Procedure

This investigation was approved by the University of California, Los Angeles Human Subjects Protection Committee and complied with all ethical, federal, and professional standards for conducting research with human participants. Schools agreed to participate in exchange for a full disclosure of their school's statistical findings. Those students who were 18 years of age or older consented to their participation, and parental consent was obtained for each student respondent under 18 years of age. Participants were given two movie passes as a small gratuity.

Most students were either recruited from an Advanced Placement course or from the

Advancement Via Individual Determination (AVID) program, which is a program that prepares traditionally disadvantaged students for college eligibility by placing them in AP classes while providing the academic support to succeed. Data were collected on the high school campus from September 2001 through June 2002.

Group interviews varied from 1 to 2 hours and were conducted by the primary research investigator, coprincipal investigators, or a graduate student researcher. Each focus group was audio-recorded, transcribed by a professional agency, and coded by project student researchers.

Qualitative and Quantitative Data Analyses

Focus group transcripts were reviewed by individual research team members for the purposes of identifying reoccurring themes in the data. Group discussions were facilitated to develop coding categories that were used in ATLAS to analyze the data. SPSS software was used to analyze survey data collected in this study. Combining both forms of data provided a more complete view of the similarities and differences in minority and majority students' school experiences.

RESULTS

Campus Integration and Belonging

> They [adults at Cove High] expect us to go to college but their expectations are not as high as what we expect of ourselves. They may say a community college, and our main focus is on a university. So by grown-ups looking down on us, saying, "Oh, you can go to community college," that brings our self-esteem down because that's all you're looking at. Like I'm only, I'm only good enough to go to a community college. Like they don't think I can go to a university. –Latina Student

> I think this school's had a pretty big influence on me because they're constantly letting you know what you need to get done in order to get in a four-year college, when the deadlines are and when to apply for financial aid. They tell us, "Do this and do that." They call you in to talk to you. They will get you prepared for college.
>
> —White Female Student

Overall, two different perceptions of campus culture emerged from these data. White and Asian students had more similar perceptions of the college-going culture than did Black and Latino students. Specifically, White and Asian students reported that Cove High was an encouraging and supportive campus that fostered a strong sense of student commitment and high academic expectations. Whites and Asians expressed that both teachers and college counselors were motivational and consistent about offering information regarding college. One White male expressed that his teacher made sure the class understood the college transition and what to expect on a college campus:

> My history teacher really talked a lot about college. He was a young guy right out of Santa Barbara and so knew what was going on. He was a really cool guy to talk to us about education. He talked about the differences between high school and college and making the transition so we know what to do. This teacher really impacted my decisions. He was pretty helpful.

Another student discussed how college counselors kept them focused on higher education by keeping them well informed about the college process:

> They never left us alone. During the year, they're really on top of us, coming in classes and telling us about dates and like what needs to be done and they wouldn't get off your back about college. They just did a great job.

When asked if race played a role in the high school experience, White students were generally convinced that campus staff were supportive of all students regardless of race because they were simply committed to helping students get to college:

> They haven't really cared about your race or anything like that. The counselors, they're the ones that seem to be determined on what you want to do without even knowing who you are. They don't know you at all. They're just making judgments on you based on what classes you're taking.

Although White students did not perceive any racial disparities in the quality of services administered across ethnic groups, Asian students did. They generally were outspoken about the racial inequalities at Cove High. Asian students were clear about the negative stereotype held by school staff about Latino and Black students. Asians repeatedly expressed that Latinos and Blacks were basically expected to achieve less than Asian and White students. Unfortunately, staff's low expectations of Latinos and Blacks had serious consequences on the quality of services and education minorities received. One Asian expressed his observation of counselors' racial prejudice:

> I know certain individuals of a particular race that automatically, even when the counselor hasn't seen their classes, they'll say, "You know, maybe a community college is an option for you." And that individual of color is going to Georgetown University. And frankly, that's never been placed on me or people that are White.

Asian students further discussed that the impact of counselors' biases against Latino and Black students' academic potential resulted in racially segregated courses:

> Academically, I know there is inequality in the expectations. I just look at my AP classes. There is only one African American individual in my AP English class. It's mostly White or Asian, but mostly White though. Counselors, when you're doing your scheduling, they push you to take those AP classes, they suggest them to you. And so as I got into this school and got into the AP classes, I saw less and less minority friends and more of my White friends. And like colored people, they all hang around the lesser, the lower classes that are not AP, not as hard.

Black and Latino students' perceptions of the campus culture were more consistent with Asians' account of racial inequalities than Whites' account of equality. Blacks and Latinos generally expressed that school staff were pessimistic about their academic potential and reported that they, themselves, were often discouraged about attending competitive colleges. One Black female discussed her negative interaction with a counselor:

> The counselor told me that it would be better for me to go to community college because people of color, they don't really achieve much in big places like universities.

It was not easy for students to communicate to school staff that they indeed had higher aspirations than those transmitted by negative racial stereotypes. Minority students often found themselves debating with school staff about their intellectual credibility. A Latina gave her account of a confrontation she had with an administrator concerning her academic potential and ambitions:

> I had a personal confrontation with one of the administrators here at the school. He was saying to me that I should have taken, not a college prep course, but a prep course for a class I wanted to take, other than a class I needed to go to college. For like 45 minutes, we were having the argument, and he was saying that I wasn't going to go to college, and it was basically based on my race, that since I was a Latina, I wasn't going to be able to succeed in college.

Black and Latino students found themselves on the defensive with school staff, making the case that they had the potential to succeed on the college track and attend a university. One Black student expressed that as a minority, she had to justify wanting information on four-year universities because she was automatically judged as a good candidate for community college:

> Being half Black has been really weird here because when I go see the regular counselors, they're like, "What do you plan to do for college?" And I'm like, "I plan on going to a four-year university." They just give me this really odd look and tell me, "Why don't you just try a community college?" Oh, great! I've been taking AP classes since my sophomore year, and how can you say that I need to go to community college? So the counselor was like, "Oh, you can get into UCLA under some Black special admissions program." I said, "I don't want to go through those programs. I can go through regular admissions." They automatically characterize you and tell you to go through a special program if you want to attend a four-year to weave you in that school. Because of my race, they assume this is the only way to get into a university. "Oh, you have a great chance." But I don't look at my color and believe, oh, I have a greater chance of getting in like all my White friends. I'm competing against others academically, not against skin color.

Many minority students expressed that they simply wanted to be accepted as part of the college-going community at Cove High. Latinos and Blacks, who eventually broke down some of their peers' racial bias, found themselves more motivated and better informed about the college process:

> Once they finally started to realize that we [minorities] had the potential not only athletically but also intellectually to go to college, then everybody started talking about college with us a little bit more. They asked us where we wanted to go to college and stuff. And so all of us just hit the books a little bit harder.

Minority students who were unable to dispel negative stereotypes about their academic potential used their stigma as a motivating factor at Cove High:

> That [negative Black stereotypes] really encourages me to do as well as I can so I can show them, but also just for myself. I don't have to be another statistic or part of the stereotype. So I can have goals based on me and not my skin color.

One student expressed how he developed a resilient and positive attitude regarding the struggles of getting through high school as a Latino male:

> I've always tried to set a "no excuses" standard. The point is it's going to be hard no matter what. Even if you conquer one obstacle, there's gonna be a thousand more. So you just have to move on and keep your head up and go forward. It's a matter of determination and mind strength about yourself and your surroundings. [You need to be] able to separate yourself from negative vibes to let yourself get a positive attitude.

Yet another Latino gave an account of how a teacher's racial prejudice encouraged him to do well in an AP course:

> And I was sitting down in my AP English class and was probably one of three Hispanics in the classroom. Two teachers shared the classroom and my teacher was there and the other teacher walks in and I was getting my work out. Then she walks up to me and was like, "Are you lost? What classroom are you supposed to be in?" And I looked at her and I was like, "What are you talking about? What classroom am I supposed to be in?" It's been like two weeks in the semester and I would think she would have seen me every day. She told me, "If you're supposed to be in another class, I suggest you get there right now." I just looked at her and was kind of upset because she said such a comment like that. She proceeded

> with stuff like that throughout the year. It just motivated me more just to get a good grade in the class and let her see that this kid is not only in the class but he's excelling in it. And being able to show them that I wasn't what they thought I was. I think negative aspects in life have motivated me to excel and do better and prove everybody wrong.

Although students of color generally perceived a hostile campus environment, Black and Latino students found refuge in the AVID program. AVID was perceived to be a positive learning space in which Black and Latino students were expected to have high academic goals, encouraged to pursue four-year universities, and validated in their potential for college success:

> I've gotten the support through the AVID program in the school. It's a group of students who are first-generation and going to college. AVID gives us the support that maybe our parents don't know exactly how to because they haven't gone to college. Knowing that [in AVID] there are other people in the same place as you is very supportive. My AVID teacher has been very amazing. Because of him, he's actually opened the doorway for me to think about getting my master's and also my Ph.D.

Similarly, a Latina student reported that AVID helped her to envision herself at a four-year institution rather than a community college:

> I was encouraged to attend a community college because we lived right across the street from it. Everyone that lives around us would go there or drop out to work. So I always had the mentality that I would go to a community college. But it was through AVID that it really hit me that there are other colleges than community colleges. Four-year colleges are competitive and you have to challenge yourself. Through AVID, I saw that UCLA is an opportunity other than community college.

Students reported that part of AVID's success was that it offered them a safe and comfortable space on campus given its ethnic diversity: "AVID has encouraged us a lot. They don't show racism. They have a lot of every race here, not like in my AP classes where everybody is White." Other students reported that AVID gave them the direction and opportunities that otherwise would not have presented themselves:

> If it wasn't for AVID, I know I would end up exactly like my sister, just taking any classes here and going to community college. If it weren't for AVID, I would probably go to community college and waste my time just like those other students. Because I've been in AVID since my freshman year, I've always been pushed and they always check our schedule to make sure you're in the right classes that you need to graduate and get into college.

In fact, the AVID program had been so successful that all students were accepted to a four-year institution. Part of the success of AVID was the student community it fostered among ethnic minority students and the college expectations it supported among all participants. One AVID student realized that minorities indeed were capable of going to a four-year institution: "We're all college-bound, too. Every one of us got into a college already! That's what this program is for."

CONCLUSION

Returning to Cremin's (1977) quote from the introduction, it is apparent from the data analysis that the students at Cove High School are being socialized, but to what end? In general, White and Asian students had full access to the educational benefits of attending a high-resourced school and were being socialized to become college educated, while their African American and Latino peers encountered many obstacles and were being socialized toward school failure. Even so, the underserved minority students in this study revealed personal characteristics that allowed them to overcome such obstacles. For instance, the students employed their problem-solving talents in different ways. Some students gained acceptance into the college-going culture by consistently displaying their intellectual prowess, while other equally successful students demonstrated autonomy by disconnecting from the negative campus climate and turning inward to find the motivation to achieve. Yet other students used negative stereotyping to develop a sense of purpose.

The distinction between personal characteristics and environmental factors was useful in that it provided a simple model for appreciating the range of resiliency. However, this distinction is limited in that it failed to capture the dynamic interplay of the person and the environment. For example, Asian and White students in this study were easily able to identify supportive and nurturing adults, whereas African American and Latino students described adults who were uncooperative and espoused low expectations. What is not fully addressed is the teachers' and counselors' racial biases and unjustified labeling based on stereotypes.

In sum, using this model has provided some insights to the next steps schools and administrators might take with the hope of creating a campus climate that engenders high school completion and postsecondary aspirations in all students, especially those traditionally underserved by the current system. The AVID program was an environmental factor that not only provided minorities with a safe space and access to supportive adults, but also helped African American and Latino students develop a sense of resiliency. The structural elements of the program, such as providing college information, developing study skills, and ensuring involvement with motivated peers, are important to achievement. However, equally important are the relationships that develop between students and AVID teachers. Providing clear and positive college-going expectations for students who have been traditionally denied access to higher education can serve as a catalyst for developing more ambitious academic goals and the confidence to pursue them. The challenge confronting U.S. schools is how to expand "opportunities to learn" (Oakes, 2005) for all students regardless of race, ethnicity, language group, or social class background. Until this challenge is addressed, public schools will continue to fall short of their ideals and promise.

REFERENCES

Adelman, C. (1999). *Answers in the tool box: Academic intensity, attendance patterns, and bachelor's degree attainment.* Washington, DC: U.S. Department of Education, Office of Educational Research and Improvement.

Balz, F. J., & Esten, M. R. (1998). Fulfilling private dreams, serving public priorities. *Journal of Negro Education, 67*(4), 333–345.

Benard, B. (1996). Fostering resiliency in children and youth: Promoting protective factors in the school. In Dennis Saleebey (Ed.), *The strengths perspective in social work practice* (pp. 167–182). New York: Longman.

Berliner, D. C., & Biddle, B. J. (1995). *The manufactured crisis: Myths, fraud, and the attack on America's public schools.* Cambridge, MA: Perseus Books.

California Postsecondary Education Commission. (2002). *Quick data.* Retrieved September 1, 2002, from http://www.cpec.ca.gov/SecondPages/QuickData.asp

College Board. (1999). *Reaching the top: A report of the National Task Force on minority high school achievement.* New York: College Board.

Cremin, L. A. (1977). *Traditions of American education.* New York: Basic Books.

Education Trust. (1999). *Dispelling the myth: High poverty schools exceeding expectations.* Washington, DC: Council of Chief State School Officers.

English, F. W. (2002). On the intractability of the achievement gap in urban schools and the discursive practice of continuing racial discrimination. *Education and Urban Society, 34*(3), 298–311.

Foster, M. (1997). *Black teachers on teaching.* New York: New Press.

Franklin, V. P. (2004). Social capital, cultural capital, and the challenge of African American education in the 21st century. In V. P. Franklin & C. J. Savage (Eds.), *Cultural capital and Black education: African American communities and the funding of Black school, 1865 to the present* (pp. 159–171). Greenwich, CT: Information Age.

Gonzalez, N., Moll, L. C., Tenery, M. F., Rivera, A., Rendon, P., Gonzales, R., et al. (1995). Finds of knowledge for teaching in Latino households. *Urban Education, 29*(40), 443–470.

Howard, T. C. (2001). Powerful pedagogy for African American students: A case of four teachers. *Urban Education, 36*(2), 179–202.

Kozol, J. (2005). *The shame of the nation: The restoration of apartheid schooling in America.* New York: Crown.

Ladson-Billings, G. (1994). *The dreamkeepers. Successful teachers of African American children.* San Francisco: Jossey-Bass.

Masten, A. S., Best, K. M., & Garmezy, N. (1990). Resilience and development: Contributions from the study of children who overcome adversity. *Development and Psychopathology, 2*(4), 425–444.

Masten, A. S., & Curtis, W. J. (2000). Integrating competence and psychopathology: Pathways toward a comprehensive science of adaptation in development. *Development and Psychopathology, 12*(3), 529–550.

National Education Association. (2003). *Status of the American public school teacher.* Washington, DC: NEA.

Oakes, J. (2005). *Keeping track: How schools structure inequality* (2nd ed.). New Haven, CT: Yale University Press.

Oakes, J., & Guiton, G. (1995). Matchmaking: The dynamics of high school tracking decisions. *American Educational Research Journal, 32*(1), 3.

Perkins, D. N. (1995). *Outsmarting IQ: The emerging science of learnable intelligence.* New York: Free Press.

Pianta, R. C., & Walsh, D. J. (1998). Applying the construct of resilience in schools: Cautions from a developmental systems perspective. *School Psychology Review, 27*(3), 407–417.

Rutter, M. (1981). Stress, coping and development: Some issues and some questions. *American Journal of Orthopsychiatry, 57,* 316–331.

Sadovnik, A. R., Cookson, P. W., & Semel, S. F. (2001). *Exploring education: An introduction to the foundations of education* (2nd ed.). Needham Heights, MA: Allyn & Bacon.

Shields, P. M., Esch, C. E., Humphrey, D. C., Young, V. M., Gaston, M., & Hunt, H. (1999). *The status of the teaching profession: Research findings and policy recommendations* [Report to the Teaching and California's Future Task Force]. Santa Cruz, CA: The Center for the Future of Teaching and Learning.

Snow, C. E. E., Burns, M. S. E., & Griffin, P. E. (Eds.). (1998). *Preventing reading difficulties in young children.* Washington, DC: National Academy of Sciences—National Research Council Commission on Behavioral and Social Sciences and Education.

Stanton-Salazar, R. D. (2001). *Manufacturing hope and despair: The school and kinship networks of U.S.–Mexican youth.* New York: Teachers College Press.

Wang, M. C., Haertel, G. D., & Walberg, H. J. (1994). Educational resilience in inner cities. In M. C. Wang & E. W. Gordon (Eds.), *Educational resiliency in inner city America: Challenges and prospects* (pp. 45–72). Hillsdale, NJ: Lawrence Erlbaum.

Waxman, H. C. (1992). Reversing the cycle of educational failure for students in at-risk school environments. In H. C. Waxman, J. Walker de Felix, J. Anderson, & H. P. Baptiste (Eds.), *Students at risk in at-risk schools: Improving environments for learning* (pp. 1–9). Thousand Oaks, CA: Corwin.

Welner, K. G. (2001). *Legal rights, local wrongs: When community control collides with educational equity.* New York: SUNY Press.

White, M. A. (2004). Paradise lost? Teachers' perspectives on the use of cultural capital in the segregated schools of New Orleans, Louisiana. In V. P. Franklin & C. J. Savage (Eds.), *Cultural capital and Black education: African American communities and the funding of Black school, 1865 to the present* (pp. 143–158). Greenwich, CT: Information Age.

Wolin, S. J., & Wolin, S. (1993). *The resilient self.* New York: Villard Books.

CHAPTER 12

The Influence of Peers on the Development of a Multicultural Worldview

CYNTHIA HUDLEY

The role of peers as socializing agents and potent influences in social development is undeniable. Some theorists (Harris, 1995; Youniss, 1980) have even argued that peers may be more important than parents in the process of socialization for peer competence. Based on substantial findings that link peer relationships to children's social and emotional functioning (Ladd, 1999), it is reasonable to presume that peers also play an important role in the development, structuring, and maintenance of a child's multicultural worldview. As our communities and schools become more culturally diverse, youth often have more opportunities and a greater need to interact across cultural, racial, and ethnic borders, and those borders are more visible than was true a generation ago (Wakefield & Hudley, in press).

Today, even children growing up and going to school in the most racially isolated schools and communities, whether by choice or by necessity, are more likely to interact with youth of other backgrounds than was true for earlier generations. Sports leagues, shopping malls, summer programs, amusement parks, and too many other settings to enumerate are often populated by children and youth from a variety of cultural, racial, and ethnic backgrounds, frequently without parents in the immediate vicinity. Because peers often represent the majority of actors and set the social agendas in contexts that provide opportunities for multicultural interaction, they also have many opportunities to provide feedback, make judgments, and generally exert influence on the development of a child's multicultural worldview.

This chapter will assess our understanding of the strength of peer influences on a multicultural worldview as well as the processes by which peer influences might be exerted. The review will begin with a brief discussion of the concept of a multicultural worldview, followed by a discussion of relevant literatures from social and developmental psychology. We will examine several theoretical perspectives that can illuminate the role of peer influences on a multicultural worldview among children and adolescents, including social identity, intergroup contact, and ethnic identity. The chapter concludes with a selective review, critical analysis, and integration of literature on peers and a multicultural worldview.

MULTICULTURAL WORLDVIEW

Over the past half-century, the idea of a multicultural worldview has been assigned an array of terms and meanings by both research and practice in a variety of domains, including education (Banks & Banks, 2004), counseling psychology (Pope-Davis & Coleman, 1997; Sue, 2001), youth violence prevention (Hudley & Taylor, 2006), and social psychology (Stephan & Stephan, 2001). Multicultural education has typically been defined by pedagogical strategies that incorporate students' and families' cultural backgrounds into effective classroom and school practices. Importantly for this discussion, multicultural education assumes that a multicultural worldview and the promotion of positive relations and interactions among individuals and groups are necessary elements of successful learning and development, for both students and teachers (Banks & Banks, 2004).

Research in counseling psychology has been concerned with the construct of cultural competence for clinicians, which involves the incorporation of a client's cultural experiences and worldview into the therapeutic relationship and treatment plan (Sue, 2001). Most models of cultural competence in counseling include the need for counselors to establish positive interpersonal attitudes and interactions across racial and ethnic lines, in both work and community settings, or what might be considered a multicultural worldview. Similar to the counseling literature, recent work in youth violence prevention has also put forward a multicomponent model of cultural competence that specifies successful interaction across cultural divides as an important strategy to reduce youth violence. According to this model, culturally competent peer interactions are fostered by acknowledging and valuing the worldview of members of groups different from one's own (Hudley & Taylor, 2006).

Finally, a large research literature in social psychology has examined both intergroup and interpersonal relations. This perspective has concluded that more positive attitudes toward the qualities and contributions of individual members of other groups as well as toward interaction with other groups in general are fostered by close, cooperative, equal status contact, when this contact is consistently maintained over time (Stephan & Stephan, 2001). Thus, major domains of study that have investigated multicultural understanding all seem to converge on a conclusion that positive attitudes and positive interpersonal and intergroup experiences are relevant components of a multicultural worldview.

Consistent with this range of conceptualizations in the literature, in this review I define multicultural worldview as a positive valuing of members of other racial, ethnic, and cultural groups as well as one's own group and a positive attitude toward interpersonal experiences with people from cultural, racial, and ethic groups different from one's own. This definition captures a set of general beliefs that should allow each member of a multicultural society to interact successfully and with minimal prejudice across racial and ethnic boundaries (Coleman, 1995). The specific concern of this chapter will be to review the theoretical and empirical evidence that bears on the influence of peers, both positive and negative, in shaping such beliefs.

THEORETICAL FOUNDATIONS

Why should we imagine that peers might play any role at all in the development and maintenance of a multicultural worldview? Several theories drawn from social and developmental psychology suggest processes by which group members reciprocally influence one another's perceptions of the world, attitudes, and behaviors. From social psychology, two influential theories of interpersonal and intergroup relations offer potentially useful insights on the role of peers in the development and maintenance of a multicultural worldview.

Social Identity Theory

Social identity theory (Tajfel & Turner, 1986) is perhaps the best-known perspective in the broad tradition of the study of social influence. Fundamentally, the core theory argues that all people derive a sense of self-worth and social belongingness from memberships in groups. People judge the appropriateness of their own beliefs and behavior with comparisons to the norms of the groups to which they belong. Group norms provide information about how group members should understand and respond to a given situation, and group members share and enforce those norms. Thus, group membership carries with it a preference for the normative standards of the group as well as a sense of obligation to fulfill those norms for members of the in-group.

A related formulation in the social identity perspective, self-categorization theory (Turner, Hogg, Oakes, Reicher, & Wetherrel, 1987) describes the processes by which individuals come to identify themselves as a part of a given group in comparison to other (out-) groups (i.e., how a person comes to "self-categorize"). In brief, people self-categorize when they identify as a member of a social group (or category) that they perceive to be relevant to their identity. When children and adolescents categorize themselves as a member of a group they perceive to be relevant to their identity ("I am a member of the football team; they are my social group"), a social identity perspective would propose that they would then be influenced by the norms of that group ("football players use profanity, racial slurs, and sexist put-downs, so I will start using that kind of speech to be an accepted member of my group"). Further, social identity theory contends that group cohesion is sometimes maintained by a positive valuing of the in-group at the expense of any out-groups. The more a given group feels itself to be under threat from a given out-group, the greater will be the possibility of bias toward the in-group, derogation of the out-group, and intergroup conflict (Hewstone, Rubin, & Willis, 2002). Thus, according to a social identity perspective, the peers in those groups with which youth identify should have a powerful influence on the development and maintenance of a multicultural worldview by establishing and enforcing group norms that either reward or sanction such beliefs and behavior.

As well, a more recent formulation of self-categorization theory, the common ingroup identity model (Dovidio & Gaertner, 1999), theorizes that peer groups comprising members of different backgrounds may be especially influential in promoting a multicultural worldview. When members of various backgrounds identify with one another by categorizing themselves within a single, superordinate group, they will feel more positive toward others who also share the backgrounds of the members of the superordinate group. Thus, a cross-ethnic peer group organized around shared interests (e.g., video games) should lead all members to have more positive perceptions (e.g., more empathy, less reliance on stereotypes) of people of other ethnicities, that is, a multicultural worldview. This model also has much in common with the well-known contact hypothesis.

The Contact Hypothesis

The contact hypothesis is a highly visible theory from social psychology that has been extensively used to understand peer influences on a multicultural worldview. Initially proposed by postwar American social science as a model for combating the entrenched prejudice and racism of the day, the contact hypothesis initially formulated a set of conditions that were necessary in intergroup encounters to foster positive rather than prejudiced interactions (Allport, 1954; Watson, 1947). This early formulation focused on four dimensions of intergroup contact. According to this model, intergroup contact that leads to positive attitudes and interaction across groups must occur in the context of cooperation to achieve shared goals, and a cooperative activity should comprise members of varying backgrounds who will interact as individuals. All participants in the contact experience must hold equal status in the cooperative activity (if not in their lives external to the activity) for cooperation to successfully produce positive beliefs and behaviors. Finally, such contact must be publicly valued and supported by respected authority figures drawn from each of the groups represented in the contact experience. However, these theorists immediately acknowledged the potential for simple contact to undermine any positive benefits of intergroup interaction (e.g., by confirming negative attitudes and stereotypes directed toward other groups), and research has continued to examine and reconsider the necessary conditions for positive interactions across groups.

Most importantly for our discussion, more recent formulations of the contact hypothesis suggest that friendship and its attendant positive emotions (rather than simple contact) across racial and ethnic lines should be a particularly persuasive influence on positive attitudes toward those of backgrounds other than one's own as well as toward intergroup contact more generally (Pettigrew, 1998). Another recent elaboration, the extended contact effect, has further theorized that simply knowing that members of one's group have personal friendships with members of other groups can predict more positive attitudes toward those groups (Wright, Aron, McLaughlin-Volpe, & Ropp, 1997). However, the knowledge or experience of a single friendship will not automatically generalize to a multicultural worldview. It is possible for a single intergroup friendship to simply confirm for each of the friends that the other friend is an exception to the rule. In order for a personal friendship, experienced either personally or vicariously via the extended contact effect, to promote a multicultural worldview, at some point the different group memberships of the two friends must be explicitly recognized (Brown & Hewstone, 2005; Wright et al., 1997) and the other-race friend must be seen as somehow typical of the larger group to which that friend belongs (Brown & Hewstone, 2005).

The implications of the social identity perspective, contact hypothesis, and extended contact effects indicate clearly that peers should play a substantial role in the development and maintenance of a multicultural worldview. If peers engage in positive, cooperative activities with members of other groups that include affectively positive personal interactions, then multicultural attitudes of the peer group in general should tend to be positive, and group norms should support such positive attitudes. If even one member of a peer group maintains a genuine friendship across racial/ethnic lines, that friendship has the potential to provide all other members of the peer group with an exemplar that creates more positive multicultural attitudes in everyone (not just the friendship pair) and group norms that support intergroup contact. In sum, social psychological theory posits that an intergroup friendship, as well as cooperative equal status contact, provides the possibility for establishing or altering group norms and individual beliefs in a manner that promotes a multicultural worldview. If these conditions are not met, group norms may reject a multicultural worldview in the face of negative stereotypes of an out-group, efforts to maintain group cohesion, or intergroup relations that are perceived as threatening.

Racial/Ethnic Identity

Recall that the definition of multicultural worldview that provides the framework for our discussion goes beyond intergroup attitudes and contact with other group members to include a positive valuing of one's own group as an important element. Turning our attention from social to developmental psychology, theoretical formulations that can shed light on the role of peers in establishing attitudes toward one's own group can be drawn from the literature on ethnic and racial identity development. Ethnic identity is often defined as the component of the self-concept that is grounded in knowledge of, a sense of belonging to, and attitude toward membership in a given ethnic group (or groups) (Phinney, 1990; Tajfel, 1981). Much of this literature has explicitly attended to youth and adults of color, seemingly exempting those of Western European background from a sense of ethnic identity (but see Alba, 1990). However, related theorizing specific to racial identity has explicitly modeled both Black (Cross, 1991) and White (Helms, 1995) racial identity development.

Although a number of conceptual models have described ethnic and racial identity development in somewhat different terms, these models share a developmental progression that moves in phases from no insight into ethnic and racial identity to a full commitment and positive valuing toward one's membership in a racial, ethnic, or cultural group (Atkinson, Morton, & Sue, 1983; Cross, 1991; Helms, 1995; Phinney, 1990). People in the earliest phase are characterized by a lack of interest in or awareness of racial or ethnic group membership. Those in an intermediate phase (or phases in some models) are characterized by an active exploration of their group's history, cultural practices, and beliefs as well as exploration of the meaning of their ethnic group membership and their relationship to other ethnic groups present in a multiethnic society. At the intermediate phase(s), people may isolate themselves from members of other groups and immerse themselves solely in intragroup activities and relationships, a move that reflects the converse of a multicultural worldview. However, as they move through this developmental task, people use newly absorbed information to construct an ethnic identity and move into the final phase. Those at this highest phase in development, referred to variously as an achieved identity, identity internalization, identity incorporation, and synergistic articulation (to name but a few terms), have a working knowledge of their ethnic heritage, a clear idea of the meaning of their ethnic group membership, and a commitment to their ethnicity and the role it plays in their lives. Parenthetically, not everyone will make the developmental passage across all phases; an individual may remain stable at any phase, and each person may revisit intermediate phases of identity development in cycles that involve further exploration or rethinking of the role or meaning of one's race or ethnicity (Parham, 1989) as life circumstances and personal reflection dictate.

All of these models posit that an achieved, internalized racial or ethnic identity is associated with successful psychological adjustment (Wakefield & Hudley, 2007) that includes positive attitudes toward other groups and successful relationships with members of other groups. Thus, consistent with our original definition, ethnic identity development theories would propose that a multicultural worldview is difficult if not impossible to attain absent an achieved ethnic identity. These theories, derived from a developmental psychology tradition, see ethnic identity development as a highly individual process that is governed by the development of cognitive structures and an increasing awareness and understanding of the social world in which the individual matures. On their face, there is little or no attention to the role of peer processes in the development of ethnic identity.

However, peers are an undeniable part of the child's social world, and their influence on developmental processes (including identity) is reflected in the principle of homophily (Berndt, 1982; Kandel, 1978). In brief, this principle states that peers seek out others who are like themselves (i.e., selective association), and once affiliated become more similar to one another due to their consistent interactions (i.e., reciprocal socialization) within the consensual norms of the peer group. Youth with a more positive ethnic identity and multicultural worldview would be more likely to initially affiliate, and over time more likely to construct group norms that support and strengthen such positive views of self and others. Conversely, a peer in such a group who has relatively more negative views and/or may be at a somewhat less advanced phase of ethnic identity than others in the peer group will either adjust previously held beliefs and behaviors or reduce the frequency of interaction with the peer group.

However, other relevant theorizing proposes processes whereby identity development and group process can move youth away from a multicultural worldview. Social identity theory, as discussed earlier, would argue that a strong ethnic identity should promote strong in-group favoritism (if not outright antipathy toward an out-group) (Hewstone et al., 2002), an attitude that would militate against a multicultural worldview. Another model, John Ogbu's (1983) cultural ecological theory of human development, attends specifically to cultural and historical barriers and affordances that shape children's development. His theory proposes that children and adolescents of oppressed groups in hierarchically stratified societies may develop an oppositional identity in which they reject the values, attitudes, and behaviors of the dominant group in order to affirm personal identity and peer group solidarity. As this definition makes plain, an oppositional identity is incompatible with a multicultural worldview. However, such an identity would not preclude positive relations with members of other socially oppressed groups or positive attitudes toward intergroup relations (although to the exclusion of members of the dominant group). Consistent with the principle of homophily, Ogbu's theory specifically identifies the peer group and its established norms as the mechanism that supports and maintains the development of an oppositional identity and an attenuated multicultural worldview (Fordham & Ogbu, 1986).

To summarize the theoretical evidence, theories of social and developmental psychology make a strong argument for the influence of peers on the development of a multicultural worldview. Although theorized influences may pull youth in a positive or negative direction, there is some consensus that peers exert nontrivial influences on beliefs and behavior in childhood and adolescence. Taken together, these theories seem to put forward a sequence of interlocking influences. Youth affiliate with self-relevant social groups (self-categorization) that comprise normative standards that youth use to define and evaluate their beliefs and behaviors (social identity). Youth make adjustments to more closely correspond to these group norms (homophily via reciprocal socialization). Given the opportunity for collaborative equal status contact, an affectively positive intergroup friendship by at least one member of the peer group should shape group norms toward favoring intergroup relations (contact effects). As well, if at least some of the group members have strong, achieved ethnic identities, peer norms should support positive intergroup attitudes and interactions. However, groups comprising influential members who are at earlier, exploration phases of identity development may construct norms that support intergroup conflict and sanction intergroup contact and relations. As well, if youth, oppressed minority youth in particular, have developed an oppositional identity, peer group norms will tend to favor intergroup interactions only with members of other oppressed groups.

Given the relative sophistication of the theoretical formulations concerning the question of peer influence on a multicultural worldview in children and adolescents, we should now consider the empirical evidence that has bearing on this question. What can the research literature tell us about the role of peers in supporting a multicultural worldview? What follows is a selective review and critical analysis of literature in the fields of education and human development that examines influences on children's and adolescents' intergroup attitudes and behavior. This review will first examine research that directly compares attitudes between friends and among peers. We then turn to the literature from social psychology to understand group norms and worldview and finally examine literature on identity development to understand the role of individual development in shaping intergroup processes.

PEERS AND A MULTICULTURAL WORLDVIEW

Attitude Research

Empirical research has measured shared attitudes toward out-groups among self-nominated friends and self-selected peer groups, with mixed results. Ritchey and Fishbein (2001), for example, examined similarities in attitudes of White, middle-class adolescent friends attending all-White high schools. Attitudes toward personal characteristics included race, sexual orientation, health status (HIV positive), body size, and gender; responses were measured individually and also collapsed into a single measure of intolerance. No relationships existed among self-nominated friends on attitudes; however, social desirability, particularly for racial attitudes, may have influenced results. For example, racial attitude items asked about beliefs that Black people are undeserving of social benefits and social status, and the belief that Black students have lower capabilities than Whites. Some students may have felt constrained in responding to some of the more transparently racist items. As well, the study was conducted in an all-White environment, suggesting that attitudes toward race may not have been particularly salient.

An examination of attitudes among early adolescents in Italy measured opinions of 11 different groups who experience greater or lesser discrimination in the Italian culture (including Black Africans, Germans, Chinese, Jews, Gypsies, Albanians, and Italians) (Kiesner, Maass, Cadinu, & Vallese, 2003). More congruence existed between respondents and their self-nominated peer groups in this sample than in the American sample. Participant and peer attitudes toward stigmatized out-groups (e.g., Gypsies) and toward in-groups (e.g., Italians) were moderately correlated, but no relationships emerged for nonstigmatized out-groups (e.g., French). These data also suggest that shared attitudes may be more likely to occur around groups that are salient, either positively or negatively, in a given context.

Aboud and Doyle (1996a) paired children, again all White, in grades 3 and 4 who had either high or low levels of out-group prejudice with a same-age friend who had a contrasting level of measured prejudice. Pairs discussed their feelings toward members of out-groups and their reasons for those feelings. Children with low levels of prejudice showed no changes in attitudes measured after the discussions; however, children with high levels of prejudice showed significant reductions in such attitudes after the discussions concluded. Apparently even relatively young children can discuss multicultural attitudes, and these data suggest that the direction of influence through overt discussions is toward a more multicultural worldview, as none of the children with low levels of prejudice were persuaded toward a more negative view of other groups.

In a related study, Aboud and Doyle (1996b) measured attitudes toward other ethnic groups with a sample of more ethnically diverse (59% White, 33% Asian, 8% Black) young students (third and fourth graders) and found mixed relations between participants' and a self-nominated best friend's attitudes. There was no correlation between individual positive or negative attributes assigned to any group by a participant and a best friend. However, for participants and a best friend, perceived attitudes of Whites toward interactions with Black peers, as measured with hypothetical stories, were significantly related. A composite ratio of positive evaluation of Black children to negative evaluation of White children was also significantly related for each participant and a best friend. Finally, this study also measured participants' perceptions of their friend's attitudes and found moderate to strong correlations (r ranging from 0.47 to 0.73). This vicarious influence is perhaps the most critical peer mechanism in shaping a multicultural worldview. Children embrace the norms of a group once they have self-identified with that group; however, norms are rarely explicitly taught but are grounded in perceptions of shared beliefs. Thus, perceptions of peers' attitudes may be more influential in the decision to affiliate with a peer group as well as an understanding of group norms. Particularly on topics that may not be frequently or openly discussed, such as racial attitudes, youth often infer peers' attitudes rather than directly asking.

Research that directly assesses shared attitudes has shed some light on our question of peer influences on a multicultural worldview. We might expect that friends would be more congruent in attitudes than peer groups, given the previously discussed prominence of friendships in the contact hypothesis. However, some evidence suggests that friends' attitudes are unrelated, although the salience of racial and ethnic concerns appears to increase attitude similarity. Even though objective measures of attitudes are not always related, children believe that their attitudes toward others and toward interaction with those of other groups are similar to those of their friends. In general, these findings from the literature on attitudes provide fairly consistent support for peer influence on a multicultural worldview, measured as either acceptance of or prejudice against ethnic groups different from one's own.

Contact Effects

The contact hypothesis was an important framework for early research that examined the effects of school desegregation. Typical of this work, one longitudinal study in the Midwest in the early 1970s (Patchen, 1982) examined high schools undergoing voluntary desegregation. In general, findings suggested that both Black and White students who reported positive interactions with other-race peers (e.g., spent time talking, did schoolwork together) also reported that their opinion of other-race peers and toward interacting with such peers had "gotten better" during high school. Conversely, students who reported avoiding other-race peers (e.g., would not sit near) and remained with only their own race peers reported that their attitudes had "gotten worse." As well, students' attitudes toward other-race peers were significantly correlated to measured attitudes of same-race peers averaged across the entire school of attendance ($r = 0.21$ and 0.24 for Black and White students, respectively), suggesting the presence of collective norms. Interestingly, Black student attitudes also correlated with the average of White student attitudes, but the reverse pattern was not significant ($r = 0.20$ and 0.01). Finally, perceived positive attitudes of same-race peers also correlated significantly with positive attitudes toward other-race peers ($r = 0.37$ and 0.58 for Black and White students, respectively) and self-reported friendships with other-race peers ($r = 0.21$ and 0.37).

More recent work with both adolescents and children has also examined contact effects on multicultural attitudes. A full-year ethnography (Peshkin, 1991) of a multiethnic school (34% Black, 32% White, 22% Latino, 12% Asian) in a multiethnic community revealed that students endorsed a multicultural worldview. Three important themes emerged from observations and interviews. Students, in general, embraced pride in ethnic identity, support for both intergroup and intragroup peer interactions (casual nods to romantic relationships), and the belief that similarities are more important than differences. Racial taunts and overt discrimination were virtually unheard of, but negative sanctions were enforced in certain situations toward Black males and South Asian "newcomers." Romantic relationships with Black males, in particular, were sufficiently sanctioned by peer norms that students had a pejorative label ("mira"; Peshkin, 1991, p. 226) for other-race girls who dated Black boys. On the other hand, casual contact and personal friendships ("mingling"; Peshkin, 1991, p. 213) were the norm rather than the exception across all ethnic groups. These data suggest that peer norms and expectations defined a fairly specific worldview that all students recognized, although followed more or less according to personal preference. Most importantly for this review, informants in this study reported that their attitudes and behaviors reflected their shared peer norms, not the dictates of their parents or teachers.

Cross-race friendships have also been studied as exemplars of an optimal form of contact, because they are ostensibly both equal status and emotionally positive. Recent research in a Canadian multicultural (50% White, 30% Black, 20% Asian) elementary school examined cross-race friendships and multicultural attitudes among students in grades 1–6 (Aboud, Mendelson, & Purdy, 2003). White children with high levels of prejudice had more racially exclusive peer groups, whereas data showed no association between peer group composition and racial attitudes for Black students. However, the data were unable to speak to direction of causality, so it is not clear whether peers influenced worldview or worldview determined selection of peers among White students.

The extended contact hypothesis has been tested in work with older adolescents (i.e., college students), examining relationships between attitudes toward out-groups and knowledge of cross-group friendships (Wright et al., 1997). Two studies, one with a White sample and a second with a multiethnic sample, demonstrated that participants who knew a same-race peer with a friend of another race showed significantly lower levels of prejudice toward that outgroup when compared to participants who did not have peers who shared cross-race friendships. The more peers a participant knew who shared cross-race friendships, the lower the levels of prejudice toward that outgroup. This extended contact effect was significant even when controlling for cross-race friendships that the participant also shared. Collectively, these data are representative of findings derived from a number of studies using a variety of research methods (see Pettigrew & Tropp, 2006, for a review) that have examined relationships among cross-ethnic attitudes, peer contact, and friendship. Studies generally find that peers often influence a multicultural worldview, through either actual close cross-race relationships or the knowledge of such relationships between same-race and other-race peers; such interpersonal relationships can foster positive feelings toward an entire out-group.

Social Identity

This brief review of research on contact effects suggests that cross-race contact under certain conditions can establish peer group norms that support a multicultural worldview. Therefore, youth who identify with peer groups whose norms support such a worldview will themselves endorse a multicultural worldview and will come to hold such attitudes even more strongly over time. Research conducted within the social identity framework has essentially come to this same conclusion, complementing the work done on contact effects. An examination of the previously described common ingroup identity model surveyed Jewish American high school students attending a 5-week educational summer program in Israel (Horenczyk & Bekerman, 1997). Students and their Israeli peers participated in structured activities designed explicitly to create a sense of common identity between the two groups. Study participants were divided between those who had already participated in these activities and those who had not. Whereas simply visiting Israel had no impact on American adolescents' in-group attitudes, those who had participated in the structured activities showed more positive change toward their Jewish Israeli peers (i.e., the out-group). Only this group of American adolescents perceived their Israeli peers as more similar to themselves and as having more positive personal characteristics, as social identity theory would predict. The structured activity apparently prompted the Jewish American youth to recategorize themselves with this former out-group into a superordinate group of familiar adolescents.

Research in a multiethnic high school has also provided support for the relationship between in-group identity and a multicultural worldview (Gaertner, Rust, Dovidio, Bachman, & Anastasio, 1994). Surveys administered to students from a variety of ethnic and racial groups (African American, Korean, Japanese, Chinese, Latino, and White) measured several perceptions of school climate, including perceived equal status treatment, group interdependence, and intergroup relations. As well, students reported the extent to which they perceived the school community as a single group working toward a common goal, several groups working together as a team, separate groups working apart, or a collection of individuals. The investigators hypothesized that the first two options represented different types of a superordinate group identity. Finally, students reported their overall attitude toward each of the ethnic and racial groups represented at the school. As predicted by the model, the greater the perception of peers as a single group (regardless of ethnicity) or several groups working on the same team, the more positive were attitudes toward members of other groups.

These studies are representative of a much larger body of research in social psychology that has been able to blend the social identity perspective and the contact hypothesis to provide clarity to our understanding of the associations between peer and intergroup relations and a multicultural worldview. However, our initial definition of a multicultural worldview included a positive attitude toward one's own group, and one might wonder how attitudes toward self might enhance this substantial body of knowledge on intergroup attitudes. This review will now turn to an examination of evidence that speaks to the ways in which attitudes toward one's own group, defined for our purposes as one's ethnic identity, can influence peer relationships, intergroup understanding, and a multicultural worldview.

Ethnic Identity

Recall that stage models of ethnic identity posit that a secure, positive sense of membership with an ethnic group will be accompanied by a more positive acceptance of other ethnic groups. However, the role that group processes or peer influences play in this relationship is not very clear. Research on ethnic identity in multiethnic schools can provide some tantalizing insights.

Much work has been done on group relations in ethnically diverse schools, and some research has examined the role of ethnic identity in group relations. Hamm and Coleman (2001) examined cross-ethnic peer relations and ethnic identity for African American and White high school students in predominately White schools. Students responded to a variety of survey items, including the kinds of things they did together with peers of other races (e.g., see a movie), the racial or ethnic background of their closest friends (as many as they wished to name), their attitudes toward cross-ethnic interactions, and their sense of belonging and commitment to their ethnic group (i.e., their ethnic identity). All students who enjoyed more cross-ethnic friendships and African American students who had a more committed ethnic identity held more positive attitudes toward cross-ethnic interactions; however, analyses did not explicitly test the combination of friendship group and ethnic identity on multicultural attitudes. The authors speculated that ethnic identity might be less salient and therefore less meaningful for White adolescents than for African American adolescents in a predominantly White school context and thus has little impact on a multicultural worldview.

Research in more ethnically diverse schools has also examined links between ethnic identity, cross-ethnic interaction, and multicultural attitudes. An examination of in-group attitudes, ethnic identity, and out-group attitudes (Phinney, Ferguson, & Tate, 1997) measured high school students' (African American, Asian, and Latino) attitudes toward their in-group peers, frequency of interactions with and attitudes toward other-race peers, and ethnic identity. Using causal modeling techniques, the authors found three distinct pathways that influenced multicultural attitudes. Ethnic identity positively influenced attitudes toward one's in-group, and these attitudes influenced out-group attitudes. Thus, ethnic identity influenced out-group attitudes only indirectly through in-group attitudes. As well, frequency of interactions with other-race peers influenced out-group attitudes, and out-group interactions showed an interaction effect with in-group attitudes. Higher levels of cross-ethnic peer interaction led to the most positive cross-ethnic attitudes for those with the most positive in-group attitudes. As ethnic identity was a causal predictor of in-group attitudes, these data suggest that adolescents with the most positive ethnic identity and the most culturally diverse peer groups also had the most positive multicultural worldview.

However, recall that ethnic identity can take on a decidedly negative tone in the case of oppositional identity. Empirical investigations of oppositional identity, typified by Fordham and Ogbu's (1986) seminal study of low-income African American high school students, reveal that an oppositional ethnic identity born out of a sense of alienation from the larger society is antithetical to a multicultural worldview and supported by powerful peer norms. Youth who maintain this kind of ethnic identity typically perceive themselves as having no place in the larger, White-dominated society (Irving & Hudley, 2005). Fordham and Ogbu found that, in an effort to protect their sense of themselves, some low-income, low-achieving African American students rejected involvement in academic and other school activities and defined themselves as the opposite of attitudes and behaviors that they perceived to be representative of White society. Rather than a multicultural worldview, these youth with an oppositional identity aligned themselves with a similar peer group that typically was exclusively African American. Fordham and Ogbu, using ethnographic data that included sustained observations and in-depth interviews, demonstrated that high-achieving African American students were accused of "acting White" and challenged by their peers to conform to peer norms that supported an ethnic-specific worldview and an oppositional ethnic identity.

CONCLUSION

This review has taken up the question of peer influence in the development and maintenance of a multicultural worldview. Although there is relatively little theoretical and empirical literature specifically on peer relations and multicultural beliefs, there is a broad theoretical and empirical literature on intergroup relations that bears directly on this question. This review draws attention to the theoretical maturity of the field. The various perspectives in social psychology (social identity and the contact hypothesis) have become progressively more complex, both independently and as a more comprehensive and unified social psychological explanation for the phenomenon of intergroup relations. Researchers have developed reciprocal linkages between the two traditions to better understand the group processes that lead to positive or negative intergroup attitudes and interactions. The expanded contact hypothesis and the common ingroup identity model are but two of the several developments that have brought theoretical order to this rapidly exploding field, and both models speak to the importance of the peer group and exposure to diverse peers in developing and sustaining a multicultural worldview. As well, both in-group affiliation and ethnic identity development are strongly implicated in the development and maintenance of a multicultural worldview, and both are heavily influenced by peer interactions and peer norms. In sum, the evidence leaves little room for doubt that peers have a great deal to say about a child's worldview through a complex network of norms and social influence. Parents, educators, and researchers will do well to take note of the strength of peer influence as we all struggle to develop strategies to strengthen cross-ethnic peer relations throughout the life span.

REFERENCES

Aboud, F., & Doyle, A. (1996a). Does talk of race foster prejudice or tolerance in children? *Canadian Journal of Behavioural Science, 28,* 161–170.

Aboud, F., & Doyle, A. (1996b). Parental and peer influences on children's racial attitudes. *International Journal of Intercultural Relations, 20,* 371–383.

Aboud, F., Mendelson, M., & Purdy, K. (2003). Cross-race peer relations and friendship quality. *International Journal of Behavioral Development, 27,* 165–173.

Alba, R. (1990). *Ethnic identity: The transformation of White America.* New Haven, CT: Yale University Press.

Allport, G. W. (1954). *The nature of prejudice.* Reading, MA: Addison-Wesley.

Atkinson, D., Morten, G., & Sue, D. (1983). *Counseling American minorities.* Dubuque, IA: W. C. Brown.

Banks, J., & Banks, C. (2004). *Handbook of research on multicultural education* (2nd ed.). San Francisco: Jossey-Bass.

Berndt, T. J. (1982). The features and effects of friendship in early adolescence. *Child Development, 53,* 1447–1460.

Brown, R., & Hewstone, M. (2005). An integrative theory of intergroup contact. *Advances in Experimental Social Psychology, 37,* 255–343.

Coleman, H. (1995). Strategies for coping with cultural diversity. *Counseling Psychologist, 23,* 722–740.

Cross, W. (1991). *Shades of black: Diversity in African-American identity.* Philadelphia: Temple University Press.

Dovidio, J., & Gaertner, S. (1999). Reducing prejudice: Combating intergroup biases. *Current Directions in Psychological Science, 8,* 101–105.

Fordham, S., & Ogbu, J. (1986). Black students' school success: Coping with the "burden of 'acting white.'" *Urban Review, 18,* 176–206.

Gaertner, S., Rust, M., Dovidio, J., Bachman, B., & Anastasio, P. (1994). The contact hypothesis: The role of a common ingroup identity on reducing intergroup bias. *Small Group Research, 25,* 224–249.

Hamm, J., & Coleman, H. (2001). African American and White adolescents' strategies for managing cultural diversity in predominantly White high schools. *Journal of Youth and Adolescence, 30,* 281–303.

Harris, J. (1995). Where is the child's environment? A group socialization theory of development. *Psychological Review, 102,* 458–489.

Helms, J. E. (1995). An update of Helms's White and people of color racial identity models. In J. G. Ponterotto, J. M. Casas, L. A. Suzuki, & C. M. Alexander (Eds.), *Handbook of multicultural counseling* (pp. 181–198). Thousand Oaks, CA: Sage.

Hewstone, M., Rubin, M., & Willis, H. (2002). Intergroup bias. *Annual Review of Psychology, 53,* 575–604.

Horenczyk, G., & Bekerman, Z. (1997). The effects of intercultural acquaintance and structured intergroup interaction on ingroup, outgroup, and reflected ingroup stereotypes. *International Journal of Intercultural Relations, 21,* 71–83.

Hudley, C., & Taylor, A. (2006). Cultural competence and youth violence prevention programming. In N. Guerra & E. Smith (Eds.), *Ethnicity, culture, and youth violence prevention programming* (pp. 249–269). Washington, DC: APA.

Irving, M., & Hudley, C. (2005). Cultural mistrust, academic outcome expectations and outcome values among African American adolescent men. *Urban Education, 40,* 476–496.

Kandel, D. (1978). Homophily, selection and socialization in adolescent friendships. *American Journal of Sociology, 84,* 427–436.

Kiesner, J., Maass, A., Cadinu, M., & Vallese, I. (2003). Risk factors for ethnic prejudice during early adolescence. *Social Development, 12,* 288–308.

Ladd, G. (1999). Peer relationships and social competence during early and middle childhood. *Annual Review of Psychology, 50,* 333–359.

Ogbu, J. (1983). Minority status and schooling in plural societies. *Comparative Education Review, 27,* 168–190.

Parham, T. (1989). Cycles of psychological nigrescence. *The Counseling Psychologist, 17,* 187–226.

Patchen, M. (1982). *Black-White contact in schools: Its social and academic effects.* West Layfayette, IN: Purdue University Press.

Peshkin, A. (1991). *The color of strangers the color of friends: The play of ethnicity in school and community.* Chicago: University of Chicago Press.

Pettigrew, T. (1998). Intergroup contact theory. *Annual Review of Psychology, 49,* 65–85.

Pettigrew, T., & Tropp, L. (2006). A meta-analytic test of intergroup contact theory. *Journal of Personality and Social Psychology, 90,* 751–783.

Phinney, J. (1990). Ethnic identity in adolescents and adults: Review of research. *Psychological Bulletin, 108,* 499–514.

Phinney J., Ferguson, D., & Tate, J. (1997). Intergroup attitudes among ethnic minority adolescents: A causal model. *Child Development, 68,* 955–969.

Pope-Davis, D., & Coleman, H. (1997). *Multicultural counseling competencies: Assessment, education and training, and supervision.* Thousand Oaks, CA: Sage.

Ritchey, P. N., & Fishbein, H. (2001). The lack of an association between adolescent friends' prejudices and stereotypes. *Merrill-Palmer Quarterly, 47,* 88–206.

Stephan, W., & Stephan, C. (2001). *Improving intergroup relations.* Thousand Oaks, CA: Sage.

Sue, D. W. (2001). Multidimensional facets of cultural competence. *The Counseling Psychologist, 29,* 790–821.

Tajfel, H. (1981). *Human groups and social categories.* Cambridge, UK: Cambridge University Press.

Tajfel, H., & Turner, J. C. (1986). The social identity theory of intergroup behavior. In W. G. Austin & S. Worchel (Eds.), *The social psychology of intergroup relations* (2nd ed., pp. 7–24). Chicago: Nelson-Hall.

Turner, J. C., Hogg, M., Oakes, P., Reicher, S., & Wetherell, M. (1987). *Rediscovering the social group: A self-categorization theory.* Cambridge, MA: Basil Blackwell.

Wakefield, W. D., & Hudley, C. (2007). Ethnic and racial identity and adolescent well-being. *Theory Into Practice, 46,* 147–154.

Watson, G. (1947). *Action for unity.* New York: Harper.

Wright, S. C., Aron, A., McLaughlin-Volpe, T., & Ropp, S. (1997). The extended contact effect: Knowledge of cross-group friendships and prejudice. *Journal of Personality and Social Psychology, 73,* 73–90.

Youniss, J. (1980). *Parents and peers in social development: A Sullivan-Piaget perspective.* Chicago: University of Chicago Press.

Part III

Media and the Development of a Child's Multicultural Worldview

Children today can press a button and instantly become a part of a multimedia and multicultural set of experiences that provide images of ethnic, religious, gender, class, and lifestyles from around the corner where they live to around the world. Part III of the *Handbook* concentrates on these influential multimedia forms and their associated learning experiences by exploring how they influence the multicultural worldview of children and youth.

Dana Mastro and Michelle Ortiz begin Part III of this volume with an overview of the theories that underlie research on the effects of media exposure on intergroup attitudes, beliefs, and behaviors. The theories reviewed include cultivation theory, drench hypothesis, social cognitive theory, social identity theory, framing and priming, parasocial contact, and uses and gratifications.

The next chapter focuses on the most long-standing of media forms—print medium. Clint Wilson and Mary Wilson assess children's exposure to multicultural messages in books, newspapers, and magazines. Each of these types of print medium are faced with challenges such as the decline in publishing new children's multicultural books, newspaper advertising that targets purchasing decisions over multicultural sensitivity, and magazines that are intended more to entertain than educate.

Sherryl Browne Graves, Jeffrey Brand, and Venita Kelley have contributed chapters that focus on children and television. Presented are chapters on programming, advertisements and commercials, and news broadcasting, respectively, and how these different forms of television exposure may contribute to children's development of multicultural attitudes and beliefs. The influence of another visual media form, cinema, is presented by Jannette Dates, Lillie Fears, and Josephine Stedman. In their chapter, they provide findings from an investigation that explores the relevance of race and/or gender to perceptions of movie characters, using an older adolescent population.

Music plays an important role in the lives of young people, particularly youth. Peter Christenson and Tom ter Bogt, and Khia Thomas, Kyla Day, and L. Monique Ward, focus on this genre of entertainment; the former chapter focuses on popular music consumption from an international perspective and the latter on music videos and socioemotional development.

Whereas Khia Thomas and colleagues focused on music videos for entertainment value, Dorothy Singer, Jerome Singer, and Harvey Bellin used videos and DVDs to prepare children from underresourced communities for school. Their chapter presents the findings from their investigation of imaginative games and emergent literacy skills.

There is nothing more 21st century than the digitally mediated environments to which we have access. Computers, interactive games, and the Internet—the "information superhighway"—provide rich opportunities for enhancing the multicultural education and development of children. But both the chapters by Adrienne Shaw and Deborah Linebarger, and Edward Palmer and Jennifer Tuttle, argue for the need to address the digital divide by institutionalizing the use of these media forms so children from all walks of life, nationally and globally, have access to their use.

Part III of the *Handbook* ends with a chapter by Darnell Hunt and Angela James in which they make a case for not only considering the "meaning" intended by those producing the media content but also taking into account the meaning children make of their mediated encounters in the design and execution of research on children and media. These contributors believe that such a research approach allows for a more authentic understanding of the intersection of child development, multiculturalism, and media.

CHAPTER 13

Media and Communication Theories

Implications for a Multicultural Perspective

DANA MASTRO

MICHELLE ORTIZ

Theories investigating the effects of media exposure on intergroup attitudes, beliefs, and behaviors posit that media content becomes incorporated into individuals' cognitions about race/ethnicity, ultimately shaping perceptions about these groups (Berry & Mitchell-Kernan, 1982; Harwood & Roy, 2005). Research on child development suggests that these outcomes are not limited to adult consumers. Indeed, children are able to visually differentiate between different groups based on race/ethnicity about the time of their first birthday (Fagot & Leinbach, 1991). By ages 3–4, they can sort themselves and others based on those categories (Aboud, 1988; Lovelace, Scheiner, Dollberg, Segui, & Black, 1994; McKown & Weinstein, 2003). By approximately 5–6 years of age, they are knowledgeable about the observable, concrete aspects of racial stereotypes (Aboud, 1988; Brown & Bigler, 2005). Although these early developments focus primarily on distinguishing among physical features, by the time they reach the age of 10, children develop an awareness and understanding of the intangible qualities associated with race, including more abstract stereotype-based constructs and discrimination (Brown & Bigler, 2005). Thus, during their elementary school years, children come to understand that the status of different racial/ethnic groups is linked to the stereotypes associated with these groups (Brown & Bigler, 2005).

Accordingly, it would be expected that alongside family members, teachers, and peers, media consumption would play a role in this process (Bar-Tal, 1996). However, scant empirical research exists that specifically addresses the relationship between children's media exposure and issues of race, ethnicity, and multiculturalism. The present chapter addresses this issue by identifying the central assumptions offered from the key media and intergroup theories, as these form much of our knowledge base in this domain. Although research on depictions of race, media effects, and media use are addressed in greater detail elsewhere in this volume, we begin by identifying overarching portrayals of race/ethnicity in the media as well as children's media consumption patterns and preferences in order to provide greater insights into the theoretically derived associations between media use and interracial outcomes.

MEDIA PORTRAYALS AND USAGE PATTERNS

In documenting media consumption rates and images of race/ethnicity in the media, focus is centered on African Americans, Asian Americans, Latinos, Native Americans, and Whites, as these groups constitute the majority of the population in the United States (U.S. Census Bureau, 2000).

Media Images

Whether looking at prime-time television programming (Children Now, 2004; Mastro & Behm-Morawitz, 2005), commercials (Coltrane & Messineo, 2000; Mastro & Stern, 2003), movies (Kelly & Smith, 2006), video games (Glaubke, Miller, Parker, & Espejo, 2001), or even children's programming (Dobrow & Gidney, 1998), the offerings provided in the media have historically been inequitable when it comes to the frequency of racial/ethnic representations. U.S. Census Bureau (2000) data indicate that among adults, Whites constitute approximately 69% of the U.S. population, Latinos 13%, African Americans 12%, Asian Americans 4%, and Native Americans 1%. Yet, the racial/ethnic distribution in the media is far from representative of these figures. In particular, White characters greatly outnumber both their mediated racial/ethnic counterparts as well as their proportion of the real-world population. Alternatively, Latinos appear at a rate well below that of their proportion of the population, at least on television (Children Now, 2004; Mastro & Behm-Morawitz, 2005). Notably, parity is found when looking at depictions of African Americans on television (who appear at a rate equivalent to their proportion of the population); however, Asian American characters are rarely depicted and Native American characters are nearly entirely absent from the television landscape (Children Now, 2004).

The racial/ethnic distribution in the U.S. population varies somewhat based on age. When looking at children and youth, Whites constitute approximately 65% of the U.S. population, Latinos 16%, African Americans 15%, Asian Americans 4%, and Native Americans 1%. This distribution is not paralleled in programming designed for children. Here, Whites dominate; appearing at a rate that greatly exceeds real-world figures (Dobrow & Gidney, 1998; Graves, 1996; Greenberg & Brand, 1993). Moreover, these characters rarely interact with members of different racial/ethnic groups (Weigel & Howes, 1982). Notably, when looking beyond children's programming to considerations of what children actually report watching, a different picture emerges. Although White characters remain in the majority (55%), they appear at a rate below their proportion of the U.S. population (Borzekowski & Poussaint, 1998). Conversely, African Americans exceed their percentage of the population, composing 32% of characters in these shows. However, Latinos lag far behind census reports at 3.2% and Asian Americans appear somewhat below their proportion of the population at 2.7% of characters in the programming watched most by children.

Despite imbalances in the frequency of racial/ethnic representations in the media, some notable advances have been revealed when it comes to the manner in which different groups are depicted (Glaubke et al., 2001; Kelly & Smith, 2006; Mastro & Behm-Morawitz, 2005). These improvements vary, however, based on the character's race/ethnicity, the medium, and the genre. To illustrate, images of African Americans in entertainment media have positively changed over time (Greenberg, Mastro, & Brand, 2002). The same cannot be said of their portrayal on television news (Dixon & Linz, 2000a, 2000b). Similarly, Latino characterizations have begun to deviate from many of the long-standing stereotypes that have traditionally been associated with this group (e.g., criminal), but Latinos regularly remain in inauspicious and unflattering roles compared with their peers (Harwood & Anderson, 2002; Mastro & Behm-Morawitz, 2005). Media depictions of Asian Americans and Native Americans are so uncommon that few conclusions can be drawn about the attributes typically associated with these groups.

Children's Media Use

Television sets can be found in nearly every household in the United States and in the bedrooms of a majority of U.S. children (Roberts, Foehr, & Rideout, 2005). Not surprisingly, then, children consume an average of over 4 hours of screen media (i.e., TV, videos/DVDs, and movies) per day (Roberts et al., 2005). However, viewing patterns vary based on the race/ethnicity of the child, with Whites consuming among the lowest levels of screen media (at approximately 3¾ hours per day) and African Americans the highest (at roughly 6 hours). Latino children fall between these two groups at about 4½ hours per day. In addition to increased levels of screen media consumption, African American children report higher levels of video game play than their peers (Roberts et al., 2005). On average, African Americans play 1½ hours of computer and console-based video games per day, whereas White and Latino children spend approximately an hour engaged in video game play.

THEORETICAL FRAMEWORKS

When the predominant theories of media effects and intergroup processing are considered alongside information regarding children's media usage patterns and images of race/ethnicity in the media, the potential influence of exposure on children's race-related cognitions and behaviors is underscored. Taken together, these theories suggest that the features of media content as well as the characteristics of child viewers each play a role in determining the outcomes associated with exposure. In particular, (a) what and how much media children consume, (b) the frequency and nature of representations of race/ethnicity in these media offerings, and (c) the child's own racial/ethnic identification and background all contribute to the complex relationship between children's media exposure and issues of race/ethnicity. The unique contributions of each of the most pertinent theories follow.

Cultivation Theory

Cultivation theory is concerned with the long-term, aggregate effects of media exposure on consumers' perceptions of reality; proposing that much of what people know comes from the stories they see on television (Gerbner, Gross, Morgan, & Signorielli, 1980; Shanahan & Morgan, 1999). From this perspective, television is a socializing agent that provides viewers with repeated, consistent messages that convey a largely homogenized conceptualization of reality (Morgan & Signorielli, 1990; Signorielli & Morgan, 1996). Through time and continuous exposure, viewers incorporate the thematic messages seen on television into their perceptions about the world (Signorielli & Morgan). In other words, cultivation theory emphasizes outcomes associated with overall exposure to the repetitive system of messages presented on television.

As theorizing in the area has progressed, greater emphasis has been directed at variations in cultivation effects based on amount of exposure to the different types of programs and genres viewers select for consumption (Cohen & Weimann, 2000; Hawkins & Pingree, 1981; Potter & Chang, 1990).

Ultimately, exposure (overall or genre specific) then influences perceptions about the tangible features of the world such as the number of different racial/ethnic groups in society (i.e., first-order effects), as well as the value placed on different social phenomena (i.e., second-order effects), such as beliefs about the status of different ethnic groups (Hawkins & Pingree, 1990; Potter, 1988, 1991).

Given this emphasis on sheer amount of exposure, the effects of consumption are expected to be most pronounced among (a) heavy, as opposed to light, viewers and (b) viewers whose real-world experiences are reflected in the thematic messages presented on television (Gerbner et al., 1980; Morgan & Signorielli, 1990). For White viewers, then, what research has revealed is that increased consumption of thematic, stereotypic messages about racial/ethnic groups is associated with the development of real-world racial stereotypes, particularly among viewers with limited real-world knowledge that may mitigate the influence of exposure (Mastro, Behm-Morawitz, & Ortiz, 2007). Genre-specific cultivation effects also have been demonstrated in terms of children's race-related belief systems. Zuckerman, Singer, and Singer (1980) found that increased exposure to violent television dramas among children was associated with stereotypic beliefs about African Americans' competence and aggressiveness. Alternatively, increased exposure to programs featuring African American characters was associated with elevated beliefs in African Americans' unique athletic prowess.

Drench Hypothesis

Whereas cultivation theory proposes a gradual effect of media on viewers' perceptions, the drench hypothesis (Greenberg, 1988) purports that certain media messages can have a dramatic, immediate impact on viewers. According to this hypothesis, exposure to even a single character can have a powerful and instant effect on viewers, under certain conditions (Greenberg, 1988). In particular, Greenberg submits that strong and significant characters may be more salient and thus better remembered by viewers. As a result, these characters may have a greater influence on the subsequent attitudes and perceptions of consumers (Reep & Dambrot, 1989). Therefore, the number of images of race/ethnicity and the race-related themes in content are secondary to the existence of meaningful and substantive representations of different groups. Notably, research in this area indicates that exposure to these commanding characters is mediated by the perceived realism of the message, identification with the character, and involvement with the message (Bahk, 2001).

Applied to consumption of media portrayals of underrepresented groups, the drench hypothesis predicts that exposure to a single representation can lead to attitudinal changes among viewers. For instance, research demonstrates that viewing a positive, meaningful portrayal of an underrepresented group member can lead to improved attitudes about that group among out-group members (e.g., Schiappa, Gregg, & Hewes, 2005). Moreover, the portrayal may lead to more positive evaluations of self among in-group members (Greenberg, 1988).

Of course, for child viewers, the potentially favorable outcomes associated with exposure to prominent representations of race/ethnicity depend on children's ability to classify the character as a member of an ethnic group and on their ability to adopt the perspective of the character, both of which develop by the age of 6 (Aboud, 1988; Brown & Bigler, 2005). In fact, research supports this association. After viewing scenes from *Sesame Street* with racial/ethnic minority children as leading characters, children report an increased eagerness to choose minority playmates (Gorn, Goldberg, & Kanungo, 1976) and increased interest in playing with a Black Barbie doll (Fisch, Truglio, & Cole, 1999).

Social Cognitive Theory

According to social cognitive theory, humans have the unique ability to learn from indirect experiences (Bandura, 2002), including from exposure to mass media. This vicarious capability allows humans to acquire cognitive, affective, and behavioral information from numerous situations that they might not otherwise experience. Individuals may then enact the learned behaviors if presented with the appropriate context (Bandura, 2002). Bandura notes that televised models are of particular import within the social cognitive model due to the tremendous volume of consumers that these messages reach. Thus, as a result of television's ubiquitous nature, one character can impact countless viewers across the country and around the world.

Bandura (2002) identifies four mechanisms that govern the process of learning from the media. The first involves attention. This entails the extent to which viewers attend to media messages, as influenced by a variety of content-based and consumer-based characteristics. The second process focuses on retention of the observed event. Exposure to a message is meaningless if it is not retained for future use. Once the message has been cognitively stored, the behavior must be refined based on feedback. This is known as the production process. The final process, that of motivation, addresses incentives to reproduce the learned behavior. Viewers certainly do not reproduce every behavior they learn from the media. Instead, actions acquired from the media are replicated when a reward is associated with the behavior. On the other hand, viewers are discouraged from reproducing a behavior if they perceive that negative consequences will be linked with the enactment.

Children's cognitive development affects each subprocess within this social learning model. For example, younger children may lack the ability to derive more sophisticated inferences from media content. Moreover, they may be unable to draw connections between the behaviors and beliefs of media models—an ability that develops around the age of 6 (Brown & Bigler, 2005; Flavell, 1992). Older children, however, should be more capable of appropriately and successfully modeling behaviors acquired from the media, as they possess the perspective-taking ability required to understand how characters' behaviors are associated with the rewards or punishments they attain.

In addition, although the media landscape affords child viewers with numerous models whose behaviors they can emulate, they nonetheless gain vicarious experience from certain characters over others (Bandura, 1977). As the social cognitive model explains, viewers are more likely to be motivated to reproduce behaviors if they perceive themselves to be similar to the model (Bandura, 2002). When viewers believe they are like the models they see in the media, they are more apt to vicariously experience the character's behaviors (Eyal & Rubin, 2003), hence facilitating their enactment of the modeled act under appropriate conditions. Given these conditions, each image of race/ethnicity gains increasing importance as children (racial/ethnic minority children in particular) may concentrate on these models due to their infrequency compared with White characters.

Social Identity Theory

According to social identity theory (Tajfel & Turner, 1979), individuals' self-concept is derived in part from their group memberships. Because these categories play an important role in self-evaluation, individuals use group comparisons in attempts to provide a comparative advantage for their in-group. That is, if the group is perceived as having a privileged status, then the positive distinctiveness associated with the group also will be associated with the individual. Alternatively, if the group is perceived as having a disadvantaged status, then the individual is also perceived as having a disadvantaged status (Abrams & Hogg, 1990). When perceiving others in terms of group memberships, individuals minimize differences between the self and the in-group and maximize differences between the in-group and the out-group, resulting in stereotypic evaluations of out-groups.

Individuals' social identities do not only come into play in real-world settings, they also may affect mediated intergroup interactions. Specifically, viewers' social identities have been found to influence individuals' selection of media messages (Harwood, 1997, 1999) as well as their evaluation of such messages (Harwood & Roy, 2005; Mastro, 2003). In particular, research demonstrates that individuals prefer media messages that serve positive social identity needs (Harwood, 1997, 1999). For example, media use can serve to advance cultural socialization (Greenberg & Atkin, 1982; Stillig, 1997) or to strengthen identification with one's culture of origin. As research demonstrates, ethnic media (i.e., media emphasizing portrayals of one's group) is used in the process of cultural maintenance, as it helps ethnic groups preserve cultural ties (Jeffres, 2000; Ríos & Gaines, 1999).

Alongside the quality of the message, the number of representations of one's in-group also may influence social identity. Data indicate that the sheer number of images in the media affects perceptions of group vitality, such that the absence of portrayals of one's in-group could result in reduced group vitality (Abrams, Eveland, & Giles, 2003; Harwood & Roy, 2005). Thus, both absence from representation in the media and negative representations in the media may have detrimental effects on in-group self-concept (Greenberg & Atkin, 1982; Fryberg, 2003).

Children's cognitive development dictates the extent to which they will engage in such categorization and social comparison processes. Although preschool-age children typically have developed the ability to classify themselves and others based on race/ethnicity, more sophisticated classification skills do not emerge until around age 7 (Inhelder & Piaget, 1964). At that time, children are able to organize objects into multiple, superordinate categories. This ability is meaningful as it may be associated with decreased stereotyping among children (Bigler & Liben, 1992) and with increased likelihood of attributing others' racially driven behaviors to discrimination (Brown & Bigler, 2005). Thus, images of race/ethnicity in the media are meaningful as they may contribute to children's perceptions about the attributes associated with their in-group as well as beliefs about how others perceive their group.

Framing and Priming

Framing refers to the conceptualization of reality that media create when presenting stories for viewers (Entman, 1993). Specifically, frames place attention on a given social phenomenon, attribute blame for the issue, make judgments regarding the causes of the issue, and offer solutions to the problem (Entman, 1993). By focusing on certain aspects of a message, frames make these characteristics salient in the mind of the receiver (Entman, 1993; Tankard, Hendrickson, Silberman, Bliss, & Ghanem, 1991), affecting later evaluations (Bargh, Bond, Lombardi, & Tota, 1986). In other words, exposure to messages presented in the media primes those constructs, temporarily increasing their accessibility for use in processing subsequent information. From this perspective, importance is not just given to what is presented, but also to what is absent (Entman, 1993) as the inclusion and exclusion of information provides a context for interpreting the issue (Tankard et al., 1991). Thus, the media dictates how the audience will process information about an issue.

This relationship gains increasing consequence when findings regarding depictions of race/ethnicity in the news are considered. Not only do content analyses indicate that local television news stories tend to be reported from a "White perspective" and to overrepresent minorities in stories about crime (Poindexter, Smith, & Heider, 2003, p. 534), but they additionally reveal that African Americans and Latinos are less likely than Whites to be depicted as victims of crime (Dixon & Linz, 2000a) and more likely than Whites to be portrayed as lawbreakers in news stories (Dixon & Linz, 2000b). It would be expected, then, that exposure to such images in the news would influence audience members' subsequent race-based evaluations. Indeed, research repeatedly demonstrates that priming negative racial/ethnic stereotypes in the minds of viewers increases the likelihood of their use in later evaluations (Hansen & Hansen, 1988), resulting in unfavorable evaluations of the racial/ethnic group (Devine, 1989; Power, Murphy, & Coover, 1996). In terms of the implications for our multicultural society, what the research on framing and priming underscores is the need for positive images of race/ethnicity in the media as these images influence viewer's perceptions of and judgments about racial/ethnic groups in society (Gandy, 1996; Poindexter et al., 2003).

Parasocial Contact

Intergroup contact, as identified by Allport (1954), can be an effective mechanism for the development of more favorable attitudes toward out-groups. In particular, the contact hypothesis stipulates that positive contact between members of different groups (e.g., racial, ethnic) can lead to positive changes in attitudes toward out-group members (i.e., reduced prejudice). According to Allport, for positive outcomes to result, the intergroup contact setting must meet several essential conditions, including equal status and shared common goals between the individuals (Allport, 1954; Gaertner & Dovidio, 2000). If these conditions are not satisfied, then the contact experience may not produce positive results. The parasocial contact hypothesis extends the contact hypothesis, applying it to interactions involving media characters. Specifically, through parasocial interaction, viewers can interact with minority group members and develop relationships that may serve to improve viewers' attitudes toward the out-group (Schiappa et al., 2005).

Parasocial interaction refers to the relationships that individuals develop with media personalities (e.g., characters). Such mediated relationships model actual face-to-face interactions (Horton & Wohl, 1956), leading to perceptions among viewers that the character is a part of his or her peer group (Levy, 1979). This bond with the character is formed in part from the perception of shared experiences with the character (Horton & Wohl, 1956), and in time, the viewer generates affective bonds with the character (Levy, 1979).

Thus, the parasocial contact hypothesis holds that if parasocial relationships are comparable to real relationships, then the relationships that viewers form with out-group characters should lead to attitude changes paralleling those emergent from real-world intergroup interactions (Schiappa et al., 2005). However, in order for mediated intergroup contact to generalize to the entire out-group, the out-group character must be perceived as representative of his or her group (Hewstone & Brown, 1986). That is, if the character is not perceived to be typical of the group, then the positive effects of the intergroup contact situation will not generalize to the out-group as a whole. In other words, for positive attitude changes to be applied to the entire out-group and not just the out-group character, the character must be deemed archetypical of the group.

Ultimately, the parasocial contact hypothesis stipulates that exposure to a single television character can lead to improved attitudes toward the out-group among viewers (Schiappa et al., 2005). However, this character must be appealing enough to encourage the development of a parasocial relationship. For child viewers, this will require the existence of media characters with whom to identify as well as the appropriate level of cognitive development.

Uses and Gratifications

Unlike most of the theories discussed to this point, which focus on how media affects individuals, the uses and gratifications (U&G) framework addresses how individuals use the media. Specifically, the U&G framework argues that audiences actively seek out media in a goal-directed way that provides them with the means of gratifying a wide variety of needs. Thus, the framework tries to understand the motivations behind individuals' media behavior (Katz, Blumler, & Gurevitch, 1974; Palmgreen, Wenner, & Rosengren, 1985; Rubin, 2002).

Although the U&G framework initially centered on media gratifications sought at the individual level (e.g., Rubin, 1983), recent applications have addressed its role with regard to intergroup outcomes (Harwood, 1997, 1999; Yang, Wu, Zhu, & Southwell, 2004). For instance, Yang et al. found that media are sought to provide gratifications dealing with acculturation; specifically, immigrants attend to mass media to learn about the host country. Among Latinos, for example, less acculturated women report higher levels of English language television consumption to learn the language and to gain knowledge about life in the United States (Johnson, 1996). In addition, research by Harwood demonstrates that individuals seek media messages that provide social identity gratifications such as maintaining and bolstering social identities.

For children to obtain race-based needs gratifications from media, they must first be able to categorize themselves and others by race/ethnicity, such that they can identify which characters belong to their racial/ethnic in-group and which do not. This ability develops by age 6 (Aboud, 1988). By this time, children should be capable of deriving racial/ethnic identity-based gratifications from the media.

CONCLUSION

The crux of the existing research on issues of media, children, and race/ethnicity has focused on documenting portrayals of children and race/ethnicity on television and on children's use of mass media. Indeed, these studies reveal that prime-time, commercial, news, and children's programming, as well as film and video games, each paint a different picture of race/ethnicity in the United States. However, questions regarding whether child viewers are more likely to be affected by one genre (or medium) than another and how these effects influence real-world outcomes remain unanswered. For example, whereas African Americans compose a proportion of the television population comparable to that of their proportion of the United States, research indicates that they continue to be overrepresented as lawbreakers on television news. Unlike African Americans, Latinos and Asian Americans are underrepresented on television, and Native Americans are virtually missing from the media landscape. Yet, the consequences of television's demographic makeup on children's perceptions about themselves and about other ethnic groups are relatively unexplored.

As the assumptions of both cultivation theory and social identity theory tell us, the fact that Latinos, Asian Americans, and Native Americans are underrepresented in the media does not imply that viewers' perceptions and attitudes toward these groups won't be influenced. In fact, quite the opposite would be predicted. From a social identity perspective, presence in the media designates the relative strength and social standing of a group. Accordingly, invisibility would be expected to have a harmful effect on group status. Based on the postulates of cultivation theory, the number of images also would play a role in shaping viewers' perceptions about outcomes such as real-world demographics and possibly even appropriate roles for different racial/ethnic group members. Each of these are critical factors in shaping children's norms and expectations about society as well as their own, personal aspirations.

Of course, the manner in which different racial/ethnic groups are presented also is critical. As the drench hypothesis (Greenberg, 1988) suggests, even a single portrayal could meaningfully influence viewers' race-based cognitions. Assumptions based on the parasocial contact hypothesis (Schiappa et al., 2005) are consistent with this assertion, suggesting that exposure to an out-group character is enough to lead to more favorable attitudes toward the out-group as a whole. According to this hypothesis, viewers can form relationships with television characters that are analogous to the relationships one would form in the real world. Thus, building a meaningful, substantive relationship with a minority character can have a profound impact on a viewer.

Equally important, the tenets of social cognitive theory further suggest that children's media exposure to images of race/ethnicity may even teach children what they perceive to be appropriate and normative race-based attitudes and behaviors, shaping their real-world actions. Here, the number of images is seen as less consequential than the manner in which different racial/ethnic groups are depicted in the media.

Finally, given the importance of new media technologies (like the Internet and video games) in the lives of children, the impact of these outlets cannot be ignored. When considering that a majority of White, African American, and Latino children have Internet access at home (Roberts et al., 2005), it would be expected that this technology also would be actively used to communicate with and learn about other groups. For example, Tynes, Reynolds, and Greenfield (2004) found that adolescents communicate their ethnic identity in chat rooms in ways that dramatically differ from such expressions in face-to-face settings. It would be of interest to further investigate how children manage their identity through the sites they visit and determine the varying influences of different media outlets on this process.

This chapter looked at the predominant mass media theories relevant to the study of the impact of media messages on children's racial/ethnic identity development and their racial/ethnic cognitions and behaviors. Despite the myriad research opportunities revealed within and across these theoretical frameworks, it is clear that more comprehensive and systematic research in this domain is vital.

REFERENCES

Aboud, R. (1988). *Children and prejudice.* Oxford, UK: Blackwell.

Abrams, D., & Hogg, M. A. (1990). An introduction to the social identity approach. In D. Abrams & M. Hogg (Eds.), *Social identity theory: Constructive and critical advances* (pp. 1–9). Hemel Hempstead, UK: Harvester Wheatsheaf.

Abrams, J. R., Eveland, W. P., & Giles, H. (2003). The effects of television on group vitality: Can television empower nondominant groups? In P. Kalbfleisch (Ed.), *Communication yearbook 27* (pp. 193–219). Mahwah, NJ: Lawrence Erlbaum.

Allport, G. W. (1954). *The nature of prejudice.* New York: Addison-Wesley.

Bahk, C. M. (2001). Drench effects of media portrayal of fatal virus disease on health locus of control beliefs. *Health Communication, 13,* 187–204.

Bandura, A. (1977). *Social learning theory.* Englewood Cliffs, NJ: Prentice Hall.

Bandura, A. (2002). Social cognitive theory of mass communication. In J. Bryant & D. Zillmann (Eds.), *Media effects: Advances in theory and research* (pp. 121–154). Hillsdale, NJ: Lawrence Erlbaum.

Bargh, J. A., Bond, R. N., Lombardi, W. J., & Tota, M. E. (1986). The additive nature of chronic and temporary sources of construct accessibility. *Journal of Personality and Social Psychology, 50,* 869–878.

Bar-Tal, D. (1996). Development of social categories and stereotypes in early childhood: The case of "the Arab" concept formation, stereotype and attitudes by Jewish children in Israel. *International Journal of Intercultural Research, 20,* 341–370.

Berry, G., & Mitchell-Kernan, C. (1982). *Television and the socialization of the minority child.* New York: Academic Press.

Bigler, R. S., & Liben, L. S. (1992). Cognitive mechanisms in children's gender stereotyping: Theoretical and educational implications of a cognitive-based intervention. *Child Development, 63,* 1351–1363.

Borzekowski, D., & Poussaint, A. (1998). *Latino American preschoolers and the media* (The Annenberg Public Policy Center Report Series No. 24). Philadelphia: University of Pennsylvania.

Brown, C., & Bigler, R. (2005). Children's perceptions of discrimination: A developmental model. *Child Development, 76,* 533–553.

Children Now. (2004). *Fall colors, 2003–2004: Prime time diversity report.* Oakland, CA: Author.

Cohen, J., & Weimann, G. (2000). Cultivation revisited: Some genres have some effects on some viewers. *Communication Reports, 13,* 99–115.

Coltrane, S., & Messineo, M. (2000). The perpetuation of subtle prejudice: Race and gender imagery in 1990s television advertising. *Sex Roles, 42,* 363–389.

Devine, P. G. (1989). Stereotypes and prejudice: Their automatic and controlled components. *Journal of Personality and Social Psychology, 56,* 5–18.

Dixon, T., & Linz, D. (2000a). Overrepresentation and underrepresentation of African Americans and Latinos as lawbreakers on television news. *Journal of Communication, 50,* 131–154.

Dixon, T., & Linz, D. (2000b). Race and the misrepresentation of victimization on local television news. *Communication Research, 27,* 547–573.

Dobrow, J., & Gidney, C. (1998). The good, the bad, and the foreign: The use of dialect in children's animated television. In A. Jordan & K. Hall Jamieson (Eds.), *The annals of the American academy of political and social science: Children and television* (pp. 105–119). Thousand Oaks, CA: Sage.

Entman, R. M. (1993). Framing: Toward clarification of a fractured paradigm. *Journal of Communication, 43,* 51–58.

Eyal, K., & Rubin, A. M. (2003). Viewer aggression and homophily, identification, and parasocial relationships with television characters. *Journal of Broadcasting & Electronic Media, 47,* 77–98.

Fagot, B. I., & Leinbach, M. D. (1991). Gender-role development in young children: From discrimination to labeling. *Developmental Review, 13,* 205–224.

Fisch, S., Truglio, R., & Cole, C. (1999). The impact of *Sesame Street* on preschool children: A review and synthesis of 30 years' research. *Media Psychology, 1,* 165–190.

Flavell, J. H. (1992). Perspectives on perspective taking. In H. Beilin & P. Pufall (Eds.), *Piaget's theory: Prospects and possibilities* (pp. 107–140). Hillsdale, NJ: Erlbaum.

Fryberg, S. (2003). Really? You don't look like an American Indian: Social representations and social group identities. *Dissertation Abstracts International: Section B: The Sciences & Engineering.*

Gaertner, S., & Dovidio, J. (2000). *Reducing intergroup bias: The common ingroup identity model.* Hove, UK: Psychology Press.

Gandy, O. H., Jr. (1996). If it weren't for bad luck: Framing stories of racially comparative risk. In V. T. Berry & C. L. Manning-Miller (Eds.), *Mediated messages and African-American culture* (pp. 55–75). Thousand Oaks, CA: Sage.

Gerbner, G., Gross, L., Morgan, M., & Signorielli, N. (1980). The "mainstreaming" of America: Violence profile no. 11. *Journal of Communication, 30,* 212–231.

Glaubke, C., Miller, P., Parker, M., & Espejo, E. (2001). *Fair play? Violence, gender, and race in video games.* Oakland, CA: Children Now.

Gorn, G. J., Goldberg, M. E., & Kanungo, R. N. (1976). The role of educational television in changing the intergroup attitudes of children. *Child Development, 47,* 277–280.

Graves, S. B. (1996). Diversity on television. In T. M. MacBeth (Ed.), *Tuning in to young viewers: Social science perspectives on television.* (pp. 61–86). Thousand Oaks, CA: Sage.

Greenberg, B. (1988). Some uncommon television images and the drench hypothesis. In S. Oskamp (Ed.), *Applied social psychology annual: Television as a social issue* (Vol. 8, pp. 88–102). Newbury Park, CA: Sage.

Greenberg, B., & Atkin, C. (1982). Learning about minorities from television: A research agenda. In G. L. Berry & C. Mitchell-Kernan (Eds.), *Television and the socialization of the minority child* (pp. 215–243). New York: Academic Press.

Greenberg, B., & Brand, J. (1993). Cultural diversity on Saturday morning television. In G. Berry & J. Asamen (Eds.), *Children and television: Images in a changing sociocultural world* (pp. 132–142). Newbury Park, CA: Sage.

Greenberg, B., Mastro, D., & Brand, J. (2002). Minorities and the mass media: Television into the 21st century. In J. Bryant & D. Zillmann (Eds.), *Media effects: Advances in theory and research* (pp. 333–351). Hillsdale: NJ: Lawrence Erlbaum.

Hansen, C. H., & Hansen, R. D. (1988). How rock music videos can change what is seen when boy meets girl: Priming stereotypic appraisal of social interactions. *Sex Roles, 19,* 287–316.

Harwood, J. (1997). Viewing age: Lifespan identity and television viewing choices. *Journal of Broadcasting & Electronic Media, 41,* 203–213.

Harwood, J. (1999). Age identification, social identity gratifications, and television viewing. *Journal of Broadcasting and Electronic Media, 43,* 123–136.

Harwood, J., & Anderson, K. (2002). The presence and portrayal of social groups on prime-time television. *Communication Reports, 15,* 81–97.

Harwood, J., & Roy, A. (2005). Social identity theory and mass communication research. In J. Harwood & H. Giles (Eds.), *Intergroup Communication.* (pp. 189–211). New York: Peter Lang.

Hawkins, R., & Pingree, S. (1981). Using television to construct social reality. *Journal of Broadcasting, 25,* 347–364.

Hawkins, R., & Pingree, S. (1990). Divergent psychological processes in constructing social reality from mass media content. In N. Signorielli & M. Morgan (Eds.), *Cultivation analysis: New directions in media effects research* (pp. 35–50). Newbury Park, CA: Sage.

Hewstone, M., & Brown, R. (1986). Contact is not enough: An intergroup perspective on the 'contact hypothesis.' In M. Hewstone & R. Brown (Eds.), *Contact and conflict in intergroup encounters* (pp. 1–44). Oxford, UK: Blackwell.

Horton, D., & Wohl, R. R. (1956). Mass communication and para-social interaction: Observations on intimacy at a distance. *Psychiatry, 19,* 215–229.

Inhelder, B., & Piaget, J. (1964). *The early growth of logic in the child.* New York: Norton.

Jeffres, L. W. (2000). Ethnicity and ethnic media use: A panel study. *Communication Research, 27,* 496–535.

Johnson, M. (1996). Latinas and television in the United States: Relationships among genre identification, acculturation, and acculturation stress. *The Howard Journal of Communications, 7,* 289–313.

Katz, E., Blumler, J. G., & Gurevitch, M. (1974). Utilization of mass communication by the individual. In J. G. Blumler & E. Katz (Eds.), *The uses of mass communications: Current perspectives on gratifications research* (pp. 19–32). Beverly Hills, CA: Sage.

Kelly, J., & Smith, S. L. (2006, May). *G movies give boys a D: Portraying males as dominant, disconnected, and dangerous.* Retrieved March 1, 2007, from http://www.seejane.org/pdf/g.movies.give.boy.a.d.pdf

Levy, M. R. (1979). Watching TV news as para-social interaction. *Journal of Broadcasting, 23,* 69–80.

Lovelace, V., Scheiner, S., Dollberg, S., Segui, I., & Black, T. (1994). Making a neighbourhood the *Sesame Street* way: Developing a methodology to evaluate children's understanding of race. *Journal of Educational Television, 20,* 69–78.

Mastro, D., Behm-Morawitz, E., & Ortiz, M. (2007). The cultivation of social perceptions of Latinos: A mental models approach. *Media Psychology, 9,* 1–19.

Mastro, D., & Stern, S. (2003). Representations of race in television commercials: A content analysis of primetime ads. *Journal of Broadcasting & Electronic Media, 47,* 635–644.

Mastro, D. E. (2003). A social identity approach to understanding the impact of television messages. *Communication Monographs, 70,* 98–113.

Mastro, D. E., & Behm-Morawitz, E. (2005). Latino representation on primetime television. *Journalism and Mass Communication Quarterly, 82,* 110–130.

McKown, C., & Weinstein, R. (2003). The development and consequences of stereotype consciousness in middle childhood. *Child Development, 74,* 498–515.

Morgan, M., & Signorielli, N. (1990). Cultivation analysis: Conceptualization and methodology. In N. Signorielli & M. Morgan (Eds.), *Cultivation analysis: New directions in media effects research* (pp. 13–34). Newbury Park, CA: Sage.

Palmgreen, P., Wenner, L. A., & Rosengren, K. E. (1985). Uses and gratifications research: The past ten years. In K. E. Rosengren, L. A. Wenner, & P. Palmgreen (Eds.), *Media gratifications research: Current perspectives* (pp. 11–37). Beverly Hills, CA: Sage.

Poindexter, P. M., Smith, L., & Heider, D. (2003). Race and ethnicity in local television news: Framing, story assignments, and source selections. *Journal of Broadcasting and Electronic Media, 47,* 524–536.

Potter, W. J. (1988). Three strategies for elaborating the cultivation hypothesis. *Journalism Quarterly, 65,* 930–939.

Potter, W. J. (1991). The relationship between first- and second-order measures of cultivation. *Human Communication Research, 18,* 92–113.

Potter, W. J., & Chang, I. C. (1990). Television exposure measures and the cultivation hypothesis. *Journal of Broadcasting and Electronic Media, 34,* 131–333.

Power, J. G., Murphy, S. T., & Coover, G. (1996). Priming prejudice: How stereotypes and counter-stereotypes influence attribution of responsibility and credibility among ingroups and outgroups. *Human Communication Research, 23,* 36–58.

Reep, D. C., & Dambrot, F. H. (1989). Effects of frequent television viewing on stereotypes: "Drip, drip" or "drench"? *Journalism Quarterly, 66,* 542–550, 556.

Ríos, D., & Gaines, S. (1999). Latino media use for cultural maintenance. *Journalism & Mass Communication Quarterly, 75,* 746–761.

Roberts, D., Foehr, U., & Rideout, V. (2005, March). *Generation M: Media in the lives of 8- to 18-year-olds* (Report No. 7251). Menlo Park, CA: The Henry J. Kaiser Family Foundation.

Rubin, A. M. (1983). Television uses and gratifications: The interactions of viewing patterns and motivations. *Journal of Broadcasting, 27,* 37–51.

Rubin, A. M. (2002). The uses-and-gratifications perspective of media effects. In J. Bryant & D. Zillmann (Eds.), *Media effects: Advances in theory and research* (2nd ed., pp. 525–548). Hillsdale, NJ: Lawrence Erlbaum.

Schiappa, E., Gregg, P. B., & Hewes, D. E. (2005). The parasocial contact hypothesis. *Communication Monographs, 72,* 92–115.

Shanahan, J., & Morgan, M. (1999). *Television and its viewers: Cultivation theory and research.* Cambridge, UK: Cambridge University Press.

Signorielli, N., & Morgan, M. (1996). Cultivation analysis: Research and practice. In M. B. Salwen & D. W. Stacks (Eds.), *An integrated approach to communication theory and research* (pp. 111–126). Mahwah, NJ: Lawrence Erlbaum.

Stilling, E. (1997). The electronic melting pot hypothesis: The cultivation of acculturation among Hispanics through television viewing. *The Howard Journal of Communication, 8,* 77–100.

Tajfel, H., & Turner, J. C. (1979). An integrative theory of intergroup conflict. In S. Worchel & W. G. Austin (Eds.), *The social psychology of intergroup relations* (pp. 33–47). Monterey, CA: Brooks-Cole.

Tankard, J. W., Jr., Hendrickson, L., Silberman, J., Bliss, K., & Ghanem, S. (1991, August). *Media frames: Approaches to conceptualization and measurement.* Paper presented at the convention of the Association for Education in Journalism and Mass Communication, Boston, MA.

Tynes, B., Reynolds, L., & Greenfield, P. M. (2004). Adolescence, race, and ethnicity on the Internet: A comparison of discourse in monitored vs. unmonitored chat rooms. *Applied Developmental Psychology, 25,* 667–684.

U.S. Census Bureau. (2000). *All across the USA: Population distribution and composition, 2000.* Retrieved January 01, 2007, from http://www.census.gov/population/popprofile/2000/chap02.pdf

Weigel, R., & Howes, P. (1982). Race relations on children's television. *Journal of Psychology, 111,* 109–112.

Yang, C., Wu, H., Zhu, M., & Southwell, B. G. (2004). Tuning in to fit in? Acculturation and media use among Chinese students in the United States. *Asian Journal of Communication, 14,* 81–94.

Zuckerman, D., Singer, D., & Singer, J. (1980). Children's television viewing, racial and sex role attitudes. *Journal of Applied Social Psychology, 10,* 281–294.

CHAPTER 14

The Influence of Print Media on the Development of a Multicultural Perspective in Children

CLINT C. WILSON, II

MARY J. WILSON

Multiculturalism as an idea—and ideal—emerged in the American popular consciousness at the dawn of the 20th century. It was an age of industrialism and the growth of a working class that epitomized the end of the "Gilded Age." However, the prevailing notion of a multicultural society during that era was the blending of various western European ethnic and national groups that had arrived as immigrants through the portal of New York's Ellis Island.

Newspapers, flush in the midst of the "yellow journalism" era, built their circulations and fortunes by ostentatiously catering to and exploiting the interests of the new immigrants. Joseph Pulitzer, publisher of the *New York World,* led a campaign among his readers to collect pennies, nickels, and dimes to raise funds to construct the pedestal upon which France's gift—the Statue of Liberty—could stand in recognition of the newly arrived people from Southern and Eastern European countries.

In fact, it was a cartoon feature that first appeared in the *World* that gave yellow journalism its name. The cartoon was called "Hogan's Alley" and depicted life in the lower East Side New York slums. The single-panel cartoon was printed in black ink except for its central character, which was colored in yellow ink. That character's name was "The Yellow Kid" and lent its name to the sordid era of sensational journalism that characterized much of the newspaper industry of the day.

The first two decades of the 20th century were marked by the reluctance of WASP (White Anglo-Saxon Protestant) citizens to accept the new arrivals who had come to America with different languages, customs, and religions. Assimilation of the immigrants was difficult despite the fact that they shared common physical characteristics with Anglo citizens. They were of the same racial stock but found the ways of the"old country" inhibited their acceptance. The solution was to shed their old identities and customs and to become Americanized.

The major corporate giants joined with popular communications media in promoting what came to be known as the *melting pot* phenomenon. The term was introduced in a play of the same name written by Israel Zangwill in 1908. Typical of the manner in which the concept was adapted was a melting pot ceremony conducted by the Ford Motor Company for graduates of its English school for immigrant automobile factory workers. The commencement ceremonies included a component wherein each student entered a large cauldron (melting pot) on the stage dressed in the clothing and carrying a sign denoting his country of origin. He would emerge minutes later dressed in "American" clothes and waving small American flags in his hands (Henry Ford Museum and Greenfield Village, n.d.).

From 1900 to the early 1980s, the melting pot was not operative for non-White persons whose skin color or shape of eyes worked against their inclusion in all aspects of citizenship. Persons whose physical appearance suggested Native American Indian, Black, Latino, or Asian heritage found stereotypical images and descriptions in print and other communications media worked against their ability to fully enjoy the benefits of American society. Their historical portrayal in popular American media was less that of blending into a melting pot and more in the context of what was termed "the White man's burden." Some observers of that circumstance have chosen to reject the notion of melting pot. Instead they have characterized American society as a salad bowl or, in the parlance of Latino cultures, a paella dish symbolized by a bowl of white rice containing a variety of colorful ingredients that stand out and give texture to the entity.

But, by the 1980s, the aftermath of the civil rights movement, enlightened social consciousness, and economic necessity ushered in by dramatic demographic shifts gave people of color a newfound status and a definition of *multiculturalism* that included them. Ironically, against this historical backdrop emerged the trend among some White persons—inspired by long-suffering racial "minorities"—to embrace distinct identities they believe are in danger of being lost to "Americanization." Thus, many descendants of European immigrants of the last century are now referring to themselves in hyphenated terms such as "I am German-American."

The term *multicultural* has also been broadened by some to include women, gay and lesbian persons, the disabled, the elderly, and religious groups that have suffered discrimination. Thus, the challenge facing educators is how to foster among children a sense of "Americanism" while accepting the broadened definition of multiculturalism that respects one's right to maintain one's cultural identity. This chapter assesses the exposure of children to multicultural messages in print media—books, newspapers, and magazines.

BOOKS

Children learn about multiculturalism and diversity through multiple avenues that begin with the parents' instructional influence as it relates to a child's self-identity in the home, the community, and eventually as a student in school. Parents and schools are able to use many methods to instruct children. Electronic media, verbal interactions, environmental print, and other direct engagement with the environment are all legitimate methods of instruction. Books, including children's literature, are an effective means of instructing children about multiculturalism and diversity and exposing them to valuable and important concepts about other cultural groups.

In education, it is a commonly held belief that parents are a child's first teacher. With that being the case, Young (2005) states that

> parents can play an important role in helping their children (and their schools) deal with the ever-increasing diversity of people they will encounter, not only in many schools today, but in everyday living. As student populations in schools become more and more diverse, educators must find ways to engage a wider range of students with different backgrounds, interests, and experiences. Educators are challenged to find new ways of creating learning environments and experiences that promote success for students who differ in many ways. As parents you can guide children in better understanding their own uniqueness and in understanding and respecting the unique and varied strengths and talents of others. Understanding one's own strengths, interests, style preferences, and values enables young people to understand and appreciate others. (p. 24)

Once students understand their values, talents, and uniqueness, they can begin to see their place in the world and where others fit. One of the major ways children "fit" into the world is for them to learn how to "get along with others." Examples among the array of resources available to parents in developing multicultural awareness in children are the books *We Can Get Along: A Child's Book of Choices* by L. M. Payne (1997) and *I'm Like You, You're Like Me* by C. Gainer (1998). Payne's work is for parents of children ages 3–8 and discusses how children in their formative years may socialize with others of different cultural backgrounds by practicing respect, kindness, tolerance, and responsibility. She helps young children learn to recognize and resolve conflict in a practical and peaceable manner. Gainer's book—also written for children ages 3–8—focuses on children understanding and celebrating each other and offers a gentle introduction to diversity and tolerance. The book helps children appreciate people who are different from themselves while at the same time helping them develop and understand their own unique skills and traits.

Multicultural children's books encourage parents to begin teaching children at home to facilitate the transition to school and interactions with persons of diverse backgrounds that they will encounter outside the home. When children are exposed during their formative years to cultures other than their own, they acquire a greater acceptance for others throughout their lives. Children's literature is one way for them to gain such exposure.

The decade of the 1980s, however, saw a disturbing trend with the decline in writing and marketing of multicultural children's literature despite its importance to developing positive self-identities for children. During the civil rights era and immediately thereafter, money was available for schools to buy children's books about "minorities" and multicultural themes. But by 1990, fewer than 8% of the approximately 5,000 children's books published yearly could be classified as multicultural (Martinez & Nash, 1990). The reason for the scarcity of newly published multicultural children's literature is complex. Many publishers believe that a limited market exists for such literature and they are unwilling to publish new titles. They believe that books depicting a specific cultural group will only be read by that particular group, whereas mainstream books will be read by everyone. Other publishers assert that they receive fewer manuscripts depicting multicultural experiences from authors.

In addition, bookstores are unwilling to stock books that do not have a wide appeal or do not appeal to White readers. It comes as no surprise, then, that the driving force is economic gain rather than altruistic reasons of empowering children and developing a society of knowledgeable, culturally aware people in a multicultural nation.

Children of color (African American, Native American, Latino, and Asian American) benefit from seeing images that look like them in literature. It affirms and empowers them to know that members of their particular group have contributed and continue to contribute to society. Seeing these images enables them to know where they and others in their culture "fit in" to forming the complete picture of this American society. Education should develop in children the knowledge, values, and contributions of their culture while creating a sense of Americanism. Teachers need to develop what Gloria Ladson-Billings calls "culturally appropriate" learning. Children need to see themselves and their cultures represented in the community. Although curriculum of this nature has been lacking for the most part in the American system of education, children's literature can fill that void. John Dewey taught that children learn best when they have authentic experiences. Educators also know that for learning to be effective, teachers should build upon each child's background knowledge in a developmentally appropriate way to construct meaning and understanding. There is no better way of accomplishing this than to write and publish authentic experiences of children of color and then expose them and others to those experiences as a means of expanding understanding and acceptance.

The curriculum in most public school systems is based on state-mandated outcomes or standards. Since enactment of No Child Left Behind legislation, teachers must strictly adhere to curricular guidelines to ensure student success on standardized tests. There is little classroom time available to be creative. One author suggests that teachers will have to become "subversive" in order to create culturally competent classrooms (Kohl, 2006, p. 4). Teachers will have to create *riffs* in their instructional programs to meet the educational needs of each child. (In jazz music, a riff is a short phrase repeated and inserted in the whole composition, usually as a way of reference to an old standard, while changing it and incorporating it into a larger musical structure.) When teachers engage in creative instruction by introducing powerful ideas such as race, culture, gender differences, and tolerance, they engage students in ways that may transform the world. Such teachers provide opportunities for intellectual, emotional, and cultural growth in their students.

In view of the paucity of new books and other published material on multiculturalism, school media centers and public libraries have an important role to play in educating the public. In schools, media specialists and librarians need to keep abreast of the cultural diversity represented in their student populations. Book offerings in the media center should reflect the curriculum and the student population. Children should be able to select books that not only reflect their culture, but the cultures of their peers and other members of their community. The greater the exposure to the ideas and ideals of a multicultural society, the greater the acceptance of all its inhabitants.

NEWSPAPERS AND MAGAZINES

Distinct differences between the natures of newspaper and magazine publishing have largely determined their approach to addressing multiculturalism. The former lend themselves to the more immediate issues of general news and current events, whereas the latter tend to focus on topical subject areas and longer articles of interest to a more finite readership. Insofar as preadolescent children are concerned, their lack of independent expendable income and limited reading discretion limits their viability as a market for commercial magazine entrepreneurs. With a few exceptions, this circumstance renders discussion of multiculturalism in the magazine medium to the slick popular culture publications that cater to adolescent interests in music, motion pictures, sports, fashion, beauty, and related celebrities. American newspapers have a much more eventful, if not noble, history as relates to people of color and issues of cultural diversity.

Multiculturalism was seared into the consciousness of mainstream American newspapers in 1968 when President Lyndon Johnson's commission on civil disorders, known as the Kerner Commission, published its report. Johnson had been motivated to create the commission to investigate causes of urban rebellions among Black citizens in U.S. cities that began in 1965 with the infamous Watts Riot in Los Angeles. Over the next several years, such uprisings had struck several cities with large Black populations, including Detroit, Newark, Chicago, and New York.

The Kerner Commission—named for its chairman, former Illinois governor Otto Kerner—began its wide-ranging probe without a clue that the news media would be among the major sources of discriminatory irritants motivating the riots. When the report was issued, however, the nation learned that its newspaper press had "too long basked in a White world, looking out of it, if at all, with White men's eyes and a White perspective" (Kerner Commission, 1968, p. 366). Newspapers were now added to the list of usual suspects complicit in the national shame of racial discrimination in housing, education, health care, and employment. Suddenly, the newspaper industry that had prided itself as the "fourth estate" and as the watchdog over private and public malfeasance, found itself the object of criticism for its complicity in racial discrimination. Particularly ironic was the role newspapers—even a few in the South—had played in chiding others about resistance to racial integration in the civil rights era.

Following a brief period of embarrassment and hand wringing, the newspaper industry began to react with a series of special training programs and "minority" scholarships and internships designed to increase the numbers of people of color in the ranks of newsroom employees. Concurrently, newspapers began publishing more balanced and sensitive feature articles on the plight of Blacks and other citizens of color in an attempt to rectify decades of neglect, distortion, and stereotypical portrayals that had been the legacy of their reportage and editorial commentary. The institutional entities charged with addressing shortcomings in newspaper industry discrimination were the American Newspaper Publishers Association (ANPA), representing publishers, and the American Society of Newspaper Editors (ASNE) and the Associated Press Managing Editors (APME), representing U.S. and Canadian editors whose newspapers are members of the Associated Press news service. In 1992, ANPA changed its name to the Newspaper Association of America (NAA).

A significant means of determining how newspapers have treated multiculturalism and diversity specifically for children among their readership is through the various Newspapers in Education (NIE) sections they publish. NIE sections have been under the purview of the NAA Foundation and its predecessor, the ANPA Foundation, since the 1970s. According to the foundation's website, formal organization of the NIE program began in 1957 as the Newspapers in the Classroom project (Newspaper Association of America [NAA] Foundation, 2007). It was the culmination of a long-standing idea among educators that newspapers could be a valuable extension of the curriculum to enhance the reading, writing, and current events abilities of students. The website quotes the following 1795 excerpt from the Portland (Maine) *Eastern Herald* on the subject:

> Much has been said and written on the utility of newspapers; but one principal advantage which might be derived from these publications has been neglected; we mean that of reading them in schools, and by the children in families. Try it for one session—Do you wish your child to improve in reading

solely, give him a newspaper—it furnishes a variety, some parts of which must infallibly touch his fancy. Do you wish to instruct him in geography, nothing will so indelibly fix the relative situation of different places, as the stories and events published in the papers. In time, do you wish to have him acquainted with the manners of the country or city, to the mode of doing business, public or private; do you wish him to have a smattering of every kind of science useful and amusing, give him a newspaper—newspapers are plenty and cheap—the cheapest book that can be bought, and the more you buy the better for your children, because every part furnishes some new and valuable information. (as cited in NAA Foundation, "History of NIE," ¶ 1)

The newspaper industry, on the other hand, also realized it could benefit from the cultivation of a newspaper-reading habit among youth who would hopefully become adult readers. For a period in the 1990s, the NAA Foundation maintained a Youth Services Committee that worked closely with NIE programs to ensure, among other matters, that NIE editorial content reflected multiculturalism and racial tolerance. These efforts coincided with recognition that the demographic composition of the U.S. population had shifted dramatically, with Black and Latino residents outnumbering Whites in several major cities where some of America's foremost daily newspapers were published.

By the beginning of the 21st century, more than 850 NIE programs were in operation and their newspaper organizational locus had shifted from the promotions and community service departments to the circulation departments. The continued growth of newspaper commitment to youth programs is reflected in the NAA Foundation's claim that more than 950 NIE programs were then serving nearly 40% of all public school students in the nation. About 94% of U.S. newspapers with daily circulations of 15,000 or more now maintain an NIE program (as cited in NAA Foundation, "History of NIE," ¶ 8). NIE editorial content is commensurate with public education initiatives such as the No Child Left Behind policies of the George W. Bush presidential administration, which places emphasis on standardized testing. Multiculturalism content in NIE is, therefore, reflective of the extent to which it is dictated in school curricula.

The age groups targeted by NIE programs vary among the newspapers and may address elementary, middle school, high school, college students, or a combination of levels. Because newspapers usually package NIE content within their sales strategy, commercial advertising that appeals to young readers is a prominent aspect of such sections. As such, the nature of advertising content has evolved to reflect the multicultural marketing messages of corporate America involved in merchandising toys, electronics, clothing apparel, video games, and music, among others. Consistent with population trends, advertising images of children and teen models have shifted from those with distinctive Anglo-American features to those with non-White ethnic features in recent decades. It is not uncommon to see children of mixed or indeterminate racial heritage portrayed in newspaper advertisements, as merchants eagerly seek to capitalize on the economic potential of America's burgeoning multicultural marketplace. The combined purchasing power of Black, Latino, and Asian/Pacific Island Americans is estimated to be 20% of U.S. buying power in 2007.

Although children's advertising in newspapers has improved in numerical representation, the content shift has not been without problems. Some merchants and/or their advertising agencies have been plagued by the same issues as their counterparts that advertise to adults. When marketing to the youngest age levels, newspaper advertisers necessarily cater to both the desires of children and the sensibilities of adults who make purchasing decisions. This circumstance has led to advertisements that have included racially insensitive representations of Black and Latino youth involved in or idolizing urban gang culture or Asian youth portrayed as academically achieving but awkward in assimilating American culture. Such ill-advised ads that portray children of color in stereotypical ways are counterproductive to the objectives of rearing children in a society that espouses multicultural and egalitarian principles.

Commercial magazines are fueled by advertising dollars, and their commitment to a multicultural editorial philosophy is directly related to popular appeal. Publisher attitudes in that regard are similar to those of book publishers noted earlier: if the content is not assumed to be of interest to a predominantly White readership, the prospects of significant multicultural articles are negligible. The result is a preponderance of articles on persons of color who are celebrities in sports and entertainment. Such imagery, when displayed consistently over time, distorts and limits the perception of social reality for children of color and their White peers.

There are, however, a few magazines devoted to children whose content speaks to the ideal of promoting multiculturalism. Foremost is *Skipping Stones,* a magazine published in Eugene, Oregon, that carries thesubtitle "An International Multicultural Magazine." The publisher's description of the magazine squarely meets the objectives of multicultural education (*Skipping Stones,* n.d.):

> *Skipping Stones* is a nonprofit children's magazine that encourages cooperation, creativity and celebration of cultural and linguistic diversity. We explore stewardship of the ecological and social webs that nurture us. We offer a unique forum for communication among children from different lands and backgrounds. *Skipping Stones* expands horizons in a playful, creative way.

Although very few magazines address multiculturalism in the manner of *Skipping Stones,* another publication that has been a part of cocurricular education for many years deserves consideration here. *Weekly Reader* first appeared in American elementary classrooms in 1902 and its inclusion of cultural diversity has generally coincided with the level of social awareness exhibited by the American public at any historical point. An item on the *Weekly Reader*'s (2007) website notes how the magazine and its ancillary enterprises serve the needs of various state educational guidelines.

CONCLUSION

Books represent the most effective means of teaching children about tolerance and understanding in preparation for growth into adulthood in a multicultural society. The decline in publishing new children's multicultural books, however, is a major concern. Efforts to be multiculturally inclusive in newspaper articles intended for children—primarily as part of the Newspapers in Education program—must be matched by the commercial advertising that surrounds them in both message content and volume. The vast majority of magazines for youth are commercial enterprises that are intended for entertainment rather than educational purposes. The fact that the most educationally sound multicultural magazine, *Skipping Stones,* is operated by a nonprofit entity is significant and reflects the nature of American commitment to the issue.

The extent and timeframe in which multicultural education becomes a national education priority will determine whether and how long it will take for America to realize the philosophical vision of equality and tolerance on which it was founded.

REFERENCES

Gainer, C. (1998). *I'm like you, you're like me.* Minneapolis, MN: Free Spirit.

Henry Ford Museum and Greenfield Village. (n.d.). *The Ford English school.* Retrieved January 14, 2007, from http://www.hfmgv.org/education/smartfun/modelt/highlandpark/fordschool/fordschool.htm/

Kerner Commission. (1968). *Report of the National Advisory Commission on Civil Disorders.* New York: Bantam.

Kohl, H. (2006). A love supreme riffing on the standards: Placing ideas at the center of high stakes schooling. *Multicultural Education, 14*(2), 4.

Martinez, M., & Nash, M. (1990). Bookalogues: Talking about children's literature. *Language Arts, 67*(6), 599–601.

Newspaper Association of America Foundation. (2007). *History of NIE.* Retrieved January 14, 2007, from http://www.naafoundation.org/NewspaperInEducation/HistoryOfNIE.aspx

Payne, L. M. (1997). *We can get along: A child's book of choices.* Minneapolis, MN: Free Spirit.

Skipping Stones. (n.d.). Retrieved January 13, 2007, from http://www.skippingstones.org/

Weekly Reader. (2007). *Our classroom magazines correlate to state standards.* Retrieved January 26, 2007, from http://www.weeklyreader.com/correlations

Young, G. (2005, March). An array of resources for diversity. *Parenting for High Potential,* 24.

CHAPTER 15

Children's Television Programming and the Development of Multicultural Attitudes

SHERRYL BROWNE GRAVES

The demographic landscape of the United States is changing dramatically. The country is becoming more diverse as the numbers of people of African and Asian descent increase and as the numbers of Latinos/as become a large proportion of the U.S. population (U.S. Census Bureau, 2002). This change is happening in the general population and can be seen in school settings as well. The school-age population will experience the "browning effect" as 50% of that group will be children of color by 2030 (U.S. Census Bureau, 2004). By 2050, 40% of students entering school will have exposure to a language other than English in their home (Lindholm-Leary, 2000).

Living in a diverse society like the United States and having access to information about a diverse world present children and adolescents with challenges. Today's youth are more likely to encounter people who look and speak differently than they do. They are more likely to encounter other young people whose life experiences may be unfamiliar. Yet, given the changing demographics, youth will find themselves with both the opportunity and the challenge of trying to engage with diverse individuals. The extent to which children are likely to embrace these opportunities and be able to interact with others will depend on their repertoire of multicultural knowledge, attitudes, and behavior.

Preparation for a multicultural society is the responsibility of family and caregivers, schools and teachers, religious institutions and leaders, and, increasingly, the media. For some children, television provides them with vicarious experiences that are not present in their everyday lives. For other children, television may present information that supports or challenges their lived experience. Children acquire knowledge about diverse groups in various ways. They learn from others around them about how each group is perceived. Children watch the behaviors of the role models in their environment. As a result of both processes, children develop attitudes by associating different characteristics with the racial/ethnic, social class, and cultural groups in the society. Attitudes are important because they influence behavior and predispose children to be more or less willing to interact with or learn more about groups other than their own.

Television is an important part of the ecology for children and adolescents. Children in the United States spend over 20,000 hours watching television by the time they graduate from high school (Aikat, 2007). Many are exposed to television within hours of their birth in hospitals or birthing centers. In a country with increasing diversity of the population in terms of race and ethnicity, language, and religion, and with widening gaps between the experience of those at the bottom and top of the socioeconomic ladder, what role does television play in crossing boundaries among individuals and groups? As almost 99% of American youth have a television and more than 87% live in homes with two or more televisions (Rideout, Roberts, & Foehr, 2005), does television live up to the promise of being a window on the world? Does television's view of the world help children become knowledgeable members of a diverse national and global society? Does television enhance or retard children's desire to learn, play, and work with others different from themselves?

This chapter will answer those questions by reviewing relevant research on (a) television usage by diverse groups; (b) television content about diverse groups; (c) exposure of diverse groups to multicultural content, including the role of preferences for content; and (d) television's role in the development of multicultural attitudes.

TELEVISION USAGE AND DIVERSITY

An international study of children in 23 countries confirms the importance of television as a powerful presence in their lives (Wartella & Knell, 2004). Given the widespread access to television for children of different ages and linguistic, ethnic, racial, and socioeconomic groups, how do children use television? What is the role of television in the world of children?

Age Differences

Among mass media, it is clear that television is the most available medium to children regardless of their demographic characteristics. It is an unusual U.S. family that does not have access to television in the home. Age affects how much children watch television. Adults control access to television for the youngest children, although 99% of children 6 months to 6 years live in a home with at least one television (Rideout & Hamel, 2006). Moreover, 51% of them have access to a TV in their bedrooms. Preschool children watch about 2 hours of television daily, with the amount of television viewing increasing to a peak at about age 9 (Vandewater et al., 2005). Total television viewing for 8- to 10-year-olds increases to 4 hours daily, including time with videos and recorded programs (Rideout et al., 2005). Between ages 9 and 13, the interest in television decreases, and it reaches its lowest level between ages 15 and 18 (Rideout et al., 2005). The amount of time with television shifts from approximately 3 hours a day at age 9 to 2 hours a day at age 15, as peer influences and other media become more prominent.

Environmental factors and developmental changes affect how much and in what way children watch television. Over two thirds of a national sample of children ages 8–18 watch nonbroadcast television, as 8 in 10 youth have cable or satellite TV service in the home. Only 49% watch broadcast television, a drop from 66% in 1999 (Rideout, Foehr, Roberts, & Brodie, 1999; Rideout et al., 2005). In addition, about one third of youth watch television programs that have been recorded on DVRs or TIVO, allowing television viewing to occur at a time of convenience. In less than a decade, cable/satellite television access and recorded programming have changed the ecology of the television experience.

There are other changes in television's ecology for children. Adolescents report a shift from exposure to general television programming on broadcast channels to more adult content on specialized channels and networks. Another change in the use of television is that viewers are doing something else while viewing television. This multitasking occurs only 17% of the time spent watching television, but affects 45% of youth engaged in television viewing (Foehr, 2006). Youth eat, do chores, talk on the phone, or do homework with television. Sometimes, youth also use another mass medium while watching television; they listen to music or play with video games (Foehr, 2006).

Gender Differences

Gender affects some aspects of television usage but not other aspects. Female and male children and adolescents tend to use television in equal amounts, although boys are somewhat more likely than girls to have access to a TV and a video game player in their bedroom between the ages of 6 months and 6 years (Rideout & Hamel, 2006). Although there are no significant differences in the types of shows young girls and boys watch (Rideout & Hamel, 2006), preschool boys tend to favor action adventure content whereas girls prefer genres that reflect relationships (Valkenburg & Cantor, 2000). With increasing age through elementary school, girls persist with educational programming longer than boys, while boys continue to favor shows with action-oriented themes (Lyle & Hoffman, 1972; Roberts & Foehr, 2004; Valkenburg & Cantor, 2000). Other studies of gender differences in content preferences found that girls watched more situation comedies and boys watched more sports programs (Rideout et al., 2005).

Media use among adolescents may be influenced by other factors. For example, television viewing varied as a function of their sexual self-concepts or how they viewed themselves in terms of dating and sex norms (L'Engle & Brown, 2007). Two groups—"curious conservatives" and "sexual sophisticates"—both had high levels of media use, but they varied by content preferences. Curious conservatives favored reality dating shows whereas sexual sophisticates used MTV and BET the most. The other two types, "virgin valedictorians" and "silent susceptibles," had lower levels of television usage relative to other media.

These are examples of the gender differences in television found in different age groups and across different television genres. The sources of these differences in television use by boys and girls may result in part from perceptions about what is appropriate gender behavior.

Racial/Ethnic Differences

There are racial/ethnic variations in the use of the television. For children between 6 months and 18 years of age, race/ethnicity has a relationship to television viewing, independent of age of the child or family income and education (Rideout & Hamel, 2006; Rideout et al., 2005). African American youth watch more television than their Caucasian and Latino counterparts (Rideout & Hamel, 2006; Rideout et al., 2005). This difference persists when there are controls for parental income and education. On a daily basis, Black youth watch an average of 4 hours compared to 3 hours for Latinos and 2½ hours for White youth (Rideout et al., 2005). Heavier television use among African American children is evident during the preschool years (Anand & Kosnick, 2005) and continues through adolescence (J. D. Brown & Pardun, 2004;

Rideout et al., 2005). Though there has been limited examination of television in the lives of Native American children, national data suggest high levels of television use compared to African Americans, Asian Americans, Caucasians, and Latinos (National Center for Educational Statistics, 1991). The reasons for variations in television use among diverse groups of children are complex. For example, in one study, child characteristics, demographics, family characteristics, and parental well-being formed a model that better predicted television use for European American and Latino children than it did for African American children (Bickham et al., 2003). In this model, educational television use was predicted by parental education for European American children but by family income for African American children (Bickham et al., 2003).

The differences in media use by racial and ethnic groups are probably the result of differences in their particular media environments. African American youth are much more likely than other youth to inhabit a media-saturated environment, including TVs, DVRs, cable or satellite access to premium TV channels, and video game devices. Moreover, these items are located in their bedrooms, thereby increasing their access to television content (Rideout et al., 2005). Latino youth are less likely to have access to premium cable television than are African Americans. Whereas African American youth watch television for more hours than Latino or Caucasian youth, all three groups are equally likely to watch television on any given day (Rideout et al., 2005; Roberts & Foehr, 2004).

There is limited information on the use of television by Asian/Pacific Islanders and Native American youth. There is evidence that Asian children spend more time in educational activities in the home than other groups (Hofferth & Sandberg, 2001). A recent study of health and physical activity deliberately sampled Asian youth as part of the California Health Interview Survey (Allen et al., 2007). In this study, immigrant Asian adolescents had higher levels of television viewing and video game playing than did White youth. Among third-generation Asian youth, the latter group was indistinguishable from White youth in the use of television. A growing number of cable networks are directed toward Asian Americans, such as the following channels: AZN (quality Asian films and dramas), MTV Desi (Bollywood offerings), MTV Chi (MTV from China, Asia, and Singapore), and ImaginAsian (high-quality Korean dramas and original material, like Comedy Zen). For Latinos, the Spanish-language channels are Telemundo and Univision.

Children from different racial and ethnic groups vary in the content they use. Generally, children favor entertainment and education programs designed for them (Rideout et al., 1999). Young people do vary in their use of entertainment programs. Latino youth (37%) watch less comedy programming than do African American youth (49%). European American youth (25%) watch television dramas more compared with Latino children (16%). African American children exhibit strong preferences for television programs that are Black oriented and that feature African Americans (Appiah, 2002; J. D. Brown & Pardun, 2004). Latino youth, in addition to mainstream programming, also watch Spanish-language television that is developed in the United States and in Latin America. One study found that 25% of viewing time for Latino youth was with Spanish-language television (Rivadeneyra & Ward, 2005).

MULTICULTURAL CONTENT ON TELEVISION

How diverse is the television landscape? How does it compare to the diversity in the American society? To answer these questions, one must examine who is presented in television programming and how they are represented. Programs vary in format, with some using fantasy representations of people and others using actors. Programs also are designed for different viewers. Some content is designed for general audiences and some targets child or adolescent audiences. This latter distinction does not prevent children from viewing adult content, because there are few barriers to limit children's access to content not designed for them.

Television's portrayals of diverse groups offer content in two ways: (a) via *recognition,* determined by the group's level of participation in the medium; and (b) via *inclusion,* determined by the nature or quality of the portrayals (Clark, 1972). The nature of racial presentations on television has been studied for over 50 years, starting with a focus on African Americans and now examining how other diverse groups are portrayed.

Age Differences

Youth of different ages are presented in different ways on television according to the genre of programming studied. Little analysis has been devoted to portrayals of youth on the media. Youth represent only a small portion of prime-time characters (16%) (Children Now, 2004). Another way to examine how youth are presented is to study programs featuring families, because they also include children. From 1950 to 1990, programs featuring families included more conflict, less control, and less cohesion than programs without children (Douglas & Olsen, 1996). A look at sibling relationships reveals that they were more positive in the 1950s but became more central to the storyline in the 1980s (Larson, 1991). News programs present children in distinct ways in the news. For example, a study of local news' portrayals indicated (a) about 45% of the local news stories associate children with crime; (b) children are generally included in about 10% of local news despite being 25% of the population; and (c) when children from visible racial and ethnic groups are presented, African American children are in most of the stories (61%) followed by Latino children (32%) (Children Now, 2001b). Asian/Pacific Islander and Native American children are rarely included.

Gender Differences

Males and females vary in how often and in what way they are included on television. Male characters continue to outnumber female characters in all types of television programming, including programs designed for children (Aubrey & Harrison, 2004; Barner, 1999; Hentges, 2007; Thompson & Zerbinos, 1995).

There are clear differences in portrayals of females and males on television. Females are underrepresented as main characters except in situation comedies, though from 1967 to 1998 there were increases followed by decreases in the rates of women in leading and supporting roles (Signorielli & Bauce, 1999). Women are more likely to be younger than males, attractive with an emphasis on thin body types, and independent characters fraught with relationship, career, and appearance problems. Men are more likely to be central to the action, and continue to be important even as they age past 65.

On children's programming, the stereotyping continues. In a recent study of preschool programs, there was less gender stereotyping than in programs for school-aged children (Hentges, 2007). Females in programs for school-aged children were more likely to help, show affection, focus on their appearance, and display domestic behaviors. In children's programs designed with prosocial themes, male characters solve problems and achieve goals more often than female characters (Aubrey & Harrison, 2004).

Television content continues to feature males over females across genres designed for adults and children. There are more types of roles for males, with female characters displaying a more limited range of roles and personality characteristics. These gender patterns have persisted over time and have extended to new television delivery systems, like cable television.

Racial/Ethnic Differences

Wide variations exist in how often and in what way diverse racial and ethnic groups are included in television programs. In general, European Americans are overrepresented and are assigned the greatest diversity and range of roles and personality characteristics. As a result, Africans, Asians, Latinos, and Native Americans are underrepresented. Of visible racial and ethnic groups, African Americans are presented in the largest numbers across the widest range of television genres, whereas Native Americans are the least likely to be included and, some would argue, have the most stereotyped images (Children Now, 2004; Geiogamah & Pavel, 1993; Sanchez, 2003).

The nature of racial and ethnic portrayals varies by program genre, time of day, type of media outlet, and racial and ethnic group. Among program genres, there are higher levels of racial diversity in programs targeting preschool children than programs designed for older children (Hentges, 2007). However, in a study of Saturday morning cartoons on the four broadcast networks, there were no female characters of color on three of those networks (Greenberg & Brand, 1993)! Situation comedies tend to be racially/ethnically homogenous. This phenomenon, sometimes referred to as the "ghetto gulch," results in programs that are all-Black, all-Latino, or all-White. Despite, for example, the popularity of African American comedians on television and the success of African American dramatic actors in movies, there is no prime-time, noncomedy program that features a main character that is not European American. There are ensemble casts in which diverse characters play important roles (e.g., *Grey's Anatomy, Lost, Law and Order*).

In prime-time programming, there is more diversity after 10 p.m. (two thirds of programs), than there is at 8 p.m. (13%), a time when children are more likely to be watching (Children Now, 2001a). There are fewer examples of interracial or intergroup interaction on programming directed at children on Saturday morning than there is for preschoolers during weekday mornings and afternoons. Cartoons have more representation of visible racial/ethnic groups than other types of noneducational children's programming (Calvert, Stolkin, & Lee, 1997).

The lack of diversity on broadcast television has sometimes been attributed to the commercial model, which requires each program to appeal to the largest part of the audience or, more recently, the most important audience segment according to advertisers, 18- to 45-year-olds. Advertising has higher levels of diversity than the programs that surround it because of the desire to reach every potential user of the product.

Most of the research reviewed has focused on broadcast television. However, in the last decade, there has been an increase in the use of cable television and the rise of cable networks. Research on cable television and diversity suggests that despite a subscription base and the existence of a few channels targeting specific diverse groups (e.g., BET, Univision), cable's record on diversity is similar to that of broadcast television (Kubey, 1995). Another study of cable networks found no African American participation in the programming (Children Now, 2002). Given these levels of recognition in television, how are specific racial/ethnic groups presented on television?

African Americans

Presentations of African Americans have received the most attention. In some comparative research on African American appearances on television, there is evidence of significant change since 1979 with the percentage of on-screen time increasing from 8% to 17%. Although African Americans were underrepresented for most of the time, they were included on television; in the middle 1990s, they reached a level commensurate with their numbers in the population (Greenberg, Mastro, & Brand, 2002; Mastro & Greenberg, 2000). African Americans are most likely to appear in situation comedies, with African American women two times more likely than African American men to participate in all-Black situation comedies (Signorielli, 2005). Although women typically function in television as sex objects, African American women are infrequently presented as sex objects in prime-time programs.

The all-Black situation comedies in the 2000s were almost exclusively found on the newer cable networks like UPN, and they accounted for 40% of African American portrayals on television (Signorielli, Horry, & Carlton, 2004). Compared to Black women, Black men have more diverse roles and appear in both racially diverse and ghetto gulch programs (Signorielli, 2005). Because they appear in a wider range of program types, African American males are associated with a wider range of occupations. Given their more limited representation, African American women are associated with occupations that have the least prestige. These all-Black programs on the newer networks are important because they are favored by African American teens over the more popular teen programs on the broadcast networks (J. D. Brown & Pardun, 2004).

African Americans are also participants in the criminal world of entertainment television (Tamborini, Mastro, Chory-Assad, & Huang, 2000). Of criminals, 11% are African Americans, whereas 13% of officers of the court, including police officers and attorneys, are African Americans. Black criminals on entertainment television are most often associated with high levels of violence, charged with murder, and presented as guilty. In addition, African American criminals are portrayed as inured to pain and injury. When African Americans are presented as officers of the court, they are overwhelmingly presented as police officers (86%) and infrequently as attorneys (9%). The criminal world of local news does not vary much from this fantasy picture. Compared to other groups, Black males, both young and old, are more likely to be shown as criminals on local news and reality cop shows (Children Now, 2001b).

Asian Americans

Asian Americans are underrepresented in all aspects of television programming (Calvert et al., 1997; Hamamoto, 1993). Asian Americans account for about 3% of all characters, 2% of recurring prime-time characters, 2% of characters on advertising for children, and 8.4% of characters in ads directed at adults (Greenberg et al., 2002; Taylor & Stern, 1997). Asian and Asian American women are still associated with stereotypes that were paramount from the 1950s to the 1970s. The earlier stereotypes included the peasant, the prostitute/geisha, and the "Dragon Lady." The latter stereotype continues to be used in contemporary programs.

The overwhelming message about Asians and Asian Americans on television is that they are present but in the background. It is a "seen but not heard" stance for this group. Thus, Asian portrayals are limited in number and Asians are passive participants in the world of television.

Latinos/as

Latinos are also underrepresented on television, though in the 2000s their numbers have been increasing to 6.5% of prime-time characters and participants in advertising (Children Now, 2004). About half of prime-time programs had at least one Latino character, and an all-Latino situation comedy was part of the 2003–2004 television season. Like African American and Caucasian American characters, about one third of Latino roles were important to the storyline. However, these were likely to include more nonrecurring than recurring roles. Despite low numbers of domestic worker characters on television, when these roles were included, they were most likely to be Latinas/os (Children Now, 2004). This compares to analyses from the 1990s, when Latino characters were portrayed as respected, the least lazy, and not dressed as professionals (Mastro & Greenberg, 2000). They were also more likely to be presented as the least articulate, with heavily accented speech, and engaged in conversations generally focused on crime and violence. In more recent studies of crime and entertainment shows, Latinos are associated with the criminal justice system as either police officers or as criminals (Mastro & Greenberg, 2000; Tamborini et al., 2000). A little more than 60% of Latino criminals are accused of murder and 80% are identified as guilty, though few or none go to trial, a common fate for most televised criminals. These images of Latinos from entertainment television are also found on reality cop shows (Tamborini et al., 2000).

There are more positive Latino portrayals in children's television. For example, *Sesame Street*, *Dora the Explorer*, and *Cyberchase* feature positive Latino portrayals using live actors and animated characters; the former two are popular with preschoolers and the latter with elementary students. It is interesting that in one study of middle-class Caucasian and lower-income Latino preschoolers, White children were more likely than were Latino children to say that Dora, a Latina animated character, was like them (Calvert, Strong, Jacobs, & Conger, 2007).

The overall trend for Latinos on television is underrepresentation despite their growing proportion of the U.S. population. Their roles are severely limited in entertainment programming. These stereotypic presentations suggest limited inclusion of Latinos in all aspects of American society, and, therefore, are of concern to those who worry that television has the power to influence multicultural attitudes, especially about Latinos (Cortes, 2004).

Native Americans

Native American portrayals are severely limited and are usually included in programming of a historic nature about the old West. They are rarely shown in contemporary settings. In a focus group study with Native American youth, the participants identified the stereotypes associated with their group (Children Now, 2001a). They reported that Native Americans are portrayed as poor, drunk, living on reservations, selling fireworks, and fighting over land.

Language Differences

With the advent of cable television, there are opportunities for children from diverse language groups to see television programming in their first language. Spanish-language programming can be found on Univision and Telemundo. AZN features content in Chinese, Japanese, Tagalog, Korean, Hindi, and Vietnamese, along with English dubbing or subtitles in some instances. Programming in languages other than English largely originates outside the United States and gives youth access to a wider range of portrayals of their language group because the programming is developed by native speakers of the language.

Intergroup/Interracial Interaction

With the presence of diverse individuals, roles, and characters on television, there is the potential for the medium to provide children and adolescents with models for how to get along and interact with individuals different from themselves. These portrayals could show interactions among diverse people who share goals, engage in joint decision making, and develop cooperative relationships.

Intergroup interactions on television have some particular characteristics. The amount of interracial interaction is limited (Huston et al., 1992). The majority of these interactions are restricted to work settings (Entman & Rojecki, 1998; Weigel, Kim, & Frost, 1995). As a result, few of the interactions take place under conditions of positive close interpersonal relationships across racial and ethnic lines (Entman & Rojecki, 1998). In entertainment programs, it is difficult to model intergroup interaction in the situation comedy genre because these programs are racially homogeneous: all-White, all-Black, or all-Latino. This is a missed opportunity for modeling because this genre is the most popular with children ages 12–17 (Nielsen Media Research, 2003). Additionally, intergroup interaction, when it does occur, almost always includes a Caucasian participant (Kubey, 1995). The inclusion of a White character may suggest different ideas to the viewers. One message might be that groups of only visible racial and ethnic group members do not work well. Another message might be that groups without Caucasians are not valued or important. Neither message supports the development of multicultural attitudes and behaviors in children.

On educational television programs designed for children, there is more intergroup interaction. These interactions are usually presented as neutral or positive (Calvert et al., 1997; M. E. Williams & Coudry, 1989). For example, intergroup interactions have been an integral part of *Sesame Street* since its inception with people from diverse backgrounds as friends and neighbors. In addition, in the 1990s, a specific race relations curriculum was developed for *Sesame Street* (Lovelace & Scheiner, 1994). Additionally, intergroup interaction goals have been included in international coproduction of the series for the Israeli-Palestinian versions (Cole et al., 2003). Other educational programs have also included intergroup interaction as a goal, including *Vegetable Soup* (Mays, Henderson, Seidman, & Steiner, 1975) and *Carrascolendas* (F. Williams & Natalicio, 1972) in the 1970s, and *Puzzle Place* (Powers, 1998) and a video series titled *Different and the Same* (Graves, 1999a) in the 1990s. Most of these programs almost never present examples of difficult interactions. *Different and the Same*, however, provides children with the opportunity to learn how to handle uncomfortable or difficult interactions.

Intergroup interactions are limited on television. The presentations do not suggest close, personal relationships across racial/ethnic groups. Rather, they suggest that the encounters are superficial and generally must include a Caucasian for a diverse group to be recognized. Because the interactions are largely positive or neutral, viewers do not learn to manage interactions among people who may come together with different experiences. In the extreme, these presentations may suggest that race or ethnicity does not matter because people on television do not talk about it. Children without opportunities in their everyday lives for such experiences are not prepared by these restricted television presentations.

MEDIA EFFECTS ON MULTICULTURAL ATTITUDES

Television does influence racial knowledge, attitudes, and behavior (Graves, 1993, 1996, 1999b) as a consequence of both underrepresentation and stereotyping of groups (G. Berry, 2000). Most of the research in this area focuses on perceptions of, attitudes about, and behavior toward African Americans. The work includes studies with young children and adolescents and content from entertainment and educational television.

Perceptions of and Identification With Television Characters

Children from diverse groups vary in their perceptions of and identification with television characters of their same racial/ethnic group. Generally, children believe that the televised portrayals of different-race/ethnic characters are more realistic than the stereotyped and limited presentations of their same-race/ethnic group (Children Now, 1998; Entman & Rojecki, 1998; Greenberg & Brand, 1994; Lichter & Lichter, 1988). Specifically, Latino and Asian children reported that portrayals of African Americans were more realistic than portrayals of their respective groups (Lichter & Lichter, 1988). Native American children in a focus group study were clear about the nature of stereotyping on television for their own group and for others like African Americans and affluent children (Chen, Haufler, & Taam, 1999). Children who have experiences with diverse individuals attribute less realism to televised portrayals than do children who lack direct experience (Greenberg & Reeves, 1976).

Adolescents tend to seek out programming that features characters like themselves. This is particularly characteristic of African American teens, though other teens (e.g., Korean and Latino adolescents) have reported similar tendencies (Huntemann & Morgan, 2001; Subervi-Velez & Colsant, 1993).

Television content can affect the viewer's identification with specific characters. Middle-class, Caucasian, preschool-age children were more likely than lower-income Latino preschoolers to identify with Dora, the Latina star from *Dora the Explorer*. This may be the result of Dora's greater use of English than Spanish and her middle-class lifestyle. There is some evidence that social class may be a more powerful influence as the basis of identification than is race and ethnicity. Latino children, after exposure to an educational program, *Vegetable Soup,* had increased identification with same-race/ethnicity characters, though there was no similar effect on other groups of children (Mays et al., 1975).

Perceptions of diverse groups can be influenced by television viewing. Sometimes the perceptions can produce unpredictable outcomes. Exposure to African Americans on *The Cosby Show* resulted in positive perceptions of the Huxtable family among Caucasian viewers. However, these viewers used the success of the fictional African American family to fault less successful real-life African Americans for their inability or unwillingness to achieve levels of success comparable to the fictional family (Jhally & Lewis, 1992)! While African American viewers acknowledged the presence of positive portrayals in *The Cosby Show,* they also evaluated the show as unrealistic in its presentation of issues affecting African Americans (Innis & Feagin, 1995). The race/ethnicity of the viewer influenced how the portrayals were perceived.

Racial/Ethnic Identification and the Self

Identity influences how youth use television. The influence can also be bidirectional, that is, television can influence the self and identity. For first- and second-grade African American children, exposure to positive portrayals of same-race television characters was associated with higher racial identification for boys than girls (Bonvillain & Huston, 2001). Higher levels of identification with same-race/ethnic characters than with different-race/ethnic characters occurred after exposure to a multiethnic animated series, *Superfriends*, among young children (LaRose & Eisenstock, 1981).

Television exposure also influences the viewers' sense of self. This effect has been seen repeatedly in African American viewers (Greenberg et al., 2002). For elementary-age African American children, television viewing was associated with more positive self-concept in girls than in boys (Stroman, 1986). Watching *The Cosby Show* led to an increase in Black self-esteem (Innis & Feagun, 1995). However, African American adolescents had a more complex reaction to televised Black portrayals than did children. Regular viewing of sports programming and music videos by Black teens resulted in lower levels of self-esteem (Ward, 2004a). Because adolescents generally name athletes and entertainers among their favorite or most admired individuals, it may be that when Black teens compare themselves to these role models in sports and music programming, they evaluate themselves as less adequate. Yet among African American youth, strong identification with same-race television characters predicted higher levels of self-esteem, including performance self-esteem and appearance self-esteem, than did strong identification with White characters (Ward, 2004a). Finally, the negative influences of television on the self were reduced for teens who were relatively high in religiosity. That is, teens who participated in a religious institution associated with African American culture were less vulnerable to the negative effects of media than teens who did not participate in similar cultural institutions.

Media can affect how young women view their bodies. In particular, the use of television by adolescent girls has been associated with an increased desire for the often unattainable, thin body image (Ward & Caruthers, 2001). However, African American women who viewed Black-oriented television were more likely to have a healthy body image than Black women who viewed mainstream television (Ward, 2004b). Is television's effect on the self-system of African Americans a result of their unique history in this country or does it have a general effect on other groups?

There is limited research on the role of television in the development of self-concept among other groups. In a study of Latino elementary children, there was no relationship between a general measure of self-concept and television viewing, including the use of Spanish-language television (Subervi-Velez & Necochea, 1990). The latter had been predicted to provide viewers with more diverse and positive Latino portrayals. On the other hand, a study of diverse 9th and 12th graders indicates that viewing television for more than 20 hours a week resulted in less complex descriptions of the self relative to appearance and body image (Harrison, 2006). This was true for Asian, Caucasian, Latina, and Native American teen girls but not for African American girls. For Black adolescent girls, an increase in television viewing was associated with a more complex description of self. Self-complexity refers to the use of a greater number of characteristics in describing the self (Linville, 1987). It is likely that for non-Black female teens, more television viewing increases exposure to the limited stereotypes of femininity, which focus on a thin body image and have limited roles and characteristics. For African American females, however, increased viewing and a higher propensity to seek out programs with Black characters will provide exposure to same-race, female body images that are more diverse. If it is the case that African Americans use same-race members for social comparison, then it is more likely that during adolescence when aspects of the self are rebuilt (Harter, 1998), African American girls are not restricted to the White normative, thin female ideal. African American girls can rebuild this aspect of self during adolescence within a more complex conception of "female." The result is the use of more complex descriptions of the self.

Television viewing has the potential to influence self-concept and identity. The research suggests that characteristics of the viewer make a difference. The characteristics include (a) developmental stage, (b) amount of television viewed, (c) television genre, (d) gender, and (e) racial/ethnic group membership. While some have suggested that exposure to the stereotypes of African Americans would lead to a negative self-concept, there is evidence that exposure to African American portrayals was associated with identification with same-race characters. Stronger racial identification led to more positive self-concept. Because African Americans and other minority group members more often use their same-race/ethnic group as their comparison group, rather than members of the dominant society, identification with the same-race/ethnic group becomes a protective factor for these youth (Huntemann & Morgan, 2001).

Racial/Ethnic Attitudes

Exposure to television portrayals of same- and different-race/ethnic characters results in changes in racial/ethnic attitudes. Let's first examine the effects on Caucasian youth. Educational and entertainment programs featuring positive or counterstereotypic portrayals have led to more positive attitudes toward African Americans and Latinos in Caucasian preschoolers (Bogatz & Ball, 1971) and more positive attitudes toward African Americans by Caucasian elementary children (Dorr, Graves, & Phelps, 1980). Also, a study of clips from *Sesame Street,* where some inserts featured White children engaged in intergroup interaction and some inserts did not, examined children's willingness to play with different-race/ethnicity children (Gorn, Goldberg, & Kanungo, 1976). Those children exposed to the different race and ethnicity inserts were more willing to play with different-race/ethnicity children than children not exposed to the cross-race/ethnicity inserts.

Positive images generally led to more positive attitudes, but under certain conditions, exposure to any type of African American portrayals resulted in more positive attitudes for Caucasian children (Dorr et al., 1980). The latter result could be the consequence of unusual and intense African American portrayals or it could be the result of limited exposure to different-race portrayals. However, a study of educational programming that used a single presentation of a 10-minute clip from either *Puzzle Place* (Weiner & Taylor, 1993) or *The Human Race Club: The Unforgettable Pen Pal* (J. Berry, 1989) did not lead to any changes in 5- and 6-year-old Caucasian children's attitudes toward African, Asian, and Caucasian stimuli (Perrson & Musher-Eizenman, 2003). Expanding exposure to 3 weeks with four repetitions of a 20-minute segment of a video, *Prevent Violence With Groark: Groark Learns About Prejudice* (Elkind + Sweet Communications, 1996), did not change attitudes of the Caucasian children. They continued to express strong pro-White bias, though their comprehension of the messages did increase with the extended viewing time.

Generally, the previous findings support a social cognitive model of effects (Bandura 1986, 1997, 2001) in which children adopt attitudes that imitate the nature of the television presentation. That simple exposure to Black portrayals, regardless of the nature of the portrayals, led to more positive attitudes could also be explained by this model. Recognition on television of an underrepresented group could be interpreted as transmitting a degree of value and importance to the group. This effect would be more likely to occur in a context where it would be unusual for the viewer to have experience with the different-race/ethnicity group. African Americans fit this criterion on television in the late 1970s and early '80s. However, other research suggests a cultivation effect on attitudes (Gerbner, Gross, Morgan, & Signorielli, 1994; Morgan & Shanahan, 1997). Heavy viewers of television, especially crime and news programs, were more likely to express negative attitudes toward African Americans than were light viewers of television and of these types of programs (Entman & Rojecki, 1998). Those who spent more time with television and had increased exposure to negative stereotypes expressed attitudes that mirrored the world according to television.

How do other racial and ethnic groups react to different-race/ethnic presentations after exposure to television? There is less research in this area and much examines educational television. Exposure to an educational television program, *Vegetable Soup*, by Latino and Native American children increased their endorsement of diverse children as potential friends, though Asian American viewers appeared to be unaffected (Mays et al., 1975). In a study using *Sesame Street* segments, African American, Asian American, Latino, and Native American children expressed positive feelings about Black, White, and Latino children who engaged in different-race and different-ethnicity home visits (Lovelace, Scheiner, & Graves, in press). After exposure to these segments, African American and Caucasian children remembered details about the encounter and thought that the children on television were happy with their cross-race/ethnicity visits.

Children's attitudes toward same-race portrayals can also be affected by television exposure. Almost all of this research has examined African American youth. For example, African American and South African Black children found same-race, middle-class characters like those on *The Cosby Show* realistic (B. M. Brown, Austin, & Roberts, 1988; D. P. Van Vuuren, Bornman, Mels, & M. Van Vuuren, 1990). African American youth generally report more positive attitude change after exposure to Black televised portrayals (Graves, 1993). What is less clear is how the nature of the portrayal, whether positive or negative, predicts the direction of the attitude change. In some instances, positive portrayals result in more positive attitudes (Dorr et al., 1980), but in some cases, any inclusion of African Americans was associated with positive attitudes for Black children (Graves, 1975). These findings may be a reflection of a particular historical context. These studies were conducted in the late 1970s and early '80s, when it was not typical for African American children to see same-race characters on television. Television's recognition of their racial group may have been a more powerful influence than the nature and direction of the portrayals. Research on contemporary portrayals of African Americans on television might yield different findings. It would be important to establish the amount of exposure of children to same-race presentations and then examine the impact of the specific types of portrayals on attitudes.

Intergroup Interaction

Educational programs for children have been designed for viewers to see members of diverse groups and to see interaction among diverse people from a positive perspective. This is evident in television programs like *Sesame Street* or a prejudice reduction video series like *Different and the Same*. During the 1990s, *Sesame Street* designed specific segments to encourage cross-racial friendships using real children and adults to serve as models of positive attitudes and behavior (Lovelace & Scheiner, 1994). African American and Caucasian preschoolers expressed caution about the interactions because none of the segments included the mother of the White child (Lovelace et al., in press). The same portrayals included the parents of the African American child. Preschoolers interpreted the absence of the White mother as an indication of her disapproval of the visit and the friendship, despite the perception that the televised children liked each other and had a good time together during the cross-race visit.

International versions of *Sesame Street* for Israeli, Israeli Arab, and Palestinian Arab children were designed to present messages of mutual respect and understanding. Although children had negative perceptions of Arab and Jewish adults, exposure to the series led to some positive outcomes. Exposure led to an increase in the use of prosocial explanations for conflict resolutions in cross-ethnic situations. Viewers were also more likely to use positive characteristics to describe cross-ethnic group members after exposure to the series (Cole et al., 2003). This series produced changes in ethnic attitudes by using the context of peer interactions focused on the everyday lives of children from different cultural groups. This familiar context appeared to make acceptance of the other accessible and influential for all three groups of children.

There is some additional evidence about the impact of intergroup interaction from other educational programming. Exposure to *Vegetable Soup* increased the acceptance of diverse racial and ethnic groups by Caucasian children and increased the willingness of Latino and Native American children to consider children from different race and ethnicity groups as potential friends (Mays et al., 1975). A prejudice-reduction series designed for classroom use was also effective in promoting intergroup interaction. *Different and the Same* increased cross-race/ethnicity friendship selections and altered the willingness to help a child, regardless of racial/ethnic group (Graves, 1999b; Katsuyama, 1997). Exposure to *Different and the Same* changed students' strategies for resolving prejudice-based interpersonal conflict (Graves, 1999b; Katsuyama, 1997).

One study offers a perspective about how television might influence intergroup interaction. In an experimental study with a group of British adolescents, participants were given varied information about the musical tastes of their own and another group (Bakagiannis & Tarrant, 2006). When the information said that the out-group had similar musical tastes, adolescents were more positive in their perceptions of the out-group than adolescents not given information about the out-group. In a similar fashion, adolescents with information about similar musical tastes of the out-group subsequently believed that the out-group teens would perceive the in-group members more positively. Consequently, they were less likely to report discrimination toward the out-group. Not only direct experience but prior knowledge about commonalities appears to shift perceptions of individuals of different groups.

Entertainment television is limited in its portrayals of intergroup interaction, and there has been almost no study of the effect of these presentations on young viewers. For example, Native American children report that television does not display how Native children interact with children from diverse groups (Chen et al., 1999). It would be useful for researchers to study how intergroup interaction in a variety of television genres, including entertainment programs, affects children. In addition, research should examine how the presence or absence of direct experience with intergroup interaction mediates the effects of exposure to televised cross-racial and cross-ethnic interactions. Prior exposure to televised intergroup interaction could also be examined in relation to the effects of specific content.

CONCLUSION

Media are an important part of the lives of American youth. Television is available to all youth across the development life course and across a wide range of demographic characteristics. There is some diversity on television, though much of it is characterized by limited and stereotypical portrayals of a wide range of groups. Educational television provides more positive portrayals, but the usage rates are more limited both in daily use and in use at particular times during development. Television's portrayals of diverse groups affect diverse children and adolescents in their perceptions, sense of self and identity, attitudes, and interest in intergroup interaction. Television, when designed to have a positive influence in these areas, has a demonstrated capacity to be effective. As the country becomes more diverse and as the lives of children and adolescents present more opportunities and challenges that come with increased diversity, will television assist or hinder their ability to be effective participants in a multicultural society?

REFERENCES

Aikat, D. (2007). Extent of and response to violence. In J. J. Arnett (Ed.), *Encyclopedia of children, adolescents and the media* (Vol. 2, pp. 852–853). Thousand Oaks, CA: Sage.

Allen, M. L., Elliott, M. N., Morales, L. S., Diamant, A. L., Hambarsoomian, K., & Schuster, M. A. (2007). Adolescent participation in preventive health behaviors, physical activity, and nutrition: Differences across immigrant generations for Asians and Latinos compared with Whites. *American Journal of Public Health, 97*(2), 337–343.

Anand, S., & Kosnick, J. (2005). Demographic predictors of media use among infants, toddlers and preschoolers. *American Behavioral Scientist, 48,* 539–561.

Appiah, O. (2002). Black and White viewers' perception and recall of occupations characters on television. *Journal of Communication, 52*(4), 776–793.

Aubrey, J. S., & Harrison, K. (2004). The gender-role content of children's favorite television programs and its links to their gender-related perceptions. *Media Psychology, 6*(2), 111–146.

Bakagiannis, S., & Tarrant, M. (2006). Can music bring people together? Effects of shared musical preference on intergroup bias in adolescence. *Scandinavian Journal of Psychology, 47,* 129–136.

Bandura, A. (1986). *Social foundations of thought and action.* Englewood Cliffs, NJ: Prentice Hall.

Bandura, A. (1997). *Self-efficacy: The exercise of control.* New York: W. H. Freeman.

Bandura, A. (2001). Social cognitive theory of mass communication. *Media Psychology, 3*(3), 265–299.

Barner, M. R. (1999). Sex-role stereotyping in FCC-mandated children's educational television. *Journal of Broadcasting & Electronic Media, 43*(4), 551–564.

Berry, G. (2000). Multicultural media portrayals and the changing demographic landscape: The psychosocial impact of television representations on the adolescent of color. *Journal of Adolescent Health, 27S,* 57–60.

Berry, J. (1989). *The human race club: The unforgettable pen pal* [Motion picture]. Woodland Hills, CA: Celebrity Home Entertainment.

Bickham, D. S., Vandewater, E. A., Huston, A. C., Lee, J. H., Caplovitz, A. G., & Wright, J. C. (2003). Predictors of children's electronic media use: An examination of three ethnic groups. *Media Psychology, 5,* 107–137.

Bogatz, G., & Ball, S. (1971). *The second year of Sesame Street: A continuing evaluation.* Princeton, NJ: Educational Testing Service.

Bonvillain, J. F., & Huston, A. C. (2001). *The effects of positive portrayals of Black television characters on Black children's racial attitudes, self-perception and racial identification.* (ERIC Document Reproduction Service No. ED455478). Retrieved June 18, 2007, from ERIC database.

Brown, B. M., Austin, E. W., & Roberts, D. F. (1988, May). *Real families versus television families: Children's perceptions of realism in* The Cosby Show. Paper presented to the International Communication Association, New Orleans, LA.

Brown, J. D., & Pardun, C. J. (2004). Little in common: Racial and gender differences in adolescents' television diets. *Journal of Broadcasting & Electronic Media, 48,* 266–278.

Calvert, S. L., Stolkin, A., & Lee, J. H. (1997, April). *Gender and ethnic portrayals in children's Saturday morning television programs.* Paper presented at the annual convention of the Society for Research in Child Development, Washington, DC.

Calvert, S. L., Strong, B. L., Jacobs, E. L., & Conger, E. E. (2007). Interaction and participations for young Hispanic and Caucasian girls' and boys' learning from media content. *Media Psychology, 9*(2), 1–15.

Chen, P., Haufler, H., & Taam, H. (1999). *A different world: Native American children's perceptions of race and class in the media.* Oakland, CA: Children Now.

Children Now. (1998). *A different world: Children's perceptions of race and class in media.* Oakland, CA: Author.

Children Now. (2001a). *Fall colors 2000–2001 prime time diversity report.* Oakland, CA: Author.

Children Now. (2001b). *The local television news media's picture of children.* Oakland, CA: Children Now.

Children Now. (2002). *Why it matters: Diversity on television.* Oakland, CA: Children Now.

Children Now. (2004). *Fall colors 2003–04: Prime time diversity report.* Oakland, CA: Children Now.

Clark, C. (1972). Race, identification, and television violence. In G. A. Comstock, E. A. Rubinstein, & J. P. Murray (Eds.), *Television and social behavior: Television's effects: Further explorations* (Vol. 5, pp. 120–184). Washington, DC: U.S. Government Printing Office.

Cole, C. F., Arafat, C., Tidhar, C., Tafesh, W. Z., Fox, N. A., Killen, M., et al. (2003). The educational impact of *rechove sumsum/shara'a simsim:* A *Sesame Street* television series to promote respect and understanding among children living in Israel, the West Bank, and Gaza. *International Journal of Behavioral Development, 27*(5), 409–422.

Cortes, C. E. (2004). Knowledge construction and popular culture: The media as multicultural educator. In J. A. Banks & C. A. M. Banks (Eds.), *Handbook of research on multicultural education* (2nd ed., pp. 211–227). Hoboken, NJ: Jossey-Bass.

Dorr, A., Graves, S. B., & Phelps, E. (1980). Television literacy for young children. *Journal of Communication, 24,* 130–137.

Douglas, W., & Olsen, B. (1996). Subversion of the American family? An examination of children and parents in television families. *Communication Research, 23,* 73–99.

Elkind + Sweet Communications. (1996). *Prevent violence with Groark: Groark learns about prejudice* [VHS]. San Francisco: Live Wire Media.

Entman, R. M., & Rojecki, A. (1998). Minorities in the mass media: A status report. In A. K. Garmer (Ed.), *Investing in diversity: Advancing opportunities for minorities and the media* (pp. 67–85). Washington, DC: Aspen Institute.

Foehr, U. G. (2006). *Media multitasking among American youth: Prevalence, predictors and pairings.* Menlo Park, CA: Kaiser Family Foundation.

Geiogamah, H., & Pavel, D. M. (1993). Developing television for American Indian and Alaska Native children in the late 20th century. In G. Berry & J. K. Asamen (Eds.), *Children and television: Images in a changing sociocultural world* (pp. 191–204). Newbury Park, CA: Sage.

Gerbner, G., Gross, L., Morgan, M., & Signorielli, N. (1994). Growing up with television: The cultivation perspective. In J. Bryant & D. Zillman (Eds.), *Media effects: Advances in theory and research* (pp. 17–41). Hillsdale, NJ: Lawrence Erlbaum.

Gorn, G. J., Goldberg, M. E., & Kanungo, R. N. (1976). The role of educational television in changing the intergroup attitudes of children. *Child Development, 47,* 277–280.

Graves, S. B. (1975). *Racial diversity in children's television: Its impact on racial attitudes and stated program preferences.* Unpublished doctoral dissertation, Harvard University, Cambridge, MA.

Graves, S. B. (1993). Television, the portrayal of African Americans and the development of children's attitudes. In G. Berry & J. K. Asamen (Eds.), *Children and television: Images in a changing sociocultural world* (pp. 179–190). Newbury Park, CA: Sage.

Graves, S. B. (1996). Diversity on television. In T. M. MacBeth (Ed.), *Tuning into young viewers: Social science perspectives on television* (pp. 61–87). Newbury Park, CA: Sage.

Graves, S. B. (1999a). *Different and the same: A final report.* New York: Carnegie Corporation.

Graves, S. B. (1999b). Television and prejudice reduction: When does television as a vicarious experience make a difference? *Journal of Social Issues, 55*(4), 707–725.

Greenberg, B. S., & Brand, J. E. (1993). Cultural diversity on Saturday morning television. In G. Berry & J. K. Asamen (Eds.), *Children and television: Images in a changing sociocultural world* (pp. 132–142). Newbury Park, CA: Sage.

Greenberg, B. S., & Brand, J. E. (1994). Minorities and the mass media: 1970s to 1990s. In J. Bryant & D. Zillman (Eds.), *Media effects: Advances in theory and research* (pp. 273–314). Hillsdale, NJ: Lawrence Erlbaum.

Greenberg, B. S., Mastro, D., & Brand, J. E. (2002). Minorities and the mass media: Television into the 21st century. In J. Bryant & D. Zillman (Eds.), *Media effects: Advances in theory and research* (pp. 333–351). Mahwah, NJ: Lawrence Erlbaum.

Greenberg, B. S., & Reeves, B. (1976). Children and the perceived reality of television. *Journal of Social Issues, 32,* 89–97.

Hamamoto, D. Y. (1993). They're so cute when they're young: The Asian-American child on television. In G. Berry & J. K. Asamen (Eds.), *Children and television: Images in a changing sociocultural world* (pp. 205–214). Newbury Park, CA: Sage.

Harrison, K. (2006). Scope of self: Toward a model of television's effects on self-complexity in adolescence. *Communication Theory, 16,* 251–279.

Harter, S. (1998). The development of self-representations. In N. Eisenberg (Ed.), *The handbook of child psychology: Social, emotional, and personality development* (Vol. 3, pp. 102–132). New York: Wiley.

Hentges, B. A. (2007, March). *Gender and racial representations in television programs targeting preschool and school aged children.* Poster session presented at the biennial meeting of the Society for Research in Child Development, Boston, MA.

Hofferth, S. L., & Sandberg, J. F. (2001). How American children spend their time. *Journal of Marriage and Family, 63,* 295–308.

Huntemann, N., & Morgan, M. (2001). Mass media and identity development. In D. G. Singer & J. L. Singer (Eds.), *Handbook of children and the media* (pp. 309–322). Thousand Oaks, CA: Sage.

Huston, A. C., Donnerstein, E., Fairchild, H., Feshbach, N. D., Katz, P. A., Murray, J. P., et al. (1992). *Big world, small screen: The role of television in American society.* Lincoln: University of Nebraska Press.

Innis, L. B., & Feagin, J. R. (1995). *The Cosby Show:* The view from the middle class. *Journal of Black Studies, 25,* 692–711.

Jhally, S., & Lewis, J. (1992). *Enlightened racism.* Boulder, CO: Westview.

Katsuyama, R. M. (1997). *An evaluation of the Springfield city schools: Reaching our children (ROC) program.* Dayton, OH: University of Dayton, Social Science Research Center.

Kubey, R. (1995). Demographic diversity on cable: Have the new cable channels made a difference in the representation of gender, race, and age? *Journal of Broadcasting & Electronic Media, 39,* 459–471.

LaRose, R., & Eisenstock, B. (1981). *Techniques for testing the effectiveness of minority portrayals in multicultural children's programming.* Paper presented at the annual meeting of the International Communication Association, Vancouver.

Larson, M. S. (1991). Sibling interactions in 1950s to 1980s sitcoms: A comparison. *Journalism Quarterly, 68,* 381–387.

L'Engle, K. L., & Brown, J. D. (2007, March). *Adolescents' sexual self-concepts and use of mass media.* Symposium paper presented at the biennial meeting of the Society for Research in Child Development, Boston.

Lichter, S. R., & Lichter, L. (1988). *Television's impact on ethnic and racial images: A study of Howard Beach adolescents.* New York: Institute of Human Relations, American Jewish Congress.

Lindholm-Leary, K. (2000). *Biliteracy for a global society: An idea book on dual language education.* Washington, DC: National Clearinghouse on Bilingual Education.

Linville, P. W. (1987). Self-complexity as a cognitive buffer against stress-related illness and depression. *Journal of Personality and Social Psychology, 52,* 663–676.

Lovelace, V., & Scheiner, S. (1994). Making a neighbourhood the Sesame Street way: Developing a methodology to evaluate children's understanding of race. *Journal of Educational Television, 20*(2), 69–78.

Lovelace, V., Scheiner, S., & Graves, S. B. (in press). Role relations and *Sesame Street*: Racial knowledge, attitudes and understanding in preschool children. In M. B. Spencer & G. K. Brookins (Eds.), *Research in minority children's development.* Hillsdale, NJ: Lawrence Erlbaum.

Lyle, J., & Hoffman, H. R. (1972). Explorations in patterns of television viewing by preschool-age children. In E. A. Rubinstein, G. A. Comstock, & J. P. Murray (Eds.), *Television and social behavior: Television in day-to-day life* (Vol. 4, pp. 257–273). Washington, DC: U.S. Government Printing Office.

Mastro, D., & Greenberg, B. S. (2000). The portrayal of racial minorities on prime-time television. *Journal of Broadcasting & Electronic Media, 44*(4), 690–703.

Mays, L., Henderson, E. H., Seidman, S. K., & Steiner, V. S. (1975). *An evaluation report on* Vegetable Soup: *The effects of multiethnic children's television series on intergroup attitudes of children.* Albany: Department of Education, State of New York.

Morgan, M., & Shanahan, J. (1997). Two decades of cultivation research: An appraisal and meta-analysis. *Communication Yearbook, 20,* 1–45.

National Center for Educational Statistics. (1991). *A profile of the American eighth grader: NELS: 88 student descriptive summary.* Washington, DC: U.S. Department of Education.

Nielsen Media Research. (2003). *Prime time day part. 2003–04 season to date program rankings from September 22, 2003 through May 30, 2004.* Retrieved June 1, 2006, from http://www.abcmedianet.com/pressrel/dispDNR.html?id=060204_11

Perrson, A., & Musher Eizenman, D. R. (2003). The impact of a prejudice-prevention television program on young children's ideas about race. *Early Childhood Research Quarterly, 18,* 530–546.

Powers, C. M. (1998). The influence of the *Puzzle Place* television program on preschoolers' social behavior. *Dissertation Abstracts International Section A: Humanities and Social Sciences, 59*(2-A), 0414.

Rideout, V., Foehr, U. G., Roberts, D. F., & Brodie, M. (1999). *Kids & media at the new millennium: A comprehensive national analysis of children's media use.* Menlo Park, CA: Kaiser Family Foundation.

Rideout, V., & Hamel, E. (2006). *The media family: Electronic media in the lives of infants, toddlers, preschoolers and their parents.* Menlo Park, CA: Kaiser Family Foundation.

Rideout, V., Roberts, D. F., & Foehr, U. G. (2005). *Generation M: Media in the lives of 8- to 18-year olds.* Menlo Park, CA: Kaiser Family Foundation.

Rivadeneyra, R., & Ward, L. M. (2005). From *Ally McBeal* to *Sabado Gigante:* Contributions of television viewing to the gender role attitudes of Latino adolescents. *Journal of Adolescent Research, 20,* 453–475.

Roberts, D. F., & Foehr, U. G. (2004). *Kids and media in America.* New York: Cambridge University Press.

Sanchez, J. (2003). How American public schools using down-linked news media shape American Indian identity. *Howard Journal of Communications, 14*(1), 39–48.

Signorielli, N. (2005, November). *Minorities in prime: A look at occupations and occupational prestige.* Paper presented at the annual convention of the National Communication Association, Boston.

Signorielli, N., & Bauce, A. (1999). Recognition and respect: A content analysis of prime-time television characters across three decades. *Sex Roles, 40*(8), 527–544.

Signorielli, N., Horry, A., & Carlton, K. (2004, November). *Minorities in prime time: Is there parity?* Paper presented at the annual convention of the National Communication Association, Chicago.

Stroman, C. A. (1986). Television viewing and self-concept among black children. *Journal of Broadcasting & Electronic Media, 30,* 87–93.

Subervi-Velez, F. A., & Colsant, S. (1993). The television worlds of Latino children. In G. Berry & J. K. Asamen (Eds.), *Children and television: Images in a changing sociocultural world* (pp. 215–228). Newbury Park, CA: Sage.

Subervi-Velez, F. A., & Necochea, J. (1990). Television viewing and self-concept among Hispanic American children: A pilot study. *Howard Journal of Communications, 2*(3), 315–329.

Tamborini, R., Mastro, D., Chory-Assad, R. M., & Huang, R. H. (2000). The color of crime and the court: A content analysis of minority representation on television. *Journal of Mass Communication Quarterly, 77*(3), 639–653.

Taylor, C., & Stern, B. (1997). Asian-Americans: Television advertising and the model minority stereotype. *Journal of Advertising, 26,* 47–61.

Thompson, T. L., & Zerbinos, E. (1995). Gender roles in animated cartoons: Has the picture changed in 20 years? *Sex Roles, 32,* 651–673.

U.S. Census Bureau. (2002). *Statistical abstracts of the United States: 2002* (122nd ed.). Washington, DC: U.S. Commerce Department.

U.S. Census Bureau. (2004). *U.S. interim projections by age, sex, race, and Hispanic origin.* Washington, DC: U.S. Commerce Department.

Valkenburg, P. M., & Cantor, J. (2000). Children's likes and dislikes of entertainment programs. In D. Zillman & P. Vorderer (Eds.), *Media entertainment: The psychology of its appeal* (pp. 135–152). Mahwah, NJ: Lawrence Erlbaum.

Van Vuuren, D. P., Bornman, W., Mels, G., & Van Vuuren, M. (1990). Children's perceptions of and identification with the social reality of *The Cosby Show:* A comparison between the USA and South Africa. *South African Journal of Psychology, 20*(2), 70–79.

Vandewater, E. A., Bickham, D. S., Lee, J. H., Cummings, H. M., Waterlla, E. A., & Rideout, V. (2005). When the television is always on: Heavy television exposure and young children's development. *American Behavioral Scientist, 48*(5), 562–577.

Ward, L. M. (2004a). Wading through the stereotypes: Positive and negative associations between media use and Black adolescents' conceptions of self. *Developmental Psychology, 40*(2), 284–294.

Ward, L. M. (2004b). Who's that girl: Television's role in the body image development of young White and Black women. *Psychology of Women Quarterly, 28,* 38–47.

Ward, L. M., & Caruthers, A. (2001). Media influences. In J. Worell (Ed.), *Encyclopedia of women and gender* (Vol. 2, pp. 687–701). San Diego, CA: Academic Press.

Wartella, E., & Knell, G. E. (2004). Raising a world-wise child and the power of media: The impact of television on children's intercultural knowledge. *Phi Delta Kappan, 86*(3), 222–224.

Weigel, R. H., Kim, E. L., & Frost, J. L. (1995). Race relations on prime time reconsidered: Patterns of continuity and change. *Journal of Applied Social Psychology, 25,* 223–236.

Weiner, E., & Taylor, T. (1993). *A world of difference. On* The Puzzle Place. Los Angeles: Lancet Media Entertainment and KCET Public Television.

Williams, F., & Natalicio, D. S. (1972). Evaluating *Carrascolendas:* A television series for Mexican-American children. *Journal of Broadcasting & Electronic Media, 16*(3), 299–309.

Williams, M. E., & Coudry, J. C. (1989, April). *Living color: Minority portrayals and cross-racial interactions on television.* Paper presented at the annual convention of the Society for Research in Children Development, Kansas City, MO.

CHAPTER 16

Advertisements, Commercials, and the Development of a Child's Multicultural Worldview

JEFFREY E. BRAND

Although not essential for the cognitive, social, and moral development of children, commercial advertising targeted to children is nevertheless a prominent feature of children's contemporary experience—regardless of its effect on their beliefs, attitudes, and behaviors. So prominent is advertising in children's lives that researchers who write about television advertising and children—in America at least—have concluded that children and adolescents view as many as 40,000 television advertisements a year, plus thousands more in other media from hundreds of magazines, films, and websites designed to target children (Committee on Communications, 2006).

However, children are not a single audience, nor are they likely to receive, understand, or respond to commercial advertising based on a common filter. For a start, cognitive development mediates children's understanding of television advertising and, therefore, subsequent effects of advertising exposure. It is rare in social research to observe a factor in a cause-and-effect model that is so clearly dominant as is the influence of cognitive development on the role of advertising in children's lives. Other factors, such as culture, parental intervention, media literacy, consumer experience, and program/advertisement separators each play a role in helping children understand and make use of television advertising directed to them. As other chapters in this volume make clear, cognitive development is the demonstrated leading mediator of many influences on children, and cognitive development also mediates advertising's role in children's multicultural development.

In reception, understanding, and consequent behavior, children begin using advertising very early in life and require more than a decade to reach the sophistication and ability of adults to know the intent, context, appropriateness, and veracity of advertisers' claims. Without help, children appear to be ready targets for manipulation by commercial advertising. Advertising directed to children, like the children themselves, is multifaceted. Commercial messages include a variety of tactics and formal features that allow them to draw the attention of, and communicate messages to, children.

IMPLICATIONS OF ADVERTISING FOR THE DEVELOPMENT OF CHILDREN

Television is the first medium from which children begin to receive advertising directed to them. They begin to pay attention to television at 2 years of age and watch for about 2 hours per day in which time they are exposed to as much as 20 minutes of commercial messages. Exposure to commercial television increases steadily to 3.5 hours a day at age 11 or 12 and then declines to 2.75 hours in late adolescence (Story & French, 2004). Roughly half of all television advertisements directed to children are for food, and most of these foods are high in fat, salt, and sugar.

Given exposure statistics such as these, one finds it hard to imagine how advertising can be a neutral force in the development of children. Therefore, notwithstanding the common view that children's cognitive capacity will determine their reception of advertising messages, it is likely that advertising to children "is, potentially, a potent force affecting children's development" (Mizerski, 2005, p. 400). For many scholars like Kunkel (Kunkel & Ford, 2005), the estimated annual expenditure of $15 billion on advertising and marketing to children in the United States and alarming increases in childhood obesity rates in media-rich countries indicates that advertising to children has a profound impact on their development, with the most obvious of advertising's effects being on their physical growth and health. Kunkel's conclusions are consistent with and likely related to macrosocial evidence presented by Reekie (1988) that the growth of advertising during a period of an evolving multicultural society has produced homogenized consumer behavior.

IMPLICATIONS OF ADVERTISING FOR THE DEVELOPMENT OF CHILDREN'S MULTICULTURAL WORLDVIEW

Much more research contributes to a picture of how the advertising directed to children may contribute to their development, particularly their multicultural development. This body of research, which is relatively robust and current, can be divided into two lots. The first lot of research is presented in the advertising content studies that demonstrate what children are exposed to when they watch, read, or hear advertisements. The second lot of research is presented in the studies that observe children or their care providers (or both) as audiences for commercial advertising.

Content Studies

Advertising directed to children portrays social diversity, multiculturalism, and pluralism surprisingly better, in many ways, than do programming and story content. Research on advertising portrayals intersects with more pressing concerns than simply what is shown in advertising to children, to encompass concerns about the effect of advertising on child audiences. Content research, then, attaches additional dimensionality to understanding the place of advertising in the lives of young audiences. Diversity and multicultural content research is situated in two groups: race and culture in one group, gender in another.

Race/Ethnicity and Culture Portrayals in Advertising to Children

Although advertising directed to children presents social diversity, it favors dominant culture. Indeed, compared with content analyses published over a decade ago, representations of minority groups (African Americans, Asian Americans, and Latinos) have increased overall, although Whites still dominate the representations seen on television. The importance of advertising for these presentations was highlighted in a qualitative study designed to explore the context of ethnic and racial portrayals on Saturday morning programs broadcast on U.S. networks ABC, CBS, NBC, and PBS (Greenberg & Brand, 1993). In over 10 hours of children's programs and over 100 commercials during that time, Greenberg and Brand found more ethnic and racial diversity in advertising to children than in the programs directed to them: "So much for racial diversity in television programming on a typical Saturday morning," they wrote. "If you want to see . . . diversity on Saturday morning television, watch the commercials and skip the programs" (pp. 133, 135).

Of the 20 programs reviewed in the Greenberg and Brand (1993) study on commercial television, three featured major characters who were African American; only one program featured a "guest" Latino character, and all minority characters were male. By comparison, nearly every commercial break featured a minority character, limited, however, to African American portrayals with only fleeting images of characters from other ethnic and racial backgrounds. On public television, however, most programs presented a range of minority lead and minor characters from a variety of backgrounds.

More recent quantitative research demonstrates that advertising to children does represent characters of different races and ethnicities, but tends to stereotype, nevertheless. For example, Bang and Reece (2003) conducted an analysis of 813 commercials shown during children's television programming to assess minority portrayals in those advertisements directed to children. Researchers reviewed materials collected from ABC, CBS, Fox, and Nickelodeon television networks during key child viewership hours (i.e., Saturday mornings) in 1997. The commercials were then coded based on a number of characteristics including network; type of program during which the ad appeared; type of product or service advertised; and presence of Caucasian, Black, Latino, and Asian American models. Age, relationships, and individual versus group were also recorded. The study found that ethnic/racial minorities are more likely to be seen in representations that perpetuate societal stereotypes. For example, Asian Americans are likely to be seen promoting technology, furthering the view that they are smart and not fun. Whites were more likely than African Americans to be seen in a family setting, thus suggesting that African American families are single-parent rather than dual-parent units.

Examining 724 commercials featuring 1,209 distinct primary characters on eight U.S. networks, Li-Vollmer (2002) found that White characters appeared more frequently than any other group. For primary human characters, 75% were White, 20% were African American, 2% were Latino and Asian American, and Native Americans and Arab Americans were only a fraction of 1% of the sample. The proportionate low-level visibility of ethnic/racial minorities was further diminished by their segregation into commercials for a limited group of products and in which minority characters or actors were presented in lower prestige roles compared with White characters or actors. Whites were more likely to be spokespeople, initiators of action, and problem-solvers.

The contemporary portrayal of race/ethnicity and interracial/ethnic relationships in television commercials directed to and featuring children was examined in a content analysis of 595 commercials shown on four U.S. networks to determine the level at which interracial/ethnic play and mixing is portrayed in different advertisements (Larson, 2001, 2002). Only commercials that featured at least one real or animated child under the age of 12 were considered. Skin tone and facial features were determinants of race/ethnicity. The dominant setting was then coded (home/indoors, home/outdoors, other/indoors, etc.). Also coded were the type of interaction (cooperative, competitive, alone, none), type of activity (playing, eating, athletic play, productive/educational, stealing, none), and type of product (toy, food/groceries, clothing/accessories, and so on).

Larson (2002) found that 42% of commercials featured only White children, 57% featured White and AHANA (African, Hispanic, Asian, and Native American) children together, and 1% featured only AHANA children. Most White-children-only commercials were set in a "home/indoor" setting, but White and AHANA children together were more likely to occur in "other/indoor" settings. When compared to commercials with White children only, commercials that featured White and AHANA children together were more likely to contain "competitive" activities, "athletic play," or "eating," as well as being featured for restaurants. Commercials for toys were more likely to feature only White children.

Similarly, in a study of 381 advertisements aired on the Turner Cartoon Network in the afternoon, afterschool time slot, Merskin (2002) found that half featured an all-White cast of characters and one third featured mixed race groups, including Whites, with over half of these targeting both boys and girls. Only occasionally did advertisements that targeted girls feature an all–African American cast. The author concluded that advertisements continue to stereotype racial groups.

Harrison (2005) conducted a study in which 380 food advertisements shown during children's programs were analyzed for type of food shown and its nutritional values as well as character race, gender, age, eating behavior, and body size. Underlying Harrison's study was the argument that (a) African American children primarily learn about food and nutrition through television advertising and (b) children learn about race and culture from such commercials. The findings illustrate how complex are the opportunities for exposure to messages that may influence the development of children. Snack and fast foods dominated the advertisements, followed by bread and cereal. Commercials featuring African American characters were more likely to advertise snack and fast foods than those featuring all other groups, which were more likely to advertise bread and cereal. African American but not other characters tended to have apparent body sizes that were positively correlated with the food they were shown eating. Moreover, eating is depicted more as a family or adult supervised activity for Whites and other characters, but not for African American characters.

When studies of media content focus on a particular ethnic, linguistic, racial, or cultural group, it is uncommon for them to concentrate on any other group than African Americans. Yet Latinos and Asian Americans are growing in population and market. Taylor and Stern (1997) claimed that Asian Americans are an attractive minority market and conducted a content analysis of 1,300 prime-time television advertisements to document both the proportion and contextual nature of commercial representations of Asian Americans. They found that Asian Americans are overrepresented in television advertising in relation to their population in the U.S., but that portrayals of Asian Americans retain a century of stereotypes and appear tokenistic.

One of the difficulties faced by attempting to understand how advertising affects children's worldview is that much of the research is distinctively American, which engenders specific American experiences and imperatives. That most content research demonstrates that African Americans are "the other group" commonly found in advertising to the exclusion of other nationalities, races, ethnicities, and cultures is testament to this argument. Yet, given the common finding that African Americans are depicted substantially as the "dominant minority" in U.S. advertising, Peterson's (2002) study on what African American children are shown doing in television commercials is compelling.

Peterson's (2002) content analysis examined commercials on three U.S. networks and a local TV station as well as five cable TV stations. Only commercials showing African American child models were included in the sample. The expectation was that African American children would be shown in fewer scholastic roles than in other roles, and when these children were shown in such a role, their portrayal would be less frequently positive and shown differently from one product class to another. However, favorable depictions were substantially larger in scholarly, personal care, and eat or drink portrayals of African American children, who were depicted engaged in eating, drinking, athletic pursuits, scholastic activities, and visits with friends. They were portrayed less frequently engaged in exercise, work, play, and family activities than in other roles. Peterson observed that African American children are depicted in scholarly activities most often in ads for toys, games, and reading materials, whereas scholarly activity was infrequent in sporting goods, personal care, food, drink, and clothing commercials. From this study, one may draw the conclusion that advertisers are attempting to promote a positive image of African American youth. Peterson, however, concluded that the findings indicated advertisers pursued sales rather than an agenda of reducing (or enhancing) stereotypes or racism, because positive scholarly portrayals were limited to product classes that would appeal to such an image of minority youth.

Given that television remains, for the moment, the dominant source of media entertainment for children, studies of television eclipse studies of other media. However, as computer games increasingly compete for child (and adult) attention, researchers are beginning to ask questions about how games and their associated media portray culture and race/ethnicity. Scharrer (2004), for example, looked at portrayals of race/ethnicity in advertisements in popular computer game magazines including *Game Informer, GameNow,* and *Electronic Gaming Monthly.* White characters appeared in 86% of the advertisements, followed by African American characters in 30.2%, Asian characters in 18%, Latino characters in 10%, and Native American characters in 2% of the advertisements. This finding is consistent with a content analysis of 130 popular computer games across the five main gaming platforms in 2002 by Brand, Knight, and Majewski (2003). The authors found that computer game characters are presented using stereotypes found in traditional mainstream media like television. Of the 168 leading characters coded, all but a few were either White or obscured by costume or suit to make determining their ethnic/racial background impossible.

One expects the emergence of more research in countries other than the United States as cultural shifts are noted in places like China, where the market is likely to accommodate competing representations and ideas. An early example of this line of research in China suggests that although Chinese children's commercials reflect traditional cultural values, there appears to be a shift from a focus on older to younger Chinese and the increasing presence of Western values (Ji & McNeal, 2001). Given that the multicultural history and experience of the United States is unlike that of other nations, this research will be useful in highlighting different concerns and approaches to the potential effects of media content on cultural diversity and advance a more complete picture of children's development around the world.

Gender Portrayals in Advertising to Children

Although gender portrayals seemingly only intersect with ethnic, race, and culture portrayals, they do offer another mechanism by which to observe diversity and pluralism in advertising to children. The literature can be reviewed economically to demonstrate this point.

Many advertising content studies consider gender alongside ethnicity and race portrayals, presumably because ethnicity/race and gender are the two fundamental axes on which diversity and plurality are presented in contemporary media (Appiah, 2001; Bang & Reece, 2003; Harrison, 2005; La Ferle & Lee, 2005; Larson, 2001, 2002; Merskin, 2002; Rose & Robbs, 2001; Scharrer, 2004). Two studies, in particular, examine gender portrayals in cross-cultural studies: (a) Neto and Furnham (2005) compared U.S., U.K., and Portuguese television commercials aimed at children and (b) Browne (1998) compared U.S. and Australian television commercials directed to children.

Across the range of studies, the unequal and stereotyped representation of gender in advertising directed to children lends weight to the argument that advertising presents children with a narrow picture of the social world. Researchers have noted that their findings, when compared to earlier findings, demonstrate a gradual equalization of representation and some gains in roles for female characters, but both males and females continue to be presented in roles and contexts that researchers interpret as stereotyped (Davis, 2003; Larson, 2001; Neto & Furnham, 2005). For example, Merskin (2002) and Chandler and Griffiths (2000) found that males are more likely to be narrators in advertisements aimed at girls than are females in advertisements aimed at boys. Male characters are more likely than female characters to be presented as active, to be portrayed as an independent agent, and to be employed (Davis, 2003). Girls in advertisements tend to be portrayed in domestic activities and boys in active and combative contexts (Larson, 2001).

Stereotyping of characters through formal features also continues. In a content analysis of 117 toy commercials by Chandler and Griffiths (2000), boys' advertisements appeared more often than advertisements directed at girls (132 times versus 94 times), and boys' advertisements used more cuts whereas girls' advertisements used more dissolves. Advertising directed to boys had shorter shot lengths and more long shots whereas advertising directed to girls had longer shot lengths and more frequent closeups.

These single-country findings hold up in the cross-cultural studies of gender portrayals in children's television advertising presented by Neto and Furnham (2005) and Browne (1998). Neto and Furnham found that men and women portrayed in advertisements demonstrated similar levels of credibility and power across U.S., U.K., and Portuguese samples, with female characters relatively less powerful and credible than male characters, although males in Portuguese advertisements more often appeared as the central figure and engaged in aggressive and action roles than they did in the U.K. and U.S. However, stereotyping in Portuguese children's television advertising is less prevalent than in advertising directed to adults in Portugal.

Consistent with the research by Larson (2001) in which 595 commercials featuring children showed boys more than girls and boys more often in active and aggressive roles compared with more stereotypical domestic and indoor play for girls, Browne's U.S. and Australian results are comparable. In Australia, boys were shown more frequently than girls, and boy characters were shown in traditional roles in which they were more agentic, informed, and dominant than girl characters.

Summary of Content Research

Advertising aimed at child audiences is laden with stereotyped ways of presenting characters. Advertising also stereotypes by virtue of excluding groups from representation. Both of these mechanisms for stereotypes exist for cultural and racial/ethnic portrayals as well as for gender depictions. These general conclusions are based on research available largely for an American television experience to the exclusion of almost every other nation other than the U.K. and other media forms. In short, researchers have examined race/ethnicity within the U.S. culture and gender on television, with few unique exceptions.

Bearing this in mind, although portrayals of females and African Americans in U.S. ads have increased, stereotyping persists, and for all other ethnic and race groups, the lack of representation continues unabated. In this way, American television advertising is not diverse, particularly because the research available demonstrates that African Americans are the only "significant other" in race representation given to children through advertising. Even though there is often a sense that African Americans are shown in numbers proportionate with their population, the contexts in which they are presented, although not perfectly uniform, would not be accurately described as diverse. Meanwhile, Latino, Asian American, and Native American portrayals are very sparse and one could argue that setting aside context of portrayal, nearly any representation would represent an improvement in condition.

AUDIENCE STUDIES

According to Bang and Reece (2003), the impact of advertising on children may range from the foods they want to their worldviews, including attitudes toward other ethnicities and nationalities. Children are naturally curious and, according to Bang and Reece, they hunger for increased diversity in representation. When given the opportunity, children verbalize their desire for television to more accurately portray real life, which includes interaction with other racial/ethnic or cultural groups.

It is problematic and probably symptomatic of the advertising industry when audience research findings indicate viewers more easily orient to characters who are more like themselves. Thus, if the audience for an advertisement is populated predominantly by one group, advertising executives and creatives are more likely to use characters that resemble the market segment. Indeed, past audience studies have illustrated same-race media characters are more likely to attract the attention and interest of children than racially different characters due to in-group favoritism, which emerges when early-school-age children develop racial consciousness (Harrison, 2005).

Studying the responses of young children proves a challenge as researchers are faced with restricted access to young research participants and these participants have limited ability to communicate their experiences effectively to researchers. As researchers include older children as participants, these limitations begin to dissipate. Most research in this area is question-asking in nature. Of these studies, many involve parents, mainly mothers, responding to questions about what they have observed in their children's experiences. Only one experimental study has attempted to establish a causal model between advertising and young audiences.

Question-Asking Studies on Child Audiences of Advertising

A potentially influential study in terms of shedding light on how children's cognitive capacity may determine their understanding of advertising centers on a series of six focus groups conducted with 30 children aged 5 to 7 years and 13 children aged 11 to 12 years (Mallalieu, Palan, & Laczniak, 2005). The authors argued that children are growing more sophisticated in their ability to understand and respond to advertising directed to them. Among the questions asked in the focus groups were those about being able to differentiate advertising from program content, the ability to recognize the sponsor or backer of the advertisement, and the ability to evaluate advertising claims when trying specific products that they have seen in advertisements. Children were also shown contemporary commercials and asked questions about these advertisements. The authors claim their qualitative data show that younger children do not have complete understanding about the persuasive intent of advertising but they do show early signs of skepticism and awareness. They also found that the current generation of children is more savvy about advertising than children in the previous generation. By age 11 to 12, participants in this research were aware of and skeptical about the intent of advertising. The study did not explicitly, however, explore children's responses to multicultural stimuli in advertising.

Focus group research commissioned and published by one of the five broadcast networks in Australia, the Special Broadcasting Service (Ang, Brand, Noble, & Sternberg, 2006), did not look explicitly at advertising but did study adolescents/young adults (but not children), media, and multiculturalism. Compared with the United States, the Australian experience with multiculturalism has focused more on linguistic and cultural diversity (if not pluralism), and less on race/ethnicity. Nevertheless, it would be misleading to argue that Australia is a more diverse nation than the United States.

The Ang et al. (2006) research included 18 focus groups of Australians aged 16 to 40 years from diverse linguistic and cultural backgrounds conducted in three states and nine different communities. Results of the study were reported for different age bands; the findings reflected here are for 16- to 20-year-olds. Clearly these results do not generalize well to younger children but offer a useful glimpse at the effects of commercial television on adolescent and young adult attitudes, particularly in light of the findings by Browne (Browne, 1998) of similar portrayals of gender diversity in Australian and American television commercials.

Ang and her colleagues (2006) found that Australians from all backgrounds think multiculturalism is a positive aspect of Australian society, and this value is most obvious in the younger age band. They also found that younger audiences (aged 16–20 in this study), in particular, want to see diversity in television portrayals and are concerned that commercial interests may compete with diversity interests. This finding is consistent with what was reported, more generally, by children in the Mallalieu et al. (2005) study. The research suggests that younger audiences welcome diversity to learn, to understand, and for its novelty. Instead of arguing that advertising to children is necessarily driven by its content and the medium, the results of the Ang et al. research suggest that audiences may be attempting to meet purposes that are, unfortunately, unmet by advertisers.

It may also be that parents determine much of their children's orientation to advertising messages. To investigate this hypothesis, Rose, Bush, and Kahle (1998) conducted a comparative international study that drew on consumer socialization research. They administered a survey that examined communication patterns in families and attitudes toward television advertising among mothers of children 3 to 8 years of age in the United States and Japan. The authors found that mothers who held pluralistic and consensual values had more negative attitudes toward advertising than laissez-faire mothers. They found that TV advertising in general is related to negative attitudes toward advertising and increased parental attempts to intervene in children's media exposure. Laissez-faire mothers, on the other hand, indicated the least control over children's television viewing of advertising. The findings illustrate that ideologically oriented parents are highly involved in child rearing and distrustful of outside influences, such as advertising. One might argue that these parents have the capacity to more directly affect their children's multicultural worldview development than the relatively narrowly constructed views of race/ethnicity and gender portrayals of advertisers.

Nevertheless, researchers tend not to design their research to look for evidence of directed and individualized uses of media portrayals; instead, they look for evidence of a relationship between exposure to advertising and attitudes (and sometimes behaviors) among many different participants. La Ferle and Lee (2005), for example, surveyed the attitudes of Whites, African Americans, and Latinos in Texas about the frequency and accuracy of ethnic/racial representations in the media as well as the desire for ethnic/racial representation in advertising. Using a mall intercept design, the researchers surveyed 871 adult respondents, including one third each of White, African American, and Latino adults. The authors found that Latinos and African Americans were positive toward the idea of their ethnicity/race being more frequently represented in advertising, whereas Whites demonstrated the highest level of satisfaction with characters presented in ads. Although these findings cannot be generalized neatly to child audiences, it does indicate what past research has shown. Audiences, particularly minorities, not only enjoy diversity in the presentation of cultures in advertising, they also enjoy their own representation in advertisements. The overwhelming conclusion, therefore, is that more diversity is likely to be more positively received by contemporary minority audiences. Given that majority audiences would experience fewer representations of themselves, it is not clear that they would express the same levels of satisfaction.

An Experimental Study on Child Audiences of Advertising

Appiah (2001) conducted a 2 × 2 factorial experiment (African American or White by low or high cultural embeddedness) to test the hypothesis that people are attracted to models in advertisements based on perceived similarities between themselves and the model. These perceived similarities lead, in turn, to perceptions that the character is similar in characteristics to the perceiver, particularly when more highly embedded in one's culture. The four criterion variables included perceived similarity to characters, identification with characters, belief that advertisements are intended for the participant, and overall rating of advertisements. The sample consisted of nearly 350 students aged 14 to 19 years that included 92 Whites, 92 Latino Americans, 84 Asian Americans, and 81 African Americans. The findings were intriguing. White adolescents identified more strongly with African American characters in advertisements than with White characters, were more likely to believe they were the target audience of African American character advertisements, and were more likely to rate African American character advertisements favorably than White character advertisements. African American participants were more likely to perceive themselves as more similar to African American characters than White characters, were more likely to believe that advertisements were intended for them when they contained African American characters than White characters, and rated advertisements with African American characters more favorably than those with White characters. Importantly, Latino and Asian American audiences also responded more positively to African American characters than to White characters.

The results of the Appiah (2001) study suggest the number of advertisements showing African Americans may have created for Whites acceptance of and interest in racial/ethnic minority group portrayals in commercial advertising. If such interest was, in fact, generated, it may be argued that advertisers can comfortably expand the cultural diversity of the characters they use in advertisements. Perhaps more importantly, for African American children, the results suggest race of the character is critical to their feeling similar to and able to identify with the character. The authors concluded that there is reasonable support for identification theory, indicating that familiarity is important to minority children to identify comfortably with ads.

Summary of Audience Research

Although a larger body of research exists on the effects of advertising on children's food, alcohol, and tobacco use (cf. Audrain-McGovern et al., 2006; Bar-on, 2000; Braverman & Aaro, 2004; Henriksen, Flora, Feighery, & Fortmann, 2002; Jensen, Hickman, Landrine, & Klonoff, 2004; Pechmann & Reibling, 2006), there is little evidence that can be brought to bear on the exploration of how advertising directed to children plays a role in children's multicultural worldview development. There is some indication from the studies presented that the children of today are more critical consumers of media and generally embrace the practice of cultural pluralism. Although the research is limited, one might also theorize that advertising with ethnically/racially diverse characters may stimulate the curiosity and provide novel content, particularly for White child audiences, whereas African American children may feel less marginalized when characters who look like themselves are present in commercials.

IMPLICATIONS OF NEW AND EMERGING MEDIA IN SOCIETY

Television broadcasting is one of over 20 channels of electronic media available to children today. Twenty years ago, it was one of five. Other channels include pay television, prerecorded content on DVD, downloadable content in the form of peer-to-peer exchanges of commercial material or community-created content (C3) including short films posted online, and commercially available television programs and films downloadable for a fee, sometimes containing overseas advertising. Thus, in addition to an incomplete picture of the implications of traditional advertising on the development of children, researchers have recognized the increased complexity that new media have introduced. Kunkel and Ford (2005) wrote,

> Another new context for advertising is the internet. Roughly one-third (34%) of children aged 8–18 use the internet on an average day. . . . Even the youngest end of this range includes large numbers of web surfers, with 21% of 8- to 10-year-olds reported as users. Thus, it is no surprise that marketers have established websites termed "branded environments" in which children can play games while constantly exposed to advertising logos and product replicas. (p. 401)

The Internet gives audiences access to text plus video and audio content in the form of online news and entertainment, access to interpersonal and public communications services, and access to photographic and video sharing services, as well as access to libraries of music both for a fee and free. These services are often available at no cost and sign-up does not require a credit card. Instead, basic demographic and personal details are requested from the user and advertising is presented to the users as part of the service, with target audiences for the advertisements based on the information provided (e.g., age, sex, postal code, and so on).

Mobile telephony offers users not only telephone calling on mobile networks, but also text exchange, picture exchange, news, entertainment, and sports in video and text form. These forms of communication are ripe, too, for advertising customization and viral (one to one, relational) marketing.

Computers and dedicated home and hand-held game consoles add more media experiences to the mix for children. Indeed, the widespread popularity of computer games married with the uptake of computers and broadband has led to the rapid increase in *advergaming*, in which small online games created to advertise a product or brand can be played by consumers. Websites associated with characters, premiums, and toys are often embedded with small games. Brands like Mattel Hot Wheels (http://www.hotwheels.com/games/index.aspx), Bandai toys (http://www.bandai.com/), Kellogg's (c.f., www.frootloops.com), and Kinder Surprise (www.kindersurprise.com) all have games and promotions, and currently run television adverts and other marketing tools directed to children. Miniclip (www.miniclip.com/advertising) is a game site that is popular with schoolchildren and features advertising by Coca-Cola, Sony, Walt Disney, Nintendo, Nike, and others.

As Millwood Hargrave and Livingstone (2006) have noted, little research is available to address the impact of new media advertising and marketing on children. However, Aikat (2005) conducted a content analysis of the four leading mainstream children's websites based in the United States—Children's Television Workshop (http://www.ctw.org/), Disney Online (http://www.disney.com/), Nickelodeon Online (http://www.nick.com/), and PBS Online (http://www.pbs.org/). Aikat found that these children's websites were full of information of interest for children of different ages and contained many content features to attract young audiences. Unfortunately, online advertising was not included in the study focus.

A content analysis of food advertisers' websites by Moore (2006) focused on advergaming and online marketing of food to children. The study included 96 brands and examined the formal features of the website, the nature of the brand's presence on a website, and the presence of one or more games on the site. The author suggested that the Internet (specifically commercially sponsored websites containing games and promotions designed for children) is an effective marketing force because children are willing consumers of these marketing communications products by virtue of their exciting, fun, interactive, and tie-in potential with toys. Because the study did not measure children's actual use of products, effectiveness of online advertising to children was assessed only in terms of intent. However, of the 96 brands studied, 82 had a website that targeted or included a point of interest for children. This suggests, perhaps, that marketers believe the child and parent audiences are attending. Websites were highly varied, with some focusing on information and others on entertainment. Unfortunately, data on children's clicking and other behaviors were not included in this study, although it may well have been available from web traffic metrics.

It is unfortunate that early studies on children's online experiences with advertisements have not included a focus on cultural diversity and multiculturalism in popular online destinations.

Children's Media Savvy

Although it may appear that the increased channels available to children may make them more susceptible to the influence of advertising messages, Karet (2004) interviewed groups of U.K. children between the ages of 6 and 16 years about their multichannel television environment and concluded that children in multichannel television homes showed more savvy, understanding, and sophisticated use of the media. Karet reasoned, but did not measure, that increased ability may be a function of the increased functionality and control in a multichannel television environment.

Children, particularly older children, are regarded for their sophistication in using the rapid expansion of technological venues in which advertising is moving (Palmer & Carpenter, 2006). Advertising approaches are expected to be more diverse, sophisticated, personal, interactive, and mobile as food and beverage marketers pursue the so-called Generation Y and M children. Palmer and Carpenter conducted a literature review on trends in food and beverage marketing to children and youth. They determined that increased integration of technological approaches (for example, advergames, seeded chat rooms, embedded celebrity marketing, and stealth and viral marketing) means it will be increasingly difficult to distinguish between noncommercial communication and marketing. While commercial and noncommercial messages become blended and more sophisticated, studies indicate that children's cognitive capacity to process advertising messages remains unchanged. On reflecting on the obesity epidemic among children, Palmer and Carpenter argue that many of the counteradvertising and counter-obesity efforts often discussed in policy research cannot compete with the sophisticated marketing and advertising venues.

Nevertheless, children are receptive to new media channels, and this receptivity can be used positively if channelled by the community. An example of their receptivity is offered by a review of literature about ways of increasing fruit and vegetable consumption among children between 6 and 12 years of age. Blanchette and Brug (2005) found that behavioural change to healthy eating can be achieved with parental and school involvement in which consistent messages are given to this effect along with technology-based interventions such as computer games.

Summary of New Media Implications

In 2000, the *Journal of Interactive Advertising* was launched to address the growing interest of industry and academics in the potential for new advertising channels. The first issue featured remains a useful framework for considering the response of all audiences to interactive advertising content. Rodgers and Thorson (2000) hypothesized that audiences approach the Internet more than traditional electronic media with goal direction and initiative. Depending on an audience member's goals for using new media, from highly directed (e.g., doing work) to playful (e.g., playing games), and skill level at using the technology, the authors argue advertising can work either very well or very poorly. Given the newness and complexity of the media environment, it is difficult to draw any conclusions about how children use new channels. And it is even more difficult to determine what impact advertising might have on them through these channels. Children tend to be receptive to technology in a way that older generations are not, so it is reasonable to hypothesize that children could be learning about cultures, languages, and races/ethnicities from online content, including advertising, but it is a hypothesis that still requires empirical validation.

DISCUSSION

Despite the limitations of the empirical evidence available on advertising and children's multicultural worldview development, there is the promise that new research is forthcoming, particularly research that explores children's advertising in all its related contexts, including a multinational perspective. Research by Rose and Robbs (2001) is an example of a study that may eventually lead to further understanding of multiculturalism and advertising. In a survey of advertising faculty in 147 colleges and universities in the United States, the authors found 66% of the respondents included a multiethnic component in their courses and 51% indicated that courses had a multicultural component. However, the amount of time spent on multiculturalism in advertising during the semester was just 3 hours on average. Only 15% reported offering full courses on the subject of multicultural media, but all of these courses were offered as electives.

The present state of knowledge is far from complete. We know that children are exposed to a large volume of advertising over the course of their development. We know that television advertising dominates, but that other media feature advertising directed to children as well. We know that most of the research in this area focuses on content rather than on the child audience directly and is situated in the United States. We also know that African Americans are the "dominant other" in advertising directed to children, but they are shown in stereotyped ways. At least in the United States, children appear to be developing their worldviews in ways that include greater sophistication about advertising and media messages, giving them tools with which to counteract the potential disadvantages of residing in a generally monocultural media world.

Given that advertising is a global business designed to create a stimulus for consumption, perhaps an apropos analogy is the marketing of medications by the pharmaceutical industry for treating the medical conditions of children. Before these medications are placed on the market, there is the assumption that they undergo rigorous clinical trials and must adhere to strict regulations that supposedly protect the welfare of those children who will consume the medications. To protect our children from the potential harmful effects of advertising messages, particularly those messages that may influence how children feel about themselves and others, it would appear prudent to subscribe to similar rigor to inform policy on this complex issue. In the meantime, we can be comforted in knowing that the children of today are remarkably sophisticated media consumers compared to the days when we were children.

REFERENCES

Aikat, D. (2005, May). *"Click here for fun, games, friends . . .": Analyses of media content characteristics of children's web sites.* Paper presented at the annual conference of the International Communication Association, New York.

Ang, I., Brand, J., Noble, G., & Sternberg, J. (2006). *Connecting diversity: Paradoxes of multicultural Australia.* Artarmon: SBS.

Appiah, O. (2001). Black, White, Hispanic, and Asian American adolescents' responses to culturally embedded ads. *The Howard Journal of Communications, 12,* 29–48.

Audrain-McGovern, J., Rodriguez, D., Patel, V., Faith, M. S., Rodgers, K., & Cuevas, J. (2006). How do psychological factors influence adolescent smoking progression? The evidence for indirect effects through tobacco advertising receptivity. *Pediatrics, 117*(4), 1216–1225.

Bang, H.-K., & Reece, B. B. (2003). Minorities in children's television commercials: New, improved, and stereotyped. *Journal of Consumer Affairs, 37*(1), 42–67.

Bar-on, M. E. (2000). The effects of television on child health: Implications and recommendations. *Archives of Disease in Childhood, 83*(4), 289–292.

Blanchette, L., & Brug, J. (2005). Determinants of fruit and vegetable consumption among 6- to 12-year-old children and effective interventions to increase consumption. *Journal of Human Nutrition and Dietetics, 18*(6), 431–443.

Brand, J. E., Knight, S. J., & Majewski, J. (2003, November). *The diverse worlds of computer games: A content analysis of spaces, populations, styles and narratives.* Paper presented at the Level Up: Digital Games Research Conference, Utrecht.

Braverman, M. T., & Aaro, L. E. (2004). Adolescent smoking and exposure to tobacco marketing under a tobacco advertising ban: Findings from 2 Norwegian national samples. *American Journal of Public Health, 94*(7), 1230–1238.

Browne, B. A. (1998). Gender stereotypes in advertising on children's television in the 1990s: A cross-national analysis. *Journal of Advertising, 27*(1), 83–96.

Chandler, D., & Griffiths, M. (2000). Gender-differentiated production features in toy commercials. *Journal of Broadcasting & Electronic Media, 44*(3), 503–520.

Communications, Committee on (2006). Children, adolescents and advertising. *Pediatrics, 118,* 2563–2569.

Davis, S. N. (2003). Sex stereotypes in commercials targeted toward children: A content analysis. *Sociological Spectrum, 23*(4), 407–424.

Greenberg, B. S., & Brand, J. E. (1993). Cultural diversity on Saturday morning television. In G. L. Berry & J. K. Asamen (Eds.), *Children and television: Images in a changing sociocultural world* (pp. 132–142). London: Sage.

Harrison, K. (2005, May). *Thinking outside the bun? Racial differences in food advertisements viewed by children.* Paper presented at the annual conference of the International Communication Association, New York.

Henriksen, L., Flora, J. A., Feighery, E., & Fortmann, S. P. (2002). Effects on youth exposure to retail tobacco advertising. *Journal of Applied Social Psychology, 32*(9), 1771–1789.

Jensen, J. A., Hickman, N. J., III, Landrine, H., & Klonoff, E. A. (2004). Availability of tobacco to youth via the Internet. *JAMA, 291*(15), 1837.

Ji, M. F., & McNeal, J. U. (2001). How Chinese children's commercials differ from those of the United States: A content analysis. *Journal of Advertising, 30*(3), 79–92.

Karet, N. (2004). Understanding children's responses to TV. *International Journal of Advertising & Marketing to Children, 5*(2), 51–59.

Kunkel, D., & Ford, J. (2005). Predicting a renaissance for children and advertising. *International Journal of Advertising, 24*(3), 401–405.

La Ferle, C., & Lee, W.-N. (2005, March). Can English language media connect with ethnic audiences? Ethnic minorities' media use and representation perceptions. *Journal of Advertising Research,* 140–153.

Larson, M. S. (2001). Interactions, activities and gender in children's television commercials: A content analysis. *Journal of Broadcasting & Electronic Media, 45*(1), 41–56.

Larson, M. S. (2002). Race and interracial relationships in children's television commercials. *The Howard Journal of Communications, 13,* 223–235.

Li-Vollmer, M. (2002). Race representation in child-targeted television commercials. *Mass Communication & Society, 5*(2), 207–228.

Mallalieu, L., Palan, K. M., & Laczniak, R. N. (2005). Understanding children's knowledge and beliefs about advertising: A global issue that spans generations. *Journal of Current Issues and Research in Advertising, 25*(1), 53–64.

Merskin, D. (2002). Boys will be boys: A content analysis of gender and race in children's advertisements on the Turner Cartoon Network. *Journal of Current Issues and Research in Advertising, 24*(1), 51–59.

Millwood Hargrave, A., & Livingstone, S. (2006). *Harm and offence in media content: A review of the evidence.* Bristol, UK: Intellect Books.

Mizerski, D. (2005). Issues concerning the effects of advertising on children. *International Journal of Advertising, 24*(3), 399–401.

Moore, E. S. (2006). *It's child's play: Advergaming and the online marketing of food to children.* Menlo Park, CA: Henry J. Kaiser Family Foundation.

Neto, F., & Furnham, A. (2005). Gender-role portrayals in children's television advertisements. *International Journal of Adolescence and Youth, 12*(1–2), 69–90.

Palmer, E. L., & Carpenter, C. F. (2006). Food and beverage marketing to children and youth: Trends and issues. *Media Psychology, 8*(2), 165–190.

Pechmann, C., & Reibling, E. T. (2006). Antismoking advertisements for youths: An independent evaluation of health, counter-industry, and industry approaches. *American Journal of Public Health, 96*(5), 906–913.

Peterson, R. T. (2002). The depiction of African American children's activities in television commercials: An assessment. *Journal of Business Ethics, 36*, 303–318.

Reekie, D. W. (1988). Market segmentation and apartheid. *European Journal of Marketing, 22*(3), 7–13.

Rodgers, S., & Thorson, E. (2000). The interactive advertising model: How users perceive and process online ads. *Journal of Interactive Advertising, 1*(1). Retrieved May 6, 2007, from http://www.jiad.org/v011/n01/rodgers/index.htm

Rose, G. M., Bush, V. D., & Kahle, L. (1998). The influence of family communications patterns on parental reactions toward advertising: A cross-national examination. *Journal of Advertising, 27*(4), 71–85.

Rose, P., & Robbs, B. (2001, Winter). Multicultural issues in the advertising curriculum. *Journalism & Mass Communication Educator*, 30–38.

Scharrer, E. (2004). Virtual violence: Gender and aggression in video game advertisements. *Mass Communication & Society, 7*(4), 393–412.

Story, M., & French, S. (2004). Food advertising and marketing directed at children and adolescents in the U.S. *International Journal of Behavioral Nutrition and Physical Activity, 1*(3), 1–17.

Taylor, C. R., & Stern, B. B. (1997). Asian-Americans: Television advertising and the 'model-minority' stereotype. *Journal of Advertising, 26*(2), 47–61.

CHAPTER 17

Children and Television News Broadcasting

An Intercultural Communication Analytical Approach

VENITA A. KELLEY

The average news story is 60 seconds long. The average news article is 400 words long. The normal child is developing the cognitive skills to read visual media until past the age of 21, extended adolescence having become a norm in the United States. Children who have been raised since the 1980s are cited as less compassionate, as having more ennui, and as looking for more cultural substance than those of previous generations. In this chapter, my approach will be from an intercultural communication viewpoint. Lustig and Koester (1996) define communication as a symbolic process by which people create meaning. Meaning is a perception, thought, or feeling expressed and communicated by a person. In communication, everything is based on an interpretive process.

Context is important in determining meaning. The contexts we create for our children around multiculturalism will be crucial to their development as citizens who believe they have agency in the societies in which they live. Kluver (2000) argues that "informatization," stemming from information and communication technologies, shapes cultural and civic discourse. For him, the implications are that globalization and informatization will have profound cultural and social consequences on societies. The positive outcome to informatization is forecast to be the empowerment of marginalized communities and the democratization of information. The negative consequences are likely to be that local autonomy, tradition, and cultural integrity are harmed.

Television news broadcasting, because its purpose is to present and explain the experiences that occur in societies, is the mass medium that, by its own definition, conveys it will offer a truthful, trustable context of information that may then be used to evaluate and understand the state of our society, ourselves, and other citizens. News broadcasting informs us and offers a context for that which affects us locally, nationally, and globally. In accordance with symbolic interaction theory, once the news is constructed for an audience, there is a symbolic and interpretive construction of message and meaning that has taken place that affects the viewer (Langer, 1960). Before the age most are allowed to enter preschool, our children are gathering information that they make sense of according to known patterns and meaning. The more those patterns and meaning are reinforced, the more the structures for interpreting those patterns are formed in the mind of the child. Therefore, an information source, such as television news broadcasts, a societal mechanism for guarding democracy and defending the public interest, affects children's development as citizens of their society and/or contributes to their competency as cultural beings in the multicultural environment that stems from globalization and intercultural contact within societies and around the world.

Intercultural communication occurs when people from different cultures work to establish understanding while interacting according to the meaning systems that inform their cultures (Lustig & Koester, 1996). An underlying principle of intercultural communication approaches to knowledge is that multiple perspectives tend to lead to the development of multiple intelligences and competencies in those that practice them. Multicultural intelligence then develops and includes an awareness of one's attitudes toward a home culture and the self, as well as toward others and their cultures. The intercultural communication focus applied herein will examine how dominant and macrocultural symbolic constructions inform television news broadcasting and the influence that news broadcasting may have on children and their multicultural understanding and competence.

SYMBOLISM AND THE SHAPING OF COGNITION

Human beings are symbol-making, symbol-synthesizing organisms. My working definition for cognition is that it is the ability to recognize, analyze, and gain perspective about the information that one observes. Symbols are the means by which human beings gain cognitive ability (Campbell, 1949; Langer, 1960). A symbol is presented; the human mind absorbs the symbol and then makes sense of what the symbol means to inform human behavior, sense, and decision making. Symbols have both the ability to shape human meaning as well as to reinforce what humans understand something to mean (Langer, 1960).

Humans use symbols to shape and develop their cultures, which are then used to build societies (Kelley, 1994). Symbols are reshaped into myths, which are stories human beings tell themselves to describe the reality they know and accept, thereby establishing a cultural foundation, shaping modes of behavior, and inculcating expectations that strengthen their society (Kelley, 1994). The myths contribute to the perception that the cultural bases of society are stable. Experiencing cultural perspectives reinforces and shapes one's membership in the society. Myths are, therefore, stories that human beings tell themselves and one another to strengthen and legitimize the culture they create.

Powerful multilevels of meaning come with the evolved structuring of symbols in which the visual gives rise to language terms that describe and stand in for the symbol and create the myths that support our view of reality (Pennington, 1985). Though we have developed verbal language that has meaning to us, we still pay great attention to the nonverbal or symbolic when living our daily lives (Langer, 1960). The interconnection of the visual and the linguistic seems to create one of the strongest tools for cementing the myths we create to reinforce our notions of culture and reality.

By nature of them being developing citizens, eager to understand the world they confront, children seek and absorb these symbolic structures at a fantastic rate because they are invested in building the reference points for how to view life, understand what they experience, and give their lives the predictability and stability said to be a foundational human need necessary for self-actualization (Maslow, 1943).

THE DEVELOPMENT OF CULTURAL AUTHENTICITY AND CULTURAL WORTH

One of the worst misconceptions of multiculturalism is that as practice, people are encouraged to celebrate their own cultures *instead of* that of a dominant or macroculture for the society. My argument is that, in fact, the multiculturalism movement is most invested in cultures being able to claim and legitimize those goods and perspectives, stemming from culturally founded philosophies, that reinforce the culture as viable and contributing to the society within which the cultural member resides. Each culture existing within a society then operates with efficacy and agency, as well as is recognized for their contributions to the overarching culture of the society. The cultural artifacts, or the particular culture, then become a resource for the overall society in terms of how it reinforces itself so as to serve the needs of all its members.

In societies made up of multiple peoples and cultures, all cultures have contributed to the massive body of philosophy, knowledge, laws and practices, behavioral expectations, and history that have shaped the society (Takaki, 1993). From these diverse contributions, a macroculture emerges that provides reference points for meaning, expectation, membership, and relevant philosophy for the society. As Takaki's work verifies, often a dominant culture also exists and absorbs and claims possession of all the cultural goods that are deemed good, meaningful, and worthwhile. Those cultural goods are redefined as stemming from the dominant culture (or those who control it), its structures, its existence, and its perspectives. A mainstream manifesto of what is respectable, meaningful, and appropriate for the society emerges. The dominant culture claims as its own the symbols, myths, and inventions that have contributed to overall societal development and considers it a right to name the meanings attached to those cultural products. Controlling the macrocultural cache of referential knowledge is a powerful means for influencing societal meaning and interpretive structures, and it serves a dominant culture well to gain and sustain control (Morris, 1993).

The problem with dominant culture absorption of the cultural goods of other cultures, in my view, is that particular cultural contributions, their meaning and intended use, cannot be fully operative in the ways the culture intended, when those goods are presented through the filters of a dominant culture. This is especially true if the dominant culture, as is the case in the United States, is marred by constructions that negate other cultures and the people who act in accordance with their cultural customs and philosophies. Viability and use are always subject to scrutiny when the culture that has created a phenomenon does not control its interpretation and use in a society.

To further my argument, those from microcultures (people of color) are also affected by their cultural frames of reference. The current focus on diversity, intercultural competency, and multicultural inclusion indicates that there is strong and relentless advocacy to have those cultural perspectives included, understood, and recognized in the daily lives of those who are from those microcultures.

Dominant cultures endeavor to retain rights to rhetorical, mythic, and symbolic definitions of reality and legitimacy (Morris, 1993). An erasure or absorption of the contributions, grounding perspectives, and philosophies of the microcultural peoples who have contributed strongly to the overall (macro)societal structure tends to occur in order to authenticate the dominant culture's legitimacy (Takaki, 1993). Of course, with the advent of multiculturalism and globalization, a dominant culture's inherent legitimacy is challenged because the enforced anonymity upon microcultures is known to not serve the needs of all the society's citizens and there is resistance to the established order being the only legitimate order (Morris, 1993).

In multicultural societies, children must see and be exposed to structures and foundations of belief that are based in their own particular cultural worldviews or cultural legitimacies in order to develop a positive sense of themselves and the social and societal worth of their cultures (Hilliard, 2007). What children see about themselves and their cultural group has a tremendous effect on how they feel about themselves and their development as citizens of a society. Why, then, is the visual so important in developing self-efficacy and cultural efficacy? The visual is the means by which we take in information that allows us to give rise to the language with which we construct the myths and other messages that maintain cultures and societies. Let us shift the focus to a brief discussion of how the visual influences learning.

VISUAL COMMUNICATION AND COGNITION

Joseph Campbell (1949) asserts that we process experience visually. Thus, the visual is what we trust most to support our sense of reality. Langer (1960) asserts that visual structures are taken in all at once without any specific rules of order. The visual is understood in the deep structures of the brain, even bypassing our created structures for meaning, such as language and intellectual decision making, no matter how complex the structures are. However, the visual is an amorphous system; we do not have a way to categorize the visual system of sense making or fully control human ability to interpret the visual.

According to Lester (2006), the brain responds to form, depth, movement, and color, and there is form, structure, convention, and rule for any pictures that we visually witness. The perception of color allows us to distinguish among what we observe and to assign meaning to it. Biederman (1987) indicates that our minds may store images symbolically within the brain in the form of geons (geometric ions) in order to make recognition (of symbols) quick and simple. Only 36 geons are needed to discern all objects we visually witness, and human beings can recognize many objects with the existence of only 3 geons. The more often we see the image, or its iconic geonic form, the more an interpretation of what we see is quick, unexamined, and accepted according to the meanings that have been attached to the symbol. Because of the regular use of vision (by most) to confer what we accept as the "truth" in our daily lives, most human beings tend to take for granted what they see and, unless they commonly practice analysis of the visual, they are apt to accept the "truth" of an established symbolic order.

The same can be said of written and language contexts. Chomsky (1968) argues that language contains surface and deep structures that we access to retrieve known information. The nature of language itself prompts us to develop a healthy skepticism about its use. Wisdom about the use of language is in evidence in axioms such as "actions speak louder than words." The visual, because it is so malleable, amorphous, and immediately absorbed, is more difficult to filter (Berger, 1989). You see what you see, and the mind begins to categorize what is seen according to known, evolving, and developed patterns upon receiving the information.

Images that have been constructed still carry this tension about them—the visual context that has been produced by human beings will be a reflection of the symbols, cultural contexts, and philosophies that have meaning for the producers of the image (Langer, 1960). This is why macrocultural and microcultural contexts for constructing meaning and cultural stability must be recognized as having an impact on culturally produced goods. Any culture tries to reproduce itself so as to provide reference points for the assumptions, behaviors, perspectives, and viable existence of its cultural members. A culture must see itself reflected in its society in order to have a sense of its own meaningfulness. Doing so gives the culture its foundations for the humanity and continued survival of its members. If the cultural means to self-validate are compromised or usurped, there are dilemmas that arise for members of the culture (Kelley, 1994).

TELEVISION NEWS BROADCASTING AS A MEDIUM OF CULTURAL SOCIALIZATION

Informal education stems from knowledge-producing contexts that may or may not be overt and intentional (Klopf, 1995). The knowledge from these contexts is absorbed through observation, repeated activities, stories, training, and lessons we are told. News broadcasters are purveyors of knowledge and public wisdom in most societies. Frankly, television news broadcasting is one of the mass mediums by which societal myths and stories are circulated to the populace, thereby constituting a large part of the informal education systems of most modern-day societies.

Dominant cultures form an invisible force that legitimizes and relegitimizes itself through sheer force of repetition (Morris, 1993). The underlying cultural assumptions about what should be important to people reflect a dominant culture orientation even though the news that is reported is ostensibly about all people who have contributed to the macroculture of the society. In multicultural societies, my view is that the informal educational structure about what and *who* are important in society becomes attached to the structures of news products. Every viewer is affected by the symbols that underlie the construction of news content. My view is that children are especially affected by the multiple constructions, whether overt or concealed, that are a part of television news broadcasting.

Ideally, news broadcasting is supposed to be a society's means of conveying public knowledge in order to create informed citizens who can then refer to the knowledge to make decisions about how best to take part in the governance and stabilization of society (Gans, 1979; Gitlin, 1980; Greco Larson, 2006). News broadcasting, therefore, has tremendous power to shape the societal structures and behaviors that citizens either support or reject. News content is supposedly shaped by a particular ethic of non-biased, objective reporting of facts (Greco Larson, 2006). Opinion does not belong in the dissemination of information that is considered traditional news broadcasting. Objectivity and balance in the information presented to society about itself and its members are the basis of an ethic for the production and reporting of news, as news broadcasting is intended to be an instrument serving the public good. The public good, by my broad definition, is that which enables the citizenry to understand and follow the edicts of the overarching document shaping the society. In the United States, that document would be the Constitution, which guarantees its citizens a right to life, liberty, and the pursuit of property, often amalgamated to "the pursuit of happiness" (ownership of property being the ultimate goal, ensuring happiness, according to those who shaped the

Constitution, who were highly influenced by John Locke's treatise on government). These are lofty and worthwhile goals for news broadcasting, yes? The intent is to solidify and support a democracy, a society where all people have worth and are enabled to pursue the goals they envision for their lives.

News content, though, is a product of those who produce and report it to society. News broadcasting, by its very nature, consists of information that is massaged and reshaped into contexts that best confirm the prevailing views of society (Kelley, 1994). Choices have to be made about what to broadcast, how to present the news, and how to convey core information using the simplest, most effective means of communication. A framework for defaulting into dominant cultural symbolic structures is inherent to the dissemination of news. The common reference points that already exist in the myths that shape and inform the society are easier to rely on to convey meaning. Novel information, interpretation, and perspective take time to present and explain. As for multicultural perspectives and population, news content often allows "presence" (unexplored visibility) to substitute for cultural substance and representation, thereby reinforcing that all cultures, and people from them, can be understood in the ways that are already known (Kelley, 1994).

When television news programming, like *Inside Edition* and *A Current Affair,* was introduced to the public, there was public outcry because news was being used for its "entertainment value." The objective, balanced, nonsensational presentation of fact for which news broadcasting aimed was set aside for a format that reinforced myths and symbols that enticed the viewer at the affective level rather than being directed at the analytical or intellectual level.

Traditional news broadcasting, though, has long followed the lead of the entertainment news formats for the benefit of retaining viewership. Ehrlich (1996) argues that mainstream and entertainment news were never fully distinct from one another. For Ehrlich, the characteristics of both are the same: they have a moralizing tone, take stands on guilt or innocence, and examine sex and crime. Traditional news broadcasting, however, uses discovered material to inform and improve the world, whereas entertainment news . . . entertains. In addition, human beings crave stories. Stories carry symbolic framings and mythologies that have undergirded societies for centuries—heroes, villains, the joy of innocent children, vilification of scoundrels and enemies, and identification of scapegoats—and are the glue that has built societies and societal predictability of normal public and private life (Campbell, 1949).

With television news broadcasting containing so much entertainment value to maintain viewership, the lines between what is real and what is fictitious news content are likely blurred. Certainly, what is worthwhile about news content is blurred. Gavin (2005) cites that children below the age of 6 do not readily distinguish fantasy from reality; therefore, by extension, young children may not readily know the difference between entertainment content and factual news content.

Children, through adolescence, are developing the cognitive ability that will allow them to analyze their cultural, societal, and relational realities and experiences (Epstein, 2007). The stories they are told while they are developing this cognitive ability affect how they shape and understand information for the rest of their lives. According to Waber et al. (2007), regardless of income or sex, children improve rapidly between the ages of 6 and 10 in terms of their cognitive growth, with less dramatic cognitive growth as they move further into adolescence. The Waber et al. findings suggest that children shift toward integrating what they already know based on what they have been exposed to as they approach adolescence, rather than learn new skills. And by extension, in my view, they also wane in learning new ways with which to interpret visual information, such as that presented on television news broadcasts.

Visual media become powerful mechanisms by which to spread myth and symbol, as human beings are already highly susceptible to, perhaps even prefer, what the visual can bring to them as opposed to other means, such as reading, that take greater effort and time to accomplish (Lester, 2006). Visual media are hypnotic, and children pay attention to visual media more actively (Comstock, 1978). Furthermore, it is important to consider that children have fewer psychological mechanisms for blocking information that may be harmful to their sense of self or that may produce anxiety (TalkingwithKids.org, n.d.). Children worry and are more often terrified by the television news content to which they are exposed (such as tornados and their potential descent upon them) than adults, who tend to have enough experience to reason about the reality of disasters. Similarly, and more pointedly relevant to this chapter, the exposure of children, particular children of microcultures, to news content that consistently says people like them are "bad" people may potentially have a profound influence on their personhood and relationship to their microculture as well as the macroculture. Obviously, these sorts of messages have an equally profound influence on how mainstream children perceive children of microcultures and themselves in relation to microculture children. The ability to comprehend visual media (i.e., develop visual literacy) requires young viewers to become aware of and proficient in identifying and understanding who has control over the symbolic structures that are used as a platform to create the visual messages to which they are exposed (Lester, 2006).

If we are to teach children to be multiculturally adept, my view is that we must teach children to understand context according to the cultural systems that are in place and relevant to the way a person is behaving, perceiving, or communicating. Our ability to contextualize responds to the complexity of an object, situation, and event. When we contextualize (compare, contrast, and evaluate what we experience within certain parameters), we allow new meanings to emerge from information we receive (Lustig & Koester, 1996). We also become more amenable to accepting that symbolic constructs can have multiple meanings from different cultural standpoints. The ability to discern context leads to greater culturally competent interactions (Lustig & Koester, 1996). Children need to learn how to contextualize what they see and experience to negotiate the complexities of a society that exposes them not only to vast technologies but also to increasing opportunity for global contact.

CHILDREN AND NEWS

Children do watch news broadcasts; 40% of children in the United States watch the news and are aware of news content (TalkingwithKids.org, n.d.). If news broadcasting, the mechanism used by society to sustain its cultural vitality, fails to present meaningful information that contributes to the *overall* public good, the greater the likelihood that we become susceptible to the images and language terms of the dominant culture whose meanings predetermine and define our social and cultural position as members of microcultures.

As servants of the public good, the press has been criticized for decades as having failed their task to be "the fourth estate" and, thus, a watchdog over government for the citizenry of the country by presenting little-known but key knowledge in order for citizens to make informed civic decisions

(Ott, 2007; "The Mass Media," n.d.). To distinguish itself from entertainment news programming, traditional television news broadcasting is supposed to consist of information that is factual and derived objectively. The news content that is delivered to its viewers should offer a balanced perspective.

Children do not necessarily have the experience to understand the societal import of corporate corruption trials, war profiteering, and the "oil for money" public outcry, but they may understand the simpler "doom, despair, and agony" words and symbols by which these stories are framed. Thus, news broadcasts may be conveying how overwhelming, unsafe, unpredictable, and dangerous life and the world are ("Modern Life," 2006). My argument here, extrapolating from intercultural communication theory, is that by passing on information about the society in which they exist through news content, news broadcasting is shaping the rhetorical framing and communication mapping that goes on for children (McDevitt, 2001).

Nick News emerged from a concern that children were not exposed to news content, thus, not given the opportunity to develop the critical thinking skills necessary to become involved citizens of society (Capriccioso, 2003). Journalist Linda Ellerbee has been the host of the television news program for children since 1991. Ellerbee comments that she and the producers design the presentation of news content to children in ways that avoid telling them what to think but rather encourage them *to* think (Capriccioso, 2003). The news program deliberately presents news content that communicates people accomplishing "something good" related to the topic on which they report.

Television programming like the *Colbert Report, The Daily News with Jon Stewart,* and *Real Time with Bill Maher* are increasingly used as sources of factual news by young people (Ott, 2007). Though the sarcastic humor, irony, and skepticism laden in these programs seem to be contributing to a reawakening of the importance of being an informed and a vocal citizen, opinion and social critique masquerading as news reporting can challenge the development of alternative ways of viewing the subjects covered by these programs among young people. The subject matter selected for each program is based on what the host and producers deem important and congruent with their own perspective, which limits the potential of engaging in a discourse that includes multiple realities and is multiculturally relevant.

Children of Color and News Broadcasting

Delgado and Stefancic (2004) argue that psychic injury and stigmatization, caused by hate speech, teach young microcultural children (children of color) to hate themselves and the phenotypic markers of their difference, such as skin color. Furthermore, Gamson (1997) points out that messages of exclusion and symbolic boundaries are part of the social constructions to which people in U.S. society are exposed. Stories that are told about children of color, and people of color in general, affect children. Microcultural children often are exposed to images and rhetorical framings that are symbolic constructions of their social place and function (Banks & Grambs, 1972; Douglas, 1997; Ehrlich, Weller, & Eden, n.d.; Sue & Sue, 1990), thus, their informal learning through media may override any formal learning they gain in school and in the home. Kiri Davis's 2005 documentary replicating the Kenneth Clark study of the 1950s, wherein Black children chose a White doll over a similar Black doll and defined the Black doll as "bad" because it was Black, indicates the damage that symbolic framings can have on children.

Children of color routinely see and hear shocking news reports about people from their own microcultures. Some examples of the types of news stories to which children are exposed include dehydrated would-be immigrants to the United States found dead in the desert between Mexico and the United States, a reporter beheaded by alleged religious extremists, trench-coat wearing teenagers hunting down and shooting an African American boy, an American Indian male found murdered with no suspects to pursue, an Arab American chased through the street and beaten, and an Asian American child who has his "accent" mocked as he pays for his lunch. The narrative details of these events are presented in television news broadcasts without offering young viewers an age-appropriate analysis for understanding such complex situations and considering what to do with the information.

Hence, the steady diet of negative news content to which they are exposed has the potential of destabilizing microcultural children's self-identity and cultural identity (Banks & Grambs, 1972; Tavares, 2007). If the "reality" that is visually and linguistically presented emphasizes the negative and does not reflect the space and agency of, or reinforce the humanity of, the children and their cultural groups, distressing reference points result for how children of color perceive their importance as members of society. If the macrocultural context continues to drive the symbols, images, and language that frame our understanding of microcultures, children of color will suffer in locating culturally legitimizing referential hooks for their citizenship and belongingness in society.

Mainstream Children and News Broadcasting

Let's not erase from the discussion that mainstream children (European American and those associated with the dominant culture) are affected by news broadcasts and symbolic constructs as well. Dominant cultural constructs can give mainstream European American children a sense of superiority and entitlement to the goods of the society. At the same time, immigrant ethnic Whites did experience histories of isolation, marginalization, and oppression, which have been erased by their absorption into the dominant culture, resulting in discounting their native cultural and ethnic practices (Banks, 1979). European American children once could identify more readily and proudly with their ethnic European heritage. Unfortunately, the nativist movement resulted in the imposition of a monolithic "Whiteness" and "Americanness" upon European Americans (Banks, 1979). In fact, the cultural and ethnic stripping has influenced some European Americans to intentionally seek a cultural identification in other cultures (Sue & Sue, 1990). In my view, when European American children differ from the dominant cultural platform, they often have few options but ones that define their perspectives and behaviors as deviant, misfit, and meaningless to the larger society. Perhaps this may, in part, explain why satirical news programming, such as *The Daily News with Jon Stewart,* appeals to mainstream adolescents in that these programs offer a means to critique the prevailing status quo while protecting one from being targeted or excluded by dominant culture mechanisms of social control.

CONCLUSION

When children are given the opportunity to analyze and discuss what they view in news broadcasts, they become more visually literate and multiculturally competent. That is to say, they develop the ability to interpret and understand that symbols and images exist within a cultural context and that multiple perspectives may explain an event. In other words, children can be taught to analyze the components of visual messages;

the rhetorical, language, and cultural texts that make up the constructed images; and the words that are used to describe news content. Parents and caregivers can be key to helping children develop these skills.

TalkingwithKids.org (n.d.) offers some suggestions for how parents and caregivers may facilitate how children process news content to which they are exposed. It is important to first help children understand that news reporting focuses on the unusual, not the typical. For example, although televised news broadcasts may overemphasize people of color engaged in negative behavior, people of color, like anyone, are doing more good than bad. And second, news broadcasts provide only brief reports of the simple facts rather than providing a more comprehensive understanding of the circumstances involved in an event. For instance, to simply report the unemployment rates among communities of color does not do justice to the sociocultural elements that influence these statistics. Naturally, the type of news broadcasting to which one exposes a child must consider age appropriateness; for example, children under the age of 6 have a limited ability to discern fantasy from reality. Just as children may develop fears from viewing violent news content, they may also become desensitized to viewing violent images, which is, perhaps, more concerning. Finally, setting limits on the amount of news to which children are exposed is encouraged, as is being prepared to disallow children from viewing news broadcasts deemed inappropriate.

We are more and more a visual society. Although the emphasis in this chapter was on televised news broadcasts, we can no longer ignore the Internet as an avenue for news access. The Internet combines our preference for visual information gathering with the linguistic and establishes stronger platforms for controlling our realities and presenting our cultural beliefs and practices to the world. The Internet has become one of the more accessible and reliable tools for gaining information, hearing diverse perspectives, and engaging in public debate and discourse. Yet, the same rule applies: the images and words used to construct knowledge cannot be separated from the worldview of the person who was behind its construction.

An intercultural approach to communication aims to teach how to become actively engaged in cocreating meaning that is multiculturally based and contextually relevant, from which understanding between parties emerges. Our focus for the future, as those interested in how children interact with news content, is to own that "our" truth is knowledge that is created within our own cultural framework. In other words, there is a multicultural foundation to the reality that underlies the "facts" that we report as newsworthy. Playing on the famous words of Frederick Douglass, concerned members of our societies must advocate for media that can support our humanity and its cultures, and in so doing, we can enable ourselves to be "forever free."

REFERENCES

Banks, J. A. (1979). *Teaching strategies for ethnic studies.* Old Tappan, NJ: Allyn & Bacon.

Banks, J. A., & Grambs, J. D. (1972). *Black self concept.* Columbus, OH: McGraw-Hill.

Berger, A. (1989). *Seeing is believing: An introduction to visual communication.* Mountain View, CA: Mayfield.

Biederman, I. (1987). Recognition-by-components: A theory of human image understanding. *Psychological Review, 94*(2), 115–147.

Campbell, J. (1949). *The hero with a thousand faces.* Princeton, NJ: Princeton University Press.

Capriccioso, R. (2003, October 6). *News from Linda Ellerbee.* Retrieved June 1, 2007, from http://www.connectforkids.org/1note/50.5

Chomsky, N. (1968). *Language and mind.* Orlando, FL: Harcourt Brace Jovanovich.

Comstock, G. (1978). *Television and human behavior.* New York: Columbia University Press.

Davis, K. (2005). *A girl like me* [Youth documentary]. Retrieved June 22, 2007, from http://www.mediathatmattersfest.org/6/a_girl_like_me/

Delgado, R., & Stefancic, J. (2004). *Understanding words that wound.* Boulder, CO: Westview Press.

Douglas, S. (1997, April). Body bag journalism—local TV news. *The Progressive.* Retrieved June 11, 2007, from http://findarticles.com/p/articles/mi_m1295/is_n4_v61/ai_ 19254725f

Ehrlich, H. J., Weller, J., & Eden, A. (n.d.). *If it bleeds it leads, if it's white it's right: Local TV news in 12 cities.* Retrieved June 11, 2007, from http://www.prejudiceinstitute.org/IfItBleeds.html

Ehrlich, M. J. (1996, February). The journalism of outrageousness: Tabloid television news vs. investigative news. *Journalism & Mass Communication Monographs,* (155), 1–20.

Epstein, R. (2007). *The case against adolescence: Rediscovering the adult in every teen.* Sanger, CA: Quill Driver Books.

Gamson, J. (1997). Messages of exclusion: Gender, movements, and symbolic boundaries. *Gender & Society, 11*(2), 178–199.

Gans, H. (1979). *Deciding what's news: A study of CBS Evening News, NBC Nightly News, Newsweek and Time.* Evanston, IL: Northwestern University Press.

Gavin, M. L. (2005). *How to talk to your kids about news.* Retrieved May 31, 2007, from http://www.kidshealth.org/parent/positive/talk/news.html

Gitlin, T. (1980). *The whole world is watching: Mass media and the making of the new left.* Berkeley: University of California Press.

Greco Larson, S. (2006). *Media and minorities: The politics of race in news and entertainment.* Lanham, MD: Rowman and Littlefield.

Hilliard, A. (2007, January). *Culturally responsive teaching.* Keynote at Central State University Center for Urban Education, Wilberforce, OH.

Kelley, V. (1994). *A different world: Striving by intention and extension to depict core African American culture.* Unpublished doctoral dissertation, University of Kansas, Lawrence.

Klopf, D. (1995). *Intercultural encounters: The fundamentals of intercultural communication* (3rd ed.). Englewood, CO: Morton.

Kluver, R. (2000). Globalization, informatization, and intercultural communication. *American Communication Journal, 3*(3). Retrieved June 12, 2007, from http://acjournal.org/holdings/v013/Iss3/spec1/kluver.htm

Langer, S. K. (1960). *Philosophy in a new key.* Cambridge, MA: Harvard University Press.

Lester, P. M. (2006). *Syntactic theory of visual communication.* Retrieved April 30, 2007, from http://commfaculty.fullerton.edu/lester/writings/viscomtheory.html

Lustig, M. W., & Koester, J. (1996). *Intercultural competence: Interpersonal communication across culture.* New York: HarperCollins College Publishers.

Maslow, A. (1943). A theory of human motivation. *Psychological Review, 50,* 370–396.

McDevitt, M. (2001). *What works in civic education? An evaluation of the kids voting USA curriculum.* Retrieved on June 8, 2007, from http://www.knightfdn.org/research/civic/kids_voting/kidsvoting_report_improved.pdf

Modern life leads to more depression among children. (2006, Sept. 13). Retrieved May 21, 2007, from http://www.telegraph.co.uk/news/main.jhtml?xml=/news/2006/09/12/nosplit/njunk112.xhtml

Morris, A. (1993). Centuries of Black protest: Its significance for America and the world. In H. Hill & J. Jones, Jr. (Eds.), *Race in America: The struggle for equality* (pp. 19–72). Madison: University of Wisconsin Press.

Ott, B.L. (2007). Some good news about the news: 5 reasons why "fake" news is better than Fox "news." Retrieved May 15, 2007, from http://jot.communication.utexas.edu/flow/?jot=view&id=812

Pennington, D. (1985). Intercultural communication. In L. Samovar & R. Porter (Eds.), *Intercultural communication: A reader* (4th ed., pp. 30–39). Belmont, CA: Wadsworth.

Sue, D. W., & Sue, D. (1990). *Counseling the culturally different: Theory and practice* (2nd ed.). New York: John Wiley and Sons.

Takaki, R. (1993). *A different mirror: A history of multicultural America.* Boston: Little, Brown and Company.

TalkingwithKids.org. (n.d.). *Talking with kids about the news.* Retrieved May 12, 2007, from http://www.talkingwithkids.org/television/twk-news.html

Tavares, M. (2007). *Should children watch news programs?* Retrieved June 1, 2007, from http://www.multirio.rj.gov.br/portal/riomidia/rm_materia_conteudo.asp?idioma=2&idMenu=3&v_nome_area=Mat%E9rias&label=News&v_id_conteudo=66975

The mass media as fourth estate. (n.d.). Retrieved June 1, 2007, from http://www.cultsockNdirect.co.uk/MUHome/cshtml/media/4estate.html

Waber, D. P., Carl de Moor, C., Forbes, P. Almli, R., Botteron, K., Leonard, G., et al. (2007). The NIH MRI study of normal brain development: Performance of a population based sample of healthy children aged 6 to 18 years on a neuropsychological battery. *Journal of the International Neuropsychological Society, 13,* 1–18.

CHAPTER 18

An Evaluation of the Effects of Movies on Adolescent Viewers

JANNETTE L. DATES

LILLIE M. FEARS

JOSEPHINE STEDMAN

One of the most important elements of adolescence is the development of an identity. As teenagers develop their values, beliefs, and ideas about behaviors, they are likely to draw from a variety of cultural and social forces in their worlds. In this regard, many look to music industry icons and figures in major sports leagues, whereas some choose celebrities who headline popular movies, and others use a mixture of such figures.

Although a healthy relationship with parents is important during the teenage years, adolescents also are confronted with a variety of other institutional, social, and cultural influences—namely those linked to school, social organizations, and the mass media. The symbols and messages a culture promotes tell a great deal about that culture's values and priorities. Although parents, educators, and religious leaders can demonstrate exemplary behaviors for teenagers to adopt, adolescents still find that they must negotiate an abundance of mediated messages, encountered either by choice or involuntarily on a daily basis.

Viewing a movie usually is a voluntary act chosen for entertainment. As such, viewers, especially youth, can count on being exposed to a variety of messages while participating in the viewing experience. What types of movies and movie characters do teens regard most favorably? Are there differences relative to teenagers' gender and ethnicity? Finally, what are the racial attitudes of adolescent

Authors' Note: The authors wish to thank Dr. Arega Negero, research methodologist at Howard University, for his assistance with statistical analyses for this chapter and Dr. James Rada, assistant professor in the Department of Radio, Television, and Film at Howard University, for reviewing and suggesting revisions for this chapter.

viewers? Using results from a survey of teenagers in late adolescence, ages 18 and 19, we conducted a descriptive investigation that addressed the following questions:

1. Are the differences that exist in adolescent perceptions of Black-oriented and general movies related to differences in race of the adolescent?
2. Are the differences that exist in adolescent perceptions of movie characters related to differences in race of the adolescent?
3. Is there a race × gender interaction effect that exists in adolescent perceptions of movie characters?
4. Are there racial attitude differences between African American and Caucasian adolescents that may help contextualize how these groups perceive their movie-viewing experience?

REVIEW OF RELEVANT LITERATURE

Social cognitive theory (Bandura, 1986), persuasion theory (Cialdini, 1984; Petty & Priester, 1994), and cultivation theory (Gerbner, Gross, Morgan, Signorielli, & Shanahan, 2002) propose that the more frequently behaviors are depicted in media, the more likely these behaviors are perceived to be prevalent. Studies (Bandura, 1994; Petty & Priester, 1994) argue that this should also increase the likelihood of imitation of these behaviors. Dixon, Borland, and Paxton (2003) tested these theories in their study of adolescents' perceptions of characters depicted smoking in videos. Their findings support the proposition that characters who smoke on-screen influence adolescents' beliefs about smoking. Results revealed that attractive, high-status characters who smoke may promote positive perceptions of the utility of smoking in youth, whereas unattractive, low-status characters may detract from the appeal of this behavior.

Research examining children and adolescents' movie-going can be traced to the Payne Fund movie studies of the early 1930s. Contemporary inquiries into these and similar issues date back to the early 1960s (Renninger, Sigel, Damon, & Lerner, 2006), and critical observers of U.S. society have attempted to assess the effects of motion pictures on viewers. This assessment has become more pronounced over the years as the number of movie-goers has multiplied and the influence of movies has grown.

Unlike the typical movie audience of the 1930s to 1970s, where many family members attended movies together in theaters, today's movie audience is much more splintered and diverse. Today's audiences consist of viewers from all life stages—childhood, adolescence, adulthood, and elderly life—with like age groups most often viewing films "appropriate" for their group with one another. Of all these age groups, the child/adolescent audience has been found to be the largest.

Additional research (Rodman, 2007) indicates that the typical movie audience consists primarily of young, Caucasian males. The fact that many of these teenagers tend to see some types of movies, such as *Matrix* and its sequels, repeatedly—as much as three times—is noticed by studios. Thus, filmmakers usually target this group by using action scenes and some female nudity in their films.

Most of the empirical research relevant to films has been conducted within the context of the debate about television. As such, little is known about how violent movies per se might affect young viewers' aggressive behavior (Moeller, 2001). Over the years, academic research has shown that at least three consequences have been empirically linked to viewing media violence—violent behavior, distorted perceptions of reality, and tolerance of "real-life" aggressive behaviors. Molitor and Hirsch (1994) cite that social learning (Bandura, 1977; Bandura & Walters, 1963) and instigation (Berkowitz, 1962) theories have offered the most support for the "media violence equals actual violence" thesis. Noteworthy investigations that support the theory that exposure to television or film violence can influence persons to commit acts of aggression include the Surgeon General's Report (Surgeon General's Scientific Advisory Committee on Television and Social Behavior, 1972), Huesmann (1982), and Molitor (1985), as well as studies by Andison (1977) and Hearold (1979).

Reith (2003) has also found a positive correlation between aggressive and criminal behavior and exposure to screen violence in Norwegian boys in their late teens. Prosecutors have even cited Martin Scorsese's 1976 film *Taxi Driver,* about a New York City cab driver stalking a political candidate, as the motive for John W. Hinckley, Jr.'s, assassination attempt on President Ronald Reagan in 1981.

Harris (2003) argues that the increase in crime over the past 40 years cannot be [solely] blamed on the absence of fathers or poor child rearing. Instead, she offers two alternative hypotheses. The first attributes the increase to the rise in the amount and vividness of movie and television violence; the second attributes the increase to the decline and fall of the cold war and the fact that Americans no longer have a common enemy that unites them.

Concerns about the effects of movies are not limited to violence, but include distorted perceptions of reality and tolerance of "real-life" aggressive behaviors. Smoking, stereotyping, and distortions of reality all pose similar concerns for those interested in the emotional and psychological well-being of teenagers. Distefan, Pierce, and Gilpin (2004) examined whether adolescents' favorite movie stars influenced their choice to start smoking. Results showed that, overall, adolescents with a favorite star who smoked on-screen were significantly more likely to have smoked by the follow-up interview. Young girls, in particular, who were highly receptive to advertising and promotions, were most likely to initiate smoking themselves when they had a favorite star who smoked on-screen.

Pechmann and Shih (1999) examined whether movie smoking scenes affected the beliefs, emotional reactions, and smoking-related thoughts and intents of nonsmoking ninth graders. Results supported the thesis that smoking (versus nonsmoking) scenes positively aroused the young viewers, enhanced their perceptions of smokers' social stature, and increased their intent to smoke. However, it is noted that showing the youths an antismoking advertisement before the film effectively repositioned smoking from forbidden to tainted social behavior, which nullified the original results.

Taveras et al. (2004) examined the relationship between adolescents wanting to look like figures in the media and their level of physical activity. Using a cross-sectional mailed survey to 11,606 boys and girls between the ages of 9 and 16, participants reported detailed information on physical activities over the previous year, and the extent to which they were trying to look like same-sex images in television, movies, and magazines. Results showed that 3,109 (46%) of the girls and 1,360 (27%) of the boys reported making at least some effort to look like figures in the media.

The foregoing theories, expectations, and concluding arguments, viewed together, provide the theoretical bases upon which the present study rests. Furthermore, the present study is an extension of previous research conducted by the first author (Dates, 1980).

METHOD

Participants

The participants were college freshmen, ages 18 to 19 years, from two universities in the United States. One university is an urban, historically Black institution located in the Mid-Atlantic region, and the other is a majority White institution located in the

Southwest. One is a public, the other a private institution.

The students were recruited from introduction to mass media courses and freshman orientation classes at the majority White institution and from freshman orientation classes at the historically Black university. Every freshman in each of the classes surveyed was invited to participate in the survey, but only the students who self-identified as Black or Caucasian and were in the 18–19 age range were included in the analysis. This sample yielded a total of 66 useable surveys from the Southwest, majority White university and 99 useable surveys from the Mid-Atlantic, historically Black university.

INSTRUMENTATION

Selection of Movies

The year 2005 was chosen to select movies that were recent enough for the 18- to 19-year-old group to have seen and still remember characters and storylines in the films. Top movies for 2005 selected for the study were obtained from the Metacritic Top Films website (Internet Movie Database, 2006). Metacritic compiles reviews from respected critics and publications for films, videos/DVDs, books, music, television, and games. Its unique metascores show the critical consensus at a glance by taking a weighted average of critic ratings. Movies that received both 1 and 2 top choice ratings were chosen and compiled in a list. The list was then pretested to find out the top movies chosen by students at the two universities. Results from each university were compiled and compared. Five movies made the final list: *The 40-Year-Old Virgin, Crash, Diary of a Mad Black Woman, Hustle & Flow,* and *Batman Begins.* Of these movies, *Diary of a Mad Black Woman* and *Hustle & Flow* may have more of an appeal to a Black-oriented audience, whereas *The 40-Year Old Virgin, Crash,* and *Batman Begins* are movies that may appeal more to a general audience.

Measurements

The measurements used in this study included (a) the Viewer-Perception Questionnaire, an instrument developed by the first author of this chapter based on the semantic differential technique (Kerlinger, 1968, pp. 564–580; Osgood, Suci, & Tannenbaum, 1971, pp. 76–126) to assess viewer perceptions of movie characters and (b) the Color-Blind Racial Attitudes Scale (CoBRAS; Neville et al., 2000).

Viewer-Perception Questionnaire

Viewer enjoyment of the selected movies and evaluative perceptions of movie characters were measured by a questionnaire developed by the lead investigator. The questionnaire allowed the participants to note enjoyment levels of the specified movies using a 5-point scale in which a higher score indicated more enjoyment of the movie. The semantic differential technique was used to evaluate participant perceptions about each of 12 movie characters by choosing a point along a 5-point continuum for each item of bipolar adjective pairs. The 13 adjective pairs for the evaluative dimension included honest-dishonest, nice-mean, attractive-ugly, fair-unfair, brave-cowardly, good-bad, successful-unsuccessful, wise-foolish, strong-weak, kind-cruel, careful-reckless, thoughtful- selfish, and boring-entertaining (evaluative dimension scores ranging from 13 to 65). There were two items that measured believability or interest in being like the character (similar-different, believable-not believable) and two items that measured identification or interest in "doing things the character does" (a lot-not at all, many things-nothing at all), with each dimension having scores ranging from 2 to 10. A composite score was then generated that ranged from 17 to 85, with a higher score indicating a generally more favorable perception of the character.

Color-Blind Racial Attitudes Scale

The Color-Blind Racial Attitudes Scale (CoBRAS) was developed by Dr. Helen Neville and her colleagues in 2000. In the article "The Construction and Initial Validation of the Color-Blind Racial Attitudes Scale (CoBRAS)," Neville and her colleagues gave detailed information concerning the reliability and validity of the CoBRAS. Factor 1, Unawareness of Racial Privilege (i.e., global belief in a just world), consists of seven items with scores ranging from 7 to 42; Factor 2, Unawareness of Institutional Discrimination (i.e., sociopolitical belief in a just world), consists of seven items with scores ranging from 7–42; and Factor 3, Unawareness of Blatant Racial Issues (i.e., denial of racism), consists of six items with scores ranging from 6–36. The 20 items were rated using a Likert scale ranging from 1 = strongly disagree to 6 = strongly agree (some items required reverse scoring). Higher scores showed greater levels of "blindness" as well as denial or unawareness of racism.

Research Procedures

The surveys were administered during regularly scheduled class meetings during the 4-day period of October 23–26, 2006 at both universities. The administration of the survey was completed in 25 to 30 minutes.

RESULTS

Table 1 presents findings regarding how much African American and Caucasian adolescent viewers liked the African American–oriented and general movies. The results from the ANOVAs indicate that African American and Caucasian adolescent viewers did not significantly differ on the degree to which they enjoyed the Black-oriented movies (*Diary of a Mad Black Woman* and *Hustle & Flow*). For the three general audience–oriented movies (*Batman Begins, 40-Year-Old Virgin,* and *Crash*), significant differences between African American and Caucasian adolescent viewers were found for *Batman Begins* and *Crash.* Whereas Caucasian adolescent viewers enjoyed *Batman Begins* significantly more than the African American adolescent viewers, the African American adolescent viewers of *Crash* liked the movie significantly more than did their Caucasian counterparts. The African American viewers' more favorable opinion of *Crash* may be, in part, due to the theme in the storylines that focused on race and racial conflicts.

What is also worthy of note is the substantial discrepancy between the percentages of Caucasian students who reported viewing the more Black-oriented movies when compared to the African American students. More than twice as many African American students viewed *Diary of a Mad Black Woman* than Caucasian students (86% and 38%, respectively) and more than three times as many viewed *Hustle & Flow* (65% African American vs. 18% Caucasian). This same imbalance in attendance was found for *Crash*, with 76% of African American students and only 36% of the Caucasian students having viewed the movie. The movies in the general category were comparable in attendance between racial groups (*Batman Begins:* 41% African American and 52% Caucasian; *40-Year-Old Virgin:* 68% African American and 71% Caucasian).

Tables 2 through 4 present the results of the two-way ANOVAs that investigated the main effects of race and gender as well as the interaction of these two subject characteristics in the adolescents' perceptions of each of the 12 movie characters. The differences due to race were not significant for any of the 12 movie characters (see Table 2). In other

Table 1 Analysis of Variance Results for Comparing African American and Caucasian Students on Movie Enjoyment

	Students								
	African American			*Caucasian*					
	M	*SD*	n^a	*M*	*SD*	n^b	df_B	df_W	*F*
Black-oriented movies									
Diary of a Mad Black Woman	4.73	.54	85	4.48	.82	25	1	108	3.16
Hustle & Flow	4.16	1.01	64	3.67	1.30	12	1	74	2. 16
General movies									
Batman Begins	3.71	1.27	41	4.41	.74	34	1	73	8.14
Crash	4.92	0.27	75	4.17	.92	24	1	97	40.27*
40-Year-Old Virgin	3.88	1.35	67	4.17	1.13	47	1	112	1.44

Note. Higher mean scores indicate a more favorable view of the movie.

[a] Sample size for the African American group differs for each movie because not all 99 students had viewed each of the movies.

[b] Sample size for the Caucasian group differs for each movie because not all 66 students had viewed each of the movies.

*$p < .01$.

Table 2 Analysis of Variance by RACE of Student Reactions to Movie Characters

Movie characters		*n*	*M*	*SD*	*F*	*p*
40-Year-Old Virgin						
Andy Stitzer	African American	63	45.7937	6.28916	.100	.752
	Caucasian	43	46.1860	6.21540		
	Total	106	45.9528	6.23261		
Trish	African American	62	61.0161	8.65266	.105	.747
	Caucasian	46	61.5435	8.00196		
	Total	108	61.2407	8.34744		
Batman Begins						
Alfred	African American	37	64.2973	8.08931	3.728	.058
	Caucasian	32	67.9063	7.31926		
	Total	69	65.9710	7.89633		
Henri Ducard	African American	35	38.8571	10.61393	1.437	.235
	Caucasian	30	41.8000	8.91492		
	Total	65	40.2154	9.90185		
Crash						
Jean Cabot	African American	70	37.0429	8.60811	.607	.438
	Caucasian	22	38.6364	7.53750		
	Total	92	37.4239	8.35245		
Cameron Thayer	African American	71	45.7324	6.65251	2.299	.133
	Caucasian	23	43.1739	8.12769		
	Total	94	45.1064	7.08242		
Christine Thayer	African American	69	50.5217	6.94645	3.222	.076
	Caucasian	23	47.3043	8.80823		
	Total	92	49.7174	7.53501		
Hustle & Flow						
Key	African American	55	48.3273	6.62223	.960	.331
	Caucasian	11	46.1818	6.66060		
	Total	66	47.9697	6.62622		
Shug	African American	58	47.8276	6.48382	3.606	.062
	Caucasian	11	43.8182	6.04679		
	Total	69	47.1884	6.54234		
Nola	African American	58	43.5690	7.94082	.062	.803
	Caucasian	10	42.9000	6.98331		
	Total	68	43.4706	7.76227		
Diary of a Mad Black Woman						
Helen	African American	84	50.5714	7.26650	.132	.717
	Caucasian	23	49.9565	6.89847		
	Total	107	50.4393	7.16145		
Orlando	African American	64	55.0938	7.49967	.274	.602
	Caucasian	14	53.9286	7.78029		
	Total	78	54.8846	7.51273		

Note. Higher mean scores indicate a more favorable view of the movie character.

Sample sizes for both the Caucasian and African American groups differ from character to character because not all the participants viewed each of the movies or elected to rate all the characters.

words, African American and Caucasian adolescent viewers experienced similar reactions to the characters, whether in the more Black-oriented movies or the movies that may have a more general appeal.

Table 3 presents findings related to the adolescents' gender. There were significant differences found for 2 of the 12 characters. Male students liked the character Henri Ducard in *Batman Begins* significantly more than did their female counterparts, whereas the female students significantly favored Christine Thayer in *Crash*. Furthermore, in analyzing the interaction of the race and gender subject characteristics, ordinal interactions appear to exist for the same two movie characters (see Table 4). Although males of both racial groups favored the Henri character more than females, the Caucasian adolescents, regardless of gender, viewed the character more positively than their African American counterparts. Just the opposite was true for Christine in that females of both racial groups viewed the character favorably, but both male and female African American adolescents reacted more positively to this character than the Caucasian viewers.

Table 5 presents the racial attitudes of the African American and Caucasian viewers. Two significant findings were found. First, the African American adolescents appeared more unaware of White privilege in society when compared to their Caucasian counterparts. And second, Caucasian adolescents were more willing to reject the notion that social policies are warranted to eliminate the negative consequences of racism. The racial groups were comparable on their beliefs about the existence of racism.

DISCUSSION

This investigation sought to describe the relationship of race to adolescent perceptions of their movie-viewing experiences and used data regarding their racial attitudes to descriptively contextualize their expressed preferences, theorizing that adolescent moviegoers would differ by race on their racial attitudes, which, in turn, would have relevance to understanding why the participants may have expressed particular preferences for movies and movie characters.

The films that targeted African American audiences, *Diary of a Mad Black Woman* and *Hustle & Flow*, did not attract a large number of Caucasian viewers. The small number of Caucasian viewers who saw the films reacted similarly to the way the African American film-goers did to the characters. Possibly, those Caucasian students who elect to attend films that target Black audiences are more similar to the African American viewers than might be expected, and this could explain the lack of a significant difference between the two racial groups' perceptions of the characters. When taking into account the African American adolescents' significant lack of awareness that White privilege exists in society when compared to their Caucasian counterparts and the fact that both racial groups did not significantly differ on their denial that racism exists in society, there may, in fact, be more similarity between these two viewing audiences than differences.

There were not many differences in adolescent perceptions of the 12 characters in the five movies used in this study. Clearly, however, the male students liked Henri Ducard in *Batman Begins* significantly more than did the female students, whereas the female students significantly liked Christine Thayer more than did male students. Perhaps these findings might imply that males prefer male action characters and females like passionate women who stand up for themselves.

But of greater relevance is the ordinal interaction effect that exists for race and gender relative to movie character preferences. Although Henri was rated more favorably by

Table 3 Analysis of Variance by GENDER of Student Reactions to Movie Characters

Movie characters		*n*	*M*	*SD*	*F*	*p*
40-Year-Old Virgin						
Andy Stitzer	Male	30	46.6000	5.53110	.722	.397
	Female	84	45.4643	6.52603		
	Total	114	45.7632	6.27582		
Trish	Male	31	61.2258	8.06106	.042	.838
	Female	84	60.8690	8.36340		
	Total	115	60.9652	8.24933		
Batman Begins						
Alfred	Male	34	66.2059	7.03144	.051	.821
	Female	41	65.7805	8.86711		
	Total	75	65.9733	8.03703		
Henri Ducard	Male	32	43.5000	10.94856	7.191	.009*
	Female	40	37.3500	8.51710		
	Total	72	40.0833	10.08241		
Crash						
Jean Cabot	Male	30	37.3667	8.78668	.037	.848
	Female	71	37.7183	8.20136		
	Total	101	37.6139	8.33663		
Cameron Thayer	Male	30	44.7667	9.17900	.022	.883
	Female	74	45.0000	6.43833		
	Total	104	44.9327	7.28779		
Christine Thayer	Male	30	46.6333	8.39739	7.443	.008*
	Female	72	50.8333	6.47204		
	Total	102	49.5980	7.30693		
Hustle & Flow						
Key	Male	16	47.3125	6.11794	.039	.844
	Female	53	47.6981	7.02081		
	Total	69	47.6087	6.78063		
Shug	Male	17	47.4118	5.59083	.009	.923
	Female	55	47.2364	6.77130		
	Total	72	47.2778	6.47470		
Nola	Male	17	45.7059	7.84829	1.943	.168
	Female	54	42.7407	7.58893		
	Total	71	43.4507	7.70118		
Diary of a Mad Black Woman						
Helen	Male	24	48.0833	6.39916	2.967	.088
	Female	95	50.9789	7.57513		
	Total	119	50.3950	7.41988		
Orlando	Male	21	53.2857	6.32568	.689	.409
	Female	66	54.8788	8.02403		
	Total	87	54.4943	7.64454		

Note. Higher mean scores indicate a more favorable view of the movie character.

Sample sizes for both the male and female groups differ from character to character because not all the participants viewed each of the movies or elected to rate all the characters.

Table 4 Analysis of Variance of RACE and GENDER of Student Reactions to Movie Characters

Movie characters		*n*	*M*	*SD*	*F*	*p*
40-Year-Old Virgin						
Andy Stitzer	African American					
	Male	12	47.58	4.38	.41	.668
	Female	51	45.37	6.62		
	Total	63	45.80	6.29		
	Caucasian					
	Male	16	46.31	5.63		
	Female	27	46.11	6.64		
	Total	43	46.19	6.22		
Trish	African American					
	Male	21	62.00	8.72	.072	.931
	Female	50	60.78	8.71		
	Total	62	62.00	8.65		
	Caucasian					
	Male	17	61.29	7.60		
	Female	29	61.69	8.36		
	Total	46	61.54	8.00		
Batman Begins						
Alfred	African American					
	Male	16	63.38	6.65	1.99	.145
	Female	21	65.00	9.13		
	Total	37	64.30	8.09		
	Caucasian					
	Male	15	67.73	6.34		
	Female	17	68.06	8.28		
	Total	32	67.91	7.32		
Henri Ducard	African American					
	Male	15	41.93	21.46	4.05	.022*
	Female	20	36.55	8.61		
	Total	35	38.86	10.61		
	Caucasian					
	Male	14	45.43	8.26		
	Female	16	38.63	8.45		
	Total	30	41.80	8.91		
Crash						
Jean Cabot	African American					
	Male	17	37.35	10.75	.329	.720
	Female	53	36.94	7.92		
	Total	70	37.04	8.61		
	Caucasian					
	Male	11	37.36	6.05		
	Female	11	39.91	8.89		
	Total	22	38.64	7.54		

Movie characters		*n*	*M*	*SD*	*F*	*p*
Cameron Thayer	African American					
	Male	16	46.06	7.72	1.152	.321
	Female	55	45.64	6.38		
	Total	71	45.73	6.65		
	Caucasian					
	Male	12	43.17	10.23		
	Female	11	43.18	5.49		
	Total	23	43.17	8.13		
Christine Thayer	African American					
	Male	16	47.89	7.15	4.17	.012*
	Female	53	51.38	6.72		
	Total	69	50.52	6.95		
	Caucasian					
	Male	12	45.33	10.60		
	Female	11	49.45	6.11		
	Total	23	47.30	8.81		
Hustle & Flow						
Key	African American					
	Male	12	47.92	6.19	.479	.622
	Female	43	48.44	6.80		
	Total	55	48.33	6.62		
	Caucasian					
	Male	3	47.00	6.93		
	Female	8	45.88	7.12		
	Total	11	46.18	6.66		
Shug	African American					
	Male	13	47.92	5.19	1.78	.176
	Female	45	47.80	6.86		
	Total	58	47.83	6.48		
	Caucasian					
	Male	3	42.67	4.93		
	Female	8	44.25	6.67		
	Total	11	43.82	6.05		
Nola	African American					
	Male	13	46.38	8.31	.675	.512
	Female	45	42.76	7.73		
	Total	58	43.57	7.94		
	Caucasian					
	Male	3	41.00	5.29		
	Female	7	43.71	7.82		
	Total	10	42.90	6.98		

(Continued)

Table 4 (Continued)

Movie characters		*n*	*M*	*SD*	*F*	*p*
Diary of a Mad Black Woman						
Helen	African American					
	Male	16	47.31	6.27	1.93	.150
	Female	68	51.34	7.31		
	Total	84	50.57	7.27		
	Caucasian					
	Male	7	49.14	7.19		
	Female	16	50.31	6.79		
	Total	23	49.96	6.80		
Orlando	African American					
	Male	13	53.31	5.51	.777	.464
	Female	51	55.55	7.91		
	Total	64	55.09	7.50		
	Caucasian					
	Male	7	52.71	8.36		
	Female	7	55.14	7.60		
	Total	14	53.93	7.78		

Note. Higher mean scores indicate a more favorable view of the movie character.

Sample sizes for the groups differ from character to character because not all the participants viewed each of the movies or elected to rate all the characters.

Table 5 Racial Attitude and Race of Viewers

Racial attitude	*n*	*M*	*SD*	*F*	*P*
Unawareness of racial privilege				68.9	.001
African American	94	28.12	4.67		
Caucasian	63	21.39	5.40		
Unawareness of institutional discrimination				32.6	.001
African American	94	21.94	4.56		
Caucasian	63	26.25	4.72		
Unawareness of blatant race issues				.094	.759
African American	94	21.56	2.72		
Caucasian	63	21.71	3.39		

Note. On the CoBRAS, higher scores on each of the three factors are related to greater (a) global belief in a just world (scores ranging from 7 to 42), (b) sociopolitical belief in a just world (scores ranging from 7 to 42), and (c) denial of racism (scores ranging from 6 to 36).

males than females, more Caucasians than African Americans viewed this character favorably. In regards to Christine, as previously observed, more females viewed this character favorably than males, but also important to note is that the African American viewers were more positive than their Caucasian counterparts. Perhaps a key consideration in making sense of these findings is that Henri is a White male and Christine an African American woman. Although these results are not unexpected, it does raise some interesting issues, given the racial attitudes data in which both racial groups appeared to experience some degree of racial unawareness. Despite the colorblindness that appears to characterize the participants in this study, the race (and perhaps gender) of the movie characters still appears to have salience in how favorably adolescents depict the characters.

It is important to note that in selecting the movies to serve as stimuli for this investigation, adolescent African American moviegoers on the East Coast and adolescent Caucasian movie goers in the Southwest chose many of the same movies as their favorites for the time period being assessed. This suggests two things: (a) the heavy mass marketing of movies means that the targeted audiences cannot readily escape the advertisements used to entice them to the marketers' age-identified movies, and (b) viewers from various racial and ethnic backgrounds are having a shared (albeit mediated) experience. Since most racial and ethnic groups are generally segregated from each other, this has implications for the multicultural worldview development of viewers. Although they are unable to often interact with each other in the real world, movie/mass-mediated experiences offer an opportunity for adolescents from varied racial and ethnic backgrounds to fill such voids.

African American and Caucasian, male and female—these viewers chose the same movies to view, and some adolescents from across the racial divide responded to some movie characters in similar ways. Although some differences were discerned between Caucasian and African American adolescent movie-goers' perceptions, for the most part, there was agreement about which movies they enjoyed and what they liked and did not like about the characters and the types of people the movie characters represented. It is clear from the findings that African American adolescent movie-goers attended movies that are more Black oriented and liked *Crash*, a movie that depicted racism and racial conflict, much more than did their Caucasian counterparts. The findings also provide supportive evidence that African American and Caucasian adolescents, at least by their movie choices, have some shared experiences, and in some instances have similar responses and reactions to the movie characters seen on the screen.

These findings have implications for educators and for filmmakers alike, who should share concern about how we as a society are shaping the worldviews of the citizens and leaders of the future. Clearly, we have a responsibility to help young viewers understand the multicultural world that is dawning just as the 21st century is unfolding before us. Moving pictures that tell compelling stories that resonate across race, class, socioeconomic status, and other artificial dividing lines should be encouraged and embraced, for they are clearly helping to shape perceptions about the world that have implications for how tomorrow's adults will support and interact with each other.

The global community and global markets are in place and thriving in today's economy, with promises for expanding and growing ever deeper as tomorrow's viewers make their way in a complex world. Adults who make the movies that young viewers watch so faithfully must assume more responsibility for helping them understand their multicultural world, a world that has sprung from the demographic and societal shifts, resulting in a new mainstream—driven by the convergence of creative and multicultural groups that are changing our world (Garcia, 2004).

REFERENCES

Andison, F. (1977). Television violence and viewer aggression: A cumulation of study results 1956–1976. *Public Opinion Quarterly, 41,* 314–331.

Bandura, A. (1977). *Social learning theory.* Englewood Cliffs, NJ: Prentice Hall.

Bandura, A. (1986). *Social foundations of thought and action: A social cognitive theory.* Englewood Cliffs, NJ: Prentice Hall.

Bandura, A. (1994). Social cognitive theory of mass communication. In J. Bryant & D. Zillman (Eds.), *Media effects: Advances in theory and research* (pp. 61–90). Hillside, NJ: Lawrence Erlbaum.

Bandura, A., & Walters, R. H. (1963). *Social learning and personality development.* New York: Holt, Rinehart and Winston.

Berkowitz, L. (1962). *Aggression: A social psychological analysis.* New York: McGraw-Hill.

Cialdini, R. B. (1984). *Influence: The psychology of persuasion.* Melbourne: The Business Library.

Dates, J. (1980). Race, racial attitudes and adolescent perceptions of Black television characters. *Journal of Broadcasting, 24,* 549–560.

Distefan, J. P, Pierce, J. P., & Gilpin, E. A. (2004). Do favorite movie stars influence adolescent smoking initiation? *American Journal of Public Health, 94,* 1239–1244.

Dixon, H., Borland, R., & Paxton, S. (2003). *Smoking in movies: Does it matter who does the smoking?* Paper presented at the annual meeting of the International Communication Association, San Diego, CA.

Garcia, G. (2004). *The new mainstream: How the multicultural consumer is transforming American business.* New York: HarperCollins.

Gerbner, G., Gross, L., Morgan, M., Signorielli, N., & Shanahan, J. (2002). Growing up with television: The cultivation processes. In J. Bryant & D. Zillman (Eds.), *Media effects: Advances in theory and research* (pp. 43–68). Mahwah, NJ: Lawrence Erlbaum.

Harris, J. R. (2003). The outcome of parenting: What do we really know? In M. Coleman & L. Ganong (Eds.), *Points and counterpoints: Controversial relationship and family issues in the 21st century (an anthology)* (pp. 136–141). Los Angeles: Roxbury.

Hearold, S. S. (1979). *Meta-analysis of the effects of television on social behavior.* Unpublished doctoral dissertation, University of Colorado, Boulder.

Huesmann, L. R. (1982). Television violence and aggressive behavior. In D. Pearl, L. Bouthilet, & J. Lazar (Eds.), *Television and behavior: Ten years of scientific progress and implications for the eighties* (Vol. 2, Technical reviews, pp. 126–137). Rockville, MD: National Institute of Mental Health.

Internet Movie Database. (2006). *All-time USA box office.* Retrieved October 16, 2006, from http://www.imdb.com/boxoffice/alltimegross

Kerlinger, F. (1968). *Foundations of behaviorial research.* New York: Holt, Rinehart and Winston.

Moeller, T. G. (2001). *Youth aggression and violence: A psychological approach.* Mahwah, NJ: Lawrence Erlbaum.

Molitor, F. (1985). *Violence on TV: A social issue release from the Board of Social and Ethical Responsibility for Psychology.* Washington, DC: American Psychological Association.

Molitor, F., & Hirsch, K. W. (1994). Children's toleration of real-life aggression after exposure to media violence: A replication of the Drabman and Thomas studies. *Child Study Journal, 24,* 191–207.

Neville, H., Lilly, R., Duran, G., Lee, R. M., & Browne, L. (2000). Construction and initial validation of the colorblind racial attitudes scale (CoBRAS). *Journal of Counseling Psychology, 47,* 59–70.

Osgood, C., Suci, G., & Tannenbaum, P. H. (1971). *The measurement of meaning.* Chicago: University of Illinois Press.

Pechmann, C., & Shih, C. (1999). Smoking scenes in movies and antismoking advertisements before movies: Effects on youth. *Journal of Marketing, 63,* 1–13.

Petty, R. E., & Priester, J. R. (1994). Mass media attitude change: Implications of the elaboration likelihood model of persuasion. In J. Bryant & D. Zillman (Eds.), *Media effects: Advances in theory and research* (pp. 91–122). Hillsdale, NJ: Lawrence Erlbaum.

Reith, M. (2003, May). *Media violence: An analysis of changing and contrasting associations with antisocial aggression among teenage boys.* Poster session presented at the conference of the International Communication Association, San Diego, CA.

Renninger, K., Sigel, I., Damon, W., & Lerner, R. (2006). *Handbook of child psychology.* Hoboken, NJ: John Wiley and Sons.

Rodman, G. (2007). Mass media in a changing world. New York: McGraw-Hill.

Surgeon General's Scientific Advisory Committee on Television and Social Behavior. (1972). *Television and growing up: The impact of televised violence.* Washington, DC: U.S. Government Printing Office.

Taveras, E. M., Rifas-Shiman, S. L., Field, A. E., Frazier, A. L., Colditz, G. A., & Gillman, M. W. (2004). The influence of wanting to look like media figures on adolescent physical activity. *Journal of Adolescent Health, 35,* 41–50.

CHAPTER 19

The Multicultural Implications of Popular Music

PETER CHRISTENSON

TOM TER BOGT

Of all the media, perhaps none is more relevant to youth than popular music. Nor is any other medium more essentially multicultural, in two senses. First, however one defines *culture*, it is possible to identify hundreds, even thousands, of them worldwide, all incorporating music into their social fabric and most producing music that is in some way culturally distinct. Thus, multiple cultures create multiple musics. Second, this rich profusion of music styles and genres creates opportunities for listeners to cross boundaries and expose themselves to music from outside their own cultural confines, leading to multicultural awareness and (perhaps) understanding.

This chapter explores some of the multicultural dimensions of popular music. First, we will outline the many ways in which cultural variables (race/ethnicity, class, nationality, gender, etc.) influence orientation to music—that is, how music preference and uses relate to social identity. Second, we explore the function of music in the formation and maintenance of subcultural distinctions within youth culture, that is, the process through which music genres and subgenres define and represent group membership and affiliation within adolescent society. Finally, the chapter looks at some of the ramifications of pop music "cultural tourism"—that is, the consumption of music produced by racial and ethnic groups other than one's own. In the United States, for instance, many White adolescents listen avidly to urban African American music (hip-hop); in Europe, youth listen to virtually all forms of American pop music. Of particular interest in this connection are the implications of such patterns for developing impressions of the "other" culture. In part, the discussion of these issues will be grounded in existing research on patterns of popular music uses and preferences in the

Acknowledgments: The research of Tom ter Bogt is supported by the Dutch music authors' rights organization Buma/Stemra.

United States. In addition, the chapter features recent and previously unreported data from surveys conducted among youth in the Netherlands. To the extent research and evidence allows, the authors, one American and one Dutch, attempt to infuse a comparative perspective throughout this treatment.

THE IMPORTANCE OF MUSIC TO YOUTH

Some years ago, Roberts and Henriksen (1990) addressed the subject of adolescent media involvement by asking a sample of several hundred high school students which of several media they would choose to take with them should they be stranded on the proverbial "desert isle." The choices included TV, books, video games, radio, newspapers, VCR/videotapes, computer, magazines, and popular music. The teens' responses provide a reasonably good gauge of the relative importance of these various media in adolescent life. At all three grade levels in the study—7th, 9th, and 11th—what one could call music media (radio and recorded music) came out well ahead of the closest competitor, television. Over 80% of the students placed music in their top three, and around 50% selected music as their *first choice*.

Because music listening can so easily slip back and forth from background to foreground, daily exposure time is extremely difficult to measure. Roberts and Christenson (2001) have argued that self-report measures, few of which make any attempt to account for background (or secondary) listening, probably underestimate the amount of time music is actually impinging on teen eardrums. It would be no surprise to most parents to learn that music is the most likely of the media to be on in the background while doing homework (Foehr, 2006). Yet the music is definitely "on" and is being listened to. Measurement problems aside, studies indicate a considerable amount of listening time, increasing from about an hour per day during early grade school to 3 hours or more by the end of high school (cf. Christenson & Roberts, 1998; Roberts & Foehr, 2004). Television use shows the opposite relationship to age, averaging about 3 hours in grade school followed by a drop to around 2 hours a day by 12th grade. Although both media are important at all ages, television can be properly called the medium of childhood, music the medium of adolescence.

The amount and nature of music use are related to both gender and race. Most studies find, for example, that girls spend somewhat more time with music than boys, and African Americans somewhat more time than Whites (cf. Roberts & Christenson, 2001; Roberts & Foehr, 2004); girls are more likely than boys to use music to work through a "down" or lonely time, boys more likely than girls to get "pumped up" or energized by music (Arnett, 1991; Larson, Kubey, & Coletti, 1989); and girls are more likely than boys to cite dancing as an important music use, and African Americans more likely than Whites (cf. Christenson & Roberts, 1998).

For all groups, however, popular music offers a multitude of functions and pleasures, both personal and social. Music supplies the atmosphere at social occasions and provides company when alone. It brings youth together in raucous communion at concerts, yet with headphones can block out the rest of the annoying world. It makes chores and homework less onerous, fills gaps in conversation, and more. Indeed, for most adolescents, popular music is the medium most intimately linked with their personal and cultural identity, the medium that constitutes their most useful "equipment for living" (cf. Christenson & Roberts, 1998).

One aspect of music use seems to apply equally to all groups as well, and that is the role of music in defining and expressing group membership in the teen social environment. As Christenson and Roberts (1998) write,

> An adolescent's music affiliation says much about his or her social affiliation. Popular music at once expresses, creates, and perpetuates the essential "us-them" distinctions that develop between groups. . . . Music may be the most highly charged "No Trespassing" sign in adolescent society. (pp. 58–59)

As much as youth love music, it is *their group's* music that they truly love—indeed, the attitude toward the music of *others* is often characterized by active scorn and disdain (ter Bogt, Raaijmakers, Vollebergh, Van Wel, & Sikkema, 2003). As we will discuss later, this aspect of music use has much to do with how the issue of multiculturalism actually plays out in youth culture; that is, although there are certainly some musical "omnivores" who see in pop music's dizzying variety a rich cornucopia from which to pick and choose, many, if not most, teens see it as a reminder of how many groups exist from which to establish cultural distance.

DIVERSITY AND DIFFERENCE IN MUSIC TASTE IN THE UNITED STATES

The multicultural strains of American popular music are well known and widely celebrated. Each wave of immigrants brought a distinct musical tradition, and of course African slaves brought a variety of traditions which taken together have provided much, if not most, of the foundation for contemporary rock and jazz forms. The list of American hybrids includes such disparate forms as spirituals, hillbilly, cowboy, bluegrass, country, gospel (White and Black), blues, jazz, zydeco, Tejano, salsa, banda, rock and roll, Motown, rhythm and blues, soul, funk, rap/hip-hop, and many more. And these are just the primary strains; embedded within each category, both past and contemporary, are a number of distinct subtypes. As Barkley (2003) notes, "jazz" by itself has a highly diverse background, evolving from ragtime and early rural blues through New Orleans and Kansas City styles, Dixieland, big band, swing, bebop, "cool" (or West Coast), avant-garde, fusion, crossover, Afro-Cuban, and so on, and encompassing artists as varied as Scott Joplin, Ella Fitzgerald, Pete Fountain, Gerry Mulligan, John Coltrane, and Chucho Valdes.

Moving to the present, *Billboard* magazine, which concerns itself with relatively mainstream and, therefore, commercially important forms, lists separate charts for R&B/hip-hop, rap, Latin, independent (indie), country, pop, rock, modern rock, jazz, contemporary jazz, classical, bluegrass, international, blues, reggae, new age, gospel, Christian, electronic, and more. *Radio and Records,* another industry magazine, posts a similar list of genres, but with some additional categories, including active rock (essentially heavy metal), Latin pop, Latin jazz, Latin rhythm, regional Mexican, and tropical. Many high school and college students could list all these as well as another 20 or 30 labels for subgenres they would consider quite distinct.

It can be argued whether or not these different genres constitute distinct cultures in and of themselves. In certain cases—heavy metal and hip-hop, for instance—music is so central to group identity that it may, in fact, be appropriate to call the subculture by the name of the music. Most other forms are less definitive in this sense; one doesn't hear reference to a "soft rock"' culture, for instance. Moreover, many of the distinctions are between closely related music types. Factor analytic studies have shown that long lists of music types can be reduced to a much shorter list of "metagenres" (Christenson & Peterson, 1988; ter Bogt et al., 2003). There is no disputing, however, that music choice matters a great deal in adolescent culture, and that by selecting one type of music over others, a teen makes a cultural choice that sends a message about individual and group identity.

Far from being random or idiosyncratic, popular music preference is strongly predicted by a number of personality and social background variables. The most interesting of these variables from the standpoint of this chapter are age, gender, and race/ethnicity. Concerning age, we noted the increasing amount of time spent and involvement with popular music over the span of the school years, and made the observation that television is probably more important than music until early adolescence. That said, popular music does factor into childhood media use, and the importance of music in childhood has probably been on the rise over the last few decades. In the United States and Europe, at least, popular music is important for most children by middle to late grade school. The primary age-related change in preferences consists of a shift from mainstream genres in grade school toward more differentiated and somewhat less centrist tastes in middle and late adolescence. The more elaborated tastes in later adolescence correspond with increasing peer group orientation and differentiation.

Given the centrality of gender identity and gender relationships in adolescent development, it is not surprising that gender maps onto popular music preferences. In their review of the research, Christenson and Roberts (1998) argue that the various studies tended to converge on three overall patterns. First, females tend to orient more to mainstream "pop" forms, and are attracted more than males to more romantic, "softer" forms of popular music. Males, in contrast, are more likely to prefer the harder-edged sounds—heavy metal, hardcore punk, gangsta rap, and so on. Second, males are more likely than females to adopt nonmainstream, fringe music choices. Third, White females show more affinity for music by African American artists than do White males—in other words, females are more likely to "cross over" in their music listening.

Christenson and Roberts (1998) based their analysis on research conducted from the 1970s through the 1990s, and robust as the major patterns have proven, they may be eroding somewhat. A recent national survey of media use commissioned by the Kaiser Family Foundation (Roberts, Foehr, & Rideout, 2005) found differences on only 2 of 14 music categories—country/western and Top 40, both of which were strongly preferred by girls—but no difference on the other 12. Two comments are in order. First, the differences on country/western and Top 40 were not only quite sizeable, but confirmed the traditional pattern of girls' preference for mainstream pop (12% of boys versus 22% of girls said they had listened to Top 40 the previous day). Moreover, the use of global labels for music categories may obscure distinctions embedded within those categories—"alternative rock" and "rap/hip-hop," the two most popular categories in the Kaiser study, contain a multitude of artists, many with quite different attitudes, styles, and messages. Our intuition is that questions about *favorite artists* would reveal gender differences within the global categories. In any case, even if gender makes less of a difference than it used to, it still figures into music taste.

Of all the demographic and background predictors of music taste, race and ethnicity are surely the most powerful. Major genres of popular music are associated unambiguously (and proudly) with specific racial and ethnic roots—R&B, soul, and hip-hop with African American culture, salsa with Latin, reggae with Jamaican. Other forms—hard rock, heavy metal, and indie, for example—are associated just as clearly with White youth culture. Taste differences based on race and ethnicity can be quite dramatic. Typical of the research is a study by Dykers (1992), who asked students to indicate their favorite music from among these categories: rock, heavy metal, pop/Top 10, country, punk, and rap. Sizeable race differences appeared for all but the pop/Top 10 category. By ratios of five to one or more, Whites were more likely than Blacks to select rock, heavy metal, and country. Blacks, in turn, chose rap as their overwhelming preference; 70% of the Blacks in the sample named it as their favorite, versus 13% of Whites.

Of course, Dykers gathered her data just as rap music was breaking into the mainstream—in fact, by far the most significant trend in pop music over the last decade or two has been the explosive penetration of rap/hip-hop into the general population of youth. The best and most recent data on racial differences in music preferences comes from the aforementioned Kaiser survey (Roberts et al., 2005), in which a national representative sample of teens were asked which of several types of music they had listened to the previous day. The data clearly reveal the powerful surge in the popularity of rap/hip-hop in recent years—indeed, this category was by far the most popular overall, outscoring the nearest competitor, alternative rock, by two to one. Nearly two thirds (65%) of the 7th to 12th graders said they had listened to rap/hip-hop the previous day. The results clearly reconfirm previous research on the importance of race differences. Indeed, statistically significant race/ethnicity differences emerged for 10 of the 14 categories, including rap/hip-hop, which was listened to the previous day by over 80% of the African American youth (versus 65% of Latinos and 43% of Whites). The differences corresponded almost perfectly with the predominant race/ethnicity of the performers: African Americans listened much more frequently than Whites or Latinos to rap/hip-hop, R&B/soul, reggae, and gospel/Christian; Latinos more than the other two groups to Latin/salsa; and Whites more frequently to alternative rock, classic rock, country/western, hard rock/metal, and ska/punk.

African American youth in this study were more likely than Whites or Latinos to "stay at home" with their music listening (Roberts et al., 2005). Their overwhelming preference for rap/hip-hop was noted. It was followed by R&B/soul (33%), reggae (24%), and gospel/Christian (19%). The highest previous-day percentage for any of the "White" music genres, alternative rock, was 9%. The Whites and Latinos tended to spread their listening out more broadly, and engaged in more "crossover" listening, as indicated by the high rates of listening to rap/hip-hop. (Note: even though there are White and Latin hip-hop artists, the genre was created and is still dominated by African Americans.)

Finally, despite the natural tendency of youth to focus on culturally relevant "in-group" music, one also sees evidence in these results that considerable numbers of youth are exposing themselves to music associated with racial and ethnic groups other than their own (Roberts et al., 2005). The most obvious phenomenon here is the attraction of Whites and Latinos to rap/hip-hop. In addition, though, among Latinos, 16% listened to alternative rock, 20% to heavy metal, 17% to reggae; among Blacks, 9% listened to alternative, 7% to heavy metal; among Whites, 9% listened to reggae, 5% to R&B. We leave our discussion of the implications of these patterns of exposure for perceptions of other groups until later in this piece.

To sum up this section, listening to popular music is a central activity of youth in our culture. In addition, popular music is tremendously diverse, consisting not of just a few divisions or styles but of scores. Finally, while music brings youth together in some ways, it also reflects—indeed, it may accentuate—their differences. At this point, we make a transition from popular music differences and diversity as reported in previous U.S.-based research to the presentation of some recent unreported data from survey research on Dutch youth. Following that, a concluding section presents some ideas related to the possible role of popular music exposure in forming youngsters' multicultural worldviews.

RACE, ETHNICITY, AND MUSIC IN THE NETHERLANDS

As a small country, the Netherlands has always been open to cultural influences from abroad, and that certainly applies in the case of popular music. Prior to the 1950s, the major influences were German and French, but since then, the Dutch charts have been dominated by various forms of American and British pop and rock: first U.S. rock 'n' roll and British "beat," followed by later American forms including soul, heavy metal, alternative rock, R&B, and hip-hop. In 2002, only 17% of all the music sold in the Netherlands was of domestic origin, although Dutch artists, like many popular artists throughout Europe, produce music that sounds indistinguishable from the corresponding American/British forms. Dutch popular music reflects the spectrum of music types present in the U.S. and the U.K., that is, artists play hip-hop, rock, heavy metal, R&B, pop ballads, jazz, and even country and gospel. Most Dutch musicians sing in English, and even when they sing in Dutch, they conform to genre-specific sound and lyrical themes established abroad. Thus, although the words of Dutch hip-hop would make no sense to a non-Dutch speaker, such a listener would immediately recognize the type of music.

To be sure, the Netherlands certainly possesses a vibrant pop music scene of its own, and some bands have acquired international fame recognition—Golden Earring, Shocking Blue, Focus, Urban Dance Squad, for example—and Dutch DJs like Tiesto, Armin van Buuren, and Ferry Corsten have played a key role in defining the trance sector within the dance field. Overall, though, it is fair to say that Dutch pop music is deeply infused with musical influences developed elsewhere. This impact, moreover, extends well beyond the music itself. The cultural elements associated with American music can be seen in fashion and street dress, hairstyles, paraphernalia of various kinds, slang, demeanor, and even worldviews.

Like the United States and Northern European countries, the Netherlands is becoming increasingly diverse racially and ethnically. The first wave of immigrants arrived from former Dutch colonies, beginning with the Dutch East Indies (now Indonesia) in the 1940s and 1950s, and later Surinam (South America) in the 1970s. Furthermore, during the last decades, many inhabitants of the Netherlands Antilles (a group of five Caribbean islands, formerly a Dutch colony and currently part of the Dutch Kingdom) have moved to the Netherlands seeking educational and job opportunities. In general, these immigrants and their children have integrated well in Dutch society, though they still maintain cultural patterns descended from the "home" region, including their choice of music. Surinam and Antillean youngsters grow up with a Caribbean mix of music and favor Surinam and Antillean music (along with Brazilian, Cuban, Jamaican, and Black American music).

The second wave of immigration began in the 1970s when large numbers came to the Netherlands to find work. Though most of these had short-term work contracts, many stayed on in the country, sent for their families, and tried to build a future in the Netherlands. The two largest of these groups are Islamic, with roots in Morocco and Turkey. Though Dutch society was and is characterized by a relatively high tolerance for minority groups and cultures, relations between the Dutch and these two groups have been more strained than relations with the groups from former colonies. Dutch participation in the war in Iraq, which is perceived by many in the Moroccan and Turkish communities as anti-Islamic, has exacerbated this tension. It is noteworthy that in a country with no history of political assassination, two high-profile figures have recently been killed for apparently political motives. In 2002, the populist politician Pim Fortuyn, who had warned against the "Islamization" of Europe, was killed by a left-wing radical; and in 2004, sharp-tongued commentator and filmmaker Theo van Gogh, who mocked Islamic religion and culture, was shot by a radical Islamist. These events put further strains on relations between the Muslim minorities and the Caucasian majority.

Youth from other "Western countries" (Germany, France, Belgium, U.S., etc., but also Japan) compose 6.6% of the adolescent population in the Netherlands. This group is described as "non-autochthonous," but it is government policy not to define them as "ethnic minorities," a classification restricted to people from developing countries. Adolescents associated with "non-Western countries," including the major minority groups mentioned in the preceding, form 15.4% of the adolescent population overall, but in large cities such as Amsterdam, Rotterdam, and The Hague, they may number up to 40% of the adolescent age group. This broad category breaks down as Surinamese (2.7%), Antillean (1.2%), Turkish (3.5%), and Moroccan (3.1%), with the rest designated as "other" (Centraal Bureau voor de Statistiek, 2007).

With some exceptions (Chinese, for example), minority adolescents are more likely than other youth to grow up in families with relatively low social and economic status. Children with Surinam or Antillean backgrounds are the most likely of all Dutch adolescents to live in single-parent families. Adolescents from minority groups tend to have lower educational attainment and demonstrate more internalizing distress and psychosomatic symptoms than majority youth, and boys—particularly those with Moroccan or Antillean backgrounds—run higher risks for externalizing behaviors such as delinquency. Interestingly, despite their lower social position and despite being subjected to discrimination, minority youth report feelings of general well-being on the same level as the White majority (ter Bogt, Van Dorsselaer, & Vollebergh, 2005).

Prior research has shown that with regard to *active* cultural participation—playing a musical instrument, singing, dancing, drawing or painting, photography, video or filmmaking, writing poetry, etc.—minority groups operate at the same level as adolescents from the majority. The picture is different, however, with regard to what one could call *highbrow receptive* cultural participation. Minority youth are significantly less likely than the majority White population to attend museums, classical concerts, operas, plays, ballet and other traditional dance performances, and buildings or other places of historical or cultural interest (Van Wel, Couwenbergh-Soeterboek, Couwenbergh, ter Bogt, & Raaijmakers, 2006). But what of Dutch youth's involvement in popular music—do race and ethnicity matter here?

The Samples

Recent survey research focusing on the social position, mental health, and consumption patterns of Dutch youth also included questions on music uses and preferences. In the following paragraphs, we present findings from three large-scale surveys of Dutch adolescents: (a) Dutch National School Survey on Substance Use (DNSSSU; 2003), N = 7,883, age range 12–17; (b) Jongeren (2005), N = 2,914, age range 12–29; and (c) Switch On (2005/06), N = 2,227, age range 12–29). DNSSSU is a government-funded national representative study conducted every 4 years to monitor substance use among Dutch adolescents. The 2003 version contained questions on lifestyle, youth culture, and music. Jongeren 2005 (biannual survey) and Switch On (Internet panel) are conducted by Qrius Research, Amsterdam, to monitor media use and consumption patterns of Dutch young people and emerging adults. The DNSSSU data closely represent the ethnic breakdown in the Netherlands. In the other two surveys, ethnic groups are underrepresented.

Due to relatively small group sizes (even within DNSSSU), all the statistical analyses reported in the following section merge the Turkish and Moroccan groups (Mediterranean/Muslim countries), and the Surinam and Antillean groups (South American/Caribbean territories, Christian countries, former Dutch colonies). The obvious advantage of these pairings is an increase in statistical power. Collapsing these groups is also justified by the fact that cultural and historical similarities exist between the paired countries. The ethnic composition of the Switch On panel is particularly biased against the inclusion of Turkish and Moroccan youth, and analyses of that data set were restricted to the White and Surinam/Antillean groups. Because nearly all young people with Dutch ancestors are Caucasian, this group will be referred to as "White." In all analyses, the effects of ethnicity were controlled for gender, age, and educational level, which are known to mediate listening habits and music taste. Education was particularly important to include as a covariate, due to the persistent tendency for Dutch ethnic youth to exhibit lower levels of attainment. When "differences" are referred to below, this indicates that in the ANCOVAs, significant differences were found between groups at $p < .05$. If salient interaction effects were found, these are reported.

Music and Ethnicity

The first issue to be dealt with is overall involvement in listening to popular music, and the measure on the survey concerned the frequency of listening to personally owned CDs, minidisks, MP3 players, or other music playback sources. In comparison to young people with Dutch origins and Turks/Moroccans, Surinamese/Antilleans listen more frequently (see Figure 1). With regard to playing an instrument or singing, no significant differences were found between the groups, thus corroborating earlier studies finding direct participation unrelated to ethnicity (Van Wel et al., 2006).

The survey also assessed frequency of music video viewing. In the Netherlands, all three major music video sources—MTV, The Music Factory, and The Box—are operated by MTV Networks. MTV caters to older adolescents and young adults, whereas The Music Factory (TMF) targets younger adolescents. The Box concentrates heavily on "urban" music (especially hip-hop). Because all three channels offer a mix of music TV and other content, it is acknowledged that the correspondence between frequency of viewing and attention to music content is only approximate. With that caveat in mind, as Figure 2 shows, the White Dutch watch less music television than the adolescents with Caribbean backgrounds (Surinamese/Antillean). For all three music video channels, the percentage of youth with Caribbean roots saying they watched 3 or more days a week was over 60%. The corresponding percentages for Dutch youth were in the low 40s.

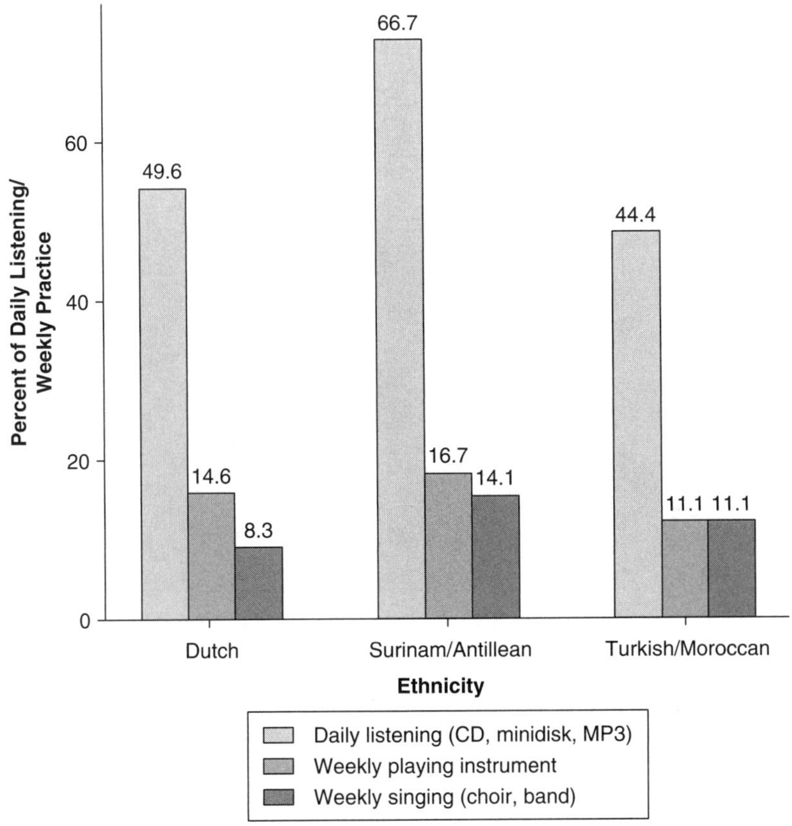

Figure 1 Ethnicity, Listening, and Music Practice

Source: Jongeren, 2005.

The adolescents were asked if they were familiar with various music categories known to be popular in the Netherlands, thus providing an additional measure of music involvement. These 16 categories were pop, Dutch pop, hip-hop, R&B, reggae, rock, heavy metal, punk/hardcore, gothic, Turkish pop, raï, classical, jazz, house/trance, techno/hardhouse, and club/mellow. Figure 3 shows the proportion of recognized music genres broken down by age and ethnicity. As one would expect, familiarity with the various categories climbed with age, although even the youngest group were familiar with most. Twelve-year-olds recognized an average of about 70%, with recognition rising to over 80% for 17-year-olds. Nearly all young people know genres such as pop, classical, and hip-hop. Levels of familiarity with other types of music, however, differ by ethnic group. Not surprisingly, knowledge of Turkish pop and raï was higher among adolescents with roots in Turkey and Morocco.

All minority groups show less knowledge of certain "White" genres—trance, techno/hardhouse, club/mellow, punk/hardcore, and gothic. Dutch adolescents have the highest level of overall genre familiarity. This may result from minority adolescents' lower awareness of "White" genres. There may also be an effect of educational level—indeed, the group differences almost disappeared after the addition of statistical control for education. The analyses also revealed an interesting interaction between education and ethnicity: whereas White Dutch youth

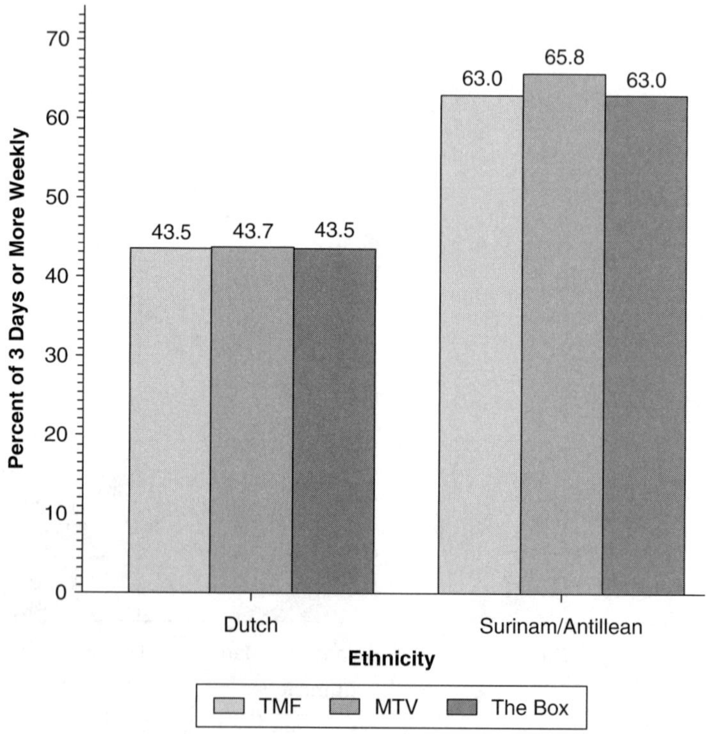

Figure 2 Ethnicity and Watching Music Television

Source: Switch On, 2005/06.

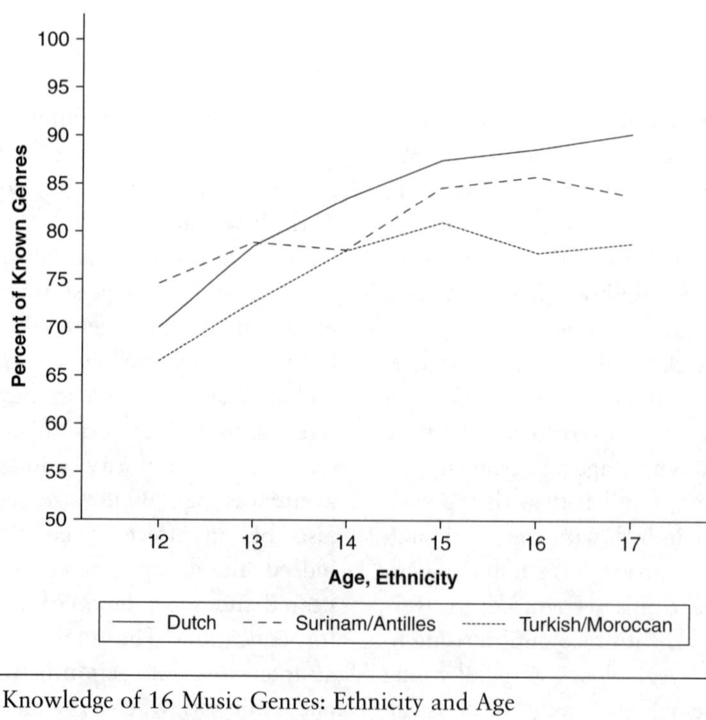

Figure 3 Knowledge of 16 Music Genres: Ethnicity and Age

Source: Dutch School Survey on Substance Use, 2003.

were the most knowledgeable of the groups, the most knowledgeable *subgroup* were minority youth with high educational attainment, who were even more familiar with the various genres than their Dutch peers.

To address differences in music preferences, we used factor analysis to reduce the complete list of 16 to 6 "metagenres"—pop (pop, Dutch pop), urban (hip-hop, R&B, reggae), rock (rock, heavy metal, punk/hardcore, gothic), highbrow (classical, jazz), dance (house/trance, club/mellow, techno/hardhouse) and Mediterranean pop (Turkish pop, raï)—and then computed mean popularity scores for each. The analysis of these scores appears in Figure 4. As one might expect almost by definition, pop is indeed the best-liked overall, and within ethnic groups, surpassed only by urban among the Surinamese/Antillean youth. In the Turkish/Moroccan group, pop was even with Mediterranean pop.

Urban music, mostly American hip-hop and R&B, was considerably more popular among the ethnic minority groups than among the White Dutch youth, even though it still is quite popular with them as well. (It should also be noted that a large proportion of "pop" music or "chart" music in the Netherlands is, in fact, hip-hop and R&B.) Though Turkish pop and raï can be heard on some radio stations in the larger cities in the Netherlands, it has not reached the mainstream. These types of music still cater to young people with Turkish or Moroccan backgrounds. The results show Rock forms to be less popular than pop or urban in the Netherlands, and rock is clearly a White-oriented metagenre. Group differences for both rock and another "White" genre—dance

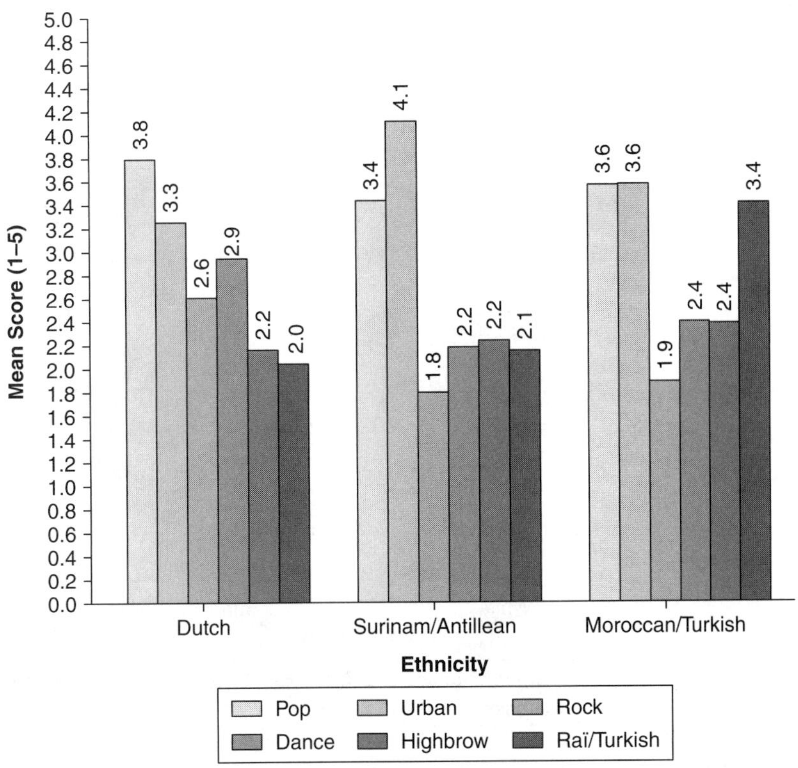

Figure 4 Popularity of Six Metagenres of Music

Source: Dutch School Survey on Substance Use, 2003.

music—are substantial. Dance has gained mainstream appeal among majority Dutch youth, but clearly not among ethnic minorities. No ethnic group differences appear for highbrow music (classical and jazz).

Differences were found in crossover listening. We examined what proportion of the different ethnic groups listened and liked both the most "White" (rock) and the most "Black" (urban) metastyles, rather than just one or the other (the definition of "liking" was a score above the natural scale mean of 3 on 1–5 point scales). Such youth can be characterized as musical "omnivores" (Peterson & Kern, 1996). Analyses revealed that Whites are much more likely to like both styles (25.6%) than are Surinam/Antillean (9.1%) or Turkish/Moroccan youth (12.1%). These differences survived controls for gender, age, and educational level. Indeed, given these findings, and given the dominance of R&B and hip-hop in the charts, on the radio, and in music videos, it is reasonable to conclude that the majority White group are more exposed to (Black) urban music than to (White) rock.

Previous research shows that although some young people are indifferent to popular music, most agree that it is important to them and fulfills several distinct functions (see Figure 5). The primary function is mood enhancement; youth rank getting into a better mood, fending off boredom, or creating atmosphere for social occasions (hitting bars, visiting rock concerts or dance events) as prime motivations for listening (Christenson & Roberts, 1998). Linked to the mood-enhancing properties of music is its function as a coping mechanism. Young

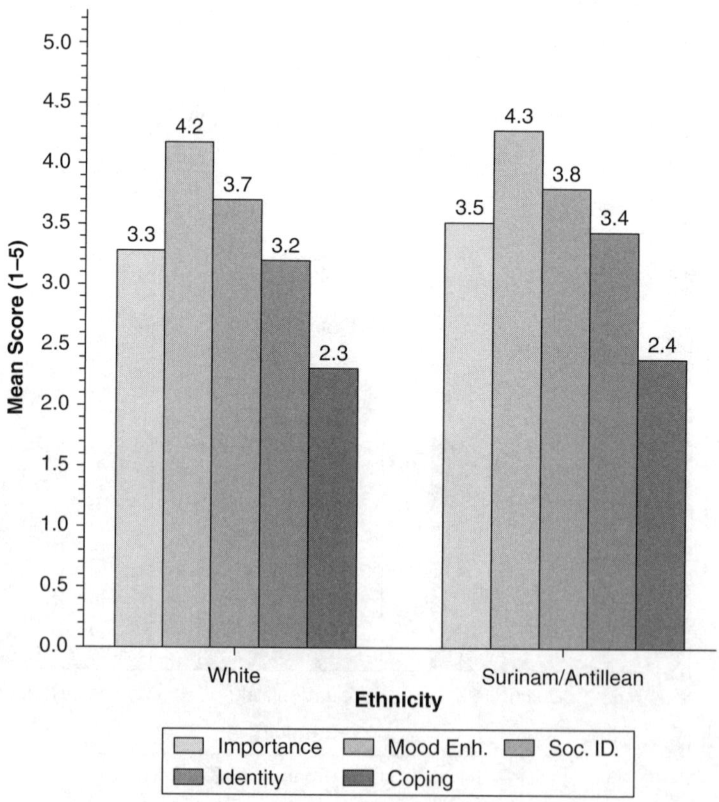

Figure 5 Ethnicity, Importance of Music, and Four Functions of Music

Source: Switch On, 2005/06.

people often report that music helps them face their problems and can be a source of comfort when sad or depressed. Music can also provide a source of knowledge and attitudes on topics ranging from politics and sex to the "dernier cri" in fashion, slang, and personal demeanor. Finally, as noted earlier, music and associated cultures contribute to both personal and group identity. Music affiliation, in particular, functions as a vehicle of social differentiation, marking the boundaries between one's own group of peers (the "ins") and other groups (the "outs").

In the Switch On sample, the White and Surinam/Antillean groups exhibited a pattern of scores very similar to the previous research, and, in fact, very similar to each other. Music is important (3.3 and 3.5 for the White and Surinam/Antillean groups, respectively), it is used by both groups to get into a positive mood (4.2 and 4.2), and it is important as a coping device (3.7 and 3.8). It is also a source of knowledge/identity and, to a lesser extent, helps define social identity. Between-group differences were not statistically significant. The Switch On sample did not contain enough Turkish/Moroccan adolescents to make valid statements about their use of music, but it is likely that they do not differ from their peers as another study (DNSSSU) showed that music effects are quite similar across groups. Within the broad category of mood or *affective* uses, three separate types can be identified: (a) positive, energizing, "up" effects; (b) heightening of aggression or anger; and (c) deepening of depressed affect, sadness. In the DNSSSU study, all groups tended to agree that music enhances positive moods, although this type of reaction is somewhat more present among Dutch (3.7) and Surinamese/Antilleans (3.8) than the Turkish/Moroccan youth (3.3). In terms of aggression/anger and depression/sadness, mean levels of agreement were well below the midpoint (around 2 on the 5-point scale), indicating that these affective effects apply less often to any given teen and/or to a lower proportion of teens. There were no differences between ethnic groups on these measures (see Figure 6).

COMMENTS ON THE MULTICULTURAL IMPLICATIONS OF POPULAR MUSIC

The American poet Longfellow once wrote, "Music is the universal language of mankind." We cannot ask him what he meant precisely by that, but surely he would not have objected to the rather obvious notion that all peoples and cultures produce some sort of music. Not that this meaning is trivial—the fact that all cultures produce some form of music says something about the power of music to provide pleasure and express important human feelings and values. Nor, one suspects, would Longfellow have objected to the notion that forms of music differ—that each "sound" is culturally unique and reflects cultural distinctions. Clearly, as we have detailed in the previous sections of this chapter, popular music is, in a sense, "all about" differences: differences between genres and subgenres, and differences between groups of young people. How youth relate to music and the kind of music they choose as their own depend importantly on age, gender, social class, and particularly race/ethnicity.

One suspects, however, that Longfellow meant something a bit broader and more "multicultural" than all this: that music somehow functions as a lingua franca, that no matter what our differences on other dimensions, we can come gather together around a good song, even if it is produced by people much different than we are, and through that song come to understand the other culture a bit better. This idea, of course, relates directly to the sense of multiculturalism *as an ideal:* the hope that exposure to the "other" will enhance, or at least coexist with,

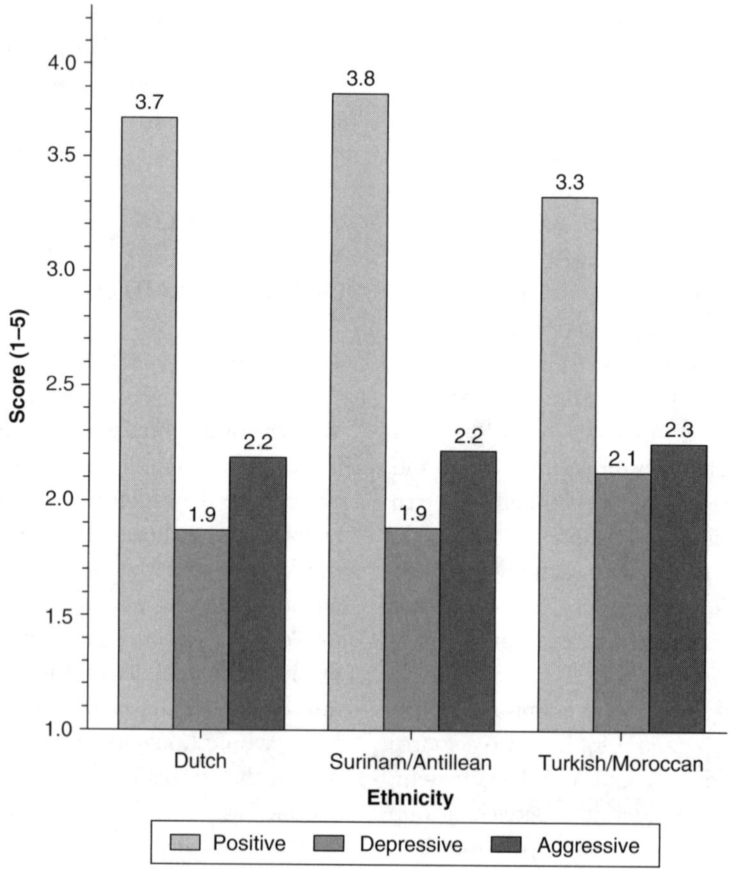

Figure 6 Ethnicity and Three Types of Music Affect
Source: Jongeren, 2005.

understanding, acceptance, and empathy (Berry & Asamen, 2001). Accordingly, this final section addresses two key questions. First, to what extent are young people *exposed to* popular music forms originating from different groups than their own? And second, for those who are so exposed, what are the *effects* of such exposure on their perceptions of the "other" group?

As for the first issue, exposure, without question a good deal of crossover listening occurs. In the United States, most of that exposure takes the form of White youth listening to Black music, primarily hip-hop. As noted earlier, in studies of the general population of teenagers in the United States, hip-hop emerges as an extremely popular genre, roughly on a par with "White" rock. The phenomenon of White youth being attracted by Black music, of course, has a long history, beginning with early rock and roll and continuing through soul, disco, and R&B. Current Billboard charts list African American artists in proportions far greater than would be predicted by mere demography, and that has been the case for decades. In the Netherlands and Europe as a whole, a huge proportion of contemporary popular music is of "foreign"—i.e., American—origin. A study in 25 European countries revealed that the proportion of music purchases accounted for by local (national) artists ranges between 10% and 59%, with a high market share for domestic repertoire (greater than 50% in Greece and France and low numbers [less than 20%] in Ireland, the Netherlands, Belgium, Portugal, and Austria) (Buma/Stemra, 2005).

A number of variables may contribute to the likelihood of crossover exposure and effects, but language is certainly one of the most important. To an extent, music is accessible regardless of language differences, and, thus, crosses borders much better than literature, film, or television. To take the example of Latin music, one can dance to salsa without being fluent in Spanish—there is just something about the sound and the beat. Yet much, if not most, of the *cultural* content of Latin music is inevitably lost on non-Spanish speakers because this content is largely embedded in the lyrics. In the United States, and in the context of youth, the question of Latin music's impact outside the Latino community is largely moot, because youth engage in very little language crossover.

Indeed, the probability that any teen will adopt a certain genre of music as a favorite depends heavily on whether the music is in a language they can understand. In the United States, the best evidence of this principle is the almost complete absence from Top 100 album or song charts of music in any language other than English. This is not surprising, of course; lyrics matter to young people, and they naturally seek music they can understand. At the same time, however, the importance of language limits the sorts of cross-cultural exposure and impact that might occur through music listening. It bears mention that the status of English as the most common second language worldwide is one of the key contributors to the tremendous advantage of English-speaking countries, particularly the U.S. and the U.K., in the international music market. Specific to the current discussion, it is much more common for youth from around the world to be exposed to U.S. rock and hip-hop than for U.S. youth to be exposed to popular music from around the rest of the world. Notwithstanding the existence of a devoted audience for "world music," this audience is in reality a narrow, and post-teen, niche in the United States. Very little enters the American mainstream from anywhere but Britain or, occasionally, Canada. The arrow of multiculturalism, in this context, is quite directional.

Studies from Europe affirm the stranglehold that American music enjoys in European markets, particularly the Black-oriented genres of R&B and hip-hop. The immense popularity of American forms in Europe exists despite a language barrier, at least of sorts. Even though European audiences generally know some English (and in many cases a great deal), they still have trouble making sense of American pop and hip-hop lyrics, especially given the singularities of American inner-city slang. Even so, this does not seem to stand in the way of hip-hop's appeal as an energizing, mood-enhancing, and danceable form. Thus, while language and lyrics matter, in Europe, at least, the sound, melody, rhythm, and *attitude* matter more.

White Youth, Hip-Hop, and Cultural Tourism

Although it would be certainly possible to find American examples of crossover listening between many groups—African Americans who listen to country/western, Mexican Americans who listen to Cajun zydeco, and so on—the dominant form of cross-cultural music listening in the United States consists of White youths' involvement in rap and hip-hop. Language poses no barrier—it's all in English, and any American hip-hop fan knows exactly what it's "about," at least superficially. Indeed, any American teen fan of hip-hop—White or Black—knows the slang.

What might be the multicultural implications of this cross-cultural exposure—specifically, how might it influence White youths' perceptions of African Americans? In their book on popular music and adolescence, Christenson and Roberts (1998) suggested that the involvement of White adolescents in rap and hip-hop might be characterized as "cultural tourism." That is, whereas African American youth see hip-hop as personally relevant and "about them," White youth's attraction, both to the music and to its cultural trappings (fashion, style, language, etc.), seems to be based on qualities such as hip-hop's edgy, defiant coolness, dynamic vocal stylings, infectious beat, outlandish modes of attire, extravagant bling, and so on. To Whites, the argument goes, hip-hop is an exciting place to visit, but whether they are conscious of it or not, their involvement is at a distance. As Christenson and Roberts put it,

> For suburban white youth an involvement with rap music amounts to a form of "cultural tourism," a way to participate in rap's vibrancy without having to live in the inner city. This suggests, in turn, that middle class audiences may select or reject rap music based on style and sound rather than on content, with the lyrics performing more of a rhythmic function than a symbolic one. (Christenson & Roberts, 1998, p. 111)

The authors further suggest, given the low levels of identification with which White youth approach hip-hop, impact on the attitudes and values of White youth should be limited: "If the music is not *about* them, presumably it will hold few important lessons *for* them" (Christenson & Roberts, p. 113). More likely, they say, are the effects on White youths' perceptions of *African Americans.*

To be sure, things have changed in the decade since Christenson and Roberts introduced the cultural tourism metaphor. The rap/hip-hop culture has become not just prominent, but *dominant,* in mainstream teen culture, and its influence on both the music charts and adolescent lifestyle has expanded accordingly. Moreover, it is now apparent that different levels of tourism exist, ranging from the very casual (e.g., listening to hip-hop only at dances or on pop radio stations) to near obsession or conversion. It is fair to say that for many White youth (from various social backgrounds), attraction to hip-hop has evolved beyond tourism into cultural emigration; they have, in essence, become *music expatriates,* with extremely deep levels of involvement not just as fans but also as performers. Notwithstanding debates about "authenticity," White youth are deeply involved as MCs and DJs in the emerging "independent hip-hop" movement.

This phenomenon of intense identification with Black culture may not be limited to the United States. American urban music has become so powerful a force in the Netherlands that it now influences the clothes young people wear, their hairstyles and makeup, and even the way they greet each other in the schoolyard. This seems to hold true particularly for young people with lower educational attainment, who may be drawn to the extravagant lifestyle ("bling") that is portrayed, and by implication advocated, in hip-hop lyrics and videos. So penetrating are these images that "to pimp up" (your car, house, face, dog, relationship) has become a household word in Dutch (albeit one used with tongue somewhat in cheek).

Given the dimensions of this phenomenon, it is remarkable how little research has emerged on the impact of White crossover on perceptions of African Americans. Indeed, it is truly impossible to say with any certainty what the nature of any such impact might be or on whom. A few experimental studies have been conducted bearing on the issue, and their results present a mixed picture, at least in terms of racial tolerance and understanding. In one study, exposure to rap music videos with politically radical, antiestablishment messages (e.g., Public Enemy's "Fight the Power") increased White students' empathy with Black political causes and positions (Zillman et al., 1995). On the other hand, a similarly designed study of the impact of listening to violent rap music showed a significant priming of negative stereotypes: White students who listened to violent rap music were more likely to attribute violent tendencies to a Black "target person" than those who heard nonviolent rap (Johnson, Trawalter, & Dovidio, 2000). These and other studies dealing generally with the impact of exposure to music and music videos (cf. Christenson & Roberts, 1998; cf. Roberts & Christenson, 2001) provide ample evidence that exposure to music media can exert short-term influences on adolescents, including the priming of racial stereotypes.

Indeed, given the predominant messages and imagery of rap and hip-hop—the emphasis on sexual exploit, jewelry, luxury cars, high-end liquor, and so on—the possibility of priming effects seems particularly troubling, especially among the "casual tourists," for whom hip-hop may provide their sole or predominant contact with African American culture. However authentically hip-hop represents the lives of the artists who perform it, it provides an extremely narrow, skewed picture of African Americans overall. This applies even more strongly to non-American listeners, who have even fewer alternative sources of information. To Dutch youth, the picture of life in the United States is of a bitter Darwinian struggle for survival in environments riddled with gang violence, dope peddling, and avaricious slumlords all pitted against a brutal, racist police force. Black culture looks to be highly eroticized and sexually exploitative, obsessed with the trappings of the pimp style, and so on.

The implications of all this for intercultural "understanding" are obviously discouraging. However, short-term studies say little about how persistent effects may be, and commonsense extrapolation from media content can be perilous. Yet, the short-term studies should not be discounted—indeed, it makes little logical sense that *short-term* exposure to the *apparent* messages in hip-hop, when replicated hour after hour and year after year as is the case with music listening, would fail to produce longer-term (and generally negative) effects on perceptions of African American (or, in Europe, American) culture. No doubt those who have conducted the various experiments on music impact would readily acknowledge the value of longitudinal research. In addition to the need for longer-term research, however, we would point out three additional factors that ought to be introduced into the research picture: fandom, age, and race/ethnicity.

As previously noted, crossover exposure in hip-hop occurs over a very wide range of involvement, and it seems quite likely that a young person's level of involvement would mediate the effects of exposure. We noted one extreme in the context of priming: if hip-hop is the sole or primary point of contact with African Americans, then given the music's most obvious, surface-level content ("bling," "booty," etc.), the effect of exposure may be more to cultivate negative stereotypes than to increase tolerance or understanding. At the other extreme, however, where involvement approaches "going native," one might expect a much different pattern. Truly devoted White hip-hop fans are not only more involved and committed to hip-hop, but they ought to be more aware of the diversity within both hip-hop and within Black culture generally, hence, these devotees should be less susceptible to the priming of negative stereotypes. At the very least, it seems likely that one's level of involvement with hip-hop—a music genre heavily identified with African Americans—would correlate with general levels of tolerance and acceptance of African Americans generally. (Interestingly, as far as we know, not even this simple hypothesis has been addressed in published research.)

Age is another mediating variable. In both the United States and Western Europe, hip-hop is extremely popular among children as early as the middle grade school years. Yet, we suspect children will be even less likely than adolescents to distinguish between the representations of American Black culture they see in hip-hop culture, on the one hand, and the richer variety of African American experience on the other. Given young children's higher persuadability, the impact on them seems particularly important. Yet, we do not know if their attraction and exposure to hip-hop translate into negative images or positive respect. Either seems possible.

Finally, the variable most central to this chapter—indeed, this volume—bears some mention. Assuredly the impact of crossover listening also depends on race/ethnicity and national background. A Surinamese youth listening to Dutch pop, a suburban White American listening to hip-hop, an African American youth listening to American indie rock, a Dutch White teen listening to Mediterranean pop—all are crossing borders. Yet, the motivations, the meaning, and the impact of these border crossings are clearly not the same from case to case. Even a casual discussion of the dynamics surrounding the interaction between race and national background, on the one hand, and cross-cultural music behavior on the other, could fill several more pages. All that can be said here is that this issue, like nearly every other important issue regarding the multicultural impact of music, remains largely unexplored. Given the centrality of popular music in the lives of children and teens, and given popular music's quintessential multiculturalism, it is curious how little attention researchers have given to the broader implications of music in the formation of young people's multicultural worldviews. Our hope is that this chapter will stimulate some attention to this critical area.

REFERENCES

Arnett, J. (1991). Adolescence and heavy metal music: From the mouths of metalheads. *Youth and Society, 23*(1), 76–98.

Barkley, E. (2003). *Crossroads: Popular music in America.* Upper Saddle River, NJ: Prentice Hall.

Berry, G., & Asamen, J. (2001). Television, children, and multicultural awareness. In D. Singer & J. Singer (Eds.), *Handbook of children and the media* (pp. 359–373). Thousand Oaks, CA: Sage.

Buma/Stemra. (2005). *Music in Europe: Sound or silence?* Utrecht: Capgemini.

Centraal Bureau voor de Statistiek. (2007). *Statistics Netherlands.* Retrieved April 4, 2007, from http://www.cbs.nl/en-GB/menu/cijfers/default.htm?languageswitch=on

Christenson, P., & Peterson, J. (1988). Genre and gender in the structure of music preferences. *Communication Research, 15*(3), 282–301.

Christenson, P. G., & Roberts, D. F. (1998). *It's not only rock & roll: Popular music in the lives of adolescents.* Cresskill, NJ: Hampton Press.

Dutch National School Survey on Substance Use. (2003). Unpublished raw data. Utrecht: National Institute of Mental Health and Addiction.

Dykers, C. (1992, May). *Rap and rock as adolescents' cultural capital at school.* Paper presented at the annual meeting of the International Communication Association, Miami, FL.

Foehr, U. (2006). *Media multitasking among American youth: Prevalence, predictors and pairings.* Menlo Park, CA: Kaiser Family Foundation.

Johnson, J., Trawalter, T., & Dovidio, J. (2000). Converging interracial consequences of exposure to violent rap music on stereotypical attributions of Blacks. *J. Experimental and Social Psychology, 36,* 233–251.

Jongeren. (2005). Unpublished raw data. Amsterdam: Qrius Research.

Larson, J., Kubey, R., & Coletti, J. (1989). Changing channels: Early adolescent media choices and shifting investments in family and friends. *Journal of Youth and Adolescence, 18*(6), 583–599.

Peterson, R. A., & Kern, R. M. (1996). Changing highbrow taste: From snob to omnivore. *American Sociological Review, 61,* 900–907.

Roberts, D. F., & Christenson, P. (2001). Popular music in childhood and adolescence. In D. Singer & J. Singer (Eds.), *Handbook of children and the media* (pp. 395–414). Thousand Oaks, CA: Sage.

Roberts, D. F., & Foehr, U. (2004). *Kids and media in America.* Cambridge, UK: Cambridge University Press.

Roberts, D. F., Foehr, U., & Rideout, V. (2005). *Generation M: Media in the lives of 8- to 18- year-olds.* Menlo Park, CA: Kaiser Family Foundation.

Roberts, D. F., & Henriksen, L. (1990, May). *Music listening vs. television viewing among older adolescents.* Paper presented at the international meeting of the International Communication Association, Dublin, Ireland.

Switch On. (2005/06). Unpublished raw data. Amsterdam: Qrius Research.

ter Bogt, T., Raaijmakers, Q., Vollebergh, F., Van Wel, F., & Sikkema, P. (2003). Youngsters and their musical taste: Musical styles and taste groups. *The Netherlands' Journal of Social Sciences, 39,* 35–52.

ter Bogt, T., Van Dorsselaer, S., & Vollebergh, W. (2005). Sociale integratie, schoolbeleving, psychosomatische problemen en welzijn van scholieren: de Nederlandse HBSC-studie. *Tijdschrift voor Jeugdgezondheidszorg, 37*(1), 2–7.

Van Wel, F., Couwenbergh-Soeterboek, N., Couwenbergh, C., ter Bogt, T., & Raaijmakers, Q. (2006). Ethnicity, youth cultural participation, and cultural reproduction in the Netherlands. *Poetics, 34*(1), 65–82.

Zillman, D., Aust., C. F., Hoffman, K. D., Love, C. C., Ordman, V. L., Pope, J. T., et al. (1995). Radical rap: Does if further ethnic division? *Basic and Applied Social Psychology, 16,* 1–25.

CHAPTER 20

Multiculturalism and Music Videos

Effects on the Socioemotional Development of Children and Adolescents

KHIA A. THOMAS

KYLA M. DAY

L. MONIQUE WARD

An entertainment favorite among adolescents and young adults, music videos became interwoven into the thread of American youth culture with the launching of MTV in 1981 (Aufderheide, 1986; Sun & Lull, 1986). The sheer popularity of the channel, which prominently featured music videos as well as entertainment news and other musically oriented programming, spawned several cable networks, including VH1, Black Entertainment Television (BET), Country Music Television (CMT), and MTV2. Over 25 years later, the mass appeal of music videos remains strong, as networks continue to proliferate and music videos become more easily accessible to the viewing public.

Given the rapid spread of music videos as a relatively newer form of media and their distinct influence on popular youth culture, questions arise concerning their role in teaching young people about culture, race, and ethnicity. To what extent are members of diverse ethnic and cultural groups represented? Perhaps more importantly, for those who are represented, what types of portrayals and messages are provided? Although created to promote songs, music videos are likely to do much more than that. Through their dynamic visual imagery, storytelling features, and appealing artists, they also provide messages about the roles and characteristics of individual peoples, ethnic groups, and cultures. Because American popular music stretches across demographic groups and across nations, parents and researchers are concerned with their racial/ethnic socialization function. Accordingly, in this chapter, we first review empirical analyses addressing the content of music videos, summarizing what little is known about the racial and ethnic makeup of music video characters and artists, and also considering the intersections of race/ethnicity and gender. We continue by discussing literature concerning effects of music video viewing on American youth of color. In our third section, we summarize existing literature on how music video viewing shapes White students' conceptions of race and ethnicity. We conclude with a discussion of future research directions.

BACKGROUND: YOUTH EXPOSURE LEVELS AND VIDEO VIEWING HABITS

Data indicate that music video networks find their primary audience within children, adolescent, and young adult demographic groups. The target audience for music videos is between the ages of 12 and 24, with a median age of 23 (Englis, Solomon, & Ashmore, 1994). Substantiating its popularity with this demographic, findings indicate that over 70% of the MTV audience is under 24 years old (Englis et al., 1994). The majority of viewers watch between 30 minutes to 2 hours of music videos per day (Sun & Lull, 1986), with many reporting watching frequently to stay abreast of current trends, fashions, and dances (Brown, Campbell, & Fisher, 1986).

Although little comparative data exist, findings across several studies suggest that usage levels are particularly high among Black and Latino youth. For example, African American high school students surveyed by Ward, Hansbrough, and Walker (2005) reported watching an average of 3.33 hours of music videos per day. Similarly, Rivadeneyra, Ward, and Gordon (in press) examined media habits among Latino high school students. Here, students reported watching music videos an average of 20.5 hours per week, which is nearly 3 hours per day. And the 176 African American high school girls surveyed by Gordon (2004) reported watching music videos for approximately 75 hours per month, which is 2.5 hours per day. These numbers greatly exceed the levels of 39.65 hours per month (or 1.2 hours/day) reported among White high school students in comparable data (Ward & Friedman, 2006). Thus, with higher exposure levels, Black and Latino youth are likely to be even more susceptible to any potential music video effects.

One unique feature of music videos is their fusion of song lyrics and visual storytelling imagery. With this combination, some researchers have questioned the relevance or salience of one aspect over the other, asking, "Aren't they just songs with pictures?" Recent research indicates that song lyrics are subordinate to the musical soundtrack and visual imagery in music videos (Vernallis, 2002). It appears as if the lyrics only intermittently occupy viewers' attention in comparison to the images and storylines contained within music videos. As a result, a strong argument can be made that visual imagery may play the most important role in the socialization function of music videos. Indeed, adolescents cite using the imagery to gain meaning or a different perspective on song lyrics (Sun & Lull, 1986). One of the implications of this study is that adolescents, as a whole, believe there is "one authentic meaning" to song lyrics, as shown through the visual imagery (Sun & Lull, 1986). This finding suggests an internalization process whereby adolescents are chiefly in tune to the images contained in music videos and that they accept, without challenge or alternative explanation, the visual representations of these images for their own judgment. Given the prominence of music videos in young people's lives, and their attention to the visual images and stories, the question then becomes, What kinds of messages and themes are conveyed about race and ethnicity (and gender)?

SECTION 1: MULTICULTURAL REPRESENTATION IN MUSIC VIDEOS

Level of Representation

Much like other forms of the entertainment media, the world of music videos appears to be sharply divided by race/ethnicity. Early research indicated that characters from diverse backgrounds were in the minority on mainstream musical programming (Brown & Campbell, 1986), which instead featured mostly European American performers and characters. Of the 102 videos played per week on mainstream music networks, only 5.5% featured African American artists (Brown & Campbell, 1986). A decade later, content analyses revealed that roughly 11% of popular music videos on MTV contained non-White characters (Seidman, 1992). As the type of music featured on these channels has changed from solely pop and rock, analyses comparing racial/ethnic representation across music video genres revealed that Black males and females were significantly more likely to appear in rap and R&B/soul music videos compared to other music genres (Tapper, Thorson, & Black, 1994). These same characters appeared much less frequently in pop music videos (approximately 18%), and at that time, Latina females appeared in only 3% of popular music videos and 1% of music videos overall (Tapper et al., 1994).

In contrast, music videos shown on ethnically oriented networks, such as BET, almost exclusively show minority characters, and if characters from the dominant ethnic group appear, they typically occupy minor roles (Brown & Campbell, 1986; Emerson, 2002). These figures may have changed somewhat in recent years, as mainstream music networks, such as MTV, broadcast videos from "crossover artists" from other ethnic backgrounds with widespread mass appeal and popularity (Peterson-Lewis & Chennault, 1986). Many of these crossover artists represent the growing popularity of musical genres such as Latin music, hip-hop, and R&B among American youth in general (Cobo, 2006; del Rio, 2007; Hughes, 2002; Moran, 2007; Sullivan, 2003). Many of these artists are lesser known within mainstream popular music, after having appeared in heavy rotation on ethnically oriented programming (Cobo, 2006; Finn, 2006).

Several premium networks have become available in recent years to fulfill the entertainment media needs of ethnically diverse Americans, such as MTV Tr3s (Latina Americans), MTV Chi (Chinese Americans), MTV K (Korean Americans), and MTV Desi (South Asian Americans) (Cobo, 2006; Finn, 2006). These networks are attempting to bridge the gap between mainstream and ethnically oriented programming for these groups of Americans, presenting videos that feature musical artists of diverse backgrounds, and music videos that are relevant to the cultural background and experiences of these ethnic groups. At this point in time, research is unavailable on how often these ethnically oriented music networks, featuring videos from artists of diverse backgrounds, are viewed by mainstream youth. However, it appears reasonable to assume that, for White youth, crossover artists that appear on mainstream music networks may represent their sole source of media exposure to people of color.

Nature of Music Video Portrayals: A Focus on African Americans

Visual representations contained throughout music videos offer viewers of all backgrounds a glimpse into how people look, act, behave, and live. The videos presented are frequently stylized, however, often depicting more of a fantasy world of the producers, directors, and artists than a snapshot of reality. Within this realm, what are some of the common themes of how people of multicultural backgrounds are represented within music videos? Surprisingly, relatively few studies exist on the content of portrayals of multicultural people within music videos. The majority of these articles describe portrayals of African Americans in music videos, with few studies focusing specifically on Latinos/as, Asian Americans, or Native Americans.

One of the few existing studies with an in-depth racial analysis is Brown and Campbell's 1986 study of early music videos. Their analysis compared Whites on 75 MTV videos to Blacks on 37 videos from BET's Video Soul. As noted earlier, they found few depictions of people of various ethnic backgrounds in mainstream videos. However, there were similar themes that appeared as far as how people of color behaved in music videos (analyses only provided for Black vs. White character depictions). They found that Blacks were more likely than Whites to be shown engaged in domestic activities (i.e., housework, yard work, child care, service work, custodial work) than in professional work. Although Black males were just as likely to hold professional jobs as White characters, Black females were most likely to be shown performing domestic work. Many of these domestic work roles appearing within music videos are stereotypically associated with Black women, such as cooking, cleaning house, and waitressing (Peterson-Lewis & Chennault, 1986). And the Black women were shown dancing more frequently than the White women (50% vs. 3%).

Indirect information about racial differences can be drawn from work comparing different genres of music videos. Coding 203 videos drawn from BET, MTV, VH1, and TNN, Jones (1997) analyzed the prevalence of violent and sexual imagery in videos of specific genres. Although information about the racial background of the artists featured was *not* provided, it is likely that the majority of artists in the country and rock videos were White whereas the majority of artists in the rap and hip-hop videos were Black. Based on these assumptions, it appears that levels of violence and sex are particularly high in video formats likely to feature Black artists. More specifically, Jones reported significant genre differences in portrayals of violence, with gun talk, drug talk, grabbing/clutching, and bleeping (over obscenities) appearing with the greatest frequency in rap videos. Alcohol use and gambling were also featured significantly more frequently in rap videos than in videos of other genres. Significant genre differences were also found across the 11 sexual behaviors coded. For 8 of the 11 behaviors (fondling, simulated intercourse, simulated masturbation, simulated oral sex, sex talk, "hot" pants, male sex dance, and female sex dance), levels were highest in the hip-hop or rap videos. For only one behavior (heavy cleavage) was the prevalence highest in the country and western videos. Similar findings were reported by Hansen and Hansen (2000) in their genre analysis of videos from MTV, CMT, VH1, and BET. Here, BET surpassed other channels in the percentage of videos containing visual images of scantily clad women (about 77%), and also led in the frequency with which both women and men were portrayed as sexually aggressive. Thus, although music videos, in general, tend to focus on sexuality, toughness, and social vices (e.g., alcohol use, gambling, cursing), videos featuring African Americans tend to do this even more, thereby creating a very skewed portrait of a people who may receive little other media coverage.

Nature of the Portrayals: African American Women

Others have studied Black videos exclusively, and have attempted to describe the dominant themes and messages conveyed about African American women and men. Emerson (2002) conducted a content analysis of 56 popular music videos featuring Black female musical artists from MTV, BET, and VH1. Using a more focused approach, Shaviro (2005) offered an in-depth analysis of the themes and symbolism in two individual music videos by Black female artists. Finally, Stephens (2003) has analyzed sexual scripts for women that dominate hip-hop culture, in general. One of the dominant themes emerging from these pieces is that music videos heavily emphasize Black women's bodies and sexual appeal over other talents and abilities (e.g., intellect, personality). The Black women that dominate music videos are generally young, thin, physically attractive, and scantily clad, with little variation in body size and type (Emerson, 2002). Because music videos tend to mimic mainstream beauty standards, even when female characters of color are shown, the majority of Black women appearing have light complexions and long, straight hair (Shaviro, 2005). Most recently, music videos featuring Black performers have "expanded" these definitions of beauty to encompass ethnic women who appear as close to White as possible, by including more multiracial, exotic-looking women (Englis et al., 1994; Shaviro, 2005). Yet nearly all women in the videos would be considered thin by mainstream standards (Emerson, 2002; Shaviro, 2005), effectively contradicting notions that the Black community allows for greater acceptance of larger body types, and conforming to the thin ideals indicative throughout television in general.

A second characteristic of African American women noted from these music video analyses is the heavy emphasis on style and materialism. The Black women appearing in music videos are often very stylized and glamorous, wearing the latest designer fashions, expensive jewelry, and elaborate hairstyles, adding to the emphasis on physical attractiveness above all other qualities (Emerson, 2002; Roberts, 1994; Shelton, 1997; Stephens, 2003). These images serve to bolster the idea of these women as objects to be adored and worshipped (Stephens, 2003). Even more so, the "gold digger" image of Black women is prevalent, as they are often depicted as prioritizing financial gain above all other pursuits in life, and as desirous of money, trinkets, and financial rewards from men (Stephens, 2003).

In contrast, music videos rarely offer images of pregnant women, mothers, older women, or women with larger body types (Emerson, 2002). Instead, music videos reflect an overall image of Black women as "decorative eye candy" rather than multidimensional beings, and emphasize the availability of these women's bodies for men's sexual desires (Emerson, 2002; Stephens, 2003). Again, we see conformity to mainstream music video standards of presenting women in highly traditional, stereotyped roles (e.g., Gow, 1996; Seidman, 1992).

A third prominent theme emerging from the existing music video analyses is the notion that these visual images confirm stereotypes of wanton sexual appetite and promiscuity of African American women. Within the context of American society, Black women actively confront stereotypes about their sexuality, from the "Mammy's" celibacy to "Jezebel's" hypersexuality (Collins, 2000; Roberts, 1994; Stephens, 2003). Music videos commonly feature an almost excessive showing of sexuality. African American women are typically highly sexualized (Emerson, 2002; Roberts; Shaviro, 2005; Stephens, 2003), their bodies objectified by the camera's gaze on their breasts, crotch, and behind. Often the gaze of the camera projects from the floor angle to maximize the view of women's bodies, shows close-ups of women's body parts rather than displaying the whole woman, or films in slow motion to emphasize the gyrating body parts of female dancers. These objectified close-ups of women's bodies are a hallmark of hip-hop videos, appearing more frequently there than in other musical video genres (Englis et al., 1994). Indeed, in her analysis of the eight types of Black women appearing in music videos, Stephens notes the prevalence of "the freak," a woman who is sexually insatiable, with little sexual inhibition. Corroborating this impression, Brown and Campbell (1986) found that Black women were more likely than Black males, White males, or White females to participate in sexual behavior in music videos.

Others note, however, that these highly sexualized images of Black women often co-occur with themes of strength, independence, streetwise nature, and toughness (Emerson, 2002). Accordingly, some speculate that perhaps these images function as a form of resistance and "reappropriation" of female sexuality in response to exploitation (Emerson, 2002; Roberts, 1994). These videos often typically stress women's sexual agency and female sexual desire, sending the message that Black women are in control of their own bodies (Emerson, 2002). As Emerson conducted analyses of videos only featuring Black female performers, one has to question whether these images of African American women are indicative of videos starring male performers as well. One also has to question whether reappropriation of female sexuality is the most common message expressed from these highly sexualized performances, especially considering the fact that hip-hop videos heavily identify with masculinity and male sexual pleasure (Emerson, 2002; Shelton, 1997). Certainly, a female music artist may intend to make a political statement through visual imagery in a particular music video, but how often do many female artists' videos indeed enact this intent? These types of resistance videos appear to be in the minority, existing among a majority that feature models, dancers, and female music artists engaged in sexually suggestive dances and provocative situations.

Although feminist portrayals of African American women are difficult to find within the music video world, these Afrocentric portrayals of Black womanhood find a small but important space within ethnically oriented musical programming. Within these contexts, Black women exemplify values such as promoting women's importance, demanding equal treatment, and demonstrating the need for women to support one another (Emerson, 2002; Roberts, 1994). However, these messages rarely stand alone within a single music video, and underlie other worrisome images of sexual suggestion and unidimensional depictions of women (Roberts, 1994). These types of music videos that deviate (or attempt to) from the predominant script of Black female sexuality are found almost exclusively on ethnically oriented networks (Brown & Campbell, 1986; Emerson, 2002).

Nature of the Portrayals: African American Men

There are few published studies of common themes and images of African American men relative to the literature on African American women's representations. African American men have been portrayed throughout the entertainment media according to stereotypes of violence, aggressiveness, and potent sexual appetite (Hall, 1993; Page, 1997). As much as Black women are portrayed with a bold, in-your-face hypersexuality, Black male sexuality is often portrayed along similar lines (Saucier, 2006). Black men are almost always portrayed as heterosexual, aggressively in pursuit of women's affections at one end of the continuum, and in pursuit of as many female sexual partners as possible at the other extreme (Powell Hammond, 2002; Ward & Rivadeneyra, 2002). Powell Hammond's content analysis of manhood portrayals in popular hip-hop videos found that 75% of the nonverbal behaviors displayed by Black male characters were related to *profiling*, emphasizing maleness as being the center of attention with females playing subordinate roles, and *pimping*, emphasizing sexual prowess, promiscuity, or objectification of women. Appearing as frequently as profiling and pimping behaviors were *bonding/backing*, or nonverbal behaviors that suggested emotional connectedness toward men as brothers, without the influence or interference of women (Powell Hammond, 2002).

A growing number of music videos appear to "flip the script" on the camera's objectifying gaze by focusing on the bodies of Black men (Emerson, 2002; Harris, 1999). This trend is perhaps best exemplified by D'Angelo's "Untitled," where the male artist appears to be nude and sings directly into the camera, with the gaze of the camera focusing on his chiseled musculature. Music videos of this nature focus on a more sensual view of Black men's bodies, usually within the confines of the hip-hop aesthetic, channeling an image of Black men that is unflinchingly heterosexual yet sensual (Harris, 1999), and available for female sexual pleasure.

In addition to being sexual, Black men are also featured as tough and aggressive. Many videos rely on hip-hop style fashions, such as multilayered, oversized shirts, sagging jeans that partially expose boxer shorts, prison-inspired uniforms, tattoos, and bandanas, in order to evoke images of "controlled aggressiveness" of Black men, and concealing men's bodies from view (Harris, 1999). Often Black men appearing in music videos are shown in prison scenes, hanging out on street corners, or emerging from jail. Similarly, research has found that approximately 38% of hip-hop videos reflect nonverbal behaviors that reinforce the message of overall resistance to authority or requiring restraint (Powell Hammond, 2002). As an overall "take-home message," Powell Hammond (2002) proposes that music videos reflect the message, "A Black man backs his brothers, has wealth, power, women, and commands respect with his physical presence" (p. 1).

Nature of the Portrayals: Latinos and Asian Americans

No published studies were found on content analyses of how Latinos or Asian Americans are portrayed within music video imagery. However, research does indicate several themes in how Latinos are depicted within the entertainment media in general. Largely underrepresented in mainstream television, Latinos most often appear in roles that are consistent with negative racial stereotypes, such as villains and other criminalized characters, sexualized lovers, and domestic workers (del Rio, 2007). Asians and Asian American women's character representations are marked with cultural stereotypes as well, such as hyperfeminine, exotic, submissive, and docile, whereas men of Asian descent are rarely represented as objects of physical attraction or sexual desire (Lee & Vaught, 2003). However, in recent years, more representation and positive images of Latinos have emerged within the media, in celebration of rich cultural, historical, and music traditions (Cobo, 2006; del Rio, 2007). Similar to the representation patterns found with African Americans, niche musical programming has emerged, for Latinos and Asian Americans alike, which may eventually offer a wider array of visual imagery and character depictions than those indicative within mainstream programming.

SECTION 2: IMPACT OF MUSIC VIDEO VIEWING ON THE PERCEPTIONS OF YOUTHS OF COLOR

Given the limited scope of adolescents' cognitive development and real-world experiences paired with their high levels of music video viewing, to what extent are they prepared to judge the realism of the media content presented? Are they equipped to understand that the images are not an accurate representation of *all* Black people, all White people, or all men and women? These questions underscore the importance of understanding the role that these inaccurate but pervasive images may play in shaping young people's developing worldviews. We argue that the images seen in music videos are likely to play an important role in youths' perceptions of themselves and others. In this section, we explore findings concerning how music videos affect Black adolescents' self-perceptions and beliefs about men, women, and sexual relationships. In the next section, we summarize findings linking music video exposure to White students' perceptions of African Americans as a whole.

Self-Perceptions/Appraisal

One area of importance is the role of viewing on individuals' beliefs about themselves. It has been suggested that the media may act in similar ways as peers in shaping youths' self-conceptions (Farrar et al., 2003). In the same way that an adolescent male might base his beliefs about his body on his perceptions of his friends' bodies, so might he turn to the media for insight into the body type that is most valued and sought after. However, basing one's self-perceptions on media characters is likely to produce some negative consequences, because TV characters and magazine photographs are perfected images, do not typically feature "average" bodies, and are mostly Eurocentric in appearance. What might the implications be of repeated exposure to this content on adolescents' assessments of the self, including body image, self-concept, and beliefs about intelligence? Will comparing themselves to an ideal that is nearly impossible to achieve or to people who do not look like them lead to lowered self-esteem, racial self-esteem, and body image? Studies directly investigating associations between music video viewing and self-concept among youth of color have found many interesting, but rather alarming, trends.

For example, Ward (2004) tested whether diverse forms of media use contribute to African American adolescents' racial self-esteem and three dimensions of their self-esteem. Here, findings indicated that more frequent viewing of music videos predicted lower performance, social, and appearance self-esteem, as well as lower racial self-esteem. In addition, when further investigations were conducted of other aspects of the viewers' backgrounds, it was found that these associations were mainly relevant for youth who report low levels of religiosity. These findings suggest that Black youth who may be less strongly tied to the Black community or Black culture (via the Church), may be especially vulnerable to buying into media images, comparing themselves unfavorably, and feeling worse about themselves as a consequence.

In a similar study, Gordon (2004) examined associations between music video exposure and self-esteem among Black high school girls. Her results indicated that students who reported a higher percentage of Black music and music videos in their media diets also expressed higher appearance self-esteem. Again, however, closer examination of specific subpopulations revealed that Black music video exposure was especially beneficial to youth who may have felt less connected with their racial identity or community. More specifically, for those low in racial centrality, having a higher percentage of Black music and music videos in their diet was associated with higher appearance and performance self-esteems yet held no connection for those higher in racial centrality. Similarly, for those low in religiosity, having a higher percentage of Black music and music videos in their diet was associated with higher appearance and social self-esteem, yet held no connection for those higher in religiosity. Together, the findings from Ward (2004) and Gordon illustrate the complex relations between types of Black viewers and media effects, highlighting the impact of preexisting racial support and identity.

In one of the few existing studies testing effects of music video viewing among Latino youth, Rivadeneyra et al. (in press) examined media habits among 40 Latino high school students ages 14 to 17. Analyses linked music video viewing to poor self-conceptions, such that frequent exposure was associated with notably lower levels of social self-esteem and with a desire to change more aspects of one's own body ($p < .09$). These findings suggest that frequent consumption of idealized images that do not include people like oneself may lead to a diminished self-esteem among Latino adolescents, but more work is needed.

Behavioral Consequences

The field has also focused its attention on the effects of music video viewing on adolescent behavior. For example, Klein et al. (1993) investigated the adverse behavior outcomes of music video viewing among African American early adolescents. Participants were asked to provide their level of media use and experience with several adverse behaviors, such as stealing, drinking alcohol, and sexual activity. Findings indicated that the adolescents with higher levels of music video viewing were more likely to exhibit risky behavior, such as stealing, cigarette use, and sexual intercourse. These results, even though preliminary, suggest that music video consumption is an important predictor of behavioral outcomes. In a related study that examined sexual behavior directly, Wingood et al. (2003) found that higher levels of music video viewing among Black female adolescents predicted an increased likelihood of engaging in risky sexual intercourse and higher incidences of sexually transmitted diseases, although these conclusions remain tentative due to concerns about the limited sample used.

In addition to being linked with students' actual behavior, music video viewing has also been associated with adolescents' endorsement of the violent behavior of others. Specifically, Johnson, Jackson, and Gatto (1995) examined African American boys' (ages 11–16) perceptions of violence after exposure to violent music videos. Participants were randomly assigned to one of three conditions (control, nonviolent, violent) and then asked to indicate their attitudes toward the use of violence and their own probability of engaging in violent behavior. The study found that those viewing a series of violent music videos demonstrated a higher endorsement of violent behavior than those exposed to nonviolent music videos. In addition, illustrating the connection between endorsement and enactment, participants in the experimental group were more likely to report a high probability of committing similar acts of violence. Therefore, music video viewing may contribute not only to the way in which minority adolescents perceive themselves, but also to their acceptance of and participation in certain negative behaviors.

Beliefs About Men, Women, and Sexual Relationships

Music videos send very specific messages about masculinity, femininity, and how the sexes relate to each other. As outlined in the previous section, these portrayals are often very narrow and conform to many existing stereotypes about Black women and men. Given this imagery, many have questioned whether Black adolescents viewing the videos are subject to an internalization of the images, and to developing beliefs about gender roles, sexual roles, and sexuality that conform to the images presented. In one investigation of these notions, Bryant and Bowman (2002) tested associations between time spent watching rap music videos and Black girls' perceptions of women shown in video imagery. For this study, 53 African American female adolescents were shown 10 minutes of music videos and were asked about their regular music video consumption. Preliminary results showed that participants who watched more than 2 hours of videos per week were more likely to accept the negative images of women shown in the music videos. These results may suggest that African American women may become desensitized to negative images of women due to high levels of exposure to these images.

A more recent study, conducted by Ward et al. (2005), provides experimental evidence for the effect of music video viewing on perceptions and stereotypes of men and women. In this study, 152 African American high school students participated in an experiment to delineate the role of music video viewing on gender role beliefs. Participants in the experimental group were asked to view four videos representing the following stereotypical notions: women are sex objects, sexual relationships are adversarial, material wealth is important, men are emotionally and physically hard, and men are "players." Participants in the control condition were asked to view four videos that did not portray these stereotypes. Gender role beliefs were assessed using three measures that examined students' endorsement of traditional gender stereotypes, their acceptance of stereotypical beliefs about sexual roles and relationships, and their ideals about masculinity and femininity. As expected, participants in the experimental condition (stereotype) were more accepting of stereotypical beliefs about sexual relationships, and attributed more importance to external qualities (e.g., beauty, sexiness) in their gender ideals. At the same time, those who more frequently watch music videos, in general, also reported greater acceptance of these gender and sexual stereotypes.

These perceptions of relationship roles also extend to perceptions of dating violence, an important adverse outcome that may be associated with more stereotypical gender role attitudes. Johnson, Adams, Ashburn, and Reed (1995) conducted a study with 60 African American youth (30 male, 30 female) ages 11–16 years to investigate the role of music video viewing on attitudes toward men and women in relationships. Female participants assigned to the experimental (video viewing) condition were more likely than those in the control (no video) condition to report acceptance of a vignette featuring violence perpetrated by a male on a female victim while the two were on a date.

Combining evidence from these correlational and experimental studies, we see significant and consistent relations between Black students' consumption of music videos and their endorsement of the gender and sexual stereotypes that dominate them. These results suggest that media, and music videos in particular, are indeed a powerful force in the gender and sexual socialization of African American youth. It appears, then, that Black adolescents may be receiving messages from music videos that in romantic relationships, men should be dominant and, when needed, violent. Meanwhile, women are expected to be submissive and accepting of any violence perpetrated against them in the context of a relationship. Adolescents' acceptance of these notions may be damaging to their own expectations of their roles in a relationship.

Conclusion

Considering the total effects of music video consumption on Black adolescents, it appears that there are several perceptual, behavioral, and attitudinal outcomes. Specifically, it can be concluded that in viewing music videos, Black adolescents are more likely to endorse and exhibit violent behavior, risky sexual behavior, and stereotypical beliefs about Black women and men. Although research in this area is beginning to tease apart the negative effects of music video viewing on the cognitive and social development of adolescents of color, much more needs to be done to understand the exact mechanisms by which these effects operate.

SECTION 3: EFFECTS OF MUSIC VIDEO VIEWING ON WHITE ADOLESCENTS

The content of music videos, and particularly their portrayal of individuals of color, can have an effect not only on the adolescents of color who view them, but also on White adolescents. The images are often stereotypical, and can serve to reinforce existing stereotypes about people from other cultural and ethnic backgrounds. In terms of the mechanism at work, it is argued that media images both trigger certain existing cognitive structures and help create new schemas. Johnson, Trawalter, and Dovidio (2000) investigated this phenomenon in the context of music videos and found that the images portrayed of Blacks activate previously stored information about racial groups. Often these beliefs take the form of stereotypes, and this process is known as *stereotype activation*. After these stereotypes have been activated, or accessed as a result of video viewing, then individuals can use this information to apply attributes to a certain racial group, a process known as *stereotype application*. According to Johnson et al., the outcome of this application is clear; adolescents both within and outside of the observed racial group will apply this information when making decisions about that group. This process can have an effect on general perceptions of persons of color, which can, in turn, have an effect on expectations of others and behavior toward others. For adolescents, this process can impact peer group selection, as well as intergroup interactions. Perhaps more importantly, however, it serves to reinforce those stereotypes that have perpetually disadvantaged certain racial groups.

The central question pursued in this line of research is whether music videos lead White viewers to adopt limited conceptions of youth of color, based on the limited images and stereotypes presented. In one of the few studies to pursue this question, Gan, Zillman, and Mitrook (1997) explored stereotyping effects as a result of viewing music videos laden with sexual imagery. After being assigned to one of three conditions (control/no videos, devoted love, and sexual enticement), 55 White men and women evaluated six photographs of Black and White women and rated the models according to a set of positive and negative qualities. Results showed significant effects of video exposure on the evaluation of Black women, but not of White women. Specifically, exposure to the sexual videos fostered distinctly unfavorable evaluations of Black women. Following exposure to sexual rap, as compared to exposure to romantic videos or no videos, Black women received lower scores on positive traits (such as attractive, beautiful, caring, considerate, faithful, intelligent, romantic, sensual, sexy, and trustworthy) and higher scores on negative traits (such as bad, cheap, cold, crude, easy, exploitative, indecent, irresponsible, obscene, promiscuous, reckless, sleazy, sluttish, and vulgar). Researchers concluded that, for White men and women, exposure to sexually enticing rap music imagery may activate perceptual primes that are generalized to other members of the same ethnic or racial group, resulting in unfavorable evaluations.

SECTION 4: IMPLICATIONS AND SUGGESTIONS FOR FUTURE RESEARCH

Music videos reflect the heart of American youth culture, readily influencing what is cool, fashionable, and important to an entire generation of young adults. At the same time, however, their lyrical and visual content also convey powerful messages about culture, gender, ethnicity, and race. At this point, most research on the cultural messages conveyed has focused on portrayals of African Americans, particularly in hip-hop music. Emerging from these analyses is a portrait of African Americans as a people whose men are dangerous and aggressive "players" and whose women are sexually promiscuous and materialistic. The potential power of these images comes not only from their presence, but also from their prevalence. When few alternative images exist, more weight is given to those that remain, and this allows them to define, for the world, who these people are. Youth of *all* cultural backgrounds may then come to adopt these images as an "authentic" representation of what it means to be a member of this community, leading Black youth to behave consistently with these images, and confirming for non-Black youth pervasive racial stereotypes that abound throughout society. Thus, content that was intended mainly to sell songs and records carries great power to shape how young viewers of diverse cultural backgrounds come to perceive themselves and each other.

Evidence, as summarized here, is slowly emerging to indicate that this dynamic is indeed the case. Findings from both surveys and experiments indicate that adolescents' behavioral, attitudinal, and perceptual outcomes can be affected by the limited and frequently stereotypical images they consume in music videos. It has been suggested that these media effects are detrimental to the developing adolescent in very specific and concrete ways. It appears that both physical behavior (e.g., engaging in violent behavior and risky sexual behavior) as well as beliefs about the world (e.g., beliefs that men and women should conform to more traditional gender roles) are affected by music video viewing.

One of the more obvious messages emerging from this study is the need for more research in this area. We see that even some of the most basic questions remain unanswered. First, systematic analysis is needed exploring the prevalence and nature of portrayals of youth of color, other than African Americans. These analyses should cover both minority-oriented and mainstream music videos, as well as videos produced in other countries and languages. Second, additional research is needed about the implications of this content on social relations and interactions. One line of research is needed addressing basic questions about how exposure to music videos affects the racial attitudes and stereotypes of youth around the world. How does this exposure shape how non-Americans view Americans? How does music video content affect how Whites view Blacks and Latinos? To what extent does music genre matter? A second line of research is needed that focuses on the effects on social relations and interactions. When considering the role of music video consumption, it is essential to include the effects of the images on stereotype activation and application, as these processes set the stage for the expectations and beliefs made about members of various racial and ethnic groups. Future research must also examine further the role of age in viewers' processing of this content. Because adolescents are susceptible to the socializing effects of the media in a unique way, their developing cognitive structures are likely to be especially affected by the narrow images that they view. In addition, as these cognitive structures are created and reinforced, adolescents may be more likely to include stereotypes in their decision making about their peers. How might this affect intergroup relations among adolescents and their ability to become open-minded, adult members of society?

In considering these and other issues, we also need to keep in mind that music videos themselves are diverse, and may serve a range of functions for youth of color. First, ethnically oriented music networks fill a niche within the market by providing representation to the diverse points of view and perspectives of people of color. Indeed, for some, they may be one of the only sources of *positive* visual content of people of color, offering a wider variety of visual representations of multicultural individuals than those shown on mainstream music programming. For many of the lesser known artists, music videos function as a "synthesis of soundtrack and visual narrative" that mediates their experiences in America, which may not be adequately represented on mainstream music programming channels (Roberts, 1994). Second, some artists use music videos as a platform for cultural expression, and resistance of racism, sexism, and classism, regardless of ethnic background (Emerson, 2002; Roberts, 1994). For those music videos that display these messages of resistance, music videos may serve as a positive socialization influence on youth of color and White youth alike.

However, perhaps the majority of artists use music videos solely as a platform to establish an image, promote celebrity, and appeal to a wider demographic group in the marketplace (Aufderheide, 1986). What are the connections between motivations behind the videos, their content, and their effects? It is troubling to many that a majority of videos reflect some of the most insidious and stereotyped characterizations of multicultural people and disseminate these messages to yet another generation of young people. One has to question why music videos that reflect negative and stereotyped images are so popular among White and ethnic minority youth alike. And when more varied or nonstereotypical images are used, they frequently appear on networks that are watched almost exclusively by ethnic minority youth. Does this trend indicate that these more positive representations in music videos are simply more appealing to ethnic minority youth? Accordingly, what does this imply for White youth whose music video diet may be composed solely of racially stereotyped images of people of color?

However, work can be done to diversify the racial, ethnic, and gender representations portrayed in music videos. There has been much debate over identifying those responsible for enacting a change in these portrayals. However, rather than assign blame for the limited and often negative portrayals found in popular music videos, what may be needed is an empirical investigation into the effect of a diverse set of representations on adolescents' beliefs, attitudes, and behavior. Might it be that having multiple images upon which to draw comparisons could make it easier for adolescents to identify potential role models? Could this broader field lead to a rejection of the negative images and more critical viewing habits? If research can demonstrate that having a wide variety of portrayals upon which to base their decisions aids in adolescents' more positive and less stereotypical schemas about race, ethnicity, and gender, then *perhaps* industry leaders may begin to advocate for an overhaul to the current state of music videos today.

REFERENCES

Aufderheide, P. (1986). Music videos: The look of the sound. *Journal of Communication, 36,* 59–80.

Brown, J. D., & Campbell, K. (1986). Race and gender in music videos: The same beat but a different drummer. *Journal of Communication, 36,* 94–106.

Brown, J. D., Campbell, K., & Fischer, L. (1986). American adolescents and music videos: Why do they watch? *Gazette, 37,* 19–32.

Bryant, Y., & Bowman, S. (2002, April). *African American female adolescents and rap music video's image women: Attitudes and perceptions.* Poster presented at the biennial meeting of the Society for Research on Adolescence, New Orleans, LA.

Cobo, L. (2006, April 15). MTV Tres aimed at U.S. Latinos. *Billboard, 118,* 12.

Collins, P. H. (2000). *Black feminist thought: Knowledge, consciousness, and the politics of empowerment* (2nd ed.). New York: Routledge Press.

del Rio, E. (2007). Media images of Latina/os. In J. J. Arnett (Ed.), *Encyclopedia of children, adolescents, and the media* (Vol. 2, pp. 471–472). Thousand Oaks, CA: Sage.

Emerson, R. A. (2002). "Where my girls at?" Negotiating Black womanhood in music videos. *Gender & Society, 16,* 115–135.

Englis, B. G., Solomon, M. R., & Ashmore, R. D. (1994). Beauty before the eyes of the beholder: The cultural encoding of beauty types in magazine advertising and music television. *Journal of Advertising, 23,* 49–63.

Farrar, K., Kunkel, D., Biely, E., Eyal, K., Fandrich, R., & Donnerstein, E. (2003). Sexual messages during prime-time programming. *Sexuality and Culture: An Interdisciplinary Quarterly, 7,* 7–37.

Finn, N. (2006, September 11). MTV Networks says "Let's play." *Television Week, 24,* 34–36.

Gan, S., Zillman, D., & Mitrook, M. (1997). Stereotyping effect of Black women's sexual rap on White audiences. *Basic and Applied Social Psychology, 19,* 381–399.

Gordon, M. (2004). *Media images of women and African American girls' sense of self.* Unpublished doctoral dissertation, University of Michigan, Ann Arbor.

Gow, J. (1996). Reconsidering gender roles on MTV: Depictions in the most popular music videos of the early 1990s. *Communication Reports, 9,* 151–161.

Hall, R. (1993). Clowns, buffoons, and gladiators: Media portrayals of African American men. *Journal of Men's Studies, 1,* 239–252.

Hansen, C. H., & Hansen, R. D. (2000). Music and music videos. In D. Zillman & P. Vorderer (Eds.), *Media entertainment: The psychology of its appeal* (pp. 175–195). Mahwah, NJ: Lawrence Erlbaum.

Harris, K. M. (1999). "Untitled": D'Angelo and the visualization of the Black male body. *Wide Angle, 21,* 62–83.

Hughes, A. (2002, May). Hip hop economy. *Black Enterprise Magazine,* 70–75.

Johnson, J. D., Adams, M. S., Ashburn, L., & Reed, W. (1995). Differential gender effects of exposure to rap music on African American adolescents' acceptance of teen dating violence. *Sex Roles, 33,* 597–605.

Johnson, J. D., Jackson, L. A., & Gatto, L. (1995). Violent attitudes and deferred academic aspirations: Deleterious effects of exposure to rap music. *Basic and Applied Social Psychology, 16,* 27–41.

Johnson, J. D., Trawalter, S., & Dovidio, J. F. (2000). Converging interracial consequences of exposure to violent rap music on stereotypical attributions of Blacks. *Journal of Experimental Psychology, 36,* 233–251.

Jones, K. (1997). Are rap videos more violent? Style differences and the prevalence of sex and violence in the age of MTV. *The Howard Journal of Communication, 8,* 313–356.

Klein, J. D., Brown, J. D., Childers, K. W., Oliveri, J., Porter, C., & Dyskers, C. (1993). Adolescents' risky behavior and mass media use. *Pediatrics, 92,* 24–31.

Lee, S. J., & Vaught, S. (2003). "You can never be too rich or too thin": Popular and consumer culture and the Americanization of Asian American girls and young women. *Journal of Negro Education, 72,* 457–466.

Moran, K. C. (2007). Media use in Latin America. In J. J. Arnett (Ed.), *Encyclopedia of children, adolescents, and the media* (Vol. 2, pp. 468). Thousand Oaks, CA: Sage.

Page, H. E. (1997). "Black male" imagery and media containment of African American men. *American Anthropologist, 99,* 99–111.

Peterson-Lewis, S., & Chennault, S. A. (1986). Black artists' music videos: Three success strategies. *Journal of Communication, 36,* 109–116.

Powell Hammond, W. (2002, April). *Made men: Manhood portrayals in hip hop videos.* Poster presented at the biennial meeting of the Society for Research on Adolescence, New Orleans, LA.

Rivadeneyra, R., Ward, L. M., & Gordon, M. (in press). Distorted reflections: Media exposure and Latino adolescents' conceptions of self. *Media Psychology.*

Roberts, R. (1994). "Ladies first": Queen Latifah's Afrocentric feminist music video. *African American Review, 28,* 245–258.

Saucier, P. K. (2006). Feminism and the Hip-Hop Conference, University of Chicago (April 2005). *Journal of Popular Music Studies, 18,* 94–101.

Seidman, S. (1992). An investigation of sex-role stereotyping in music videos. *Journal of Broadcasting and Electronic Media, 36,* 209–217.

Shaviro, S. (2005). Supa dupa fly: Black women as cyborgs in hiphop videos. *Quarterly Review of Film and Video, 22,* 169–179.

Shelton, M. L. (1997). Can't touch this! Representations of the African American female body in urban music videos. *Popular Music and Society, 21,* 107–116.

Stephens, D. P. (2003). Freaks, gold diggers, divas and dykes: The socio-historical development of adolescent African American women's sexual scripts. *Sexuality & Culture: An Interdisciplinary Quarterly, 7,* 3–49.

Sullivan, R. E. (2003). Rap and race: It's got a nice beat, but what about the message? *Journal of Black Studies, 33,* 605–622.

Sun, S., & Lull, J. (1986). The adolescent audience for music videos and why they watch. *Journal of Communication, 36,* 117–128.

Tapper, J., Thorson, E., & Black, D. (1994). Variations in music videos as a function of their musical genre. *Journal of Broadcasting and Electronic Media, 38,* 103–113.

Vernallis, C. (2002). The functions of lyrics in music video. *Journal of Popular Music Studies, 14,* 11–31.

Ward, L. M. (2004). Wading through the stereotypes: Positive and negative associations between media use and black adolescents' conceptions of self. *Developmental Psychology, 40,* 284–294.

Ward, L. M., & Friedman, K. (2006). Using TV as a guide: Associations between television viewing and adolescents' sexual attitudes and behavior. *Journal of Research on Adolescence, 16,* 133–156.

Ward, L. M., Hansbrough, E., & Walker, E. (2005). Contributions of music video exposure to Black adolescents' gender and sexual schemas. *Journal of Adolescent Research, 20,* 143–166.

Ward, L. M., & Rivadeneyra, R. (2002, August). *Dancing, strutting, and bouncing in cars: The women of BET music videos.* Paper presented at the annual meeting of the American Psychological Association, Chicago, IL.

Wingood, G. M., DiClemente, R. J., Bernhardt, J. M., Harrington, K., Davies, S. L., Robillard, A., et al. (2003). A prospective study of exposure to rap music videos and African American female adolescents' health. *American Journal of Public Health, 93,* 437–439.

CHAPTER 21

Electronic Media and Learning Through Imaginative Games for Urban Children

Dorothy G. Singer

Jerome L. Singer

Harvey F. Bellin

In *Ready to Learn: A Mandate for the Nation,* the late Ernest L. Boyer (1991), then president of the Carnegie Foundation for the Advancement of Teaching, commented on the sorry state of education in the United States. Approximately one third of American children who entered kindergarten were ill prepared. This finding was repeated about a decade later in a report by West, Denton, and Germino-Hausken (2000), indicating that 34% of kindergarten children had difficulty recognizing letters and 71% had difficulty understanding the beginnings of sounds. In the Boyer report, teachers also cited that language difficulties were the most glaring deficit, and that parent education would be one of the deciding factors in helping improve their children's school readiness. Many of the children Boyer referred to were in the lower social strata of America. These are the same ethnic and socioeconomic groups that we have worked with during the past 5 years. The focus of this chapter is on the need for preparing children from under-resourced communities for school. Our approach was through the use of videos and DVDs as well as written materials that contain imaginative games, a program called *My Magic Story Car.* Embedded in these games are opportunities to acquire cognitive and social skills needed for emergent literacy.

Boyer (1991) offered many recommendations for improving education for young children and among them was his suggestion that television could be a teacher. He cited a quote by E. B. White as follows:

> I believe television is going to be the test of the modern world, and that in this new opportunity to see beyond the range of our vision, we shall discover either a new and

> unbearable disturbance of the general peace or a saving radiance in the sky. We shall stand or fall by television—of that I am quite sure. (as cited in Boyer, p. 79)

Certainly, there are many educational programs on television that could lead to "a saving radiance" or at least improvements in language acquisition and in social skills on the part of young viewers, but unfortunately, most children tend to watch commercial broadcasting. Research, for example, by Huston, Anderson, Wright, Linebarger, and Schmitt (2001) suggests that children who were viewers of educational broadcasting when in preschool fared much better academically in high school in English, math, and science than children who rarely viewed educational programming.

According to Anand and Krosnick (2005), children's time spent watching television increases steadily as their age increases, up to 4 years. Children less than 1 year old view TV about 35 minutes per day; by 1 year, children view TV about 55 minutes per day; 70 minutes at 2 years; and more than 70 minutes per day at 3 and 4 years. In a nationally representative, random-digit-dial telephone survey of 1,065 parents of children ages 6 months to 6 years old, it was found that many young children are also using computers, but although computer usage has expanded, television is still the most favored medium for children today (Rideout, Vandewater, & Wartella, 2003). In a report prepared for Congress (J. Singer & D. Singer, 1993), one of the suggestions made was to use television as an outreach medium to help ready children for kindergarten. At the time of the report, there were about 15 million preschool children in America ages 2 to 5 years. The parents, relatives, and home care providers were the majority caring for children in their own homes during the day. Only about 28% of children were in a nursery, preschool, or child care center. Thus, it seemed fruitful to propose that the Public Broadcasting System offer specially designed programs geared to these children that contain material related to cognitive and social skills. In addition, we suggested that special programs aimed at parents could offer developmental information, and approaches for dealing with problems that children face such as sibling rivalry, discipline, aggression, sleep disturbances, and bed-wetting, among others. A public TV station, KCET in Los Angeles, has recently launched such a program, called *A Place of Our Own*, for homecare providers—the primary audience for a national ready-to-learn service—that focuses on many of the typical problems parents and teachers face in dealing with preschoolers (Drachkovitch & Brook, 2006). The program has now been adopted by many other public television stations.

THE TARGETED AUDIENCE FOR OUR TRAINING PROGRAM, *MY MAGIC STORY CAR*

If you walk into a poor, working-class neighborhood in a large urban center, you will find many of the problems that Wandersman and Nation (1998) describe in an article dealing with urban neighborhoods and mental health. The structural characteristics, such as the percentages of residents living below the poverty level, number of female-headed households, rate of population turnover in a given neighborhood, juvenile delinquency, amount of violence against children, impoverishment of resources, instability, and child care burden, are all associated with social problems. Of particular interest in this chapter is the minority preschool population in such urban centers and the effect of such structural conditions on children's ability to enter school well prepared in terms of cognitive and social skills.

Despite the fact that many of these children may be in preschool programs, a recent study suggested that boys are 4.5 times more likely than girls to be expelled for behavior problems and that African Americans experience the highest rate of expulsion at twice the rate for White and Latino children (Gilliam & Shabar, 2006). The quality of the preschool is one factor in determining how well a child will function both in learning and in social behavior. In a recent study, observers in more than 100 randomly selected classrooms found that children of color were recipients of hostility from teachers and peers more than White children were. Punishment and reward also depended on the race of children (Barbarin & Crawford, 2006). In one study (Bridges, Fuller, Rumberger, & Tran, 2006), it was reported that nearly two thirds of the children in California attend a center-based child care or Head Start program prior to kindergarten. Latino children, however, are half as likely as White children to attend center-based programs in the year prior to kindergarten entry. Among the children who do attend center-based programs, Latino children spend 7 hours per week, Asian American children spend 12 hours per week, and White children spend 14 hours per week. African American children participate for 20 hours per week, the largest amount of time. The Latino children, according to this study, are about 30 points below the White children on early language and preliteracy assessments at age 5 years. Unfortunately, the Latino children also entered preschool a year later than other children. It is found that the *earlier* a child enters preschool, the more cognitive gains will be made (Lewin, 2005). In a sample of 14,000 kindergartners, youngsters who came from poor families made more gains in early language and mathematics learning than middle-class children if they had entered preschool at ages 2 to 3 years. However, there was less advantage in social gains for high-income children who entered preschool early compared to similar children who remained at home with a parent. It appears that parents can be valuable in offering children help in social skills whereas the classroom with many children may be a more difficult setting for a one-to-one approach.

According to the National Institute of Child Health and Human Development (NICHD; 2006), in a study of 1,000 ethnically and demographically diverse children, most children during the first 2 years of life were in the care of relatives or child care homes. The average child spent 27 hours a week in nonmaternal care during the first 4.5 years of life (NICHD, 2006). Children who were in higher-quality nonmaternal child care had somewhat better language and cognitive development during their preschool years. In terms of social skills such as cooperation, the children in high-quality centers fared better than those children in centers of lesser quality. Family variables such as education, higher incomes, emotional support, cognitive enrichment, and reduced maternal stress predicted developmental outcomes that were not determined by the kind of child care. "Family and parenting experiences were as important to the well-being of children who had extensive child care experiences as families and parenting experiences were for children with little or no child care experience" (NICHD, 2006, p. 1).

Certainly in programs where parents are involved, children manage to do better in school. In one kindergarten program dealing with children of diverse backgrounds, especially children of immigrant parents who were approached not only with parent-teacher conferences, but also with a systematic plan concerning the classroom routine, the children improved significantly in acquisition of language skills (Lee, 2006). One of the important features of the program was the emphasis on parents' interaction with their children in their home language, and the need for teachers to value cultural and linguistic diversity. As an example of this approach, Lee describes an Asian family and the intense effort the parent made to help her son gain skills in English. One of the benefits of family child care is the investment made by the provider in *each* child and *each* family. This is similar to the suggestions of Lee on reaching out for the individual child with English language deficits and who may be of a different cultural perspective.

Children who do not engage in rich language interactions with their parents will have low levels of vocabulary and conceptual development, and this will affect their later reading and academic achievement (Whitehurst, 2001). The *Meaningful Differences* study by Hart and Risley (1995) recorded naturally occurring conversations in the homes of professional, working-class, and welfare families with young children for 2.5 years. They found that professional parents exchanged nearly 300 more spoken words per hour with their children than did welfare parents. As a result, by age 3, professional-family children had larger recorded vocabularies than the welfare-family parents. By first grade, linguistically advantaged children are likely to have vocabularies four times the size of their linguistically disadvantaged peers, and these differences widen in elementary school (Whitehurst, 2001). A longitudinal study of African American Head Start students by Storch and Whitehurst (2002) demonstrated the equally significant role of home literacy environments in fostering children's emergent literacy and subsequent reading achievement. The findings highlight the importance of factors such as the frequency of shared book reading and trips to a library, the number of age-appropriate books in the home, and parental expectations for their child's learning to read and write. Therefore, providing parents/caregivers easy and effective ways to enhance children's emergent literacy is another key component of a comprehensive strategy for preventing reading difficulties among at-risk children.

HOW ELECTRONIC MEDIA CAN HELP CHILDREN LEARN

The question is often asked, Can television truly help children learn? We know from our research over the years that when the content of a television program is of high quality, age appropriate, and carefully paced, children understand and retain the material more effectively. In addition, when a parent or other adult serves as a mediator, that is, explains the content if a child seems confused, and then uses material from the program to reinforce the concepts, television can indeed be a teacher (D. Singer & J. Singer, 2005). In terms of digital media, computer and Internet use begin early for most children in the United States. About two thirds of children in nursery school and 80% of kindergartners use computers, and 97% of students in grades 9–12 do so. About 23% of children in nursery school use the Internet, and this number rises to 50% by grade 3 and to 79% in grades 9–12. However, socioeconomic factors impact access to these technologies, with higher usage by children who live in two-parent households and whose families are White or Asian and have higher income and/or higher educational attainment. For example, only 44% of Hispanic children and 47% of African American children use the Internet, in contrast with 67% of White children and 58% of Asian children. Also, the Internet is used by 73% of children of parents with graduate degrees but only 37% of children whose parent(s) did not graduate from high school (DeBell & Chapman, 2006). Nonetheless, African Americans, especially teenagers, are steadily gaining access to the Internet and closing what has been called the digital divide. As a result, many more children will have the opportunity to view some of the educational websites (Marriott, 2006).

Preschoolers not only need help in processing information from television but they also, if they use computers, require an adult to help them make sense of the computer games and Internet websites. At this young age, they miss some concepts in television program content, make incorrect inferences, do not infer relations between scenes well, and often retain stereotypical information (Doubleday & Droege, 1993).

Would young children learn more from television if they had reinforcement for the story ideas by adults after viewing a program? We conducted a national study of 474 low-income urban and rural ethnic preschool children including Latinos, African Americans, and Native Americans in five regions of the United States to test the learning potential in the *Barney & Friends* television series. Teachers were trained in how to use lesson plans that we had prepared and were related to each of 10 episodes. We assessed children in the experimental and control (children with no Barney exposure and who followed the regular school routine) groups, and found that those children exposed to *Barney & Friends* and also receiving lessons after each program made the most cognitive gains. Those who viewed Barney without the additional reinforcement of the lesson plans also made modest gains compared to the control group (J. Singer & D. Singer, 1998).

In an earlier study of 250 low-income families with young children, sizable numbers of African American (40%) and Latino (20%) children were included in the sample. They were evaluated four times each year in a 2-hour visit in which the parent was interviewed and the child assessed. For those children who watched educational programming such as *Sesame Street, Mister Rogers' Neighborhood,* and *Reading Rainbow,* it was found that television appears to play a positive role in the development of readiness for school. This contribution occurs between the ages of 2 and 5 years and is independent of parents' education, quality of home environment, and family income (Wright & Huston, 1995). The children who were the viewers of educational television performed better than nonviewers on tests of reading, math, vocabulary, and school readiness as much as 3 years later. Using a Spanish version of *Sesame Street, Plaza Sesamo,* with 173 poor children ages 3 to 5 years in Mexico City who were randomly assigned to watch either *Plaza Sesamo* or cartoons and other noneducational programs, researchers found that children in the experimental group who watched *Plaza Sesamo* made significant gains in general knowledge, numbers, letters, and words. They also performed significantly better than the control group in cognitive and oral comprehension (Diaz-Guerrero & Holtzmann, 1974).

Finally, it is important to examine how television affects attitudes about minority groups. Entman and Rojecki (1998) suggest that the cognitions and emotions of the majority of White Americans are based on their mass media experiences. Some White Americans tend to associate ethnic/racial groups with negative values and antisocial behavior. Many content analyses of television programs demonstrate that ethnic groups are underrepresented and often negatively portrayed. Children's programs, as well as commercials, are highly segregated, and ethnic groups such as Latinos, Asians, and Native Americans are nearly invisible (Hunteman & Morgan, 2001). Although newer programming is reversing this trend, ethnic groups are often presented in more homogeneous and less differentiated ways than members of the dominant group, and one rarely sees intimate or even moderately positive relationships with Whites.

There is evidence, however, that educational shows that emphasize diversity can change children's racial attitudes. Multiracial inserts in *Sesame Street,* for example, changed the short-term intergroup attitude of preschool children in a study conducted with White preschoolers in Canada. Children exposed to *Sesame Street* with the multiracial inserts were more likely to choose a photograph of a non-White child as a playmate than control group participants who did not see the inserts (Gorn, Goldberg, & Kanungo, 1976). Same-race portrayals on television, however, can have mixed results (Graves, 1980). In one study, Graves (1975) found that cartoons featuring African American characters, regardless of type of portrayal, produced positive racial attitudes in African American participants. This positive effect was strongest when the same-group characters were presented in an integrated setting. In another study that featured prime-time programming, exposure to same-group characteristics resulted in negative attitudes (Dorr, Graves, & Phelps, 1980).

MY MAGIC STORY CAR: A PROJECT TO REACH AT-RISK CHILDREN

Television has the potential to be a teacher for all children regardless of race, ethnicity, and income. For the past decade, we have developed a series of video-based programs to foster the cognitive and socioemotional development of ethnically diverse preschool children from low-income families. Games used in the program are based on ideas from a book, *Make-Believe: Games and Activities for Imaginative Play* (D. Singer & J. Singer, 2001). Each video is designed for implementation in culturally diverse child care settings, features children and adults of diverse ethnicities and races, and includes a full spectrum of approaches to learning. The videos and DVDs can be used in the home, preschools, or home care settings, and can be downloaded from the Internet to help prepare children with the skills needed for entry into kindergarten. Our early videos, *Learning Through Play* and *Circle of Make-Believe,* concentrated on social and cognitive skills (for a detailed description, see Bellin, Singer, & Singer, 1999, 2001; D. Singer & J. Singer, 2004). Our latest program, *My Magic Story Car,* features imaginative games that foster emergent literacy. Testing over the years with 1,443 preschool children and 829 of their parents, teachers, and home care providers indicates that all three programs achieved their learning objectives. Research documents how make-believe play, a natural feature of early childhood development, peaking at ages 3 to 5, is an intrinsically motivating modality for engaging preschoolers in activities to enhance a plethora of cognitive, socioemotional, and motor skills (Segal, 2004; Simms, 2003; D. Singer & J. Singer, 1990, 2005). Through play, children practice vocabulary and new ways to express themselves. They verbalize plot sequences with increasingly complex situations that often evoke correcting responses from adults or peers. The narrative sequences of imaginative play can also enhance socioemotional skills such as cause-and-effect thinking, empathy, cooperation, patience, civility, and self-regulation (D. Singer & J. Singer 1990, 2005; J. Singer, 2002).

The program's title, *My Magic Story Car,* is derived from the findings of our previous video-based programs that demonstrated preschool children's fascination with driving make-believe vehicles. In this program, adults help children assemble their own Magic Story Cars (chairs, cushions, or cardboard boxes decorated with alphabet letters) with a "license plate" on which children are assisted in writing their name or initials. The children shown in the video and the young viewers drive their Magic Story Cars to play five learning games with make-believe narratives designed to strengthen specific emergent literacy skills (see Figure 1). The five

My Magic Story Car games and their targeted emergent skills are the following:

1. *Rhyme Store Game.* Children practice rhyming, then use rhymes to buy toy animals at a discount in the Rhyme Store.
2. *Lost Puppy Game.* Children "drive" to a library, get library cards, and borrow a book that tells how to help a sad lost puppy go home—they must guess the first letter, then the name of the puppy's owner. The puppy barks positive or negative feedback to the children's choice of letters.
3. *Octopus Treasure Game.* To raise funds for a neighborhood playground, children transform their cars into submarines to retrieve a treasure in a sunken ship. A giant octopus guarding the ship requires them to answer several compound-word riddles to win the treasure.
4. *Birthday Presents Game.* Children match pictures of birthday presents that start with the same first letter and sound. At the party, they give the birthday person these sets of presents as well as the special present of learning alphabet letters.
5. *Trip to Mars Game.* In response to a make-believe inquiry from children on Mars, an adult helps children make their own book about their life on earth. Children change their cars into spaceships, fly the book to Mars, and teach Martian children (who have never seen books) how to use the book.

The *My Magic Story Car* program presents the five learning games in two components:

1. Printed manuals for parents/caregivers with comprehensive instructions in user-friendly text that is clear to all adults, including those with limited literacy skills or for whom English is a second language. Included are a list of materials needed for playing each game so that no purchases are necessary and tips on helping preschoolers prepare to become good readers, as well as resource lists.
2. Video/DVD program for preschool children with depictions of playing the five learning games that interweave live action, playful animations, and interactive challenges to preschoolers. Viewers stop the program after watching each game, and then play that game using guidelines and materials in the printed manuals. The video component incorporates several approaches that proved effective in our previous programs, *Learning Through Play for School Readiness* and *Circle of Make-Believe.*

TESTING *MY MAGIC STORY CAR*: RESEARCH QUESTIONS

To assess the program's efficacy in enhancing emergent literacy of 4- to 5-year-olds from low-income families, *My Magic Story Car* was tested in underresourced communities in six states with a representative sample of 434 preschoolers in the care of 259 parents, teachers, and home care providers. The program was tested in two phases, Year One, Local Testing (New Haven, CT) in representative parent, teacher, and home care settings, and Year Two, National Testing in five geographically and demographically diverse states (California, Illinois, New York, Ohio, and South Carolina).

Each phase of the testing addressed the following research questions: Can representative parents, home care providers, and teachers of 4- to 5-year-olds from low-income families use the video-based program in their respective child care settings without any prior training; and do they find it effective after playing the games for just 2 weeks? Does the program engage preschoolers and motivate them to play the learning games? Do preschoolers demonstrate measurable gains in targeted emergent literacy knowledge and skills embedded in the learning games? Do adults show gains in their own skills for enhancing the emergent literacy of children in their care? After the 2-week

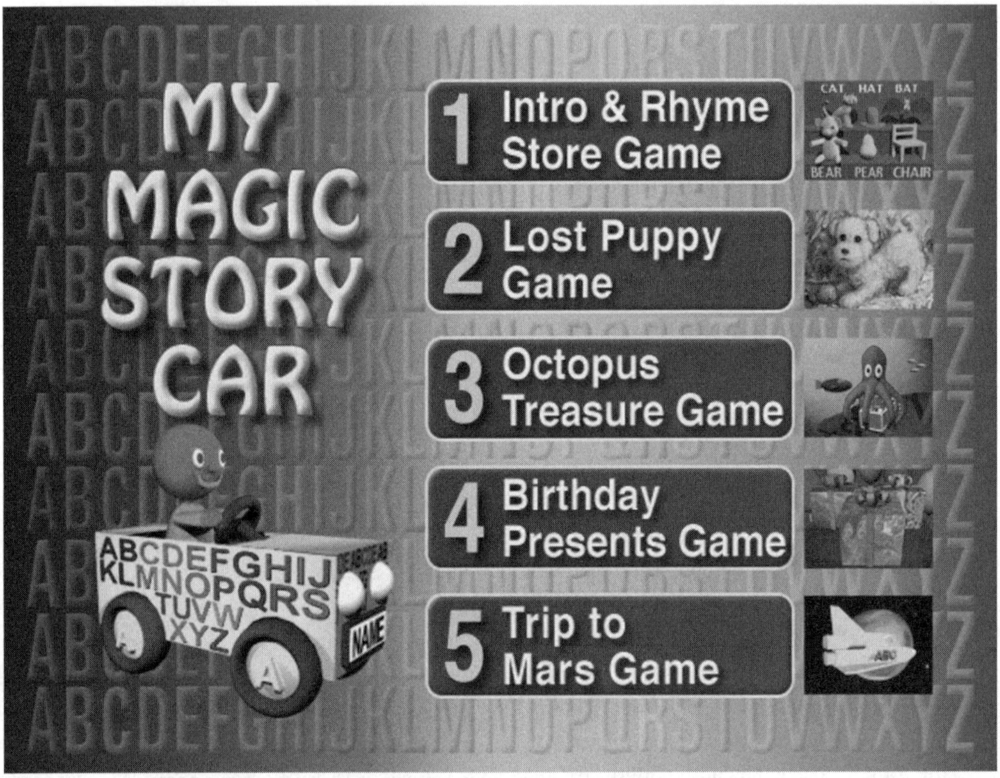

Figure 1 Children Driving *My Magic Story Car*

Source: Reprinted with permission from Harvey Bellin.

test period, do preschoolers continue to play the games on their own without adult intervention, engage other children in playing the games, and/or incorporate skills demonstrated in the games into their daily activities?

TESTING *MY MAGIC STORY CAR*: PARTICIPANTS

Participants in Year One (Local) Testing

Following the positive outcomes of testing a prototype program, in the first year of the study, the program was tested in representative urban child care settings in New Haven, CT, using random assignment, before-and-after measures, and statistical controls. Testing was conducted with 267 participants: 176 preschool children in the care of 91 adults—33 parents, 35 teachers, and 23 home care providers. The *M* age of the 176 participating children was 4.07 years (SD = 0.40). Each parent tested the program with one child. Teachers tested it with a *M* of 2.74 preschoolers, and home care providers tested it with a *M* of 2.04 preschoolers.

Demographic features of participating parents reflected those of the program's targeted communities—nearly all were mothers (92%), and over half (56%) were unmarried. Eighteen percent spoke Spanish as their first language; and some parents presented the program to their child in a mixture of English and Spanish. Participating teachers and home care providers reflected the greatly varied levels of educational attainment and teaching experience among these professions in underresourced communities.

For ethical reasons, participants were not asked to identify their race/ethnicity or that of children in their care. However, in order to test the program in settings representative of targeted end-users, participants were recruited from predominantly African American and Latino preschools.

Participants in Year Two (National) Testing

The second year of the study focused on the extent that positive outcomes from Year One testing in Connecticut (see following) could be replicated in representative low-income child care settings in five other states. Through the cooperation of other universities, participants were recruited in Los Angeles, CA; Chicago, IL; New York City; Cleveland, OH; and Greenville, SC. Testing was conducted with 303 participants: 180 preschool children in the care of 123 adults—44 parents, 45 teachers, and 34 home care providers.

Demographic features of the national testing participants were similar to those of the participants in Year One local testing. Participants were recruited from predominantly African American and Latino preschools and communities in order to test the program in settings representative of targeted end-users. The *M* age of the 180 participating children was 4.00 years. Eleven percent of children spoke a first language other than English. Ninety-one percent of participating parents were mothers.

Participants' Use of Information Technologies

Among Year One (local testing) participants, 62% of parents, 83% of teachers, and 78% of home care providers had some access to computers. One year later, participants in national testing reflected even stronger gains in access to computers. Eighty-nine percent of adult participants—89% of parents, 87% of teachers, and 91% of home care providers—had some access to computers. About half of participants in both years (56% and 44%, respectively) used computers at home, about a fourth (21% and 29%, respectively) accessed computers at work, about 15% (13% and 17%, respectively) in public libraries, and the remainder (10% and 8%, respectively) in other settings.

Participants' use of DVD players reflected the accelerated adaptation of this technology in all segments of the U.S. population. In 2002, only 2% of adult participants (1 out of 50) had requested a DVD copy of the program's prototype version; 98% had requested videocassettes. By 2004, the first year of the full study, nearly a third (32%) of adult participants requested the program in DVD rather than videocassette format. In 2005, the second year of the full study, 60% of participants in national testing requested the program in DVD format.

TESTING *MY MAGIC STORY CAR*: METHODOLOGY

In both years of the study, adult participants and parents of preschoolers in the care of participating teachers and home care providers signed informed consent forms; all participants were assigned code numbers to preserve their anonymity.

Testing in the first year of the study was conducted in representative urban child care settings in New Haven, CT, using random assignment, before-and-after measures, and statistical controls. A written instrument and telephone interviews were employed to assess children's preintervention emergent literacy skills, including the number of alphabet letters the child could name, print knowledge (e.g., parts of a book, direction in which English text is read, the meaning of terms such as *author* and *title*), phonological awareness (e.g., child's ability to make rhymes), and emergent writing (e.g., child's ability to write his or her name). Adults' current practices to foster emergent literacy (e.g., frequency of taking children to a library) were also assessed prior to intervention.

Participants were randomly assigned to an experimental group (n = 136, 45 adults and 91 children) that used the program with children in their care for 2 weeks, and a control group (n = 131, 46 adults and 85 children) that did not receive this intervention. The two groups were evenly matched in terms of demographic features and children's preintervention scores on the multiple emergent literacy measures.

The video/DVD for children and printed manuals for adults were distributed to parents, teachers, and home care providers in the experimental group. In order to simulate how the final version of *My Magic Story Car* would be used in child care settings, participants had no prior training in how to use the program. Participants were simply asked to present the program to children in their care and play its emergent literacy learning games for 2 weeks. After the 2-week test period, experimental group outcomes were recorded on three instruments: (a) Children's Postintervention Emergent Literacy Skills: children's scores for the same skills previously scored on the preintervention instrument and telephone interviews (e.g., the number of letters the child can name); (b) Record of Play Form: a log of the frequency (times/week) and amount of time spent playing the games, which games were played most often and were "favorite games," and the extent to which children continued to play games on their own without adult intervention; and (c) Feedback Form: participating adults rated the program's usefulness on a 5-point scale, and provided qualitative comments on any enhancements in children's emergent literacy and/or their own practices for fostering emergent literacy after using the program. Experimental group adults also attended one of several 90-minute focus groups to provide additional qualitative feedback on their experiences using the program with children in their care and to offer suggestions for any refinements needed.

For ethical reasons, to increase the number of participants testing the program, and to examine whether their experiences would replicate the outcomes of the experimental group, the same intervention was then provided for the control group (n = 46 child care settings) subsequent to testing the program with the experimental group. Testing procedures were the same as those conducted with the experimental group, including asking adults to present the program to children for 2 weeks with no prior training in the program's use.

Quantitative and qualitative data were compiled and analyzed to determine whether (a) as a result of using the program for 2 weeks, the experimental group children showed measurable gains in targeted emergent literacy skills when compared with the control group, and (b) the combined pre/post scores of all participants (experimental group and former control group) showed significant gains after the intervention.

Year Two national testing in the five additional states was conducted with similar protocols of assessing children's targeted emergent literacy skills prior to intervention; asking parents, teachers, and home care providers to present the program to children in their care for 2 weeks with no prior training in the program's use; assessing children's targeted emergent literacy skills after the intervention; and conducting focus groups to compile adults' qualitative feedback. However, due to logistical considerations, national testing participants were not divided into experimental and control groups. Instead, all national testing participants received the same intervention at the same time.

RESULTS: ASSESSMENTS OF PROGRAM EFFICACY AND USE

The data indicated that participating low-income parents, teachers, and home care providers were able to use the program with no prior training. Participants also had no difficulties in providing children some form of the Magic Story Cars needed for playing the learning games. The majority reported they had used cushions, pillows, chairs, or decorated cardboard boxes. Some participants evolved rather creative solutions such as giving children laundry baskets, mop buckets, diaper boxes, carpet squares, or large stuffed animals to drive as their Magic Story Cars.

Adult participants were asked to rate the usefulness of the *My Magic Story Car,* and gave it very high scores. They rated the video/DVD and printed manuals on a 5-point scale, in which 1 = not useful, 2 = somewhat useful, 3 = fairly useful, 4 = very useful, and 5 = extremely useful. In Year One, 85% of participants scored both the video/DVD and the printed manuals "4" (very useful) or "5" (extremely useful) on the 5-point scale. Among Year Two national testing participants, 85% rated the video/DVD and 82% rated the printed manuals scores of "4" (very useful) or "5" (extremely useful).

As one measure of the extent to which the program engaged and motivated children, participants recorded how much time children spent playing the emergent literacy games during the 2-week test period. Their responses indicated that despite the adults' hectic schedules, participants devoted considerable time engaging in the games. In Year One (local) testing, children in home care played the games for a *M* of 9.5 hours, children played the games with parents for a *M* of 7.7 hours, and those with teachers played for a *M* of 4.4 hours. Teachers attributed their lower number of hours playing the games to their more limited opportunities within the highly structured school schedule.

Year Two testing employed slightly different measures, but indicated that the 303 national testing participants devoted considerable time to playing the games. On average, participants played the games 4.5 times per week, with 95% of the sessions lasting 20 minutes or more, and more than half of the sessions (53%) lasting 30 minutes or more.

Pre-/Posttest Scores: Knowing Letters

Year One (Local Testing) Results

After exposure to the program for 2 weeks, the experimental group children's postintervention *M* score of knowing 16.79 letters ($p < .01$) was more than one third higher than the control group children's *M* preintervention score of knowing 12.32 alphabet letters. The most significant difference was among children in home care settings, where the experimental group's postintervention *M* score of knowing 16.35 letters ($p < .01$) was more than two thirds higher than the control group's preintervention *M* score of knowing 9.73 letters.

After the control group also used the program and played its games for 2 weeks, their pre/post scores were combined with those of the experimental group children. Again, there were significant gains when comparing pre/post scores for all participants (experimental group and former control group)—a postintervention gain from a *M* of knowing 12.35 letters to a *M* of knowing

17.51 letters ($p < .01$). The largest pre/post gain was among home care children, who increased their ability to name alphabet letters by more than 50%, from a *M* of identifying 10.93 letters to a *M* of identifying 16.57 letters ($p < .01$; see Table 1).

Year Two (National Testing) Results

It is important to note that Year Two national testing occurred later in the academic year (April–May) than Year One local testing (November–December). This resulted in many children having higher preintervention scores and somewhat lower rates of gain than Year One participants for skills such as identifying alphabet letters. Nonetheless, after children participating in Year Two national testing played the games for just two weeks, they showed a statistically significant postintervention gain from a *M* of knowing 14.21 letters to a *M* of being able to identify 17.19 letters ($p < .01$).

Pre-/Posttest Scores: Words Related to Books

Year One (Local Testing) Results

The Trip to Mars Game and the Lost Puppy Game incorporate definitions and narrative examples of the words *author, title, library,* and *borrow* (as in *borrowing* library books). Pre-/posttest scores indicated significant gains in children's understanding and use of these four words. The experimental group children's postintervention *M* score, correctly identifying 2.98 of the four

Table 1 Pre-/Posttest Scores, *My Magic Story Car*

Year 1: Local Study		
Outcome variable	*Pretest M score* ($n = 208$)	*Posttest M score* ($n = 176$)
Alphabet letters (of 26)	12.35	17.51
Book words (of 4)	1.59	3.08
Book use (of 3)	2.25	2.76
Make rhymes (%)	54.8%	84.4%
Write names (%)	59.6%	71.9%
Year 2: National Study		
Outcome variable	*Pretest M score* ($n = 188$)	*Posttest M score* ($n = 180$)
Alphabet letters (of 26)	14.21	17.19
Book words (of 4)	1.37	2.48
Book use (of 4)	3.37	3.69
Make rhymes (%)	42.8%	76.0%
Write names (%)	43.3%	58.1%
Compound words (of 8)	3.73	5.75
Letter sounds (of 3)	1.33	1.90

Note. All differences between pretest and posttest scores are significant at $p < .05$ or less.

literacy-related words ($p < .01$), was more than two thirds higher than the control group children's preintervention *M* score (correctly identifying 1.76 of the four words). The experimental group children in home care settings showed particularly strong gains; their postintervention *M* score of knowing 3.35 words of the four words ($p < .01$) was more than double the home care control group's score of knowing only 1.57 of the four words.

After the control group also used the program and their pre/post outcomes were combined with those of the experimental group children, even stronger gains were evident when comparing pre/post scores for all participants (experimental and former controls)—a postintervention score of knowing 3.08 words of the four words ($p < .01$), which nearly doubled their preintervention score of knowing only 1.58 of the four words.

Year Two (National Testing) Results

Preschoolers who participated in national testing in five additional states also demonstrated statistically significant gains in their understanding of the literacy-related words *author, title, library,* and *borrow*. Their postintervention *M* score of knowing 2.48 of the four words ($p < .01$) was more than three fourths higher than their preintervention *M* score of identifying only 1.37 of the four words.

Pre-/Posttest Scores: Using Books

Year One (Local Testing) Results

The Trip to Mars Game, and to some extent the Lost Puppy Game, demonstrate and provide young viewers interactive challenges to practice how to use books and identify the parts of books. In Year One, preschoolers were scored for their understanding of three elements of print knowledge: (a) identifying a book's front cover; (b) identifying a book's back cover; and (c) indicating the direction in which we read English text (top to bottom, left to right).

Children also showed gains in this skill after exposure to the program. The experimental group children's postintervention *M* score, correctly answering 2.80 of the three book use questions ($p < .01$), contrasted with the control group children's *M* score of 2.16 correct answers to the three questions. After the control group also played the program's games for 2 weeks, and their pre/post scores were combined with outcomes of the experimental group, the *M* postintervention score for all participants (experimental group and former control group) increased from a *M* of 2.25 correct answers to a *M* of 2.76 correct answers to the three book use questions ($p < .01$).

Year Two (National Testing) Results

Because national testing was conducted later in the school year than Year One local testing, children began with higher preintervention scores, and, therefore, showed smaller resultant gains for the book knowledge measure. On average, children participating in national testing demonstrated a modest gain in their correct answers to four book knowledge questions: (a) identifying a book's front cover, (b) identifying a book's back cover, (c) identifying which elements of a printed page are "words," and (d) indicating the direction in which we read English text. Their preintervention *M* score, correctly answering 3.37 of the four questions, rose to a postintervention *M* score of 3.69 correct answers to the four book use questions ($p < .01$) after playing the program's games.

One objective of the Lost Puppy Game is to motivate children to want to use libraries and to obtain their own library cards. Participants' feedback indicated strong increases in children's (and parents') interest in libraries and books after playing the program's games.

Pre-/Posttest Scores: Rhyming

Year One (Local Testing) Results

The Rhyme Store Game demonstrates rhyming and gives young viewers many interactive challenges to practice rhyming, an important phonological sensitivity skill. Pre-/posttesting indicated statistically significant gains in children's abilities to rhyme after exposure to the program for just 2 weeks.

The experimental group children's postintervention score, a *M* of 77.8% who could make rhymes, was 16.7% higher than the control group children's preintervention *M* score of 61.1% who could rhyme. After the control group also used the program for 2 weeks and their pre/post scores were combined with those of the experimental group children, the *M* postintervention score for all participants (experimental group and former control group) increased by 27.84% from a *M* of 56.5% to a *M* of 84.4% of children who could make rhymes.

Year Two (National Testing) Results

Children who played the program in the five additional states showed an even stronger 33% *M* gain, an increase from 43% to 76% of children who could make rhymes after exposure to the program for 2 weeks.

Pre-/Posttest Scores: Compound Words—Year Two Results

The primary learning objective of the Octopus Treasure Game is demonstrating and providing young viewers interactive challenges to practice recognizing and manipulating compound words such as *cowboy, sunshine,* and *popcorn.* Children's abilities to recognize and manipulate compound words were not fully assessed until Year Two national testing. The Year Two national testing instrument included a set of eight questions to score children's understanding of compound words before and after intervention (e.g., "What two words do you hear when I say the word *doorbell*? What word is left when I take the word *door* away from the word *doorbell*?).

Understanding compound words is the program's most challenging emergent literacy skill. Several participants noted children experienced difficulties on their first attempts with compound words; however, the vast majority experienced gains in this skill after playing the game again. Before exposure to the program, children had a *M* score of correctly answering less than half, only 3.73, of the eight compound word questions. After playing the games for 2 weeks, children's *M* score rose by over 50% to a *M* of correctly answering 5.57 of the eight compound word questions ($p < .01$).

Participants' qualitative feedback reinforced these findings. For example, one teacher noted, "I have seen a change in the children's vocabulary. They are using words from the games. They loved compound words. They broke up words by syllable. They also tried to put two words together, like *dollhouse, doghouse, classroom, basketball, bathtub, bathroom,* and *boxcar.* I was amazed and excited about their progress."

Pre-/Posttest Scores: Letter Sounds—Year Two Results

The primary emergent literacy objective of the Birthday Presents Game is demonstrating and providing young viewers interactive challenges to practice alliterations—words that begin with the same sound (and letter). Children in the video and young viewers are asked to match sets of make-believe birthday presents that begin with the same sound and letter, such as *ball, bat, balloon,* and *book.* At the same time, they practice naming alphabet letters.

Children's abilities to recognize and manipulate letter sounds were not fully assessed until Year Two national testing. In three questions on the national testing instruments, two words that start with the same sound (e.g., *dog* and *doll*) were read aloud to a child, and the child was asked to say those two words aloud and then say another word that begins with the same sound. After playing the program's games for 2 weeks, participating children showed a statistically significant gain in this skill, going from a preintervention *M* of correctly answering 1.33 of the three letter-sound questions, to a postintervention *M* of correctly answering 1.99 of the three letter-sound questions ($p < .01$).

Pre-/Posttest Scores: Emergent Writing

Year One (Local Testing) Results

The program provides children opportunities to practice emergent writing when playing the Lost Puppy Game (writing their names on library cards), when playing the Trip to Mars Game (writing their name as the "author" of a book for children on Mars), and when writing their names on "license plates" for their Magic Story Cars. Writing is a complex skill involving cognitive as well as motor skills that develop over a longer time frame than other emergent literacy variables, such as learning the meanings of the book-related words (*title, author, library,* and *borrow*). Nonetheless, in both years of testing, children showed statistically significant gains in emergent writing after using the program for just 2 weeks. The percentage of experimental group children who could write their names after playing the games (74.2%) was 13.6% higher then the percentage of the control group who could write their names before using the program (60.6%). After the control group also used the program, and their pre/post scores were combined with those of the experimental group children, the *M* postintervention score for all participants (experimental group and former control group) increased by 12.3%, from a preintervention *M* of 59.6% to a postintervention *M* of 71.9% of children who could write their names.

Year Two (National Testing) Results

Children who participated in national testing showed a comparable 15% postintervention gain. After exposure to the program, their *M* score increased from 43% to 58% of children who could write their names.

Playing the Learning Games on Their Own

Year One (Local Testing) Results

An important measure of the product's efficacy is the extent to which, after playing the games for 2 weeks with adults, children continued playing the games on their own without adult intervention, engaged other children in playing the games, made up variations of the video games, and/or incorporated skills they learned in the games into their daily activities.

Adult participants (n = 91) rated the extent to which children (n = 176) continued playing the games on their own on a five-point scale, in which 1 = not at all, 3 = sometimes, and 5 = many times. Sixty-five percent of all adult participants (73% of home care providers, 70% of parents, and 54% of teachers) reported children continued to play the games on their own, that is, they gave scores of "3" (sometimes) to "5" (many times) for this measure.

Year Two (National Testing) Results

Adults participating in national testing (n = 123) reported somewhat higher scores for this measure. Sixty-eight percent of participants (84% of home care providers, 82% of parents, and 49% of teachers) reported that children continued to play the games on their own without adult intervention after the 2-week test period. In both years, teachers attributed their lower scores for this measure to children's more limited free time during the highly structured hours they spend with teachers.

CONCLUSION

Within a short time, 2 weeks of exposure to videos/DVDs using five imaginative games, our sample of ethnically diverse, urban at-risk children from low-income families made significant gains in key emergent literacy skills. In both the local site and in national testing, children were able to learn about books and the vocabulary associated with books such as author and title, and to understand that we read from left to right in English. They were able to increase their ability to learn alphabet letters, understand rhyming and alliteration, and understand how to compose compound words. Some of the children were able to make strides in emergent writing. They were able to use expressive language as they dictated stories to the adults while they played specific games. Subsequently, after the training period, teachers reported that children played games on their own, were pretending to read, looked at more picture books, told stories about them, and asked for stories to be read to them. It is apparent that with further exposure to training, even greater gains could be made in emergent literacy by at-risk children than those we found in so brief a time.

It is interesting to note that the children in the care of home care providers, who feel somewhat isolated, made even stronger gains in specific areas compared to children in the care of teachers in day care centers. The providers actually played the games for longer times than the teachers and the parents. This may be due to the fact that these providers have fewer children in their care than the teachers, have a less structured curriculum, and are eager to have material that is new in their homes. Many of the parents in the study were single, working, and feeling the stress of not having enough time to spend with their children. Nevertheless, even these parents reported that they enjoyed the games and were eager to play more with their children using play as a method to teach basic skills.

Our qualitative data suggest that adults gained in understanding on how to use electronic media in an interactive manner. They also found that through imaginative play, children can learn easily and with great pleasure. Many of the parents and teachers were reading more to the children, and many parents reported joining their local library.

We believe that Boyer's recommendation to use television as a teacher has been implemented in this study, and we hope that this project can serve as a model for future efforts using electronic media as effective tools to foster essential school entry skills among at-risk young children of diverse backgrounds.

REFERENCES

Anand, S., & Krosnick, J. A. (2005). Demographic predictors of media use among infants, toddlers, and preschoolers. *American Behavioral Scientist, 48*(5), 539–561.

Barbarin, O., & Crawford, G. M. (2006). Acknowledging and reducing stigmatization of African American boys. *Young Children, 61*(6), 79–86.

Bellin, H. F., Singer, D. G., & Singer, J. L. (1999). *Learning through play for school readiness.* Unpublished report to the United States Department of Education Early Childhood Institute.

Bellin, H. F., Singer, D. G., & Singer, J. L. (2001). *Circle of make-believe.* Unpublished report to the United States Department of Education Early Childhood Institute.

Boyer, E. L. (1991). *Ready to learn: A mandate for the nation.* Princeton, NJ: The Carnegie Foundation for the Advancement of Teaching.

Bridges, M., Fuller, B., Rumberger, R., & Tran, L. (2006). *Preschool in California: Promising benefits, unequal access.* Retrieved November 28, 2006, from http://pace.berkeley.edu/packardfoundationstudy.html

DeBell, M., & Chapman, C. (2006). *Computer and Internet use by students in 2003* (NCES 2006–065). Washington, DC: U.S. Department of Education, National Center for Education Statistics.

Diaz-Guerrero, R., & Holtzman, W. H. (1974). Learning by televised *Plaza Sesamo* in Mexico. *Journal of Educational Psychology, 66,* 632–643.

Dorr, A., Graves, S. B., & Phelps, E. (1980). Television literacy for young children. *Journal of Communication, 30*(3), 71–83.

Doubleday, C. N., & Droege, K. L. (1993). Cognitive developmental influences on children's understanding of television. In G. L. Berry & J. K. Asamen (Eds.), *Children and television: Images in a changing world* (pp. 23–37). Thousand Oaks, CA: Sage.

Drachkovitch, S. (Executive Producer), & Brook, S. O. (Coexecutive Producer). (2006). *A place of our own* [KCEd Television series]. Los Angeles: KCET, Public Broadcasting Service.

Entman, R. M., & Rojecki, A. (1998). Minorities in mass media: A status report. In A. K. Garner (Ed.), *Investing in diversity: Advancing opportunities for minorities and the media* (pp. 67–85). Washington, DC: Aspen Institute.

Gilliam, W. S., & Shabar, G. (2006). Preschool and child care suspension rates and predictors in one state. *Infants and Young Children, 19*(3), 228–245.

Gorn, G. J., Goldberg, M. E., & Kanungo, R. N. (1976). The role of educational television in changing the intergroup attitudes of children. *Child Development, 47,* 277–280.

Graves, S. B. (1975). *Racial diversity in children's television: Its impact on racial attitudes and stated program preferences.* Unpublished doctoral dissertation, Harvard University, Cambridge, MA.

Graves, S. B. (1980). Psychological effects of black portrayals on television. In S. B. Withey & R. P. Abeles (Eds.), *Television and social behavior: Beyond violence and children* (pp. 259–289). Hillsdale, NJ: Lawrence Erlbaum.

Hart, B., & Risley, T. R. (1995). *Meaningful differences in everyday experiences of young American children.* Baltimore: Paul H. Brooks.

Huntemann, N., & Morgan, M. (2001). Mass media and identity development. In D. G. Singer & J. L. Singer (Eds.), *Handbook of children and the media* (pp. 309–322). Thousand Oaks, CA: Sage.

Huston, A. C., Anderson, D. R., Wright, J. C., Linebarger, D. L., & Schmitt, K. L. (2001). *Sesame Street* viewers as adolescents: The recontact study. In S. M. Fisch & R. T. Truglio (Eds.), *"G" is for growing* (pp. 131–143). Mahwah, NJ: Lawrence Erlbaum.

Lee, S. (2006). Using texts to communicate with parents of English-language learners. *Young Children, 61*(5), 18–25.

Lewin, T. (2005, November 1). 3 new studies assess effects of child care. *New York Times,* p. A21.

Marriott, M. (2006, March 31). Blacks turn to Internet highway, and digital divide starts to close. *New York Times,* pp. A1, A15.

National Institute of Child Health and Human Development. (2006). *The NICHD study of early child care and youth development* (NIH Publication No. 05–4318). Washington, DC: U.S. Department of Health and Human Services.

Rideout, V. J., Vandewater, E. A., & Wartella, E. (2003). *Zero to six: Electronic media in the lives of infants and toddlers.* Menlo Park, CA: The Henry J. Kaiser Family Foundation.

Segal, M. (2004). The roots and fruits of pretending. In E. F. Zigler, D. G. Singer, & S. J. Bishop-Josef (Eds.), *Children's play: Roots of reading* (pp. 33–48). Washington, DC: Zero to Three Press.

Simms, E. M. (2003). Play and the transformation of feeling: Niki's case. In S. Olfman (Ed.), *All work and no play: How educational reforms are harming our preschoolers* (pp. 177–191). Westport, CT: Praeger.

Singer, D. G., & Singer, J. L. (1990). *The house of make-believe: Children's play and the developing imagination*. Cambridge, MA: Harvard University Press.

Singer, D. G., & Singer, J. L. (2001). *Make believe: Games and activities to foster imaginative play in young children.* Washington, DC: Magination Press.

Singer, D. G., & Singer, J. L. (2004). Encouraging school readiness through guided pretend games. In E. F. Zigler, D. G. Singer, & S. J. Bishop-Josef (Eds.), *Children's play: The roots of reading* (pp. 175–187). Washington, DC: Zero to Three Press.

Singer, D. G., & Singer, J. L. (2005). *Imagination and play in the electronic age.* Cambridge, MA: Harvard University Press.

Singer, J. L. (2002). Cognitive and affective implications of imaginative play in childhood. In M. Lewis (Ed.), *Child and adolescent psychiatry: A comprehensive textbook* (3rd ed., pp. 252–262). Philadelphia: Lippincott, Williams and Wilkins.

Singer, J. L., & Singer, D. G. (1993, February 5). *Public broadcasting; Ready to teach.* Report presented to the 103rd Congress and the American people, Washington, DC.

Singer, J. L., & Singer, D. G. (1998). *Barney & Friends* as entertainment and education: Evaluating the quality and effectiveness of a television series for preschool children. In J. K. Asamen and G. L. Berry (Eds.), *Research paradigms in the study of television and social behavior* (pp. 305–367). Beverly Hills, CA: Sage.

Storch, S. A., & Whitehurst, G. J. (2002). A structural model supporting home literacy activities with African American children. In B. Bowman (Ed.), *Love to read* (pp. 31–45). Washington, DC: National Black Child Development Institute.

Wandersman, A., & Nation, M. (1998). Urban neighborhoods and mental health: Psychological contributions to understanding toxicity, resilience, and interventions. *American Psychologist, 53*(6), 647–656.

West, J., Denton, K., & Germino-Hausken, E. (2000). *America's kindergartners: Findings from the early childhood longitudinal study, kindergarten class of 1998–99* (NCES 2000–070, Revised), Washington, DC: U.S. Department of Education, National Center for Education Statistics.

Whitehurst, G. J. (2001). *White House summit on early childhood cognitive development.* Retrieved January 27, 2007, from http://www.ed.gov/news/pressreleases/2001/07/07262001_whitehurst.html

Wright, J. C., & Huston, A. C. (1995). *Effects of educational TV viewing of lower income preschoolers on academic skills, school readiness, and school adjustment one to three years later.* Report presented to Center of Research on the Influences of Television on Children, Department of Human Development, University of Kansas, Lawrence.

CHAPTER 22

The Influence of Computers, Interactive Games, and the Internet on a Child's Multicultural Worldview

Adrienne Shaw

Deborah L. Linebarger

Computer programs, video games, and Internet sites, as immersive interactive environments, allow children to interact directly with multicultural messages. Instead of watching a movie about the lives of people in Russia, they can use an interactive CD-ROM to create their own day in St. Petersburg. Rather than watching a show in which other children enjoy the Chinese New Year celebration, children can actively experience a celebration through an avatar. In addition to learning about the different cultural backgrounds of their classmates, students can use the Internet to connect with real children around the world to learn about their lives (e.g., by asking questions). Children can identify and experience other cultures in a much more complex way than they might otherwise. As Anna Kindler (1994) encourages, "In a multicultural society we should allow children to construct their own heritage from all cultural traditions to which they are exposed while growing up in a culturally diversified society" (p. 59). Rather than merely teaching children about the ways and rituals of other people, digitally mediated environments allow them the chance to actually live in new cultures and even potentially create their own multicultural culture. Moreover, by inhabiting these cultures, the children may form attachments and develop complex understandings that help curb the development of stereotypical thinking about other cultures.

Although there is little empirical research supporting it, digitally mediated environments have a unique ability to affect multicultural education. Soska (1994), for example, lists multicultural education as one of the potential uses of computer-mediated education. Moreover, several authors have noted that teachers can simultaneously address the need for multicultural literacy and digital literacy by using digital media in diversity lessons (D'Andrea, 1995; Damarin, 1998). A number of theoretical claims have been made about the ability of digitally mediated environments (including video/computer games, handheld electronic games, CD-ROMs, and the Internet) to enhance learning (Clem, 2004; Condry & Keith, 1983; Dahlen, 2006; DeVillar & Faltis, 1991; Foreman, 2004; Gee, 2003; Livingstone, 2003; Meyer & Rose, 1998; Sewell, 1990; Wartella, O'Keefe, & Scantlin, 2000). The ability of play to enhance learning makes environments that invite playfulness particularly useful educational tools (Gros, 2003). In particular, three characteristics play key roles in shaping worldviews through computer-mediated environments: identification, immersion, and reflexivity (Gee, 2003). Internet-based communications also create a distinctive environment for multicultural learning. It must be noted, however, that socioeconomic status influences access to these technologies. Such discrepancies in access only lend credence to arguments for institutionalizing this type of education and making it more readily available to children from all walks of life.

COMPUTERS AND VIDEO GAMES

The bulk of the literature about digitally mediated learning refers to self-contained games with distinct objectives and/or endpoints (Bauserman, Cassady, Smith, & Stroud, 2005; Ellis & Blashki, 2004). A digital game provides visual digital information or substance to one or more players, takes input from players, processes the input according to a set of programmed game rules, and alters the digital information provided back to the players (Kirriemuir & McFarlane, 2004). Damarin (1998) points out, however, that when considering the applicability of these games to multicultural education, one cannot ignore the fact that cultural values are often encoded in the software. Moreover, before making broad claims about video/computer games and learning, one must first acknowledge the diversity of forms digital games and their platforms take as well as the ability of each of these forms to influence learning. There are four main platforms on which educational games currently appear:

> 1. Edutainment: These are games explicitly designed to be educational in nature. Edutainment software has predominantly appeared on PCs, this being the information technology platform of choice in the classroom.
> 2. Console games: These are "pure" games developed for video game consoles, such as the Nintendo GameCube, Sony Playstation 2, and Microsoft Xbox.
> 3. PC (and Apple) games: These are "pure" games developed for use predominately on a PC (though increasingly, multiplatform games are developed for the PC and console).
> 4. Internet-based games: These are constructed in application languages such as Flash, and are typically much simpler than PC and console-based games. (Dumbleton & Kirriemuir, 2006, p. 225)

Many popular games, particularly those designed for educational purposes, are often very linear and potentially restrictive. But it is possible to create more open-ended exploratory learning environments that are not necessarily games. For example, CD-ROMs such as *A Brief History of Time,* console environments like *The Sims*, Internet sites with interactive activities, and massively multiplayer online games (MMOGs) are all types of this sort of learning environment.

PLAY AS LEARNING

The literature about children's learning and computer-mediated environments consists primarily of claims based on cognitive learning theory and anecdotal evidence on digital game play. These claims do not necessarily theorize about teaching specific skills; rather, the emphasis is on how the act of playing the game leads to learning, particularly social learning (e.g., Gee, 2003). Although these ideas may involve a new medium, it is not a new claim. Prior research suggests that play is a powerful learning tool. Bergen (2002), for example, notes, "There are clear links between pretend play and social and linguistic competence" (Abstract section).

Rieber (1996) uses two different learning theories to describe how play leads to learning: Piaget's cognitive developmental theory and Csikszentmihalyi's flow theory. Both theories are also useful for thinking about how computer games, in particular, can support learning. If a presented situation conflicts with one's experience, cognitive developmental theory asserts that a child will either attempt to fit this new information into an established mental structure (i.e., assimilation) or form a new structure (i.e., accommodation). Multicultural education, therefore, can occur when a computer-mediated stimulus conflicts with internal stereotypes held by the child. Through the child either assimilating or accommodating this conflict, learning takes place.

The simplistic view that video games can make learning fun simply because they are games is problematic (Kirriemuir & McFarlane, 2004). Kirriemuir and McFarlane argue,

> Rather than aiming for an experience that superficially resembles leisure based "fun" activities, or one which attempts to conceal the educational purpose, it might be argued that we should understand the deep structures of the game play experience that contribute to "flow" and build these into environments designed to support learning. (p. 5)

The relationship to which Kirriemuir and McFarlane refer between digital gaming and learning is situated in flow theory. Flow theory asserts that by increasing an individual's involvement and attention to an activity, he or she becomes self-motivated to learn, that is, learning becomes intrinsic. Intrinsic learning occurs when one is fully engaged in an activity that has clearly defined goals, is challenging, provides feedback on one's progress, and allows one to feel free to experiment in the course of performing the activity, all of which can be achieved through computer-mediated environments (Rieber, 1996). By being actively engaged in a computer-mediated environment, then, children can explore and learn about various cultures at their own pace. Gros (2003) argues that digital games can induce a flow state more readily than traditional educational methods because as learning environments they are flexible, adaptable, and more easily distributed. Plowman and Stephen (2003) emphasize, however, that traditional play is generally seen as an embodied activity, that is, occurring in a physical space, rather than one mediated by technology. Therefore, drawing parallels between play as an embodied activity and one that is a digital activity may not necessarily be appropriate.

Digitally mediated environments can be integrated into a school context. Clements (1985) offers a number of principles for the integration of computers into early childhood education. First and foremost, computers should only be used in contexts in which they are supportive of current educational goals and situate the child in the role of an active learner. Although drill and skill, tutorial, and experiential programs can be useful in some instances, children should also use programs that either provide or elicit higher-level cognitive experiences. Further, programs should be well integrated into the curriculum and mindful of teachers' styles and technical abilities. Sanford and

Williamson (2005) suggest that games used in schools should present authentic challenges, allow exploration of alternative possibilities and consequences, imbue cultural appropriateness, provide meaningful assessments of performance, and afford time and opportunities for reflection. The teacher's role is critical to the successful creation of an optimal computer-mediated learning experience. Similar recommendations are echoed by Galarneau (2004) and Pittman (2003).

Informal learning opportunities (via games played outside school) are increasingly available through a game's structure rather than a game's content (Sanford & Williamson, 2005). In other words, "computer games are designed 'to be learned' and, therefore, provide models of good learning principles" (Sanford & Williamson, p. 2). Papert (1980), Malone (1980), Johnson (2005), and Gee (2003) have argued that these informal learning opportunities can be derived from high-quality video and computer games. Vicarious interaction with computer-mediated environments can also lead to learning via the cognitive reprocessing of content regardless of whether the learning is derived from someone else's primary experiences (Andrews, Jannasch-Pennell, & DiGangi, 2005). Similarly, the social and collaborative aspects of games (both online and off) allow opportunities for children to teach one another how to play games more effectively. Collaborative learning is among the most important benefits of using computer-mediated programs for teaching multiculturalism, as playing with children from various backgrounds via computer, video, and Internet games or programs can encourage cross-cultural sharing and identification.

Not all research supports open-arm adoption of computer games. Literature encouraging the use of video games for educational gains is balanced with the acknowledgement that games used outside school are tied to issues of childhood obesity (Vandewater, Shim, & Caplovitz, 2004), violent and aggressive behavior (Anderson, 2003; Gentile & Anderson, 2006), and inadequate representations of diverse populations such as women and ethnic minorities (Cassell & Jenkins, 2000; Wilburn, 2005). In addition, others have pointed to potential problems with using digital games in education, including the distance between the learning objectives of a game and its general objectives (D. Clark, 2003; Mitchell & Savill-Smith, 2004). If this distance is sizable (i.e., the learning objective is tangential to the general objective), then children will default to the general objective (Fisch, 2005). Moreover, even if the game goals and learning objectives are the same, the act of playing the game may distract the child from learning the intended information. Because games are fictional, the association between lessons learned in the game and the real world may not always be achieved.

Though these are important concerns, research has demonstrated many positive influences of digital games on learning and cognitive development. Mitchell and Savill-Smith (2004) propose that digital games are capable of creating more engaging learning environments and encouraging social learning, both of which can contribute to multicultural education. Gee (2003), in his influential book *What Video Games Have to Teach Us About Literacy and Learning*, has argued that video games lead to learning by way of 36 learning principles. These principles are drawn from cognitive science and semiotics, as well as research on "situated" cognition, New Literacy Studies, and connectionism. Similar to flow theory, Gee argues that the game must encourage active engagement with the medium. He also emphasizes the importance of using games that encourage transfer of learning. A true hallmark of learning is the child's ability to learn a specific set of objectives, internalize these objectives, and subsequently transfer or generalize these internalizations to novel situations (Fisch, 2004). It is one thing to learn that stereotypes do not hold true in a particular game world; however, true learning has not taken place unless the information can then be used in a novel situation inside the game world and, more importantly, in life within the real world.

Gee (2003) further argues that overly structured learning experiences stifle children's intrinsic learning motives. Rather, children should be free to explore inside the learning experience and be allowed to engage in proactive rather than passive learning. Moreover, it is important that the games allow players to explore options without reprisal or judgment, that is, the ability to play with cultural identities in a "safe" space is important. Creating a space where children can feel free to actively engage in a multitude of cultural identities and experiences is an important component in the deconstruction of stereotypes. Finding a space to play within various cultures is not only important for teaching children about other cultures, but it is also important in allowing them to understand their own conceptions of culture in more depth.

CHARACTERISTICS OF COMPUTER-MEDIATED ENVIRONMENTS

Identification

Identification, or the extent to which a child feels connected to the game experience, is one of the processes that makes computer-mediated environments well suited to multicultural education. Unlike other media forms, these environments create an atmosphere similar to diversity training exercises where participants can act out scenarios in order to deconstruct stereotypes and educate participants about tolerance. As seen in a set of studies evaluating the effectiveness of diversity training seminars on college students, Rudman, Ashmore, and Gary (2001) argue that "because evaluation, making friends, and fear reduction are suggestive of affective processes, one route to implicit orientation change may be emotional" (p. 866). The proactive deconstruction of stereotypes and emotional investments in counterstereotypical individuals/characters are methods by which both explicit and implicit stereotypes can be influenced. If one were to create an invested attachment with a character (whether with a real person or artificial intelligence) in a computer program, video game, or via the Internet that disconfirmed stereotypes, this experience might lead to implicit stereotype change.

Identification is a major tenet of Gee's (2003) argument for the application of video games to learning. He discusses this process as a "tripartite play of identities" composed of the player's own identity, the identity of the avatar she or he plays, and the interplay between the two, which is expressed as a projection of her or his own identity on a virtual character. These identities exist simultaneously and are symbiotic in nature. By encouraging active participation and reflexive thinking about their video game characters, games allow children to learn in a way that other media do not. Children's sustained interactions with game texts and other children teach them how to participate in "semiotic domains" (Kirriemuir & McFarlane, 2004, p. 16).

McDonald and Kim (2001) assert that there may be a relationship between how much children identify with characters in electronic games and their development of a social self in that they found considerable evidence that children do identify with these characters. Further, these identifications are complicit in children's emotional and personality development. Although the authors note that their study was limited in scope, the results do demonstrate an interesting relationship worthy of further investigation.

Immersion and Role-Play

Computer worlds are also uniquely immersive environments. As previously mentioned, much like diversity training exercises, computer worlds allow for active role-play that can be used to deconstruct stereotypes and allow children to experience a new culture in an interactive way. Using virtual reality to study social psychological processes is useful for understanding how computer-mediated environments might be used for multicultural education (Blascovich, Loomis, Beall, Swinth, Hoyt, & Bailenson, 2002). Elaborate scenarios result in more compelling and authentic experiences. Because physical role-play can often feel false, moving this exercise into an arena (e.g., video games and online arenas) where children are used to playing different roles may be a more effective educational experience. Immersive virtual environment technology can allow scientists (or teachers) to "manipulate participants' group identity experimentally rather than quasi-experimentally" (Blascovich et al., p. 120).Walking in the shoes of a member of another culture takes on a whole new meaning in digital environments.

One model for this type of immersive environment is online role-playing games. In these games, players create their own avatars and play with others (whom they may or may not know personally) in a virtual environment. For the most part, one does not know the "true" identity of the other players. This allows for interesting learning effects to occur, as Yee (2001) found in his study of the game *Everquest*. Although the relevant data from this study only discusses gender, it is conjectured that it could apply to ethnicity/race, sexuality, religion, or any other component of cultural identity. Yee's data indicate that 47.9% of male and 23.3% of female players have at least one game character that is of the opposite gender (Gender Bending section). Furthermore, women were much more likely to play male characters for reasons of gender exploration whereas men played female characters for in-game advantage.

Particularly interesting in Yee's (2001) data are the quotes from participants' open-ended question responses. These excerpts demonstrate that players actually think about the way gender stereotyping affects how their gender-bending avatars are perceived. For example, several players noted that when they played female avatars, male players tended to give them more free items and unsolicited help. Conversely, when playing male avatars, they found that they were treated with more respect by male players. One respondent also noted that when the other players in her group found out that she was a woman in real life (she played a male avatar), they began treating her differently and giving her less dangerous tasks to perform. Thus, there is evidence to suggest that computer worlds (including video games, MMOGs and other Internet based games, and Internet communities) are related to the formation and reflexive modification of identity. Similar interaction in which ethnicity/race, sexuality, religion, and so on are made important could yield similar results.

MMOGs are not the only forum in which digital technology could be used to teach multiculturalism. Another option is having the children play a game in which various cultural markers matter. *Runaways*, a CD-ROM developed by Marsha Kinder, accomplishes this task (although from the information available, it did not appear to make it past the prototype stage). "The computer game 'Runaways' challenges the notion of gender by splintering it, demonstrating that biological sex and gender are not the same, and that neither is the same as self-perceived gender identity or sexual orientation" (as cited in Cassell & Jenkins, 2000, p. 28). The game also allows the players to identify their body shape/size, sexual orientation, and ethnicity/race. There is a strong link between the deconstruction of stereotypes and the narrative aspect of the game. As Kinder describes it in an interview,

> To link this narrative premise with issues raised on the ID card, we designed it so that whatever information players give about themselves has narrative consequences within the game, it helps determine how they are treated and what kind of information they get about the runaway. . . . The game puts you in the uncomfortable role of being treated as a stereotype and having other characters make all sorts of false assumptions about you. (Cassell & Jenkins, p. 219)

This type of game allows children to explore varied expressions of identity and to see how one's identity affects one's interaction with others. Like MMOGs, games like *Runaways* allow players to interact with the issues of culture, race, gender, and so forth in an immersive environment where choices they make have implications during the game.

The Sims has often been noted as the hallmark of open-construction games. Consalvo (2003) notes, for example, that the game allows for an exploration of a multitude of sexual identities in a way not allowed in most video games. In contrast, Beavis and Charles (2005) investigated gender play and the use of *The Sims* in Australian classrooms and caution against being too hasty in celebrating the openness of these games.

> Whilst the game offered both male and female students an arena for living out fantasies, pushing boundaries, and experimenting in ways not necessarily possible in their own homes, they nonetheless acted out gendered identities in the classroom as they constructed domestic space in gendered ways. (Beavis & Charles, p. 360)

In other words, despite the ability of the game to allow the open construction of gender identities, students continued to operate from what they know and perpetuated hegemonic gender beliefs. Furthermore, the students in Beavis and Charles's study worked in pairs, which may have inhibited their ability to freely engage in their own gender expression. As Gee (2003) notes, learning through the use of video games requires being able to interact with the gamespace on one's own.

The Sims games have been used in other educational contexts as well. For example, Purushotma (2005) uses modification software to alter the content of the game to help develop second-language skills in high school students. The ability to communicate in languages other than those with which one is familiar is another important aspect of developing a multicultural worldview as it offers the opportunity to connect with individuals from diverse cultures.

Video and computer games have the ability to teach different skills and allow for exploration into the unfamiliar. Furthermore, these gamespaces are not simply "play worlds" that are separate from the "real world," as there exists an interplay between the two. It is through this interplay that children can learn about themselves and others.

Reflexivity

Although a child playing a video game independently of others can learn, learning is enhanced by engaging in a larger discussion with others, that is, cooperative learning experiences (Bjorklund, 2005). For example, Francis (1998) emphasizes the importance of getting children to talk about gender in nonhegemonic ways. She found that children drew on four main sources in their discussions of gender to demonstrate how females and males are similar or different: (a) family (particularly parents), (b) their communities,

(c) anecdotal evidence, and (d) the media. Although the ability to identify instances in which gender stereotypes are disconfirmed is an important exercise, this act, in and of itself, will not deconstruct gender stereotypes. Francis is not discouraged, however.

> Although the discussion of gender in this context may not lead to immediate, dramatic change in children's oppositional gender constructions, it might serve to stem the excesses of gender category maintenance (such as sexist incidents) and to empower children intellectually to challenge them. It will enable them to challenge constructions and assumptions emanating from the dominant discourse of gender dichotomy if they wish. Moreover, it will provide children with extra information, fantasies and discursive resources which they can draw on to create more flexible constructions of their own gender identity if they want to. (p. 181)

Gee's (2003) second learning principle promotes the type of discourse encouraged by Francis: "Learning involves active and critical thinking about the relationships of the semiotic domain being learned to other semiotic domains" (p. 208). Furthermore, "Meaning/knowledge is dispersed in the sense that the learner shares it with others outside the domain/game, some of whom the learner may rarely or never see face-to-face" (Gee, p. 212).

Reflexivity has been found to occur in online role-play environments. In Yee's (2001) study, when asked if they learned anything by playing the opposite gender, male players often noted how much other male players harassed their female avatars, particularly with sexual advances. Female players playing male characters, on the other hand, noted the difficulties men in the game faced as they were socialized not to ask for help and forced to be more independent. Respondents also noted the ways in which the online gender-bending experiences forced them to question their real-life adherence to gender stereotypes. One 25-year-old, male respondent stated, "As I got to see how the rest of Norrath treats males and females, I came to realize that, try as I might, I don't treat men and women equally in [real life] myself" (Yee, 2001). This study provides evidence that Internet games may encourage players to *think* reflectively about gender stereotypes.

There is also potential for reflexivity in CD-ROM or platform video games. Returning to the *Runaways* example, placing the game in a classroom context would allow for more reflexive learning to take place. It would be possible to have children discuss, after having played the game, the way certain identity expressions led to particular outcomes. They could then relate these outcomes to their own lived experiences and discuss the fairness or bias of these practices. Played individually and used as the basis for mediated discussion, *Runaways*, or a similar game, could be used to help children learn to deconstruct stereotypes, thereby nurturing the development of an inclusive and a just multicultural worldview.

INTERNET

Collaborative gaming with children locally and globally can provide a uniquely reflexive learning experience. One of the ways computers can uniquely affect teaching multiculturalism is by allowing children to discuss their cultures directly with one another rather than relying on textbook examples. Internet communities or MMOGs, for example, give children opportunities to communicate across geographic and cultural boundaries. Thanks to the online capabilities of newer gaming consoles, these opportunities are not limited to Internet-connected computers.

Unlike the research on computer- and console-based learning with digital games, the data on learning and the Internet is, like the Internet itself, more complex. There is research on virtual versus real-world museums, for example. Prosser and Eddisford (2004) investigated children's use of virtual museums and the effect of these environments on children's learning. They found that children were able to transfer what they learned in the virtual experience to the physical experience of the museum and vice versa. On the other hand, a study by Calvert, Strong, and Gallagher (2005), using an online storybook, found that "children who controlled the computer demonstrated more attention and involvement than those who watched an adult control the experience. . . . Control, however, had no effect on children's memory of visual or verbal content" (p. 578). Plowman and Stephen (2003) point out that there are some potential problems with using the Internet in children's education. First, they note that the fixed boundaries of CD-ROM (and potentially console-/handheld-based games) are preferable, as "children do not face straying into unsuitable sites" (p. 158). Moreover, they cite research by Gilutz and Nielsen (2002) that found children had difficulty with sites that were not designed to be user friendly or used extensive amounts of text that posed problems for young readers.

St. Amant (2002) discusses two potential Internet-based approaches that can be used in multicultural education. The first approach is based on a "unidirectional" model in which students are asked to use the Internet to find materials produced by people from other cultures. To overcome linguistic barriers, he suggests that the focus be on visual content. Students can compare the culture to their own, compare different sites from the same culture, or use the sites as a way to talk about access issues in other countries. The basis of the second approach is "bidirectional" and encourages communication between different cultures, that is, cross-cultural collaboration. In this approach, students focus on connecting through language and overcoming cultural barriers that impede communication, both of which Kim and Bonk (2002) indicate can limit the extent to which groups engage in cross-cultural collaboration.

DIGITAL LITERACY/DIGITAL DIVIDE/ACCESS

The usefulness of computer-mediated environments in developing a multicultural perspective is inextricably tied to children's ability to use and access digital technology. Physical disability, social class, race, and gender have all been noted as potential factors influencing access to computers (C. Clark & Gorski, 2002a, 2002b; Gorski & Clark, 2001, 2002). Moreover, the influence of culture on the creation of digital environments is rarely considered (Damarin, 1998). Clem (2004), for instance, asserts that culture has largely been ignored in research on online learning although cognition, motivation, and values are deeply intertwined with culture. Similarly, St. Amant (2002) notes that when using computer-mediated technology to communicate across cultures, cultural differences must be taken into account to avoid problems in online interactions.

One issue that is often unaddressed when extolling the transformative potential of digital games on learning is whether or not children have the capabilities to use the hardware and input devices (Plowman & Stephen, 2003; Revelle, Zuckerman, Druin, & Bolas, 2005). As was postulated during a 2003 conference on Interaction Design and Children, "usability issues are crucial to the development of effective interactive materials for children" (Gilutz, Bekker, Druin, Fisch, & Read, 2003). Only a handful of studies have addressed this issue. An early study by Strommen (1994) found that children were successfully able to use three different mouse interfaces, but the click go, click stop model of interface was the most useable. A more recent study by Revelle and Medoff (2002), discussed in Revelle (2003), found that preschool children were able to use Playstation 2 controllers effectively as long as the "kinds of inputs and choices that must be made by the child are limited"(p. 6). Another study by Wood et al. (2004) analyzed preschoolers' success and preferences across four conditions: (a) mouse, (b) touch screen, (c) touch pad, and (d) enlarged mouse (EZ ball). The children generally preferred the EZ ball and made the fewest errors when using either the EZ ball or the mouse.

Clark and Gorski (2002) also note children with disabilities are often ignored when computer technology is used to learn. Adaptive technologies are one solution to this problem, as is incorporating disabilities into discussions of diversity.

Plowman and Stephen (2003) list several digital literacy skills that must be addressed in developing age-appropriate software:

- Interpreting the computer's interface, including familiarity with the screen conventions and how to map icons onto user actions and screen events
- Navigating the text, including understanding different representations of space and the structure of multimedia documents
- Knowing how to "read" texts with contiguous media components
- Locating and retrieving appropriate information
- Having the ability to produce multimedia texts
- Understanding the provisionality of texts
- Understanding shifts in relationships between reading and writing
- Differentiating between texts in terms of their provenance and verifiability
- Having sensorimotor skills necessary for computer interaction. (p. 156)

Beyond whether or not a child can use the hardware, we must also ask whether the child requires adult intervention to play the digital game and, likewise, whether the digital game requires adult involvement to keep the child playing. For example, Bauserman et al. (2005) found that an otherwise effective learning program was technically too difficult for children to use. In contrast, a study by Ellis and Blashki (2004) found that a sample of young children (ages 2–3 years) were quite capable of interacting independently of adult supervision when playing a game that used a customized software program that specifically targeted this age group of children.

A final but often ignored issue is whether or not learning on school computers can be correlated to learning on home computers. Cuthell (2002) found, during a 6-year longitudinal study at a comprehensive school in England, that the way students used computers at school was distinguishable from their use of computers at home. The use of computers at home was viewed as more of a dynamic experience whereas the school experience was more narrowly defined and static. Unfortunately, studies on digital games and learning are conducted almost entirely in school contexts. Whether the same results can be achieved in a home setting as what has been found in schools has yet to be determined.

A major concern in any study of digital game use and digital literacy, especially in low-income and urban student populations, is children's access to and experience with technology (Wartella et al., 2000). As Dumbleton and Kirriemuir (2006) observe, schools in underresourced communities lack the financial basis with which to implement such technology. The monies required to purchase the necessary hardware and games as well as the investment of time and the acquisition of competency to make sound curricular changes that incorporate the use of technology often limit the feasibility of using popular games in school contexts. But the need to bring digital technologies to children from all walks of life is essential to narrow the gap between the haves and have-nots lest we risk creating "a permanent underclass" (Bolt & Crawford, 2000, p. 124).

In a literature review by Wartella et al. (2000) for the Markle Foundation, they note that four demographic variables have been analyzed for their effect on digital literacy and access: sex, age, socioeconomic status, and ethnicity/race. The complex interplay that exists among these variables makes it difficult to isolate the effect of any one factor. For example, the effect of ethnicity/race or sex cannot always be disentangled from the effects of socioeconomic status as these relationships are often mediated by other influences, such as the socialization experiences of children. One's developmental age group and the related cognitive abilities is the only variable that has the potential of being addressed in isolation, that is, research findings do advocate for the use of software that is age appropriate.

A recent national survey by Calvert, Rideout, Woodlard, Barr, and Strouse (2005) found that although there was no gender divide in early computer use, family income and education level were strong indicators of computer ownership and Internet access. Moreover, race/ethnicity was found to be related to technology use in the home as it was found that Latinos were the least likely to have computers in their homes and Caucasian families were more likely to have Internet access in their homes when compared to Latino and African American families. Ba, Tally, and Tsikalas's (2002) 1-year comparative investigation of children's computer use in low- and middle-income homes studied the digital divide relative to digital literacy rather than focusing on technological resources. They found several differences between the two groups, all of which showed middle-income children as having a significant advantage over low-income children in the area of digital literacy. However, when children from different socioeconomic (SES) backgrounds were questioned regarding what medium they would use for learning (from a set of pictures that included a TV, computer, books, video game console, handheld game, phone, and radio), low-SES children more often identified computers while middle- to upper-middle-SES children indicated books (Linebarger, Royer, & Chernin, 2003). The authors speculated that this difference in perceptions may be due to the context in which the child uses the computer. Low-SES children (who did not have computers in the home) used computers only at their schools, whereas middle- to upper-SES children used computers just as often in their homes. The contexts (school and home) in which children have access to computers led them to make different assumptions about the ways in which one learns.

CONCLUSION

Several authors have indicated that multicultural education is imperative to being an effective participant in our current global society. According to D'Andrea (1995), multicultural literacy involves "being knowledgeable and respectful of the history, traditions, and values of persons from diverse backgrounds" (¶ 4). There are three distinct digitally mediated environments in which multicultural education could potentially take place: personal computers, video game consoles, and the Internet. These technologies create useful environments for multicultural education via three qualities: identification, immersion, and reflexivity. The Internet, moreover, provides a unique space for cross-cultural communication that can further foster the development of a multicultural worldview.

Digital multicultural education focuses on teaching students about other cultures, and does so in an open-ended, less static manner. Through computer-mediated role-play and online exchanges, children can develop a better understanding of themselves while becoming more familiar with others from diverse cultures and walks of life. Moreover, through virtual experiences, children can move beyond just learning about cultures to actually living the cultural experiences of others. Despite the potential value of these technologies, access continues to be a challenge that must be overcome so that all children have the opportunity to avail themselves of the resources that will support their success in our increasingly tech-savvy society.

REFERENCES

Anderson, C. A. (2003). An update on the effects of playing violent video games. *Journal of Adolescence, 27,* 113–122.

Andrews, S. S., Jannasch-Pennell, A., & DiGangi, S. A. (2005). The digital divide: Focused research results on peer mentoring, scalability and occupational self efficacy in a home-based technology integration program. *Association for Educational Communications and Technology, 27,* 35–48.

Ba, H., Tally, B., & Tsikalas, K. (2002). *Children's emerging digital literacies: Investigating home computing in low- and middle-income families.* New York: Education Development Center for Children and Technology.

Bauserman, K., Cassady, J., Smith, L., & Stroud, J. (2005). Kindergarten literacy achievement: The effects of the PLATO Integrated Learning System. *Reading Research and Instruction, 44*(4), 49–60.

Beavis, C., & Charles, C. (2005). Challenging notions of gendered game play: Teenagers playing *The Sims. Discourse: Studies in the Cultural Politics of Education, 26*(3), 355–367.

Bergen, D. (2002). The role of pretend play in children's cognitive development. *Early Childhood Research & Practice,* 4(1). Retrieved May 3, 2007, from http://ecrp.uiuc.edu/v4n1/bergen.html

Bjorklund, D. F. (2005). *Children's thinking: Developmental function and individual differences* (4th ed.). Belmont, CA: Wadsworth.

Blascovich, J., Loomis, J., Beall, A. C., Swinth, K. R., Hoyt, C. L., & Bailenson, J. N. (2002). Immersive virtual environment technology as a methodological tool for social psychology. *Psychological Inquiry, 13*(2), 103–124.

Bolt, D., & Crawford, R. (2000). *Digital divide.* New York: TV Books.

Calvert, S., Rideout, V., Woodlard, J., Barr, R., & Strouse, G. (2005). Age, ethnicity, and socioeconomic patterns in early computer use: A national survey. *American Behavioral Scientist, 48*(5), 590–607.

Calvert, S., Strong, B., & Gallagher, L. (2005). Control as an engagement feature for young children's attention to and learning of computer content. *American Behavioral Scientist, 48*(5), 578–589.

Cassell, J., & Jenkins, H. (2000). *From Barbie to* Mortal Kombat: *Gender and computer games.* Cambridge, MA: MIT Press.

Clark, C., & Gorski, P. (2002a). Multicultural education and the digital divide: Focus on gender. *Multicultural Perspectives,* 4(1), 30–40.

Clark, C., & Gorski, P. (2002b). Multicultural education and the digital divide: Focus on socioeconomic class background. *Multicultural Perspectives,* 4(3), 25–36.

Clark, D. (2003, November 20). *Computer games in education and training.* Paper presented at the Learning Skills Research Center Seminar, London.

Clem, F. A. (2004). Culture and motivation in online learning environment. *Association for Educational Communications and Technology, 27,* 183–192.

Clements, D. H. (1985). *Computers in early and primary education.* Englewood Cliffs, NJ: Prentice Hall.

Condry, J., & Keith, D. (1983). Educational and recreational uses of computer technology: Computer instruction and video games. *Youth and Society, 15*(1), 87–112.

Consalvo, M. (2003). *It's a queer world after all: Studying* The Sims *and sexuality.* New York: GLAAD Center for the Study of Media & Society.

Cuthell, J. P. (2002). *Virtual learning: The impact of ICT on the way young people work and learn.* Burlington, VT: Ashgate.

Dahlen, C. (2006). Playing to the test. *The Escapist, 59,* 8–12.

Damarin, S. K. (1998). Technology and multicultural education: The question of convergence. *Theory Into Practice, 37*(1), 11–19.

D'Andrea, M. (1995). Using computer technology to promote multicultural awareness among elementary school-age students. *Elementary School Guidance & Counseling, 30*(1), 45. Retrieved May 4, 2007, from Academic Search Elite database.

DeVillar, R. A., & Faltis, C. J. (1991). *Computers and cultural diversity: Restructuring for school success.* Albany: State University of New York Press.

Dumbleton, T., & Kirriemuir, J. (2006). Digital games and education. In J. Rutter & J. Bryce (Eds.), *Understanding digital games* (pp. 223–240). London: Sage.

Ellis, K., & Blashki, K. (2004, January). Toddler techies: A study of young children's interaction with computers. *Information Technology in Childhood Education Annua1,* 77–96.

Fisch, S. M. (2004). *Children's learning from educational television:* Sesame Street *and beyond.* Mahwah, NJ: Lawrence Erlbaum.

Fisch, S. M. (2005, June). *Making educational computer games "educational."* Paper presented at the conference on Interaction Design and Children, Boulder, CO.

Foreman, J. (2004). Game-based learning: How to delight and instruct in the 21st century. *Educause Review, 39*(5), 50–66.

Francis, B. (1998). *Power plays: Primary school children's constructions of gender, power and adult work.* Staffordshire, UK: Trentham Books.

Galarneau, L. (2004, October). *The eLearning edge: Leveraging interactive technologies in the design of engaging, effective learning experiences.* Paper presented at the e-Fest, Wellington, New Zealand.

Gee, J. P. (2003). *What video games have to teach us about learning and literacy.* New York: Palgrave Macmillan.

Gentile, D. A., & Anderson, C. A. (2006). Violent video games: Effects on youth and public policy implications. In N. E. Dowd, D. G. Singer, & R. F. Wilson (Eds.), *Handbook of children, culture, and violence* (pp. 225–246). Thousand Oaks, CA: Sage.

Gilutz, S., Bekker, M., Druin, A., Fisch, S. M., & Read, J. (2003, July). *Children's online interfaces: Is usability testing worthwhile?* Paper presented at the conference on Interaction Design and Children, Preston, UK.

Gilutz, S., & Nielsen, J., (2002). *Usability of web sites for children: 70 design guidelines.* Nielsen Norman Group. Retrieved May 3, 2007, from http://www .nngroup .com/reports/kids/

Gorski, P., & Clark, C. (2001). Multicultural education and the digital divide: Focus on race. *Multicultural Perspectives, 3*(4), 15–25.

Gorski, P., & Clark, C. (2002). Multicultural education and the digital divide: Focus on disability. *Multicultural Perspectives, 4*(4), 28–36.

Gros, B. (2003, July). The impact of digital games in education. *First Monday, 8*(7). Retrieved on May 3, 2007, from http://firstmonday.org/issues/issue8_7/xyzgros/

Johnson, S. (2005). *Everything bad is good for you: How popular culture is making us smarter.* London: Allen Lane/Penguin.

Kim, K.-J., & Bonk, C. J. (2002). Cross-cultural comparisons of online collaboration. *Journal of Computer-Mediated Communication, 8*(1). Retrieved May 3, 2007, from http://jcmc.indiana.edu/vol8/issue1/kimandbonk.html

Kindler, A. M. (1994). Children and the culture of a multicultural society. *Art Education, 47*(4), 54–60.

Kirriemuir, J., & McFarlane, A. (2004). *Literature review in games and learning.* Bristol, UK: NESTA Futurelab.

Linebarger, D. L., Royer, S., & Chernin, A. (2003). Young children, parents, perceptions and technology. *IT and Society, 1*(4), 87–106.

Livingstone, S. (2003). Children's use of the Internet: Reflections on the emerging research agenda. *New Media and Society, 5*(2), 147–166.

Malone, T. (1980). *What makes things fun to learn? A study of intrinsically motivating computer games.* Palo Alto, CA: Xerox.

McDonald, D., & Kim, H. (2001). When I die, I feel small: Electronic game characters and the social self. *Journal of Broadcasting and Electronic Media, 45*(2), 241–258.

Meyer, A., & Rose, D. H. (1998). *Learning to read in the computer age.* Cambridge, MA: Brookline Books.

Mitchell, A., & Savill-Smith, C. (2004). *The use of computer and video games for learning: A review of literature.* London: Ultra Lab.

Papert, S. (1980). *Mindstorms: Children, computers and powerful ideas.* New York: Basic Books.

Pittman, J. (2003, January). Preparing teachers to use technology with young children in classrooms. *Information Technology in Childhood Education Annual,* 261–287.

Plowman, L., & Stephen, C. (2003). A "benign addition"? Research on ICT and preschool children. *Journal of Computer Assisted Learning, 19,* 149–164.

Prosser, D., & Eddisford, S. (2004, January). Virtual museum learning. *Information Technology in Childhood Education Annual,* 281–297.

Purushotma, R. (2005). Commentary: You're not studying, you're just . . . *Language Learning and Technology, 9*(1), 1–17.

Revelle, G. (2003). Educating via entertainment media: The Sesame Workshop approach. *ACM Computers in Entertainment, 1*(1), 1–9.

Revelle, G., & Medoff, L. (2002). Interface design and research process for studying the usability of interactive home-entertainment systems by young children. *Early Education and Development, 13*(4), 423–434.

Revelle, G., Zuckerman, O., Druin, A., & Bolas, M. (2005, April). *Tangible user interfaces for children.* Paper presented at the CHI Conference on Human Factors in Computing Systems, Portland, OR.

Rieber, L. (1996). Seriously considering play: Designing interactive learning environments based on the blending of microworlds, simulations, and games. *Educational Technology Research and Development, 44,* 43–58.

Rudman, L., Ashmore, R., & Gary, M. (2001). "Unlearning" automatic biases: The malleability of implicit prejudice and stereotypes. *Journal of Personality and Social Psychology, 81*(5), 856–868.

Sanford, R., & Williamson, B. (2005). *Games and learning: A handbook from Futurelab.* Bristol, UK: Futurelab.

Sewell, D. F. (1990). *New tools for new minds.* New York: St. Martin's Press.

Soska, M. (1994). An introduction to educational technology. *Directions in Language and Education, 1*(1), 10.

St. Amant, K. (2002). Integrating intercultural online learning experiences into the computer classroom. *Technical Communication Quarterly, 11*(3), 289–315.

Strommen, E. (1994, April). *Children's use of mouse-based interfaces to control virtual travel.* Paper presented at the CHI conference on Human Factors in Computing Systems, Boston, MA.

Vandewater, E. A., Shim, M.-S., & Caplovitz, A. G. (2004). Linking obesity and activity level with children's television and video game use. *Journal of Adolescence, 27,* 71–85.

Wartella, E., O'Keefe, B., & Scantlin, R. (2000, May). *Children and interactive media.* New York: Markle Foundation.

Wilburn, T. (2005, October 18). Guns, gangs and greed: Gaming's hip hop diversity gap. *The Escapist.* Retrieved October 31, 2006, from http://www.escapistmagazine.com/issue/15/4

Wood, E., Willoughby, T., Schmidt, A., Porter, L., Specht, J., & Gilbert, J. (2004, January). Assessing the use of input devices for teachers and children in early childhood education programs. *Information Technology in Childhood Education Annual,* 261–280.

Yee, N. (2001). *The Norranthian Scrolls: A study of EverQuest.* Retrieved December 1, 2006, from http://www.nickyee.com/eqt/report.html

CHAPTER 23

Multicultural Perspectives, Developing Children, and Access to the Information Superhighway

EDWARD L. PALMER

JENNIFER A. TUTTLE

Few technological developments in our societal history have had an impact comparable to that experienced with the advent of the Internet and its information superhighway. From interpersonal communication to information access to scholarship to banking, bill paying, and purchasing, it has revolutionized the way our society functions, operates, and transacts business. While libraries contemplate its implications for hard copies of reference works and journals, and traditional news outlets assess its meaning for newspapers and newscasts, even retirement communities and their residents—long wedded to the typewriter—are seeking to access this new tool, its potentials, and its opportunities.

Potentials and opportunities, however, vitally hinge upon familiarity and access, and nowhere is this contrast more dramatically apparent than among families of differing educational, social class, income, and ethnic backgrounds. This chapter will examine the many facets of the *digital divide* and their implications for children and youth, their development, their worldview, and their capacity to become knowledgeable, effective participants in this rapidly moving technological environment.

MARKETABILITY AND THE ROLE OF CHILDREN

The Television Prologue

Marketing a new communications technology carries with it a twofold dilemma and—within it—a delicate dance. The first partner in this "dance" is the marketer, who must have a viable product to interest the consumer. That product, however, is useless unless and until the second "dance" partner—the consumer—has a way to receive it. To make the partnership happen, the marketer must take a leap of faith, investing in product with little or no assurance that return and profitability will follow. Hence, the second partner in the dance. This model played out dramatically in the early days of television. Following World War II, a proud, new television set owner would have seen only test patterns on the screen for much of any given day.

There was little reason to turn a set on, and even less reason to buy one. Marketers recognized the importance of underscoring the educational value of television programming for children, and that appeal—coupled with quality children's and family programming—transformed television from a marketer investment gamble to a lucrative market success. Where only 1 household in 100 had a television set in 1947, 1 in 10 had a set by 1950, and 9 out of 10 households had acquired a set by 1960. The child-based educational appeal to families had been instrumental in achieving virtually total market saturation within a very brief span of time (Palmer, 1987; Sterling & Haight, 1978).

While marketers successfully attained total market saturation within this brief span of time, cable and satellite brought what one could term the *connectedness divide*—those families who could afford the basic connection and program-package fees compared with those families who could not afford them. Inability to afford and to access meant inability to share a large buffet of family- and child-based channel selections such as *Nickelodeon*, the *Discovery Channel, Arts and Entertainment Channel,* and the *Family Channel.* If one lived in an area of the country where reception of Public Broadcasting Service (PBS) was either spotty or impossible, the socioeconomic differential left "have-nots" and their children at a distinct disadvantage.

In the 26-year period from 1980 to 2006, the percentage of American homes with basic cable penetration jumped from 22.6% to 58.9% (National Cable and Telecommunication Association, 2006). As more and more children's family programming shifted from commercial television networks to cable addresses, the magnitude of the "have-not" disadvantage deepened.

The Computer/Internet Sequel

Compared with television, one finds notable similarities and equally notable contrasts in the onset and development of computer ownership and Internet accessibility among U.S. households. Again, the appeal to children and educational value has taken a major role and, correspondingly, the pattern of acquisition and connectedness has followed closely households with children. A 2003 census comparison of personal computer penetration for households with children ages 6–17 compared with households without children revealed a computer-in-household differential of 76.2% to 56.6% based on child presence and a similar Internet-connectedness differential of 67% to 50.2%, respectively. This slightly narrowed the 20% differential between the two groups found in 1997 (U.S. Census Bureau, 2000, 2005).

Educational level of parent or primary caretaker, family income, and race/ethnicity served as much more dramatic predictors of computer ownership and Internet connectedness. In only 20.2% of households whose parent/caretaker had less than a high school degree did children have access to both a home computer and the Internet, whereas 76.8% of the children in households whose parent/caretaker had a bachelor's degree or higher had both home computer and Internet access (U.S. Census Bureau, 2005). The pattern of Internet access followed a systematic, steadily increasing pattern of connectedness relating to educational attainment of householder from the low point of 20.2% connectedness outlined previously to a peak of 81.1% connectedness among householders with advanced degrees.

The educational attainment of householder pattern is intricately interwoven with a corresponding pattern relating to family income. For families with less than $25,000 annual income, only 30.7% were Internet connected, compared with 92.2% of families with incomes of $100,000 or more (U.S. Census Bureau, 2005). Again, as with householder educational attainment, the Internet access curve increased smoothly and markedly on the basis of income. As Table 1 outlines, the $25,000–$49,999 income group had 57.3% connectedness; $50,000–$74,999, 77.9%; and $75,000–$99,999, 85.8%. As income and educational level increase, a household is significantly more likely to be Internet connected.

Race/ethnicity of householder also factored into major differences in connectedness. African American households were only 36% connected whereas Asian American households were 66.7% connected. Anglo-American connectedness approached the higher end of that range at 59.9% (U.S. Census Bureau, 2005).

Each of these patterns—taken individually—provides prominent evidence of critical variables contributing to the digital divide, and the intricate interweaving of relationships between householder education, income level, and race/ethnic origin must be acknowledged as well. The disadvantaged and, correspondingly, the have-nots, are disadvantaged on a combination of levels and dimensions. Key aspects of this

Table 1 Households With Computer and Internet Access in 2003 by Selected Characteristics

	Characteristic	*Computer in household* %	*Internet access* %
Presence of school-aged children	With children 6–17 years	76.2	67.0
	Without children 6–17 years	56.6	50.2
Educational attainment of householder	Less than high school graduate	27.9	20.2
	High school graduate	51.1	43.1
	Some college	70.7	62.6
	Bachelor's degree	81.9	76.8
	Advanced degree	85.8	81.1
Family income (annual)	Less than $25,000	41.0	30.7
	$25,000–$49,999	66.9	57.3
	$50,000–$74,999	83.7	77.9
	$75,000–$99,999	89.8	85.8
	$100,000 or more	94.7	92.2
Race/Hispanic origin of householder	White alone	63.9	57.0
	White alone, non-Hispanic	66.6	59.9
	Black alone	44.6	36.0
	Asian alone	72.9	66.7
	Hispanic (any race)	44.3	36.0

Source: U.S. Census Bureau (2005).

disadvantage will be examined later in the chapter.

CHILDREN'S USE OF THE INTERNET

Home Based

For children and adolescents who are connected at home, the nature of use varies by age. Preschoolers (3- to 5-year-olds) access the Internet primarily to play games. Game playing accounts for 85.2% of preschooler use. Game-playing use continues at this high level throughout the elementary, tween, and early teen years, peaking at 87.7% among 6- to 9-year-olds (U.S. Census Bureau, 2005). Only among the 15- to 17-year-olds does game playing drop below this level as use for school assignments takes on greater prominence.

Briefly profiling each of these age groups, one gains a clearer picture of what users are most likely to be doing with their home computer and online access. Reading the statistics as a percentage of those with home computers and Internet access (U.S. Census Bureau, 2005), these are the activities my age-mates and I are most likely to be doing online:

- As a *3- to 5-year-old,* I most likely—and virtually exclusively—will be game playing (game playing accounts for 85.2% of preschooler use). There will be a bit of e-mailing (10.8%) and a bit of word processing (12.5%), but only a bit in each instance.

- As a *6- to 9-year-old,* I will increase my game playing while doubling the time I spend e-mailing and instant messaging (20.3%) and doubling the time I spend word processing (24.7%). School assignments Internet time will take on the largest increase (45.8%).

- As a *10- to 14-year-old,* I will maintain a high level of game playing while dramatically increasing my school assignments time (84.0%), my word processing (56.4%), and my e-mailing and instant messaging (52.8%).

- As a *15- to 17-year-old,* my age-mates and I will reduce slightly our game-playing use (73.9%) while increasing our school assignment use (90.8%) and our word processing (69.2%). Almost half of us will be manipulating graphics and audios (43.4%) while a fifth of us will be venturing into spreadsheets (21%) and a few will be managing household finances (4.4%). By age 15 to 17, the overall trend across the age range will have been one of steadily increasing Internet use, e-mail/instant messaging, word processing, and school assignments, while still finding time for game playing.

Put in the context of a typical day—and taken collectively—the young person at home will spend slightly more than an hour in computer use (both online and offline) while spending almost 2 hours listening to music and almost 4 hours watching TV, videos, DVDs, and prerecorded shows. "Those young people who spend the most time using computers or playing video games also spend more time watching TV and listening to music" (Rideout, Roberts, & Foehr, 2005, p. 39).

School Based

By surface appearance, census data suggest that the income and ethnicity gaps in computer/Internet access and use narrow within school settings. At 83.8% and 90.5%, only 6.8% separated reported school use by the lowest and highest income levels, respectively. Ethnic differentials also narrowed, as 83.5% of Hispanic children and 85.1% of African American children reported school access and use compared with 89.2% of Anglo-American children (U.S. Census

Bureau, 2005). Fisch (2003) is quick to point out that the appearance of wide cross-cultural availability in schools and libraries must be viewed with caution. The data neither reflect the number of computers present within a given school nor the age of the computers and their capability to run current versions of software. Nor is it clear how frequently and under what circumstances a school child or teen is able to have computer use and Internet access. When the United Kingdom carefully examined data indicating that the number of computers per school had more than doubled within a brief 2-year time frame, limited bandwidth connections revealed a very different on-site picture from initial appearances. Only six children per school could access streaming websites simultaneously. Though one cannot discount the value of school and library access, the translation of its meaning for the digital divide must be made very cautiously.

INDICATORS OF EARLY HOME-BASED EXPOSURE IMPORTANCE

Ching, Basham, and Fang (2005) examined what they termed "the legacy of the harshest *digital divide*" (p. 394, italics added). Surveying young adults who had grown in tandem with the early development of computers and Internet access, the authors set out to explore the impact of gender, socioeconomic status, and early exposure as predictors of full-spectrum technology use. Full-spectrum technology use was defined as computer/Internet use across the three categories of "Communication Technologies" (synchronous or asynchronous, text- or voice-based, . . . via computer or handheld [e.g., e-mail, chat, cell phones, message boards]); "Construction Technologies" (creating and manipulating in contexts including web pages, spreadsheets, text documents, web authoring software, digital cameras, scanners, PowerPoint, etc.); Entertainment Technologies (recreational use [e.g., computer and video games, DVD players, digital music technologies and downloads]).

For purposes of this chapter focus, the most salient results outcome pertained to the three demographic variables of household income status, gender, and age of first home computer use. All three variables attained stepwise regression significance (gender—.005; income—.007; age of first home computer use—.014; Ching et al., 2005). The child who had first experienced computer access and use in the home before age 10 was significantly more likely than post-age-10 counterparts to use full-spectrum technology as a young adult. By contrast, no school-based use variable attained significance. The outcome warrants replication with a larger sample, but the early indications—if they hold—suggest early home exposure to computers and the Internet as critical predictors of full-spectrum use as adults. With recent census data revealing a continuing gap—and in some instances, chasm—in home access likelihood as a function of family income, educational background, and ethnicity, perhaps the divide becomes formidable, if not impossible, to fully bridge if young children have missed a critical period of exposure within the home context.

GENDER-BASED CHARACTERISTICS OF THE DIGITAL DIVIDE

Current estimates indicate that 25% of all new jobs in the United States will be technology based by the year 2010 (American Association of University Women Educational Foundation Commission on Technology, Gender and Teacher Education, 2000). This technology prevalence in the careers sector poses special challenges for those groups without computer/Internet access or access that is limited and inadequate. Particularly disturbing has been the widening of the computer-ownership gap between economically privileged and the working poor, African Americans and Anglo-Americans, and Hispanics and Anglo-Americans. Computer ownership and access at an early age are surfacing as fundamental links in the chain to academic success, and the new-jobs landscape cited underscores the importance of this linkage (Atwell & Battle, 1999; Cooper, 2006).

The reality poses special challenges for each group just cited, but the challenge becomes especially acute and deleterious for women. Cooper and Weaver (2003) brought close-up focus to this gender divide, concluding that women are severely disadvantaged in receiving the benefits of the technological revolution. The advantage for men begins early, follows age-old stereotypical patterns, and continues throughout adulthood. Virtually across the board, statistics on ownership and attitudes toward computer/Internet use paint a dramatic story of gender-divide difference and disadvantage. Compared to men, women own and use computers less frequently (Pinkard, 2005; Yelland & Lloyd, 2001) and are less likely to enroll in high school technology classes (Pinkard, 2005) or to attain a degree in an information technology (IT) field (Mitra et al., 2001). Women enjoy computer/Internet interaction far less than do men—a pattern that follows women longitudinally from their earliest socialization with a presumed "boy toy" and boy software. Wilder, Mackie, and Cooper (1985) first noted this computer interest/enjoyment difference. As early as kindergarten, the attitudinal/interest difference was apparent and became all the more so through middle and high school. The researchers hoped they were witnessing an anomaly that was either locally based or an artifact of early years of computer use—an anomaly that would dissipate with time. Sadly, their hope was not to be realized.

The fun and enjoyment men find in computer/Internet use is not shared by women. Compared to men, women are more computerphobic—feeling anxious and uncertain about the prospect of computer/Internet use. This level of anxiety and negative association has been found in studies spanning the age range from kindergarten to the university (Brosnan, 1998; Colley & Comber, 2003; Colley, Gale, & Harris, 1994; Todman & Dick, 1993; Whitley, 1997). It is compounded by gender differences in attribution when experiencing success or failure. On a computer task—as in the broader attribution context—men are more likely to attribute their success to ability whereas women are more likely to attribute their success to luck. Conversely, for men a failure experience means simply trying it again or working a bit harder whereas women interpret a failure as lack of ability (Cooper & Weaver, 2003). The net effect of this gender difference exacerbates women's computerphobia, discourages them from working with computers or taking computer classes, and prompts them to drop out and move away from IT career pathways. The loss to them and to society is a telling and major one.

A gender-based digital divide has been found throughout the world. Countries reporting its presence have included Australia, Canada, Egypt, Italy, Romania, Spain, and the UK (Abdelhamid, 2002; Colley et al., 1994; Dundell & Haag, 2002; Farina, Arce, Sobral, & Carames, 1991; Okebukola & Woda, 1993; Temple & Lips, 1989). Evidence of the divide has spanned both time and nationality.

The roots of this gender-based difference reach far into children's early socialization. Just as dolls and toy trucks are gender stereotyped, so too are computers and the Internet. While young boys receive positive reinforcement for following and adopting the stereotype, young girls are not reinforced or are outwardly discouraged from doing so. Both wittingly and unwittingly, the self-fulfilling prophecy (Rosenthal & Jacobsen, 1968) comes into play with teachers shaping the gender-based behaviors consistent with the stereotype. Another facet of this complex socialization phenomenon relates to primary avenues through which most children, notably boys, are introduced to the computer/Internet arena—the video game and, a bit later, the video arcade. In each instance, the stimulus is action packed, aggression/violence based, and carries the series of ingredients long-known to appeal uniquely to boys within children's television programming. As schools and their classrooms adopt software patterned after the video game and the arcade, they automatically tilt heavily toward boys while closing the door to girls (Lepper & Malone, 1987).

Again, a carryover from television advertising to children has found its way into this computer/Internet realm. While television ads have cast boys as the players with action and outdoor toys and male voice-overs have been the norm, arcade/video game–patterned software has adopted action-type or male titles and words (e.g., *Demolition Division)* for instructional software. While boys find excitement in the competitive, action-packed adventure, girls meanwhile are turned off, anxious, and lose self-confidence (Littleton & Hoyles, 2002). The difference a name and format can make in performance results is quite striking. Transforming a warrior-based *King and Crown* into one that was gender neutral and nonaggressive, Littleton, Light, Joiner, Messer, and Barnes (1998) found that girls and boys proved equally proficient in learning the skills. In the action-adventure format, girls had been far less proficient than boys (Littleton et al., 1998). This notable difference and comparable findings in other research contexts (e.g., Cooper, Hall, & Huff, 1990) create a meaningful and constructive guideline for enabling girls to close the gender gap in learning computer-/Internet-based skills.

An ongoing challenge will be that of sensitizing and instilling in software creators/providers both the knowledge and the desire to create gender-neutral materials. In a creative community that itself is primarily male dominated, action-based patterns and creative avenues can prove resistant to change. But the male-based default-style attribution spans both female and male creators of instructional programming. Huff and Cooper (1987) demonstrated this male-attribution tendency with three groups of seventh-grade public school teachers in New Jersey. One group was asked to design software helping seventh-grade boys learn the correct usage of commas. The resulting designs focused heavily on aggressive action, warfare, weaponry, and sports. A second group of teachers was asked to design software helping seventh-grade girls learn correct comma usage. By contrast, the girl-based designs featured shopping, conversing, and learning. Most revealing of all was a third group of teachers being asked to design software helping seventh-grade students to learn correct comma usage. The resulting designs closely paralleled those created for boys. In the absence of gender indicators, the attribution assumption becomes male (Huff & Cooper, 1987). This male-default tendency continues to be one of our greatest challenges in bridging the gender divide. Unlike its ethnic-based counterparts, it cuts across all income groups.

COST OF INTERNET DISCONNECT FOR THE HAVE-NOTS

Internet connectedness is, admittedly, a mixed blessing. While it connects families and their children to 800 million web pages, countless games, and library resources, it also connects these families to 12 million pornographic pages and violent game sites unsuitable for children (Paik, 2001). The blend calls upon parents to be vigilant and to institute safeguards to insulate their children from the "seedy" side of Internet access while providing opportunities for the prosocial and educational access. On the face of it, this responsibility appears quite straightforward with the purchase and installation of one of the family-based firewall programs. But "setting it and forgetting it" is not a parental option. With an emerging population of children more techno-savvy than their parents, the challenge of access shaping becomes an ongoing parental responsibility. With television as the historical precedent, it was apparent that the majority of American families had relinquished viewing control to their children. Comstock, Chaffee, Katzman, McCombs, and Roberts (1978) observed that for all practical purposes, television and its viewing scheduling appeared to be much more within the province of the authority of children than their parents. Even in the early decades of that era, children were considered more knowledgeable than their parents, and multiset households with television, computer, and Internet connections in children's bedrooms have served to exacerbate that pattern and reality. With unsuitable websites cleverly named to shadow or parallel established sites (e.g., whitehouse.com), children can stumble upon them quite by accident. There never has been a more critical time for parental responsibility. It is essential to all households with children connecting to the Internet and its information superhighway.

While disconnected households and their children are missing the problem of pornographic sites and other unsuitable material, they also are missing the opportunity to share the many positive, prosocial, and educational resources at their web fingertips. The advantages of being connected include

1. Developing the knowledge and technological skills necessary to compete and gain employment in an increasingly technological marketplace
2. Accessing websites and resources that can broaden multicultural vistas and appreciation of diversity
3. Increasing knowledge of one's cultural heritage and pride in one's identity

Knowledge and Technological Skill Development

With a predicted 25% of new jobs being technology based in 3 years (American Association of University Women Educational Foundation Commission on Technology, Gender and Teacher Education, 2000), it is essential that children attain the tools they will need to participate and to contribute. The costs of anything short of that participation will be exceedingly high—both societally and personally. Several initiatives have recognized the vital importance of averting this cost by investing in technological preparation of children. The Bill & Melinda Gates Foundation (2007, Creating Opportunities for All, ¶ 1) goals statement speaks centrally to this concern and this chapter's focus:

> As a nation, it's critical we ensure equitable access to opportunities for America's most vulnerable people. Nearly one-third of high school students won't graduate on time, and the rate is worse for Latino, Native American, and African American students. Millions of people do not have access to the powerful information that others readily access through computers and the Internet. In the Pacific Northwest, a growing number of families struggle to get by. The mission of the United States Program is to reduce these inequities and improve access to opportunities by:
>
> - Significantly increasing the number of students who graduate from high school with the skills needed to succeed in college and work

- Improving the lives of at-risk children, youth, and families in Washington state and Greater Portland, Oregon
- Expanding access to information through technology in public libraries that serve low-income and disadvantaged communities

From a flagship company on the cusp of technological innovation and change, the foundation is uniquely positioned to prepare students in the ways outlined. Their approach also recognizes the vital importance of focusing both regionally and nationally with a multifaceted approach that includes schools, service agencies to at-risk families/children in the foundation's region, and public libraries.

The Children's Partnership provides a comprehensive *Parents' Guide to the Information Superhighway* (Lazarus & Lipper, 1998) with its "rules and tools for families online." A project of the Tides Center, the Partnership is a joint initiative with the National PTA and the National Urban League. Its elite group of advisers spans the broad spectrum of public and private foundations, educational institutions, library associations, educational/ethnic media outlets, national ethnic leadership, and community organizations. At the frontlines level, the Partnership mirrors goals expressed in the Gates Foundation Mission Statement—"[to] help children learn skills using information resources and technology . . . [to] open up new worlds of rich learning experiences to children through schools, libraries, and home . . . [to] increase access to children who have been shut out" (Lazarus & Lipper, 1998, p. 2). The "shut out" are described as "children in poor or rural school districts," providing them the online opportunity "to visit museums, cities, and wildlife preserves they would not otherwise get to see" (Lazarus & Lipper, 1998, p. 2).

A third initiative comes from the Corporation for Public Broadcasting. Titled *Connected to the Future* (Corporation for Public Broadcasting, 2002), it compares U.S. Census data on Internet use from 2000 to 2002 and underscores the need to bridge the digital divide at school. To quote their byline message, "Under-served Children Get an 'A' for Attitude, Not Access" (Corporation for Public Broadcasting, 2002, p. 6). The report underscores the income and ethnic disparities in home access and, like the Gates Foundation, the Corporation for Public Broadcasting considers school to be a critical link in the disparity chain. Hispanic and African American children who access the Internet at school report increased liking for school, and similar enthusiasm is expressed by Hispanic children's parents and—to a lesser degree—African American children's parents (Corporation for Public Broadcasting, 2002, p. 6). Until the digital divide is bridged, school will play an essential role in connecting disadvantaged children.

Website Access to Broaden Vistas and Diversity Exposure

Once children are Internet connected, they have a broad-ranging cornucopia of websites to access. Virtually all the popular children's television programs have a corresponding website with games and other program character–related materials. The 2- to 5-year-olds rate their top programs to be *Clifford, Arthur, Dragon Tales, Barney & Friends, Caillou, Dora the Explorer, Sesame Street, Bob the Builder,* and *Teletubbies.* For the broader 2–11 age range, *Arthur* and *Clifford* again top the list (in reverse order), followed by *Dragon Tales, Rugrats, Barney & Friends,* and *SpongeBob* (Crane & Chen, 2003). Children in the 2- to 5-year age range relate naturally and easily to their program characters, and diversity appreciation is taught both explicitly and implicitly. For example, the *PBS Kids* website describes Clifford as "an every dog kindness . . . approaching the world with an open heart and mind" (*Clifford,* 2006, FAQ section, "What are the programs' goals?," ¶ 7). Big-hearted and fun-loving, standing up for what is right, he models the hopes, dreams, and fears of his preschool viewers (*Clifford,* 2006). Similar lessons are taught by *Arthur,* reinforcing themes of reading as fun, creative problem solving, being a good friend, connecting to family, respecting and appreciating diversity, and generally having fun. As with *Clifford,* the qualities of kindness, courage, cooperation, collaboration, and conflict resolution are modeled along with those of identifying with feelings such as being left out, the joy of helping others, one's body image and gender, and the satisfaction in group accomplishment (*Arthur,* 2007a, 2007b). With a generally younger target audience than *Clifford* or *Arthur, Dragon Tales'* animated fantasy adventure conveys the comparable lessons of caring about and supporting one another, taking turns, celebrating small and partial successes, learning to cope with fears, understanding and expressing one's feelings, and helping the newcomer feel welcome. It models looking beyond physical limitations and accepting differences in children's abilities, and its compassionate characters learn how to get along with others, resolve conflicts, and develop patience and empathy (*Dragon Tales,* 2006). Among the remaining top program selections, the most explicitly cross-cultural is *Dora the Explorer,* a cartoon format from Nickelodeon targeting preschool 3- to 4-year-olds. It features a young, bilingual Latina girl and her monkey companion, Boots, who are always on the go. They get directional help from her talking backpack and make a point of "talking to viewing children" and asking them to "Say it again." Upon their arrival at a destination, they sing and dance in the spirit of "We did it, we did it." The program fosters a "can do!" attitude, teaches basic shapes and numbers and Spanish vocabulary and phrases. It teaches "diversity in a world where people are still so blinded by where someone is from that they can never seem to see who that person is" (Winston, 2006, p. 1).

Sesame Street and *Barney* teach diversity appreciation both explicitly and implicitly. The explicit message generally is conveyed through a song or dance whereas the implicit message is conveyed through the ethnicity, gender, and disability diversity of program children guests. In *Barney,* a group of children representing diverse ethnic groups dance, sing songs, role-play, problem-solve, practice politeness and manners, and learn to identify and express their feelings. The signature song, "I love you/you love me/we're a happy family," spreads Barney's general "feel-good"/acceptance message (Marsh, 2006). From its very inception, *Sesame Street* embraced diversity. Premiering in November, 1969, this program was designed to prepare urban, low-income preschoolers for their entry into first grade. Along with letter and word recognition, number concepts, geometric forms, cognitive processes, and basic classification, it also teaches life skills for road-crossing safety, personal hygiene, healthy eating patterns, and the prosocial skills of cooperation and respectful acceptance of diversity. Its adult-oriented parodies and humor foster shared coviewing by grownups with their children. Now televised in 120 countries and over 20 international versions, it is the longest-running American children's program (*Sesame Street,* 2006).

Knowledge of One's Cultural Heritage/Pride in One's Identity

If one were to Google four children's heritage search terms—African American, American Indian, Hispanic, and Latino—each search would produce hits exceeding one million and spanning a diverse range of topics and children's interests. A child would find books by children for children, the celebration of respective heritage months, and so forth. The child curious about Hispanic heritage, for example, could go to hundreds of public library websites (e.g., the Newark Public Library site) and find a variety of fascinating questions such as "Do you know the words to 'De Colores'?" or "What does a vejigante look like?" Website guidance would be provided for Spanish-speaking children ("Habia una vez," 2007). This is but one example of the wealth of information at a young person's fingertips when—and if—connected to the information superhighway. One can readily see the positive contribution this resource can make to a child's understanding of his or her cultural heritage and pride in his or her identity. The key, of course, is having access, and therein lies the challenge foundations such as Bill & Melinda Gates and The Children's Partnership Initiative seek to address.

THE GLOBAL DIGITAL DIVIDE

The U.S. digital divide landscape is but a faint harbinger of the far more gaping global digital divide in developing and underdeveloped countries. In addition to the problems of poverty and isolation, authoritarian political structures restrict any open access to information beyond the leadership's control. Add to these elements the absence of infrastructure such as phone lines and electricity, and one quickly begins to see the harshly gaping nature of this divide. Less than 1% of the populations in underdeveloped countries of Africa, Central America, and South Asia have Internet access and use, compared with 50% to 60% access and use in Scandinavia, Singapore, South Korea, and the United States (International Telecommunication Union, 2003). A child in an underdeveloped country will be unlikely to gain any cross-cultural or diversity worldview beyond the bounds of his or her own village. "Windows" to the world beyond the village will be tightly closed. Meanwhile, the child in upper-income households within developed countries will have full-spectrum access and familiarity with the Internet. As with the U.S. discussion earlier in this chapter, global use and access closely follow income lines.

With the Internet heralded early in its emergence as a decentralizing and empowering force (Negroponte, 1995), the scope of the divide has prompted more recent cautions and warnings from international, governmental, and university agencies and scholars (e.g., Horrigan, 2003; UCLA Center for Communication Policy, 2000; U. S. Department of Commerce, 1999). In a sobering analysis, Guillen and Suarez (2005) concluded that developed countries that participated centrally in the creation of the Internet and its knowledge base are likely to benefit disproportionately from its use. If this analysis proves true and the use/access divide continues to widen, the little child in the remote village will have scant opportunity to see and experience the broader and more diverse world. But efforts modeled after *Sesame Workshop*'s global outreach in children's television programming and major international foundation/agency commitments lend hope that the village "window" will remain ajar. It may begin with a generator or a village kiosk, but once the window has opened and a child has peered through it, there dare be no turning back.

FAMILIARITY—THE KEY AND THE CHALLENGE

To bridge the digital divide both domestically and globally, familiarity becomes a key and essential ingredient. The weight of research evidence in the context of prejudice consistently has confirmed that prejudice functions and thrives in the abstract. When "the different from" can be kept at a distance, grouped, and labeled, the prejudicial attitudes will be formed and maintained.

These prejudicial attitudes break down and change once familiarity develops with individuals in the stereotyped group (e.g., Sherif, Harvey, White, Hood, & Sherif, 1961; Zajonc, 1965, 1968). In children's television programming history, programs such as *Big Blue Marble* spanned cultures, introduced viewing children in different cultures to one another, and developed pen pal relationships. The Internet carries the potential to bring this introduction and familiarity to yet another level. But that level can only be reached if a second dimension of familiarity within the monumental divide challenge can be addressed. The "jury is out" and the questions are daunting:

- Can children gain access to Internet tools early enough in their lives to become "natural" and full-spectrum participants in the digital revolution, its careers, and its opportunities?
- Can teaching and mentoring support be provided for disadvantaged children who gain access, enabling them to make effective use of the Internet?
- Will the gender divide be addressed, bridged, and eliminated?
- Will the overall digital divide narrow and bridge both nationally and globally, or will the haves continue to leap farther, faster, while leaving the have-nots farther behind?

Positive response to these—and related—questions will hold enormous potential for educating our world's youth and instilling the familiarity so essential to appreciating, respecting, and embracing diversity. Monumental indeed is the challenge. So, too, is the hope for our children, their cross-cultural familiarity, and their commitment to friendship and a more peaceful world.

REFERENCES

Abdelhamid, I. S. (2002). Attitudes toward computer: A study of gender differences and other variables. *Journal of the Social Sciences, 30*, 285–316.

American Association of University Women Educational Foundation Commission on Technology, Gender and Teacher Education. (2000). *Tech-savvy: Educating girls in the new computer age.* Washington, DC: Author.

Arthur. (2007a). Retrieved January 31, 2007, from http://en.wikipedia.org/wiki/Arthur_(TV_series)#About_Arthur

Arthur. (2007b). Retrieved January 31, 2007, from http://www.pbs.org/arthur/parentsteachers

Atwell, P., & Battle, J. (1999). Home computers and school performance. *The Information Society, 15*, 1–10.

Bill & Melinda Gates Foundation. (2007). *United States mission statement.* Retrieved January 9, 2007, from http://www.gatesfoundation.org/UnitedStates

Brosnan, M. J. (1998). The impact of psychology gender, gender-related perceptions, significant others, and the introducer of technology upon computer anxiety in students. *Journal of Educational Computing Research, 18*, 63–78.

Ching, C. C., Basham, J. D., & Fang, E. (2005). The legacy of the Digital Divide: Gender, socioeconomic status, and early exposure as predictors of full-spectrum technology use among young adults. *Urban Education, 40*, 394–411.

Clifford. (2006). Retrieved June 30, 2006, from http://pbskids.org/clifford/parentsteachers/about_program/faq.html.q.11

Colley, A., & Comber, C. (2003). Age and gender differences in computer use and attitudes among secondary school students: What has changed? *Education Research, 45,* 155–165.

Colley, A. N., Gale, M. T., & Harris, T. A. (1994). Effects of gender role identity and experience on computer attitude components. *Journal of Educational Computing Research, 10,* 129–137.

Comstock, G., Chaffee, S., Katzman, N., McCombs, M., & Roberts, D. (1978). *Television and human behavior.* New York: Columbia University Press.

Cooper, J. (2006). The digital divide: The special case of gender. *Journal of Computer Assisted Learning, 22*(5), 320–334.

Cooper, J., Hall, J., & Huff, C. (1990). Situational stress as a consequence of sex-stereotyped software. *Personality and Social Psychology Bulletin, 16,* 419–429.

Cooper, J., & Weaver, K. D. (2003). *Gender and computers: Understanding the digital divide.* Mahwah, NJ: Lawrence Erlbaum.

Corporation for Public Broadcasting. (2002). *Connected to the future.* Retrieved January 4, 2007, from http://www.cpb.org/stations/reports/connected_report.pdf

Crane, V., & Chen, M. (2003). Content development of children's media. In E. L. Palmer & B. M. Young (Eds.), *The faces of televisual media: Teaching, violence, selling to children* (2nd ed., pp. 55–81). Mahwah, NJ: Lawrence Erlbaum.

Dragon Tales. (2006). Retrieved June 30, 2006, from http://www.pbs.org/teachersource/prek2/progarticles/dragontales.shtm

Dundell, A., & Haag, Z. (2002). Computer self-efficacy, computer anxiety, attitudes toward the Internet and reported experience with the Internet, by gender, in an east European sample. *Computers in Human Behavior, 18,* 521–535.

Farina, F., Arce, R., Sobral, J., & Carames, R. (1991). Predictors of anxiety towards computers. *Computers in Human Behavior, 7,* 263–267.

Fisch, S. M. (2003). Challenges for the future of educational media. In E. L. Palmer & B. M. Young, (Eds.), *The faces of televisual media: Teaching, violence, selling to children* (pp. 125–139). Mahwah, NJ: Lawrence Erlbaum.

Guillen, M. F., & Suarez, S. L. (2005). Explaining the global digital divide: Economic, political and sociological drivers of cross-national Internet use. *Social Forces, 84,* 681–708.

Habia una vez y dos son tres: Hispanic children's literature in the U.S. Retrieved January 8, 2007, from http://www.npl.org/Pages/ProgramsExhibits/Exhibits/habia.html

Horrigan, J. B. (2003, May 18). *Adoption of broadband to the home.* Retrieved February 5, 2007, from http://www.pewinternet.org/pdfs/PIP_Broadband_adoption.pdf

Huff, C., & Cooper, J. (1987). Sex bias in educational software: The effect of designers' stereotypes on the software they design. *Journal of Applied Social Psychology, 17,* 519–532.

International Telecommunication Union. (2003). *World telecommunications indicators database.* Retrieved January 10, 2007, from http://www.itu.int/ti/publications/world/world.htm

Lazarus, W., & Lipper, L. (1998, May). *The parents' guide to the information superhighway.* Santa Monica, CA: The Children's Partnership.

Lepper, M. R., & Malone, T. W. (1987). Intrinsic motivation and instructional effectiveness in computer-based education. In R. E. Snow & M. J. Farr (Eds.), *Aptitude, learning and instruction: Conative and affective process analysis* (pp. 255–286). Hillsdale, NJ: Lawrence Erlbaum.

Littleton, K., & Hoyles, C. (2002). The gendering of information technology. In N. Yelland & A. Rubin (Eds.), *Ghosts in the machine: Women's voices in research with technology* (pp. 5–32). New York: Peter Lang.

Littleton, K., Light, P., Joiner, R., Messer, D., & Barnes, P. (1998). Gender, task scenarios and children's computer-based problem solving. *Educational Psychology, 18,* 327–340.

Marsh, T. (2006). *Barney and Friends.* Retrieved June 30, 2006, from http://www.bookrags.com/history/popculture/barney-and-friends-sjpc-01/html

Mitra, A., Lenzmeier, S., Steffensmeier, T., Avon, R., Qu, N., & Hazen, M. (2001). Gender and computer use in an academic institution: Report from a longitudinal study. *Journal of Educational Computer Research, 23,* 67–84.

National Cable and Telecommunication Association. (2006). *Statistics.* Retrieved January 29, 2007, from http://www.ncta.com/ContentView.aspx?contentId=54

Negroponte, N. (1995). *Being digital.* New York: Knopf.

Okebukola, P. A., & Woda, A. B. (1993). The gender factor in computer anxiety and interest among some Australian high school students. *Educational Research, 35,* 181–189.

Paik, H. (2001). The history of children's use of electronic media. In D. G. Singer & J. L. Singer (Eds.), *Handbook of children and the media* (pp. 7–27). Thousand Oaks, CA: Sage.

Palmer, E. (1987). *Children in the cradle of television.* Lexington, MA: Lexington Books.

Pinkard, N. (2005). How the perceived masculinity and/or femininity of software applications influences students' software preferences. *Journal of Educational Computing Research, 32,* 57–78.

Rideout, V., Roberts, D. F., & Foehr, U. G., (2005, March). *Generation M: Media in the lives of 8–18 year-olds, Executive summary.* Menlo Park, CA: The Henry J. Kaiser Foundation.

Rosenthal, R., & Jacobson, L. (1968). *Pygmalion in the classroom: Teacher expectation and pupils' intellectual development.* New York: Rinehart and Winston.

Sesame Street. (2006). Retrieved July 4, 2006, from http://en.wikipedia.org /wiki/Sesame_Street

Sherif, M., Harvey, O. J., White, B. J., Hood, W., & Sherif, C. (1961). *Intergroup conflict and cooperation: The Robbers Cave experiment.* Norman: University of Oklahoma Institute of Group Relations.

Sterling, C. H., & Haight, T. R. (1978). *The mass media: Aspen Institute guide to communication industry trends.* New York: Praeger.

Temple, L., & Lips, H. M. (1989). Gender differences and similarities in attitudes toward computers. *Computers in Human Behavior, 5,* 215–226.

Todman, J., & Dick, G. (1993). Primary children and teacher's attitudes to computers. *Computers and Education, 20,* 199–203.

UCLA Center for Communication Policy. (2000). *Surveying the digital future: Year three.* Retrieved January 10, 2007, from http://www.ccp.ucla.edu

U.S. Census Bureau. (2000). *Access to a home computer and use of the Internet at home by children 3 to 17 years: August 2000.* Retrieved January 31, 2007, from http://www.census.gov/prod/2001pubs/p23-207.pdf

U.S. Census Bureau. (2005). Current population reports (CPR): *Computer use in the United States: October 2003.* Retrieved January 4, 2007, from http://www .census.gov/prod/2005pubs/p23-208.pdf

U.S. Department of Commerce. (1999). *Falling through the net: Defining the digital divide.* Washington, DC: Author.

Whitley, B. E., Jr. (1997). Gender differences in computer-related attitudes and behavior: A meta-analysis. *Computers in Human Behavior, 13,* 1–22.

Wilder, G., Mackie, D., & Cooper, J. (1985). Gender and computers: Two surveys of computer-related attitudes. *Sex Roles, 13,* 215–228.

Winston, J. (2006, June 30). *Dora the Explorer cartoon: Teaching diversity.* Retrieved June 30, 2006, from http://articles.simplysearch4it.com/article/00025/29652.html

Yelland, N., & Lloyd, M. (2001). Virtual kids of the 21st century: Understanding the children in schools today. *Information Technology in Childhood Education Annual, 13,* 175–192.

Zajonc, R. B. (1965). Social facilitation. *Science, 149,* 269–274.

Zajonc, R. B. (1968). The attitudinal effects of mere exposure [Monograph]. *Journal of Personality and Social Psychology,* 9, 1–27.

CHAPTER 24

Making Sense of Kids Making Sense

Media Encounters and "Multicultural" Methods

Darnell Hunt

Angela James

Some families connect over dinner. In our family, the most intense conversations occur on the ride home from school. Today, the subject is whether or not "The Undertaker" is better than "Bautista," as well as the question of how tall "Rey Mysterio" really is. We ask whom our 9-year-old twin sons are talking about and learn that these characters are professional wrestlers, a televised sport that up to now they have not been allowed to watch. We listen, amazed, as they patiently explain seemingly every facet of the pantheon of characters that inhabit the World Wrestling Federation. We are impressed by the thoroughness with which they describe and assess each character's strengths and weaknesses. We know they have never actually seen any of the wrestlers perform, and yet they passionately communicate detailed knowledge about each of them.

Then we learn that both of our sons have friends who regularly watch wrestling on television. It is from these friends, as well as on the playground, that they have learned and begun to share in the world of power, teamwork, intrigue, and double-cross depicted in professional wrestling. We wonder if it is merely coincidence that they detest one of the few Black characters, a muscular, dreadlocked, dark-skinned villain named "King Booker." We worry that his "queen" Charmelle (as well as the other scantily clad women who exist to cheer on the wrestling warriors) will teach them it's okay to objectify women. Our sense that we have been protecting them from the various problematic racial and sexual images we see embedded in professional wrestling is immediately shattered. We suddenly realize that the reach of television extends far beyond the boundaries of the viewing room. All we have done with our efforts to control what they watch, it is now clear, is make it more difficult for them (though obviously not impossible) to participate in the meaning making around a spectacle that drives the imaginations of boys their age. After a few more of these conversations, and seemingly endless lectures from us about the dangers of wrestling with each other, we relent and allow them to watch Friday Night Smackdown.

As African American parents, we are acutely sensitive to the messages our children take away from their encounters with media. Although our sons are good kids who make friends easily, excel in school, and rarely exhibit any behavioral problems, we find ourselves constantly guarding against the socializing effects of media that most people fear and take for granted. Our childhood world of prime-time television, comic books, and matinees has morphed into our children's hyper-mediated world of satellite television, video games, and the Internet. Youth today watch between 1.8 to 2.8 hours of television per day, depending on age and gender. Boys and girls with access to video games spend about 60 and 23 minutes per day, respectively, with these media. Youth spend an additional 30 minutes per day with computers (Marshall, Gorely, & Biddle, 2006). Media are indeed everywhere today; their boundaries, as our sons' example illustrates, are beyond specification. It's no wonder that we fear the worst.

Because race is arguably "the central axis of social relations" in America (Omi & Winant, 1994), a cultural "representation" that serves to account for (and even legitimate) difference and stratification in society (S. Hall, 1997), American media have always been saturated with racial meanings. Recent studies of prime-time television, for example, show that White characters continue to dominate in terms of time on the screen and prominence in show narratives (Hunt, 2000, 2005; Bang & Reece, 2003). Despite the strict regulation of children's programming and the relatively high degree of diversity that has come to characterize most of this programming, studies show that subtle messages in these programs sometimes work to reinforce traditional gendered roles (Powell & Abels, 2002). This finding, it seems, raises important questions about the ideological work of racial imagery in the programs. An important goal of what might be termed "multicultural" research methodologies is to examine how minority children read these media patterns. What sense do they make of their encounters with media and how might these meanings resonate with their understandings of race?

Race in America is a multifaceted phenomenon. At the level of society, it refers to the classification of persons into groups that differ in terms of the degree of access their members have to opportunities, power, and privilege. On a more personal level, it refers to an important aspect of identity, one that emanates from a consciousness of membership in one of these groups and an awareness of certain commonsense "truths" about the group that must be negotiated (if not embraced). An important question confronting any student of media and minority children involves the subject position of these children. Research shows, for example, that Black children of all ages are more likely than their White counterparts to have well-developed ideas about racism and to talk about these ideas in ways that explicitly implicate power relations in society (McKown, 2004). To what degree does this tendency shape how minority children engage with media? That is, to what degree do they interact with media *as minorities?* How might "multicultural" research methodologies be employed to get at this meaning-making process and to identify the role that race plays?

We both recall growing up in the 1960s and 1970s, noticing how the villain was usually dark and dark-haired and the hero White and blond. We also remember how a grandparent might reframe the narrative by suggesting that the dark-haired princess was actually prettier or that the Indians were really the heroes. There existed a clear social context of dissent and criticism around the media encounter then, one in which minority children as well as adults were imbedded. Race was front and center on the national agenda, and it seemed that the parents of minority children were ever vigilant in their attempts to mediate the impact of racial imagery on their children's psyches.

In today's supposedly color-blind era, minority children confront the mediated imagery of a society that continues to be racialized, despite official discourses that minimize the centrality of race (Hunt, 2005). What analytical framework(s) do these children bring to their media encounters when making sense of what they see? What language and verbal tools do they have at their disposal? How can we know what to make of these encounters, particularly as they relate to our concerns about the continuing impact of race in society?

In this chapter, we attempt to make a case for the importance of studying what media encounters *mean* to minority children—as opposed to what they *do to them*. In order to do so, we feel it first necessary to briefly review how children and media traditionally have been studied. With this grounding in place, we hope to clarify what's distinctive about a meaning-based, "multicultural" research approach, as well as consider some methodological tools particularly suited to it.

STUDYING WHAT MEDIA DO TO CHILDREN

Research on children and media was born in an era of rising fears about the negative effects of media on the morals and behavior of American youth. Early studies concentrated on film, a medium that had suddenly forced itself front and center in American culture during the 1920s. These studies examined the degree to which the images circulated in popular films encouraged imitation by youth, influenced childhood play, and framed adolescent daydreaming and fantasy. Findings suggested that film had indeed become a central component of the cultural environment in which youth were immersed and that the potential for influencing their lives was substantial (Lowery & DeFleur, 1995).

The first comprehensive studies of the effect of television on children emerged in the late 1950s and early 1960s, after television viewing began to erode film attendance and the small screen became the dominant American media form. In many respects, the concerns about television were more pressing than those concerning film because commercial television was conceived and built upon the ideal of the nuclear family. Television inserted itself directly into the home in ways that film never could, apparently increasing the opportunities for influence, as well as the associated stakes. Schramm, Lyle, and Parker (1961), however, questioned the commonsense notion that children were passive viewers waiting to be acted upon by television. Consistent with the emerging "uses and gratifications" paradigm of the period, these researchers conceived of children as active viewers who have specific uses for television (e.g., entertainment and information) and who receive gratifications from television based on important underlying needs. Their study thus focused on *how* and *when* children use television as opposed to what television *does to* children; its findings worked to assure parents that a nurturing home environment would offset any possible negative effects emanating from television exposure.

But longstanding concerns about the harmful effects of media on children did not die easily. Indeed, as the field of media effects research progressed, it eventually adopted a rather schizophrenic position on the power of media and the vulnerability of audiences: on the one hand, the "limited-effects" model associated with the "dominant paradigm" (Gitlin, 1978) proclaimed that media have only a marginal impact on the lives of most Americans; on the other hand, an increase in violent images in film and television continued to spawn studies seeking to establish any links between the images and aggression in youth. The 1972 Surgeon General's Report, for example, focused on televised violence and concluded that there was indeed a statistically significant relationship between violent imagery and increasing aggression in youth. The study also offered the caveat that its findings—which were largely based on laboratory experiments and surveys—should be considered further in the context of the total home environment, which includes exposure to other forms of media.

These concerns about harmful effects, it should be noted, were heightened by the realization that children had primarily watched television intended for the general audience (Comstock & Cobbey, 1979). Saturday morning programming was the exception to this rule in the 1970s. During the decade, minority children were "either a minority within the majority for the modest portion of children's viewing represented by Saturday morning, or a minority within a minority most of the time" (Comstock & Cobbey, 1979, p. 104).

As mass media came to be identified as a major source of learning for youth, other studies focused on children's viewing and cognitive processing. A meta-analysis of studies from the 1970s showed that these issues dominated mass media effects research during the decade (Emmers-Sommer & Allen, 1999). Findings suggested that media can influence attitudes, which can, in turn, shape social behaviors, and that a major motivation for watching is the gratification children associated with the media encounter.

The studies also found that age was related to processing ability—that is, as children grow older, they understand media better. Of course, this finding begs the question of what *understand* means, particularly if the researcher is interested in the meanings *children make* of their media encounters. This question, we contend, is central for researchers studying *how* race intervenes in the process of media consumption. Indeed, whereas a more recent study identifies media use as a dominant childhood activity and an increasingly important cultural influence, it maintains that youth are active media consumers who interpret the meanings of these encounters in strikingly different ways (Brown & Cantor, 2000).

Nonetheless, research on media stereotyping grew out of a persistent concern about media's power to socialize. If stereotypes are understood as (re)circulated generalizations or "representations" used by groups to reduce other targeted groups to a few (often undesirable) qualities (S. Hall, 1997), then the question was to what degree and in what ways were minority children affected by these images? Research on children and television suggests that exposure to certain types of programming can promote the acceptance of stereotypes (Graves, 1999). This is significant because content studies of television found that portrayals of minorities were traditionally more "negative"[1] than those of their White counterparts (Hunt, 2000, 2002, 2003, 2005). Indeed, Tan and Tan (1979) found a positive relationship between heavy television usage and low self-esteem among African Americans adults, which they theorized might have been due to the negative impact of Blacks regularly watching "white-oriented" television (p. 131). This theory seems consistent with research suggesting that Black viewers—due to the relatively high salience of race in their lives—tend to be more attuned to racial cues than their White counterparts when they engage with media (Beaudoin & Thorson, 2006).

At the same time, studies show that minority children may be quite resilient in their engagement with stereotypes. One study of fourth-, sixth-, and eighth-grade African Americans found that the children eschewed stereotypes that reflected negatively on their racial group in favor of those that rendered the group in more positive terms (Rowley, 2002). Moreover, research has shown that minority children traditionally have distinctive tastes and preferences in their television programming choices and generally indicated more favorable attitudes toward television than their White counterparts (Comstock & Cobbey, 1979). Another study, which focused on "wishful identification," concluded that Black high schoolers were more likely to identify with characters that had the higher-prestige jobs in television. It also found that they were more likely to aspire to college degrees if the characters with which they identified had themselves completed college (Hoffner et al., 2006). Television, the authors concluded, can be an important source of knowledge about the work world of youth, even if its images are a bit distorted. Considered together, these findings raise important questions about what minority children might take away from their experiences with media, about the meanings that they make from the encounters. As Berry (1998) notes, we have to understand the needs children bring to these encounters to really get at the meanings they make of them. Oversimplified theories about *the effects* of different types of media content on children—as if media influences are fixed—won't do.

STUDYING WHAT CHILDREN DO WITH MEDIA

In the final analysis, a compelling case can be made for the importance of approaching minority children's encounters with media as open-ended questions, each encounter representing a new opportunity for meanings to be made, a new case to be studied. A quarter of a century ago, Berry and Mitchell-Kernan (1982) argued that race and ethnicity are likely to be intervening variables in the process of media socialization for minorities because minorities traditionally have been either the targets of stereotyping in media or profoundly marginalized by them. Minority children, the scholars pointed out, bring distinctive cultural consciousnesses to the media encounter that must be taken into account—even if it is understood that ethnic and racial groups are not monolithic (see also Comstock & Cobbey, 1979).

But Berry and Mitchell-Kernan (1982) also concluded that it might be impossible to predict the impact of these consciousnesses on media socialization because of the influence of other intervening factors and processes. This latter point about prediction is key. It points to a fundamental divide in the literature between researchers driven to document replicable media effects and those more interested in exploring the meanings associated with particular media encounters (Jensen, 1991). The first approach, we argue, characterizes quantitative studies of media "effects," whereas the latter is more descriptive of qualitative, interpretive studies of "meaning." The two approaches are rarely brought together in empirical studies of media, despite the growing acceptance within the academy of the "postpositivist" perspective (Tashakkori & Teddlie, 1998, p. 8). As a result, what we know about minority children and media—particularly concerning the role that racial meanings play in these encounters—is riddled with theoretical, methodological, and empirical gaps.

"Multicultural" Research Methods

Researchers who privilege the role of racial meanings in their analyses necessarily embark on what we will term "cultural" approaches, approaches that recognize racial meanings as possessing varying degrees of autonomy from economic and other structural factors (Hunt, 2006). Race cannot be reduced to these factors—they are far from perfect proxies, despite the clear associations between these factors and racial status. Racial meanings inform our actions, simultaneously shaping and transcending the particulars of material existence. For example, although it may be relatively easy to measure racial differences in household income, it is much more difficult to determine *how* the racial meanings that saturate a child's home environment shape his or her experiences with media. This is because racial meanings are not easily rendered in numbers or a priori categories. Researchers interested in getting a handle on how a minority child's encounter with media relates to the racial order require a research toolkit stocked with a variety of quantitative *and* qualitative methodological tools.

Researching children is generally seen as a problematic enterprise for four reasons: (a) children are not competent enough to narrate their own lives, (b) children will not tell the truth, (c) children will only say things to please the researcher, and (d) children are silly and unreasonable (Ali, 2006). Although some of these concerns can be managed and others may be somewhat overstated, all are reasonable considerations for those designing studies of children and their media encounters. Much of what happens in the audience/media encounter happens within the minds of audience members, which creates serious challenges for researchers attempting to generate data for studying the resulting meaning-making process.

On the other hand, research has convincingly shown that audience members are not isolated entities who make sense of media in a vacuum (Hunt, 1997, 1999). A growing body of literature makes a compelling case for conceptualizing media consumption as social activity, which expands the domain of activity (and observable data) that may be associated with the media encounter. This is particularly true for children, who regularly consume media within the family setting, sometimes in accordance with influence from their peers, but usually under the supervision of adults. For example, one ethnographic study of how families watch television found that social interaction is the most common concurrent activity for all television viewers (Schmitt, Woolf, & Anderson, 2003). Playing and eating were particularly common concurrent activities for children television viewers. Contrary to theories that conceive of television viewing as an isolated experience, the study showed television viewing to be a profoundly social experience, particularly among the youngest viewers. Indeed, the researchers found that 2-year-olds were engaged in social activity 39% of the time they watched.

The specific actions and behaviors associated with children's media consumption—talking before, during, and after; play; imitation; and so on—lend themselves to study with a variety of methodological tools. Although no one methodological tool is likely to provide a whole rendering of the meaning-making process, of complete truth, each has a valuable perspective to contribute. Used in combination, the researcher may more effectively use different tools to triangulate in on the most salient meanings minority children take from their media encounters, as well as the role that race and ethnicity likely play in the process. Both quantitative and qualitative methods may have something to offer in the analysis of cultural values and beliefs, and triangulation should be an integral part of any "holistic research perspective" (Berry, 1998). The most nuanced studies are often multidisciplinary in approach, based on conceptual models that benefit from the best insights of different disciplines (Brown & Cantor, 2000).

In the next section, we discuss several methodological tools that may aid researchers in their quest for more holistically studying the meanings minority children make from their media encounters. Our goal here is not to provide an exhaustive narrative about how to employ these tools. Rather it is to discuss some of the issues associated with using them for navigating the tricky terrain of understanding how minority children make meaning from their media encounters, which involves being sensitive to the role race may play in the process.

Observation and Ethnography

From time to time, we observe our 9-year-old twin boys as they watch professional wrestling on television. On one particular occasion, their eyes and ears are so glued to the action unfolding on the screen that they do not hear their mother calling them to dinner. Suddenly, one leaps over the top of the sofa and onto the footrest closest to the television in a move shadowing one of the wrestlers, who flings his body from the ropes and onto his opponent in the ring. Two seconds later, his brother jumps from the same sofa and lands on a pink, toddler-sized, stuffed starfish named Patrick (a character from a popular cartoon the boys frequently watch). He bends one of the stuffed animal's legs back close to its head and pins it in a three-count—just as the wrestler on the television screen is declared the winner. What do we make of this activity? Should we be terrified that our sons are being socialized into violent, aggressive behavior?

It would be very tempting for us, as parents, to be driven by concerns about the glorification of violence in our society and to assume that this particular media encounter was helping to socialize our children into this culture (cf. Messner, Hunt, & Dunbar, 1999). But to succumb to this temptation too quickly may channel us into an overly narrow understanding of the "meanings" of the encounter. Perhaps an alternative understanding of how our boys responded to this encounter with televised wrestling is that they, like other children, were engaged in a form of free play that goes hand in hand with what it means to be a kid. Growing up, after all, is a process of "reining in the bodily and imaginative possibilities" (Thorne, 1993, p. 16). Maybe their imitation of the activity they saw on the screen had more to do with conquering fears and fashioning a strong sense of self than lessons learned about behavior appropriate for the "real" world (cf. Jones, 2002).

Researchers who use observation and other ethnographic techniques to study the meanings children make from their media encounters face the same challenge that confronts all ethnographers: how to understand the reality of the encounter from the informant's perspective so that it is this understanding that frames the researcher's narrative about the encounter. This is a particularly thorny issue for researchers studying children. As adults, researchers usually assume they know better than the children themselves "the meaning" of the situations they observe and describe. It is important to note that this issue is not just a case of the researcher privileging his or her theoretical frame over the accounts of informants. Rather, it also has much to do with the fact that adult researchers were once children themselves, which makes it tempting for them to project their own pasts and related understandings onto their informants. Thorne (1993) articulates this issue in compelling terms:

> To learn *from* children [emphasis original], adults have to challenge the deep assumption that they already know what children

> are "like," both because, as former children, adults have been there, and because, as adults, they regard children as less complete versions of themselves. When adults seek to learn about and from children, the challenge is to take the closely familiar and render it strange. (p. 12)

In order to understand observations of the media encounter from the perspective of children—to "render it strange"—researchers must search for patterns in the observed actions and behavior of their informants and then find ways to relate these patterns to how their informants experience the encounter. This task requires that researchers work hard to step outside of their own preconceived notions about the meaning of the encounter so that understandings flowing from the "social worlds" of the informants might be considered and incorporated into study narratives (Dunn, 2005, p. 87). It calls for a substantial amount of reflexivity regarding the "authorial power" researchers necessarily exert on the data in their pursuit of truth (Jordan, 2006, p. 480).

One strategy for exploring the role race may play in these encounters involves first analyzing the racial cues embedded in the media text and then exploring how children respond to these cues. That is, an ideological analysis of the pattern of assumptions and imagery embedded in the media text often provide the researcher with a compelling account of what was intended by the producers of the text. Once the researcher completes this benchmark reading, the question becomes to what degree do the meanings made by children converge with or diverge from it. For example, the researcher may observe that children "go along with the narrative" by cheering for the established heroes and routing against the implied villains. Imitation also may be involved as children act out important fantasies associated with what they see on the screen. Alternatively, children may rebel against the narrative by siding with the villain and making fun of the hero. Children also may "negotiate" the narrative in ways that demonstrate their support for certain embedded assumptions and their rejection of others (cf. S. Hall, 1973). In any event, in order to reach reasonable conclusions about the role race plays in the encounter, the researcher will have to somehow connect patterns in the observable behavior of his or her informants to the racial cues revealed by the ideological analysis of the media text. The validity of the researcher's interpretation of these patterns—the degree to which it fits with the meanings made by the children themselves—can be tested in one-on-one interviews.

Interviews

One-on-one interviews constitute a valuable technique for exploring the ways in which children make meaning (Westcott & Littleton, 2005). With this method, the researcher employs an interview schedule designed to elicit informant responses to questions central to the study. Care must be taken, however, not to impose the researcher's interpretive frame on the informant by relying too heavily on leading questions. At the very least, the interviewer should reserve these questions for the latter stages of the interview, after she or he has exhausted the use of more open-ended questions better suited for providing peeks into the social worlds of the informants.

The age of the informant is likely to figure prominently in the interview context. Not only will age impact the verbal skills children have at their disposal to describe their world to the researcher, but age also shapes how children determine what's "real" in their world—particularly when assessments of media credibility are involved (Eastin, Mong-Shan, & Nathanson, 2006). Indeed, before about age 5, children do not typically distinguish advertising from other types of media content. By 7 or 8, they can usually distinguish between information and persuasive intent. By 12 or so, they can critically analyze commercials and talk about the producer's intent (Livingstone & Helsper, 2006). In other words, age usually will have a significant impact on the type of talk and analysis children are able to produce about their encounters with media. For younger informants, the researcher is often put in the position of having to "read between the lines" more aggressively—a practice that necessarily increases the risk of the researcher's interpretive frame crowding out the informant's.

When we talk to our 9-year-old sons about their favorite wrestlers, it immediately becomes clear to us that race is not foremost in their minds. Instead, they tend to talk about how successful their favorite wrestlers are in defeating their foes, about how many titles the men have won. They revel in the physical prowess the wrestlers possess, in their agility, and the skills with which they subdue their adversaries. They are clearly attuned to the producers' attempts to cast certain wrestlers as heroes and others as villains, and they more often than not embrace these designations.

When we begin to probe more directly about race, they deny that the race of the wrestlers has anything to do with how they see the men. They dislike the Black villain named King Booker because "he thinks he's all that," an overly boastful wrestler "who never really shows it." His costume, they add, is just "kind of average," not nearly as interesting and intimidating as the one worn by the Undertaker, for example. We should note here that one of our sons begged us for over a year to allow him to wear his hair in dreadlocks; ever since growing them, he has proudly identified with athletes who wear their hair in the style. When we ask him how he feels about King Booker's dreadlocks, however, he surprises us by complaining that the wrestler's locks are too long. "I like them kind of medium."

But our sons complicate what may be shaping up for some readers as a simple equating of Black with villain. They also affirm their admiration for Bobby Lashley, another muscular African American wrestler whom—unlike King Booker—they consider a hero. Lashley, they note, is "very strong, very fit" and "the crowd likes him." They go on to explain that Lashley has a "lot of courage" and that he is a "good friend" of their favorite wrestler, the Undertaker.

What, then, can we say about the role race might play in our sons' encounters with televised wrestling? Examining how they talk about these encounters with their peers may shed more light on this question.

Focus and Discussion Groups

Media interpretation is inherently social activity (A. Hall, 2003). When people talk in focus groups, they are simultaneously defining themselves and interacting with others. Focus groups—as well as the variant that we refer to as discussion groups—are group interviews that may facilitate the researcher's exploration of important meanings children make of their media encounters. Both types of interview involve multiple informants who are simultaneously engaged in a discussion related to the phenomena under study. In the case of focus groups, the theme and trajectory of the discussion is controlled by an interviewer/moderator who seeks to elicit responses to specific questions or propositions from a group of 7 to 10 participants (Krueger, 1994). Discussion groups, by contrast, are designed to encourage the more natural progression of talk between informants and, thus, to downplay the interviewer's role in shaping the discussion agenda. Thematic focus is sacrificed in these interviews in the name of privileging the issues informants find salient, which may actually facilitate attempts to minimize the narrative intrusions of the researcher and foreground the meanings informants actually make of the encounter (Hunt, 1997, 1999).

As is the case with one-on-one interviewing, informant age is an important consideration when employing these methods. Young children may not have the vocabulary to address themes or topics of interest to the researcher without the type of prompting and follow-up specific to the focus group approach. Discussion group interviews, in which informants themselves largely set the discussion agenda, may be more valuable when used to study older children. In any event, researchers can generally increase the usefulness of discussion group interviews by pairing them with more focused interview techniques, such as the focus group interview or one-on-one interviews. Study designs that triangulate in on meaning are generally more powerful than those that attempt to render meaning from a single vantage point.

When our sons talk to us together about their encounters with televised wrestling, the nature of the talk is different from that flowing from our interactions with them individually. In the group setting, our sons interact with one another as much as they do with us (if not more), reliving the media encounters jointly in ways that expand upon an open-ended question and provide us with a sense of how they are cocreating the meanings they associate with wrestling. The social dynamics of a focus group or discussion group setting in which peers participate may simulate the meaning-making process that regularly takes place on the playground. In these research settings, the researcher can often discern patterns in the positions adopted by differentially positioned informants (e.g., by race), which may implicate racial influences sometimes missed by direct questioning.

Experiments

What, in the final analysis, are the racial implications of our sons' encounters with televised wrestling? Has their dislike for King Booker, combined with the obvious racial cues embedded in the character by the show's producers, caused them to associate Blackness with the undesirable? Have their encounters with televised wrestling caused them to think and feel about themselves in ways that might be detrimental to their healthy psychosocial development as 9-year-old African American boys? How might the other media encounters that saturate our sons' social worlds influence their experience of televised wrestling?

An age-old problem in media research is how to control for the myriad factors that likely influence the way people think and behave so that any possible media influences can be isolated (Lowery & DeFleur, 1995). Part of the problem is rooted in the existence of intertextuality—the notion that the reading of a given media text is necessarily influenced by the reader's previous encounters with other media texts (Fiske, 1989). That is, readers bring with them to the media encounter a host of experiences related to their engagement with the countless media messages that saturate the modern social environment. These experiences literally shape how readers relate to, frame, and ultimately make sense of what they see in the current encounter (cf. Hunt, 1997, 1999). It thus becomes difficult to say that a particular way of thinking or behaving is *caused* by a given encounter when it is far from clear where to locate the boundaries of the relevant media text or texts.

In theory, at least, experimental design is an important methodological approach for addressing difficult questions of causality like these. Experiments are research designs that allow the analyst to control for certain variables, thereby isolating from other possible influences the impact of a particular variable of interest (i.e., the independent variable), which is suspected of *causing* the phenomenon under study (i.e., the dependent variable). Classic stimulus-response experiments tend to be quite rigid in design and conducted in a laboratory setting that necessarily sacrifices naturalness for rigor and analytical control (Tashakkori & Teddlie, 1998). This reality poses a significant challenge for researchers interested in studying the *meanings* children make from media because the controls inherent in any experimental design will necessarily truncate the range of possible reader interpretations the researcher considers when he or she takes stock of informant responses to the different experimental treatments. That is, though the researcher may be able to employ experimental designs to make some compelling inferences about the effect of a given variable on the reader (e.g., race), she or he may end up missing the forest for the trees when it comes to considering what informants *themselves* feel is most salient about the media encounter.

Although a rigid application of the experimental method to the media encounter is likely to block from view important meanings informants themselves may be making, elements of the method can be employed in order to say something about possible causal relationships between the reception of media texts and attitude or behavioral change. One such strategy involves examining any changes on attitude scales or in observed behavior before and after the treatment (e.g., the media encounter or group discussion *about* the media encounter). Used in conjunction with ethnography, interviews, and group discussions, before-and-after designs may help the researcher read between the lines without completely rewriting the stories told by informants.

CONCLUSION

It may be tempting for some readers to conclude that we are arguing media don't really matter, that a focus on meaning making places all the control in the hands of children. No need to worry about stereotypes circulated in the media or how racial meanings embedded in our culture work to position children in their media encounters. Children are free to make whatever meanings they choose to make in these encounters, unencumbered by the constraints our society and culture may try to impose upon them. But this was not our intention.

To be sure, we continue to monitor our sons' encounters with televised wrestling, the imagery embedded in the spectacles, and the meanings our sons make of the encounters. Although children can be quite resourceful in their active engagements with media, there is no guarantee they will make sense of and respond to these encounters in ways that are self-affirming and healthy. Our point is that researchers cannot assume a priori that a particular type of media content (e.g., racial stereotypes) will be read by children in a particular way. The outcome of the interaction between media texts and readers is always an open, empirical question. It is analytically useful to understand how these texts function ideologically, to identify, if possible, the intentions embedded in them by their producers. But these meanings must always be considered in relation to the meanings children make of the encounters, not in place of them.

In the final analysis, negotiating seemingly opposed research imperatives—identifying the ideologies embedded in media *without* discounting the meanings children make because of (or despite) them—is no easy task. It is an enterprise that calls out for a synthesis of positivist and interpretive approaches, for a methodological toolkit equipped with a mix of quantitative and qualitative approaches. It requires a holistic analysis, where triangulation is a central strategy and where media encounters are subjected to multicultural methods. It is this approach, we argue, that best equips us to intervene in the meaning-making process, if necessary, and facilitate the healthy development of minority children.

NOTE

1. It should be noted that Hunt (2005) discusses problems associated with concepts like "positive" and "negative" when applied to media imagery. As the meaning of an object is always established in relation to some other object, in a particular socio-historical context, and by the "reader" of the object, it is always an open, empirical question.

REFERENCES

Ali, S. (2006). Racializing research: Managing power and politics? *Ethnic and Racial Studies, 29*(3), 471–486.

Bang, H., & Reece, B. B. (2003). Minorities in children's television commercials: New, improved, and stereotyped. *Journal of Consumer Affairs, 37*(1), 42–67.

Beaudoin, C. E., & Thorson, E. (2006). The social capital of Blacks and Whites: Differing effects of the mass media in the United States. *Human Communication Research, 32,* 157–177.

Berry, G. L. (1998). Black family life on television and the socialization of the African American child: Images of marginality. *Journal of Comparative Family Studies, 29*(2), 223–244.

Berry, G. L. & Mitchell-Kernan, C. (Eds.). (1982). *Television and the socialization of the minority child.* New York: Academic Press.

Brown, J. D., & Cantor, J. (2000). An agenda for research on youth and the media. *Journal of Adolescent Health, 27,* 2–7.

Comstock, G., & Cobbey, R. E. (1979). Television and the children of ethnic minorities. *Ethnic Studies in Black and White, 29*(1), 104–115.

Dunn, J. (2005). Naturalistic observations of children and their families. In S. Greene & D. Hogan (Eds.), *Researching children's experience: Approaches and methods* (pp. 87–101). London: Sage.

Eastin, M. S., Mong-Shan, Y., & Nathanson, A. I. (2006). Children of the Net: An empirical exploration into the evaluation of Internet content. *Journal of Broadcasting & Electronic Media, 50*(2), 211–231.

Emmers-Sommer, T. M., & Allen, M. (1999). Surveying the effect of medial effects: A meta-analytic summary of the media effects research in human communication research. *Human Communication Research, 25*(4), 478–497.

Fiske, J. (1989). *Understanding popular culture.* London: Routledge.

Gitlin, T. (1978). Media sociology: The dominant paradigm. *Theory and Society, 6*(2), 205–253.

Graves, S. B. (1999). Television and prejudice reduction: When does television as a vicarious experience make a difference?" *Journal of Social Issues, 55*(4), 707–725.

Hall, A. (2003). Reading realism: Audiences' evaluations of the reality of media texts. *Journal of Communication, 53*(4), 624–641.

Hall, S. (1973). *Encoding and decoding in the television discourse.* Centre for Contemporary Cultural Studies working paper, University of Birmingham, UK.

Hall, S. (1997). *Representation: Cultural representations and signifying practices.* London: Sage.

Hoffner, C. A., Levine, K. J., Sullivan, Q. E., Crowell, D., Pedrick, L., & Berndt, P. (2006). TV characters at work: Television's role in the occupational aspirations of economically disadvantaged youths. *Journal of Career Development, 33*(1), 3–18.

Hunt, D. M. (1997). *Screening the Los Angeles "riots": Race, seeing, and resistance.* Cambridge, UK: Cambridge University Press.

Hunt, D. M. (1999). *O.J. Simpson facts & fictions: News rituals in the construction of reality.* Cambridge, MA: Cambridge University Press.

Hunt, D. M. (2000). *The African American television report: Progress and retreat.* Los Angeles: Screen Actors Guild.

Hunt, D. M. (2002). *Prime time in black and white: Making sense of the 2001 fall season.* Los Angeles: Ralph J. Bunche Center for African American Studies, UCLA.

Hunt, D. M. (2003). *Prime time in black and white: Not much is new for 2002.* Los Angeles: Ralph J. Bunche Center for African American Studies, UCLA.

Hunt, D. M. (2005). *Channeling blackness: Studies on television and race in America.* New York: Oxford University Press.

Hunt, D. (2006). Race and ethnicity. In B. Turner (Ed.), *The Cambridge dictionary of sociology* (pp. 490–496). Cambridge: Cambridge University Press.

Jensen, K. B. (1991). Humanistic scholarship as qualitative science: Contributions to mass communication research. In K. B. Jensen & N. W. Jankowski (Eds.), *A handbook of qualitative methodologies for mass communication research* (pp. 1–15). London: Sage.

Jones, G. (2002). *Killing monsters: Why children need fantasy, super heroes, and make-believe violence.* New York: Basic Books.

Jordan, A. B. (2006). Make yourself at home: The social construction of research roles in family studies. *Qualitative Research, 6*(2), 169–185.

Krueger, R. A. (1994). *Focus groups: A practical guide for applied research.* Thousand Oaks, CA: Sage.

Livingstone, S., & Helsper, E. J. (2006). Does advertising literacy mediate the effects of advertising on children? A critical examination of two linked research literatures in relation to obesity and food choice. *Journal of Communication, 56*(3), 560–584.

Lowery, S. A., & DeFleur, M. L. (1995). *Milestones in mass communication research: Media effects* (3rd ed.). White Plains, NY: Longman.

Marshall, S. J., Gorely, T., & Biddle, S. J. H. (2006). A descriptive epidemiology of screen-based media use in youth: A review and critique. *Journal of Adolescence, 29,* 333–349.

McKown, C. (2004). Age and ethnic variation in children's thinking about the nature of racism. *Applied Developmental Psychology, 25,* 597–617.

Messner, M., Hunt, D., & Dunbar, M. (1999). *Boys to men: Sports media.* Oakland, CA: Children Now.

Omi, M., & Winant, H. (1994). *Racial formation in the United States: From the 1960s to the 1990s.* New York: Routledge.

Powell, K. A., & Abels, L. (2002). Sex-roles stereotypes in TV programs aimed at the preschool audience: An analysis of *Teletubbies* and *Barney & Friends*. *Women and Language Urbana, 25*(2), 14–23.

Rowley, S. (2002, April). *The development of race, gender, and social class stereotypes in Black and White adolescents.* Paper presented at the biennial meeting of the Society for Research on Adolescence, New Orleans, LA.

Schmitt, K. L., Woolf, K. D., & Anderson, D. R. (2003). Viewing the viewers: Viewing behaviors by children and adults during television programs and commercials. *Journal of Communication, 53*(2), 265–281.

Schramm, W., Lyle, J., & Parker, E. (1961). *Television in the lives of our children.* Palo Alto, CA: Stanford University Press.

Tan, A. S., & Tan, G. (1979). Television use and self-esteem of Blacks. *Journal of Communication, 29*(1), 129–135.

Tashakkori, A., & Teddlie, C. (1998). *Mixed methodology: Combining qualitative and quantitative approaches.* Thousand Oaks, CA: Sage.

Thorne, B. (1993). *Gender play: Girls and boys in school.* London: Taylor and Francis.

Westcott, H. L., & Littleton, K. S. (2005). Exploring meaning in interviews with children. In S. Greene & D. Hogan (Eds.), *Researching children's experience: Approaches and methods* (pp. 141–157). London: Sage.

Part IV

Perspectives on Media Literacy and the Forces That Shape the Media Experiences of Children

Part IV brings the many research and theoretical themes of the *Handbook* together with the concepts and practices of various constituent groups that have the power to influence what children learn from the media and what various forms of media will broadcast. A core theme of Part IV centers on the role of media literacy because what children and youth learn about the media during their early or formative years will serve as a springboard for how they will use and understand them in adulthood.

Congruent with the ontological assumptions of a postmodernist, James Anderson offers a cultural analysis of the media literacy literature from the last 100 years and proposes that the concepts and practices of media literacy are cultural responses to media in society at any given point in time. In other words, as media change and our sensibilities about media change, media literacy "reconfigures" itself in response.

Given the importance of the school setting in the lives of children and youth and the abundance of media forms available to them, Kevin Clark explores the use of technologies in the educational setting. He suggests ways educators can maximize the positive capabilities of technologies and media while minimizing the potential negative effects as a means to influence the intellectual and multicultural development of children.

Laurie Trotta carries the discussion to a grassroots level in a discussion of how advocacy groups can influence the quality of entertainment for children, particularly the on-screen representation of diverse groups and multicultural media content. She describes a "new breed of activism" where celebrities and others use their power and fame as well as the Internet and new technologies to promote social causes.

The final chapter in Part IV, written by Christina Romano Glaubke and Patti Miller, addresses how parents and child caregivers can create healthy multicultural media environments in their homes as well as how they can influence their children's media consumption outside their homes. These contributors offer a list of resources to organizations and websites that offer useful information on children and media.

CHAPTER 25

Media Literacy, the First 100 Years

A Cultural Analysis

JAMES A. ANDERSON

Media literacy is the current term[1] for (generally) school-based instruction for (mostly) K–12 students that is intended to advance something from: content analytical skills, social process analytical skills, and media production skills, as well as audience liberation and empowerment—all in the service of right-thinking media use and appreciation, discriminating consumerism, civic responsibility, and social justice. But wait, there's more. Not only a course of instruction, media literacy is also a field of study tied to media production, media criticism, cultural studies, and critical rhetoric. It is also a state of being, as each of us is more or less literate in each of the many media that we attend to, create with, and use for some purpose.

Media literacy may be the current term, but there has been a consistent focus of educational and scholarly initiatives on media education since the 1850s, when Benjamin Day's promotion of the newspaper story combined with the invention of the cylinder press to create the first truly mass medium (Brazeal, 2005). The issues were much the same: violence in the press and our enjoyment of it ("Crime of Adultery," 1868; "Remarkable," 1860), the distortions and exploitations of the political process (Yarros, 1899), and its influence on our children (Fenton, 1910). Wilcox (1900), first warning that school children are often urged to read the newspaper, counted three evils of the practice:

> First the waste of much time and mental energy in reading unimportant news and opinions, and premature, untrue, or imperfect accounts of important matters; second, the awakening of prejudices and the enkindling of passions through the partisan bias or commercial greed of newspaper managers; third, the loading of the mind with cheap literature and the development of an aversion for books and sustained thought. Thus the daily newspaper often tends to make the intellectual life of its readers one continuous series of petty excitements. (p. 57)

Like much of our concern about the media, media literacy appears to be a dynamic issue within society that requires regular attention to rehearse its characteristics and importance. This description follows the cultural analytic work of Anderson and

Colvin (2008, in press), who have been addressing the media literature. They argue that topic areas that regularly appear in the literature over an extended period of time, such as media violence and media literacy, are not resolvable through scientific study. Rather, these topics provide a venue for cultural work that manages the realities and relationships (to borrow the phrase from Gergen, 1995) of the social organization. Consequently, media literacy is a topic whose time has come, is coming, and will come again.

AN INVESTIGATION OF THE LITERATURE

This study is based on a review of the literature extending from 1900 to 2007 in media education and its collaborative fields. It is based on a found sample of journal articles published in communication, education, psychology, sociology, and adjunct fields as made available in full-text databases. A found sample can be considered a systematic convenience sample of the materials available to the researcher. In this case, the sample was based on full-text databases such as PsychInfo, JStor, CMMC, and the archives of the International Communication Association and the National Communication Association. In addition, 30 articles from the turn of the 20th century from the education, sociology, and psychology journals available for that period were digitally copied.

Sample

Two hundred and eight articles from 68 different journals were identified and entered into the analysis. The articles are listed in the appendix and the journals in Table 1.

A found sample of this size and diversity can be relied on to present the range of topics or "conversations" in the literature but is less secure in making claims about the relative rates of kinds of articles or discussion topics in the whole of the literature. We can, therefore, be comfortable about representing the diversity of the literature but not necessarily the proportions.

Coding

The 208 articles were converted to searchable RTF files, descriptors were entered for their overall characteristics, and then the articles were coded across their content. Though time-consuming, the advantage of the conversion is that computer analysis can be added to traditional interpretive approaches. For example, once the descriptors and codes were developed using the grounded approach of "close reading," the database could be searched across key words to identify the files that might qualify for codification under those terms. The researcher still has to open the file and judge each occurrence of the key terms, but the procedure eliminates fatigue, misreadings, and the like that are common to unsupported coding. There are other advantages in analysis discussed below.

The descriptors and codes used in this study followed the methodology developed by Anderson and Colvin (2008, in press). Six descriptors (each with several values) were used to categorize each case (article): (a) approach (analytical, critique, didactics, evidentiary, pedagogics), (b) article type (advocacy, critical/analytical[2], instructional, review, theoretical), (c) decade of publication, (d) discipline represented (aesthetics, communication, cultural studies, education, psychology, sociology), (e) medium of interest, and (f) thematic (advancing knowledge/skill, civic practice, cognitivist, critical/skeptical, pragmatist/rationalist, protectionist/interventionist, responsibility of the school, social justice).

Table 1 Journals Appearing in the Review (68 Total)

American Behavioral Scientist	*American Journal of Sociology*	*American Political Science Review*
American Psychologist	*American Quarterly*	*American Sociological Review*
Annals of the Am. Ac. of Political and Social Science	*Annual Review of Anthropology*	*AEJMC*
British Journal of Educational Studies	*California Journal of Elementary Education*	*Child Development*
Cinema Journal	*Clearing House*	*College Composition and Communication*
Communication Education	*Communication Review*	*Communication Theory*
Communication Yearbook	*Critical Studies in Media Communication*	*Discourse*
EDRS	*Educational Research Bulletin*	*Educational Review*
Elementary English	*Elementary School Journal*	*English Journal*
ERIC Digest	*ETC*	*Future of Children*
Health Communication	*Hollywood Quarterly*	*HCR*
International Journal of Ethics	*JADE*	*Journal of Adolescent and Adult Literacy*
Journal of Adult and Adolescent Literacy	*Journal of Aesthetic Education*	*Journal of Applied Psychology*
Journal of Applied Sociology	*JOBEM*	*Journal of Communication*
Journal of Consumer Research	*Journal of Educational Media*	*Journal of Educational Sociology*
Journal of Health Communication	*Journal of Higher Education*	*Journal of Media and Religion*
Journal of Personality and Social Behavior	*Journal of Sex Research*	*Journal of Social Issues*
Journal of Visual Literacy	*Journalism and Mass Communication Educator*	*Language and Education*
Media Psychology	*Media, Culture and Society*	*New Literary History*
Oxford Review of Education	*Peabody Journal of Education*	*Pedagogical Seminary*
Public Opinion Quarterly	*Quarterly Journal of Speech*	*School and Society*
School Review	*Screen Education*	*Social Forces*
Theory and Society	*Yearbook of English Studies*	

Content coding further adopted the cultural approach of Anderson and Colvin (2008). They argued that the cultural positioning of an article is most likely to appear in the more open, less conventionalized sections, namely, the statement of the problem and the implications and conclusions sections. Consequently, the first-level coding selected the content of these sections. This is coding based primarily on structure, which usually followed the designated headings but, in the absence of marker headings, meant taking the first and last set of paragraphs in an article. Second-level coding engaged the content of each section.

Second-level coding was done at the paragraph level, and codes were developed using the "next unique paragraph approach" until there were sufficient codes to cover the content. In coding the paragraphs, a code that continued across contiguous paragraphs was counted as a single occurrence. A code that reappeared in a subsequent but separated paragraph was counted as a new occurrence. As writers do not always follow the "rules" of good paragraph construction, multiple codes could be attached to a single paragraph. Consequently, there is little correspondence between the number of paragraphs and coding occurrences, but every paragraph has at least one code attached to it, even if not separately counted.

ANALYSIS

Descriptives Case Attributes

Overall

Analysis of the case attributes indicates that the most common article was from education (42%), took an analytical approach (45%) that argued for the need for media literacy (29%), focused on media in general (34%), was most likely to be protectionist (24%) and, as might be expected, declared media literacy to be an appropriate province of the school (22%). Within this framework, the motion picture is the dominant medium until the mid-1940s; radio peaks in the mid-1930s; print picks up the comic book scare of the mid-1940s to mid-1950s; television is supreme by 1980, but then loses out to a concern for all media as convergence begins in the late 1990s.

By Decade

Advocacy is the only type of article that has had a consistent appearance across the 11 decades of this analysis. Table 2 presents the article types by decade.

There are several other interesting findings shown in Table 2. Not only is advocacy the primary form of article, but also empirical studies represent slightly less than 17% of the total, and the majority of those are content analyses. There is simply very little empirical analysis available. The lack of empirical evidence is doubly matched by the absence of theory (6%). A search of all files surfaces only one reference to media literacy

Table 2 Article Types by Decade

Decade	*Advocacy*	*Instructional*	*Critical analytical*	*Review*	*Empirical*	*Theoretical*	*Totals*
To 1919	5	0	1	0	1	0	7
To 1929	1	1	4	0	1	0	7
To 1939	4	8	8	3	4	1	28
To 1949	5	6	6	4	2	1	24
To 1959	4	1	3	0	7	0	15
To 1969	4	0	1	1	0	0	6
To 1979	2	1	0	0	2	2	7
To 1989	5	4	5	3	5	2	24
To 1999	13	12	5	7	4	3	44
To 2009	17	5	6	6	9	3	46
Totals	**60**	**38**	**39**	**24**	**35**	**12**	**208**

theory (Hart, 2002) and that is in a passing reference to the difficulties of developing it (p. 31). Media literacy seems to be one of those "of course it's true" topics. Kruger (1998), while citing her lack of empirical evidence, for example, nonetheless defends what she "believes so strongly: media literacy does work" (p. 16). And clearly, most of the community simply agrees.

There is an interesting slump in media literacy articles in the 1960s and 70s. These were the decades of U.S. scholarly interest in media violence and aggression. Elsewhere, the United Nations Educational Scientific and Cultural Organization (UNESCO) was pursuing its media education objects established in the early 1950s (UNESCO, 1951) and there was an active program in the Catholic school system in Australia. But in the United States, government money was flowing toward violence studies, which peaked in 1979 (Anderson, 2006, in press). The exit of that period, however, was the funding of five critical viewing projects (Anderson, 1980), and the trajectory has remained upward since.

By Discipline

Disciplines took characteristic approaches to media literacy and represented different thematics. Table 3 presents the number of articles by discipline for approach with the categories of analytical and critique combined and the categories of didactics and pedagogics combined. As Table 3 shows, (a) education focuses on the problems and techniques of teaching as does aesthetics; (b) psychology has the majority of its few studies in the evidentiary column; and (c) communication, cultural studies, and sociology take analytical approaches.

Table 4 presents the number of articles by discipline for thematic in which the values for each pair of civic practice and social justice, pragmatist and rationalist, and protectionist and interventionist have been combined.

The thematics in Table 4 represent the motives that underlie each article. They represent two different types. The thematics of advancing knowledge, civic practice (social justice), pragmatist (rationalist), and protectionist (rationalist) are outcome themes; they describe the goals of media literacy—increased knowledge, better citizens, smarter consumers, and so forth. Cognitivism and school responsibility are closer to explanatory themes—media literacy makes sense because of cognitive processes or because of the societal responsibilities of the school. Given that difference, the data in Table 5 indicate that (a) protectionism/interventionism is the most important goal across education, communication, and psychology; (b) citizenship and social justice is paramount in cultural studies and sociology; and (c) knowledge is the primary goal

Table 3 Approach by Discipline

	Aesthetics	*Education*	*Communication*	*Cultural studies*	*Psychology*	*Sociology*	*Totals*
Analytical	5	26	29	11	6	16	93
Evidentiary	0	10	14	0	10	5	39
Teaching	6	52	13	4	0	1	76
Totals	**11**	**88**	**56**	**15**	**16**	**22**	**208**

Table 4 Thematic by Discipline

	Aesthetics	*Education*	*Communication*	*Cultural studies*	*Psychology*	*Sociology*	*Totals*
Advancing knowledge/skill	5	17	7	1	1	4	35
Civic practice	1	8	7	6	2	10	34
Cognitivist	0	1	6	0	4	1	12
Critical/skeptical	0	3	2	3	1	2	11
Pragmatist	2	10	2	4	1	2	21
Protectionist	2	21	16	1	7	2	49
Responsibility of school	1	28	16	0	0	1	46
Totals	**11**	**88**	**56**	**15**	**16**	**22**	**208**

for the relatively few studies in aesthetics. While there are more cognitivist explanations in communication than in psychology, the percentage is much higher in psychology (25% vs. 11%).

By Thematic

Table 5 presents the cross-break for approach by thematic. Good citizenship is the primary goal of analytical approaches followed closely by protectionism. Teaching advances knowledge in both rationale and methods. And finally, the primary evidence that is generated is in support of protectionism.

Descriptives: SOP Codes

Table 6 presents the codes used to classify 10 or more instances of content from the statement of the problem (SOP) section from each of the cases. All 208 cases qualified in this analysis. As can be seen from the table, the majority of the introductions begin with some comment about the state of the media, generally as it poses a level of threat, continue by describing the circumstances of being a child within this media environment, and then move to the resolution of this potentially volatile situation that is offered by media literacy. Nearly 36% of all coding occurrences had something to do

Table 5 Approach by Thematic

	Analytical	*Evidentiary*	*Teaching*	*Total*
Advancing knowledge/skill	9	4	22	35
Civic practice	21	4	9	34
Cognitivist	4	7	1	12
Critical/skeptical	9	1	1	11
Pragmatist	14	3	4	21
Protectionist	20	18	11	49
Responsibility of school	16	2	28	46
Total	**93**	**39**	**76**	**208**

Table 6 Codes and the Number of Occurrences for the "Statement of the Problem" (SOP) Sections

SOP codes (10 or more occurrences)	*Number of occurrences*
Conditions of the child	64
Conditions of the media	71
Consumer/consumerism	23
Critique	28
Didactics	28
Intervention/mediation	25
Media production skills	10
Media literacy definition	51
Media literacy results/goals	31
Need for media literacy	52
Pedagogics	63
Social/cognitive processes	25
State of media literacy	35
Theory of/for media literacy	28
Total all occurrences	**548**

with media literacy, which is hardly remarkable, but the fact that 26% of the media literacy occurrences were connected to definitions suggests that the concept is far from conventionalized. Renee Hobbs in her 2005 review of contemporary texts and the state of media literacy comments:

> Whereas the diversity and number of scholars with interests in media literacy have grown rapidly in recent years, the infighting and fragmentation that result from the collision of multiple disciplines and fields continue to create a cacophony of voices that, to a non-specialist, can make the growth in knowledge and theory about media literacy seem inconsistent and incoherent. (p. 865)

She goes on not to deny this inconsistency and incoherence but to note the "fertile opportunity" for advancement that it provides.

Exemplars of SOP Coded Content

Unfortunately, space does not permit me to provide exemplars for each of the 14 codes. Let me rather provide exemplars for just two—definitions and pedagogics—as these two provide a good look at the very elastic boundaries of the field.

Definitions

Definitions of media literacy generally contain some notion of critical skill or ability as related to media texts and a recognition of the impact of media, often include knowledge of the industries, and occasionally include the ability to produce messages in media. Rosenbaum (2003) provides an overview of these definitional efforts. Some recent, diverse examples from the archive:

> Media literacy (ML) may be thought of as the ability to critically understand, question and evaluate how media work and produce meaning, how they are organized, how they mediate and construct reality, and how they impact our lives. ML may include the ability to create media products. (Abdullah, 2000, p. 1)

> [Media literacy] aims to develop metacognitive reflective strategies by means of study and critical responses towards the content of the media and its messages. (Feuerstein, 1999, p. 44)

> And I wish to suggest that at the core of such media literacy should be a moral agenda, always debated, never fixed, but permanently inscribed in public discourse and private practice, a moral discourse which recognizes our responsibility for the other person in a world of great conflict, tragedy, intolerance and indifference, and which critically engages with our media's incapacity (as well as its occasional capacity) to engage with the reality of that difference, responsibly and humanely. (Silverstone, 2004, p. 440)

> The "New Literacy Studies" . . . takes a sociocultural view of literacy, emphasizing the description of literacy practices of everyday life, and challenging approaches which emphasize decontextualized basic skills. (Stephens, 2000, p. 10)

> The major argument is that contextual media aesthetics is the necessary foundation of media literacy and that we need to know how the basic aesthetic building blocks are used to create and shape our cognitive and affective mental maps. The media literacy model proffered here attempts to show the hierarchical relationship of four levels: (a) the basic aesthetic image elements and their aesthetic fields, (b) how they are structured for specific purposes, (c) how we perceive them and how they affect us, and (d) how they fit into the various intellectual and cultural frameworks for media analysis. (Zettl, 1998, p. 81)

Pedagogics

Media literacy pedagogics refers to the rationale that governs the content, methods, and goals of media literacy instruction. As we look across the 11 decades of the archive, we see both the struggle and the certainty that mark media literacy.

> We see evidences on all sides of attempts to develop curricula, to organize administrative programs, to develop teacher improvement movements, to set up child accounting, without a fundamental understanding of major problems or ultimate functions. In the consideration of the program of audio-visual instruction we must begin with the question "What is the function of an audio-visual program?" (Arnspiger, 1936, p. 143)

> In humanistic education the future lies with film. Of this I am firmly convinced. I do not mean by this either "audio-visualism" or educational filmstrips. I mean that film will be not only the future medium of instruction, but that film also will challenge and eventually claim the place and prestige accorded to literature and the arts in the traditional curriculum. In short, film not merely as medium but as curriculum, too. This conviction rests upon a faith that human society cannot do without the humanities, cannot forsake its faith in the project of making men [sic, but also appropriate] more fully human, helping men to "become the thing they are." If real education—and not merely the transmission of knowledge—is to take place, a curriculum is required which corroborates and exemplifies moral discovery, the making of a fate, the hunger for identity. (Arrowsmith, 1969, p. 75)

> For those who seek a self-contained unit, I suggest using an advertising theme. Why advertising? First, the impact of advertising provides a common experience for teacher and student. Second, advertising emphasizes the economic motivations of the media messages. By exploring the business aspect of media and the structure of the communication industry sending messages, students can be engaged in higher thinking skills. And third, advertising is commonly used by all the media, so it provides a basis for comparing magazines, newspapers, billboards, radio, and television. (Lowenstein, 1981, p. 88)

> There are four interrelated dimensions of media literacy:
>
> - Cognitive: understanding how the message was produced and the symbols it used
> - Emotional: understanding the cues that are used to trigger emotional response in the audience
> - Aesthetic: understanding and appreciating the craft of the creators of the media
> - Moral: the ability to infer value underlying the messages
>
> Age, level of cognition, the social domain of the viewer, culture of the viewer, and media skills and knowledge are all important. Like verbal and written literacy, media literacy cannot be studied in isolation from the meanings that readers produce. The language of the media is as complex and interesting as our verbal and written languages. It is just as important to become articulate in it. (Burton, 2005, p. 95)

As the four quotations demonstrate, recommendations for teaching drip readily off the pen, but consistency across the recommendations is clearly missing.

Descriptives: I & C Codes

Table 7 presents the codes used to classify 10 or more instances of content in the implications and conclusions (I & C) sections of the cases in the archive. The analysis is based on 204 cases, as 4 cases did not have this structural component. It is interesting that the largest value occurs with recommendations rather than an outcome code. When all of the "should" codes (call, civic, promise, recommendations, requirements, school) are combined, they represent 44% of all the coding occurrences. On the other hand, the outcome codes (intervention, goals, findings) account for only 18% of occurrences. This result corresponds to a field that has not matured, as it references the work that ought or needs to be done, not what has been accomplished.

It is also interesting that even at this late moment in their arguments, 14 authors felt the need to initiate or reprise a definition of what they had been writing about. Messaris (1996) offers a somewhat eyebrow-raising example:

> As used in this discussion, the term visual literacy refers to the assumption that the ability to recognize the meaning of visual images (both still pictures and movies) is dependent on prior experience (and is therefore roughly analogous to linguistic competence). (p. 158)

Basically, this definition says that visual literacy is learned and not innate. That would seem to be a bottom-line assumption for any program of instruction in literacy. That it needs to be said anywhere points to a reaction to a typical trivialization of nonprint literacies: "I know it when I see it."

Exemplars of I & C Coded Content

Because of their most frequent status, this section will provide exemplars from each of the "should" categories (call, civic, promise, recommendations, requirements, school). There is, of course, much to be gleaned from the other 14 codes of this content. I will try to offer some insights into unmarked codes in the interpretation section that follows these descriptives.

Call for Action

The following are two examples from opposite ends of the time frame:

> These evidences of a widespread demand for reform indicate recognition of the tremendous influence of the press in the molding of public opinion. The situation is more serious for the child than for the

Table 7 Codes and the Number of Occurrences for the "Implications and Conclusions" (I & C) Sections

I & C codes	*Number of occurrences*
Call for research/action	66
Civic responsibility	24
Conditions of the child	23
Conditions of the media	35
Consumer/consumerism	21
Critique	26
Didactics	18
Intervention/mediation	21
Media production skills	12
Media literacy definition	14
Media literacy goals	37
Media literacy research findings	44
Need for media literacy	19
Pedagogics	27
Promise of media literacy	23
Recommendation	69
Requirements of media literacy programs	33
School responsibility	36
State of media literacy	11
Theory of/for media literacy	14
Total occurrences	**573**

adult. Children are more likely to accept what they read uncritically and indiscriminately than are adults. Suggestion is a potent factor during the formative period of youth. What the child reads in the news-papers will condition how and what he thinks as the citizen of tomorrow. Society cannot afford to be indifferent to the nature of the subject matter which school children read in the newspapers. . . . The problem of how to train intelligent readers is obviously one that is to be solved only by experimentation. It is the hope of the writers that this article will stimulate further experimentation in this regard. (Lehman & Witty, 1927, p. 101)

In sum, the goal of creating a quality digital media culture for children must be placed at the forefront of public debate. If this debate is to be an intelligent and reasoned discussion, however, it must be informed by a full range of research on the cognitive, emotional, and social-development effects of the new interactive media, and it must strive for a notion of quality that encompasses the development of responsible citizens for the future. (Montgomery, 2000, p. 161)

Civic Responsibility

As one can see in the foregoing exemplars, citizenship, or civic engagement as it is now being called, is a foundational motive of media literacy. Undoubtedly the strongest statement of civic responsibility comes from Wirth (1948), writing during the cold war's "duck and cover" days:

> The atomic bomb will not, we are told, yield to a physical defense or a counterweapon which will neutralize its destructive potential. The only defense we have is social—the creation of world consensus. Since the mass media of communication are capable of providing the picture of social reality and the symbolic framework of thought and fantasy and the incentives for human action on an enormous scale, the knowledge of their effective use should become the most important quest of social science, and particularly of sociology. The circumstances under which we live do not any longer allow the saints to sit in their ivory tower while burly sinners rule the world. (pp. 14–15)

Promise

It is hard to top the promise of saving the world from an atomic holocaust, but authors have not been shy in offering what might be the results of a media literacy program: from a reform of the entire system of pedagogy (Hobbs, 1996), to classrooms filled with power and vitality (May, 1937), to the "richest possible contribution the minds, hearts, and souls of the children" (Mersand, 1952, p. 147), to a rebirth of the high influence of poetry (Matthews, 1945), to the ecumenical union of the arts and sciences (O'Grady, 1969), to a solution to the unequal distribution of wealth (Parker, 1973–74), and to the empowerment of all children (Shields & Behrman, 2000). All this is apparently available from just a few hours of classroom instruction. Bazalgette (1996) brings us back to earth:

> Reflecting upon such questions [of industry practices] revives the radical aspirations of earlier media education campaigners in a new guise: will it be the agile button punching of network-surfing kids that finally brings the Murdoch and Berlusconi empires to their knees? And if it does, what will the kids be doing for a living? As usual, we don't really know what we are doing—but then, neither does anyone else. (p. 77)

Recommendations

The unknowing, nonetheless, do offer a number of recommendations. These recommendations cover the school, society, the media, scholarship and scholars, media pedagogy, and classroom practice. Two examples:

> Finally, and most important of all, we must equip our citizenry with the understanding, the insight, the discrimination necessary to evaluate critically what they see on the screen, hear on the radio, or read in the press. We have learned in America and elsewhere to make and distribute propaganda faster than we have learned how to resist and evaluate it. It comes to us in a constant stream from the press, the radio, and the movies. We need a Consumers Research Organization to evaluate its factual accuracy, its biased sources. We need to put the easy stereotypes of racial and nationalistic prejudice under the microscope to determine whether they are false, half-truth, or truth. We need, in short, to inoculate the American public with the vaccine of critical judgment. (Dale, 1938, p. 42)

> Ethical values are inherent in any serious study of media. Values should be neither narrowly instructional nor exclusively moralistic in a single tradition. Media training should not be valueless, however, because it relates to the broad humanistic

> heritage and to the Judeo-Christian ethic. Educators should not proselytize on behalf of a given value system. Values and assessments should be identified by eliciting from individuals' reflection and judgment, building on values already embraced. (Brown, 1998, p. 50)

Requirements

The following two examples show the range of guidance that appears in the archive:

> We can and should, too, help children learn to discriminate among the comics as among other forms of reading. We cannot choose children's comics for them, since their choices will be guided by their own particular interests. But we can help them to evaluate differences in quality and worth, remembering, however, that taste and discrimination develop slowly. (Frank, 1944, p. 222)

> It is not enough to merely understand media, students need to be empowered to critically negotiate meanings, engage with the problems of misrepresentations and under-representations, and produce their own alternative media. Addressing issues of inequality and injustice in media representations can be a powerful starting place for problem-posing transformative education. Critical media literacy offers the tools and framework to help students become subjects in the process of deconstructing injustices, expressing their own voices, and struggling to create a better society. (Kellner & Share, 2005, p. 382)

Responsibility of the School

This content tended to break along what the school ought to be doing and that the school has the appropriate societal authority to be doing it. Four examples:

> Television is now so pervasive a feature of daily life and of the growing child's world that it must become a subject for the regular educational curriculum. Our study suggests that children can be taught about the medium in the regular school curriculum by tying in their natural interest in TV with exercises in reading, writing, and critical thinking. (Singer, Zuckerman, & Singer, 1980, p. 93)

> Schools must be in the media literacy business as an important adjunct to their core business of ensuring every child can read. Reading should include the media and visual imagery. We don't want George Orwell's 1984 to come true: a society controlled by those who have access to technology and the ability to create any history or knowledge it desires for the purpose of manipulation, creating a schism between those with access and those without. (Krausz, 2001, p. 108)

> Media teachers should see themselves in the 1990s as one constituency amongst many who are concerned to preserve, and where possible extend, democratic values. (Masterman, 1996, p. 61)

> For an institution that has historically clung to the concept of [print] literacy as the central organizing force of education, we must respect the time it will take to create the support for sustained, rigorous, and meaningful change that is necessary for schools to embrace this expanded vision of literacy for twenty-first century schools. (Hobbs, 1996, p. 181)

INTERPRETATION OF THE LITERATURE

Throughout this continuing era of concern, media literacy has been a peculiar mixture of science, educational imperative, technological attraction, political ideology, protectionist impulse, and emancipatory longings.

Science

As science, there have been scattered efforts to demonstrate that children and adults become more competent media users (Anderson & Ploghoft, 1981), make better consumer decisions (Livingstone & Helsper, 2006), and are protected from the putative effects of exposure to media violence (Eron, 1986; Huesmann, Eron, Klein, Brice, & Fischer, 1983) as well as those from alcohol (Austin & Johnson, 1997), smoking (Pinkerton, Austin, Marilyn, & Miller, 2003), and sex (Keller & Brown, 2002) as a result of media literacy training. There have also been several efforts to demonstrate that children and adults can learn to be more media literate (Kruger, 1998; Singer, Zuckerman, & Singer, 1980), which is to say that they can give the right answers on a media literacy test. There has been almost no investigation of whether that knowledge makes any difference in socially important ways (Bazalgette, 1996).

Whether that difference occurs is, of course, the crucial question. If media literacy training makes no difference in the everyday engagement of media and their texts, then what is the value of media literacy training (Masterman, 1996)? In the apparently one study of its kind, Anderson and Ploghoft (1981) demonstrated that the gains in rational media interpretation skills achieved through media literacy training were also achieved by simple maturation processes. Trained third graders scored better than untrained third graders but no better than untrained fourth graders. Want your third graders to be as media literate as fourth graders? One can embark on a one-year course of study or simply wait a year.

On the other hand, if it makes a difference, whose difference should it make? Is it enough to increase the participants' aesthetic pleasure (Deboer, 1959)? Or should the difference be the replacement of enjoyment and pleasure with so-called objective and rational evaluation in a rebirth of Cartesian rationality, which constitutes the audience, as Bignell (2002) puts it, "as irrational, illiterate, immoral, and violent" (p. 131).

Education

But the questions of effectiveness and to what end anyway are beside the point in terms of the educational imperative, because certainly children (and adults) need to "access, analyze, evaluate and use media" to become "civically engaged" citizens (United States Department of State, September 19, 2006, press release). Lagging only slightly behind the technological advance, education has always been in media, both in media didactics (instruction through media) and in media pedagogics (instruction about the media). By the mid-1930s, the education journals were regularly featuring lesson plans and instructional approaches for the movies, newspapers, radio dramas, and even comic books (Eldridge, 1937).

John Dewey's experiential education was in full throat (Dopp, 1902; Thomas, 1936), so many of the approaches involved training by doing—making the motion picture, putting out the school newspaper, creating the radio drama. Today, an Internet search on the term *media lesson plans* returns nearly 9,000 sites, including everything from creating your own cooking show to critiquing commercials and government censorship to defending against sex and violence to examining Internet and gaming addictions. Other fields such as communication, psychology, and sociology discover and rediscover media appreciation, receivership skills, media education, and media literacy, as it has been called over the years in a cyclical fashion, but education is the consistent player.

Education may be a consistent player, but it and all other disciplines appear to be in a constant state of discovery. The literature supports two reasons for this recycled discovery. Those curricular approaches (e.g., Fleischman & Woellhaf, 1942; Gordon, 1956; Hobbs, 2004) by some necessity are typically tied to the contemporary media technology, products, and techniques. Each change in any of those three initiates a change in the curricular approach. One cannot teach radio today (Hobbs, 2004; Orfanella, 1998) as one did in the 1940s (Bartlett, 1947; Matthews, 1945). I cannot easily explain why each revision is often seen as entirely new unless it is a re-mediation in which the reasoning goes something like "No one is teaching digital music; I will create the curriculum."

Meyrowitz (1998), in his usual perceptive way, illuminates the second reason. He suggests "that there is no finite set of knowledge that will make someone media literate, and that it is unrealistic to expect any given media literacy program to teach all that we could hope children and adults would know about media" (p. 107). As scholarship changes, media literacy changes. What media literacy was to Lloyd-Kolkin, Wheeler, and Strand in 1980 is not what media literacy is to Kellner and Share (2005) today.

To no small extent this chameleonesque character suggests that media literacy is more of a venue for the educator and media scholar than it is a field of study. It is a convenient stage on which we can demonstrate the practical accomplishments of our scholarship. From my reading and 30 years of practice in media literacy, I am led to suspect that we (the community of scholars) need media literacy programs more than the individuals enrolled in its courses. Media literacy gives us relevance, legitimacy, and work to do.

Techno-Attraction

Two scholarly conversations invariably accompany the introduction of some new technology: Social commentators see the end of the world as we know it and educators get excited about the latest gizmo's ability to turn the bored into the brilliant. It seems to be a great disappointment to both that neither happen. Writing in the *Educational Review,* Freeman (1926) stated,

> It is with mingled feelings of discouragement and hope that I think of the problem of the [media] in education—discouragement because of the present deplorable conditions, but hope because of the undeveloped possibilities. *The [media] are today the most important single destructive force in our civilization* [italics original]. (p. 115)

Freeman was writing in 1926, and her media were limited to the newspaper and the motion picture (radio was still trying to discover its business model).

Seven years earlier, however, Blanchard (1919) was celebrating the arrival of the motion picture in the classroom, by exclaiming,

> There is little doubt that its advent will be hailed with enthusiasm alike by progressive teachers and long-suffering pupils, because it will afford better pedagogical results at the same time that it makes memory an unconscious function instead of a labored effort involving all the agony of concentration on an uninteresting piece of work. (p. 287)

Ninety years later, we have neither been destroyed nor been significantly relieved of the labored effort of learning, as any group of PowerPointed students will attest.

One of the principles of dominance is to co-op the pleasures of the subjugated and put those pleasures to work in the interests of the dominant. The school's attraction to and rejection of technology are, consequently, inevitable. We recognize that the iPoded student is deliberately disconnected and, therefore, work both to rationalize that medium's use and to exploit the student interest for the purpose of our goals. We put our lessons in a podcast. Now, indeed, we are supposed to know better than our students, but there is more than a little hypocrisy in our typical refusal to open ourselves up to the same critical review that we expect our students to conduct across media texts. In 1969, I sat across from a principal of a school in downstate Michigan. I had just finished pitching a proposal for in-service training for his teachers on media literacy. He immediately grasped the concept and told me he would have none of it because it would lead to questioning of textbooks and teachers as well. He was an honest man.

Political Ideology

One can get rapidly caught up on the political ideology of media literacy by searching nearly any Internet site with the word *family* in the title (only a slight exaggeration). Again, it is easy to be misled into holding this to be a contemporary condition, not a continuation of our history. But that misperception occurs only because the historical record is difficult to access. The Internet of yesterday was composed of the pamphlets, newsletters, ringing pulpit denunciations, and rousing political addresses that took the media on for its glorification of crime, celebration of sex, and insidious propaganda, and warned of the growing addictions of our young people to the movies and the radio (Geiger 1923; Preston, 1941), all the while 88 million movie tickets were being sold each week and there were more radio households than homes with electricity.

Most of this was and is "huff and puff" politics or what is more academically termed *symbolic politics* (Edelman, 1971). The Family Research Council boasts of its success in denying Internet URLs ending in *.xxx* and warns its members to gird its loins because the issue is coming back.[3] Congress holds yet another hearing on media, this time on a remote control device that will allow the adults their lascivious pleasures while denying children access. It's important stuff because as Grimes, Anderson, and Bergen (2007) put it, the work gets votes and energizes memberships without expecting us to sacrifice any of our own guilty pleasures or changing any of the fundamental power structures that define our society.

From Geiger (1923) to Brown (1998), there is more than a streak of puritanism in U.S. media literacy. But British and European initiatives (Bazalgette, 1996; Buckingham, 1998; Masterman, 1996) have their own ideological cant. As a postmodernist, I find this all to be expected. What is amusing is the scholarly pretense of neutrality. As Masterman points out, there is no one way of using the media, and as Meyrowitz (1998) argues, there are not only multiple bases for media literacy, there are also multiple media literacies that are embedded in multiple media ecologies. Anything that is taught, therefore, is the consequence of choice. Media literacy is not mathematics. It is not a formal system of logic with one right answer. It is value saturated and ideologically constructed. It is not the business of creating some universal critical media user; it is the business of creating media users like us.

Protectionism

If there is any common denominator other than media in media literacy, it is the notion of protectionism (Hobbs, 2005). But the concept is more nuanced than simply protecting our children from the ill effects of media. Anderson and Colvin (2008) have shown in their cultural analysis of media violence research that the primary recipient of that protection is us—the dominant interests of society. The most frequent justification for concern offered in the 100-plus year history of media violence research has been what the Other might do. It is the fear of what the Other, in the person of our children and those of less, will be motivated to do to us in the form of violence, crime, or sexual disruption, or in some other way denying our rightful place or the peace and tranquility of our neighborhoods.

According to Anderson and Colvin (2008), media violence research is primarily concerned with the level of aggression in society and little concerned with the lost souls captured in the webs of media violence. The rhetoric to our children is "don't watch that; don't listen to that; don't look at that; don't play that; or if you do, don't enjoy that," because if you do you may become different from us or equally as bad exactly like us. Fear of the Other and self-hatred are two very strong motives in protectionism.

My reading of the media literacy literature suggests that protectionism works the same in many of these media literacy initiatives from *School and Society*'s call for a board of movie censors in 1917 ("School Children") to Wartella and Jennings's (2000) discussion of children's peril at the site of the computer as it does in our concerns over media violence. The underlying theory of protectionist media literacy describes the child as "vulnerable, unruly, and driven by excessive urges" (Bignell, 2002, p. 128). We protect the child but we protect ourselves from the child as well. And should we fail, as we often seem to do, it will be the media's fault, not our own.

Emancipation

The emancipatory longings of media literacy arise from a heady cocktail of German critical theory (Adorno, Hockheimer, Marcuse), French poststructuralism (Lacan, Derrida, Foucault), British cultural studies (Williams, Hoggart, Hall), and American critical pedagogy (Friere, Giroux, McLaren). The positions advanced there are represented in the media literacy work of Buckingham, (1998), Gitlin (1978), Kellner and Share (2005), and Masterman (1996). Masterman sounds the call:

> Teachers and journalists are both concerned with one of contemporary societies' most important functions: the production, circulation, distribution, and (crucially) the legitimation of information and ideas. Both are powerful creators and mediators of public consciousness, of social knowledge. Both have an important ideological role in the societies they serve, hence, the interest taken in the sphere of education and media by political and social elites. Workers in each of these spheres are faced with often quite stark choices. Their work may have either a liberating or an enslaving function. (p. 63)

Emancipation is, of course, a tricky business. It presumes that the emancipators know the true path to freedom and that the emancipatees will willingly follow. Because I have identified myself as a postmodernist, you can understand my discomfort with the principles of emancipation. Postmodernism is the antithesis of utopianism (while attempting to avoid dystopianism). Emancipation smacks too much of spreading freedom through preemptive advocacy advanced within a questionable certainty. On the other hand, the critique of postmodernism is that it is too self-absorbed, too delighted by its wordplay that it cannot act and that in that inaction and in denying the identity of the oppressed it colludes with their oppressors (Atkinson, 2002, p. 83).

But for postmodernists, it is centralization and unification that poses the greatest danger. When we act in unison, we can accomplish great things but at a great cost to social justice. Far better to preserve our differences. This brings this chapter full circle as I began by noting media literacy as a dynamic, irresolvable field. Media literacy will continue to invent its material form because whatever material expression is produced cannot be sustained. What survives is the idea that the world around us—now mostly a mediated world—is to be critically examined. For a postmodernist, that's right where we ought to be.

CONCLUSION

Media literacy is an unstable conglomerate idea whose elements are under constant tension. A tremor in the mediascape, in the practice of the classroom, or in communication or educational theory causes these elements to break their bonds and to re-form in a new configuration. This configuration has the remarkable power to obscure its past, and we greet this configuration as a discovery of its era. In this chapter, I have attempted to show first that the past is the present and will provide the future and, second, that the concepts and practices that form media literacy, in whatever its current configurations, are a necessary cultural response to the force of media in society.

In each instance for the past 150 years, the appearance of the first to the latest popular medium has forced the appearance of the literacy response. So, to paraphrase Klaus Bruhn Jensen (1991), the answer to the question of what is media literacy is "when." As our media change, as our sensibilities change, and as our sensibilities about the media change either through ideological location or through time, media literacy will reconfigure itself in response, sometimes in surprising, but always unpredictable, ways. For a practitioner and postmodern commentator like myself, there is both comfort and security in that.

NOTES

1. Historically, it has gone under reading skills or just plain literacy, journalism education, motion picture appreciation, discriminating listening, critical reading, critical thinking, critical viewing skills, receivership skills, visual literacy, film criticism, media criticism, and the like.
2. "Critical" refers to an implicative analysis approach rather than a review of limitations, errors, or failings, which is the purview of "critique."
3. More to the truth of the matter is that the adult entertainment industry does not want the designation and has, at the time of this writing, been denied again by the authorities for that reason.

APPENDIX: LITERATURE ENTERED INTO THE ANALYSIS

Abdullah, M. H. (2000). Media literacy. *ERIC Digest, D152,* 1–6.

Alexander, A., Hoerner, K., & Duke, L. (1998). What is quality children's television. *Annals of the American Academy of Political and Social Science, 557*(May), 70–82.

Anderson, J. A. (1980). The theoretical lineage of critical viewing curricula. *Journal of Communication, 30*(Summer), 64–70.

Anderson, J. A. (1981). Receivership skills: An educational response. In M. E. Ploghoft & J. A. Anderson (Eds.), *Education in a television age* (pp. 19–27). Springville, OH: Charles Thomas.

Anderson, J. A. (1983). Television literacy and the critical viewer. In J. Bryant & D. R. Anderson (Eds.), *Children's understanding of television: Research on attention and comprehension* (pp. 297–330). New York: Academic Press.

Anderson, J. A., & Ploghoft, M. E. (1981). Receivership skills: The television experience. *Communication Yearbook, 4,* 293–307.

Arnspiger, V. C. (1936). The educational talking picture. *Journal of Educational Sociology, 10*(3), 143–150.

Arrowsmith, W. (1969). Film as educator. *Journal of Aesthetic Education, 3*(3), 75–83.

Aufderheide, P. (1996). Media literacy: From a report on the National Leadership Conference on Media Literacy. In R. Kubey (Ed.), *Media literacy in the information age: Information & behavior* (pp. 79–86). New Brunswick, NJ: Transaction.

Austin, E. W., & Johnson, K. K. (1997). Effects of general and alcohol-specific media literacy training on children's decision making about alcohol. *Journal of Health Communication, 2,* 17–42.

Austin, E. W., & Johnson, K. K. (1997). Immediate and delayed effects of media literacy training on third graders' decision making for alcohol. *Health Communication, 9*(4), 323–349.

Austin, E. W., Pinkleton, B. E., Hust, S. J. T., & Cohen, M. (2005). Evaluation of an American Legacy Foundation/Washington State Department of Health media literacy pilot study. *Health Communication, 18*(1), 79–95.

Averill, L. A. (1915). Educational possibilities of the motion picture. *Educational Review, 50*(June–December), 392–398.

Bair, F. H. (1938). Exploring the educational possibilities of motion pictures. *Clearing House, 12*(9), 515–518.

Barth, R. J. (1976). ERIC/RCS report: Popular culture, the media, and teaching English. *English Journal, 65*(3), 84–88.

Bartlett, K. G. (1947). Social impact of radio. *Annals of the American Academy of Political and Social Science, 250,* 89–97.

Bazalgette, C. (1996). An agenda for the second phase of media literacy development. In R. Kubey (Ed.), *Media literacy in the information age: Information & behavior* (pp. 69–78). New Brunswick, NJ: Transaction.

Bender, L. (1944). The psychology of children's reading and the comics. *Journal of Educational Sociology, 18*(4), 223–231.

Bernays, E. L. (1947). The engineering of consent. *Annals of the American Academy of Political and Social Science, 250,* 113–120.

Bignell, J. (2002). Writing the child in media theory. *Yearbook of English Studies, 32,* 127–139.

Blanchard, P. (1919). The motion picture as an educational asset. *Pedagogical Seminary, 26*(3), 284–287.

Brooks, J. (1998). Teenagers evaluating modern media. *English Journal, 87*(1), 21–24.

Brown, F. J. (1937). Media of propaganda. *Journal of Educational Sociology, 10*(6), 323–330.

Brown, J. A. (1998). Media literacy perspectives. *Journal of Communication, 48*(1), 44–57.

Broz, S. L. (2001, August, 2001). *Media literacy: A review and critical assessment of its diverse literature.* Paper presented at the Association for Education in Journalism and Mass Communication, Washington, DC.

Brucker, H. (1942). The newspaper, the community, and the citizen. *Annals of the American Academy of Political and Social Science, 219,* 1–6.

Buckingham, D. (1998). Media education in the UK: Moving beyond protectionism. *Journal of Communication, 48,* 33–43.

Buckingham, D. (1999). Young people, politics and news media: Beyond political socialisation. *Oxford Review of Education, 25*(1/2), 171–184.

Burton, L. (2005). What is this media literacy thing? *Screen Education, 36*, 93–98.

Byrne, S. (2005, May). *Effective and lasting media literacy interventions.* Paper presented at the International Communication Association, New York City.

Cantor, J., & Wilson, B. J. (2003). Media and violence: Intervention strategies for reducing aggression. *Media Psychology, 5*, 363–403.

Chauvin, B. A. (2003). Visual or media literacy. *Journal of Visual Literacy, 23*(2), 119–128.

Christ, W. G., & Potter, W. J. (1998). Media literacy, media education, and the academy. *Journal of Communication, 48*, 5–15.

Christenbury, L. (1998). From the editor. *English Journal, 87*(1), 13.

Chung, S. K. (2007). Media literacy art education: Deconstructing lesbian and gay stereotypes in the media. *JADE, 26*, 98–107.

Cohen, J. R. (1994). Critical viewing and participatory democracy. *Journal of Communication, 44*(4), 94–113.

Collins, J. (1995). Literacy and literacies. *Annual Review of Anthropology, 24*, 75–93.

Collins, W. A. (1970). Learning of media content: A developmental study. *Child Development, 41*(4), 1133–1142.

Collins, W. A., Wellman, H., Keniston, A. H., & Westby, S. D. (1978). Age-related aspects of comprehension and inference from a televised dramatic narrative. *Child Development, 49*(2), 389–399.

Cooper, E., & Dinerman, H. (1951). Analysis of the film *Don't Be a Sucker*: A study in communication. *Public Opinion Quarterly, 15*(2), 243–264.

Corder-Bolz, C. R. (1980). Mediation: The role of significant others. *Journal of Communication, 30*(Summer), 107–118.

Cressey, P. G. (1934). The motion picture as informal education. *Journal of Educational Sociology, 7*(8), 504–515.

Curry-Tash, M. W. (1998). The politics of teleliteracy and adbusting in the classroom. *English Journal, 87*(1), 43–48.

Dale, E. (1938). Motion pictures and human relations: The motion picture and intergroup relationships. *Public Opinion Quarterly, 2*(1), 39–42.

Deboer, J. J. (1959). What shall we teach in high-school English. *School Review, 67*(3), 305–319.

Dopp, K. E. (1902). A new factor in the elementary-school curriculum. *American Journal of Sociology, 8*(2), 145–157.

Dorr, A., Graves, S. B., & Phelps, E. (1980). Television literacy for young children. *Journal of Communication, 30*(Summer), 71–83.

DuBreuil, A. J. (1915). The moving picture and the school: The first organized visual instruction and what preceded it. *Educational Review, 49*, 203–211.

Dunne, P. (1946). The documentary and Hollywood. *Hollywood Quarterly, 1*(2), 166–172.

Edman, M. (1940). Attendance of school pupils and adults at moving pictures. *School Review*, December, 753–763.

Eldridge, D. A. (1937). Motion-picture appreciation in the New Haven schools. *Journal of Educational Sociology, 2*(3), 175–183.

England, D. A., & Eisele, C. (1981). Bait/rebait: English teachers have a responsibility to teach about and from television. *English Journal, 70*(7), 18–21.

Eron, L. D. (1986). Interventions to mitigate the psychological effects of media violence on aggressive behavior. *Journal of Social Issues, 42*(3), 155–169.

Erskine, J. (1935). The future of radio as a cultural medium. *Annals of the American Academy of Political and Social Science, 177,* 214–219.

Fehlman, R. H. (1992). Making meanings visible: Critically reading TV. *English Journal, 81*(7), 19–24.

Feuerstein, M. (1999). Media literacy in support of critical thinking. *Journal of Educational Media, 24*(1), 43–54.

Fleishchman, E. E., & Woellhaf, R. (1942). The motion picture: A neglected "liberal art." *Quarterly Journal of Speech, 28*(2), 182–184.

Fleming, P. J. (1911). Moving pictures as factor in education. *Pedagogical Seminary, 27,* 336–352.

Foster, H. M. (1981). Electronic media: Teaching television literacy. *English Journal, 70*(8), 70–72.

Foster, H. S., Jr., & Friedrich, C. J. (1937). Letters to the editor as a means of measuring the effectiveness of propaganda. *American Political Science Review, 31*(1), 71–79.

Frank, J. (1944). What's in the comics? *Journal of Educational Sociology, 18*(4), 214–222.

Freeman, B. (1926). The movies in education. *Educational Review,* 72(June–December), 115–118.

Freeman, G. L. (1940). The motion picture and informal education. *Journal of Educational Sociology, 13*(5), 257–262.

Geiger, J. R. (1923). The effects of the motion picture on the mind and morals of the young. *International Journal of Ethics, 34*(1), 69–83.

Geller, R., & Kula, S. (1969). Toward filmic literacy: The role of the American Film Institute. *Journal of Aesthetic Education, 3*(3), 97–111.

Gitlin, T. (1978). Media sociology: The dominant paradigm. *Theory and Society,* 6(2), 205–253.

Glock, C. Y. (1952–1953). The comparative study of communications and opinion formation. *Public Opinion Quarterly, 16*(4), 512–523.

Goodwyn, A. (1993). News from nowhere: Reading the media. *English Journal, 82*(5), 60–65.

Gordon, S. S. (1956). Recent developments in communication courses. *College Composition and Communication,* 7(1), 13–16.

Gould, J. (1946). Television: Boon or bane? *Public Opinion Quarterly, 10*(3), 314–320.

Gould, K. M. (1928). Cinepatriotism. *Social Forces,* 7(1), 120–129.

Goulden, N. R. (1998). The roles of national and state standards in implementing speaking, listening, and media literacy. *Communication Education, 47,* 194–208.

Gray, J. (2005). Television teaching: Parody, *The Simpsons,* and media literacy education. *Critical Studies in Media Communication, 22*(3), 223–238.

Gruenberg, S. M. (1935). Radio and the child. *Annals of the American Academy of Political and Social Science, 177,* 123–128.

Gruenberg, S. M. (1944). The comics as a social force. *Journal of Educational Sociology, 18*(4), 204–213.

Hart, E. M. (2002). *Teens, sex, and media.* Retrieved March 8, 2007, from http://www.frankwbaker.com/MediaLitEd.pdf

Hazard, P., & Hazard, M. (1961). The public arts: Multi-media literacy. *English Journal, 50*(2), 132–133.

Heiligmann, R., & Shields, V. R. (2005). Media literacy, visual syntax, and magazine advertisements: Conceptualizing the consumption of reading by media literate subjects. *Journal of Visual Literacy, 25*(1), 41–66.

Hendrix, M. (1998). Media literacy. *English Journal, 87*(4), 9.
Hettinger, H. S. (1935). Broadcasting in the United States. *Annals of the American Academy of Political and Social Science, 177,* 1–14.
Hettinger, H. S. (1941). Organizing radio's discoveries for use. *Annals of the American Academy of Political and Social Science, 213,* 170–189.
Higgins, H. W. (1999). Community television and the vision of media literacy, social action, and empowerment. *Journal of Broadcasting & Electronic Media, 43*(4), 624–644.
Hobbs, R. (1996). Expanding the concept of literacy. In R. Kubey (Ed.), *Media literacy in the information age: Information & behavior* (pp. 163–183). New Brunswick, NJ: Transaction.
Hobbs, R. (1998). The seven great debates in the media literacy movement. *Journal of Communication, 48*(1), 16–32.
Hobbs, R. (2004). Media literacy, general semantics, and K–12 education. *ETC, 61*(1), 24–28.
Hobbs, R. (2005). The state of media literacy education. *Journal of Communication, 55*(4), 865–871.
Hoffmann, G. (1999). Media literacy study. *ETC, 56*(2), 165–171.
Hoffmann, G. (2004). Media literacy and general semantics. *ETC, 61*(1), 29–31.
Hoffmann, G., & Brecklin, T. (1996). A media literacy course for middle school students. *ETC, 53*(1), 39–46.
Huesmann, L. R., Eron, L. D., Klein, R., Brice, P., & Fischer, P. (1983). Mitigating the imitation of aggressive behaviors by changing children's attitudes about media violence. *Journal of Personality and Social Behavior, 44*(5), 899–910.
Hunt, S. (1997). Film and media education, K–12. *Cinema Journal, 36*(2), 106–109.
Huston, A. C., Watkins, B. A., & Kunkel, D. (1989). Public policy and children's television. *American Psychologist, 44*(2), 424–433.
Huston, A. C., & Wright, J. C. (1998). Television and the informational and educational needs of children. *Annals of the American Academy of Political and Social Science, 557,* 9–23.
Jonassen, D. H. (1981). Learning from television: What are the limits? *Peabody Journal of Education, 58*(4), 242–250.
Jordan, A. B., & Jamieson, K. H. (1998). Preface. *Annals of the American Academy of Political and Social Science, 557,* 7–8.
Karl, H. (1974). Guest editorial: Media literacy: The right to know. *English Journal, 63*(7), 7–9.
Katz, E. (1936). Making movies in the classroom. *Clearing House, 11*(1), 153–156.
Keliher, A. V. (1938). The motion picture and problems of youth. *Public Opinion Quarterly, 2*(1, Special Supplement: Public Opinion in a Democracy), 53–54.
Keller, S. N., & Brown, J. D. (2002). Media interventions to promote responsible sexual behavior. *Journal of Sex Research, 39*(1), 67–72.
Kellner, D. (1995). Media communications vs. cultural studies: Overcoming the divide. *Communication Theory, 5*(2), 162–177.
Kellner, D., & Share, J. (2005). Toward critical media literacy: Core concepts, debates, organizations, and policy. *Discourse: Studies in the Cultural Politics of Education, 26*(3), 369–386.
Kenney, E. A. (1938). Administrative problems in the use of radio in the classroom. *California Journal of Elementary Education, 7*(2), 101–108.

Key facts: Media literacy. (2003). Retrieved March 7, 2007, from http://www.kff.org/entmedia/Media-Literacy.cfm

Kirkton, C. M. (1971). Media literacy: Focus on film. *English Journal, 60*(6), 831–838.

Krausz, P. (2001). Children and the new media literacy. *Screen Education, 25*, 106–108.

Kruger, E. (1998). Media literacy does work, trust me. *English Journal, 87*(1), 17–20.

Kubey, R. (1996). Introduction: Media education: Portraits of an evolving field. In R. Kubey (Ed.), *Media literacy in the information age: Information & behavior* (pp. 1–11). New Brunswick, NJ: Transaction.

Kubey, R. (1998). Obstacles to the development of media education in the United States. *Journal of Communication, 48*(1), 58–69.

Lawton, S. P. (1930). The principles of effective radio speaking. *Quarterly Journal of Speech, 26*(3), 266–277.

Lazere, D. (1987). Literacy and mass media: The political implications. *New Literary History, 18*(2), 237–255.

Lehman, H. C., & Witty, P. A. (1927). The compensatory function of the movies. *Journal of Applied Psychology, 11*(1), 33–41.

Lehman, H. C., & Witty, P. A. (1927). Newspaper vs. teacher. *Educational Review, 73*(February), 97–102.

Lewis, J., & Jhally, S. (1998). The struggle over media literacy. *Journal of Communication, 48*(1), 109–120.

Livingstone, S. (2004). Media literacy and the challenge of new information and communication technologies. *Communication Review, 7*, 3–14.

Livingstone, S., & Helsper, E. J. (2006). Does advertising literacy mediate the effects of advertising on children? A critical examination of two linked research literatures in relation to obesity and food choice. *Journal of Communication, 56*, 560–584.

Lloyd-Kolkin, D., Wheeler, P., & Strand, T. (1980). Developing a curriculum for teenagers. *Journal of Communication, 30*(Summer), 119–125.

Lowenstein, R. B. (1981). Nonprint media: Forward to the fundamentals. *English Journal, 70*(3), 88–90.

Maccoby, E. E. (1951). Television: Its impact on school children. *Public Opinion Quarterly, 15*(3), 421–444.

Maguire, F. W., & Spong, R. M. (1949). Journalism in the liberal arts. *Journal of Higher Education, 20*(6), 295–298, 337–338.

Marsh, J. (2006). Emergent media literacy: Digital animation in early childhood. *Language and Education, 20*(6), 493–514.

Masterman, L. (1996). A rationale for media education. In R. Kubey (Ed.), *Media literacy in the information age* (pp. 15–68). New Brunswick, NJ: Transaction.

Matthews, W. (1945). Radio plays as literature. *Hollywood Quarterly, 1*(1), 40–50.

May, M. A. (1937). Educational possibilities of motion pictures. *Journal of Educational Sociology, 2*(3), 149–160.

McMullan, L. (1938). The newspaper goes to school. *Clearing House, 13*(1), 103–104.

Merrill, I. R. (1961). Broadcast viewing and listening by children. *Public Opinion Quarterly, 25*(2), 263–276.

Mersand, J. (1952). The English teacher and guidance. *English Journal, 41*(3), 141–147.

Messaris, P. (1996). Visual "literacy" in cross-cultural prespectives. In R. Kubey (Ed.), *Media literacy in the information age* (pp. 135–162). New Brunswick, NJ: Transaction.

Messaris, P. (1998). Visual aspects of media literacy. *Journal of Communication, 48*(1), 70–80.

Meyrowitz, J. (1998). Multiple media literacies. *Journal of Communication, 48*(1), 96–108.

Mihailides, P. (2006). Media literacy in journalism/mass communication education: Can the United States learn from Sweden. *Journalism & Mass Communication Educator, 60*(4), 416–428.

Miller, E. (1999). Twelve basic principles for incorporating media literacy into any curriculum. *EDRS,* 1–12.

Montgomery, K. (2000). Children's media culture in the new millennium: Mapping the digital landscape. *Future of Children, 10*(2), 145–167.

Morris, B. S. (1998). Toward creating a TV research community in your classroom. *English Journal, 87*(1), 38–42.

Morrow, J. (1980). Media literacy in the 80s. *English Journal, 69*(1), 48–51.

Motomura, K. (2003). Media literacy education in art: Motion expression and the new vision of art education. *Journal of Aesthetic Education, 37*(4), 58–64.

Moving pictures and school children. (1934). *School and Society, 39,* 837–838.

Nabi, R. L., & Krcmar, M. (2004). Conceptualizing media enjoyment as attitude: Implications for mass media effects research. *Communication Theory, 14*(4), 288–310.

Nathanson, A. I. (2004). Factual and evaluative approaches to modifying children's responses to violent televison. *Journal of Communication, 54*(2), 321–326.

Norton-Meier, L. A. (2005). Trust the fungus: Lessons in media literacy learned from the movies. *Journal of Adolescent and Adult Literacy, 48*(7), 608–611.

The N.S.S.C. and the C.C.C.C. (1951). *College Composition and Communication,* 2(2), 13–15.

Objectives and organization of the communication course: Report of workshop no. 4. (1950). *College Composition and Communication, 1*(2), 15–18.

O'Grady, G. (1969). The preparation of teachers of media. *Journal of Aesthetic Education, 3*(3), 113–134.

Olson, D. R. (1988). Mind and media: The epistemic function of literacy. *Journal of Communication, 38*(3), 27–36.

Olson, W. C. (1934). Social significance of the cinema. *School Review, 42*(6), 466–470.

Orfanella, L. (1998). Radio: The intimate medium. *English Journal, 87*(1), 53–55.

Organization of the communication course: The report of workshop no. 4. (1951). College Composition and Communication, 2(4), 8–11.

O'Rourke, B. (1981). Nonprint media: Whatever happened to visual literacy? *English Journal, 70*(2), 71–73.

Owen, D. B., Silet, C. L. P., & Brown, S. E. (1998). Teaching television to empower students. *English Journal, 87*(1), 28–33.

Palmer, C. (1947). Cartoon in the classroom. *Hollywood Quarterly, 3*(1), 26–33.

Parker, E. B. (1973–1974). Implications of new information technology. *Public Opinion Quarterly, 37*(4), 590–600.

Patton, C. S. (1938). Moving pictures in the church. *Journal of Applied Sociology, 3*(1), 59–64.

Pease, K. (1937). Hamden's course in appreciation of movies and radio. *Clearing House, 12*(1), 39–43.

Phillips, D. (1937). A unit on the use of radio. *English Journal, 26*(1), 33–38.

Piette, J., & Giroux, L. (1996). The theoretical foundations of media education programs. In R. Kubey (Ed.), *Media literacy in the information age* (pp. 89–134). New Brunswick, NJ: Transaction.

Pinkerton, B., Austin, E. W., Marilyn, C., & Miller, A. (2003, May). *Media literacy and smoking prevention among adolescents: A year 2 evaluation.* Paper presented at the International Communication Association, San Diego, CA.

Potter, G. (1936). A study of the use of the radio in a group of California schools. *California Journal of Elementary Education, 5*(1), 59–64.

Quigley, M. (1938). The function of the motion picture. *Public Opinion Quarterly, 2*(1, Special Supplement: Public Opinion in a Democracy), 47–49.

Rachford, H. F. (1944). Developing discrimination in radio listening. *English Journal, 33*(6), 315–317.

Reid, S. (1940). Hollywood hokum: The English teacher's responsibility. *English Journal, 29*(3), 211–218.

Reisman, L. (1949). Cinema technique and mass culture. *American Quarterly, 1*(4), 314–329.

Remmers, H. H. (1938). Propaganda in the schools: Do the effects last? *Public Opinion Quarterly, 2*(2), 197–210.

Roberts, D. F., Christenson, P., Gibson, W. A., Mooser, L., & Goldberg, M. E. (1980). Developing discriminating consumers. *Journal of Communication, 30*(Summer), 94–105.

Rosenbaum, J. (2003, May). *How media literacy is defined: A review.* Paper presented at the International Communication Association, San Diego, CA.

Ross, J. (1940). The speech teacher keeps abreast of the radio and the motion picture. *Quarterly Journal of Speech, 26*(3), 431–437.

Rosten, L. C. (1947). Movies and propaganda. *Annals of the American Academy of Political and Social Science, 254,* 116–124.

Rowland, H. (1944). Radio crime dramas. *Educational Research Bulletin, 23*(8), 210–217.

Ruben, A. M. (1998). Editor's note. *Journal of Communication, 48*(1), 3–4.

Saiyidain, K. G. (1955). Secondary education: A statement of objectives, purposes, moral and spiritual values. *Journal of Educational Sociology, 28*(5), 205–209.

Scharrer, E. (2003). Making a case for media literacy in the curriculum: Outcomes and assessment. *Journal of Adolescent and Adult Literacy, 46*(4), 354–458.

School children and motion pictures in England. (1917). *School and Society, 6*(134), 78–80.

Shannon, P., & Fernie, D. E. (1985). Print and television: Children's use of the medium is the message. *Elementary School Journal, 85*(5), 662–672.

Shields, M. K., & Behrman, R. E. (2000). Children and computer technology: Analysis and recommendations. *Future of Children, 10*(2), 4–30.

Shrum, L. J. (2001). Processing strategy moderates the cultivation effect. *Human Communication Research, 27*(1), 94–120.

Silverstone, R. (2004). Regulation, media literacy, and media civics. *Media, Culture & Society, 26*(3), 440–449.

Singer, D. G., & Singer, J. L. (1998). Developing critical viewing skills and media literacy in children. *Annals of the American Academy of Political and Social Science, 557,* 164–179.

Singer, D. G., Zuckerman, D. M., & Singer, J. L. (1980). Helping elementary school children learn about TV. *Journal of Communication, 30*(Summer), 84–93.

Skornia, H. J. (1969). What TV is doing to America: Some unexpected consequences. *Journal of Aesthetic Education, 3*(3), 29–44.

Smythe, D. W. (1954). Reality as presented by television. *Public Opinion Quarterly, 18*(2), 143–156.

Sones, W. W. D. (1944). The comics and instructional method. *Journal of Educational Sociology, 18*(4), 232–240.

Stephens, H. B. (1926). The relation of the motion picture to changing moral standards. *Annals of the American Academy of Political and Social Science, 128*(The Motion Picture in its Economic and Social Aspects), 151–157.

Stephens, K. (2000). A critical discussion of the "new literacy studies." *British Journal of Educational Studies, 48*(1), 10–23.

Stout, D. A. (2002). Religious media literacy: Toward a research agenda. *Journal of Media and Religion, 1*(1), 49–60.

Sutz, R., Warren, M. W., & Williams, H. (1998). How to break through technoshock and build multi-media units. *English Journal, 87*(1), 25–27.

Thoman, E. (1998). Media literacy: A guided tour of selected resources for teaching. *English Journal, 87*(1), 34–37.

Thoman, E. (2004). Media literacy: A national priority for a changing world. *American Behavioral Scientist, 48*(1), 18–29.

Thomas, F. W. (1936). Radio: An instrument in progressive education. *Clearing House, 10*(5), 402–406.

Thrasher, F. M. (1936). The motion picture: Its nature and scope. *Journal of Educational Sociology, 10*(3), 129–142.

Verkaik, N., & Gathercoal, P. (2001). Lessons in media literacy and students' comprehension of television and text advertisements. *EDRS,* 1–15.

Wallendorf, M. (2001). Literally literacy. *Journal of Consumer Research, 27*(4), 505–511.

Waples, D. (1930). Propaganda and leisure reading. *Journal of Higher Education, 1*(2), 73- 77.

Warren, R. (2003). Parental mediation of preschool children's television viewing. *Journal of Broadcasting & Electronic Media, 47*(3), 349–417.

Warren, R. (2005). Parental mediation of children's television viewing in low-income families. *Journal of Communication, 55*(4), 847–863.

Wartella, E., & Jennings, N. (2000). Children and computers: New technology, old concerns. *Future of Children, 10*(2), 31–43.

Wehmeyer, J. (2000). Critical media studies and the North American media literacy movement. *Cinema Journal, 39*(4), 94–101.

Wilcox, D. F. (1900). The American newspaper: A study in social psychology. *Annals of the American Academy of Political and Social Science, 16*(July), 56–92.

Willey, M. M. (1935). Communication agencies and the volume of propaganda. *Annals of the American Academy of Political and Social Science, 179,* 194–200.

Williams, A. S. (1956). Television in education: Possibilities and obstacles. *School Review, 64*(4), 187–190.

Williams, B. T. (2003). What they see is what we get: Television and middle school writers. *Journal of Adolescent and Adult Literacy, 46*(7), 546–554.

Williams, T. M. (1981). How and what do children learn from television? *Human Communication Research, 7*(2), 180–192.

Williamson, D. (1999). Media education in the university: Enhancing media literacy through first-year undergraduate coursework. *Journal of Educational Media, 24*(3), 203–215.

Wirth, L. (1948). Consensus and mass communication. *American Sociological Review, 13*(1), 1–15.

Witty, P. (1953). Children's reactions to TV: A fourth report. *Elementary English, 1953*(30), 444–451.

Witty, P. (1955). Children and TV: A sixth report. *Elementary English, 32,* 469–476.

Witty, P. A., & Sizemore, R. (1954). Reading the comics: A summary of studies and an evaluation II. *Elementary English, 31,* 43–49.

Witty, P. A., & Sizemore, R. (1954). Reading the comics: A summary of studies and an evaluation III. *Elementary English, 31,* 109–114.

Yates, B. L. (2001, May). *Applying diffusion theory: Adoption of media literacy programs in schools.* Paper presented at the International Communication Association, Washington, DC.

Zettl, H. (1998). Contextual media aesthetics as the basis for media literacy. *Journal of Communication, 48*(1), 81–95.

Zorbaugh, H. (1944). The comics: There they stand! *Journal of Educational Sociology, 18*(4), 196–203.

REFERENCES

Abdullah, M. H. (2000). Media literacy. *ERIC Digest, D152,* 1–6.

Anderson, J. A. (1980). The theoretical lineage of critical viewing curricula. *Journal of Communication, 30*(Summer), 64–70.

Anderson, J. A. (2006, February). *The production of media violence and aggression research: A cultural analysis.* Paper presented at the annual conference of the Western State Communication Association, San Francisco.

Anderson, J. A. (in press). The production of media violence and aggression research: A cultural analysis. *American Behavioral Scientist.*

Anderson, J. A., & Colvin, J. W. (2008). Is it just science? A cultural analysis of media violence and aggression research. In T. Grimes, J. A. Anderson, & L. Bergen, (Eds.), *Media violence and aggression: Science and ideology* (pp. 93–152). Thousand Oaks, CA: Sage.

Anderson, J. A., & Colvin, J. W. (in press). Media research 1900–1945. In D. Park & J. Pooley (Eds.), *Media research and its histories: New perspectives on the contested memory of the field.* New York: Peter Lang.

Anderson, J. A., & Ploghoft, M. E. (1981). Receivership skills: The television experience. *Communication Yearbook, 4,* 293–307.

Arnspiger, V. C. (1936). The educational talking picture. *Journal of Educational Sociology, 10*(3), 143–150.

Arrowsmith, W. (1969). Film as educator. *Journal of Aesthetic Education, 3*(3), 75–83.

Atkinson, E. (2002). The responsible anarchist: Postmodernism and social change. *British Journal of Sociology of Education, 23*(1), 73–87.

Austin, E. W., & Johnson, K. K. (1997). Immediate and delayed effects of media literacy training on third graders' decision making for alcohol. *Health Communication, 9*(4), 323–349.

Bartlett, K. G. (1947). Social impact of radio. *Annals of the American Academy of Political and Social Science, 250,* 89–97.

Bazalgette, C. (1996). An agenda for the second phase of media literacy development. In R. Kubey (Ed.), *Media literacy in the information age: Information & behavior* (pp. 69–78). New Brunswick, NJ: Transaction.

Bignell, J. (2002). Writing the child in media theory. *Yearbook of English Studies, 32,* 127–139.

Blanchard, P. (1919). The motion picture as an educational asset. *Pedagogical Seminary, 26*(3), 284–287.

Brazeal, D. K. (2005). Precursor to modern media hype: The 1830s penny press. *Journal of American Culture, 28*(4), 405–414.

Brown, J. A. (1998). Media literacy perspectives. *Journal of Communication, 48*(1), 44–57.

Buckingham, D. (1998). Media education in the UK: Moving beyond protectionism. *Journal of Communication, 48,* 33–43.

Burton, L. (2005). What is this media literacy thing? *Screen Education, 36,* 93–98.

The crime of adultery. (1868). *American Law Register, 16*(12), 769–777.

Dale, E. (1938). Motion pictures and human relations: The motion picture and intergroup relationships. *Public Opinion Quarterly, 2*(1), 39–42.

Deboer, J. J. (1959). What shall we teach in high-school English. *School Review, 67*(3), 305–319.

Dopp, K. E. (1902). A new factor in the elementary-school curriculum. *American Journal of Sociology, 8*(2), 145–157.

Edelman, M. (1971). *Politics as symbolic action.* Chicago: Markham.

Eldridge, D. A. (1937). Motion-picture appreciation in the New Haven schools. *Journal of Educational Sociology, 2*(3), 175–183.

Eron, L. D. (1986). Interventions to mitigate the psychological effects of media violence on aggressive behavior. *Journal of Social Issues, 42*(3), 155–169.

Fenton, F. (1910). The influence of newspaper presentations upon the growth of crime and other anti-social activity. *American Journal of Sociology, 16*(3), 342–371.

Feuerstein, M. (1999). Media literacy in support of critical thinking. *Journal of Educational Media, 24*(1), 43–54.

Fleishchman, E. E., & Woellhaf, R. (1942). The motion picture: A neglected "liberal art." *Quarterly Journal of Speech, 28*(2), 182–184.

Frank, J. (1944). What's in the comics? *Journal of Educational Sociology, 18*(4), 214–222.

Freeman, B. (1926). The movies in education. *Educational Review, 72* (June–December), 115–118.

Geiger, J. R. (1923). The effects of the motion picture on the mind and morals of the young. *International Journal of Ethics, 34*(1), 69–83.

Gergen, K. J. (1995). *Realities and relationships: Soundings in social construction.* Cambridge, MA: Harvard University Press.

Gitlin, T. (1978). Media sociology: The dominant paradigm. *Theory and Society, 6*(2), 205–253.

Gordon, S. S. (1956). Recent developments in communication courses. *College Composition and Communication, 7*(1), 13–16.

Grimes, T., Anderson, J., & Bergen, L. (2007). *Media violence and aggression: Science and ideology*. Thousand Oaks, CA: Sage.

Hart, E. M. (2002). *Teens, sex, and media.* Retrieved March 8, 2007, from http://www.frankwbaker.com/MediaLitEd.pdf

Hobbs, R. (1996). Expanding the concept of literacy. In R. Kubey (Ed.), *Media literacy in the information age: Information & behavior* (pp. 163–183). New Brunswick, NJ: Transaction.

Hobbs, R. (2004). Media literacy, general semantics, and K–12 education. *ETC, 61*(1), 24–28.

Hobbs, R. (2005). The state of media literacy education. *Journal of Communication, 55*(4), 865–871.

Huesmann, L. R., Eron, L. D., Klein, R., Brice, P., & Fischer, P. (1983). Mitigating the imitation of aggressive behaviors by changing children's attitudes about media violence. *Journal of Personality and Social Behavior, 44*(5), 899–910.

Jensen, K. B. (1991). When is meaning? Communication theory, pragmatism, and mass media reception. *Communication Yearbook 14*, 3–32.

Keller, S. N., & Brown, J. D. (2002). Media interventions to promote responsible sexual behavior. *Journal of Sex Research, 39*(1), 67–72.

Kellner, D., & Share, J. (2005). Toward critical media literacy: Core concepts, debates, organizations, and policy. *Discourse: Studies in the Cultural Politics of Education, 26*(3), 369–386.

Krausz, P. (2001). Children and the new media literacy. *Screen Education, 25*, 106–108.

Kruger, E. (1998). Media literacy does work, trust me. *English Journal, 87*(1), 17–20.

Lehman, H. C., & Witty, P. A. (1927). Newspaper vs. teacher. *Educational Review, 73*(February), 97–102.

Livingstone, S., & Helsper, E. J. (2006). Does advertising literacy mediate the effects of advertising on children? A critical examination of two linked research literatures in relation to obesity and food choice. *Journal of Communication, 56*, 560–584.

Lloyd-Kolkin, D., Wheeler, P., & Strand, T. (1980). Developing a curriculum for teenagers. *Journal of Communication, 30*(Summer), 119–125.

Lowenstein, R. B. (1981). Nonprint media: Forward to the fundamentals. *English Journal, 70*(3), 88–90.

Masterman, L. (1996). A rationale for media education. In R. Kubey (Ed.), *Media literacy in the information age* (pp. 15–68). New Brunswick, NJ: Transaction.

Matthews, W. (1945). Radio plays as literature. *Hollywood Quarterly, 1*(1), 40–50.

May, M. A. (1937). Educational possibilities of motion pictures. *Journal of Educational Sociology, 2*(3), 149–160.

Mersand, J. (1952). The English teacher and guidance. *English Journal, 41*(3), 141–147.

Messaris, P. (1996). Visual "literacy" in cross-cultural prespectives. In R. Kubey (Ed.), *Media literacy in the information age* (pp. 135–162). New Brunswick, NJ: Transaction.

Meyrowitz, J. (1998). Multiple media literacies. *Journal of Communication, 48*(1), 96–108.

Montgomery, K. (2000). Children's media culture in the new millennium: Mapping the digital landscape. *Future of Children, 10*(2), 145–167.

O'Grady, G. (1969). The preparation of teachers of media. *Journal of Aesthetic Education, 3*(3), 113–134.
Orfanella, L. (1998). Radio: The intimate medium. *English Journal, 87*(1), 53–55.
Parker, E. B. (1973–1974). Implications of new information technology. *Public Opinion Quarterly, 37*(4), 590–600.
Pinkerton, B., Austin, E. W., Marilyn, C., & Miller, A. (2003, May). *Media literacy and smoking prevention among adolescents: A year 2 evaluation.* Paper presented at the International Communication Association, San Diego, CA.
Preston, M. I. (1941). Children's reactions to movie horrors and radio crime. *Journal of Pediatrics 19*(2), 147–168.
Remarkable criminal trial: The watchman of Eldagsen. (1860). *American Law Register, 9*(12), 1–22.
Rosenbaum, J. (2003, May). *How media literacy is defined: A review.* Paper presented at the International Communication Association, San Diego, CA.
School children and motion pictures in England. (1917). *School and Society, 6*(134), 78–80.
Shields, M. K., & Berrman, R. E. (2000). Children and computer technology: Analysis and recommendations. *Future of Children, 10*(2), 4–30.
Silverstone, R. (2004). Regulation, media literacy, and media civics. *Media, Culture & Society, 26*(3), 440–449.
Singer, D. G., Zuckerman, D. M., & Singer, J. L. (1980). Helping elementary school children learn about TV. *Journal of Communication, 30*(Summer), 84–93.
Stephens, K. (2000). A critical discussion of the "new literacy studies." *British Journal of Educational Studies, 48*(1), 10–23.
Thomas, F. W. (1936). Radio: An instrument in progressive education. *Clearing House, 10*(5), 402–406.
United Nations Educational Scientific and Cultural Organization. (1951). *International Orgaization, 6*(3), 451–453.
United States Department of State. (2006, September 19). Retrieved March 27, 2007, from http://usinfo.state.gov/
Wartella, E., & Jennings, N. (2000). Children and computers: New technology, old concerns. *Future of Children, 10*(2), 31–43.
Wilcox, D. F. (1900). The American newspaper: A study in social psychology. *Annals of the American Academy of Political and Social Science, 16*(July), 56–92.
Wirth, L. (1948). Consensus and mass communication. *American Sociological Review, 13*(1), 1–15.
Yarros, V. S. (1899). The press and public opinion. *American Journal of Sociology, 5*(3), 372–382.
Zettl, H. (1998). Contextual media aesthetics as the basis for media literacy. *Journal of Communication, 48*(1), 81–95.

CHAPTER 26

Educational Settings and the Use of Technology to Promote the Multicultural Development of Children

KEVIN CLARK

The early days of technology in education focused on films, with television and computers becoming the focus in recent years (Clark, 1998). Technology presents the greatest potential for underresourced ethnic communities to begin to improve their conditions and get their needs met through rich learning environments that act as scaffolds to learner performance (Laffey, Musser, & Tupper, 1998; Clark, 2005). There are many educational theories and approaches that allow for the use of instructional technologies like television, computers, and the Internet. The newest instructional technology paradigm involves the visual capabilities of television and the interactivity and processing capabilities of computer-based technologies (Clark, 1998). As a result, there are instructional strategies that are more conducive and appropriate for the use of these instructional technologies.

Roschelle, Pea, Hoadly, Gordin, and Means (2000) suggest that technology enhances learning in children by supporting four essential characteristics of learning: (a) active engagement, (b) participation in groups, (c) frequent interaction and feedback, and (d) connections to the real world. According to Jonassen, Howland, Moore, and Marra (2003), students do not learn from television and/or computing technology, but because students learn from thinking, these technologies should be used to engage and facilitate thinking and knowledge construction. The ways that technologies (television, computers, the Internet, etc.) can be used as tools to facilitate and support learning include supporting knowledge construction, acting as a vehicle for the exploration and access of information, supporting contextual and real-life learning situations, acting as a medium for collaboration and dialogue, and providing a mechanism to reflect on and represent their knowledge (Jonassen et al., 2003). Regardless of the theoretical perspective—behaviorism, cognition, or constructivism—there are some common elements of successful instruction such as active participation, practice, individualized instruction, reinforcement, realistic context, and cooperative groups (Heinich, Molenda, Russell, & Smaldino, 2002) that can be supported and accentuated by using instructional technologies and media.

Researchers (Clark, 1998; Peck & Dorricott, 1994) have identified 10 reasons to use technologies in educational settings: (a) to individualize instruction; (b) to help learners become proficient at accessing, evaluating, and communicating information; (c) to foster an increase in the quantity and quality of a learner's thinking and writing skills; (d) to encourage learners to solve complex problems by independently organizing, interpreting, developing, and evaluating solutions and strategies; (e) to appeal to learners and encourage their artistic expression; (f) to help learners reach the world outside their physical location; (g) to provide opportunities for learners to create meaningful work through publication, postings, and other media outlets; (h) to provide access to high-level and high-interest educational materials; (i) to help learners feel comfortable with the tools of the Information Age; and (j) to make instruction more productive and efficient.

Although technologies and media can be effectively integrated into most instructional situations, there are educational settings where the use of technologies is more appropriate. Characteristics of effective educational technologies and media are (a) age-appropriate content, (b) gender- and ethnic-appropriate content, (c) stimulating effects (action, sound, etc.), (d) language that is easy to understand, (e) repetition, (f) interactive format, (g) likeable cast and characters, (h) familiar setting, (i) theme-based content, (j) fun activities, and (k) support from complementary materials such as books and manipulatives (Calvert, 1999).

INSTRUCTIONAL STRATEGIES

Although it is important to have access to effective educational technologies and media, the strategies used to present the content are just as important. Instructional strategies refer to the approaches used to achieve the learning objectives. The instructional strategies that are most conducive for the use and support of educational technologies are (a) direct instruction, (b) collaborative learning, (c) constructivist-based strategies, and (d) discovery learning (Conway, 1997).

The direct instruction strategy is grounded in behaviorist theory and focuses on the transmission of knowledge (Conway, 1997). Direct instruction is a structured approach that presents content in small steps with opportunities to check for learner understanding so as to elicit active successful participation from all learners. This form of instruction is particularly effective with facts, concepts, and procedures. The types of educational strategies that support direct instruction are (a) information gathering, (b) drill and practice, and (c) tutorials (Conway, 1997). Information gathering focuses on obtaining access to content and knowledge. Technology and media tools that may provide this access include but are not limited to Internet search engines (e.g., Google, Yahoo, MSN, and AOL), multimedia encyclopedias (e.g., MSN Encarta, Britannica, Grolier, World Book, and Wikipedia), education software (e.g., Plato Learning, The Learning Company, Sunburst), and television programming (e.g., PBS and Discovery). Drill and practice is the simplest and most common instructional strategy and is used to review and reinforce knowledge that has already been acquired. Examples of drill and practice include the use of didactic questioning, reading guides, and compare and contrast activities in educational software (e.g., Math Blaster).

Tutorials offer a one-to-one learning experience that provides opportunity for immediate feedback. This strategy typically presents or reviews new information with the goal to help the learner acquire basic facts and concepts. Examples of tutorials include the use of demonstrations, structured overviews and reviews, and guided viewing and listening activities (e.g., Mavis Beacon Teaches Typing).

The collaborative learning strategy is grounded in cognitive theory and emphasizes working in a group to acquire content knowledge or to achieve a task (Conway, 1997). The essential components of the collaborative learning strategy are (a) learners work in teams to acquire content knowledge, (b) teams are composed of individuals with diverse backgrounds and abilities, and (c) rewards/assessments are based on team achievements. Educational technologies that support the collaborative learning strategy are referred to as productivity tools. Productivity tools may include but are not limited to word processors (e.g., Microsoft Word, WordPerfect, or Apple's Pages), spreadsheets (e.g., Microsoft Excel and Corel Quattro Pro), databases (e.g., Microsoft Access and Filemaker Pro), drawing and paint software (e.g., CorelDraw, Adobe Photoshop and Illustrator, and Tux Paint), and presentation software (e.g., Microsoft PowerPoint and Apple's Keynote).

Constructivist strategies are based on the belief that one constructs knowledge in the context of creating personally meaningful artifacts (Nurrenbern, 2001). The collaboration and information/research software mentioned previously may be used to create instructional artifacts that are relevant and identified with specific students, groups, or communities. Learning occurs when learners create meaning based on their own past experiences and prior knowledge, rather than acquiring knowledge based on someone else's interpretation. Learners should be actively involved in choosing the instructional objectives. When working toward these learning goals, scaffolding or support should be provided as needed for each learner, depending on his or her ability and prior knowledge. The learning environment in which the subject material or content is delivered must connect the skills to which the learner is being exposed to its applicability and relevance in real-world situations (Ertmer & Newby, 1993). These learning environments should support discovery or inquiry-based learning, and allow for social interactions and role-playing (Dabbagh & Bannan-Ritland, 2005). Inquiry-based learning provides students with the opportunity to experience and learn about the world around them by questioning. Emphasis is placed on the process of thinking, and divergent thinking is not only supported but encouraged. Constructivist strategies include cognitive apprenticeship and situated learning.

Cognitive apprenticeship emphasizes teaching processes or learning through guided experience or discovery (Dabbagh & Bannan-Ritland, 2005). Components of cognitive apprenticeship include modeling, coaching, articulation, reflection, and exploration. Media can be used to enable students to work with experts in the completion of a task. The expert can model and provide feedback to the students by using technologies such as electronic mail, messaging, and chat. Additionally, webcasts may be used by the expert to provide students with demonstrations and modeling of specific tasks or content.

Situated learning is a constructivist strategy in which the learning takes place in an environment where the skills can be applied and practiced. Situated learning environments "provide instruction through the exploration of authentic scenarios, cases, or problems" (Dabbagh & Bannan-Ritland,

2005, p. 170). Media such as graphics, audio, and video can be used to realistically depict and represent cases and scenarios as well as embed them with relevant resources and information (Dabbagh & Bannan-Ritland, 2005). A multisensory constructivist strategy promotes transfer to real-life situations by not only helping students acquire knowledge but also showing them how to use it in the real world.

Discovery learning is based in cognitive theory and approaches instruction by having the learner interact with his or her environment or manipulate objects (Dabbagh & Bannan-Ritland, 2005). Discovery learning encourages problem solving and critical thinking skills. The learners are given tools in an environment and they are encouraged to experiment and explore. They are able to create their own goals or learning objectives and outcomes. Discovery learning can be implemented through the use of simulations or virtual environments. Simulations reproduce realistic situations in which the student is able to manipulate different variables and make decisions that will determine the outcome. These types of instructional strategies help integrate one's skills and knowledge and also help the learner develop problem-solving skills. Computer games have become popular vehicles for computer simulations. These computer simulation games (e.g., *RollerCoaster Tycoon, SimCity, The Sims, MS Flight Simulator,* and *Civilization*) are extremely popular and cover a variety of topics. For example, *SimCity* is a very popular game that allows students to build and maintain cities. *Civilization* is another simulation game that allows students to build and manage empires.

Simulations that allow the user to interact in the environment are referred to as virtual environments or virtual reality (Dabbagh & Bannan-Ritland, 2005). Virtual environments have the same benefits of simulations with the added feature of allowing students to become immersed in the learning environment. By taking a first-person view in the virtual environment, content, skills, and tasks become relevant and vital to the success of the student in the virtual space. One of the most popular virtual environments is *SecondLife* (and *Teen SecondLife*). *SecondLife* is an Internet-based virtual world in which users interact with one another through avatars to explore, meet others, socialize, participate in individual and group activities, and buy items and services from one another.

The use of direct instruction, collaborative, constructivist, and discovery-based strategies are key in the use of technology in educational settings. Technology provides opportunities for practice as well as the acquisition of new knowledge and skills. Technology also facilitates and supports collaboration through the use of tools like e-mail, chat, blogs, and file sharing. Last, the ability to learn in a multisensory, contextualized, simulated environment is possible through the use of educational technologies and media. Technology combined with the use of instructional strategies may also have a positive impact on the multicultural development of children.

MULTICULTURAL DEVELOPMENT

The use of technology has been shown to be effective with developing the multicultural development of young children by helping them (a) gain knowledge of the traditions, rituals, and practices of their own culture; (b) form an awareness of self and explore their individuality in relation to their place in a larger group; (c) build a sense of identification with others through the recognition of commonalities and an appreciation of differences; and (d) recognize unfair characterizations of groups and have the ability to empathize with them (Meadows & Murphy, 2004).

Calvert (1999) asserts that providing children of color with access to quality television programming and the latest information technologies may introduce them to new careers, create greater racial equality, and allow them to gain information about their own as well as other cultures. Direct instructional strategies may be used to teach children about their culture through tutorial and drill and practice activities. In addition to video, music, books, and magazines, technology and media provide access to multicultural content through online encyclopedias like *Encyclopedia Smithsonian, Wikipedia,* and *Digital Schomburg*. Providing children with access to quality media and technologies can help them obtain information about their culture and the culture of others (Calvert, 1999).

To help children form an awareness of self, explore their place in a larger group, and build a sense of identity with others, they should be exposed to technologies and media that reflect and affirm diverse cultures, languages, and heritages (Haugland & Shade, 1994). Technologies and media can positively influence the multicultural development of children by eliminating unfair characterizations of people, known as stereotypes. There is evidence that stereotyping may undermine a child's academic achievement in important ways (Aronson & Steele, 2005). Just knowledge of a stereotype can influence the thoughts and behavior of a person as well as impact the child's academic performance (Aronson & Steele, 2005). Steele and Aronson (1995) refer to this phenomenon as stereotype threat, which is the fear of confirming a negative stereotype associated with one's identified group. In addition to exerting extra pressure on the stereotype target, confirming a negative stereotype such as low performance poses a threat to three human motives: the need for competence, the need to appear competent to others, and the need to belong socially in a domain that is valued (Aronson & Steele, 2005). Black and Latino students are especially susceptible to stereotype threat and its effects because their identified groups are often the targets of negative stereotypes. Research has shown that Black students performed dramatically better in nonstereotype threat situations versus stereotype threat situations (Aronson & Steele, 2005).

There are two triggers for stereotype threat: ability evaluation and the salience of a social identity that is stereotyped as inferior in the ability domain (Aronson & Steele, 2005). Technologies and media can mitigate stereotyping and its triggers by presenting positive portrayals of groups, depicting people of color and women in roles of leadership and intelligence, and eliminating instances where a person's ability is evaluated based on his or her inclusion in a particular group. When children create their own images and depictions of themselves and their communities, they become more metacognitive about the content and how it is interpreted by others. By allowing students to use cultural contexts that are familiar and relevant to them, it may create a better link to academic content and support their multicultural development. Digital cameras and audio recorders are examples of hardware that allow children to create their own media. Software applications that allow children to create their own media include website tools (e.g., Adobe Dreamweaver, iWeb, and HTML) and digital content creation tools (e.g., iTunes, iPhoto, Adobe Photoshop, and iMovie). Virtual environments like SecondLife allow users to participate with others without regard for appearance, spoken language, or physical capability. You can create your own likeness or avatar, which may or may not be a true representation of your actual appearance. Additionally, the role-playing aspect of virtual environments allows users to experience the "life" of someone else from another gender or culture, which may result in increased sensitivity and understanding. Simulations allow users to have experiences and interactions that may be otherwise inaccessible. Having access to these "simulated experiences" may increase awareness, comfort level, and expertise of those who may have traditionally lacked access and exposure to these experiences.

In addition to mitigating stereotyping, technologies and media may also be useful in encouraging and supporting collaboration between and among groups. Collaboration between groups helps eliminate misconceptions about one another, whereas collaboration among groups has been found to have a positive impact on the acquisition of content knowledge. In Treisman's (1985) landmark study, he observed African American and Chinese American students to determine the practices that resulted in the achievement of or difficulty with mathematics. Treisman found that African American students were more likely to study alone, separated their study lives from their social activities, and did not seek assistance from each other or the teaching assistants/professors. The use of collaborative technologies (e.g., chats, blogs, e-mail, instant messaging, and webcasts) allows students to create communities and connect with people with whom they would otherwise not have been able to connect, such as potential role models, mentors, and peers from diverse groups. Through these connections, students can learn more about themselves, explore their relationship to others, and recognize commonalities between themselves and others as well as appreciate differences. Examples of these collaborative technologies include social networking websites like MySpace, FaceBook, and BlackPlanet. Although collaborative technologies have beneficial attributes, their possible misuses should also be acknowledged. If in the wrong hands, these technologies can be used to inappropriately gain access to children, allow children to have access to inappropriate people and information, and allow people to conceal their identities and misrepresent their motives. With that said, the use of collaborative technologies with children requires the guidance of parents, teachers, and other caregivers.

Students are constantly exposed to the messages conveyed and materials created by the ever-changing and abundance of media forms readily available to them. Furthermore, youth are willing consumers of all that these technologies have to offer. It is for these reasons that the use of technologies and media in educational settings has the potential of having a significant influence on the intellectual as well as multicultural development of children. Therefore, the driving force for educators should be to maximize the positive capabilities of technologies and media while minimizing potential negative effects.

REFERENCES

Aronson, J., & Steele, C. M. (2005). Stereotypes and the fragility of academic competence, motivation, and self-concept. In A. Elliot & C. Dweck (Eds.), *The handbook of competence* (pp. 436–456). New York: Guilford Press.

Calvert, S. (1999). *Children's journey through the information age.* Boston: McGraw-Hill College.

Clark, K. (1998). Intersection of instructional television and computer assisted learning: Implications for research paradigms. In J. Asamen & G. Berry (Eds.), *Research paradigms in the study of television and social behavior* (pp. 287–304). Thousand Oaks, CA: Sage.

Clark, K. (2005). Serving underserved communities with instructional technologies: Giving them what they need not what you want. *Urban Education, 40*(4), 430–445.

Conway, J. (1997). *Educational technology's effect on models of instruction.* Retrieved December 16, 2006, from http://copland.udel.edu/jconway/EDST666.htm

Dabbagh, N., & Bannan-Ritland, B. (2005). Online learning: Concepts, strategies, and application. Upper Saddle River, NJ: Pearson Merrill Prentice Hall.

Ertmer, P. A., & Newby, T. J. (1993). Behaviorism, cognitivism, constructivism: Comparing critical features from a design perspective. *Performance Improvement Quarterly, 6*(4) 50–72.

Haugland, S. W., & Shade, D. D. (1994). Software evaluation for young children. In J. L. Wright & D. D. Shade (Eds.), *Young children: Active learners in a technological age* (pp. 63–76). Washington, DC: National Association of the Education of Young Children (NAEYC).

Heinich, R., Molenda, M., Russell, J., & Smaldino, S. (2002). *Instructional media and technologies for learning.* Upper Saddle River, NJ: Merrill Prentice Hall.

Jonassen, D., Howland, J., Moore, J., & Marra, R. (2003). *Learning to solve problems with technology: A constructivist perspective.* Upper Saddle River, NJ: Merrill Prentice Hall.

Laffey, J. M., Musser, D., & Tupper, T. (1998). A computer-mediated support system for project based learning. *Educational Technology Research and Development, 46*(1), 73–86.

Meadows, M., & Murphy, F. (2004). Using technology in early childhood environments to strengthen cultural connections. *Information Technology in Childhood Education Annual, 1,* 39–47.

Nurrenbern, S. C. (2001). Piaget's theory of intellectual development revisited. *Journal of Chemical Education, 78*(8), 1107–1110.

Peck, K. L., & Dorricott, D. (1994). Why use technology? *Educational Leadership, 51*(7), 11–14.

Roschelle, J. M., Pea, R. D., Hoadley, C. M., Gordin, D. N., & Means, B. M. (2000). Changing how and what children learn in school with computer-based technologies. *Children and Computer Technology, 10*(2), 76–101.

Steele, C. M., & Aronson, J. (1995). Stereotype threat and the intellectual test performance of African-Americans. *Journal of Personality and Social Psychology, 69,* 797–811.

Treisman, P. (1985). *A study of the mathematics achievement of Black students at the University of California, Berkeley.* Unpublished doctoral dissertation, University of California, Berkeley.

CHAPTER 27

The Changing Landscape

Media Advocacy for the New Millennium

LAURIE A. TROTTA

The 2001 Academy Awards represented an exciting moment for African Americans. For the first time in history, a Black woman, Halle Berry, swept up to the sainted stage and accepted her award for Best Actress. Minutes later, another Black thespian, Denzel Washington, joined Ms. Berry, becoming the first African American to take home the coveted Best Actor Oscar in almost 40 years. To make the scene all the more poignant, Sidney Poitier—who won the Best Actor statuette in 1963 for the film *Lilies of the Field*—was in the audience, wife and family around him, smiling down beneficently. This was indeed a historic day, one that Black and media activists could only have dreamed of after decades of protesting, among other inequities in the entertainment business, the lack of nonstereotyped, challenging roles for people of color.

Was the opening of roles for these talented actors the result of advocates working in Hollywood to promote entertainment that reflects the complexion of society? Could it be that Hollywood was changing? Five years later, in the 2006 Academy Award race, as many as eight Black, Latino, and Asian artists were all leading contenders for Oscars. "As studios expand their worldview beyond the West—and see the potential for ticket sales overseas—minority actors and racially diverse themes are increasingly finding their way onto the big screen," says Scott Bowles (2007, p. D1) of *USA Today*. "The industry is willing to accept globalization and that we are all connected. . . . People are interested in stories beyond their own culture" (Bowles, 2007, p. D1).

This may well be heartening news for activists interested in a more diverse media environment. Unfortunately, the multiculturalism described in the previous paragraph is not the regular fare of many films and other media, including television news. One study finds that news media unduly connects youth to crime and violence and that youth of color are overrepresented as perpetrators and underrepresented as victims of crime (Dorfman & Schiraldi, 2001).

Film and television provide many children with their first exposure to people of other ethnicities, religions, and cultures. What they see on-screen can and does impact their attitudes about and treatment of others (Valenti, 2000). Children who grow up seeing endless negative images of themselves in the media can experience self-perception and self-esteem problems. "It hurts and has a negative impact when you don't see your own people onscreen," says Michael Smith (personal interview with Stephanie Carbone for Mediascope, July 9, 1997), founder and director of the American Indian Film Institute.

For more than six decades, media activists have been working to create a more equitable media environment. During the 1960s and 1970s, disgruntled members of society took radical action to change what they saw as disturbing images emanating from their television sets and on the big screen. Gay rights advocates stormed the offices of network executives to protest poor representation of their group. Latinos, Italian Americans, Asian Americans, German Americans, Native Americans, Gray Panthers, women's groups, children's groups, people with disabilities—all organized over complaints about negative imagery onscreen (Montgomery, 1989). In one famous case, a group of Boston mothers were so angered by the regular diet of violence and mayhem on children's TV, they took their complaints to the halls of Congress, eventually winning legislation designed to curb violence and enhance the educational nature of children's television fare. When members of the public unite in opposition or support of a certain issue, an advocacy group is born. One Washington-based group characterizes advocacy as such:

> All advocacy involves is making a case in favor of a particular cause (such as comprehensive sex education) and trying to get others to support it as well. . . . A comprehensive advocacy campaign will first and foremost influence political support for a program by educating policy makers. Policy makers can include national, state, or local legislators, county or city council members, school board members, or anyone else in a position to promote or reject proposals that you care about. Another important target for advocacy campaigns is the public, since public desires affect political decisions. A campaign aimed at the public could target a general community or a specific group such as parents in a particular neighborhood. The only prerequisite to being an advocate is being committed to the issue. (Advocates for Youth, 2007, ¶ 1–3)

Such impassioned individuals and groups have led landmark campaigns that helped in many ways to change what we see in the media, and we will examine their continuing efforts more fully in this chapter. Their work often hinges on tactics that involve taking on the existing power structure: the networks, studios, judicial system, and federal government. They court established print and electronic news media to report on their issues, form coalitions with like-minded organizations, and fight what is akin to hand-to-hand combat with those who wield the power to create, legislate, and change media.

And yet today, advocacy, as we know it, is evolving. Perhaps the most powerful force driving that change can be described in two words: the Internet. Global communications have brought about seismic shifts in how change can occur. No longer are people held hostage to the Powers That Be in the media, for just about anyone can create their own alternative. If you do not like a Hollywood film, you can make your own and show it on Google Video. Or, you can respond to the images, put that on YouTube, and invite others to build on your ideas. Today, advocacy groups who want to reach, for example, Asian American youth, can create their own content and put it on their website and market that website through grassroots outreach, thereby circumventing big media entirely. While traditional media outlets certainly remain important to spreading messages and influencing viewers, the need to depend solely on the conglomerates has simply fallen away.

Further, a shift in approaches to funding advocacy efforts is slowly taking shape. Some advocates are moving away from philanthropies that provide funding and toward a model wherein their organizations are more like corporations that are designed to do good but also to be self-sustaining entities, forming a snowball effect for social change. Indeed, the Internet—which has already opened up pathways to media access never before imagined—also is making new funding sources available for advocates. Literally billions of dollars wielded by post–baby boomer entrepreneurs who have built vast fortunes around innovative ideas for using this new technology have become available. A new breed of technologically savvy philanthropists is emerging who want to apply the knowledge gleaned from online business success to address today's problems. As one of these new waves of advocates proudly states in its advertising campaign, "Social Change is Changing" (Hollywood Hill, 2006/2007, p. 12).

Have the efforts of media advocates made a difference in what we see in filmed entertainment? Is our media landscape somehow a better place because they toiled? Where does the future lie for media advocacy? This chapter will trace the roots of children's media advocacy since the beginning of the television era. It will use texts, interviews, Internet data, and journalistic and scholarly reports, as well as personal accounts from professionals, to trace the trajectory and nature of media advocacy and the challenges for the future of these organizations. Finally, we will look at the new breed of social issues workers raised on the Internet with goals designed to carry media advocacy well into the mid-21st century. It is hoped that the exploration of where we have been will help illuminate the road ahead for future generations.

INTRODUCTION

When television swept through American living rooms in the late 1940s, a small percentage of people, mostly parents, educators, and religious leaders, expressed concern over what influence this new medium might have on viewers. But the voices of these early advocates were no match for the glamour and novelty of the light-emitting wooden boxes turning up in millions of American homes seemingly overnight. Indeed, Americans' love affair with television had begun; from 1948–1952, the number of sets in American households rose from 250,000 to 17 million (Head & Sterling, 1982).

As the old radio networks seized primary control of television programming and the medium more deeply penetrated American lives, parents and education, social, and religious groups were left to their own devices to meaningfully respond to the offerings and images they found troublesome for young viewers (Trotta, 2001). But over time, key media advocacy groups emerged to serve as voices on socially relevant issues such as on-screen violence or stereotyping (Trotta, 2001), and later spokespeople for policy issues surrounding Internet privacy and universal access. Eventually, people from the full spectrum of groups have protested to the television and film community regarding racial stereotypes, sexual and gender health, cultural issues, public health issues, violence, and disabilities issues. All have voiced concern over how the media portrays them and how those portrayals affect perceptions of them in real life.

These nonprofit advocacy groups adopted a variety of approaches, both radical and conservative, for working to change what we see on TV, inform the public about its rights, and educate the public on the effects of media on viewers (Trotta, 2001). Although variances in type, audience served, focus, budget, and size are the norm in media advocacy groups, some commonalties of approach do exist. Most of the organizations tend to weave together several of these approaches to create a mosaic of activities and initiatives that span audiences as well as methodologies. The following methods for initiating change on television and other forms of screened entertainment have been used by media advocates (Trotta, 2001, pp. 700–701):

1. Working through government channels to effect policy change, e.g., lobbying Congress and the Federal Communication Commission (FCC), testifying before government hearings, and filing FCC petitions to deny broadcast licenses or petitions of proposed rule making
2. Mobilizing the public around its rights under public interest clauses of broadcasting regulations
3. Sponsoring informational opportunities (e.g., conferences, workshops, and seminars) for industry executives and creative professionals to raise awareness and offering positive reinforcement in the forms of awards and seals of approval for perceived excellence in programming
4. Conducting research of parents on media-related issues in which the results are used to inform the public, parents, government, journalists, and the creative community and broadcasters
5. Offering technical and consultative services or referrals to the entertainment industry to provide information on sensitive depictions in early stages of a project's development
6. Educating parents, teachers, and children of the hazards of media consumption through media literacy efforts (e.g., publishing and training)
7. Organizing consumer-based initiatives (e.g., letter writing campaigns, boycotts) to exert pressure on advertisers, sponsors, and broadcasters to prohibit screening of individual episodes or movies
8. Orchestrating news media campaigns against individual programs, networks, or issues to help build awareness among the general public as well as in pressuring advertisers and broadcasters to effect change

EFFECTIVENESS OF ADVOCACY EFFORTS

The effects of these advocacy groups on influencing entertainment have been sporadic, and have historically ebbed and flowed along with the tides of popular opinion, politics, and personal relationships with individuals in the entertainment industry. It is difficult to gauge [progress made by advocacy efforts], as much of the social change in the broadcast industry has occurred slowly, the results of a gathering of many forces and pressures over time. Government has displayed a history of voicing concern over programming issues but has taken a very precautionary approach towards regulation (Trotta, 2001, p. 701).

The commitment an advocate brings to the issue is often fraught with challenges. The often underfunded nonprofit consumer groups are engaging politically with some of the largest media corporations in the world, which possess the economic and political infrastructure that present formidable obstacles (Montgomery, 2007).

Yet progress has been made. For example, individual producers and writers have come forth with truly educational and entertaining programming for children, especially preschoolers. Nickelodeon/Noggin now offers 24 hours of commercial-free programming for young children; most PBS stations dedicate a portion of their broadcast day to notable children's programming, while the networks provide a host of weekend and afternoon shows for young viewers that is largely devoid of the ultraviolent and consumer-oriented content that was, during the 1980s, regular fare. Programs such as Nickelodeon's *Dora the Explorer,* PBS's *Cyberchase*, which teaches math concepts to middle schoolers, and Discovery's *Magic School Bus* are just a few that have proven that television can be both educational and entertaining. As one veteran children's producer said,

> When I was working in children's programming in the 80s, it was really more about selling to the kids, and there was a lot of violence. But there has been a pulling back from this way of thinking today and there is some truly fine programming out there now. It may have been the results of advocacy groups in part, but these changes really must come down from the top. (N. Steingard, personal interview, January 12, 2007)

Clearly, the advocacy movement has had an effect on building awareness of issues, motivating and inspiring industry professionals, and utilizing government processes to lobby for change. It must be noted that the underlying commerciality of the television business will—unless enormous structural changes to the system are made—most likely remain a primary consideration in the industry. However, advocates represent the public, which votes by its viewing selections, supporting quality programming for children when available. Advocates have successfully exerted government pressure in the past, and as their ranks grow, those changes may happen more quickly (Trotta, 2001, p. 701).

Meeting the expenses of advocacy work remains a struggle. Advocates have been resigned to spending a percentage of their time writing grants, hiring development professionals, and cultivating relationships with philanthropic organizations to fund their efforts. Far-sighted organizations such as the Carnegie Corporation, the Robert Wood Johnson Foundation, the Markle Foundation, the Henry J. Kaiser Family Foundation, and dozens of others fund media advocacy work, either on a project-by-project scale or through general program support. But this model requires an ongoing dependence on outside funding, leaving some advocates at the mercy of changing winds in the philanthropic world. Kathryn C. Montgomery, now a professor at American University, is the former director of the powerful Center for Media Education, now defunct. She recalls,

> It was hard to raise money. We were successful at it, but it was a real challenge. Some funders may simply not be interested, others change their focus, leadership, and missions, and so you constantly have to be very creative and develop projects that are attractive to them. And sometimes this means that your core projects are only held together by your own passion and dedication. (K. C. Montgomery, personal interview, January 19, 2007)

Further complicating the issue is the sense that the funding world constitutes a "small pond," wherein many of the advocates working toward similar goals are, in fact, competing for the same pot of money from key philanthropies.

Another challenge for media advocacy has been the lack of continuity among organizational leaders. Nonprofits rise and fall as issues come to the fore and then recede, and follow-up efforts can be neglected. In 2000, a survey was conducted of 33 media advocacy organizations working in the United States (Trotta, 2001). Of these, nine were regarded as having a visible presence in Hollywood and were considered the major groups working to effect change. Of these, only four are still working in entertainment industry advocacy as of January 2007, two no longer exist, and the others have changed focus away from Hollywood or work in media literacy only. Each of these organizations had expertise in advocating in a focused area. When they moved on, if no remaining group stepped in to fill the gap, a vacuum ensued.

"An organization has its time," says Kathy Montgomery (personal interview, January 19, 2007), who has gone on to teach what she sees as the next generation of advocates. She states,

> But continuity is an ongoing concern. When we first formed CME we saw a void in the media reform leadership, which had been so strong in the 1970s. Why did this happen? Strong leaders had gone to work in the Carter administration, deregulation cut them down, funders left. . . . There was major jockeying on the part of the powerful media corporations in the policy arena, but very little representation of the public interest. So we formed CME. When we closed, several organizations picked up aspects of our work, but not all of it continued. It's a real problem.

A BRIEF HISTORY OF CHILDREN'S MEDIA ADVOCACY

Debating whether electronic communications have educational value or are simply vehicles of commercialization goes back to the time when radio became readily available after World War I (Trotta, 2001). Commercial enterprises (e.g., Westinghouse and AT&T) as well as educational, community, and religious groups were granted government licenses to broadcast over the public airwaves. However, public service stations were soon outdone by the wealthier commercial stations as the latter could offer listeners professional quality and continuous programming. As public service stations surrendered their licenses to broadcast, mass commercialization of the medium resulted. In response to this turn of events, "the government ruled that commercial stations must offer airtime to serve the public interest" (Trotta, 2001, p. 702).

Television soon replaced radio as America's source of broadcast entertainment. During the nascent era of the television industry, primary concern was centered on the effects of viewing violence. Some 30 years passed before media advocates added such issues as diversity and multiculturalism, sexual and gender issues, unbridled consumerism, mediocrity of programming, and universal access to their efforts.

Concern regarding the viewing of violent TV content emerged in the early 1950s as a way to explain the rise in juvenile crime and crime in general experienced during this time period, drawing attention to the need for quality programming for children (Trotta, 2001). This was during a time when only 23.5% of families owned a television set and visual broadcasts were confined to major metropolitan areas (Turow, 1981). In fact, popular magazines such as *Time* and *Newsweek* published research indicating children's programming was among the most violent on the air, and the National Association for Better Radio and Television (NAFBRAT), an advocacy group, reported that the amount of crime on television should concern parents (Turow, 1981).

In 1952, Congress held hearings on broadcast violence to examine whether radio and television could account for real-world violence (Turow, 1981). The networks argued there was no established causal relationship that tied on-screen violence to society's mayhem. In the first edition of the Television Code of 1952, the National Association of Broadcasters (NAB) included a section titled "Responsibility to

Children." But this section did not provide specific rules to assist broadcasters in making responsible choices in the children's programming they elected to air (Turow, 1981).

In 1960, the Federal Communications Commission (FCC) also acknowledged the special needs of children in regards to television programming, but like the NAB Television Code, the FCC did not offer specific guidelines regarding content (Head & Sterling, 1982). One year later, FCC Chairman Newton Minow coined the description "a vast wasteland" in referring to the state of television programming when he spoke before the attendees of the national NAB conference (Minow & Lamay, 1995). He admonished programmers "for failing to create a range of informative and inspirational programs that served the public interest" (Trotta, 2001, p. 702). Also in 1961, Senator Thomas Dodd of Connecticut led more television violence hearings on Capitol Hill, which were again countered by networks disputing that a contributory relationship exists between action-adventure violence and juvenile crime (Trotta, 2001).

In 1967, University of Pennsylvania professor George Gerbner began his 30-year study of TV violence (Trotta, 2001). Then, in 1972, the Surgeon General issued a major report documenting a link between screen violence and aggressive behavior (Trotta, 2001).

Action for Children's Television (ACT) was formed in 1968 by a group of women in the Boston area who wanted to increase the television programming choices available to children (Trotta, 2001). ACT persuaded the FCC to hold hearings of proposed rule making that would govern facets of children's programming. "People say the FCC was impenetrable, but in reality, we went to Washington in 1970 and were able to meet with six of the seven commissioners," says Peggy Charren, ACT's long-time president (personal interview, August 17, 1999, as cited in Trotta, 2001). ACT wanted rules requiring at least 7 hours of children's programming throughout the week, not just on weekend mornings, but this rule-making request was rejected by the FCC. In lieu of rule making, the FCC issued a policy statement in 1974 that urged broadcasters to voluntarily improve children's programming. An outgrowth of this urging by the FCC was the NAB Television Code Board's adoption of special advertising rules for children's programs (Head & Sterling, 1982).

Several years later, ACT and other groups, such as the national PTA, appointed a Children's Television Task Force to investigate the extent to which broadcasters had complied with the 1974 FCC policy statement. Although the task force found some improvement in advertising practices, marginal progress was found in children's television programming (Head & Sterling, 1982). In 1980, incoming FCC chair Mark Fowler ended efforts toward regulation, and, instead, supported deregulation for all forms of television programming, including children's programming. Advocates took the cause to Congress, and the Children's Television Act of 1990 (CTA) was passed to improve educational broadcast programming for children (Trotta, 1998).

The FCC was tasked with the responsibility to develop the guidelines to enforce the CTA, resulting in the Children's TV Rules of 1996 (Trotta, 2001). The rules included the following: (a) number of hours children's educational programming must air, (b) definition of educational programming, and (c) measures to improve public access to the programming. Television stations that do not comply with the rules risk losing their licenses to operate. But with no government oversight of compliance, it falls to citizens and advocates to monitor the progress of broadcasters.

In 2004, the FCC unanimously ruled on the ways in which broadcasters will provide educational programming to children as TV transitions from analog to digital. As a result, broadcasters must label educational/informational programming with a uniform "E/I" symbol throughout the duration of a show (Children Now, 2006).

MULTICULTURALISM ON-SCREEN

Generally, activists are concerned about two issues in media content: first, the lack of representation on-screen, witnessed by an imbalance in the depictions of their group; and second, the nature of the representations that are depicted, which are too often considered stereotypical. For example, in the 2003–2004 broadcast season, Latino characters were more likely to appear on real-life shows such as *Cops* and *America's Most Wanted,* often as criminals, than on situation comedies. They are also more likely to hold low-status jobs than members of other racial groups (Children Now, 2004).

In a 1998 report, media researcher George Gerbner followed up on the results of a 1993 study commissioned by the Screen Actors Guild. It was found that characters on prime-time and daytime television had incrementally improved in regards to diversity, although men still outnumbered women and most minority groups remained underrepresented. More specifically, for every one female character, there were two male characters (Gerbner, 1998). Viewers saw African American male characters increased to 171% of their proportion to the U.S. population from 1994–1997, although this same change did not occur for African American female characters; Asian/Pacific Islander and Latino characters, as well as characters 65 and older, were seen well under their proportional rate in the U.S. population (Gerbner, 1998). Characters with disabilities decreased, and low-income characters were virtually nonexistent (Gerbner, 1998). Some years later (2003–2004 broadcast season), the advocacy group Children Now (2004) reported, "The vast majority of programs shown on prime time—especially those most watched by youth audiences—depicted a world . . . where some racial groups remain non-existent and where males significantly outnumber females" (p. 12).

Employment figures released by the Screen Actors Guild (SAG) in 1998 showed that the percentage of SAG roles going to Native Americans, Latinos, and African Americans had actually declined from the prior year (Valenti, 2000). In 1999, it came to light that not one person of color had a starring role in any of the 26 network shows of the 1999 television season (Valenti, 2000). Activist groups—led by the National Association for the Advancement of Colored People's (NAACP) president, Kweisi Mfume—organized and demanded action. In 2000, Mfume and other minority leaders reached groundbreaking diversity agreements with television networks to bring more people of color to both the creative and the business sides of the television industry (Valenti, 2000). The coalition also threatened government intervention. Mfume, a former Maryland congressman, broached the need for government regulation for a "content-neutral rule" in an interview with Connie Chung at the National Association of Television Programming Executives Conference in New Orleans (Lorenz, 2000).

Formed in New York in 1985 to protest the *New York Post* AIDS coverage, the Gay & Lesbian Alliance Against Defamation (GLAAD) reports that prior to their founding, representations of lesbians and gay men tended to fall into one of two categories: "defamatory or non-existent." Since its inception, GLAAD claims to have changed the way lesbians and gay men are portrayed on the screen and in the news. "*Entertainment*

Weekly named GLAAD one of Hollywood's most powerful entities, and the *Los Angeles Times* described GLAAD as 'possibly the most successful organization lobbying the media for inclusion'" (GLAAD, 2007, ¶ 2).

The granting of high-profile awards for positive depictions is another technique employed by advocates. Among the host of prizes are GLAAD's annual Media Awards; the National Council on La Raza's ALMA Awards, celebrating the contributions of Latinos; the Prism Awards for accurate portrayals of substance abuse; and the Sentinel for Health Awards sponsored by the federal Centers for Disease Control, which congratulate accurate and entertaining public health information on-screen.

INFLUENCING CONTENT—PUBLIC HEALTH REACHES OUT TO MEDIA

Public health experts have long established the value of communicating with the public through entertainment products. Studies have shown that learning occurs through storytelling, and the learning is heightened when lessons are voiced by characters viewers care about (Trotta, 1998). Thus, it remains vital for advocacy groups to bring their messages to established media.

During the 1980s and 1990s, many advocacy groups—and even the federal government—began to internalize the importance of these ideas. A number of nonprofit organizations exist today whose primary mission is to work with the entertainment industry on depictions of a variety of social and health issues. These range from gender and race, to teen sexuality and violence, to population, environment, and mental health. These organizations generally work directly with the creative community, providing accurate information on health issues in a positive, industry-friendly fashion. National organizations whose primary mission is directly health-care related, such as the American Medical Association, the American Academy of Pediatrics, and the Centers for Disease Control and Prevention, strongly believe in the value of reaching out to the entertainment industry and have created media information programs (W. E. Duke & Company, 2001).

Many health and nonprofit groups hired people with various backgrounds—from academia, entertainment, marketing, public relations, and journalism—to begin to reach out to entertainment industry professionals who create content. The mission of these entertainment resource professionals, as they are known, is to encourage the creative community to incorporate storylines and characters into their products that will, in an entertaining way, educate the viewing public about a certain issue. In this way, public health information can reach the public, and television and film creators could serve not only as entertainers, but—albeit as a secondary byproduct—educators as well.

But the points of entry are sometimes difficult to determine. Filmed entertainment is collaborative. It is created through a unique amalgamation of associations, partnerships, and alliances between the major studios, mini majors, networks, distribution companies, the stars themselves, and a group of writers, directors, and producers who drive the creative process. Advocates attempting this work need to first and foremost understand the business to which they are attempting to gain entry as well as the nature of most of television and film: to entertain. Personal relationships are key. For example, a Mediascope executive met the executive producer of a hit network police show at a cocktail party. During the course of their conversation, the executive mentioned her work in violence and public health, and the producer expressed interest. Information was sent to him the next day, and a link was forged between the issue of violence depiction and a prime-time program.

Sensitive issues can emerge when any outside force attempts to influence an artist or artistic endeavor. Concerns over censorship can arise, especially when one of the nonprofit organizations has government affiliations. This was illustrated in the experiment by the Office of National Drug Control Policy in the 2000 programming year to offer tax incentives to programs that used antidrug messages. Most writers consider themselves artists, and any whiff of attempting to unduly influence their work, as opposed to offering helpful ideas, will be rebuffed immediately.

The professionals working to supply the entertainment industry with information for many multicultural and health issues have begun to build a methodology for success in their field. In 2006, they formed a collegial association, the Entertainment Resources Professional Association (ERPA), in which colleagues share information, strategies, and ideas. Members of ERPA range from GLAAD to the National Youth Anti-Drug Campaign, to the American Association of Pediatrics, to Suicide Awareness Violence in Education.

"Nonprofits attempting to bring their issue to the entertainment industry must first understand the special audience they are attempting to reach," says Lisa Cho Allen (personal interview, January 3, 2007), who cofounded ERPA in 2006 with Deborah Glick, Sc.D., Director of the Health and Media Research Center, University of California, Los Angeles, School of Public Health, and Rachel Flores, also of UCLA. Furthermore, Allen observes,

> Writers for entertainment products are interested in emotional truth. If an issue cannot be dramatized and integrated into a story, then it most likely will not make it into programming. Executives at advocacy organizations must also realize that the types of communications in entertainment outreach are different from a more traditional outreach campaign. The entertainment industry has the ability to dramatize an issue, to create empathy, a sense of shared understanding, as no other outreach work can do. But advocates will not get the message across in the same manner as they will in a traditional print or outreach campaign.

Allen also suggests that success in this field does not have to be entire programs or storylines built around issues. Simply having a character in passing comment on the importance, for example, of a health issue, can "reach literally millions of viewers and has the potential to open a window for them."

Allen (personal interview, January 6, 2007) observes that entertainment resource professionals now have years of experience working with the industry. And unlike a decade ago, where caution was exercised to gain access to the industry, today the work of advocates is more valued. She adds,

> At the same time, people working in entertainment and health recognize that media is constantly changing and evolving, and we are becoming more savvy about keeping up with those changes. There are more ways to get at media than there were before, and if you are smart and want to be involved in advocacy you can reach around Hollywood as well.

Allen continues,

> Youth are multiconsuming media at a much faster rate than ever before—instant messaging and web surfing and watching TV and talking on their cell all at the same time. Being aware that this is happening and taking advantage of these opportunities is important to keep in mind. You can work with filmmakers at all different levels, post your own series of animation on your own site, and create your own content. This is an exciting time to be working in this field. The possibilities are endless.

A NEW BREED OF ACTIVISM

As the 21st century pulses forward, a new breed of activists may be just on the horizon. Celebrities such as Bono, Drew Barrymore, Geena Davis, and others are using the power of fame to push social activism to the fore. Others working behind the scenes in Hollywood are using the power of global media to promote their causes. These new organizations are self-sustaining, savvy, and run as for-profit businesses. Their ideas are bold, and even their language represents a new dramatic approach. Ariel Hauter is a 20-something Los Angelino who cofounded The Hollywood Hill, a group of entertainment industry heavy hitters prepared to use the power of entertainment, the Internet, and new technologies to help solve social ills. Their website states,

> A new generation of Hollywood activists is taking over. But their focus is not on the Democratic Party . . . they have set their sights much higher. The world is now small and flat. And with new technologies, sciences, and the Internet, these world-renowned creators and powerbrokers are exercising their muscle to truly change the world. Considering the current threats against humanity, it's not a minute too soon. (Hollywood Hill, n.d.)

Hauter and his colleagues are building "a combination think-tank, event facility, media production studio, technology innovation lab, and a multi-pronged fundraising operation to provide a . . . self-sustaining social change machine to . . . effect global responsibility" (Hollywood Hill, n.d., ¶ 8). According to Hollywood Hill (n.d.), "Hollywood is in transition" and "[leaders] are looking for the corporate version of marching down the streets" (¶ 1). "Hollywood has matured into a business savvy industrial complex complete with large financial resources, tremendous influence, and yet a strong sense of social responsibility" (Hollywood Hill, n.d., ¶ 7). Hollywood Hill (n.d.) further says,

> Such an ambitious project is not for the faint of heart. It's for those who understand the days of "Save the Whales" are over. Affecting change in a global community controlled by many far-reaching power centers requires having a solid foundation, a self-sustaining model, and serious talent and resources. It also requires a new mode of thinking . . . a hybrid approach, based on proven techniques, but adapted to a new marketplace with new tools. (¶ 11)

Another exciting model for social change that utilizes the power of media is that of Participant Productions. This film production company blasted onto the scene in 2004 and in just 3 years has produced such critically acclaimed films as *Chicago 10; Syriana* (in partnership with Warner Bros.); *An Inconvenient Truth; Good Night, and Good Luck* (with Warner Independent Pictures, Section 8 and 2929 Entertainment); and *Fast Food Nation*. Participant Productions (n.d.) believes,

> A good story well told can truly make a difference in how one sees the world. Whether it is a feature film, documentary or other form of media, Participant exists to tell compelling, entertaining stories that also create awareness of the real issues that shape our lives. We seek to entertain our audiences first, then to invite them to participate in making a difference next. (Participant Productions, ¶ 1)

Furthermore,

> Integral to Participant's mission is our commitment to creating specific social action campaigns for each film and documentary. These campaigns are designed to give a voice to issues that resonate in the films. We partner with social sector organizations, non-profits and corporations who are committed to creating an open

> forum for discussion, education and who can, in partnership with Participant, offer specific ways for audience members to get involved and to take action. (Participant Productions, ¶ 8)

The force behind this company is Internet millionaire Jeff Skoll, the first president of ebay.

Time will tell whether these groups and others like them will use the power of media to effect real social change. Whatever their successes, they represent a new breed of entrepreneurial-style activists ready to harness the power of corporate America and technology to circumvent the traditional paths of advocacy and spur change on a massive scale.

CONCLUSION

The struggle between advocates and the media will continue, and now includes broader definitions of entertainment such as video, computer games, and all digital media. As the forms of media become more engaging, and the time spent interacting with media is ever increasing, the efforts of advocacy groups must keep pace. Advocates must find ways to keep the flame burning from one leader to the next, and they must continue to keep abreast of new ways of reaching audiences through nontraditional methods such as entertainment industry outreach and direct campaigns through new media. They must find new modes of funding, ideally self-sustaining, that allow them to focus on the important work at hand. At the same time, bold new forms of advocacy are bringing new tactics to activism, using entertainment products and the Internet and adopting corporate models to bring causes directly to millions of potential allies on a global scale. Time will see what accomplishments they will bring and where they will take us.

REFERENCES

Advocates for Youth. (2007). Advocacy for adolescent reproductive and sexual health. Retrieved February 22, 2007, from http://www.advocatesforyouth.org/advocacy.htm

Bowles, S. (2007, Jan. 22). Oscar catches up with world culture. *USA Today,* p. D1.

Children Now. (2004). *Fall colors: 2003–2004 report.* Oakland, CA: Author.

Children Now. (2006, Winter). Educational TV policy timeline. *Children & the Media Issue Brief, 1*(1). Retrieved from http://www.childrennow.org/assets/pdf/issues_media_issuebrief_winter2006.pdf

Dorfman, L., & Schiraldi, V. (2001, April). *Off balance: Youth, race, and crime in the news executive summary.* Retrieved February 22, 2007, from http://www.buildingblocksforyouth.org/media/exec.html

Gay & Lesbian Alliance Against Defamation. (2007). *Our history.* Retrieved February 22, 2007, from http://www.GLAAD.org/about/history.php?

Gerbner, G. (1998). *Casting the American scene: A look at the characters on prime time and daytime television from 1994–1998* [Screen Actors Guild report, December 1998]. Retrieved April 5, 2007, from http://www.media-awareness.ca/english/resources/research_documents/reports/diversity/american_scene.cfm

Head, S. W., & Sterling, C. H. (1982). Broadcasting in America: A survey of television, radio, and new technologies (4th ed.). Boston: Houghton Mifflin.

Hollywood Hill. (2006/2007, Dec./Jan.). *Moving Pictures Magazine, 12.*

Hollywood Hill. (n.d.). *Our mission.* Retrieved February 22, 2007, from http://www.hhill.org/hill/about_mission

Lorenz, L. (2000, January 27). NAACP vigilant to minorities. *Extra, Extra, the NATPE 2000 Newsletter.*

Minow, N. N., & Lamay, C. L. (1995). *Abandoned in the wasteland: Children, television and the first amendment.* New York: Hill and Wang.

Montgomery, K. C. (1989). *Target: Prime time.* New York: Oxford University Press.

Montgomery, K. C. (2007). Advocating children's television. In J. A Bryant, *The children's television community* (pp. 229–257). Mahwah, NJ: Lawrence Erlbaum.

Participant Productions. (n.d.). *About Participant.* Retrieved February 23, 2007, from http://www.participantproductions.com/company/About+Participant/

Trotta, L. (1998). *Building blocks: A guide for creating children's educational television.* Studio City, CA: Mediascope Press.

Trotta, L. (2001). Children's advocacy: A history and analysis. In D. G. Singer & J. L. Singer (Eds.), *Handbook of children and the media* (pp. 699–719). Thousand Oaks, CA: Sage.

Turow, J. (1981). *Entertainment, education, and the hard sell: Three decades of network children's television.* New York: Praeger.

Valenti, F. M. (2000). *More than a movie: Ethics in entertainment.* Boulder, CO: Westview Press.

W. E. Duke & Company. (2001). *Developing a Hollywood health information service for the entertainment industry.* Retrieved March 29, 2007, from http://www.rwjf.org/reports/grr/038104.htm?gsa=1#int_grantinfo

CHAPTER 28

The Role of Parents and Caregivers in Creating a Healthy Multicultural Media Environment for Children

CHRISTINA ROMANO GLAUBKE

PATTI MILLER

Young children in the United States are growing up in an increasingly diverse society. In fact, they will be the first generation to become adults in an America where people of color are the numeric majority (Children Now, 1999). According to the 2000 census, 39% of children in the United States are children of color, compared with 31% in 1990 (O'Hare, 2001), and that number is steadily increasing. Three fourths of children say they have best friends of other races or ethnicities (Children Now, 1999). In this multiracial, multiethnic world, it is essential that children not only develop positive racial and ethnic identities but also develop an appreciation and respect for diversity as well. While clearly there is a confluence of factors that contribute to children's racial and ethnic identity and attitudes, there is no question that exposure to media is one significant factor (Huntemann & Morgan, 2001).

Children of all ages, races, and ethnicities are affected by the power and ubiquity of media in their lives. They spend more time engaging with media than they spend doing anything else except for sleeping. For six and a half hours a day, they watch their favorite television shows, listen to music on their iPods, surf the Internet, and play video games (Roberts, Foehr, & Rideout, 2005). As a result, media serve as some of society's primary cultural storytellers and powerful cultural forces. The images and messages children experience through media influence their ideas, attitudes, values, and behaviors in both superficial and substantive ways. They provide inspiration for fashion trends, create and promote role models, teach about important current events, and even help children develop their self-concepts and identify how they fit into the world around them (Children Now, 1999).

One way that mass media provide children with information about themselves and their world is through the quantity and quality of media portrayals of members of their own racial or ethnic group. Children pick up on the sometimes blatant, but often subtle, media messages about race and ethnicity (Children Now, 1999). What children see and hear in the media shapes their earliest opinions and perceptions of themselves, of others in their own racial/ethnic group, and of those in other racial/ethnic groups as well, in both negative and positive ways (Berry & Asamen, 2001).

When the images and messages from a medium are taken as a whole, the absence or underrepresentation of characters of color implies that people belonging to that group are not important or valued enough to deserve attention or that they do not hold any social power (Gross, 1994). Alternately, when characters from a particular racial or ethnic group are present but are cast in negative or stereotyped ways, it can negatively affect not only the self-concepts of viewers who are members of that group, but also nongroup members' attitudes toward people from that racial or ethnic group (Graves, 1993).

Television's effect on children's attitudes and beliefs was illustrated clearly in a series of Children Now focus groups with young people ages 10–17 (Children Now, 1999). When asked to cast television roles from a collection of photographs of diverse people, children had very definite ideas of what a "good" person and a "bad" person looked like. After choosing an African American for the part of a criminal, one White boy said, "He just looks like the type of criminal that would probably steal or something." Children who chose a Latino for the criminal role explained it was because he "looked mean" or "like he could kill someone." When casting a White person for the part of a police officer, one African American boy stated that he did so because "he looks intelligent" (Children Now, 1999).

Yet television also has the ability to inspire children's positive attitudes about members of other racial and ethnic groups. Research has shown that seeing characters of color on television results in positive attitude changes for White children (Dorr, Graves, & Phelps, 1980), especially if they are shown in a multiracial setting (Graves, 1993). In addition, White, Latino, and Native American children all increased their acceptance of other racial and ethnic group members after viewing a positive, racially integrated television program (Mays, Henderson, Seidman, & Steiner, 1975). Though most of the research on the effects of media messages about race and ethnicity on children has been done with television, it is likely that other forms of media, such as movies, music, the Internet, and video games have similar effects on children.

For these reasons, all children must not only see positive representations of people of different races and ethnicities in the media they consume, but they must also have opportunities to discuss the reasons for and the implications of the negative or stereotypical images they see. Doing so will help protect them from internalizing the harmful messages about their own racial/ethnic group and it will also teach them not to unfairly judge the character of others based on their experiences with the media. It is, therefore, imperative that parents and caregivers recognize the influence of multicultural media messages so that they can make choices and take action to ensure a media diet for their children that will support their social and identity development. This chapter was designed to offer resources and tools for parents and caregivers in their efforts to create a positive multicultural media environment for their children, both inside and outside their homes.

THE STATE OF MULTICULTURAL MEDIA

The amount of diversity and the quality of multicultural portrayals featured in the media that children consume appear to vary depending on the media platform and content. In an analysis of children's television programming on broadcast and cable, one recent study found that characters in English-language children's television programs closely mirrored the diversity of the United States population, with the exception of Latino characters, who remained greatly underrepresented at only 5.5% of the children's television population (Kelly & Smith, 2007).

Children Now's (2004) study of prime-time programming on commercial broadcast television showed that Latino and Asian/Pacific Islander characters were dramatically underrepresented, accounting for only 6% and 1% of primary characters, respectively. In contrast, 18% of primary characters were African American while White characters made up the vast majority of television roles, accounting for 73% of the prime-time population. In addition to their small numbers, the study found that when characters of color were shown, they often held low-status jobs such as domestic workers or criminals (Children Now, 2004).

Another study conducted by Children Now (2001) looked for racial diversity in video games and found that more than half (56%) of all human characters in the top-selling video games were White. African Americans composed the second-largest group, representing about one fifth of all characters (22%). Asian/Pacific Islanders accounted for 9% of all characters, whereas Latinos composed 2% of the population. There were no Latina characters in any of the games. Native Americans and multiracial characters each accounted for 0.2% of the characters.

The roles of these characters were stereotyped as well. All Latino characters were athletes, usually in baseball games. Nearly all African American characters (83%) were athletes as well and were most likely of all the characters to exhibit aggressive behavior. Asian/Pacific Islander characters were found primarily in wrestling or fighting games, usually as antagonists; and while White characters were found in every game in nearly every type of role, they composed the vast majority (87%) of heroes (Children Now, 2001).

RECOMMENDATIONS FOR PARENTS AND CAREGIVERS

Just as parents and caregivers should take great care in monitoring the nutritional value of the food their children eat and teaching their children the benefits of healthy eating, so too should parents and caregivers actively participate in their children's media consumption. Although parents do recognize the importance of their role as family media manager, many have not made a commitment to doing so. In fact, almost two thirds of parents (65%) state that they could make improvements in supervising their children's media use (Rideout & Hamel, 2006). The following three simple rules, *Minimize, Monitor,* and *Mediate,* were designed to help parents and caregivers implement a system to create a healthy, multicultural media environment for their children.

Minimize—Set limits for how much time children spend with media. Almost half of children (42%) live in households where the TV is on almost around the clock, even when no one is actually viewing (Common Sense Media, 2007). While more than half of parents (57%) say that they are "very" or "strongly" concerned about how much time their children spend with media (Common Sense Media, 2007), they still have few rules about its use in the home environment (Rideout, 2004). In addition, research shows that more children say they have time limits for going online (59%) than they do for playing video games (42%) or watching TV (39%) (Rideout, 2004). Given the lack of quality multicultural content in video games and television programming, setting time limits can help parents reduce children's exposure to racially and ethnically homogenous and stereotypical portrayals.

One of the best ways to limit children's media exposure is to take televisions, computers, and video game consoles out of their bedrooms. Two thirds of 8- to 18-year-olds (68%) have television sets, half have VCRs or DVD players (54%) and video game players (49%), and one out of five (20%) have Internet access in their bedrooms (Roberts et al., 2005). Research shows that children who have a TV in their bedroom spend almost an hour and a half more each day watching television than those who don't (Roberts et al., 2005).

By taking media out of the bedroom and reducing the amount of media their children consume in general, parents will be better able to both *monitor* the content to which their children are exposed and *mediate* their children's media use by engaging their children in conversations about what they are seeing or not seeing when it comes to multicultural portrayals.

Monitor—Be aware of the media content to which children are exposed. Beyond setting basic rules for their children's media use, parents and caregivers should actively monitor their children's media for multicultural content. Parents should turn off television shows, video games, websites, or music that they feel offer negative images or stereotypes of people of color. Alternately, they should actively search for media content that offers quality portrayals of a diverse array of characters beginning in their children's early preschool years, as soon as they start engaging with media. Acceptable content should include the following criteria:

- Features a range of multicultural characters
- Shows characters of color in leading roles
- Provides a diversity of occupations for all racial and ethnic groups
- Does not reinforce negative stereotypes
- Balances negative portrayals among different racial and ethnic groups

Sometimes it can be difficult to determine whether or not a television show, video game, or website meet these criteria. The following are several actions parents can take to try to get as much information as possible about the quantity and quality of racial and ethnic depictions in media content.

- Watch television shows or movies, play a video game, or visit a website to experience the content firsthand before allowing children to do so.
- Visit the official website of the television show, video game, or movie to learn more about the program content and characters.
- Talk to other like-minded parents to find out what types of multicultural programs they choose for their children.
- For videos and video games, look at the language and imagery on the packaging to get an idea of the presence of racial and ethnic diversity or stereotypes in the movie or video game.
- Read reviews to see if there is any discussion of the racial or ethnic content, or visit websites that provide independent, family-oriented ratings for media.

One additional benefit of supporting quality multicultural shows is that it often results in the creation of even more diverse programming. After *Dora the Explorer* became a huge hit, garnering an audience of 22.6 million viewers per month and generating a total of $3 billion in *Dora*-related merchandise (Winslow,

2005), Nickelodeon created *Go, Diego, Go!* a spin-off show featuring Dora's cousin that has also been a great success in terms of viewership and merchandising. Wanting to mimic Nickelodeon's success with *Dora* and *Diego* and recognizing the growing Latino youth population, other children's channels began to offer shows with Latino lead characters such as PBS's *The Misadventures of Maya and Miguel*, Disney Channel's *Handy Manny*, and the WB's *Mucha Lucha*.

Mediate—Coview and discuss media content with children. In addition to choosing appropriate multicultural content, ideally parents and caregivers should proactively mediate their children's media use—joining their children as they engage with media (coviewing) and talking with them about the images and messages they perceive (Nathanson, 2001).

Research shows that coviewing can have positive effects (Salomon, 1977). Yet coviewing can also have adverse effects such as fostering beliefs and attitudes that television characters are like "real-world" people (Messaris & Kerr, 1984). Thus, coviewing by itself could reinforce stereotypes or negative portrayals of people of color by signaling parental approval or endorsement of specific content (Austin, Bolls, Fujioka, & Engelbertson, 1999; Nathanson, 2001). Therefore, this research points to the need for parental coviewing to be coupled with discussions about what children see on the screen. Talking with children about what they see in the media is perhaps the most effective strategy, especially when it comes to issues related to multiculturalism.

Unfortunately, parents don't engage in mediation with their children very often. When they do use it, however, they are more likely to report using this mediation style with younger children than older children (Barkin et al., 2006). Further, some Latino and African American parents also are less likely to use this strategy than are White parents. This fact, coupled with the fact that Latino and African American families watch more television than White families, could mean that Latino and African American children are "at greater risk for the problematic effects of media content" (Barkin et al., 2006, p. 398).

Not only should parents talk to their children about what they see in the media, they should focus their interactions in specific, targeted ways. Researchers note that when parents talk to their children, they generally use "unfocused guidance," where the parent coviews with the child, encourages certain viewing behaviors, and talks generally about what the child sees on the screen (Van den Bulck & Van den Bergh, 2000). A considerably more effective strategy is "evaluative guidance," where the parent specifically discusses the content, for example, by commenting on how certain characters behave and what they say, by explaining that certain things are not real, or providing perspectives on certain actions or events (Van den Bulck & Van den Bergh, 2000).

As parents think about how to actively engage children using an evaluative guidance strategy, it is essential that they have the necessary tools to do so. The advocacy organization The Geena Davis Institute on Gender in Media has developed a set of questions for parents to use when actively engaging their children in discussions about media content (See Jane, 2007).

- Compare the numbers of characters of different races and ethnicities and talk about what impact you think that has.
- In the content, what behaviors are most common for African Americans? How about for Latinos? Asian/Pacific Islanders? Whites? Native Americans?
- How often do characters of color have White characters in their circle of friends?
- How often do White characters have characters of color in their circle of friends?

- Do you think it is okay for the characters to have a circle of friends that doesn't include another ethnicity or race? Why or why not?
- What kinds of occupations do characters of color have? What kinds of jobs do White characters hold?
- Are more of the aggressive or violent characters a certain race or ethnicity? Why do you think the program has this ratio? What impact do you think that has?
- Who created the story? Was the writer White or a person of color? How about the director? If you don't know, what would you guess?
- What would you do differently if you were making this TV show?

PARENT TIPS FOR OUTSIDE THE HOME

Every parent knows that their responsibilities to care for their children are not contained solely within the walls of their home. This is certainly true when it comes to creating a healthy media environment for their children. First, children are exposed to media in many other places than just their homes, most notably in their friends' homes and at school. In addition, in order to change the amount of diversity in the media that is offered to children, parents need to broaden their influence beyond the confines of their homes to reach the people who create the media. The following are some tips for influencing children's media experiences outside the home.

- Parents should talk with the parents of their children's friends about their family's media rules if their children are going to use media at a friend's house. In addition to sharing rules concerning the amount of time their children may watch TV or play video games and the media ratings their children are allowed to consume, parents should tell other parents about their feelings concerning their children's exposure to media with negative racial and ethnic imagery or messages.

- Parents should be sure that older children understand family rules about race and ethnicity in the media and help them find ways to talk with their friends about it so they can choose positive media in the absence of adult supervision. Doing so could also help children initiate discussions about media images of race and ethnicity with their friends, potentially leading to greater awareness and audience demand for multiracial/multiethnic programming.

- At school, parents should ask what kinds of video games, videos, television programs, and books are used in the classroom. If they find that the classroom media lacks racial and ethnic diversity or positive images and messages about different racial/ethnic groups, or that the media simply is unrepresentative of the student population, parents should share their concerns about the need for diverse media images and suggest media programs and products that contain positive multicultural messages.

- Volunteering in the classroom to help teach media literacy and to moderate discussions about race and ethnicity in the media messages is an effective way to teach an entire group of children about the need for, and effects of, multicultural media (see the following section, "Parent and Caregiver Resources," for ideas on media literacy curricula and activities).

- Parents can introduce the idea of media education to their local afterschool programs, scout organizations, religious education programs, etc., and help the adult leaders of those groups incorporate a media education plan into their programs.

- To effect change on a larger scale, parents should send a letter or e-mail to their local television broadcaster, cable network, movie studio, video game maker, website developer, or book publisher to complain if they find that the material created or distributed by the company lacks diversity or includes negative racial and ethnic images or messages. Likewise, parents should be sure to let the companies know if they especially appreciated the diversity or positive racial and ethnic messages in their programs or products. Consumers' thoughts and opinions are very important to the media companies and can be a powerful way to effect change in the media.

CONCLUSION

Much of parents' time and effort is consumed with protecting their children and taking every possible measure to ensure their healthy development. It is fairly easy to understand the importance of fastening seat belts, providing a good education, and creating opportunities for positive social interactions with playmates. Yet the need for establishing a healthy multicultural media environment—although incredibly important to a child's self-esteem, identity formation, and social development—is not always so obvious. Despite the pervasiveness of the media and the powerful influence they have on children's lives, there are many things parents can do to protect their children. By minimizing, monitoring, and mediating their children's media use in the home and actively supporting the production of quality multicultural media, parents can make great strides in creating a media environment that contributes to their children's healthy development.

PARENT AND CAREGIVER RESOURCES

- American Academy of Child & Adolescent Psychiatry (www.aacap.org)

The American Academy of Child & Adolescent Psychiatry provides information on the effects of media exposure on children and teenagers and offers recommendations for parents to ensure a positive media experience for their children.

- American Academy of Pediatrics (www.aap.org)

The American Academy of Pediatrics (AAP) website contains published research on the use of media by different racial and ethnic groups as well as the effects of media messages, including racial/ethnic messages, on children's health and development.

- American Psychological Association (www.apa.org)

The American Psychological Association website contains up-to-date information on many issues related to children's emotional and psychological development, including those concerning race/ethnicity and the media.

- Center for Media Literacy (www.medialit.org)

The online store at the Center for Media Literacy contains a multitude of books on media literacy and kits to help parents and teachers implement a media literacy program in their home or school.

- Children Now (www.childrennow.org)

Children Now provides downloads of their research studies on the diversity of television and video games as well as their national polls exploring the effects of media diversity and messages about race and ethnicity on young children.

- Common Sense Media (www.commonsensemedia.org)

In addition to their useful kid-appropriate reviews of popular television shows, movies, DVDs, video games, websites, music, and books, Common Sense Media provides tools for parents to help them create a healthy media environment for their children as well as a weekly newsletter on hot topics in children's media.

- MAGIC: Media Activities and Good Ideas by, with and for Children (www.unicef .org/magic)

Born out of the UN Committee on the Rights of the Child, MAGIC is an internationally focused website that provides information and resources to help parents, teachers, the media, government, and children use the media to support the healthy development and promote the rights of all children.

- Media Awareness Network (www.media awareness.ca)

Media Awareness Network offers a comprehensive collection of media education and Internet literacy resources, including "Exploring Media & Race" as well as resources for both teachers and parents.

- MediaLiteracy.com(www.medialiteracy .com)

A portal to media literacy sites on the web, MediaLiteracy.com is a well-organized site that provides information, ideas, and materials to both teachers and parents interested in teaching children media literacy skills.

- National Institute on Media and the Family (www.mediafamily.org)

The National Institute on Media and the Family provides research and information on the effects and safe use of media with children. Their *Mediawise* newsletter provides valuable information and tips for parents.

- National Parent Teacher Association (www.pta.org)

National Parent Teacher Association provides information for both parents and teachers, such as "Navigating the Children's Media Landscape" to help those who work with and care for children use media wisely.

- PBS Kids (www.pbskids.org/parents/children andmedia/)

PBS Kids has information for parents about how media shapes child development, how to create a media-literate household, and how to educate children about stereotypes they see in the media.

- The Geena Davis Institute on Gender and Media (www.gdigm.org)

The Geena Davis Institute on Gender and Media was founded by actress Geena Davis to help create gender equity in media for children. They have conducted several studies analyzing the racial, ethnic, and gender diversity in television and movies and offer many useful tips for parents on how to use media to talk with children about issues of race, ethnicity, and gender.

- Talking With Kids (www.talkingwith kids.org)

A partnership between Children Now and the Kaiser Family Foundation, Talking With Kids offers parents helpful tips for ways to use the media to discuss tough issues with children.

- Tolerance.org (www.tolerance.org)

A project of the Southern Poverty Law Center, Tolerance.org offers resources for parents, teachers, adolescents, and children to deal with issues of tolerance. "Planet Tolerance" offers games, stories, and information on tolerance for young children, and "Mix it up" provides a place for teens to discuss and think about issues of diversity and tolerance.

REFERENCES

Austin, E. W., Bolls, P., Fujioka, Y., & Engelbertson, J. (1999). How and why parents take on the tube. *Journal of Broadcasting and Electronic Media, 43*(2), 175–192.

Barkin, S., Ip, E., Richardson, I., Klinepeter, S., Finch, S., & Krcmar, M. (2006). Parental media mediation styles for children aged 2 to 11 years. *Archives of Pediatric and Adolescent Medicine, 160,* 395–401.

Berry, G. L., & Asamen, J. K. (2001). Television, children, and multicultural awareness: Comprehending the medium in a complex multimedia society. In D. G. Singer & J. L. Singer (Eds.), *Handbook of children and the media* (pp. 359–374). Thousand Oaks, CA: Sage.

Children Now. (1999). *A different world: Children's perceptions of race and class in the media.* Oakland, CA: Author.

Children Now. (2001). *Fair play: Violence, race and gender in video games.* Oakland, CA: Author.

Children Now. (2004). *Fall Colors 2003–2004: Prime time diversity report.* Oakland, CA: Author.

Common Sense Media. (2007). *The 2007 poll of American parents: Parents speak out on the impact of media on their kids' health.* San Francisco: Author.

Dorr, A., Graves, S., & Phelps, E. (1980). Television literacy for young children. *Journal of Communication, 30*(3), 71–83.

Graves, S. B. (1993). Television, the portrayal of African Americans, and the development of children's attitudes. In G. L. Berry & J. K. Asamen, (Eds.), *Children and television: Images in a changing socio-cultural world* (pp. 179–190). Newbury Park, CA: Sage.

Gross, L. (1994). What is wrong with this picture? Lesbian women and gay men on television. In R. J. Ringer (Ed.), *Queer words, queer images: Communication and the construction of homosexuality* (pp. 143–156). New York: New York University Press.

Huntemann, N., & Morgan, M. (2001). Mass media and identity development. In D. G. Singer & J. L. Singer (Eds.) *Handbook of children and the media* (pp. 309–322). Thousand Oaks, CA: Sage.

Kelly, J., & Smith, S. (2007). *Now you see 'em, now you don't: Gender and racial disparity in television for children.* Duluth, MN: See Jane Program of Dads & Daughters.

Mays, L., Henderson, E. H., Seidman, S. K., & Steiner, V. S. (1975). *An evaluation report on* Vegetable Soup: *The effects of a multiethnic children's television series on intergroup attitudes of children.* Unpublished manuscript, New York State Department of Education.

Messaris, P., & Kerr, D. (1984). TV-related mother-child interaction and children's perceptions of TV characters. *Journalism Quarterly, 61,* 662–666.

Nathanson, A. (2001). Parent and child perspectives on the presence and meaning of parental television mediation. *Journal of Broadcast and Electronic Media, 45*(2), 201–220.

O'Hare, W. P. (2001). *The child population: First data from the 2000 census.* Baltimore, MD: Annie E. Casey Foundation and Population Reference Bureau.

Rideout, V. (2004). *Parents, media and public policy: A Kaiser Family Foundation survey.* Menlo Park, CA: Kaiser Family Foundation.

Rideout, V., & Hamel, E. (2006). *The media family: Electronic media in the lives of infants, preschoolers, toddlers and their parents.* Menlo Park, CA: Kaiser Family Foundation.

Roberts, D. F., Foehr, U. G., & Rideout, V. (2005). *Generation M: Media in the lives of 8- to 18-year-olds.* Menlo Park, CA: Kaiser Family Foundation.

Salomon, G. (1977). Effects of encouraging Israeli mothers to co-observe *Sesame Street* with their five-year-olds. *Child Development, 48,* 1146–1151.

See Jane. (2007). *Tips for parents of kids ages 8–15: Film and TV.* Retrieved July 23, 2007, from http://www.seejane.org/parents/tips8–15.aspx

Van den Bulck, J., & Van den Bergh, B. (2000). The influence of perceived parental guidance patterns on children's media use: Gender differences and media displacement. *Journal of Broadcasting & Electronic Media, 44*(3), 329–348.

Winslow, G. (2005, March 14). *The great kids' debate.* Retrieved July 23, 2007, from http://www.multichannel.com/article/CA510087.html?industryid=47286&q=Winslow%2c+March+14%2c+2005

Epilogue

The Realities of Growing Up in a Multicultural and Multimedia World

JOY KEIKO ASAMEN

Through the multitude of media forms available to children and youth and their families and the ongoing quest to develop new or renewed electronic technologies, we can now irrevocably claim that we live in a "small world." As the world shrinks, young people of the 21st century have opportunity to acquaint themselves with people from diverse cultures and walks of life who may hold beliefs and present with behaviors quite different from their own. Although some might question the value of such opportunity and others are perhaps even threatened by the idea, the editors and contributors of this volume categorically embrace multiculturalism as an enriching and necessary experience in the lives of young people. The challenge is the quality and nature of the information that is communicated to children and youth, and how what is communicated may be processed by young people and influence their perceptions of self as well as their worldview of others. The reality is that children are exposed to what media offer whether we support the experience or not. There is good reason for describing the current generation of children and youth as *Generation M* (Rideout, Roberts, & Foehr, 2005).

Despite the extensive use of media by young people, media content has yet to reflect the real-world diversity to which children and youth are exposed in their everyday lives. There is a problem not only with media representation, but also with the nature of portrayals found in media content. Both these points are consistently reiterated by contributors to this volume. Hence, access to media content that is relevant to children and families from diverse cultures and walks of life still has a long way to go. The reality of this observation is palpable when one considers print medium still faces some of the same challenges despite a much longer existence than that of other media forms.

THE CHALLENGES FACING SOCIAL SCIENTISTS: FUTURE RESEARCH CONSIDERATIONS

Research on media has existed since the early 1920s, when cinema became a major pastime for families (Paik, 2001). As new media forms came into existence and were embraced by families, research on the influences of these new technologies on children and youth also emerged. As the available technologies continue to evolve, social scientists continue to investigate the relationship of these media on young people. But investigating the relationship of media content to the development of children and youth, particularly the multicultural development of the young, faces challenges that were raised in this volume and are worthy of recapping here.

First, although there exists more than half a century of research on the effects of television on children as well as a growing body of research on the influence of television on the multicultural development of children, the influence of computer and Internet usage, for example, is less studied and the findings to date are preliminary. And studies specifically on the playing of video games and the use of digitally mediated environments for enhancing the worldview development of children are even more uncommon. Therefore, there is still much to learn about what and how diverse media forms, including television, teach children about themselves and their cultures as well as the development of their worldview toward others.

Second, how and the degree to which children's worldview development is influenced by media content must take into consideration moderating effects, for example, the type of medium, parental supervision in the use of the medium, and media literacy education regarding the use of the medium. Furthermore, the demographics, personal attributes, and culture of individuals who use the medium, as well as the social systems in which they exist, are factors relevant to how children are influenced by the media content to which they are exposed. Further complicating the situation are the ever-changing attitudes, values, and beliefs that emerge as the nation and world become more culturally diverse. In this volume, contributors have considered these dynamic influences and the layers of complexity that are added through these sources of influence. As a consequence, the complexity of the moderating effects on the relationship of media content to multicultural development introduces methodological challenges to investigations of this phenomenon. In response to these challenges, contributors to this volume recommend that the phenomenon be approached from diverse research paradigms and the findings from these investigations triangulated to produce scientifically valid and culturally relevant findings while addressing questions of function as well as process. In other words, we must not only study what media do to children and their development but what children might do with the media to which they are exposed.

Finally, the research on the relationship of media content on the development of children and youth, and multicultural development in particular, tends to emphasize the negative. But there is also a lot that is positive to gain from the use of media to facilitate the development of a worldview that embraces diversity and multicultural understanding, about which we have done less research, and, as a consequence, know less. Wartella and Knell (2004) make a case for "harnessing the power of television to inform children about the world around them" (p. 222), but one could substitute television for any of the electronic technologies of which children avail themselves, as all these media forms have the power to influence children "to build mutual respect" (p. 224). Research on current media forms as well as on new media that arrive on the scene must attempt to provide a more balanced understanding of this phenomenon. The influence of media is inescapable. Children and youth exist in a media-saturated world; therefore, determining its benefits is as critical as identifying its pitfalls.

CONCLUSION

In this volume, we have assembled scholars from multiple disciplines and various theoretical perspectives with diverse beliefs about the ontological, epistemological, and methodological assumptions that underlie the scholarship they produce. But the one issue on which they all share common ground is the importance of a multicultural worldview, particularly for a generation that must coexist with diverse cultures domestically and with the reality of globalization, which places us in contact with cultures worldwide. As is evident from reading the contributions of these scholars, a number of systems—family, community, religious, school, and peers—are influential in the worldview development of children and youth. Yet, the media to which young people have access are among the most powerful contemporary agents of socialization influencing their worldview development.

To expand their worldview and develop a multicultural sensibility, children must be exposed to diverse people, cultures, and experiences in ways that build ties and nurture respect for one another. Children must also have access to media content where characters look and behave like them as well as are portrayed in nonstereotypic ways. No child can escape the lure of some form of media, and most children engage a number of media forms on a day-to-day basis. Therefore, the media diet offered the young must be given thoughtful consideration, as what they witness and experience has the potential of profoundly influencing how they feel about themselves as individuals and behave as citizens of the world.

REFERENCES

Paik, H. (2001). The history of children's use of electronic media. In D. G. Singer & J. L. Singer (Eds.), *Handbook of children and the media* (pp. 7–27). Thousand Oaks, CA: Sage.

Rideout, V., Roberts, D. F., & Foehr, U. G. (2005). *Generation M: Media in the lives of 8- to 18-year-olds.* Washington, DC: Henry J. Kaiser Family Foundation.

Wartella, E., & Knell, G. E. (2004). Raising a world-wise child and the power of media. *Phi Delta Kappan, 86*(3), 222–224.

Author Index

Subject Index

About the Editors

Joy Keiko Asamen, PhD, is Professor of Psychology at Pepperdine University, Graduate School of Education and Psychology. Her research interests are in the areas of multicultural issues in education and psychology, at-risk youth, and research paradigms for the study of television effects on social behavior. In addition to publishing in professional journals in the areas of counseling psychology, psychiatry, and education, as well as contributing chapters to the edited volumes of colleagues on the intersection of media, children, and multiculturalism, she has coedited three books with Gordon L. Berry: *Black Students, Psychological Issues and Academic Success; Children and Television, Images in a Changing Sociocultural World;* and *Research Paradigms, Television, and Social Behavior.*

Mesha L. Ellis (PhD, the University of Alabama) is a licensed clinical psychologist and Intervention Research Fellow at Vanderbilt University. Her research interests include evaluating the role of temperamental, cognitive, and familial factors in the development and maintenance of childhood antisocial behavior. Her research interests also include the examination of factors impacting therapist adherence to treatment protocols for antisocial youth. She is currently investigating the utilization of culturally centered treatment interventions in reducing behavioral difficulties in African American youth. She has coauthored articles in professional journals and book chapters as well as presented her research at national conferences. Prior to her work at Vanderbilt, she was an Assistant Professor at Pepperdine University, Graduate School of Education and Psychology, where she taught courses in child development. She is a member of the American Psychological Association as well as the American Psychology-Law Society.

Gordon L. Berry, EdD, is Professor Emeritus in the Graduate School of Education and Information Studies at UCLA. He also holds the same title in the Department of Communication Studies at this institution. Prior to joining UCLA, he was Assistant to the Academic Vice President at Marquette University. His special areas of research are in counseling psychology and the study of media and social behavior. He has been the senior consultant for the CBS network and its programs designed for children for over 20 years. In addition, he has consulted for such programs as *Fat Albert and the Cosby Kids, Barney and Friends, That's So Raven, Liberty's Kids,* and many others. He has authored or coedited a number of books, and has published papers in many scholarly journals. He is a member of the American Psychological Association, the Association of Black Psychologists, and a charter member of the American Psychological Society. He received the 2003 Carolyn Attneave Award from the National Multicultural Conference and Summit for his dedication to learning and studying about cross-cultural issues. He served for a number of years on the Academy of Television Arts and Sciences Foundation Board and the Southwest Regional Laboratory for Educational Research.

About the Contributors

Walter R. Allen, PhD, is Allan Murray Cartter Professor in Higher Education, Graduate School of Education and Information Studies at UCLA. He is also Professor of Sociology and codirector of CHOICES, a longitudinal study of college attendance among African Americans and Latinos in California. His research interests include higher education, race and ethnicity, family patterns, and social inequality. He has worked as a consultant to courts, communities, foundations, business, and government.

James A. Anderson, PhD, is Professor of Communication and Director of the Center for Communication and Community at the University of Utah. He is the author/coauthor/editor of 16 books, including *Communication Research: Issues and Methods* (1987), *Mediated Communication: A Social Action Perspective* (1988), *Communication Theory: Epistemological Foundations* (1996), *The Organizational Self and Ethical Conduct* (2001), and *Media Violence and Aggression: Science and Ideology* (2008). His 100-plus chapters, articles, and research monographs are in the areas of family studies, cultural studies, media literacy, organizational studies, communicative ethics, methodology, and epistemology. He is a fellow and past president of the International Communication Association. He has been the editor of *Communication Yearbook* and *Communication Theory*, associate editor of *Human Communication Research*, and guest editor of *Communication Studies* and *American Behavioral Scientist*. He is currently executive editor of the *Rocky Mountain Communication Review*. His forthcoming titles from Sage include works on mediated communication research methods and theory.

Harvey F. Bellin (MA and MFA, Yale University), President of The Media Group of Connecticut, Inc., is an Emmy Award–winning director, author, and producer of PBS programs and other educational programs filmed around the world. He served as project director of 10 video-/DVD-based projects funded by United States Department of Education grants, including the early childhood education programs *Learning Through Play for School Readiness, Circle of Make-Believe,* and *My Magic Story Car.*

Sha'kema M. Blackmon is a doctoral candidate at Loyola University Chicago in the department of Counseling Psychology. Her academic work focuses on multicultural and social justice issues as they relate to people of color and the professionals who serve them.

Jeffrey E. Brand (PhD, Michigan State University) is Associate Professor and Head of School, Communication and Media at Bond University in Queensland, Australia. He is coauthor (with Mark Pearson) of the book *Sources of News and Current Affairs* (2001), and has published in the *Journal of Communication,* the *Journal of Advertising Research, Educational Leadership, Asia Pacific Media Educator,* and in edited texts in the communication field. His research focuses on cognitive effects of electronic media on youth audiences, including studies on stereotyping in the media and stereotypic attitudes of youth, effects of advertising on youth, and effects of news on youth knowledge about social and political reality. He now conducts most of his research on computer games and has consulted to the Australian Broadcasting Authority, the Office of Film and Literature Classification, the Special Broadcasting Service, Interactive Entertainment Association of Australia, and the Australian Communications and Media Authority.

Peter Christenson (BA, Dartmouth College; PhD, Stanford University) is Professor of Communication at Lewis and Clark College. His primary areas of research are health communication and the impact of media on children and adolescents, and he has published a variety of articles and book chapters on those subjects. He is coauthor of *It's Not Only Rock & Roll—Popular Music in the Lives of Adolescents* (1998, with Donald Roberts), *Substance Use in Popular Movies and Music* (1999, with Donald Roberts and Lisa Henriksen), and *Substance Use in Popular Prime Time Television* (2000, also with Roberts and Henriksen). Recently, he completed a major report on the world of teen-oriented television titled *Prime Time Teens? Perspectives on the New Youth-Media Environment,* which was funded by the W.T. Grant Foundation.

Kevin Clark (PhD, Pennsylvania State University, 1994) is Associate Professor and Program Coordinator of the Instructional Technology Program at George Mason University. His interest in educational media includes the design and development of innovative educational software and online learning environments, the use of technology in nonformal learning environments, and the role of educational technologies in underserved communities. He has published in journals such as the *British Journal of Educational Technology, Information Technology in Childhood Education Annual, Journal of Computers in Mathematics and Science Teaching, Journal of Interactive Online Learning, Journal of Negro Education, Journal of Technology and Teacher Education,* and *Urban Education.* He has been honored by the Congressional Black Caucus Education Braintrust for outstanding technology leadership in the community and has been selected as a Fulbright Senior Specialist Roster Candidate.

Robert Cooper, PhD, is Assistant Professor at UCLA and the Director of the UCLA EASE Project. His research focuses on the implementation and scale-up of school change models in urban schools. Employing an interdisciplinary approach, his research explores how the technical, normative, political, and social-cultural dimensions of the schooling process are altered in the implementation of school reform, particularly as they relate to issues of race, equity, and micropolitics. His areas of specialization include educational policy analysis, qualitative research methods, intergroup relations, and race and education.

Jannette L. Dates, PhD, is Professor and Dean in the John H. Johnson School of Communications at Howard University. Her research examines media effects, with particular attention to race, class, and gender issues. In addition to articles and book chapters in various publications, she coedited (with Dr. William Barlow) *Split Image: African Americans in the Mass Media* (1993). Her work has appeared in the *Journal of Broadcasting & Electronic Media* and the *Journal of Popular Film & TV* (*JPFTV*). She coedited (with Dr. Thomas Mascaro) the August 2005 edition of the *JPFTV*'s "African Americans in Film and Television: 20th Century Lessons for the New Millennium." She has served as president of the Association for Education in Journalism and Mass Communication and as president of the Broadcast Education Association, and she is a board member of the *Howard Journal of Communications*.

Kyla M. Day (MA, University of Michigan, Ann Arbor) is a doctoral student in the Developmental Psychology program at the University of Michigan, Ann Arbor. Her academic research interests focus on the developmental precursors to positive sexuality as well as sexual socialization and communication between parents, peers, the media, and African American adolescents.

Evellyn Elizondo (PhD, University of California, Santa Cruz, 2003) was a Postdoctoral Fellow in Education at the UCLA Graduate School of Education and Information Studies, at the time of writing the chapter. She has since accepted a position as the Director of Research and Evaluation at the Bakersfield City School District in California. Her work focuses on Latino academic achievement throughout the educational pipeline, identity, efficacy, and institutional racism.

Lillie M. Fears (PhD, University of Missouri, 1997) is Associate Professor in the Journalism Department at Arkansas State University, College of Communications. She teaches and researches in the areas of race, gender, and media; propaganda and media; and media history. She was a Fellow in the National Endowment for the Humanities Black Film Studies Summer Institute for College Teachers in 2001 and has served as associate editor of the *Southwestern Mass Communication Journal*. A former head of the Minorities and Communications Division of the Association for Education in Journalism and Mass Communication, she has also chaired the Gender Studies Division of the Southern States Communication Association. She was recently elected to the Arkansas Humanities Council, which is funded by the National Endowment for the Humanities. Her term began January 2008 and lasts for three years.

Miguel E. Gallardo, PsyD, is Assistant Professor of Psychology at Pepperdine University, Graduate School of Education and Psychology. He is also a licensed psychologist in private/consultation practice. He has written and presented in the areas of Chicano/Latino mental health, Latinos and substance abuse, integrative health care, evidenced-based practices with diverse populations, and culturally responsive therapy with diverse populations, and he has two internationally distributed educational videos that examine the intersection of ethnicity and disability. He is a statewide and nationally recognized community and social activist for the Chicano/Latino community and has been honored locally, statewide, and nationally for his commitment to the field of psychology.

Christina Romano Glaubke (MA in Education, UCLA) is the Director of the Children and the Media Program at Children Now. The Children and the Media Program is dedicated to using research and advocacy to create a healthy media environment for all children. She served as the project director for *Fair Play? Violence, Gender and Race in Video Games* and *Fall Colors 2003–04*, and was the lead researcher on *Big Media, Little Kids*, the first study to explore the impact of media consolidation on children's programming. Recently, she completed a follow-up to *Big Media, Little Kids* that evaluates the children's program offerings in eight markets across the country and is working on a research study to assess the quality of children's educational television programming. Current policy efforts include working with the Federal Communications Commission and Congress to ensure that the nation's media laws and regulations adequately serve the unique needs of children, specifically with regard to advertising, violence, media ownership, and educational programming. Prior to joining Children Now, she worked for the Walt Disney Company, developing products for the feature film, interactive games, and online divisions.

Daren A. Graves (EdD, Harvard University) is Assistant Professor in Education at Simmons College. He is Director of the Urban Education Program, a master's program geared toward first- to fifth-year teachers who teach in urban districts. His dissertation research, which he has presented at various conferences, involves the roles of school culture and racial identity on the academic performance of Black adolescents. Coupled with his role as a teacher educator, his dissertation research has driven his interest to theorize and implement innovative school cultures that promote the academic performance and resilience of adolescents of color.

Sherryl Browne Graves (PhD, Harvard University) is Professor of Psychological Foundations in the Hunter College School of Education and Director of the Urban Center for Assessment, Research and Evaluation at Hunter College. Her research focuses on the impact of television on children's racial attitudes, the role of diversity in the teaching-learning process, and the preparation of teachers to integrate technology into pedagogy. Her work appears in the *Encyclopedia of Children, Adolescents and the Media; Journal of Social Issues; Tuning Into Young Viewers: Social Science Perspectives on Television;* and *Children and Television, Images in a Changing Sociocultural World.* She has served as an advisor to children's television, including *Johnny and the Sprites; Arthur; Sesame Street;* Discovery Kids *Ready, Set, Learn;* and the PBS Ready to Learn Service.

Shelly P. Harrell (PhD, UCLA, 1988) is Professor of Psychology at Pepperdine University, Graduate School of Education and Psychology. Her areas of specialization include multicultural psychology and community psychology. Specifically, her work has focused on the comprehensive conceptualization and measurement of racism-related stress, multicultural competence, and diversity training. Currently, she is exploring intersections of constructivism, transpersonal, narrative, and positive psychology within a broader cultural-ecological paradigm. Her work has been published in journals and books, including the *American Journal of Orthopsychiatry; American Journal of Community Psychology; Expanding Our Understanding of the Psychosocial Work Environment: A Compendium of Measures of Discrimination, Harassment, and Biases;* and the *Encyclopedia of Multicultural Psychology.* Most recently, she coedited a special issue on diversity for the *American Journal of Community Psychology* and coauthored the paper "Listening to Diversity Stories: Diversity Principles for Community Research and Action" for the special issue.

Khiela J. Holmes (PhD, University of Alabama, 2007) is a Postdoctoral Fellow at the University of Michigan–Department of Psychiatry. Her research examines the role of ethnic identity, religiosity, social goals, and parenting in aggressive behavior among youth.

Jason L. Huang (MA, University of Tulsa, 2006) is a doctoral student in the Industrial/Organizational Psychology program at Michigan State University. His research interests include personality in the workplace, team effectiveness and team leadership, psychological measurement, training, and cross-cultural issues.

Cynthia Hudley (PhD, UCLA) is Professor in the Gevirtz Graduate School of Education at the University of California, Santa Barbara, where she has also served as Associate Dean of the UCSB Graduate Division. Her research addresses the effects of peers on achievement motivation and aggressive behavior, with a special interest in ethnicity and culture. She has published widely on the topics of youth social and academic behavior in journals such as *Child Development, Journal of Educational Psychology,* and *Psychology in the Schools.* She has developed an aggression-reduction curriculum, the BrainPower Program (www.brainpowerprogram.com), to improve peer relations in elementary school. The curriculum, designated a "Promising Program" by the Substance Abuse and Mental Health Services Administration, is the subject of her recently completed volume for Yale University Press.

Cheong R. Huh, PhD, is Assistant Director of the UCLA EASE Project and is interested in the academic aspirations of minority students and the ways in which they actualize those aspirations throughout the schooling process. Specializing in a mixed-methods research approach, her research focuses on how educational policy in the United States can be made more inclusive by adding student voice to the policy-making process. As the founding director of the Korean language program at the University of California, Riverside, she is particularly sensitive to and knowledgeable about the issues facing language minority students. As a scholar of the Asian American experience, she teaches courses on this topic at the University of California, Irvine.

Darnell Hunt (PhD, UCLA, 1994) is Director of the Ralph J. Bunche Center for African American Studies and Professor of Sociology at UCLA. He has written extensively on race and media, including three recent books and numerous book chapters and articles. He also is author of *The Hollywood Writers Report,* issued by the Writers Guild of America in 2005 and 2007, and author of *The African American Television Report,* released by the Screen Actors Guild in June of 2000. Prior to his academic positions, he worked in the media and as a media researcher for the U.S. Commission on Civil Rights' 1993 hearings on diversity in Hollywood.

Angela James (PhD, Sociology) is Assistant Dean in the UCLA Graduate Division. Her research interests include race, demography, family sociology, and higher education. She has published in numerous journals such as *Journal of Comparative Family Studies, Journal of Race and Society, Journal of Personality and Social Psychology,* and the *Journal of Marriage and Family.*

Venita A. Kelley, PhD, is a consultant with expertise in media, intercultural communication, and leadership development. Her professional experiences include fellowships at Harvard University and Cornell University; Associate Dean of Leadership and Student Development at Spelman College; teaching courses in intercultural communication, mass communication, and ethnic studies at the University of Nebraska, Lincoln, and the University of San Diego; and intercultural communication consultation and training with local and federal government, K–12 and university systems, and medical educators. Her scholarly foci include intercultural and inter-/intragender competency, images of culture and gender in media, African American rhetoric and culture, African American women's communication strategies, and leadership development.

Frederick T. L. Leong, PhD, is Professor of Psychology at Michigan State University in the Industrial/Organizational and Clinical

Psychology programs and Director of the Center for Multicultural Psychology Research. He has authored or coauthored over 115 articles in various counseling and psychology journals and 80 book chapters, and also edited or coedited 10 books. He is Editor-in-Chief of the *Encyclopedia of Counseling* (in press). He is a Fellow of the APA, APS, Asian American Psychological Association, and the International Academy for Intercultural Research. His major research interests center on culture and mental health, cross-cultural psychotherapy (especially with Asians and Asian Americans), and cultural and personality factors related to career choice and work adjustment. He is the Past President of APA's Division 45 (Society for the Psychological Study of Ethnic Minority Issues) and also serves on their Board of Scientific Affairs, the Minority Fellowship Program Advisory Committee, and the Commission on Ethnic Minority Recruitment, Retention, and Training (CEMRRAT2) Task Force.

Deborah L. Linebarger (PhD, University of Texas, Austin, 1998) is Assistant Professor of Communication in the Annenberg School for Communication at the University of Pennsylvania. Her research focuses on the relationships among children's developmental status, their use of media, and their larger social worlds. Her research combines descriptive work evaluating relationships between children's media use and their cognitive and social development, microlevel experimental work to detect the features used in media that elicit attention and contribute to comprehension of content, and macrolevel program evaluation and intervention work that combines the knowledge gained through both descriptive and basic research and applies it in various real-world contexts. Her research has been presented at numerous conferences and published in psychology, communication, education, and pediatric medicine books and journals. Courses taught include children's cognitive development and media use, childhood and play, and research methods and challenges unique to children and families.

John E. Lochman, PhD, ABPP., is Professor and Doddridge Saxon Chairholder in Clinical Psychology at the University of Alabama, where he directs the Center for Prevention of Youth Problem Behavior. He is also an Adjunct Professor in the Department of Psychiatry and Behavioral Sciences at the Duke University Medical Center as well as a Special Professor in Interdisciplinary Behavioral Research, and a Visiting Professor in the Rudolf Magnus Institute of Neuroscience at the University of Utrecht from 2007–2009. He received the Blackmon-Moody Outstanding Professor Award at the University of Alabama in 2005, and was awarded an honorary doctorate by the University of Utrecht in the Netherlands in 2004 for his prevention research. He has over 240 publications on risk factors, social cognition, and intervention and prevention research with aggressive children. He is Editor-in-Chief of the *Journal of Abnormal Child Psychology,* serves on the NIH study section on Psychosocial Development, Risk and Prevention, is a Fellow in the American Psychological Association and in the Academy for Cognitive Therapy, is a member of the Board of Directors of the Society for Prevention Research, and is President-Elect of the American Board for Clinical Child and Adolescent Psychology.

Dana Mastro (PhD, Michigan State University, 2000) is Associate Professor and Director of Graduate Studies in the Department of Communication at the University of Arizona. Her research examines the role of the media in processes of racial/ethnic stereotype formation and application. Her work has appeared in journals such as *Communication Monographs*, *Communication Research*, *Human Communication Research*, *Media Psychology*, and *Journal of Broadcasting & Electronic Media*, as well as in books such as *Media Effects: Advances in Theory and Research*.

Harriette Pipes McAdoo is a Distinguished Professor in the Department of Sociology at Michigan State University. She earned her PhD at the University of Michigan and did postdoctoral study at Harvard University. She was a professor at Howard University for 20 years and was a visiting lecturer at Smith College, the University of Washington, and the University of Minnesota. She was editor of *Black Families* (4th edition) and *Black Children* (2nd edition) and coauthor of *Women and Children, Alone and in Poverty* and *Services to Young Families*. She was president of the National Council on Family Relations.

Patti Miller (BA, University of California, Berkeley; MA, Stanford University) is Vice President of Children Now, a national child advocacy organization. She oversees independent research projects on children and the media and monitors public policy development in the communications field as it affects children. She cochairs the Children's Media Policy Coalition, a broad group of public health, education, and advocacy organizations, working to create a healthy media environment for the nation's children. She also has testified before the Senate Commerce Committee and the Federal Communications Commission on various children and media issues. Prior to joining Children Now, she worked as a project manager at a San Francisco–based research firm, evaluating children's educational programs for PBS. She also spent several years working in research and production for *CBS News* in Washington, DC.

John P. Murray, PhD, is Professor of Developmental Psychology in the School of Family Studies and Human Services at Kansas State University and a Senior Scientist-Visiting Scholar in the Center on Media and Child Health at Children's Hospital Boston, Harvard Medical School. He began his interest in children and television in 1969 when he served as Research Coordinator for the U.S. Surgeon General's Scientific Advisory Committee on Television and Social Behavior at the National Institute of Mental Health. Since that time, he has published 13 books and more than 80 articles on children and media. His most recent book, *Children and Television: Fifty Years of Research*, was published in 2007.

Michelle Ortiz (MA, University of Arizona) is a doctoral student in the Department of Communication at the University of Arizona. Her research interests include intergroup processes and media effects.

Edward L. Palmer (PhD, Ohio University) is Wayne M. and Carolyn A. Watson Professor of Psychology at Davidson College in North Carolina. His research has focused on the advertising, violence, and prosocial aspects of children's televisual media. He has been a Visiting Scholar at Harvard University, Center for Research in Children's Television; UCLA; the University of North Carolina at Chapel Hill; the University of Exeter (UK); and the College of Communication at the University of Alabama. His professional works include *Children and the Faces of Television: Teaching, Violence, Selling* (with Aimee Dorr); *Children in the Cradle of Television; How to Prepare for the GRE in Psychology* (with Sharon Thompson-Schill); *Faces of Televisual Media: Teaching, Violence, Selling to Children* (with Brian Young); *Food and Beverage Marketing to Children and Youth: Trends and Issues* (with Courtney Carpenter);

and several other research articles and book chapters in the children's televisual media field. He served on the American Psychological Association's Task Force on Advertising and Children, authoring their report on commercialism in schools.

Erylene Piper-Mandy, PhD, is President and CEO of the Center for Cross Cultural Competence, a consultant agency through which she and her colleagues train public and private agencies in a variety of issues related to ethnic diversity and community relations. She is a psychocultural anthropologist who specializes in cross-cultural competence and American ethnicity. She has been the recipient of numerous awards and fellowships, including the prestigious Fulbright Fellowship, through which she worked and studied in Senegal, West Africa. She has given presentations and taught seminars in over 100 institutions and agencies on practical skills and competencies required to live and work effectively in an ethnically diverse California. She has served in a number of universities in California and abroad, teaching undergraduate and graduate students in a variety of areas, including anthropology, psychology, and African American studies, and is currently teaching Black studies at California State University, Long Beach.

Desirée Baolian Qin (EdD, Harvard University, 2004) is Assistant Professor of Human Development at Michigan State University. The main question underlying her work is how immigration, culture, gender, and ecological contexts (e.g., family and school environments) impact adolescent development. She is particularly interested in alienation in immigrant families and psychological adjustment of Asian American students. She is coeditor (with Marcelo Suárez-Orozco) of *Globalization: Education and Culture in the New Millennium* (UC Press, 2004). Her work appears in *Anthropology and Education Quarterly*, *International Migration Review*, and *New Directions in Youth Development*. Her most recent paper on family and peer influences on the psychological adjustment of Chinese American adolescents will appear in *Youth and Society*.

Daryl M. Rowe, PhD, is Professor of Psychology at Pepperdine University, Graduate School of Education and Psychology. He teaches courses on sociocultural influences on human behavior and theories and strategies of clinical intervention, and provides clinical supervision to both master's and doctoral students. He was the recipient of the Howard A. White Teaching Award for Teaching Excellence from Pepperdine University in 2004. He is the National Chair of the African Psychology Institute, the training arm of the Association of Black Psychologists. He regularly consults with various local, state, and national agencies and organizations regarding cultural diversity issues, working with different clinical populations, alternative approaches to psychotherapy, and other issues that aid the social and interpersonal functioning of persons of African descent. He is the author of numerous publications and has presented at professional organizations, nationally and internationally. As a licensed psychologist, his practice emphasizes the psychological and communal needs of persons of African descent, with special focus on marital and family relationships.

Adrienne Shaw is a doctoral candidate at the Annenberg School for Communication at the University of Pennsylvania. She studies video games, gaming culture, online communities, and minority representation in video games, as well as media representation of gender and sexuality. She has also done research on children's learning and video games with regard to both gender stereotypes and literacy.

Dorothy G. Singer, EdD, is Senior Research Scientist, Department of Psychology, Yale University. She is also Co-Director, with Jerome L. Singer, of the Yale University Family Television Research and Consultation Center. Her research is in the area of early childhood development, television effects on youth, and parent training in imaginative play. Her latest books with Jerome L. Singer are *Handbook of Children and the Media, Make-Believe: Games and Activities for Imaginative Play,* and *Imagination and Play in the Electronic Age.* Her most recent edited books are *Children's Play: Roots of Reading; Children, Culture and Violence;* and *Play=Learning.*

Jerome L. Singer, PhD, is Professor Emeritus of Psychology at Yale University. He is a specialist in research on the psychology of imagination and daydreaming. He has authored articles on thought processes, imagery, personality, and psychotherapy as well as on children's play and the effects of television. Recent books include *The House of Make-Believe, Repression and Dissociation, Imagination and Play in the Electronic Age,* and *Imagery in Psychotherapy.*

Josephine Stedman is a recent telecommunications management graduate of Howard University, John H. Johnson School of Communications, in Washington, D.C. She has participated in several research conferences where she reported the findings from her research pertaining to the negative effects of television viewing on the individual. Her accolades include the National Deans List and the Howard University School of Communications Dean's List as well as acceptance in the National Society of Collegiate Scholars (NSCS) and in the Annenberg Honor's Program. She was also the recipient of three Trustee Scholarships from Howard University—the President's Student Service Award, the McNair Post-baccalaureate Grant, and Americorps NCCC Educational Grant.

Ronald Takaki, PhD, has been Professor of Ethnic Studies at the University of California, Berkeley, for 35 years, and has taught over 10,000 students. He is the author of 11 books. *Strangers From a Different Shore: A History of Asian Americans* and *A Different Mirror: A History of Multicultural America* are read in college courses across the country. Currently, he is writing a revised and updated edition of *A Different Mirror* with new chapters on Jewish Americans and the Holocaust, Vietnamese refugees, recent immigrants from Mexico, and Muslims in the U.S. post–9/11.

Tom ter Bogt is Professor of Popular Music and Youth Culture at the University of Utrecht, the Netherlands. He studied cultural psychology and philosophy at the University of Nijmegen, and received his PhD with a study on Weber's Protestant Work Ethic in the Netherlands. He has published on work ethic, youth culture, and substance use. He has written several books and a television series on the history of youth culture and pop music in the Netherlands. Recent research covers substance use, music taste development, and the link between media preferences and adolescent problem behavior.

Khia A. Thomas (MS, University of Michigan) is a doctoral candidate in developmental psychology at the University of Michigan. Her current academic research interests include gender and sexual socialization of adolescents and young adults, particularly the role of media, in the form of music lyrics and videos, in these developmental processes for African

American women and men, as well as how hip-hop culture informs the development of multicultural youth.

Laurie A. Trotta is a writer and public relations professional specializing in social issues in entertainment. Her interests include children's television, artists' rights and responsibilities, professional ethics in the entertainment industry, violence in the media, media ratings, and diversity onscreen. She is the author of *Building Blocks: A Guide for Creating Children's Educational Television* (Mediascope Press, 1998). Her work in media issues has included developing guidelines for creating quality children's programming with members of the entertainment industry and serving as Volume Editor for *More Than a Movie: Ethics in Entertainment* (Westview Press, 2000). She has produced, participated in, and/or moderated dozens of panel discussions on media and society. Currently, she is organizing film festivals around such issues, including the Moving Pictures Magazine Short Film Contest series and the E2 Film Festival at Arizona State University. She is the former Executive Director of Mediascope, a public policy and media research organization that worked for open communication among academia, government, and the entertainment industry.

Jennifer A. Tuttle is a student at Davidson College in North Carolina. She is majoring in psychology and is particularly interested in child and social psychology.

Elizabeth M. Vera is Professor in the School of Education at Loyola University Chicago. She received her PhD from the Ohio State University in 1993. Dr. Vera has published in the areas of ethnic identity development of Latino and African American children, the prevention of violence in urban adolescents, culturally responsive prevention programming, and social justice and multiculturalism. She teaches courses in adolescent development, human development, clinical supervision, and prevention.

L. Monique Ward, PhD, is Associate Professor of Psychology at the University of Michigan. Her research examines children's and adolescents' developing conceptions of both gender and sexuality, and explores the contributions of these notions to their social and sexual decision making. She is particularly interested in the role of the media in the process of sexual socialization, and has published extensively on this topic in several academic journals, including *Developmental Review, Psychology of Women Quarterly,* and the *Journal of Research on Adolescence.* She served as a member of APA's Task Force on the Sexualization of Girls, and serves on the editorial board of the *Journal of Adolescent Research* and *Media Psychology.* She was also an associate editor for the *Encyclopedia of Children, Adolescents, and the Media.*

Farrell J. Webb (PhD, University of Minnesota, 1994) is a Community Sociologist and Social Psychologist, who serves as Associate Professor of Family Studies in the School of Family Studies & Human Services. He has taught courses in diversity in families, family studies, family theory, statistics (basic and advanced), sampling, research methods, advanced research methods, program evaluation, and computerized data analysis. He recently completed postdoctoral/sabbatical training at the Pennsylvania State University-University Park in the Center for Human Development and Family Research in Diverse Contexts in the areas of ethnography, spatial demography, and epidemiological research methods. He has extensive experience in data collection among hidden communities and served as the principal investigator on two Centers for Disease Control investigations that examined HIV knowledge, attitudes, and behaviors among MSM, IDU, and at-risk heterosexuals. His upcoming publications focus on the role of families in the production of prejudice across race, ethnic, and sexually varying groups.

Kimberly A. White-Smith, EdD, is Assistant Professor of Education at Chapman University. Her scholarship is focused on uncovering systems and strategies that promote quality educational opportunities for traditionally underserved students. As a former public school teacher, her expertise is in integrated curriculum design and instruction. In addition, she has extensive experience in creating, implementing, and evaluating exemplary models of teacher professional development.

Clint C. Wilson, II (EdD, University of Southern California) is Professor of Journalism and Graduate Professor of Communication at Howard University. He is author of *Racism, Sexism and the Media: The Rise of Class Communication in Multicultural America* with coauthors Felix Gutierrez and Lena Chao. He has published four other books and numerous articles exploring aspects of the relationship between people of color and mass communications media in the United States.

Mary J. Wilson (MA, California State University, Los Angeles; MS Pepperdine University) is a doctoral candidate at Bowie State University and Supervisor, Linkages to Learning and School Based Health for Montgomery County Public Schools in Maryland. Her interests include reading achievement for preschool and elementary school students in urban school environments.

Mary Wojnaroski is a doctoral student in the Child Clinical Psychology program at the University of Alabama in Tuscaloosa. Her research focuses on the relation between parenting, social cognitions, and aggression. She is currently working on her dissertation, which examines the relation between outcome expectations and inconsistent discipline in aggressive youth.

Sinead N. Younge (PhD, Michigan State University, 2005) is Assistant Professor in the Department of Psychology at Morehouse College in Atlanta, Georgia. Her research takes an ecological approach to examining the cultural antecedents of health behavior with particular attention to HIV/AIDS risk and protective behaviors. Her work has appeared in such forums as *Patterns of Marriages and Family Socialization in Native African Americans, Caribbean and African Immigrants; Handbook of Child Behavioral Issues: Evidence-Based Approaches; Journal of Adolescence;* and *Race and Society*.